Stravinsky

Eric Walter White

STRAVINSKY

The Composer and his Works

UNIVERSITY OF CALIFORNIA PRESS

Berkeley and Los Angeles

First published in 1966
by University of California Press
Berkeley and Los Angeles
Second edition 1979

First Paperback Printing 1984
ISBN 0-520-03985-8

Printed in the United States of America

To my daughter

SARAH SWINBURNE WHITE

with love

Contents

Illustrations

PLATES

11

Illustrations

Preface to the First Edition, 1966

I first fell under the spell of Stravinsky about 1923 when as a schoolboy I heard a concert performance of *The Firebird* suite at the old Colston Hall, Bristol. At that time the composer was unknown to me; but while I was immediately captivated by his music, I was astonished to notice that part of the audience was upset and scandalised by what they heard. This led me to make a mental note that I must memorise Stravinsky's name and follow up any further opportunities of hearing his music that might come my way.

At that moment such opportunities were comparatively few. It is true that there was always a chance of hearing one of his ballet scores if one happened to be in London or Paris or some other important city during one of the Russian Ballet seasons; but his compositions were included in concert programmes only for exceptional reasons – and for a provincial amateur like myself, such performances were difficult to attend. Few of his works had been recorded for gramophone; and broadcasts on the sound radio, which was still in its infancy, were rare occurrences and had the disadvantage that, apart from the quality of the actual performance – and some of these performances left a lot to be desired – the sound that emerged through earphones or amplifiers was apt to be so crude and distorted as to make it extremely difficult to arrive at a balanced judgment. In any case, a great deal of preliminary study had to be done on the scores at the piano; and here it proved fortunate that most of Stravinsky's actual composing had been carried out at the piano too, for it meant that the pianistic approach to his works was sometimes quite a helpful and sensible one.

In these ways I familiarised myself with the early ballet scores; and I also heard performances of some of the new neo-classical compositions of the 1920's, including the first performance of the *Concerto for Piano and Wind Instruments* in Paris in 1924. Although to someone like myself who had only just caught up with *The Rite of Spring*, the change to a neo-classical idiom was surprising and slightly bewildering, I was completely reassured a few years later by the magnificent performances of *Oedipus Rex* that I had the good fortune to hear under Klemperer's direction at the Krolloper, Berlin. I then felt certain that, despite the great weight of hostile criticism currently directed against his music, particularly in Great Britain, he was one of the great composers of all time. It was in this spirit of admiration and confidence that I wrote my early book *Stravinsky's Sacrifice to Apollo* (1930).

The decade that followed was a period when his increasing activity as a conductor and performer led to numerous tours of Europe and America, and a slight falling-off in the actual volume of his composition was noticeable. This trend seemed to be reversed, however, on the outbreak of the Second World War, when removal from France to America, followed by his second marriage, brought about a renewal of his composing activities on quite an extensive scale. Wartime conditions naturally delayed performances in Europe; but when peace was declared and works like the *Symphony in C* and the *Symphony in Three Movements* became easily accessible, it was realised that in the intervening years his mind had lost none of its power and cunning. At this point I published *Stravinsky: a critical survey* (1947), in which I tried to amalgamate a sketch of his life with a study of his works. This appeared in Great Britain and the United States. The German translation (published three years later) had a wide circulation in Central Europe where his music was enjoying the sort of post-war boom it had experienced twenty years earlier.

After *The Rake's Progress*, which represents the culmination of his neo-classical period, Stravinsky had the courage to move in a totally different direction; and his recent involvement in serial music has resulted in the production of new masterpieces and opened up important new vistas. In fact, it can be justly claimed that he has been a vital influence on successive generations of composers and musicians for over half a century.

The present book has been designed for those who are interested in the man and his music. The opening section is a sketch of his life, which draws on material derived from a variety of sources, including Stravinsky's own autobiographical writings and other persons' reminiscences. The following section deals with his original compositions and arrangements of other composers' works. These now total over a hundred; and I have endeavoured to treat each work faithfully by recounting the circumstances in which it was conceived and written, briefly analysing some of the music where that seemed helpful, giving a short account of productions and first performances, examining revisions, adaptations, and transcriptions, and relating the works to each other and to the general course of Stravinsky's career as a composer. I have aimed at making the text both readable and reliable; and I have used musical quotations to illustrate some of my points, especially when dealing with the serial works. The appendices reprint nine of his occasional writings, the texts of which have hitherto not been easily accessible, and contain a list of his arrangements for player-piano, and a bibliography of books by and about him.

It is a pleasure to thank the numerous persons who have helped me in my task.

First and foremost are Mr. Robert Craft, whose initial suggestion in 1958 led to the writing of this book, and the composer himself who encouraged me to go ahead and gave me generous permission to quote from his published writings.[1] I am deeply grateful to both of them for finding time, despite their multifarious

---

[1] References to the *Chronicle* and to the first four volumes of his Conversations with Robert Craft are usually given in abbreviated form, *viz. Chr, Con, Mem, Exp,* and *Dia.* In the case of quotations from the *Chronicle*, I have revised the anonymous English translation wherever that seemed appropriate.

commitments in different parts of the world, to answer queries and help resolve doubtful points that were referred to them. In addition they have made available the text of Robert Craft's *Catalogue of Manuscripts (1904–1952) in Stravinsky's Possession* and allowed me to print it as an appendix. This is a document of prime importance, and I am honoured to have been allowed to sponsor its first publication.

Among Stravinsky's music publishers, my sincere thanks are due to Boosey & Hawkes Ltd., J. & W. Chester Ltd., and Schott & Co. Ltd.

I gratefully acknowledge valuable help received from M. Paul Collaer in Belgium; from Mrs. Rakel Wihuri in Finland; from Mlle. Nadia Boulanger, M. André Meyer and M. Roland-Manuel in France; from Sig. Fedele d'Amico, and Signorina Emilia Zanetti in Italy; from M. Ernest Ansermet, Herr Balthasar Reinhart, Dr. Erwin Rosenthal, Dr. Paul Sacher, and M. Daniel Simond in Switzerland; from Mrs. Robert Woods Bliss, Mr. John N. Burk of the Boston Symphony Orchestra, Mr. Frank G. Burke of the University of Chicago Library, and Dr. Harold Spivacke of the Library of Congress, Washington D.C. in the United States; and from Sir Isaiah Berlin, Sir Arthur Bliss, Sir George Rostrevor Hamilton, Mr. Peter Stadlen, and Dr. Frederick Sternfeld in this country.

I owe a special debt to my friend, Mr. Donald Mitchell, whose advice has invariably been of the greatest value and whose encouragement has made the writing of this book such a pleasant task.

And finally, to my dear wife, who cheerfully typed a quarter of a million words or more, and put up with the dislocation caused by an undertaking of this scale, my loving thanks.

London, 11 January 1964   E. W. W.

P.S.—While this book was passing through the press, a number of unpublished letters addressed to Stravinsky by some of his French friends and all dating from 1913 (the year of the first performance of *The Rite of Spring*) came to light in the composer's house in Hollywood. These letters—from Claude Debussy (and his wife), Frederick Delius, Maurice Ravel and Jules Romains—are additional to the letters already printed in the first volume of the Stravinsky/Craft *Conversations* (1959). Mr. Stravinsky kindly offered me the right to print them in this book; and they appear here (in the original French) by permission of the various copyright owners concerned, *viz.* Madame de Tinan, the Delius Trust, Monsieur A. Taverne, and Monsieur Jules Romains. The footnotes are based on information supplied by Mr. Stravinsky.

14 August 1965   E.W.W.

Preface to the Second Edition, 1979

In 1966 when the original edition of this monograph on Stravinsky was published, the composer had another five years to live. For the second edition not only has the original text been revised, but a new chapter added to the Life, and the Register of Compositions brought up to date by including entries for his last two compositions, *Requiem Canticles* and *The Owl and the Pussy-Cat*.

During recent years, fresh information about Stravinsky's early life and adolescent compositions has come to light in the U.S.S.R., and this has been incorporated in the new edition.

I have continued to receive invaluable help from Robert Craft, who has become a key centre of Stravinsky studies and research. I am particularly indebted to David Atherton, who on the basis of his experience as a conductor has made practical suggestions about the best way of presenting information about the percussion sections of some of Stravinsky's scores.

London, 1978   E.W.W.

Part One

THE MAN

CONTENTS

1. The Child and his Environment
(1882 - 1902)

Igor Fedorovich Stravinsky was born at Khudyntzev Cottage, 137 Shveitzarsky Street, Oranienbaum, on the Gulf of Finland opposite Kronstadt on 5 June 1882 (O.S.) or 17 June (N.S.).[1] He was baptized by a prelate of the Russian Orthodox Church a few hours after his birth, and on 29 June (O.S.) he was ceremonially joined to the Church in the Nikolsky Cathedral, St. Petersburg.

The name Stravinsky is thought to be derived from Strava, a tributary of the River Nieman in eastern Poland; and the family is said to have moved from Poland to Russia sometime during the reign of Catherine the Great.

Igor's father, Feodor Ignatievich Stravinsky, was born in Chernigov and went as a student to the Niéjinsky Lyceum, St. Petersburg. When it was discovered that he had a fine natural bass voice and a good ear for music, he joined the Conservatory, becoming a pupil of Professor Everardi, and in 1873 after graduation he went to Kiev where he was engaged as the first bass in the Opera House. He made a considerable reputation for himself as an opera-singer, for it was quickly realised that, in addition to his musical gifts he had great dramatic talent. Soon after arriving in Kiev, he met and married Anna Kholodovsky. Three years later he was offered an engagement at the Imperial Opera House: so the Stravinsky household returned to St. Petersburg where they took a third-floor apartment at 66 Krukov Canal. This was quite near the Maryinsky Theatre; and one of the curious sights from their front windows was that of opera scenery being transported by barge to and from the theatre.

Igor was the third of a family of four boys: Roman (born in 1874), Yury (in 1879), and Gury (in 1884). His life as a child seems not to have been a happy one. He was afraid of his father, who seems to have had an uncontrollable temper. His attitude to his mother was governed merely by a sense of duty. He disliked his elder brothers, Roman and Yury, who annoyed him intensely. Only for his younger brother, Gury, did he have feelings of real affection. These two found in each other the love and understanding denied them by their parents.

In this household the servants provided a refuge and support for the unhappy child. He was particularly fond of Simon Ivanovich, the butler, who helped him out of many a scrape, and of Bertha his nurse. In his *Memories*, he wrote:

---

[1] Because the difference between the Gregorian and Julian Calendars increased by one day each century, he celebrated his birthday on 18 June (N.S.) from 1901 onwards.

Stravinsky's parents, Feodor Ignatievich and Anna Kholodovsky, *c.* 1873, shortly after their wedding

The Stravinsky family in their St. Petersburg apartment, *c.* 1894. Seated clockwise round the table are two of the boys, Igor and Roman; the mother (standing) who pours the tea; Simon Ivanovich, the family retainer; the father (seated) and the two remaining boys, Yury and Gury

Bertha was an East Prussian who knew almost no Russian; German was the language of my nursery. Perhaps I should blame Bertha for corrupting me (somewhat as Byron must have been corrupted in Aberdeen by Mary Gray), but I do not. She lived on to nurse my own children and was forty years in our family when she died, in Morges, 1917. I mourned her more than I did, later, my mother.

Igor's first school was the Second St. Petersburg Gymnasium, which he attended until he was fourteen or fifteen. He seems to have hated the classes and to have made very few friends. From there he went on to the Gonrévitch Gymnasium, which he equally loathed. He studied history, mathematics, Latin, Greek, French, German, Russian and Slavonic, and from his own account was an indifferent pupil.

St. Petersburg he loved. In later years he remembered with affection the sights, colours and smells of his native city, and particularly its sounds – street noises of droshkies on cobbles or wooden block roads, of trams grinding along rails, the knife-grinder's cry, other street cries of Russian and Tartar vendors, and cannonades of bells. He also recalled 'the morning vision of the Imperial sleighs of Alexander III, the giant Tsar, and his giant coachman',[1] with one horse in front of the sleigh and a blue net behind to catch the snow, and a second horse galloping at the side. And in autumn he enjoyed watching the gulls by the Neva, 'especially when the water rose in the rivers and canals; when the city stood up to its nose in water, the fish swam closer to the surface and the birds gyrated lower' (*Exp*). Years later when he had not seen the city for about half a century, he confessed that it was dearer to his heart than any other city in the world.

The summer months were usually spent in the country. He remembered visiting the Lzys – two villages, Big Lzy and Little Lzy, surrounded by birch forests near the Valdye Hills about 100 miles south east of St. Petersburg – in the summer of 1884 when he was only two, and from this holiday date his earliest conscious musical impressions.[2]

The following year he made his first visit to a vast estate called Pavlovka belonging to his uncle Alexander Ielachich, who had married his mother's sister Sophie. Pavlovka was in the Samara Government: and it took a four days' river trip, mainly on the Volga, to get there. Uncle Ielachich was a passionate amateur of music, and from the beginning there seems to have been a bond of affection between him and his nephew.

Other relations were not so sympathetic. There was Aunt Catherine, one of his mother's sisters, who owned a large estate at Pechisky, near Proskurov, in the western part of the Ukraine, where the Stravinsky family spent the summers

---

[1] See Appendix A(1), *The Sleeping Beauty*: letter to Diaghilev dated Paris, 10 October 1921.
[2] See p. 555.

of 1891 and 1892. Her nephew describes her as 'an orgulous and despotic woman', and it is clear that he noticed and resented her numerous unkindnesses. He says that he found Pechisky a dull place. Nevertheless, there were certain compensations.

In the first place, during these two summers he had an opportunity of visiting the neighbouring fair of Yarmolintsi, which (in his mature judgment) rivalled the great fair of Nizhni-Novgorod. It had exhibitions of peasant handicrafts, and competitions for livestock and grain; and he enjoyed the bright peasant costumes and found the people in them gay and attractive. But his chief delight was in the dancing contests; and there he saw for the first time the *trepak*, and also the *presiatka* (heel dance) and *kazachok* (kicking dance), both of which were to feature in the last scene of *Petrushka*.

At Pechisky too, he first met Catherine Gabrielovna Nossenko, who was later to become his wife. Catherine's mother, Maria, was his mother's eldest sister; so the two children were first cousins. Catherine, who was a year older than Igor, soon became his dearest friend and playmate; and years later he wrote (in his *Expositions*):

> From our first hour together we both seemed to realize that we would one day marry – or so we told each other later. Perhaps we were always more like brother and sister. I was a deeply lonely child, and I wanted a sister of my own. Catherine . . . came into my life as a kind of long-wanted sister in my tenth year. We were from then until her death extremely close, and closer than lovers sometimes are, for mere lovers may be strangers though they live and love together all their lives.

The link with the Nossenkos soon led to vacations in a new part of Russia – Volhynia. Sometime in the 1890's, Catherine's father, Dr. Gabriel Nossenko, bought a distillery and a large estate at Ustilug. This little village, with an entirely Jewish population, was at the confluence of the Luga and the Bug, a few miles west of Vladimir Volynsk in a part of Russia that was later ceded to Poland (after the Treaty of Brest Litovsk). The Nossenko estate was surrounded by forests, rivers and cornfields, and its climate was considered to be so salubrious that Igor, who had been looked on by his parents 'as a disaster area of illness susceptibility' ever since his birth[1] and had had a bad attack of pleurisy in 1895, was sent there with Gury during the summers of 1896–1901.

After Igor's birth in 1882, his parents did not return to Oranienbaum. In fact, he did not revisit his birthplace until 1962 when the name of the little town had been changed to Lomonosov. Nor as a boy did he see the sea, though he had been born so near it and had lived his early life so close to it, until he

---

[1] His taste for medicines dates from his childhood. 'There was a cupboard of homeopathic remedies, aconite and belladonna and such, in his parents' home in St. Petersburg, and he used to climb up to it regularly and unhinge himself.' Letter from Vera Stravinsky to Vladimir Petrov, dated 10 December 1962.

visited Hungerburg on the Gulf of Finland in his seventeenth year and, gazing at it from a hill, was astonished to find it looked so 'vertical'! But his family were accustomed to travel abroad in the summer, and Igor accompanied them on numerous occasions.

The first of these trips was to Bad Homburg, probably in the summer of 1893. Two years later he paid his first visit to Switzerland, where he was fascinated by the English tourists who came to Interlaken and looked at the Jungfrau through their telescopes. This was the summer when his father took him again to Bad Homburg. They called on Clara Schumann in her villa in Frankfurt; and shortly afterwards news reached them that Roman had just died at Pechisky. They returned to Pechisky immediately for the funeral.

As a child Igor loved music; and the flame of his interest was fanned in various ways. From his nursery he frequently heard his father two rooms away, practising one of the roles from his extensive operatic repertory. He had appeared in numerous foreign operas such as *Il Barbiere di Siviglia*, *Guillaume Tell*, *Les Huguenots*, *The Merry Wives of Windsor*, *Rigoletto*, *Mefistofele* and *Faust*; and his Russian repertory included *A Life for the Tsar*, *Russlan and Ludmila*, *Judith*, *Prince Igor*, *Boris Godunov*, *Dubrovsky*, *The Enchantress*, *Mazeppa*, *The Maid of Orleans* and various operas by N. Rimsky-Korsakov. The boy was allowed the run of his father's library and, when his musical technique improved, spent a lot of time sight-reading many of his father's vocal scores.

His first visit to the Maryinsky Theatre seems to have occurred when he was about seven or eight, and on that occasion he saw Chaikovsky's ballet *The Sleeping Beauty* and was enchanted by it. This was the beginning of two life-long devotions – to ballet generally, and to the music of Chaikovsky in particular. A little later he was taken to his first opera, *A Life for the Tsar*, and promptly fell in love with the sound of Glinka's orchestra. In 1893 (when he was eleven) he attended a special gala performance of Glinka's *Russlan and Ludmila* to mark the fiftieth anniversary of the opera's first performance; and on this occasion his father sang the role of Farlaf. Years later he remembered how in the first interval he and his mother stepped from their box into the small foyer behind, where a few people were already walking, and suddenly his mother said: 'Igor, look, there is Chaikovsky.' 'I looked,' he writes in his *Expositions*, 'and saw a man with white hair, large shoulders, a corpulent back, and this image has remained in the retina of my memory all my life.'[1]

At the age of nine, he received his first regular piano lessons from a Mlle. Snetkova, who was replaced a few years later by Mlle. Kashperova, a pupil of Anton Rubinstein. Under her tuition he made considerable progress, in the course of time becoming a sufficiently good pianist to play the Mendelssohn G Minor concerto, as well as a wide selection of pieces by Clementi, Mozart,

---

[1] Chaikovsky's death from cholera followed two weeks later.

1. The Man

Haydn, Beethoven, Schubert and Schumann; and he seems to have enjoyed playing four-handed arrangements of Rimsky-Korsakov's operas with her. Certain aspects of her teaching left a permanent mark on his piano technique, e.g., she forbad him all use of the pedals, and he had to sustain entirely by the fingers. But in the course of time he felt a growing resentment at the narrowness of her musical outlook; and the way in which he ultimately asserted his freedom was accordingly all the more violent.

About this time he was receiving harmony lessons from Feodor Akimento and, later on, instruction in both harmony and counterpoint from Vassily Kalafaty.

He was a frequent visitor at his Uncle Ielachich's house. Ielachich adored Beethoven, had 'discovered' Brahms and Bruckner for himself, and admired Mussorgsky because of his so-called 'naturalism'. He had five children, several of whom were also musical. Igor was not fond of his cousins, but he particularly enjoyed playing piano duets with his uncle; and the uncle must have been proud of his nephew's musical prowess, for some years later he presented him with a special medal to commemorate the first performance of his *Symphony in E flat*.[1]

Much of the boy's free time was spent at the Maryinsky Theatre. His father got him a pass that enabled him to attend most of the opera rehearsals; and by the time he was sixteen he was spending five or six nights a week at the theatre. About this time he also formed a close attachment to Ivan Pokrovsky, who was eight years his senior, a lover of art in general and of music in particular. Together they played four-handed arrangements of much French music, and in this way Igor became familiar with such composers as Gounod, Bizet, Delibes and Chabrier, and with works like *Coppélia*, *Lakmé* and *The Tales of Hoffmann*.

But despite his obvious bent for music, his parents refused to allow him to pursue a musical career and insisted on his going to St. Petersburg University. He was supposed to read criminal law and legal philosophy; but, by his own account, he was a bad student, and it is unlikely that he attended more than fifty lectures during the whole of the four years he was there.

Meanwhile, his interest in music was turning gradually towards composition. At first it had been merely a question of improvising at the piano; but in his teens he began to write transcriptions. At this time he was a fervent admirer of the music of both Glazunov and Rimsky-Korsakov; and about 1897, he transcribed one of Glazunov's string quartets for piano and, acting on the impulse of the moment, took the score to the composer's house to show him. 'Though I

---

[1] This performance was given on 27 April 1907 (N.S.), and a day or two later Rimsky-Korsakov presented Stravinsky with the manuscript full score of his opera, *The Tale of Tsar Saltan*, to commemorate the occasion. The manuscript was presumably lost with the rest of Stravinsky's papers at Ustilug during the Russian Revolution.

had never been presented to him,' says Stravinsky,[1] 'he knew my father, in spite of which he received me ungraciously, perfunctorily flipping through my manuscript and pronouncing my work unmusical. I went away thoroughly discouraged.' A few years later, the young law student was writing short piano pieces, 'andantes', 'melodies' and so on, and was determined, if possible, to break through the barrier caused by his parents' indifference to his musical ambitions. One of his fellow students at the university was Vladimir Rimsky-Korsakov, the youngest son of the composer; and at some point Igor had the idea that he might consult Vladimir's father about his aspirations.

An opportunity to do so occurred in the summer of 1902 when Igor, who had accompanied his parents to Bad Wildungen, discovered that the Rimsky-Korsakov family was in the neighbourhood at Heidelberg, where Andrei, another of the composer's sons, was at that moment a student at the university. He accepted an invitation from Vladimir to go over and stay with them, and in the course of this visit found an opportunity to tell Rimsky-Korsakov of his longing to become a composer and asked his advice. An interesting account of this interview is given in Stravinsky's *Chronicle*.[2]

> He made me play some of my first attempts. Alas! the way in which he received them was far from what I had hoped. Seeing how upset I was, and evidently anxious not to discourage me, he asked if I could play anything else. I did so, of course, and it was only then that he gave his opinion.

Rimsky-Korsakov advised him not to think of entering the Conservatory, but to continue his studies in harmony and counterpoint. He thought his work should be systematically supervised and suggested this should be done by private lessons, adding that he would always be ready to offer advice if consulted. Stravinsky says:

> Although in my ingenuousness I was somewhat downcast over the lack of enthusiasm which the master had shown for my first attempts at composition, I found some comfort in the fact that he had nevertheless advised me to continue my studies, and so demonstrated his opinion that I had sufficient ability to devote myself to a musical career.

Shortly after this meeting, Stravinsky's father died. He had been suffering from cancer for well over a year; and the end came on 21 November 1902 (O.S.) or 4 December (N.S.). There seems to be a slight confusion over where he was buried. In his *Memories*, Stravinsky says he was buried 'in the Novodevitchy (the New Maiden) cemetery, but was reburied in the Alexandro-Nevsky cemetery in 1917'; but in *Expositions* he says the grave was in the Volkov Cemetery, and the reburial in the New Nuns' Cemetery.

---

[1] From a letter to *The Observer*, dated 27 November 1961, printed in that newspaper on 20 May 1962 and reprinted in *Dialogues and a Diary*.
[2] A slightly different and not so detailed account is given in *Expositions*, with the surely erroneous suggestion that this meeting took place in 1900.

2. The Pupil and his Master (1902 - 1909)

Immediately after his father's death, Stravinsky made a determined effort to assert his independence and live his own life. He even went so far as to leave home, seeking refuge with one of his Ielachich cousins who had recently married; but his mother staged a sufficiently serious illness for him to feel obliged to return to 66 Krukov Canal. He comments in his *Memories*: 'she did behave slightly less egoistically after that, however, and her delight in torturing me seemed slightly less intense'.

At this period the circle of his acquaintances and interests began to widen. He gradually became a regular attendant at the weekly gatherings at Rimsky-Korsakov's house, where he was known familiarly as 'Guima'. These meetings were held on fixed days when compositions by Rimsky's pupils were performed and discussed. He also became close friends with Stepan Mitusov, a young man a few years older than himself, whom he found a most stimulating companion.[1] He was an excellent judge of music, painting and literature; and together the two friends read the works of Hoffmann, Maeterlinck and Oscar Wilde and visited the theatre, seeing many productions of plays by Chekhov, Gorki and others that the recently founded Moscow Art Theatre brought on its occasional visits to St. Petersburg. This was the period when the review, *Mir Isskustva* ('The World of Art'), which Serge Diaghilev[2] had founded in 1898, served as a rallying point for young Russian artists of the vanguard, especially those who took part in its exhibitions in St. Petersburg (held between 1899 and 1903). About the same time, three of Stravinsky's other friends – Pokrovsky, A. P. Nourock and V. F. Nouvel – established the 'Evenings of Contemporary Music', a concert series which concentrated on works by young Russian composers, but also included contemporary French and German music in its programmes, by César Franck, Dukas, d'Indy, Debussy, Ravel, Brahms, Richard Strauss, Max Reger and others. It was at one of these concerts that Nicolas Richter played Stravinsky's *Piano Sonata in F sharp minor*, the first of his compositions to be performed in public.

---

[1] In V. Yastrebtzev's *Recollections of Rimsky-Korsakov*, Vol. II (Moscow, 1962) there is an amusing reference to the fact that at one of the regular Rimsky-Korsakov gatherings on 17 February 1904, Nicolas Richter horrified Rimsky-Korsakov's wife by playing a cakewalk, while Mitusov and Stravinsky demonstrated how it should be danced.

[2] Diaghilev was a distant cousin of Stravinsky's – they had a common relation in Stravinsky's mother's maternal grandfather, Roman Furman – but they do not appear to have met much, if at all, before 1909.

The Pupil and his Master (1902 – 1909)

This Sonata was composed in the summer of 1903[1] during Stravinsky's second visit to his Uncle Ielachich's Pavlovka estate in Samara. On this occasion he was accompanied by Vladimir Rimsky-Korsakov, and the two of them sent Rimsky-Korsakov greetings postcards from every stopping-place on their river trip – Rybinsk, Jaroslav, and Nizhni-Novgorod. When the Sonata was finished, Stravinsky felt he needed advice on some of the formal problems that had arisen in the course of composition and, remembering Rimsky's promise the previous year, decided to consult him. At that moment the composer was staying in the country at Lzy because of his asthma: so Stravinsky called there on his return journey from Pavlovka, and remained about a fortnight, during which Rimsky-Korsakov instructed him in the principles of sonata form and made him compose the first part of a sonatina under his supervision.

From this moment dated the regular instruction that Stravinsky received from Rimsky-Korsakov, and which covered a period of about three years. There were usually two lessons a week, each lasting about an hour. Rimsky taught him the compass and registers of the different instruments of the orchestra, and the first elements of orchestration. The practical work consisted in the orchestration of various piano pieces. Stravinsky says:

> I worked with him in this way. He would give me some pages of the piano score of a new opera he had just finished (*Pan Voyevoda*), which I was to orchestrate.[2] When I had orchestrated a section, he would show me his own instrumentation of the same passage. I had to compare them, and then he would ask me to explain why he had done it differently. Whenever I was unable to do so, it was he who explained (*Chr*).

Rimsky also gave him pieces of classical music to orchestrate such as sonatas and quartets by Beethoven and marches by Schubert; and this exercise was made the excuse for an analysis of the works' form and structure.

During these early years, a number of light-hearted compositions of Stravinsky's seem to have been performed at the Rimsky-Korsakov weekly gatherings. V. Yastrebtzev, mentions a group of 'plaisanteries musicales', which Stravinsky played on 6 March 1903, a 'chanson comique' (17 February 1904), and a piece called *Conductor and Tarantula* (6 March 1906), which was probably inspired by a book of humourous verse written by Alexei Tolstoy and the brothers Jemchooshnikov under the pseudonym of Kozma Prootkov. There is also reference to a cantata, which he composed and dedicated to Rimsky-Korsakov, and which was performed during dinner on 6 March 1904

---

[1] This is the date given in Stravinsky's *Chronicle*. *Expositions* has 1902.

[2] V. Yastrebtzev (*op. cit.*) recalls under the dates 22 and 23 August 1904, that Rimsky-Korsakov, then in Vehchasha near Lzy, was 'forcing' Stravinsky to work at the orchestration, for wind instruments, of the Polonaise from *Pan Voyevoda*.

[3] V. Yastrebtzev, *op. cit.*

by 'the young Rimsky-Korsakovs [i.e., Andrei and Vladimir] with Stravinsky at their head. . . . The cantata was repeated by audience request.' None of these juvenilia has survived. Among the manuscripts in Stravinsky's personal possession, however, was an unpublished song for bass and piano entitled *The Mushrooms going to War* and dated 1904.

In 1905 his university career came to an end. This was a moment when all Russia was reeling under the disasters of the Russo-Japanese War. At no point in his life does Stravinsky seem to have taken an active interest in politics – all he has ever wanted has been sufficient security to be able to pursue his professional career without hindrance or interference – but there is one anecdote about him during the period of the Russo-Japanese War that deserves quotation here.

> I was walking through the Kazansky Place one afternoon in the politically tense months following the Russo-Japanese War, when a group of students began to stage a protest. The police were prepared, however, and the protestants arrested, myself with them. I was detained seven hours, but seventy years will not erase the memory of my fears (*Mem*).

The summer seems to have been spent in Ustilug, and in October his engagement to Catherine Nossenko, who had spent the previous three years studying singing in Paris, was announced from the Nossenko family house. He experienced considerable difficulty in finding a train to get him back to St. Petersburg that autumn. The strikes and outbreaks following the Potemkin mutiny and the August ukase had made travelling difficult. Soldiers stood guard everywhere in St. Petersburg; and for a time the postal service was disrupted. His own anxieties at that moment, however, were religious rather than political, for there was an Imperial statute forbidding marriage between first cousins, and he had to find a priest who would officiate at the ceremony without insisting on the production of documents that would expose the close relationship between Catherine and himself. At last, a suitable priest was found in the village of Novaya Derevnya near St. Petersburg; and the marriage took place at noon on 11 January (O.S.) or 24 January (N.S.) 1906. No relatives were present; and the only attendants were Stravinsky's best men, Andrei and Vladimir Rimsky-Korsakov. When the married couple reached home after the ceremony, Rimsky-Korsakov was waiting for them at the door. He blessed Stravinsky, holding over his head an icon, which he then gave him as a wedding present. (According to *Expositions*, another of his wedding presents was the gift of his teaching.) A fortnight's honeymoon was spent at Imatra, 'a small Finnish Niagara, dreamily populated by newly weds'; and on their return to St. Petersburg, the newly married couple settled down in the Stravinsky apartment at 66 Krukov Canal, where they took over two adjoining rooms that had formerly been occupied by Roman and Yury. Here they remained for about a year before moving to an apartment of their own on the English

The Pupil and his Master (1902 – 1909)

Prospekt. Their eldest child, Theodore, was born in 1907; and a daughter, Ludmila, followed in 1908. It was their custom to visit Ustilug every summer; but now instead of staying at the Nossenko family house, they decided to build their own house to live in. This was situated directly on the Luga, about one kilometre from Ustilug proper and was constructed to Stravinsky's own design. He found this spot an ideal haven for composition and had his Bechstein grand piano moved there from St. Petersburg.

After his marriage, his music lessons continued; but they now consisted mainly in his showing Rimsky-Korsakov his own compositions and discussing them with him movement by movement, so that the whole of his early works, including their instrumentation, was to a certain extent under his master's control. This was the case with the *Symphony in E flat*, which had been begun in 1905 before his marriage, but was not finished until 1907 – and also with the *Faun and Shepherdess* song cycle, which he began to compose during his honeymoon. The Symphony was dedicated to Rimsky-Korsakov who, thinking his pupil ought to have a chance to hear for himself what he had written, arranged for a private performance of both the Symphony and the song cycle to be given by the Court Orchestra under H. Wahrlich (27 April 1907). Later that year Stravinsky showed him the manuscript score of his *Scherzo Fantastique* and the preliminary sketches for the first act of his opera *The Nightingale*, the libretto of which he had drafted in collaboration with Mitusov; and both works apparently met with his master's approval.

But it must not be thought that Rimsky-Korsakov was lavish with his praise. Quite the contrary. At the first performance of the *Symphony in E flat*, Stravinsky remembered his saying:[1] 'This is too heavy; be more careful when you use trombones in their middle register'; and the master seems to have been highly suspicious of the one or two 'modernist' touches that his pupil had introduced in the *Faun and Shepherdess* song cycle. This fits in with Yastrebt-zev's entry in his *Recollections* under the date 4 November 1907.

> In the opinion of Rimsky-Korsakov, the talent of Igor Stravinsky has not yet taken clear shape. Rimsky thinks that the fourth part of his Symphony imitates Glazunov too much, and Rimsky himself. And he considers that in the new romances on words of Gorodetsky, Igor Fedorovich puts himself too much on the side of *modernism*.

It should also be remembered that Rimsky-Korsakov did not make any mention of Stravinsky in his Autobiography. Stravinsky explains that this was because he did not want to show him any mark of deference – 'he had many pupils and was always careful to avoid favouritism' (*Mem*).

Among the numerous people whom Stravinsky met at the Rimsky-Korsakov household about this time should be mentioned the conductor Serge

---

[1] Quoted in *Memories*.

Koussevitzky. Later on, when he founded the Russischer Musik Verlag (Edition Russe de Musique) he was to become Stravinsky's publisher.

Towards the end of 1907 Rimsky-Korsakov's health began to fail; and during the winter of 1908 he suffered from a number of bad attacks of asthma. Stravinsky still saw him frequently; and when April came, he and his wife paid a formal visit to the Rimsky-Korsakov household in St. Petersburg before setting out for the country. Rimsky-Korsakov's daughter Nadezhda had just become engaged to be married to the composer Maximilian Steinberg; and Stravinsky told Rimsky-Korsakov of his intention to write a short orchestral fantasy to be called *Fireworks* to celebrate their wedding. Once he had settled down at Ustilug, he finished the new score in about six weeks and dispatched it by registered post to Lzy where the Rimsky-Korsakov family had gone to spend the summer. A few days later a telegram came informing him of his master's death. He immediately set out for Lzy, where he joined the Rimsky-Korsakov family and accompanied the coffin back to St. Petersburg for the funeral on 23 June. Rimsky-Korsakov was buried near Stravinsky's father in the Novodevitchy Cemetery. The tomb, a handsome affair with a Maltese cross, was designed by Nicolas Roerich.

There is no doubt that Rimsky-Korsakov had become a sort of father figure in Stravinsky's life since his own father's death in 1902, and he deeply and sincerely mourned him. On returning to Ustilug, he composed a *Funeral Dirge*, and this was performed in St. Petersburg at the first Belaiev concert of the autumn season, which was entirely dedicated to Rimsky-Korsakov's memory. Unfortunately the score of this work was lost in the Russian Revolution; but if Stravinsky's memory could be trusted, it was the best of his works before *The Firebird*.

From now onwards, Stravinsky's relations with the rest of the Rimsky-Korsakov family began to deteriorate. In the first place, there was an unhappy incident that occurred at the time of the funeral.

> I will remember Rimsky in his coffin as long as memory is. He looked so very beautiful I could not help crying. His widow, seeing me, came up to me and said: 'Why so unhappy? We still have Glazunov.' It was the cruellest remark I have ever heard and I have never hated again as I did in that moment (*Con*).

Later his friendship with Andrei and Vladimir was affected. Although he was fond of both of them he felt that their kindness towards him had lasted only so long as their father was alive. In fact, after the success of *The Firebird*, the entire family seemed to turn against him – or, rather, against his music – and a few years later, when reviewing *Petrushka* for a Russian newspaper, Andrei dismissed it as 'Russian vodka with French perfumes'. As for the Steinbergs, they did not appear to appreciate the dedication of *Fireworks* either at the time of their marriage or in later years. When Stravinsky returned to Russia in 1962 after nearly half a century's absence, the programme of his first concert in St. Petersburg (8 October) included *Fireworks* and *The Firebird*: so he arranged for the Composers' Union to send Nadezhda Rimsky-Korsakov a special invitation to the concert, which she declined because (according to Robert Craft[1]) 'she had always known that I.S. was not fond of her husband,[2] or, for that matter, herself.'

However apathetic the Steinbergs may have felt about their wedding present, *Fireworks* was about to win for Stravinsky the admiration and patronage of an important new friend.

---

[1] From Robert Craft's Diary, printed in the American edition of *Dialogues & a Diary*.

[2] She was right, for there was certainly no love lost between the two men. Steinberg was in Paris in 1924 at the time of the first performance of the *Piano Concerto*; and in his *Memories* Stravinsky relates that when they met, Steinberg wanted to lecture him about the whole of his mistaken career. Ten years later I myself met Steinberg in Leningrad and, in reply to my asking him whether Stravinsky ever visited Russia those days, he replied, 'Non – il habite toujours Paris et ne veut pas venir en Russie. Sans doute il a ses motifs; mais quand même c'est dommage'. Stravinsky's final word (in *Expositions*) was that Steinberg 'was one of these ephemeral, prize-winning, front-page types, in whose eyes conceit forever burns, like an electric light in daytime.'

3. The Composer and his Patron
(1909 - 1914)

The performance of *Scherzo Fantastique* and *Fireworks* at a Siloti concert at St. Petersburg on 6 February 1909 marked a turning point in Stravinsky's career. Now that Rimsky-Korsakov was dead, he needed a new protector and a patron who would know how to present him to the public. By a stroke of great good fortune, the audience at this concert included just such a person – Serge Diaghilev, who was immediately struck by the promise revealed by these two works – and particularly the dynamic verve and flashing tone-colour of *Fireworks*.

Since the demise of his art magazine *Mir Isskustva*, Diaghilev had begun to look to Paris rather than St. Petersburg as a suitable setting for his activities as an artistic impresario. In 1906 he had organised an exhibition of Russian art in the galleries of the Grand Palais. In 1907 he presented a series of five orchestral concerts of Russian music at the Paris Opera House, on which occasion Shaliapin sang, Rachmaninov appeared as pianist, and Nikisch conducted works by Mussorgsky, Glazunov, Rimsky-Korsakov and Scriabin. The following year he concentrated on opera; and Rimsky-Korsakov's version of *Boris Godunov* was heard for the first time in Paris with Shaliapin in the title role. By the winter of 1909 he was deeply involved in plans for presenting a mixed season of Russian opera and Russian ballet the following summer. Among his advisers were Michel Fokine, the dancer and choreographer, two artists, Léon Bakst and Alexandre Benois, but no musician; and when he heard Stravinsky's new works, the idea occurred to him that here might be the composer he needed as a collaborator in his new venture.

The programme for the 1909 ballet season was to consist of five ballets in all. There were to be two new ballets – the Polovtsian Dances from Borodin's *Prince Igor*, and *Les Sylphides* which had hitherto only been seen in St. Petersburg in a very much shorter version called *Chopiniana*; two ballets to *pasticcio* scores – *Cléopâtre*, described as a choreographic drama, and *Le Festin*, a suite of divertissements; and a revival of *Le Pavillon d'Armide* with music by N. Cherepnin. Some of the Chopin pieces for *Les Sylphides* had already been scored by Glazunov, Liadov and Cherepnin; but Diaghilev now invited Stravinsky to orchestrate the opening *Nocturne* in A flat and the *Valse Brillante* in E flat which formed the finale. He also asked him to orchestrate Grieg's *Kobold* for inclusion in *Le Festin*. These commissions were promptly carried out; and at the end of April Diaghilev and his company left for Paris, and Stravinsky and his family made their usual move to Ustilug for the summer. While the Russian dancers – particularly Anna Pavlova, Tamara Karsavina and Vaslav Nijinsky – were scoring a remarkable series of triumphs at the Théâtre du Châtelet, Paris, Stravinsky was working steadily on his opera, *The Nightingale*, the first act of which was ready in full score by the end of the summer.

On his return to St. Petersburg in the autumn, Diaghilev immediately began to make plans for a further Russian Ballet season in Paris in 1910. This time, in addition to the ballets already presented in 1909, he intended to present three new ballets, together with a *pasticcio* called *Les Orientales*, and a revival of *Giselle*. The new ballets were to be *Le Carnaval* to the music of Schumann, *Sheherazade* to Rimsky-Korsakov's tone poem, and a ballet with a new score to be based on the Russian fairy-tale of the Firebird. His first idea was to commission Liadov to write the music for *The Firebird*; but when approached, Liadov, who in any case had a reputation for being excessively dilatory, said he thought it would take him about a year to finish: so Diaghilev decided to transfer the commission to Stravinsky. Though somewhat alarmed by the fact that this was a commission for a fixed date and afraid lest he might fail to complete the work in time, Stravinsky felt flattered at being chosen to collaborate with artists of established reputations, such as Fokine who was to be responsible for the choreography and A. Golovine who was to design the scenery and costumes; and he accepted the invitation.

Before starting the work of composition, he decided to give himself a short holiday 'in birch forests and snow-fresh air' (*Exp*), and accordingly at the beginning of November he joined Andrei Rimsky-Korsakov[1] on a *dacha* belonging to the Rimsky-Korsakov family near Lzy. But as soon as he arrived, he felt a compulsion to start composing at once, and when he returned to St. Petersburg in December, he had made considerable progress with the opening of the score. He continued to work intensively during the winter months, finishing the short score in March 1910 and the full orchestral score the following month.

Now for the first time it becomes possible to glimpse him through other persons' eyes.

Fokine could not recall in later years whether he first heard Stravinsky's music or first met the composer personally at a concert performance or during a rehearsal; but he remembered standing with Diaghilev (and, possibly, Benois) when an excited young man approached them.

He was angered by the attitude of the musicians to his work. The concert was played by the magnificent orchestra of the Imperial Theatre. Many of

---

[1] The score of *The Firebird* is dedicated to Andrei.

the musicians were also professors of the Imperial Conservatory of Music. The orchestra was great but somewhat conservative, and the bold experiments of the young composer shocked the sedate musicians. The composer complained that they treated his music with utter contempt, as if they were ridiculing it.[1]

S. L. Grigoriev, the *regisseur* of the Russian Ballet, who was always present at meetings of 'Diaghilev's committee' as the regular informal gathering of Diaghilev's friends and advisers was called, wrote:[2] 'From now on Stravinsky began to be present at our committee meetings, and so I met him for the first time. He was rather short, with prominent features and a very serious expression. He took an active part in the discussions, especially those on the production of *The Firebird*'.

Benois, who also attended these meetings, wrote:[3]

> One of the binding links between us, besides music, was Stravinsky's cult of the theatre and his interest in the plastic arts. Unlike most musicians, who are usually quite indifferent to everything that is not within their sphere, Stravinsky was deeply interested in painting, architecture and sculpture. Although he had had no grounding in these subjects, discussion with him was very valuable to us, for he 'reacted' to everything for which we lived. In those days he was a very willing and charming 'pupil'. He thirsted for enlightenment and longed to widen his knowledge. . . . But what was most valuable in him was the absence of the slightest dogmatism.

R. Brussel, the French critic, wrote a vivid account of a piano run-through of the ballet score that Stravinsky gave at Diaghilev's apartment that winter; and Karsavina has described his patience and concentration at rehearsals.[4]

After completing his score on time, he retired to Ustilug for a short rest before joining the Russian Ballet in Paris at the end of May. His mind was already busy with the idea of a new work, for, while finishing the last pages of *The Firebird* at St. Petersburg, he had had a dream or vision, which gave him the clue for a kind of symphony. In his imagination he had seen 'a solemn pagan rite: wise elders, seated in a circle, watching a young girl dance herself to death. They were sacrificing her to propitiate the god of spring' (*Chr*). The new symphony was to be the musical equivalent of a spring rite in pagan Russia; and he even started to compose the final movement straight away.[5] A little later he played it to Diaghilev, who immediately grasped its possibilities as a ballet and wanted to reserve it for his company. Stravinsky agreed; and it was

---

[1] *Fokine: Memoirs of a Ballet Master*, translated by Vitale Fokine. London, Constable, 1961.
[2] S. L. Grigoriev, *The Diaghilev Ballet 1909–1929*. London, Constable, 1953.
[3] Alexandre Benois, *Reminiscences of the Russian Ballet*. London, Putnam, 1941.
[4] Both of these accounts are quoted in the Register of Compositions.
[5] This is the movement which he explains (in *Expositions*) he could play, but did not, at first, know how to write down.

decided that the scenario should be worked out with the painter, Nicolas Roerich, who was a specialist in Russian prehistory.

When Stravinsky reached Paris at the end of May for the final rehearsals of *The Firebird*, he felt immensely elated. This was his first visit to Paris; it was also the first performance of a work of his for the stage. 'Mark him well,' said Diaghilev during one of the rehearsals in the Opera House. 'He is a man on the eve of celebrity.' And so he was. When the first performance came (25 June 1910), he received a tremendous ovation; and next day the press was full of his praise. At one bound he had become an international figure.

On this and subsequent visits to Paris during the next few years, he met a number of celebrities. Claude Debussy was one of the first to compliment him on his music. The French composer was brought on to the stage of the Opera at the end of the first performance of *The Firebird* by Diaghilev, and later that summer presented Stravinsky with his photograph with an autograph dedication 'à Igor Strawinsky en toute sympathie artistique'. Stravinsky also got to know other composers, including Maurice Ravel, Florent Schmitt, Maurice Delage, Erik Satie, Giacomo Puccini, Alfredo Casella and Manuel de Falla. He met Sarah Bernhardt at one of the Russian Ballet performances, and also Marcel Proust, Jean Giraudoux, Paul Morand, St. John Perse, and Paul Claudel.

At the end of June 1910 he returned to Ustilug to fetch his family so that his wife could hear *The Firebird* at the final performance at the Paris Opera on 7 July; and then they all moved to a beachside hotel at La Baule in Brittany. Here he wrote two songs to poems by Verlaine, which he intended for his brother Gury, who had an attractive baritone voice. As his wife was pregnant, it was decided not to return to Russia at the end of the summer, but to go to Switzerland to await her confinement. At the end of August they accordingly moved to Chardon Jogny near Vevey and subsequently to Lausanne, where their second son, Sviatoslav Soulima, was born in a clinic on 23 September.

During the Russian Ballet season in Paris that June Diaghilev had invited Stravinsky to compose a new ballet based on a theme by Edgar Allan Poe; and this led the young composer to tell Diaghilev about the pagan rite symphony which he had started to discuss with Roerich. But when Diaghilev and Nijinsky, on returning from their holiday in Venice, visited him at Lausanne, they were confronted somewhat to their surprise with the first movement and part of the second movement of a completely new work, a kind of *Konzertstück* for piano and orchestra. As a result of the great success of the recent season of the Russian Ballet, Diaghilev had decided to form a permanent company, and he was determined to have a new score from Stravinsky for his 1911 season. If it couldn't be the pagan rite symphony, he was quite prepared to accept the new composition, provided it could be fitted to a ballet scenario. The solution was provided by Stravinsky proposing the name of

Petrushka as a suitable title. Diaghilev now saw that the new work could be turned into a ballet with a puppet theme, and he suggested Benois as the ideal collaborator. This was agreed, and the work proceeded apace.

During the autumn, Stravinsky made considerable progress with the score of *Petrushka*, first at Clarens (in the Hôtel Chatelard) where he and his family moved shortly after Soulima's birth, and then from October onwards at Beaulieu near Nice. Diaghilev, who was staying at Monte Carlo for part of the time, kept in close touch, and when he returned to St. Petersburg for Christmas, invited Stravinsky to join him for a fortnight so that Benois and Fokine could hear the music he had written to date. The composer found this visit rather upsetting. Not only was he daunted by the rapid transition from the sunny warmth of the Riviera to the fog and snows of the north; but the success of *The Firebird* had affected his scale of values, and the city he had known 'only a few months before as the grandest in the world now seemed sadly small and provincial' (*Exp*).

On his return journey he spent his fifth wedding anniversary (24 January) in Genoa. Back in Beaulieu, he suddenly fell ill with intercostal neuralgia caused by nicotine poisoning, and it took him a month to recover. He was naturally nervous about the fate of *Petrushka* because he was working to a deadline; but by April when his wife left Beaulieu with their children to return to Russia, he had completed the orchestral score of over three-quarters of the ballet. He then joined Diaghilev, Nijinsky, Fokine, Benois and the Russian painter Serov in Rome, where the Russian Ballet was giving performances at the Costanzi Theatre during the International Exhibition; and the score was finished there on 26 May. As soon as the music had been played over to Diaghilev and Benois, the ballet was put into rehearsal in the theatre restaurant.

The first performance of *Petrushka* took place at the Théâtre du Châtelet, Paris, on 13 June 1911; and the ballet proved just as popular with the public and critics as *The Firebird* had been the previous year. Nijinsky's performance as Petrushka was outstanding. In his *Chronicle*, Stravinsky paid homage to the 'perfection with which he became the very incarnation of this character'; and it is said that Sarah Bernhardt's comment on seeing him was 'J'ai peur, j'ai peur, car je vois l'acteur le plus grand du monde'. This further triumph consolidated Stravinsky's reputation in France as one of the most advanced young composers of the day; and from his personal point of view, this success was important for two special reasons. In the first place, he felt that whereas with *The Firebird* he had had to accept a scenario devised by Fokine and others in which he was not personally involved, with *Petrushka* he had been able to exercise an important measure of control through all the various planning stages of the ballet so that he could almost unreservedly approve the final product. Secondly, he found that he liked the sound of his music. While the score of *The Firebird* had merely been an attempt – and a very successful one at that – to outshine Rimsky-Korsakov at his own game of colourful instrumentation, *Petrushka* was the first score to reveal Stravinsky's idiosyncratic way of handling an orchestra. As he said in *Expositions*, the success of the ballet 'was good for me in that it gave me the absolute conviction of my ear just as I was about to begin *The Rite of Spring*'.

Petrushka was the first work of his to be published by the Russischer Musik Verlag, the new music publishing house which Serge Koussevitzky had just founded with the help of his wife, Natalie, the daughter of a wealthy Moscow merchant. The composers Koussevitzky took on were to be partners in this enterprise 'where profits were divided in such a way as to bring the composer a share of royalties far more generous than those of any other music publishing house of its time'.[1] Stravinsky's active co-operation with this firm was to last for about a quarter of a century.

The Russian Ballet season at the Théâtre du Châtelet that spring was a brief one (no longer than a fortnight), for the company had to be in London shortly after mid-June to take part in the Coronation Gala (26 June) at the Royal Opera House, Covent Garden. This was the company's first visit to England; but as Diaghilev in an excess of caution had decided to exclude *The Firebird* and *Petrushka* from the repertory on the ground that these novelties were likely to overtax the receptivity of the London public, there was no need for Stravinsky to accompany the dancers and he returned to Ustilug in July, determined to get down to the composition of his pagan rite symphony.

His first move was to work out the scenario of the new work with Roerich, who was staying with the Princess Tenisheva at her country estate near Smolensk. He journeyed there from Ustilug via Brest-Litovsk; and after a few days' collaboration, the plan of action and the titles of the various movements were agreed on. Back in Ustilug, he started the composition of *The Rite of Spring* with the Auguries of Spring movement. During the summer months, he also found time to set some poems by the symbolist poet Konstantin Balmont, in the form of two songs for high voice and piano, and a cantata for male voice choir and orchestra (*Zvezdoliki*). Work on *The Rite of Spring* continued until the autumn and was not even broken by the family removal from Ustilug to Clarens ('Les Tilleuls'). By Christmas the whole of Part One had been completed, including the pastoral introduction which was written last.

All this was done on the assumption that the new work would be produced by the Russian Ballet during its 1912 Paris season: but various things occurred to upset this idea.

In the first place, as the Russian Ballet was now on a permanent footing, Diaghilev was anxious to secure engagements for his dancers throughout the year; and an important part of his plans for the 1911/12 season had been to take the company to St. Petersburg where they were to appear at the Narodny Dom during December and January, the other big theatres not being available.

---

[1] Nicolas Nabokov, *Old Friends and New Music*. London, Hamish Hamilton, 1951.

1. The Man

Unfortunately the Narodny Dom was burned to the ground just before they were due to set out for Russia; and this seriously dislocated the company's schedule, because it meant that other engagements would have to be made at short notice. In the event, a tour of Berlin, Dresden, Vienna and Budapest was negotiated; but this change of plan upset the rehearsal schedule. Fokine was fully occupied with the choreography of three new ballets – *Le Dieu Bleu*, *Thamar*, and *Daphnis and Chloe* – but even had he been free, Diaghilev had other ideas for *The Rite of Spring*. He was anxious to give Nijinsky a chance to win his spurs as a choreographer and had decided that Stravinsky's new ballet should be entrusted to him. Meanwhile Nijinsky had been given Debussy's *L'Après-midi d'un faune* as a trial choreographic essay; but although this ballet lasted only nine minutes, his progress was so slow that it took 120 rehearsals before the work was ready. For these reasons Diaghilev found himself compelled to put off the première of *The Rite;* and as his heart was set on producing the new ballet during one of his company's summer seasons in Paris, this meant a year's postponement from 1912 to 1913.

Stravinsky was naturally disappointed; but at least this change of timetable meant that he need not hurry with the orchestration. In May he left Switzerland to attend the Russian Ballet season in Paris, in the course of which he saw the first performances of *L'Après-midi d'un faune* and *Daphnis and Chloe*. The latter ballet he praised unreservedly: but it is a little difficult to know exactly what he thought of *L'Après-midi*. It will be recalled that part of the first-night audience was scandalised by the Faun's simulated act of sexual penetration with the Nymph's abandoned scarf. In his *Chronicle* Stravinsky says that at the date of writing that book (i.e., 1935), the esthetics and the whole spirit of that kind of scenic display seemed so stale that he had not the least desire to discuss them further. But a quarter of a century later he recalled in his *Memories* that 'Nijinsky's performance was such marvellously concentrated art that only a fool could have been shocked by it – but then, I adored the ballet myself'.

The Paris season of the Russian Ballet was a brief one. It opened at the Théâtre du Châtelet on 13 May and closed after sixteen performances. The company then went on to the Royal Opera House, Covent Garden, London. Diaghilev had decided that the time had now come for him to introduce one of Stravinsky's ballets to an English audience; and *The Firebird* accordingly had its London première on 18 June. This was the occasion of Stravinsky's first visit to London. Among the people he met that summer were Queen Alexandra, to whom he was presented in her box at Covent Garden after one of the *Firebird* performances, Thomas Beecham the conductor, and Edwin Evans the music critic. Some years later the latter recalled that *The Rite of Spring* 'was practically complete, though partly in pencil' at the time of this London visit.[1]

After Paris and London he returned to Ustilug for the summer; but no

---

[1] Edwin Evans, *Stravinsky: 'The Fire-Bird' and 'Petrushka'*. Oxford University Press, 1933.

The Composer and his Patron (1909 – 1914)

sooner had he settled down than an invitation arrived from Diaghilev to join him at Bayreuth for a performance of *Parsifal*. Wagner's music had been an early love of his, and as a teenager he had acquainted himself with most of the music dramas from their piano reductions and defended them from the disapproval of his piano teacher, Mlle. Kashperova. He had even imitated Wagner's idiom in certain passages of his *Faun and Shepherdess* song cycle and the *Scherzo Fantastique*. But now *Parsifal*, which hitherto he had never seen on the stage,[1] was revealed as a long-winded bore; and he particularly resented the arrogant assumption that such an inflation of Celtic mythology in terms of music drama was to be regarded as the equivalent of a solemn piece of Christian ritual. After this visit to Bayreuth, his growing distrust and hatred of the Wagnerian conception of music drama lay fallow for a number of years, but finally found remarkably trenchant expression in his Harvard lectures on the *Poetics of Music* (1939/40).

In accordance with their usual custom, Stravinsky and his family moved from Ustilug to Clarens in the early autumn of 1912, where they stayed at the Hôtel du Châtelard with Ludmila Beliankin (Stravinsky's sister-in-law) and her husband. Stravinsky was still busy with the composition of the final movement of *The Rite of Spring;* and one of the last sketches[2] is dated 17 November. Three days later, he arrived at the Adlon Hotel, Berlin, to join Diaghilev for the Russian Ballet season at the Kroll Theater. The first night, when *Cléopâtre* and *Petrushka* were included in the bill, was attended by the Kaiser who was particularly impressed by the former ballet.

During this visit, he met Arnold Schoenberg several times. Apparently Schoenberg and his wife joined Stravinsky and Diaghilev in the theatre for one of the performances of *Petrushka*; and on Sunday 8 December Stravinsky attended the fourth performance of Schoenberg's *Pierrot Lunaire* in the Choralion-saal[3] and was favourably impressed by the work. Eduard Steuermann, who was the pianist in those *Pierrot Lunaire* performances, remembers a dinner party at Schoenberg's house in Zehlendorf when Stravinsky also met Alban Berg and Anton Webern; but writing in 1963, Stravinsky admitted he had forgotten this occasion – his 'First and Last Supper with the hypostatic trinity of twentieth century music' (*Dia*).

Shortly after this Berlin visit, Stravinsky was in London, and in the course of an interview with the press[4] he made a quick survey of the contemporary music field, praising the French contemporary composers, Debussy, Ravel and Florent Schmitt, and stigmatising Russian musical life as stagnant. Turning to Central Europe, he said: 'And what of Austria? The Viennese

---

[1] The production of *Parsifal* was confined to Bayreuth until thirty years after the composer's death (viz., 1913).
[2] The big percussion ostinato at figure 174 *et seq.*
[3] The first performance had taken place on 16 October 1912.
[4] From *The Daily Mail*, 13 February 1913.

are barbarians. Their orchestral musicians could not play my *Petrushka*. They hardly know Debussy there, and they chased Schoenberg away to Berlin. Now Schoenberg is one of the greatest creative spirits of our era.'

The friendship between the two composers, which had started so auspiciously, failed to mature; and after this Berlin encounter they never met again as friends. It is true that in 1919 Schoenberg wrote a cordial letter about the possibility of including some of Stravinsky's chamber music in the concerts of the Viennese 'Society for Private Performances', and in 1920 or 1921 Stravinsky attended a further performance of *Pierrot Lunaire* (conducted by Darius Milhaud) in Paris. But on his first visit to America early in 1925, he gave an interview to S. Roerig, in the course of which he referred to so-called 'modern music', explaining that he wrote neither modern music nor music for the future – he wrote only for today – and going on to say that he could point to composers who spent their whole time in trying to discover the music of the future, a pursuit he described as presumptuous and possibly insincere. Although he named no names and later referred to experiments in quarter-tone music, Schoenberg was undoubtedly the composer he had in mind; and it is hardly surprising that Schoenberg recognised the reference to himself and construed it as an unfriendly act. There are two unpublished papers in Schoenberg's literary legacy referring to this, viz., 'Comment on a subjoined newspaper article: *Igor Stravinsky on his music*, a conversation with N. [*sic*] Roerig' and 'The Restaurant Owner' (dated 24.7.26) attacking a statement by Stravinsky 'who makes fun of musicians who (while he wants only to compose the *music of the present*) are striving to write the *music of the future*'.[1] In view of this it was understandable, but unfortunate, that when in 1925 both composers were in Venice for the I.S.C.M. Festival, neither of them made the slightest attempt to meet the other. Stravinsky did not hear the performance of the *Serenade* (op. 24), which Schoenberg conducted on 7 September; nor did Schoenberg hear Stravinsky play his *Piano Sonata* the following day. Stravinsky's adoption of a neo-classical idiom for his 'music of the present' triggered off a squib of Schoenberg's, a poem called 'Der neue Klassizismus' that he set in 1925/26 as the third of his *Three Satires* for mixed chorus (op. 28); and the Russian composer can hardly have relished the reference to himself as 'der kleine Modernsky'.[2]

Early in 1928, Schoenberg attended a performance of *Oedipus Rex* at the Kroll-oper, Berlin – 'feeling *abgekühlt*', according to Stravinsky (*Dia*) – and there is an unpublished manuscript note on the opera (dated 24 February 1928)[3] in Schoenberg's literary legacy.

It is interesting to find that another juxtaposition of works by Stravinsky

---

[1] Numbered II.D.104 and II.D.60 respectively in Josef Rufer's *The Works of Arnold Schoenberg*. London, Faber, 1962.
[2] See page 320.
[3] Numbered II.D.55 in Josef Rufer's *The Works of Arnold Schoenberg*.

and Schoenberg occurred at the Venice Festival of 1937, which Casella directed. On that occasion *The Card Party* ballet score of Stravinsky's and Schoenberg's *Suite* op. 29 were performed on consecutive days. Stravinsky was present at both performances: Schoenberg was not. Peter Stadlen, who conducted the Vienna Ensemble from the piano in the Schoenberg *Suite*, recalls that after the performance, which scandalised the audience, Stravinsky came into the Green Room and said: 'I didn't know that one could already perform this music so well. As for the audience, they don't seem to have liked it; but perhaps this music was not written to please.'

By the end of the Second World War, when the two composers had become near neighbours in Hollywood, their relationship seemed to have reached a state of armed neutrality. In 1945 they met again for the first time in nearly a third of a century. The occasion was the death of Franz Werfel. As Stravinsky stood in a mortuary mourning his departed friend, he was confronted 'with the angry, tortured, burning face of Arnold Schoenberg' (*Exp*).

The audition of *Pierrot Lunaire* in Berlin in 1912 seems to have been a traumatic experience so far as Stravinsky was concerned; and no other work of Schoenberg's ever made so deep an impression. At various stages of his career, he has referred to it in varying terms. In 1935 he wrote rather grudgingly in his *Chronicle*:

> I did not feel the slightest enthusiasm about the esthetics of the work, which appeared to me to be a retrogression to the out-of-date Beardsley cult. But, on the other hand, I consider that the merits of the instrumentation are beyond dispute.

In 1959, eight years after Schoenberg's death his comments were more explicit, his tone more generous.

> The instrumental substance of *Pierrot Lunaire* impressed me immensely. And by saying 'instrumental' music I mean not simply the instrumentation of this music but the whole contrapuntal and polyphonic structure of this brilliant instrumental masterpiece (*Con*).

By 1963, his praise had become almost lyrical.

> The real wealth of *Pierrot* – sound and substance, for *Pierrot* is the solar plexus as well as the mind of early twentieth-century music – were beyond me as they were beyond all of us at that time, and when Boulez wrote that I had understood it *d'une façon impressioniste*, he was not kind but correct. I *was* aware, nevertheless, that this was the most prescient confrontation in my life . . . (*Dia*).

And by 1964 he was almost back to where he had stood in 1913, for he was prepared to recognise in Schoenberg 'the conscience-mind of the era'.[1]

---

[1] Review of Schoenberg's *Letters* in *The Observer*, 18 October 1964.

1. The Man

After Berlin and the meeting with Schoenberg, he returned to Clarens for a few days – just long enough to finish his set of *Three Japanese Lyrics* for soprano and chamber orchestra. He then rejoined the Russian Ballet in Hungary and Austria. His ballets met with considerable success in Budapest; but in Vienna, *Petrushka* ran into trouble with the orchestra – 'schmutzige Musik' ('dirty music') they called it at rehearsal and did their best to sabotage the actual performances.

All this time, rehearsals of *The Rite of Spring* were in full swing;[1] and he attended them, whenever he had a chance. He was particularly alarmed by Nijinsky's ignorance of the rudiments of music; and although he did his best to help him, there is no doubt that the rhythmic and metrical complications of the score presented the choreographer with a very difficult task. In particular, he found himself exasperated by Nijinsky's tendency to complicate the dancers' steps with all sorts of unnecessary details, thereby unconsciously slowing down the tempo of the music. In fairness to Nijinsky, however, it must be said that he was feeling his way towards a new kind of ballet technique; and in order to help him, Diaghilev had engaged Marie Rambert, an expert in eurhythmics from the Jacques Dalcroze School at Hellerau near Dresden. Nijinsky considered the subject of *The Rite* gave him a perfect excuse for reversing the classical positions so that the dancers' movements would be made *en dedans* instead of *en dehors*; but this break with tradition aroused great hostility among the dancers, and the atmosphere of the rehearsals became increasingly stormy and quarrelsome. The effect on the choreographer was unfortunate. 'Seeing he was losing prestige with the company, but being strongly supported by Diaghilev, he became presumptuous, capricious, and unmanageable. Not unnaturally this led to a number of painful scenes, which made the work of rehearsal no easier' (*Chr*).

After Vienna, the Russian Ballet returned to London some weeks before its winter season was due to open at Covent Garden; and Thomas Beecham put the Aldwych Theatre at their disposal so that rehearsals of *The Rite* could continue without interruption. The opening programme (4 February 1913) of the fortnight's season at the Royal Opera House included the first performance in England of *Petrushka*. Cyril Beaumont, who was present that evening wrote:[2] 'I well remember the startled expressions on the faces of the audience, and my own surprise, at the first hearing of Stravinsky's music, so wonderfully expressive of the raucous sounds and bustling movements of a fair, but which then sounded incredibly daring and uncouth to ears attuned to the melodies of classic composers'. After London the company went on to Monte Carlo, where Nijinsky put the finishing touches to *The Rite* and started on his choreography for the new Debussy ballet, *Jeux*.

---

[1] They had started in Berlin on 13 December 1912.
[2] Cyril Beaumont, *The Diaghilev Ballet in London*. London, Putnam 1940.

The Composer and his Patron (1909 – 1914)

Stravinsky could not remain with the company throughout the winter, as he had various jobs to do at Clarens. First of all he had to complete the orchestral score of *The Rite*; and this was finally achieved in March. Then Diaghilev had invited him to prepare a new version of Mussorgsky's *Khovanshchina* for production in Paris that summer. Mussorgsky had never completed the score of this opera himself; and a performing edition had been made by Rimsky-Korsakov. Diaghilev wanted Stravinsky to undertake the orchestration of such parts as had not been orchestrated by Mussorgsky, and to compose a chorus for the finale, where Mussorgsky had merely indicated the main theme. When Stravinsky realised how much work there was to be done, and fearing lest he could not be ready in time, he suggested the task should be shared with Ravel. Diaghilev readily agreed; and Ravel accordingly joined Stravinsky in Clarens during March and April, staying at the Hôtel des Crêtes.[1] During their collaboration, Stravinsky showed Ravel his *Three Japanese Lyrics*, the second and third of which had been composed immediately after his visit to Berlin the previous autumn; and Ravel composed and played to Stravinsky the first two of his *Trois Poèmes de Mallarmé*.

This year the Russian Ballet was to inaugurate the opening of the newly built Théâtre des Champs-Elysées in Paris. The new Debussy-Nijinsky ballet *Jeux* was included in the programme of the first night of the season (15 May 1913) when it was conducted by Pierre Monteux; but its choreography did not please, and the public received it coolly. A week later *Boris Godunov* was performed, with Shaliapin in the title role and superb scenery and costumes brought from St. Petersburg. This scored a great success. On 29 May came the first performance of *The Rite of Spring*. As the new ballet's choreography consisted almost entirely of dance ensembles, Diaghilev had decided to make up the rest of the programme by displaying his star dancers – Karsavina, Nijinsky, Bolm – in *Les Sylphides*, *The Spectre of the Rose*, and the Polovtsian Dances from *Prince Igor*, hoping thereby to ensure the success of the evening as a whole. As Grigoriev said,[2] 'he clearly had misgiving about the reception of Stravinsky's music and warned us that there might be a demonstration against it. He entreated the dancers, if so, to keep calm and carry on, and asked Monteux on no account to let the orchestra cease playing. "Whatever happens," he said, "the ballet must be performed to the end." '

His fears were well founded. Shortly after the orchestral introduction had started, mild protests against the music could be heard from part of the audience. The expressions of indignation were renewed when the curtain rose on the dancers – a group of 'knock-kneed and long-braided Lolitas jumping up and down' (*Exp*) – and the uproar redoubled as another section of the audience started to retaliate against the demonstrators by appealing for order.

---

[1] See Ravel's correspondence with Stravinsky in Appendix B.
[2] In *The Diaghilev Ballet 1909–1929*. London, Constable, 1953.

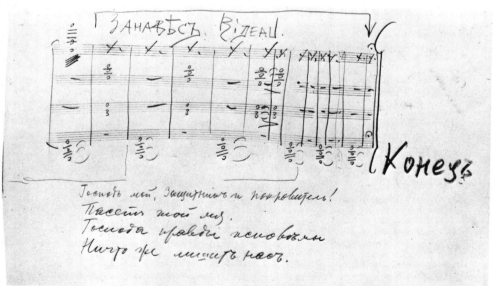

Khovanshchina: two pages from a sketch book showing Stravinsky's version of the finale of Mussorgsky's opera (1913)

The Composer and his Patron (1909 – 1914)

The hubbub became so deafening – and this seems incredible, but is vouched for by nearly every eye- and ear-witness – that scarcely a note of the music could be heard.

Shortly after the outbreak of this commotion, Stravinsky left the auditorium in a fury and went backstage, where he found Nijinsky standing on a chair in the wings and counting out loud to help the dancers keep time. Diaghilev, who was also in the wings, was extremely agitated, and when the first part of the ballet ended, he put the house lights up in the auditorium during the playing of the introduction of part two, 'so that the police, who had been called in, could pick out and eject some of the worst offenders. But no sooner were the lights lowered again for the second scene than pandemonium burst out afresh, and then continued till the ballet came to an end'.[1] The only persons who seem to have been comparatively unmoved by the behaviour of the audience were the dancers, who after so many months of rehearsing were now movement-perfect and gave a remarkably good performance.

At the end of the evening, everyone was exhausted. Jean Cocteau, who was in the audience, wrote a rather romantic account[2] of how at two o'clock in the morning Stravinsky, Diaghilev, Nijinsky and himself piled into a cab and were driven to the Bois de Boulogne in search of fresh air and quiet. But Stravinsky's recollection is that he and Diaghilev and Nijinsky were 'excited, angry, disgusted and . . . happy' and that Diaghilev's only comment was 'Exactly what I wanted' (*Con*).

The scandal of the first night was not repeated at subsequent performances; and *Khovanshchina* which was produced a week later (5 June), with Emile Cooper as conductor and Shaliapin in the cast, achieved an outstanding success with the public. But by then Stravinsky was indifferent to the fate of both works, because a few days after the première of *The Rite* he had fallen ill with typhoid fever and had been sent to a nursing home in Neuilly. To begin with, Diaghilev called on him daily; but so strong was his fear of contagion that he never entered the sick-room. Other visitors included Debussy, Ravel, de Falla, Florent Schmitt, Maurice Delage, Casella, and the critic M. D. Calvocoressi, the author of monographs on Mussorgsky and Glinka.

This six-weeks illness meant that Stravinsky was unable to attend the Russian Ballet season in London, which was held at the Theatre Royal, Drury Lane, where *The Rite of Spring* had its London première on 11 July. In an access of caution, Diaghilev had arranged for Edwin Evans to appear in front of the curtain immediately before the performance to explain the music and intention of the new ballet; 'but the audience, excited by the atmosphere of a first night and all eagerness to see *The Rite* for themselves, became restive, and Evans was forced to curtail his lecture'.[3] The performance seems to have

---

[1] S. L. Grigoriev, *op. cit.*
[2] Appendix to *Le Coq et l'Arlequin* as reprinted in *Le Rappel à l'Ordre*. Paris, Stock, 1926.
[3] Cyril Beaumont, *The Diaghilev Ballet in London*.

been an excellent one; and Marie Piltz as the Chosen Maiden scored a great triumph in her final dance, which was frequently interrupted by bursts of frenzied applause. She and the conductor, Monteux, were called before the curtain and given a great reception; but the audience's attitude to the ballet as a whole was ambivalent. Those 'who had gone to the theatre expecting to be charmed with light and graceful movements, and, instead, found themselves caught up in a maelstrom of rhythm, immensely vital and as dominating, as remorseless, and as irritating to the nervous system as the continuous thudding of a savage's tom-tom, bitterly resented Nijinsky's new production. . . . Others, none the less startled by this attempt to reproduce in terms of choreography the stark mood of primitive man, appreciated the sincerity of both composer and choreographer and applauded with fervour. It would be a fair estimate to say that the audience were about equally divided in their dislike and their appreciation'.[1]

The powerful originality of *The Rite of Spring* represented an important personal victory gained by Stravinsky over the inhibitions of his miserable childhood. For years he had tried to revolt from the stultifying restrictions of his family life; and now that he had succeeded in doing so in terms of artistic expression, it was particularly appropriate that the image that precipitated his release should have been that of spring – 'the violent Russian spring that seemed to begin in an hour and was like the whole world cracking', and which, by his own admission,[2] was the most wonderful event of every year of his childhood.

(A marginal comment on this personal victory of his is provided by the violinist, Samuel Dushkin, who met Stravinsky's mother in the 1930's when she was living with her son's household in France. Dushkin recalls how she was persuaded to attend a special concert in Paris to commemorate the twenty-fifth anniversary of *The Rite of Spring*, which she had never heard before except on gramophone records. When Mrs. Dushkin asked whether she was thrilled at the prospect of hearing a live performance of her son's masterpiece in a concert hall, she received the following reply: 'Je pense que ça ne sera pas de la musique pour moi.' Mrs. Dushkin said, 'J'espère que vous ne sifflerez pas'; to which old Mrs. Stravinsky replied 'Non, parce que je ne sais pas siffler'.[3])

Diaghilev had negotiated a South American tour for the Russian Ballet after its London season; and on 15 August the dancers embarked from Southampton on the *Avon*. Twelve members of the company remained behind, in addition to Diaghilev himself, who had an exaggerated dislike of the sea. Those who were on the liner included Nijinsky and a new young Hungarian

---

[1] Cyril Beaumont, *op. cit.*
[2] In *Memories*.
[3] 'I don't think it will be my sort of music.' – 'I hope you won't whistle.' – 'No, because I don't know how to.' From Dushkin's article 'Working with Stravinsky' in *Stravinsky*, edited by Edwin Corle. New York, Duell, Sloan & Pearce, 1949.

dancer called Romola Pulsky, with whom Nijinsky spent a considerable amount of time; and after about a fortnight, to everyone's astonishment, their engagement was announced, the wedding taking place in Buenos Aires only two days after the company's disembarkation. This event was bound to prove a great shock to Diaghilev, whose relations with Nijinsky during the last few years had been particularly intimate; and it happened that Stravinsky was with him in the Montreux Palace Hotel when the news arrived. 'I watched him,' says Stravinsky in his *Memories*, 'turn into a madman who begged me and my wife not to leave him alone.'

After his recovery from typhoid fever, Stravinsky returned to Ustilug for a brief period. As he did not feel strong enough to undertake any major work of composition, he looked out some tunes of his that were about seven years old and fitted them to Russian popular texts. These *Three Little Songs*, subtitled 'Recollections of my Childhood', were dedicated to his three children. His health became the subject of gossip in France, and early in October *Comoedia* announced that it had heard on good authority that he had been removed to a nursing home in St. Petersburg. His numerous friends in Paris were alarmed; but fortunately the rumour was false.

Earlier that year he had received a letter from the recently founded Free Theatre of Moscow asking him to complete his opera *The Nightingale* for production there the following year. He found this request rather embarrassing despite the large commission fee involved, for the orchestral score of Act I had been completed in 1909 (before *The Firebird*), but the other two acts were as yet untouched. To begin with, he put up a counter-suggestion that Act I should be presented on its own as an independent lyrical scene; but the theatre directors refused, and he found himself faced with the necessity of completing the opera after an interval of four years or more.

On his way from Ustilug to Switzerland, he broke his journey at Warsaw in order to visit Mitusov and discuss with him various details concerning the libretto; and back in Clarens, he started to compose the opening of Act II. From the beginning, it seems to have been intended that Benois, who was then acting as consultant to the Moscow Arts Theatre, should be responsible for the scenery and costumes; and Stravinsky was in correspondence with him throughout the autumn and winter.

Early in the New Year, his wife fell ill with tuberculosis and entered a sanatorium at Leysin, where their fourth child (and second daughter), Maria Milena, was born. The family moved from Clarens to the Grand Hotel, Leysin, in order to be near her; and here Stravinsky was visited by Cocteau, who had just completed an album of drawings called *Le Potomak* which he dedicated to Stravinsky, and was now anxious to interest the composer in an idea he had for a new ballet to be entitled *David*. The scene was to be a fair; and outside one of the booths an acrobat was to parade up and down, while a clown vaunted the prowess of David through a megaphone and tried to entice the public to see the show inside.

Shortly after Cocteau had left, Diaghilev arrived from Russia. First of all, he wanted to discourage the *David* project. (This in fact proved abortive, though three years later Cocteau was to use a similar idea as the basis for his ballet *Parade*, which Diaghilev mounted with music by Erik Satie and scenery and costumes by Pablo Picasso.) And then, having recently heard that the Moscow Free Theatre enterprise was bankrupt and would be unable to produce *The Nightingale* as originally planned, he was anxious to ask if the Russian Ballet might present it instead during the company's summer seasons in Paris and London. Stravinsky agreed and shortly afterwards accompanied Diaghilev to Paris, where he played through the score, as far as he had composed it, to a group of friends including Ravel and Jacques Rivière, the editor of the *Nouvelle Revue Française*. The discrepancy in idiom between Act I and the rest of the opera must have been quite striking; and at some point or other Diaghilev tried to persuade him to revise the first Act in order to achieve a greater effect of unity.[1] But Stravinsky refused.

During this winter there were several important concerts where his music was performed. In the first place, Koussevitzky included *The Rite of Spring* in the programmes of his concerts in Moscow and St. Petersburg. Benois, who was present at the Moscow concert in February, was deeply impressed, though slightly bewildered, by the new work. He reported to Stravinsky that some of the audience applauded in advance 'in defiance of Paris', and that at the end of the first part only about a hundred persons walked out adding that he found it a consolation that 'the Rimsky-Korsakov clan hissed it violently'.[2] In Paris, Monteux conducted the same score at a concert at the Casino de Paris in April, which turned into a kind of rehabilitation ceremony. In *Expositions*, Stravinsky wrote:

> At the end of the Danse sacrale the entire audience jumped to its feet and cheered. I came on stage and hugged Monteux, who was a river of perspiration; it was the saltiest hug of my life. A crowd swept backstage. I was hoisted to anonymous shoulders and carried into the street and up to the Place de la Trinité.

Earlier that month he had attended a performance of his *Symphony in E flat* conducted by Ernest Ansermet at Montreux on 2 April. Ansermet, who was his junior by one year, had formerly been professor of mathematics at Lausanne University; but his innate interest in music and an intensive study of counterpoint had led him to decide to take up music as a career, and early in 1914 he succeeded M. de Lacerda as conductor of the Montreux Kursaal Orchestra. He

---

[1] Mentioned by A. Benois in *Reminiscences of the Russian Ballet*. London, Putnam, 1941.
[2] See the letter from Benois dated 14–17 February 1914 reprinted in Stravinsky's *Memories*.

already knew Stravinsky at this date – in fact, they had been neighbours at Clarens, for Ansermet's house 'La Pervenche' was next door to the *pension* 'Les Tilleuls', and they had also met at the house of the French composer, Henri Duparc, who was then living in retirement near Clarens. During the rehearsal for this particular concert at Montreux, Ansermet handed the baton to Stravinsky and persuaded him to take the orchestra through his early Symphony. This was Stravinsky's first attempt at conducting.

Diaghilev had succeeded not only in getting Sir Joseph Beecham[1] to meet the whole cost of the production of *The Nightingale* which was to be included in the Russian Ballet's summer season at the Theatre Royal, Drury Lane, but also in reserving the première for his Paris season at the Opera House, where it was given on May 26. The opera provoked no scandal or incident; but neither did it make any great impression on the public. In fact, far greater interest and enthusiasm were aroused by one of the other novelties of the season – the special ballet arrangement of Rimsky-Korsakov's *The Golden Cockerel* which Fokine had made as the result of a suggestion by Benois. Andrei Rimsky-Korsakov came to Paris from St. Petersburg specially for this; and Gury Stravinsky came specially for *The Nightingale*. This was the last time the two brothers met.

Immediately after his trip to Paris, Stravinsky returned to Switzerland and moved his family to a '*bois de Mélèze*' châlet near Salvan in the Valais. He was working on the *Pribaoutki* songs and three short pieces for string quartet which he decided to dedicate to Ansermet. He ran over to London for the opening performances of *The Nightingale* at Drury Lane (18 June); and it was there that the young Osbert Sitwell first saw him appear on the stage:

> At the end of the performance I was excited to see the Russian composer, the master of the epoch, walk before the curtain. Slight of frame, pale, about thirty years of age, with an air both worldly and abstracted, and a little angry, he bowed back with solemnity to the clustered, nodding tiaras and the white kid gloves that applauded him sufficiently to be polite . . .[2]

During this London visit, he happened to be in a taxi with Edwin Evans one Sunday afternoon, when the two of them came upon St. Paul's just as the bells were pealing. According to Evans,[3] 'Stravinsky stopped the cab and listened intently to the "changes", taking occasional notes on a back of an envelope. He was most enthusiastic about the inexhaustible variety of the sequences in which he claimed to hear the most wonderful music.' And this moment may well have had a seminal influence on the conception of his next major work — a cantata celebrating Russian wedding customs. In order to

---

[1] Thomas Beecham's father.
[2] Osbert Sitwell, *Great Morning*. London, Macmillan, 1948.
[3] Edwin Evans, *Music and the Dance*. London, Herbert Jenkins, n.d. [1948].

construct a libretto for this score, he realised that he needed to obtain a copy of Kireievsky's collection of Russian folk poetry. So shortly after his return to Switzerland he took train to Ustilug and went on from there to Warsaw and Kiev where he found the volume he wanted. On his way back, through Warsaw, Berlin and Basel, he noticed the political atmosphere was becoming very tense; and a few days after his return to Salvan, war was declared.

To begin with, most people believed the conflict was unlikely to last long and thought life would continue on much the same lines as before; but in reality the outbreak of hostilities marked the end of an epoch.

In Stravinsky's case, he had been closely attached to Diaghilev and the Russian Ballet for nearly five years. In that period, all his major works had been produced in Paris and London, and his two most popular ballets (*The Firebird* and *Petrushka*) had been played in many other countries too. It was understood that his next work (the Wedding cantata) would be offered to the Russian Ballet as usual. The financing of the company was always something of a conjuring trick; and it should not be thought that the financial returns to Stravinsky, whether from commission fees or performing rights, were necessarily on a lavish scale. But it looks as if Diaghilev was generous in meeting his expenses when he joined the company during its Paris or London seasons or when on tour; and its brilliant artistic successes during those pre-war years certainly boosted Stravinsky's reputation like a rocket. By 1914 his name was familiar all over Europe as one of the most exciting and gifted of the younger generation of composers.

For all this, he owed a big personal debt to Diaghilev; and on the whole the relationship between patron and composer was still a friendly one. But the war was to prove a difficult testing time.

50

4. The Russian Exile in Switzerland (1914 - 1920)

To begin with, there was no question of exile. For the last four years, Stravinsky and his family had spent the greater part of the autumn and winter months in Switzerland, returning to Russia for the summer: and Switzerland was like a second home to them. Shortly after the outbreak of war, they came down from their mountain chalet in Salvan to Clarens, where they rented Ansermet's house 'La Pervenche' for part of the winter. Stravinsky had been exempted from military service because of his health: so there was no immediate need for him to go back to Russia. His mother, however, was anxious to return. There were not many routes remaining open; but ultimately she managed to make the journey by boat from Brindisi to Odessa. Stravinsky was short of ready cash; and he recalls how at that moment he unexpectedly received 2,500 Swiss francs from Thomas Beecham, who was afraid he might be in financial difficulties because of his growing isolation from Russia. 'The money came like manna,' he says,[1] 'and it paid my mother's passage.' At the same time he arranged for Bertha, his old nurse and 'second mother', to leave Russia and join his family in Switzerland.

His first preoccupation during the early months of the war was to steep himself in the various collections of Russian folk poetry and popular stories that he had brought out of Russia.[2] For musical purposes, he ignored differences of region and period, perfecting a kind of eclectic pan-Russian 'dialect'. He was attracted, not so much by the stories themselves, their images and metaphors, as by the sequence of words and syllables, and their varied cadences, 'which produce an effect on one's sensibility very closely akin to that of music' (*Chr*). Synthetic texts of this kind were prepared for *The Wedding* and *Reynard*, and also for various groups of songs – the *Pribaoutki*, the *Cat's Cradle Songs*, the *Three Tales for Children*, the *Four Russian Peasant Songs* called 'Saucers', and the *Four Russian Songs*. All these works were composed in Switzerland during the next few years.

---

[1] In 'Conductors: Good, Bad and Unspeakable', *The Observer*, 24 June 1962.

[2] In addition to Peter Kireievsky's *Sobrannyie Piésni* (10 vol., Moscow, 1868–74) which he had found in Kiev in July 1914, he had access to Sakharov's collection and Dal's Dictionary of Russian Phrases, both of which he had borrowed from his father's library. In his collection of manuscripts, under the title *Chants Georgiens*, there is a collection of sixteen songs that he copied out in 1915 from a Russian anthology (Georgia and Caucasus).

1. The Man

Despite the temporary disbanding of the Russian Ballet – (the original intention had been that the dancers should reassemble in Berlin on 1 October for their autumn season) – Diaghilev, who had gone to Italy, was trying to negotiate a contract for the company to visit North America. The two friends spent a fortnight together in Florence that autumn, discussing their difficulties and trying to console each other. As for new works, Diaghilev was looking to Stravinsky, not only for the score of *The Wedding*, but also for music for a new ballet he was planning with Mestrović called *Liturgie*, to be based on the Mass. This he intended to present with a profusion of ikons and religious vestments; and his idea was that it should be danced without music, but that there should be musical interludes. Stravinsky resisted this proposal, however, partly because he disapproved of the idea of presenting the Mass as a ballet spectacle, and partly because Diaghilev wanted him to do both works for the price that had originally been agreed for *The Wedding* alone (*Mem*).

During the winter Stravinsky thought it would suit his wife's health if he took her to Château d'Oex for the mountain air; and there they spent about two months at the Hotel Victoria. At the end of January (1915) he had to return to Clarens to discuss his responsibility as lessee of 'La Pervenche' for decorations and repairs, and while descending to Montreux by train he found himself in the same compartment as two drunken Vaudois revellers who between them roared out an extraordinary syncopated song, which he noted down and later made good use of in the last scene of *The Wedding*.[1]

A few days later, he undertook another trip to Italy, joining Diaghilev in Rome, and arriving in time to attend the first Italian concert performance at the Augusteo of *Petrushka* conducted by Casella (14 February). He had brought with him a new composition, a little piece for piano duet with easy left hand called Polka, and in due course persuaded Diaghilev, who was an amateur of four-handed piano music, to play the left-hand part with him, explaining that in composing it he had thought of his friend 'as a circus ring-master in evening dress and top-hat, cracking his whip and urging on a rider' (*Chr*). The impresario was at first rather taken back and uncertain whether he ought to be offended or not; but finally he saw the humourous side of it and enjoyed the joke.[2]

It was on this visit that Stravinsky met Gerald Tyrwhitt, who later became Lord Berners, and Serge Prokofiev, who had just arrived from Russia. He also discussed with Diaghilev and Casella the problem of publication as it affected

---

[1] See page 255.

[2] There are discrepancies between the two accounts of this incident given in the *Chronicle* and in the *Dialogues*. The *Chronicle* says that Stravinsky took all three *Easy Pieces for Piano Duet* (*March*, *Waltz*, and *Polka*) with him to Rome: the *Dialogues* state categorically that he took only one (the Polka) and that the March and Waltz were added after his return to Switzerland. The *Chronicle* implies that Diaghilev played through all three pieces with Stravinsky in Rome: the *Dialogues* state that Stravinsky played the Polka only to Diaghilev and Casella in a hotel room in Milan.

'Svadebka': a page of the MS full score of an early discarded version of *Svadebka* (*Les Noces*) for large orchestra

his music. Since 1912, the Russischer Musikverlag, had been his regular publisher; but as its headquarters were in Germany (Berlin and Leipzig), with only branches or agencies in Russia and France, he now found himself cut off from all the promotional benefits accruing from such works of his as had already been issued by them and unable to get any of his new works published. In his dilemma he asked Casella if he would introduce him to Tito Ricordi, and when Casella did so, he offered the Milanese publishing house his *Three Easy Pieces for Piano Duet*. Apparently Ricordi took fright at Stravinsky's terms, which (according to Casella) were by no means exaggerated; and so the Ricordi firm lost what might have proved a very lucrative asset.[1]

At the end of March, Diaghilev came to Switzerland and settled at Bellerive, Ouchy, where he was surrounded by a little group of artists whom he had collected together in view of the forthcoming visit of the Russian Ballet to the Metropolitan Opera House, New York. These included the young dancer Massine, the painters Bakst, Larionov and Goncharova, and Cecchetti the famous old dancing master. Ansermet, who had just succeeded Stavenhagen as conductor of the Geneva Symphony Orchestra, was to be in charge of the orchestra. When Stravinsky and his family returned to Clarens from the snows of Château d'Oex, where he had been working on the preliminary sketches for *The Wedding* and also a duet between a cat and a goat which was later incorporated in the score of *Reynard*, his meeting with Diaghilev was delayed for some time because his younger daughter, Maria Milena, caught measles, and Diaghilev was afraid of contagion. Once the period of quarantine was over, Stravinsky played him the music for the first two scenes of *The Wedding*. 'He was so moved,' he writes in his *Chronicle*, 'and his enthusiasm seemed so genuine and touching that I could not do otherwise than dedicate the work to him'.[2]

Before leaving for America, Ansermet decided to introduce Stravinsky to one of his close friends, the Swiss author C. F. Ramuz, who was then living at Le Treytorrens near Cully. One September afternoon Ramuz met the two visitors at the station of Epesses; and after climbing the hillside through the vines, the three men sat drinking Dézaley and talking on the terrace of La Crochettaz with its splendid view of the terraced vineyards falling steeply towards the lake. So began a friendship that was to grow in strength and intimacy during the remaining years of Stravinsky's Swiss exile.

Ramuz, who was descended from peasants and vine-growers in the canton of Vaud, immediately welcomed Stravinsky, not so much as a foreign composer of international repute, but as a man of perception who recognised and loved the significance and beauty of the ordinary things of life. Fourteen years

---

[1] See A. Casella, *Strawinski*. Brescia, 'La Scuola', 2nd ed. 1951. Stravinsky paid a special visit to Milan on 1 April 1915 to meet Tito Ricordi.

[2] This was the third of Stravinsky's works to be dedicated to Diaghilev, the first being his adaptation of *Khovanshchina* and the second the Polka from the set of *Three Easy Pieces* for piano duet.

later, he wrote a sensitive and moving record of their friendship – a worthy tribute by one great artist to another[1] – and in it he tried to define the reasons for the innate sympathy that proved a bond between them from their first meeting:

> What I recognized in you was an appetite and feeling for life, a love of all that is living; and for you all that is living is potentially music . . . Our similarity of tastes gave me the right to enjoy a music, which I saw was situated for you first in material things and then came into existence within your mind, entering through all the inlets of the body: touch, taste, smell, sight, and all the open and docile senses.

The live reactions of a foreigner to the common things of life were all the dearer to Ramuz, because his own artistic vision had had to contend with the stifling prejudices of the Swiss middle classes. 'It was always to the significant, the true and the authentic,' he writes, 'that you instinctively turned, and always to the raw materials of life, the things that were unclassified, unperceived and disapproved of – particularly by our own little native community.' And this led him to make a very shrewd comment on Stravinsky's possessiveness:

> The objects that made you act or react were the most commonplace, the most disdained and neglected, the most humble . . . a felt hat, a glass measure, a box of matches, a wall, a house, a drunkard's song . . . While others registered doubt or self-distrust, you immediately burst into joy, and this reaction was followed at once by a kind of act of possession, which made itself visible on your face by the appearance of two rather wicked-looking lines at the corner of your mouth. What you love is yours, and what you love *ought* to be yours. You throw yourself on your prey – you are in fact a man of prey.[2]

Shortly after this meeting at Epesses, Stravinsky and his family moved from Clarens to Morges where they settled in the Villa Rogie Vue, while Ramuz and his family moved to a house just outside Lausanne, which meant that the two friends were now within easy distance of each other.

Another dear friend and close companion of these war years was Charles-Albert Cingria[3], 'an itinerant scholar, a kind of bicycle troubadour, who would suddenly disappear in Greece or Italy and return as suddenly months later, poor and empty . . .' (*Exp*).

Ansermet also introduced Stravinsky to Aladar Racz, the Hungarian cimbalom player. Sometime in 1915, probably in the late autumn, he took Stravinsky over to Geneva, where Racz was playing at Maxim's.[4] Not only

---

[1] C. F. Ramuz, *Souvenirs sur Igor Strawinsky*. Paris, N. R. F./Lausanne, Mermod, 1929. (The translation of this and of subsequent extracts is by E. W. W.)
[2] C. F. Ramuz, *op. cit.*
[3] In 1917 Stravinsky began to set a Dialogue of his; but this was never completed, and only a few manuscript sketches remain in the composer's collection.
[4] For a fuller account of this meeting, see p. 242.

was the composer favourably impressed by Racz's playing, but he forthwith fell in love with the instrument and bought one for his own use. He learnt to play it well and wrote important parts for it in two of his scores: *Reynard* and *Rag-Time*.

Meanwhile, Diaghilev had been remarkably successful in reassembling his new company despite wartime difficulties. Grigoriev, his *régisseur*, made several journeys to and from Russia (via France, England, Norway, Sweden, and Finland) to recruit dancers. The only important person missing was Nijinsky, who had been interned in Hungary on the outbreak of war. Otto H. Kahn, who was backing the American tour, made it a condition of the contract that the company should include Nijinsky; and Diaghilev hoped that with the intervention of some of his friends (including possibly the King of Spain) the dancer would be allowed to leave Hungary. The Americans were also anxious for Stravinsky to go over to conduct his ballets; but in the absence of a definite contract he refused.

Diaghilev wished to arrange a trial performance for his company before it left for the United States, and he also wanted to see Massine's first choreographic essay, *The Midnight Sun*, a setting of the dances from Rimsky-Korsakov's opera, *The Snow Maiden*. He accordingly arranged two charity matinées for the Red Cross, one at Geneva (20 December) and one in Paris (29 December). It was agreed that Stravinsky should conduct *The Firebird* in both programmes – the concert suite at Geneva and the ballet in Paris – and these were his first public appearances as a conductor. The Paris gala at the Opera House was a triumphant success, raising a total of four hundred thousand gold francs. Immediately afterwards, the company (including Diaghilev, but excluding Nijinsky, who had not yet been released from internment) left Paris for Bordeaux and set sail for New York on 1 January 1916.

A little time before this, Stravinsky had received a letter from his friend the Princess Edmond de Polignac asking him to call on her when he was next in Paris. He did so shortly after Diaghilev's departure and discovered that she had had the idea of inviting various composers to write something for a small orchestra of about twenty players. The suggestion appealed to him, for though at that moment he thought he might need a monster orchestra of about 150 players for the score of *The Wedding*, a small chamber orchestra was what he had in mind for *Reynard*. He described the plot of this animal burlesque to the Princess, who expressed her approval: so on his return to Morges he set aside *The Wedding* for the moment in order to concentrate on the new chamber work.

Although there was no definite production in view, it became necessary to make a French version of the Russian libretto. At this point he thought of Ramuz. The Vaudois writer, though he didn't know a word of Russian, allowed himself to be persuaded; and the result was a close and successful collaboration with Stravinsky. In his *Souvenirs*, Ramuz describes these sessions at Morges:

The Russian Exile in Switzerland (1914 – 1920)

We met almost daily in the blue room which dominated the garden, surrounded by side drums, kettle drums, bass drums, and every kind of percussion instrument . . . The wallpaper was an extraordinary blue – like that of a laundry blue bag; we occupied the interior of a cube which seemed to have been hewn out of a glacier. Below was an attractive fruit garden with a lawn and flowering trees where four fine children laughed and played all day long. About five o'clock we were served with strong black coffee, fresh bread and various jams. I had a sheet of paper and a pencil. Stravinsky would read me the Russian text verse by verse, taking care each time to count the number of syllables which I noted down on the margin of my sheet of paper and then made the translation – that is to say, Stravinsky translated the text for me word by word. . . . Then there was the question of quantities (longs and shorts); vowels (one note was intended for an o, another for an a, a third for an i); finally, and above all, came the well known and insoluble problem of the tonic accent and its coincidence (or non-coincidence) with the musical accent.[1]

It was soon agreed between them that there were to be no hard and fast rules, but that each difficulty would be tackled on its merits. After a good dinner (in the Russian style) at the Villa Rogie Vue, Ramuz would return to Lausanne by the last train with his notebook crammed full of notes, hints and indications to help him in drafting the French version.

When the translation was finished, Stravinsky copied it in red ink into his manuscript score. At different times, there have been different descriptions of his manner of writing and his work-table; but Ramuz's is still the best.

Stravinsky's scores are magnificent. He is above all (in all matters and in every sense of the word) a calligrapher. . . . His writing desk resembled a surgeon's instrument case. Bottles of different coloured inks in their ordered hierarchy each had a separate part to play in the ordering of his art. Near at hand were india-rubbers of various kinds and shapes, and all sorts of glittering steel implements: rulers, erasers, pen-knives, and a roulette instrument for drawing staves invented by Stravinsky himself. One was reminded of the definition of St. Thomas: beauty is the splendour of order. All the large pages of the score were filled with writing in different coloured inks – blue, green, red, two kinds of black (ordinary and Chinese), each having its purpose, its meaning, its special use: one for the notes, another the text, a third the translation; one for titles, another for the musical directions. Meanwhile, the bar lines were ruled, and the mistakes carefully erased.[2]

About the end of March 1916, Stravinsky received a visit from Nijinsky and his wife, Romola, whom he had not met before. Through the good offices of Diaghilev, the dancer had been released from his internment in Hungary, and

[1] C. F. Ramuz *op. cit.*
[2] C. F. Ramuz *op. cit.*

he and his wife were now passing through Switzerland on their way to join the Russian Ballet for its second season that winter in New York. All three persons left different accounts of this meeting. Nijinsky referred to it in his *Diary*; and Romola described it as follows in her biography of her husband:[1]

> As soon as Stravinsky heard of our arrival, he came over to Lausanne and took possession of Vaslav. . . . He was dressed like a dandy, with the most indescribable taste. He thought it was very chic, and there was something touching in his naïvety and conceit. He seemed extremely sure of himself and was fully convinced of his genius, which he undoubtedly had, but the way he spoke of it seemed rather childish and at the same time charming. One would have thought a man as great as he would have been more dignified. When he came to see Vaslav, he was extremely courteous to me. . . . He immediately made friends with Kyra. He was a father and rather an expert in handling children. We went around Lausanne to the different cafés with Stravinsky as our guide. Vaslav was like a boy of seven; at last he was with a friend, a fellow artist, somebody to whom he could speak the same language, somebody who understood him fully and completely.

She then describes their visit to the Stravinsky household at Morges and how upset Stravinsky was at not having heard anything from Diaghilev about the suggestion that he should conduct some performances of his ballets in New York.

> He insisted that if Vaslav was a real friend, he would make it a condition to go to America only if Stravinsky was asked also. I thought this was rather stretching the bonds of friendship. Stravinsky talked, raged and cried; he paced up and down the room cursing Diaghilev: 'He thinks he is the Russian Ballet himself. Our success has gone to his head. What would he be without us, without Bakst, Benois, you, myself? Vaslav, I count on you.'

And the two of them went off to the post-office to send a telegram to Otto Kahn; but as their knowledge of English was limited they had to call in Romola to help draft it, and she was able to ensure that it was couched in sufficiently diplomatic terms. Even so, the hoped-for invitation for Stravinsky did not arrive; and a few days later the Nijinskys had to leave for Paris.

Stravinsky's comment on this episode is to be found in his *Chronicle* (written in 1935).

> I was at that time in great need, and in my ingenuousness even begged Nijinsky to make his own participation in the performances depend on my engagement. Needless to say, nothing came of it. As for Diaghilev, I learned later that he was much distressed at being unable to get the Metropolitan to engage me, as he had confidently counted upon it and it was no less important to him than to me.

---

[1] In *Nijinsky*. London, Gollancz, 1933.

Stravinsky's disappointment at his non-participation in the Russian Ballet's American visit cannot have lasted long. Their first season at the Metropolitan Opera House, New York, had opened on 17 January with a programme that included *The Firebird*. A fortnight later they went off on tour, returning to New York for a second season which opened on 3 April. Four days later, Nijinsky arrived from Europe, and his first appearance (in *Petrushka* and *The Spectre of the Rose*) was on 12 April. About this time Diaghilev accepted an invitation for the company to visit Spain and dance at the Teatro Real, Madrid. So when the American visit ended on 29 April, he and the members of his company sailed for Europe a week later on the *Dante Alighieri*, whose mixed cargo consisted mainly of ammunition and horses. The crossing was smooth; the boat made Cadiz without alarm; and the company opened in Madrid on 26 May.

'I have been waiting for you like a brother' – this was Diaghilev's greeting to Stravinsky when the composer joined him in Madrid. It was Stravinsky's first visit to Spain.[1]

> Right at the frontier, the smell of frying in oil was perceptible. When I reached Madrid at nine o'clock in the morning, I found the whole town still fast asleep, and I was received at my hotel by the night porter with a lantern in his hand. Yet it was spring. The people rose late, and life was not in full swing until after midnight (*Chr*).

Like many other Russians, he discovered an instinctive liking for the country and its people and their way of living. At the same hour every day he heard from his room the distant sound of a *banda* playing a *pasodoble*, and it appeared that military exercises always ended with this sort of music. He enjoyed the mechanical pianos, the *cante jondo* singers and the *toque jondo* guitarists. He visited Toledo and the Escurial, which made a deep impression on him as a 'revelation of the profoundly religious temperament of the people and the mystic fervour of their Catholicism, so closely akin in its essentials to the religious feeling and spirit of Russia' (*Chr*). He also had occasion to meet Alfonzo XIII, his consort Queen Maria, and the Queen Mother.

After his return to Switzerland, he paid tribute to Spain in a number of different compositions. He wrote an Española for piano four hands, with an easy right hand part so that it could be played by his two elder children, Theodore and Mika. The *Study for Pianola* (1917) was inspired by the rattletrap noise of the mechanical pianos and orchestrinas in the Madrid streets and midnight taverns. And the Royal March in *The Soldier's Tale* (1918) recalled a *pasodoble* he had heard played by a tiny 'bullfight' band, consisting of cornet, trombone, and bassoon, in Seville.

Part of the summer and autumn was spent in finishing the score of *Reynard* and working on some of his other compositions; but just before Christmas he

---

[1] This visit, which occurred in May 1916, is misdated March in Stravinsky's *Chronicle*.

had to interrupt everything because of an excruciatingly painful attack of intercostal neuralgia, as a result of which his legs were nearly paralysed. Diaghilev, who had elected to spend the winter in Rome with a small group of dancers including Massine while the rest of the company were absent on their second visit to the United States, came to visit him during his convalescence with a proposal that he should produce *The Nightingale* in ballet form, with the singers in the orchestra, as had already been the case with *The Golden Cockerel* in 1914. Stravinsky countered with a suggestion that the homogeneous music of the second and third acts should be turned into a symphonic poem without voices, which could be used for ballet purposes. Diaghilev accepted this proposal; and as soon as Stravinsky had sufficiently recovered his health, he set to work to revise the scenario and rearrange the music under the title *The Song of the Nightingale*.

It must have been about this time that the Princess Edmond de Polignac, who was then staying at Lausanne, visited the Stravinsky family at Morges. When writing her *Memoirs*[1] during the second World War, she recalled the occasion in vivid detail:

> One night he asked me to dine, and came to fetch me, as it was half an hour's journey by train from Lausanne to Morges. Everything was covered with snow and so quiet in the clear moonlight night, so still, that it was not very cold. I shall always remember the happy impression I had as Stravinsky took me into his house, for it looked to me like a Christmas tree, all brilliantly lit up and decorated in the warm colours that the Russian Ballet had brought to Paris.

> Madame Stravinsky was a striking figure: pale, thin, full of dignity and grace, she at once gave me the impression of nobility of race and grace that was confirmed by all she did in the following years. In the warmth of her charming house she looked like a princess in a Russian fairy tale; surrounded by her delicate children, then of course, very young. But although everything was so friendly and kind, there was an atmosphere of tragedy about the family which turned out to be only too justified, for all were more or less inclined to suffer from lung trouble, which ended pitifully for Madame Stravinsky and one of her daughters recently.

> I can never forget the delight of that evening at Morges: the table brilliantly lit with coloured candles, and covered with fruit, flowers and desserts of every hue. The supper was a wonderful example of Russian cuisine, carefully prepared by Madame Stravinsky and composed of every form of zakousky, then bortsch, tender sterlets covered with delicious transparent jelly and served with a perfect sauce, various dishes of fowls and every sort of sweet, making it a feast to be always remembered.

This delectable party must have taken place almost at the time of the Russian

---

[1] 'Memoirs of the late Princess Edmond de Polignac', *Horizon*. August, 1945.

The Russian Exile in Switzerland (1914 – 1920)

'Liberal' Revolution in February 1917. In his *Souvenirs*, Ramuz recalled how Stravinsky reacted to the news. He remembered going for a walk with him up the Petit-Chêne on a day when the *bise* was blowing strongly from the north under a clear blue sky. Stravinsky talked about Russia – the new Russia – and Ramuz in his enthusiasm shared his friend's hopes (and illusions). The exile had decided that his place was 'back there' – in the true Russia, the Russia that had woken from her winter sleep and would at long last assert her proper native genius. He even started to make travelling plans.

Meanwhile, Diaghilev was still in Rome, planning a spring season for the Russian Ballet in Paris and in Spain. Before he left Italy, however, his friends urged him to show *The Good-Humoured Ladies*, the new ballet Massine had been working on to music of Domenico Scarlatti arranged by Vincenzo Tommasini. He accordingly arranged four performances at the Teatro Costanzi, the first of which (on 12 April) was a gala in aid of the Italian Red Cross. As well as *The Good-Humoured Ladies*, the opening programme included *The Firebird* and *Fireworks*, both conducted by the composer. For the latter score, a special setting was provided by the Italian futurist painter, Giacomo Balla, consisting 'of various geometrical structures, such as cubes and cones, made of some transparent material that allowed of their being lit from within in accordance with a complicated lighting plot, which Diaghilev devised and worked himself'.[1] An early form of *son et lumière* it appears! Normally this gala programme would have begun with the Russian National Anthem; but in view of the recent revolution, 'God Save the Tsar!' was out of the question. At Diaghilev's express request, Stravinsky undertook to adapt *The Song of the Volga Boatmen* for this purpose. He instrumented it for wind instruments and percussion and, as time was short, dictated the score to Ansermet in Lord Berners's flat the evening before the performance.

(Although Diaghilev professed himself a monarchist, he favoured the change of government in Russia and wished to pay it tribute: so a few weeks later just before the opening of the company's Paris season at the Théâtre du Châtelet (11 May) he announced he had decided to alter the finale of *The Firebird*, which was to be included in the opening programme. 'Instead of being presented with a crown and sceptre, as he had hitherto, the Tsarevich would in future receive a cap of Liberty and a red flag.'[2] But this innovation did not please his friends and backers or the public, and it was soon withdrawn.)

Stravinsky's visit to Rome was particularly memorable, because it marked his first meeting with Pablo Picasso.[3]

Cocteau had long wished to bring Picasso and other French painters into

---

[1] S. L. Grigoriev, *The Diaghilev Ballet, 1909–1929*.

[2] S. L. Grigoriev, *op. cit*.

[3] In his *Conversations*, Stravinsky says that he has a vague recollection of having first met Picasso at Prince Argutinsky's about 1910.

61

the Russian Ballet fold. His voice was becoming increasingly important in Diaghilev's inner councils; and now that it had been decided to go ahead with preparations for his own ballet *Parade*, he had been able to persuade Diaghilev to commission Picasso to design its scenery and costumes. He took Picasso off to Rome, where the painter started to work on his designs in a studio opposite the Villa Medici. In their spare time, Cocteau, Picasso and Stravinsky explored Rome together; and when the company went to Naples, they followed the dancers there and continued their explorations, visiting the aquarium and combing the antique shops for old prints and gouaches. Together they saw a *commedia dell'arte* performance in a crowded little room reeking of garlic. 'The Pulcinella', says Stravinsky in his *Conversations*, 'was a great drunken lout, whose every gesture, and probably every word if I had understood, was obscene. The only other incident of our Neapolitan holiday I can remember is that we were both arrested one night for urinating against a wall of the Galleria.'

Numerous commentators have been struck by the points of resemblance between the work and careers of Picasso and Stravinsky. Though their painting and music are deeply rooted in tradition, their enquiring minds have never been content merely to mark time. Instead, they have been ready to experiment, to explore new directions, and to push the boundaries of their arts far into unknown fields. They are interested in the raw materials of their arts for their intrinsic esthetic value, and not for their capacity to communicate representational or emotional content. Many parallels can be drawn between their work. For instance, the violence of Picasso's reaction against impressionism can be seen in his *fauve* masterpiece, *Les Demoiselles d'Avignon* (1906/07). According to Roland Penrose, this was the first painting 'in which Picasso became entirely himself and assimilated all influences so as to let his own genius triumph. It is the battlefield on which he won his own liberty'.[1] Similar views could be expressed about Stravinsky's *fauve* masterpiece *The Rite of Spring* (1911/13). A comparison might be made between the calligraphic quality of some of Picasso's paintings and drawings and Stravinsky's strictly syllabic treatment of words in vocal settings; and it might also be maintained that there is a close relationship between Picasso's use of comparatively flat colours in his two-dimensional synthetic cubist phase (e.g., the two versions of *The Three Musicians* painted in 1921) and Stravinsky's use of pure instrumental colour to achieve tonal depth as exemplified in the score of *The Soldier's Tale* (1918).

At the time of their meeting, many of these similarities were already implicit in their work; but shortly afterwards both artists, travelling independently, were to reach a new stage of development, which was distinguished by frequent references to classical subjects and classical procedures. The great classical

---

[1] Catalogue of the Picasso Exhibition. London, The Arts Council of Great Britain, 1960.

nudes that Picasso painted between 1920 and 1923 are the pictorial counter-part of Stravinsky's scores for *Oedipus Rex* (1926/27), *Apollo Musagetes* (1927), *Persephone* (1933), and *Orpheus* (1947). At a somewhat later stage, both artists found pleasure and stimulus in recalling earlier masterpieces by other artists (e.g., Grunewald, Cranach, Velasquez, Ingres etc. – Gesualdo, Pergolesi, Bach, Chaikovsky, etc.) and using them as a peg on which to hang a series of inventive variations.

From their meeting in Rome in 1917 dates the first of the three portrait drawings of Stravinsky[1] that Picasso was to execute. Picasso drew it in the Hôtel de la Russie near the Piazza del Popolo and presented it to Stravinsky, who had considerable trouble with it later when he came to cross the Italian frontier on his return journey to Switzerland.

> When the military authorities examined my luggage they found this drawing, and nothing in the world would induce them to let it pass. They asked me what it represented, and when I told them that it was my portrait, drawn by a distinguished artist, they utterly refused to believe me. 'It is not a portrait, but a plan,' said one of them. 'Yes, the plan of my face, but of nothing else,' I replied. But all my efforts failed to convince them (*Chr*).

At this point he suddenly thought of Lord Berners, who had given him some Mandorlati figs to eat on the train journey. These had just been confiscated by one of the border police, who was starting to split them open with his sabre, presumably in search of contraband. Stravinsky managed to persuade the authorities to send back the portrait to the British Embassy in Rome, where in due course Berners arranged for it to leave Italy in the diplomatic bag, and ultimately it reached Stravinsky safely at the Maison Bornand, 2 rue St.-Louis, Morges, to which he had recently moved from the Villa Rogie Vue.

He had turned one of the attic rooms of this seventeenth-century building into a studio, which was reached by a half-hidden wooden staircase, well barricaded by doors. There after his return from Rome he added a Napolitana to the set of *Easy Pieces for Piano Duet* (with easy right hand) and continued to work on the last part of *The Wedding*. Ramuz, who had again been enlisted to make the French translation of the Russian text, expressed his admiration for this cantata in no uncertain terms. He compared the sound of the com-poser, working at the piano in the afternoon and using one or more percussion instruments whenever he had a free hand, to a storm breaking out 'above the little square outside, where the pigeons strutted about unperturbed in the dust and the women sitting on a bench and knitting in the shade of the trees raised their heads for a moment in bewilderment and then, with an indulgent "C'est le monsieur russe!" resumed their knitting'. He added:

> I reflected that many things were permitted to you, not because you were

---

[1] The other two Picasso portraits of Stravinsky are dated 24 May 1920 and 31 December 1920.

a stranger, but because, quite the contrary, you could nowhere be a stranger on this earth, for you were so closely linked with nature, mankind, and life itself, and nowhere separated from human beings or from existence itself – which is the greatest gift of all.[1]

One day when Stravinsky returned to Morges after lunching at Ramuz's house at Cour, Lausanne, he noticed a stranger wearing a top hat and morning coat in his garden. He asked him what he wanted and to his astonishment was told that there had been a death in the house. Apparently his beloved nurse Bertha, who had been in the service of the family for about forty years, had just been carried off by the bursting of a blood vessel. Stravinsky had always been devoted to her, and now he mourned her with genuine grief. Perhaps he had her in mind when a few years later he composed an encomium for a dead cook in his opera buffa, *Mavra*.[2]

The family moved to a chalet in Les Diablerets for the summer months; and while Stravinsky was staying there he met André Gide at the Chalet du Revenandray, which was situated above the village and belonged to the Société d'étudiants de Belles-Lettres de Lausanne. Gide was visiting that part of Switzerland in the company of a friend, whose romantic liaison with a handsome young student is sympathetically described in Gide's Diary. The only entry referring to Stravinsky is a rather sombre one under the date August 19th – 'I force myself to read Tolstoy's *Intimate Diary*, which I've sent for on the advice of Igor Stravinsky: but I get neither pleasure nor profit from it.' But according to an eye-witness account[3] of their meeting, which took place in the presence of a bunch of young students, the composer was in a very gay and somewhat facetious mood.

I can still see him drinking punch, covered with cloaks and shawls despite the heat, playing a mouth-organ which he had picked up somewhere, and announcing 'I'm going to play you some Wagner . . .' A moment later he was photographed with André Gide in front of the chalet, holding a bottle and proclaiming that it symbolised the Franco-Russian alliance.

The punch must have been strong, for another student remembered him commenting 'Je suis comme un samovar, je fume par les narines, comme dans Wagner . . .'

But this mood of levity was destined to pass quickly. A little later that summer a telegram from Russia reached him to say his brother Gury had died from typhus at Jassy on the Rumanian front – not far south of Pechisky where the two brothers had spent so many of their boyhood holidays together. With

---

[1] C. F. Ramuz, *Souvenirs sur Igor Strawinsky*.
[2] *Mavra*, fig. 34 *et seq.*
[3] Article by Rodolphe Faessler in *Revue de Belles-Lettres*, Lausanne, July-August 1956, quoted by Pierre Meylan in *Une amitié célèbre*. Lausanne, 1961. (Translation by E. W. W.)

The Russian Exile in Switzerland (1914 – 1920)

Gury and Bertha both dead, two of the few persons connected with his youth for whom he really cared, his links with Russia were dissolving fast. True, his mother was still there, together with Yury his remaining brother. But these were only nominal ties; and after the October Revolution, when it became clear that his income from Russia had dried up and he was unlikely to see his property in St. Petersburg and Ustilug again, he reached the conclusion he must accept the fact of his wartime exile and do his best to earn a living for himself, his wife and children outside Russia. Money had always been important to him; but now it was scarce. The position was aggravated by the fact that as he was still a Russian citizen and as Russia and the United States had not ratified the Berne Copyright Convention, his scores were not properly protected in the United States and the payment of fees that were rightfully his was not always legally enforceable. In the future he would find ways and means of overcoming this difficulty – by the subterfuge of using an American 'editor' for his published music in the 'twenties, and by adopting French nationality in 1934 – but meanwhile he had to do the best he could. In the course of time, he was to earn and deserve the reputation of being a shrewd and canny businessman – Diaghilev said that the 'or' in his Christian name surely stood for 'gold' – but at that dark moment in the First World War, it was difficult to know where he could look for help.

By the end of 1917, he had added a *Balalaika, Galop* and *Andante* to form another set of *Easy Pieces for Piano Duet*, composed one or two of the *Tales for Children* (for voice and piano), all four of the *a cappella* Russian Peasant Songs, and completed the *Study for Pianola*. He was much gratified when a group of his friends underwrote the cost of a project whereby the concert agency Ad. Henn of Geneva published some of his recent works (the *Pribaoutki*, the *Cat's Cradle Songs, Reynard*, and the two sets of *Easy Pieces for Piano Duet*). He had also finished the short score of *The Wedding*; but as there seemed to be no likelihood of its being produced in the near future, he decided to postpone the instrumentation.

Diaghilev was, in fact, experiencing increasing difficulty in securing engagements for the Russian Ballet. After its spring season in Paris, Madrid and Barcelona, it had paid a second visit to South America. As before, Nijinsky was with the dancers, while Diaghilev stayed behind; but this time it was clear that the great dancer was mentally ill. His condition deteriorated rapidly during the summer; and the last time he ever danced with the company was at Buenos Aires on 26 September 1917 in *The Spectre of the Rose* 'in which he sprang out of the window never to return, and *Petrushka*, in which he was slain, for ever, by the cruel Moor'.[1] After this he retired from professional life and entered the long period of decline that took him into the underworld of insanity. Meanwhile, after its return to Europe, the company carried out a

---

[1] S. L. Grigoriev, *op. cit.*

1. The Man

brief tour of Spain and Portugal; but at the beginning of 1918 it was stranded in Lisbon without a single firm engagement in prospect.

This was one of the darkest moments in Stravinsky's life: but he was not alone in his difficulties. Neighbours like Ramuz and Ansermet were equally affected. One day, in the course of a discussion between Stravinsky and Ramuz, the idea came to them – 'Why not do something quite *simple*? Why not write together a piece that would need no vast theatre or large public? something with two or three characters and a handful of instrumentalists.' As no theatres were available because of the war, a special mobile theatre would have to be devised for the purpose, with scenery that could easily be set up in any hall or building, or even in the open air – in fact, a travelling theatre that would tour Switzerland and give performances in towns or villages. But even so modest a plan needed financial backing; and here the two collaborators were in luck. Early in March Ramuz approached Werner Reinhart of Winterthur, who signified his interest in the project and put up sufficient money to commission the work and underwrite its production.

As Ramuz was not a man of the theatre, he proposed to write a story that could be read, played, and danced – in fact, a kind of mimed narration – while Stravinsky decided to compose incidental music that would be independent of the text and could be performed separately as a concert suite. A suitable subject was found in one of Afanasiev's tales of the soldier and the Devil. These tales belong to the period of forced recruitment for the Russo-Turkish wars under Nicholas I; but the collaborators decided to departicularise the treatment and transpose the period style of the play to any time or 1918, and to many nationalities or none.[1]

The libretto and the score of *The Soldier's Tale* were finished by the summer; and arrangements were made to hire the theatre at Lausanne for the first performance on Saturday 28 September. The two collaborators invited René Auberjonois to design the scenery and costumes and cast three students from Lausanne University in the parts of the Soldier, the Devil, and the Reader. Stravinsky then called in Georges Pitoëff and his wife Ludmila (who were living at Geneva) to dance the parts of the Devil and the Princess and to take over the general stage direction. Ansermet was put in charge of the orchestra.

The months before the first performance were full of bustling activity. Both Ramuz and Stravinsky were concerned from the start with details of organisation and rehearsals, and the first volume of Ramuz's collected letters bears striking witness to the way the two collaborators immersed themselves in these preparations. There were also proposals for playing elsewhere after the Lausanne performance – Geneva is mentioned in particular, and also Basel – but these plans, alas! were doomed to be thwarted by the epidemic of Spanish

---

[1] A fuller account of the collaboration between Stravinsky and Ramuz over *The Soldier's Tale* is to be found in the Register p. 264 *et seq.*

influenza that was then sweeping through Europe. The first performance of *The Soldier's Tale* at Lausanne was a great success; and in his *Chronicle* Stravinsky expressed his satisfaction with every detail of it. But during the following days the musicians, actors and stage-hands succumbed to flu, and the idea of touring the little mobile theatre had to be completely abandoned. Five years were to elapse before Stravinsky saw another production of the work; but for him the score remained an important landmark, for it demonstrated his will and ability to discard the Russian element in his music and embrace a more eclectic international idiom.

When Ansermet returned to Switzerland from the 1917 American tour of the Russian Ballet, he brought Stravinsky a selection of new jazz material in the form of piano reductions and instrumental parts. Stravinsky copied these out in score; and though he had never heard any of the music performed, he 'borrowed its rhythmic style not as played but as written' (*Exp*) and wrote the Ragtime (the third of the three dances) in *The Soldier's Tale*. He continued his jazz researches, writing another *Rag-Time* which was like a concertino for cimbalom and nine solo instruments with percussion. This was composed in March 1918, and the instrumentation finished on 11 November. In his *Dialogues*, he recalls how, sitting at his cimbalom that morning in his garret at the Maison Bornand, he became aware of a buzzing in his ears. Going down to the street, he was told that everyone was hearing the same noise and it came from a cannon along the French frontier. The armistice had been signed, and the war was over.

In his *Dialogues* he rightly says that this *Rag-Time* and the one in *The Soldier's Tale* are 'essays in jazz portraiture'. By the following year he had heard live bands and discovered that jazz performance is more interesting than jazz composition, particularly in view of the element of improvisation it contains. Nevertheless, the *Piano-Rag-Music* and the *Three Pieces for Clarinet Solo* (both belonging to 1919) though written partly without bar lines, are not real jazz improvisations, but merely the portraits of such improvisations.

When the piano version of *Rag-Time* was published by Editions de la Sirène, Paris, in 1919, Stravinsky asked Picasso to design a cover. The artist drew six figures – each a single uninterrupted line – and chose the published design himself. (Two of the variants are illustrated in the English edition of *Memories*.)

At the beginning of 1919, feeling rather exhausted by his recent bout of flu, Stravinsky decided not to undertake any major work for the time being, but to make a new concert suite for medium-sized orchestra from *The Firebird*, which he dedicated to Ansermet and his recently founded Orchestre de la Suisse Romande. He also made up a group of Four Songs for Mme. Maja de Strozzi-Pecic from material left over from his Russian popular period. In the spring he visited Paris and had a number of business talks with Diaghilev whom he had not seen for over a year.

By then the Russian Ballet had recovered from the doldrums. Its Portuguese

Stravinsky and Andre Gidé at Les Diablerets, 1917

Stravinsky and C. F. Ramuz at Talloires, 1929

season at the end of 1917 had run into a revolution, which meant that the dancers were stranded in Lisbon until a further Spanish tour could be negotiated in May and June 1918. There was then another enforced interval, until Diaghilev succeeded in negotiating a special season with Oswald Stoll at the Coliseum, London, starting on 5 September. The Coliseum was a music-hall which gave two performances daily with a change of programme every week; and the arrangement was that one ballet would be included in each bill. When the company reappeared in London after an absence of four years, it received a rapturous reception from public and press; and for the first time for many months the dancers began to enjoy a sense of security. The Coliseum engagement came to an end in March 1919; and after a fortnight's visit to Manchester, the company reopened at the Alhambra, London, (on 30 April) with a season devoted entirely to ballet.

When Stravinsky and Diaghilev met in Paris, their talks were no longer free and untroubled as in previous years. Stravinsky tried to interest the impresario in his latest major composition, *The Soldier's Tale*; but Diaghilev was jealous and refused to recognize his friend's right to work apart from him and the Russian Ballet, looking on such action as a breach of faith, and expressing withering contempt for Ramuz and Stravinsky's other Swiss colleagues. For his part, he talked with enthusiasm about his plans to produce *The Song of the Nightingale* as a ballet with scenery and costumes by Henri Matisse and choreography by Massine: but it was the composer's turn to evince lack of interest. He made it clear that he considered *The Song of the Nightingale* to be a symphonic poem and intended it for concert performance rather than stage production.

Diaghilev now tried a different tack. The recent success of *The Good-Humoured Ladies* had led him to plan another ballet with an adapted score; and Ottorino Respighi was busy orchestrating a selection of Rossini's little known *Péchés de ma Vieillesse* for *La Boutique Fantasque*. Would Stravinsky like to perform the same sort of operation with music by Pergolesi for a ballet on a *commedia dell'arte* theme? At first the composer was dumbfounded, because at that moment he was not very familiar with Pergolesi's music, and what little he knew did not appeal to him. But Diaghilev had collected copies of some Pergolesi manuscripts during his recent visits to Italy and explained that he would place these at Stravinsky's disposal and if he cared to work them up into a score, the argument of the ballet could be adapted from a manuscript dating from about 1700 which he had found at Naples and which contained a number of sketches featuring Pulcinella, the traditional hero of the Neapolitan popular stage. Stravinsky looked at the material and promptly fell in love with it. He agreed to write the score for the fun of it and was delighted when Diaghilev decided to commission the scenery and costumes from Picasso, who was at that moment working on *The Three-Cornered Hat*. Returning to Morges he started work on the score, composing directly on to the Pergolesi manuscripts as if he were correcting an old work of his own. *Pulcinella* was the last important work to be written in his studio in the Maison Bornand.

About this time he sold the manuscript full score of *The Firebird* to Jean Bartholoni of Geneva, who later presented it to the local Conservatoire de Musique. It was Bartholoni too who helped Otto Kling of Messrs. J. & W. Chester of London to acquire the publication rights of his recent compositions. Most of these works were published in 1920, though the vocal score of *The Wedding* and the piano reduction of the suite from *The Soldier's Tale* did not appear until 1922 and the *Four Russian Peasant Songs* ('Saucers') were delayed till 1932.[1] Shortly after the signing of this agreement with Chester's, his relations with his pre-war publishers, the Russischer Musikverlag (Edition Russe de Musique), were renewed, with the curious result that whereas the vocal score of *Pulcinella* was published by Chester's and the piano chorale written for *Le Tombeau de Claude Debussy*[2] appeared as their copyright, the full score of *Pulcinella*, together with the concert suite from that ballet, and also the *Symphonies of Wind Instruments*, were published by the Edition Russe de Musique.

Towards the end of 1919, certain important concerts, featuring Stravinsky's music, took place in Switzerland. Werner Reinhart underwrote the cost of three concerts of his recent chamber music that were given in Lausanne (8 November), Zurich (20 November) and Geneva (17 December). Mademoiselle Tatianova sang the *Pribaoutki* and the *Cat's Cradle Songs* with piano accompaniment; José Iturbi played the *Piano-Rag-Music* and the piano transcription of the *Rag-Time*; Edmond Allegra played the *Three Pieces for Clarinet Solo*; José Porta joined Allegra and Iturbi in the transcription of the Suite from *The Soldier's Tale* for violin, clarinet and piano; and Iturbi was joined by the composer in the *Eight Easy Pieces for Piano Duet*. On 6 December Ansermet conducted the first performance of *The Song of the Nightingale* at Geneva in one of the subscription concerts of the newly formed Orchestre de la Suisse Romande. In his *Chronicle*, Stravinsky writes:

> I enjoyed the performance greatly, for the rendering was careful and highly finished. I reached the conclusion – very regretfully, since I was the author of many works for the theatre – that a perfect rendering can only be achieved in the concert hall, because the stage presents a combination of several elements upon which the music has often to depend, so that it cannot rely upon the exclusive consideration which it receives at a concert. I was confirmed in this view when, two months later,[3] under the direction of the same conductor, Ansermet, *The Song of the Nightingale* was given as a ballet by Diaghilev at the Paris Opera House.

[1] See p. 249.
[2] See p. 291.
[3] On 2 February 1920.

But this attitude was hardly likely to commend itself to Diaghilev so long as he was committed to the fortunes of the Russian Ballet.

Nevertheless, the work on *Pulcinella* progressed fairly satisfactorily, despite a number of misunderstandings. First of all, Diaghilev was shocked by Picasso's designs. His first sketches were for 'Offenbach-period costumes with side-whiskered faces instead of masks' (*Con*); and Diaghilev was so upset that he threw the drawings on the floor and stamped on them in rage. Then he was disappointed with Stravinsky's music. 'He had expected a strict, mannered orchestration of something very sweet' (*Con*) and disliked its satirical tang. Massine composed his choreography from a piano reduction of the score; and when he came to the Gavotte and Variations, Diaghilev misled him by explaining that here Stravinsky intended to use a large orchestra with harps, whereas in fact he instrumented this movement for a small wind ensemble. The result was that in one or two places the choreography was out of scale with the music and had later to be altered and adapted. Doubtless certain adjustments were made when Stravinsky paid a flying visit to Monte Carlo sometime in March or April to see how the company's rehearsals were progressing. Nevertheless, when the ballet was performed for the first time at the Paris Opera House on 15 May 1920, it achieved a genuine success with the public, and in his *Chronicle* Stravinsky expressed his satisfaction with the way everything harmonised together and 'all elements – subject, music, dancing, and artistic setting – formed a coherent and homogeneous whole'. This success was repeated a few weeks later when it was given for the first time in London at the Russian Ballet's opening performance at the Royal Opera House, Covent Garden (10 June 1920). But the composer was not present on this occasion because he had had to return from Paris to Morges to supervise his family's imminent removal.

Now that the war was over he found that permanent residence in Switzerland meant that he was too isolated from the main centres of musical activity in Europe. At first he had thought of settling in Italy; and during the Russian Ballet's season at the Teatro Costanzi, Rome, in the winter of 1920 he wrote to G. F. Malipiero, saying:[1]

> I am most upset by your telegram with the news that the flat on which I was counting was let the day before my telegram arrived. I beg everyone to do their best to find me a flat in Rome. I count on all of you. B[2] tells me that in Rome there are flats that can be bought outright. Is this true?

But in the event it was in France that he decided to make his future home.

---

[1] This letter dated 3 March 1920 written from Morges is quoted in Malipiero's *Strawinsky*. Venice, Cavallino, 1945. (Translation by E.W.W.)
[2] Presumably Lord Berners.

5. The Russian Exile in France (1920 - 1929)

The summer of 1920 was spent at Carantec in Brittany; but Stravinsky did not find it a very congenial spot. Writing to Ramuz, he complained:

> I can't say I like Brittany very much – not as I liked the country in the canton of Vaud. In the first place, the weather's always bad; and then, for my part, I don't find the place at all French. . . . It's true the peasants are good fellows; but that's so everywhere. . . . I'm bored by the 'picturesque'; and everyone spends their time strolling up and down the streets of this village of fishermen. The place is full of conventional middle-class trippers, who can't afford to go to Deauville. It's not at all amusing – people who start singing outside our windows when we're in bed, and louder than is necessary in the streets at night; but apparently they think they're justified in letting themselves go when on holiday. I'm sleeping badly and composing music.[1]

The music referred to was a *Concertino* for string quartet intended for the use of the Flonzaley Quartet, a group of Vaudois musicians who already had the *Three Pieces for String Quartet* in their repertory, and a piano chorale for the *Revue Musicale*, which was planning a special number to be devoted to the memory of Debussy, who had died on 25 March 1918.

A real friendship had existed between Debussy and Stravinsky since their initial meeting in Paris after the first performance of *The Firebird* in 1910. The following year Stravinsky dedicated his cantata *Zvezdoliki* to the French composer who found the new work somewhat puzzling in its transcendentalism. Perhaps this was Plato's harmony of the eternal spheres he suggested in his letter of thanks, adding 'except on Sirius or Aldebaran, I do not foresee performances of this "cantata for planets".'[2]

In the spring of 1913 Debussy, who was already familiar with the four-handed piano arrangement of *The Rite of Spring*, attended rehearsals of the ballet; and Stravinsky got the impression that he was enthusiastic about the music. But Debussy had his reservations. Writing to André Caplet on the date of the first public performance (29 May 1913), he said, '*The Rite of Spring* is an extraordinarily savage affair. . . . If you like, it's primitive music with every modern convenience'. St.-John Perse, who was with Debussy before and after the première, told Stravinsky in 1962 that he remembered 'how excited

---

[1] Quoted in *Souvenirs sur Igor Strawinsky* by C. F. Ramuz. (Translation by E.W.W.)
[2] Letter of 18 August 1913 to Stravinsky, printed in *Conversations*.

The Russian Exile in France (1920 – 1929)

[Debussy] was by the music at first and then how he changed when he understood that with it you had taken the attention of the new generation away from him'.[1] And talking to Ansermet shortly after the outbreak of the First World War, Debussy said: 'You know how much I admire *Petrushka*, but *The Rite* disturbs me. It seems to me that Stravinsky is trying to make music with non-musical means, just as the Germans apparently pretend to be able to make beef-steaks out of sawdust.'[2]

As the war continued, his misgivings seemed to multiply; and he was particularly outspoken in his correspondence with his Swiss friend Robert Godet. In a letter of 4 January 1916 he calls Stravinsky a 'spoilt child, who sometimes cocks a snook at music. He's also a young barbarian who wears flashy ties and treads on women's toes as he kisses their hands. As an old man he'll be insupportable – that's to say, he won't support any other music: but for the moment he's unprecedented'. A few months later (14 October 1916) he wrote to Godet again: 'At this moment one wonders into whose arms the music of our day is going to fall. The young Russian school holds out its arms; but in my view they've become as little Russian as possible. Stravinsky himself leans dangerously in the direction of Schoenberg – nevertheless, he remains the most marvellous orchestral craftsman of our time.'

No hint of this slightly peevish critical attitude is to be found in Debussy's correspondence with Stravinsky, which contains expressions of warm continuing affection right up to the last published letter (dated 24 October 1915).[3] This is signed 'your always devoted old Claude Debussy' and bears the postscript: 'All our affectionate thoughts to your dear family. I have received news from the Société des Auteurs saying that you have chosen me as godfather for your entry in that society. I thank you.'

During these years, Debussy was dying of cancer. In his *Expositions*, Stravinsky says: 'I saw him rarely during the war, and the few visits I did pay him were very extremely painful. His subtle, grave smile had disappeared, and his skin was yellow and sunken; it was hard not to see the future cadaver in him . . . I saw him last about nine months before his death. This was a *triste* visit, and Paris was grey, quiet, and without lights or movement.' On this occasion Debussy apparently did not mention that he intended to dedicate the third of his three pieces for two pianos, *En Blanc et Noir*, to his Russian friend; and the news did not reach Stravinsky until about a year after Debussy's death. He was then deeply moved by his old friend's thought and delighted to find the piece such an excellent composition.

In these circumstances, the commission from *La Revue Musicale* met with a

---

[1] Quoted in Robert Craft's Diary printed in the American edition of *Dialogues and a Diary*.
[2] Quoted by Ernest Ansermet in *L'Expérience musicale et le Monde d'aujourd'hui*. La Baconniére, Neuchâtel, 1948.
[3] Printed in *Conversations*.

ready response. A chorale for piano, described as 'Fragment des *Symphonies pour instruments à vent à la mémoire de Claude Achille Debussy*' appeared in *Le Tombeau de Claude Debussy*;[1] and this ultimately became the final section of the *Symphonies of Wind Instruments* which he finished at Gabrielle Chanel's house at Garches, near Paris, in the autumn of 1920.

Although Stravinsky's musical development quickly took him to a point where he found the esthetics of Debussy's music had become completely foreign to him, he still remembered with pleasure the personality of the man, the course of their friendship, and the warmth of his regard. It was accordingly with a sense of puzzled astonishment that years later, as some of Debussy's letters to his friends were released for publication,[2] he found what seemed to be evidence of a rather unfriendly attitude towards himself and his music. 'Was it duplicity,' he asked in his *Conversations*, 'or was he annoyed at his incapacity to digest the music of *The Rite* when the younger generation enthusiastically voted for it?' Whatever the answer to this question may be, nothing can alter the fact that the *Symphonies of Wind Instruments* is one of the finest tributes ever paid by one great composer to another.

Stravinsky and his family stayed at Garches during the autumn of 1920 and winter of 1921; and during this period he wrote *Les Cinq Doigts*, eight easy pieces for piano. He also started to sketch out *Cinq Pièces Monométriques* for an instrumental ensemble; but this work was never completed.[3] Meanwhile, Diaghilev had decided to revive *The Rite of Spring* during the Russian Ballet's winter season at the Théâtre des Champs-Elysées. After seven years or more, Nijinsky's choreography had been completely forgotten; so Massine was invited to make a new version, which was danced for the first time on 15 December 1920. This revival had a very favourable reception from the public.

At the end of the winter, Stravinsky and his family moved to a beach house at Anglet, near Biarritz. The Russian Ballet was now in Spain; and he joined the company in Madrid, where he conducted a performance of *Petrushka* which was attended by Alfonso XIII and the two Queens. Easter was spent with Diaghilev at Seville. Throughout the *Semana Santa* the two friends mingled with the crowds; and Stravinsky was astonished to find that these half-pagan, half-Christian celebrations seemed to have lost no whit of their freshness and vitality.

That year the company's spring season at the Gaieté Lyrique, Paris, was quite a short one, and it was followed by a London season at the Prince's Theatre. Stravinsky came over to London on 7 June, arriving just in time to attend the first concert performance in England of *The Rite of Spring* conducted by Eugene Goossens at the Queen's Hall. Like the Paris concert performance

[1] Printed in *La Revue Musicale* for December 1920.
[2] Particularly the *Lettres à deux amis*, Paris, 1942.
[3] There are some manuscript sketches of this unfinished work in the composer's collection. [C 37].

of 1914, this proved to be a remarkable rehabilitation ceremony. According to Goossens,[1] 'the last explosive chord of the "Danse Sacrale" had barely erupted before the audience sprang to its collective feet and gave an exhibition of hysterical enthusiasm which put the fiercest demonstration of the Parisians quite in the shade'. The composer was called to the platform and enthusiastically cheered. But to some sensitive listeners on this occasion it seemed that the audience's acceptance of the music was almost more scandalous than the actual storm of protests and counter-protests at the ballet première in 1913; and this view was vigorously expressed in Siegfried Sassoon's poem 'Concert-Interpretation'.[2] The first London performance of Massine's new version of the ballet was given by the Russian Ballet at the Prince's Theatre on 27 June.

At this moment Koussevitzky, who was in London too, decided at comparatively short notice to include the first performance of the *Symphonies of Wind Instruments* in a concert he was conducting on 10 June.[3] An account of this *débâcle* is given in Stravinsky's *Chronicle*.[4] The score and parts of the new work reached London from Paris only a few days before the actual performance, and Koussevitzky made an extraordinary error of judgment when he came to the actual performance of the *Symphonies of Wind Instruments* (which followed Rimsky-Korsakov's march from *The Golden Cockerel* in his programme) by letting the twenty-one wind players remain at the back of the platform in their normal seats while the rest of the orchestra filed out. It seems incredible that this mistake should have been allowed to prejudice the successful presentation of so delicately balanced an ensemble; and in the circumstances it is hardly surprising that the London audience and critics were baffled by what they heard.

In spite of his natural distress at this calamitous performance, Stravinsky seems to have enjoyed his stay in London. The summer was hot, the town very full, and he was constantly surrounded by friends and new acquaintants. 'It was one continuous round of lunches, teas, receptions, and weekend parties' (*Chr*). Nevertheless there was sufficient time for him and Diaghilev to make plans for the future. In the first place, Diaghilev intended to revive Chaikovsky's full-length ballet, *The Sleeping Beauty*,[5] for a run in London; and Stravinsky, who was a devoted admirer of the composer, agreed to help with the orchestration of some of the numbers that had been cut in the original production in St. Petersburg and were to be found only in the piano reduction. The second project originated in the mutual admiration both Stravinsky and

---

[1] Eugene Goossens, *Overture and Beginners*. London, Methuen, 1951.
[2] Included in Siegfried Sassoon, *Satirical Poems*. London, Heinemann, 1926.
[3] It had been Goossens's original intention to include this new work in his *Rite of Spring* concert on 7 June.
[4] See p. 295.
[5] Owing to a whim of Diaghilev's the title of this ballet was changed to *The Sleeping Princess* for its London production.

Stravinsky in the Savoy Hotel, London, summer of 1921. Photograph by Alvin Langdon Coburn

The Russian Exile in France (1920 – 1929)

Diaghilev felt for the Russian poet Pushkin, and Stravinsky's wish to write an *opera buffa* in the musical tradition of Glinka and Dargomisky to a libretto based on Pushkin's rhymed story, *The Little House in Kolomna*. Diaghilev expressed his approval; and a young Russian named Boris Kochno whom he had recently met through Serge Soudeikine and taken on as his personal secretary, was engaged to write the libretto.

Towards the end of the summer Stravinsky returned to Anglet, where he made a virtuoso piano transcription of *Three Movements from Petrushka* for Artur Rubinstein; and in the autumn he and his family definitely settled in Biarritz, renting the Villa des Rochers in the centre of the town. There his work on *Mavra*, as the new *opera buffa* was called, had to be interrupted in order to carry out the various bits of orchestration that Diaghilev wanted for the forthcoming revival of *The Sleeping Beauty*. In order to aid the preliminary publicity, he wrote a warm tribute to Chaikovsky and his music in an open letter to Diaghilev from Paris dated 10 October,[1] and a few days later he was back in London.

Diaghilev was preparing this revival with loving care. Three famous ballerinas from the Maryinsky Theatre, St. Petersburg, who had emigrated to Paris, namely, Vera Trefilova, Liubov Egorova, and Olga Spesivtseva, were invited to share the title role. The part of the wicked Fairy Carabosse was to be taken by Carlotta Brianza, who had created the part of Princess Aurora in the original Maryinsky production in 1890. Scenery and costumes had been entrusted to Bakst; and Bronislava Nijinska (Vaslav's sister) had been invited to do the choreography for the extra dance numbers.

Stravinsky attended a number of the rehearsals at the Alhambra Theatre; and Cyril Beaumont remembered seeing him in the stalls, seated next to Diaghilev, with 'coat-collar turned up and felt hat pulled over his eyes'.[2] At the end of a dance number, 'Diaghilev consults with his lieutenants. . . . Stravinsky is displeased with the tempo; it must be accelerated; and he emphasises his remarks with a flourish of his cigarette.'[3]

Artistically, this revival of *The Sleeping Beauty* was an enormous success. Stravinsky paid a warm tribute to Diaghilev, who 'had worked at it passionately and lovingly, and once more displayed his profound knowledge of the art of the ballet. He put all his soul, all his strength into it' (*Chr*). In addition to the encomium of Chaikovsky contained in his open letter of 10 October, he stressed his admiration for his music in an interview with a correspondent of *The Times*, making it clear that in his view *The Sleeping Beauty* combined vivid stage imagination with true orchestral imagination. 'Every incident and every entrance' he said, 'is always individual to the character concerned, and every

---

[1] See Appendix A (1).
[2] Cyril W. Beaumont, *Complete Book of Ballets*. London, Putnam, 1937.
[3] Cyril W. Beaumont, *op. cit.*

77

number has its own special character.' Writing in his *Chronicle* fourteen years later, he went further and explained that he had enjoyed taking part in this production, not only because of his love for Chaikovsky, but also because of his profound admiration for classical ballet, which he looked on as 'the perfect expression of the Apollonian principle' in art.

With the benefit of hindsight, it can now be seen that Diaghilev's plan to present a full-length ballet for a run in a commercial theatre, whether in London, Paris, or any other big city, was doomed to failure from the start. At that moment, the ballet public in Western Europe was a very limited one and it had been fed by the Russian Ballet on an almost exclusive diet of one-act ballets, few of which were couched in a truly classical idiom. Even so, *The Sleeping Beauty* ran for 105 performances, from 2 November 1921 to 4 February 1922. But the receipts were not sufficient to recoup the initial costs of production, which had been advanced by Sir Oswald Stoll:[1] so at the end of the run the scenery and costumes were impounded, and Diaghilev was unable to take the production over to Paris. Not until a permanent British ballet company had been built up seventeen years later under the direction of Ninette de Valois (who was a dancer in the Russian Ballet during the years 1923–26), was Chaikovsky's masterpiece seen again in London in its entirety.

Stravinsky spent the remainder of the autumn and the winter, partly in Biarritz working on the score of *Mavra*, and partly in Paris where he had signed a six-year contract with the Pleyel Company covering the transcription of most of his major works for Pleyela mechanical piano.[2] The company allowed him the use of one of their Paris studios in the Rue Rochefouart, which he was able to treat as a kind of *pied à terre*. His movements were also affected by Diaghilev's plans for the Russian Ballet's late spring season in Paris.

Deprived of the possibility of mounting the London production of *The Sleeping Beauty* and faced (as always) by the necessity of offering several novelties to his Parisian public, Diaghilev thought he might salvage some of the best dances from *The Sleeping Beauty* and present them as a one-act divertissement under the title *Aurora's Wedding*. As he had no funds for a new décor, he decided to use that of *Le Pavillon d'Armide*, which had not been seen since the Russian Ballet's pre-war seasons. Then he had the idea of producing Stravinsky's *Reynard*, which was the property of the Princess Edmond de Polignac. She readily gave her permission. Scenery and costumes were entrusted to Larionov, and the choreography to Nijinska. As had been the case with the ballet version of *The Golden Cockerel*, the singers (this time only

---

[1] According to Cyril W. Beaumont (in *The Diaghilev Ballet in London*), the original sum guaranteed by Sir Oswald Stoll for *The Sleeping Beauty* was £10,000; but Diaghilev's pre-production expenses soon exceeded that figure, and in the end Sir Oswald had to put up a total of £20,000.
[2] See Appendix D.

four of them) were placed in the orchestral pit. The third novelty was *Mavra*.

Stravinsky finished the composition of his *opera buffa* in March and attended some of the rehearsals of *Mavra* and *Reynard* during the Russian Ballet's spring season at Monte Carlo. On its way to Paris, the company stopped at Marseilles to give a few performances at the Colonial Exhibition. (Stravinsky was probably with them on this occasion, for the Overture to *Mavra*, which was the last part of the music to be composed, is dated from Monte Carlo, Marseilles and Paris.) The opening programme at the Paris Opera House (18 May 1922) contained *Reynard*. Ansermet conducted; and in his *Chronicle*, Stravinsky says that the production gave him the greatest satisfaction, both musically and scenically, and regrets that Diaghilev never saw fit subsequently to revive it in that form.

Mavra was mounted with great care. A good cast was assembled under the direction of Gregor Fitelberg; scenery and costumes were designed by Léopold Surväge; and Nijinska produced. A preliminary run-through, with the composer at the piano, was held at the Hotel Continental on 29 May; but on its first public performance at the Opera House on 3 June, when it formed part of a 'Stravinsky Evening' being flanked by *Petrushka* and *The Rite of Spring*, it fell completely flat. Stravinsky thought that the main reason for this flop was an error of scale caused by the decision to produce so intimate a chamber work in the inappropriate and overpowering setting of the Paris Opera House. But there was also a psychological factor involved. By 1922 the Parisian audience had fastened on certain romantic and 'revolutionary' elements in his earlier music that appealed to them. They looked for something similar in *Mavra* and were disillusioned when they didn't find it.

Many of Stravinsky's intimates shared his disappointment over the tepid reception of *Mavra*. Among them was his elder son, Theodore, then a boy of fifteen. In his view,[1] the première of this *opera buffa* was just as scandalous in its different way as that of *The Rite of Spring*.

> The modest and intimate character of *Mavra*, together with its melodic idiom, which is related both to gypsy songs and to Italian *bel canto*, was bound to upset a public which over a period of years had become accustomed to look on Stravinsky as a revolutionary from whom it could not, and would not, expect each new work to be other than 'sensational'. Such a public was bound to feel frustrated, and to look on Stravinsky as having failed in his duty. The disappointment was great; and the most annoying part of it was that *Mavra* contained absolutely nothing to justify an uproar.
>
> Insofar as an artist aims at communion and is aware of having said

---

[1] As expressed some years later in *Le Message d'Igor Strawinsky*. Lausanne, 1948.

something essential that has not been said before, it can easily be imagined how heart-breaking it must be for him not to be understood – or, worse still, to be understood in the wrong way. Neither before nor after *Mavra* did Stravinsky suffer so severely from incomprehension and misunderstanding. On this occasion he can be said to have experienced in his innermost being what it is to be 'a voice crying in the wilderness'.[1]

The première of *Mavra* at the Opera House was followed by a party at the Hotel Majestic, which was attended by a large number of famous guests. It is only too likely that after the tepid reception of his *opera buffa*, Stravinsky was feeling rather disgruntled; and Clive Bell, who was present, recalled[2] how at a somewhat late stage in the proceedings Marcel Proust dropped in, 'clad in exquisite black with white kid gloves. . . . He was given a chair on his host's left, and found himself next to Stravinsky to whom, in his polite way, he tried to make himself agreeable. "Doubtless you admire Beethoven," he began. "I detest Beethoven," was all he got for answer. "But, mon cher maître, surely those late sonatas and quartets. . . . ?" "Pire que les autres," growled Stravinsky. Ansermet intervened in an attempt to keep the peace; there was no row but the situation was tense'. Stravinsky's own version of this meeting is contained in his *Conversations* and is clearly intended as a corrective. There he says, 'I talked to Proust about music and he expressed much enthusiasm for the late Beethoven quartets – enthusiasm I would have shared, were it not a commonplace among the intellectuals of that time and not a musical judgment but a literary pose'.

Towards the end of the summer he went to Berlin to await the arrival of his mother who, after petitioning the authorities since the Revolution for permission to emigrate from the Soviet Union, had at last secured a permit to do so and was due to arrive by boat at the port of Stettin on the Baltic. His original intention had been to remain in Berlin only a week; but in the event the sailing was postponed several times, and his stay there was prolonged by nearly two months. During this enforced period of waiting, he saw various people, including Ernest Oeberg of the Russischer Musikverlag, Leopold Stokowski the conductor, and Pavel Tchelichev the painter. He also met the young American pianist and composer, George Antheil, then aged twenty-two, who had just given his first European concert in the Wigmore Hall, London. To follow Antheil's exploits as narrated in his musical biography, *Bad Boy of Music*,[3] is to gain the impression of a volatile, spoilt, unreliable youth of considerable charm and promise. His record of his meetings and talks with Stravinsky must be received with caution. Nevertheless, it seems that during the boring period of enforced waiting Stravinsky got a certain amount of enjoyment out of the company of this lively, extrovert American.

---

[1] Translation by E. W. W.
[2] In *Old Friends*. London, 1956.
[3] Published by Hurst & Blackett, London (1947).

For some years Antheil had idolised Stravinsky's music, and when he saw the Russian composer standing near the reception desk in the Russischer Hof, Berlin, he had no hesitation in accosting him and introducing himself. Stravinsky was friendly and obviously intrigued at meeting a young American composer who appeared to be writing in a neo-Stravinskian idiom. (Antheil showed him the manuscript score of his *Symphony for Five Instruments* which, he says, he had made as nearly similar as he could to Stravinsky's own *Symphonies of Wind Instruments*.) Stravinsky expressed interest in America and asked numerous questions about musical conditions there, in the obvious expectation of being able to carry out a tour of the United States in the near future. He must also have been favourably impressed by the young American's piano playing, because before leaving Berlin he offered to arrange a piano recital for him in Paris the following Christmas. Antheil accepted this invitation but, when the time came, failed to turn up.

This was the period of post-war inflation in Berlin; and hordes of women of every class were to be found on the streets at night. Antheil recalls[1] how one night when he and Stravinsky were walking home through the Brandenburger Tor, they were accosted by about fifty girls in the Tiergartenallee.

I would not have known how to get out of such a jam. But Stravinsky was about twenty years older than I and he knew. He said that we had just come from entertaining six girls, three apiece and that we were really very, very tired. They would, he felt sure, understand. They did.

When finally Stravinsky's mother arrived, she brought with her a quantity of her son's earlier music from the years of his residence in St. Petersburg, and also a 'faint contempt for his present "mercurial" (as she considered it) reputation in Paris'.[2] Antheil describes what may well have been a typical clash between mother and son.

Her idea, then, of a *really* important modern composer was Scriabine, to whose music she was apparently devoted. . . . Stravinsky, on the other hand, cordially hated Scriabine's music . . . with all of its voluptuousness, its fat, juicy orchestration. . . . One evening, while I was sitting with both of them, I heard Mrs. Stravinsky and her son break into a heated prolonged argument. She would not give in and finally Stravinsky almost broke into tears, so wrathful did he become. At last he turned to me and translated: he, Stravinsky, no longer able to stand his mother's inordinate admiration for Scriabine (when, after all, she had a son destined to become more famous than Scriabine would ever become!), admonished her, criticising her taste and finally admitting to hating Scriabine. Whereupon she had answered:

---

[1] George Antheil, *op. cit.*
[2] George Antheil, *op. cit.*

1. The Man

'Now, now, Igor! You have not changed one bit [in] all these years. You were always like that – always contemptuous of your *betters*!'[1]

On his return to Biarritz, Stravinsky started to compose an instrumental sonata that later became the *Octet for Wind Instruments*; and when Koussevitzky visited him in order to heal the musical breach caused by his calamitous London performance of the *Symphonies of Wind Instruments*, he agreed to let him have the first performance of this new work for one of his orchestral concerts at the Paris Opera House on condition that he (Stravinsky) and not Koussevitzky should conduct it. After a few months, the composition of the *Octet* was interrupted by the necessity of completing the instrumentation of *The Wedding*, which Diaghilev had decided to produce during the 1923 season of the Russian Ballet. Various attempts, all of them abortive, had been made to solve the instrumental problem during the years 1914–17. Now that a date was fixed for the cantata's production as a ballet, a final solution had to be found. The composer saw clearly that the sung element in the work 'would be best supported by an ensemble consisting exclusively of percussion instruments'[2] (including four pianos); and the definitive instrumentation was finished at Monaco on 6 April 1923. (The *Octet* was finished on 26 May.)

The scenery and costumes for *The Wedding* were entrusted to Goncharova, who to begin with produced elaborately realistic designs; but she was persuaded to revise these until they became simplified to a point of near-austerity. The choreography was by Nijinska. As the dancers found the music difficult to assimilate, the Princess Edmond de Polignac agreed on Diaghilev's suggestion to hold a preliminary concert performance at her house; and this proved most helpful.

After the débâcle of *Mavra*, the success of *The Wedding* went some way towards restoring the public's confidence in Stravinsky as a composer, though few of them realised how remote its idiom was from his current neoclassical style, its initial inspiration being nearly ten years old and the vocal score having been completed as long ago as 1917. The first performance at the Gaieté Lyrique (13 June 1923) was conducted by Ansermet. As a tribute to Stravinsky, three contemporary French composers – Georges Auric, Francis Poulenc and Vittorio Rieti – agreed to join Marcelle Meyer as the four pianists in the orchestra.

Since meeting Antheil in Berlin, Stravinsky had made other American friends, including Gerald and Sara Murphy. This couple had been living in Paris for about two years, during which time they became friendly with many of the persons connected with the Russian Ballet. They attended all the rehearsals of *The Wedding* and were so excited by the new work that they felt

---

[1] George Antheil, *op. cit.*
[2] From Stravinsky's *Chronicle*.

compelled to throw a party to celebrate its première. As setting they chose a large converted barge on the Seine that was moored in front of the Chambre des Députés. The party was timed to begin at 7 p.m. on Sunday 17 June; and 'the first person to arrive was Stravinsky, who dashed into the *salle à manger* to inspect, and even rearrange, the distribution of place cards. He was apparently satisfied with his own seating – on the right hand of Princess Edmond de Polignac'.[1] In addition to Stravinsky and the Princess, the guests included Picasso, Milhaud, Cocteau, Ansermet, Diaghilev, Kochno, Larionov, Goncharova, Germaine Tailleferre, Marcelle Meyer, Tristan Tzara, Blaise Cendrars, Schofield Thayer, and a sprinkling of dancers. The prolonged dinner party was interspersed with music, provided by Ansermet and Marcelle Meyer at a piano, and dancing. Cocteau donned the barge captain's uniform and went about the barge with a lantern, putting his head in at portholes to announce the ship was sinking ('On coule!'). At one point Ansermet and Kochno 'managed to take down an enormous laurel wreath, bearing the inscription "Les Noces – Hommages" that had been hung from the ceiling and were holding it for Stravinsky, who ran the length of the room and leaped nimbly through the centre'.[2] Cocteau's final comment on the party is said to have been 'Depuis le jour de ma première communion, c'est le plus beau soir de ma vie'.

The invitation list at this party did not include George Antheil and his Hungarian friend Boski, who later became his wife. The two of them had arrived in Paris on 13 June just in time to attend the première of *The Wedding*. Antheil had taken steps to reconcile himself with Stravinsky in advance for his failure to turn up in Paris the previous Christmas to give the piano recital Stravinsky had offered to sponsor; and the Russian composer had suggested that if Antheil came to Paris for *The Wedding*, he should look him up. So, after the première, Antheil took Boski backstage, where Stravinsky received them warmly and invited them to visit him at Pleyel's the following day to hear the Pleyela version of *The Wedding*. Antheil writes:[3]

> The next day we went to see him at Pleyel's, the great piano warehouse rooms where Chopin had often practised; and Stravinsky himself played *Les Noces*, this time on an electric pianola. I liked the second version even better than the one which we had heard last night; it was more precise, colder, harder. . . . Stravinsky talked with us quite a while before we departed; I knew that I was still on the old terms with him, that my failing to appear at Christmas had not injured our relationship.

But a day or two later, when Stravinsky was with some Americans, the question of his acquaintance with this young American musician came up. He was told

[1] Calvin Tomkins, 'Living Well is the Best Revenge'. *The New Yorker*, 28 July 1962.
[2] Calvin Tomkins, *op. cit.*
[3] George Antheil, *op. cit.*

that Antheil was going about the place saying that Stravinsky had spent most of his time in Berlin in Antheil's company because he was so impressed by his compositions. 'That,' answered Stravinsky,[1] 'was not quite literally correct; I thought him a fine pianist, but I scarcely know his compositions.' 'Ah,' cried the American and his wife, 'that's just what we suspected, a four-flusher.' The result of this attack on Antheil's character and reputation was that the next time the two musicians met at a concert, Stravinsky drew 'himself up coldly, fixed his monocle in his eye, and cut [him] dead'.[2] This was a traumatic experience for a person who revered Stravinsky so profoundly as the young Antheil did; and the wound was not healed until 1941 when Stravinsky met and recognized Boski Antheil at the local market in Hollywood and sent the Antheils tickets for the Los Angeles première of his *Symphony in C*. The renewed friendship was sealed when Stravinsky came to dinner and the Antheils' son, Peter, then a boy of about eight, sang him excerpts from *The Rite of Spring* which he knew from Walt Disney's film *Fantasia*.

Two meetings – with Vladimir Mayakovsky and Ferrucio Busoni – deserve mention here.

In 1922 Mayakovsky visited Paris; and the two Russians saw quite a lot of each other. In his *Conversations*, Stravinsky remembered him 'as a somewhat burly youth . . . who drank more than he should have and who was deplorably dirty.' Mayakovsky spoke no French: so Stravinsky sometimes acted as his interpreter. On one such occasion Stravinsky interpreted a discussion between Mayakovsky and Cocteau; but the interview was not a success. Cocteau discovered that the two of them belonged to such different worlds and their thoughts were couched in such different terms that communication was almost impossible. Stravinsky apparently found the French for everything Mayakovsky said very easily, but not the Russian for Cocteau's remarks. Cocteau said[3] that after Mayakovsky's departure it was as though a foreigner had gone, leaving two compatriots together who were in complete understanding with each other.

In August 1923, Stravinsky was invited by the organisers of the Bauhaus Exhibition in Weimar to attend a production of *The Soldier's Tale* that was to form part of the festival. To reach Weimar, he had to travel through the occupied zone of Germany; and the journey as described in his *Chronicle* was by no means a comfortable one. The performance of *The Soldier's Tale*, which was conducted by Hermann Scherchen, was warmly received by an audience that included Klee and Kandinsky as well as Busoni. Stravinsky had never met Busoni before, and as he understood him to be an irreconcilable opponent

---

[1] This conversation is quoted by George Antheil in *Bad Boy of Music*.
[2] George Antheil, *op. cit.*
[3] In *Appendice 1924* (*Stravinsky Dernière Heure*) to *Le Coq et l'Arlequin* as printed in *Le Rappel à l'Ordre*. Paris, Stock, 1926.

of his music, he was all the more delighted to find him completely captivated by *The Soldier's Tale*. A few days later Busoni wrote in a letter to a friend:

> One had become a child again; one forgot music and literature, one was simply moved. There's something which achieved its aim! But let us take care not to imitate it![1]

Stravinsky conducted the first performance of his new *Octet* at one of Koussevitzky's Symphony Concerts at the Paris Opera House on 18 October 1923. Although the published score bears no dedication, he has stated (in his *Dialogues*) that the work was in fact dedicated to Vera de Bosset, who seventeen years later became his second wife. At that moment she was married to the Russian artist Soudeikine, who had designed *The Tragedy of Salome* for the Russian Ballet in 1913, and she had recently appeared in the non-dancing role of the Queen in the London production of *The Sleeping Beauty*. She is mentioned in Ramuz's correspondence with Stravinsky the following year (1924) when Ramuz accepted a commission to send her chocolate from Switzerland.

Stravinsky was now in the final year of his sixth septennium – a year that in some ways was to prove climacteric. Whether Diaghilev realised it at the time or not, the long promised ballet cantata of *The Wedding* was the last score Stravinsky would write specifically for the Russian Ballet.[2] The ties that bound him to the stage were weakening, partly because he found performances of his music by theatre orchestras unsatisfactory, and partly because of an impending spiritual crisis in his life. Lifar writes: 'Then in 1923 we find him finally repudiating the ballet, his religious convictions no longer permitting him to employ his art in anything so base as theatrical ballet. (Indeed a letter to Diaghilev at this time speaks of the ballet as "l'anathème du Christ".)'[3] This letter does not seem to have been released for publication; but the phrase quoted is sufficient to show that Stravinsky was then in a state of acute religious tension.

He had been born and baptised into the Russian Orthodox Church; but at the age of seventeen or eighteen he had abandoned the practice of his faith. Now his attitude was beginning to change, and a mood of acceptance was developing in him. In 1924, when he and his family left Biarritz and moved to 167 Boulevard Carnet, Nice, a certain Father Nicolas came into his life – and even into his home. 'He was practically a member of our household during a period of five years,' says Stravinsky in his *Expositions*.

At the same time as he underwent this spiritual crisis, he had to review his

---

[1] Quoted in Edward J. Dent's *Ferruccio Busoni*. London, Oxford University Press, 1933.
[2] Stravinsky wrote five ballet scores for Diaghilev and the Russian Ballet, viz., *The Firebird*, *Petrushka*, *The Rite of Spring*, *The Wedding*, and *Pulcinella*. The ballet score of *Apollo Musagetes* (1928) was written for Mrs. Elizabeth Sprague Coolidge and received its first performance in America; but Diaghilev was allowed to have the 'second rights'. At times Diaghilev used other suitable material by Stravinsky for theatrical purposes, viz., *Fireworks*, *The Nightingale* (and also *The Song of the Nightingale*), *Reynard*, *Mavra*, and *Oedipus Rex* (1927).
[3] Quoted in Serge Lifar's *Diaghilev*. London, Putnam, 1940.

professional career. If in the future he could not rely on the stage to the same extent as in the past, he would have to find some compensation. Although he had felt extremely nervous about conducting the first performance of the *Octet* – this was the first time he had launched one of his new compositions himself – the comparative success of the performance led him to think that he might develop his potential as a conductor. Koussevitzky was so pleased by the success of the *Octet* that he invited him to write another work for one of his concerts in 1924; and the composer, perhaps with the idea of an American tour in the back of his mind, suggested a piano concerto. It was Koussevitzky who, in the course of a visit to Biarritz in the winter of 1924, proposed that Stravinsky himself should play the solo part at the first performance. Stravinsky says:

> I hesitated at first, fearing I should not have enough time to perfect my technique as a pianist, to practise enough, and to acquire the endurance necessary to perform a work demanding sustained effort. But I am by nature rather tempted by anything needing prolonged effort, and prone to persist in overcoming difficulties; and as also the prospect of creating my work myself, and thus establishing the manner in which I wanted it to be played, greatly attracted me, I decided finally to accept the proposal (*Chr*).

Stravinsky rehearsing the *Piano-Rag-Music, c.* 1924

The Russian Exile in France (1920 – 1929)

The life of a conductor and executant could easily be dovetailed into that of a composer; but it meant that for the next fifteen years or so his concert tours and engagements would take up a considerable amount of each year and leave him less time for composition than in the past.[1]

This was also the moment when critical opinion began to focus on him. Although the first monographs on his music were not published until the late twenties, the *Revue Musicale* devoted a special issue to him as early as December 1923. His music was producing enthusiastic advocates as well as determined opponents.

His first concert tour was in Belgium in January 1924 (Antwerp and Brussels), followed by a brief Spanish tour (Barcelona and Madrid) in March.

The new *Piano Concerto* was brought out, first at a private audition at the house of Princess Edmond de Polignac and then a week later (22 May) at one of Koussevitzky's concerts at the Paris Opera House, where it scored a considerable success. It was in no way dwarfed by its neighbours in the programme (which included *The Firebird* and *The Rite of Spring*); and Stravinsky's own performance as soloist was excitingly dry, nervous, and percussive, the long cadenza of the first movement inducing just the right mood of vertigo in the minds of the audience. At the end of the first movement the composer picked up a clean handkerchief from a small pile at the side of the piano to dry his hands, and there was a longish pause before he embarked on the slow movement; but it wasn't until his *Chronicle* was published that he disclosed that this pause was due to a momentary black-out. He recovered from this, however, with the help of a cue from Koussevitzky, and finished the Concerto without further incident. Thereafter, he reserved for himself the exclusive rights of its performance for five years.

When he returned to Biarritz that June, he started to compose a *Sonata* for piano; but he had only just completed the first movement, when he was interrupted by his family's removal from Biarritz to Nice. He finished the work at Nice in October and then embarked on a European concert tour that took him to Warsaw, Prague, Leipzig, Berlin, Amsterdam, the Hague, Geneva, Lausanne, and Marseilles.

Early in 1925 he paid his first visit to America. On his arrival in New York, the usual collection of journalists came down to the boat to interview him. When one of them asked what he thought of modern music, he received the disconcerting reply, 'I detest it!' When another had the temerity to pursue the subject, 'But you, maestro . . .?' Stravinsky said, 'I don't write modern music – I only write good music.'[2]

This American tour lasted two months and covered New York, Boston,

---

[1] His *Chronicle* is the main authority for particulars about these concert tours, which are accordingly given in some detail for the decade 1924/34, but no attempt has been made to follow them up throughout his subsequent career.

[2] Quoted in Casella's *Strawinski*.

1. The Man

Chicago, Philadelphia, Cleveland, Detroit, and Cincinnati. As Stravinsky wrote in his *Chronicle*:

> The public was already acquainted with my most frequently performed works, which they had heard in many concerts; but what was a novelty was to see me in the roles of pianist and conductor. Judging by the full houses and the acclamations which I received, I flattered myself that I had achieved an undoubted success.

On his return to Europe, he had to go, first to Barcelona and Rome to take part in festival concerts of his music, and then to Paris where he appeared in another Koussevitzky concert at the Opera House, conducting his *Rag-Time* and playing his *Piano Concerto*.

That summer the Russian Ballet was giving a lengthy season in London at the Coliseum (from 18 May to 1 August); but this was broken for a week in June to enable the company to appear at the Gaieté Lyrique in Paris. There Stravinsky saw a new choreographic version of *The Song of the Nightingale* (17 June), which had been made by a young dancer called Georges Balanchivadze (later known as Balanchine), a former pupil of the Maryinsky Theatre, Leningrad, who had left Russia and joined Diaghilev's company the previous year. The Massine version of this ballet had not been seen for five years, and this new version was much liked by Diaghilev and the Parisian audiences.[1]

During his visit to America he had arranged with a gramophone firm to make records of some of his music; and this gave him the idea of composing a work, each movement of which would literally fit one side of a gramophone record. He planned his *Serenade in A* for piano accordingly. It was to have four movements, the last of which (Cadenza Finale) was written first (in April 1925), the remaining movements being added during the summer and early autumn.

This was the moment when the automobile stage of his life began. During that summer, he spent quite a lot of time motoring about the Riviera in his new Renault; and in September he drove as far as Venice where he was due to appear at the I.S.C.M. Festival to perform his *Piano Sonata*. Malipiero has written a curiously acid and slightly malicious account of the atmosphere during this visit:[2]

> The flower of international snobbism was reunited in Venice that September. In the salon of the Princess de P. at the Palazzo Contarini dal Zaffo, men and women paid court to the Russian composer. He was surrounded by a perpetual buzz of 'Mon cherrr. . . .' Someone asked 'Another cup of tea?' and everyone stopped talking to hear his answer. 'For a Russian, tea-

---

[1] In view of the close balletic collaboration that was to develop later between Stravinsky and Balanchine, it is curious to find that in his *Chronicle* Stravinsky erroneously refers to this new version as being by Massine instead of Balanchine.

[2] G. F. Malipiero, *Strawinsky*. Venice, 1945. (Translation by E. W. W.).

drinking is the focus of nostalgia.' (At this, there passed before our eyes the vision of a rapid succession of cossacks and sleighs, followed by packs of wolves moving across an immense snow-covered plain.) 'In the West,' he continued, 'in the absence of the samovar, tea-drinking is quite a different matter. C'est un autre goût.'

This festival was the occasion on which Stravinsky and Schoenberg so signally failed to meet each other.

On his return journey he made a short tour of northern Italy in his car, his last stopping place before Nice being Genoa. For some time he had had the feeling that after the *Sonata* and *Serenade* for piano he ought to concentrate on a large-scale composition – perhaps 'an opera or an oratorio on some universally familiar subject' (*Chr*) – but he was uncertain how to resolve the problem of language. As he explains in his *Dialogues*, Russian, the exiled language of his heart, had become musically impracticable, and French and German were temperamentally alien to him. At that moment he happened to find in a book kiosk in Genoa a life of St. Francis of Assisi, which he bought and read the same night. This gave him the idea that just as St. Francis had used Provençal, the poetic language of the renaissance of the Rhône, for hieratic purposes in contrast to his daily demotic use of Italian, so he might choose Ciceronian Latin, instead of a vernacular modern language, for his libretto in order to endow the text with a certain monumental, almost incantatory character.

The decision to base his opera oratorio on the *Oedipus Rex* of Sophocles followed quickly on his return to Nice. He picked Cocteau as his librettist because he particularly admired his recent adaptation of *Antigone* 'and the manner in which he had handled the ancient myth and presented it in modern guise' (*Chr*). The Latin translation was entrusted to Jean Daniélou.

Even now the link with the Russian Ballet was not entirely broken, for the two collaborators intended that this new opera/oratorio should be performed as a tribute to Diaghilev, the twentieth anniversary of whose theatrical enterprise would occur in the spring of 1927.

Leaving Cocteau to rough out the libretto of *Oedipus Rex*, Stravinsky undertook a tour in the autumn of 1925 that took him to Zurich, Basel and Wiesbaden for performances of his *Piano Concerto*, Winterthur and Berlin for chamber music concerts, Frankfort-on-Main for a festival of two concerts devoted to his music, and Copenhagen where he conducted a concert and also a performance of *Petrushka* by the Royal Danish Ballet. Back in Paris, he heard with grief of the death of Oeberg, director of the Edition Russe de Musique, and returned to Nice to celebrate Christmas with his family.

In 1926, he rejoined the Russian Orthodox Church, becoming a communicant for the first time since 1910.[1] In this year too he enjoyed one of the most

---

[1] This is referred to in Diaghilev's last letter to Stravinsky dated 7 April 1926 and printed in *Memories*.

1. The Man

powerful religious experiences of his whole life. A spring concert tour had taken him to Amsterdam, Rotterdam and Haarlem; and later to Budapest, Vienna and Zagreb. On his way back to Nice, he undertook his first aeroplane flight – from Trieste to Venice – and then joined a group of pilgrims going to Padua to celebrate the 700th anniversary of St. Anthony. 'I happened to enter the Basilica,' he writes in his *Dialogues*, 'just as the Saint's body was exhibited. I saw the coffin, I knelt, and I prayed. I asked that a sign of recognition be given when and if my prayer was answered, and as it was answered, and with the sign, I do not hesitate to call that moment of recognition the most real in my life.' An immediate result of this experience was the composition of the first of his religious works, the *Pater Noster* for mixed choir *a cappella*,which was not published until 1932.

At the beginning of May, his work on *Oedipus Rex* was interrupted by a message from the management of the Scala, Milan, saying that Toscanini who was rehearsing *The Nightingale* and a new production of *Petrushka* with choreography by Boris Romanov, had fallen ill and inviting him to take his place at the Scala in conducting these two works. He consented, and a little later that summer returned to Milan to play his *Piano Concerto*.

The rest of the year and the first months of 1927 were devoted to the composition of *Oedipus Rex*, the score of which was finished on 14 March. As has already been mentioned, Stravinsky and Cocteau intended that the new work should be heard in Paris as part of the celebrations of the twentieth anniversary of Diaghilev's theatrical activity. In his *Chronicle* Stravinsky says:

> We, his friends, wished to commemorate the rare event in the annals of the theatre of an undertaking of a purely artistic nature, without the least hope of material gain, which had been able to continue for so many years and to survive so many trials, including the world war, and had, moreover, continued solely owing to the indomitable energy, the persistent tenacity, of one man passionately devoted to his work. We wanted to give him a surprise, and were able to keep our secret to the last moment, which would have been impossible in the case of a ballet. . . .

Nevertheless, the moment came when Diaghilev had to be let into the secret so that arrangements could be made for the production of *Oedipus Rex*. At first Diaghilev seems to have contemplated a full stage production: but then he changed his mind, and Grigoriev recalls him saying on the terrace at Monte Carlo early in 1927: 'Well – I've thought of the way to do *Oedipus*. We'll simply give it a concert performance – no décor, and the cast in evening dress, sitting on the stage in front of black velvet curtains. Musically it will even gain.'[1] But even a concert performance entailed so large an expenditure on soloists, chorus and orchestra that it would have proved impossible, had not the Princess Edmond de Polignac come to the rescue once more.

---

[1] Quoted in Grigoriev's *The Diaghilev Ballet 1909–1929*.

90

She paid Stravinsky 12,000 francs for a private preview of the work at her house, with the composer accompanying the singers at the piano; and Stravinsky gave this fee to Diaghilev to help finance the public performances.[1]

The première took place at the Théâtre Sarah-Bernhardt on 30 May with the composer conducting: but the reception was cool; the public was not entertained; the critics were hostile; even Diaghilev was reserved – *un cadeau très macabre*' was his description of the offering. Once again Stravinsky complained that his new work had suffered from being inappropriately placed next to 'a very colourful ballet' (*Dia*),[2] and Grigoriev's verdict was that, compared with *The Firebird, Oedipus Rex* seemed very tame. No wonder Stravinsky was becoming increasingly annoyed by the public's fixation on his early ballet music; and this exasperation could be clearly felt when a few weeks later he conducted in a rather intransigent style gala performances of *Petrushka*, *Pulcinella* and *The Firebird* at the Prince's Theatre, London. As Grigoriev said,[3] the dancers were dismayed on that occasion, because they never knew what tempo he might adopt next, especially in *The Firebird* and *Petrushka*.

As for the critics, there was so much ill-considered talk about a return to Handel and the eighteenth century that Stravinsky found it necessary to issue a public warning that 'the use of certain technical devices which were current in so-called classical music' was insufficient to constitute neo-classicism, but that true neo-classicism like true classicism should be judged by its constructive values – the successful interrelation of its constituent parts.[4]

Early that summer he received his first American commission. It came from Mrs. Elizabeth Sprague Coolidge, a wealthy patroness of music, who wanted a thirty-minute ballet score for a festival of contemporary music to be held at the Library of Congress, Washington, D.C., in the spring of 1928. Diaghilev was upset by Stravinsky's defection from the Russian Ballet and, according to Stravinsky (in his *Dialogues*), the following not very edifying conversation took place:

DIAGHILEV: Cette Américaine est complètement sourde.
STRAVINSKY: Elle est sourde, mais elle paye.
DIAGHILEV: Tu penses toujours à l'argent.

The commission fee was a modest $1,000. Stravinsky was quite prepared for Diaghilev to enjoy the European rights of this ballet; and he decided to fashion the main role so that it would fit the special talents of Serge Lifar, whose

---

[1] Prokofiev ridiculed the 'supra-national' aspect of the production in a letter written to Mayakovsky – 'The librettist is French, the text Latin, the subject Greek, the music Anglo-German (after Handel), the performance will be in Monaco [*sic*] paid for by American money – indeed the height of Internationalism.'
[2] The ballet in question was *The Firebird*.
[3] S. L. Grigoriev, *op. cit.*
[4] See Appendix A (3).

performance in *The Cat* he had greatly admired that summer. This commission also gave him a chance to carry out an idea that had attracted him for some time, namely, 'to compose a ballet founded on moments or episodes in Greek mythology plastically interpreted by dancing of the so-called classical school' (*Chr*). As theme, he chose Apollo, leader of the Muses, and for the purpose of this brief ballet reduced their number to three, viz., Calliope, Polyhymnia, and Terpsichore – poetry, mime, and dance. His score would be an exercise in the metrics of versification; his idiom would be non-chromatic as being appropriate for a *ballet blanc*; and his instrumentation would be restricted to strings in view of the lack of dramatic contrast in the treatment of the subject.

Part of the summer was spent with his family at Echarvines on the shores of the Lac d'Annecy; and on returning to Nice, he devoted the whole of the autumn to writing the score of *Apollo Musagetes*, which was finished by the end of 1927. About this time, Gabriel Paichadze who was Oeberg's successor at the Edition Russe de Musique received an enquiry from Madame Ida Rubinstein, who was preparing a repertory of ballets for a new company she was about to launch. Being informed that *Apollo* was not available as Diaghilev had a prior claim, she agreed to commission an entirely new ballet from Stravinsky for the fee of $7,500. He was free to choose subject and treatment and the score would have to be ready for her projected season at the Paris Opera House at the end of November 1928.

The early part of 1928 was taken up with concerts and tours. First of all, there were two concerts at the new Salle Pleyel in the Faubourg St. Honoré, Paris,[1] at which he conducted *The Rite of Spring*. Then he went to Berlin in February for the first performance of the stage production of *Oedipus Rex* at the Krolloper under Klemperer's direction. The programme included *Petrushka* and *Mavra*;[2] and on this occasion *Oedipus Rex* made its full impact and was in no way dwarfed by its neighbours. Later that spring Stravinsky conducted concert performances of *Oedipus Rex* at Amsterdam and in London and Paris. He also conducted two concerts at Barcelona, the programmes of which included *The Rite of Spring*, and went on to Rome where he directed a production of *The Nightingale* at the Royal Opera (formerly the Costanzi Theatre).

Apollo Musagetes was produced at Washington, D.C., on 27 April with choreography by Adolph Bolm. For the Russian Ballet production at the Théâtre Sarah-Bernhardt, Paris (12 June), Diaghilev chose Balanchine to do the choreography; and the settings were after paintings by André Bauchant, whose naïve work in the style of le douanier Rousseau was fashionable in Paris at that moment. Stravinsky conducted the Paris performances and expressed particular satisfaction with the work of Balanchine.

Georges Balanchine, as ballet-master, had arranged the dances exactly as

---

[1] The Pleyel firm gave Stravinsky a studio in their new premises.
[2] In some of the later performances, *The Soldier's Tale* took the place of *Mavra*.

The Russian Exile in France (1920 – 1929)

I had wished – that is to say, in accordance with the classical school. From that point of view it was a complete success, and it was the first attempt to revive academic dancing in a work actually composed for the purpose. Balanchine . . . had designed for the choreography of *Apollo* groups, movements and lines of great dignity and plastic elegance as inspired by the beauty of classical forms. As a thorough musician – he had studied at the St. Petersburg Conservatoire – he had had no difficulty in grasping the smallest details of my music, and his beautiful choreography clearly expressed my meaning (*Chr*).

Stravinsky also conducted the London première of the ballet on 25 June.

Apollo scored a considerable success in both Paris and London: but it is difficult to know what Diaghilev's real view of it was. While the music was in course of composition, he wrote quite enthusiastically about it to Lifar; but when it came to the Paris production, he seems to have disapproved of the Terpsichore Variation and tried to have it cut.[1] This led Stravinsky to think he disliked the whole score; but Grigoriev assures us that he 'considered it the best of all Stravinsky's works, for the limpidity and calm of the music, which particularly moved him'.[2]

Stravinsky and his family returned to Echarvines on the Lac d'Annecy for the summer. It was now time to concentrate on the score Ida Rubinstein had commissioned; and Benois, who was advising her on her company's artistic policy, submitted two plans, one of them for a ballet to be inspired by the music of Chaikovsky. This suggestion appealed to Stravinsky – particularly since the date fixed for the first performance would coincide with the thirty-fifth anniversary of Chaikovsky's death – and he set to work to find an appropriate subject. As he had decided not only to dedicate his score to Chaikovsky's memory, but also to base it on a selection of Chaikovsky's music, he turned to the literature of the nineteenth century and, after a brief search found that one of Hans Andersen's longer tales, *The Ice Maiden,* would exactly suit his purpose.

In order to work on the score of *The Fairy's Kiss* as the new ballet was to be called, he hired a room in a mason's cottage where he installed a piano. Here he hoped to find peace and solitude for his composition.

> The workman who had let the room to me occupied the rest of the house with his wife and child. He went out in the morning, and all was quiet till he returned at noon. The family then sat down to dinner. An acrid and nauseating smell of garlic and rancid oil came through the chinks of the partition which separated me from them, and made me feel sick. After an exchange of bitter words, the mason would lose his temper and begin to swear at his wife and child, terrifying them with his threats. The wife would start by

---

[1] See p. 345.
[2] Grigoriev, *op. cit.*

93

answering, and then, bursting into sobs, would pick up the screaming infant and rush out, followed by her husband. This was repeated every day with hopeless regularity, so that the last hour of my morning's work was always filled with agonising apprehension (*Chr*).

Despite this rather surcharged atmosphere, the composition prospered. The only interruption he allowed himself was a visit to Scheveningen for a concert. On his return to Paris, his train was held up by the end-of-the-holiday-season traffic and shunted on to a siding at Nevers. Being unwilling to waste time, he utilised the enforced four hours' delay by working on the score in his compartment.

The orchestral score was finished so late that he was unable to spend much time with Nijinska, who had been engaged to do the choreography. When finally he saw her work, he found its quality uneven; but it was then too late to alter it. The first performance of *The Fairy's Kiss* took place at the Paris Opera House on 27 November, with Stravinsky conducting. Diaghilev, who had been with the Russian Ballet on tour in Edinburgh, made a special visit to Paris in order to see what sort of show this rival company was capable of mounting and wrote a scathing account of the production and performance to Lifar,[1] complaining that Stravinsky had given himself up 'entirely to the love of God and cash'. Shortly afterwards, the Russian Ballet returned to Paris, following Ida Rubinstein's company at the Opera House, and Diaghilev announced a special 'Stravinsky Evening' for Christmas Eve with a programme consisting of *The Firebird*, *Apollo* and *Petrushka*.

In the winter of 1928/29, Ansermet founded a new orchestra called the Orchestre Symphonique de Paris. Stravinsky was invited to conduct two of their concerts and found the players' standards so high that he agreed to entrust them with the first performance of his next composition. As he had already given more than forty performances of his 1924 *Piano Concerto*, he now decided to write another work for piano and orchestra to be entitled *Capriccio*. As was the case with the *Piano Concerto*, he intended to reserve for himself the exclusive performing rights for a period of five years. The work of composition was spread out over the first nine months of 1929; but it was interrupted by a number of engagements.

In February he conducted a concert performance of *Oedipus Rex* at the Dresden Opera House. In March he took part in a programme of his chamber music at a concert of the Société Philharmonique de Paris, conducting *The Soldier's Tale* and the *Octet* and playing his *Sonata* and *Serenade* for piano. A new version of *Reynard* was mounted by Diaghilev at the opening of the Russian Ballet season at the Théâtre Sarah-Bernhardt, Paris, that spring, (21 May) with fresh choreography by Lifar, who used acrobats as well as dancers; but this was not particularly liked by the public, and Stravinsky

---

[1] This letter is quoted on p. 352.

made it clear that he preferred the original Nijinska version. He visited Berlin that summer to play his *Piano Concerto* under Klemperer, and London to play his *Piano Concerto* and conduct *Apollo* in a concert directed by Eugene Goossens, and to conduct a broadcast performance of *The Fairy's Kiss* for the B.B.C.

While in London, he had an opportunity of meeting Willy Strecker of the German firm of music publishers, Schotts Söhne of Mainz. Schotts' already handled in Germany some works of his that were not published by the Edition Russe de Musique and in view of the increasing interest being shown in his music in Germany, he may have felt it would be useful to be in close touch with a German firm.

Back with his family at Talloires on Lac d'Annecy, he resumed work on the *Capriccio* in a two-room prefabricated summer-house. One evening he went out with his two sons to visit Prokofiev who was staying in the neighbourhood, and on returning home was met by his wife who had waited up to tell him that a telegram had just arrived from Venice saying that Diaghilev had died there that morning (19 August). This news affected him deeply.

It was true that recently the two men had become estranged. Diaghilev had never been able to reconcile himself to the idea that Stravinsky was free to write music for stage performance by companies other than the Russian Ballet, and the production of *The Fairy's Kiss* by Ida Rubinstein and her dancers had been the last straw. At first he tried to find compensation for Stravinsky's so-called defection in the discovery of a young Russian boy musician in whose precocious talents as pianist and composer he had unbounded confidence. Igor Markevich, born at Kiev in 1912, had studied counterpoint under Nadia Boulanger and orchestration under Vittorio Rieti; and that summer Diaghilev arranged for his Concerto for Piano and Orchestra in F to be performed as an interlude in one of the Russian Ballet programmes at Covent Garden (15 July). But the new work failed to make any special impression on audience or critics to Diaghilev's bitter disappointment.

Stravinsky had been completely unmoved by Diaghilev's talk of his boy prodigy's genius; and this had not improved their relations. Their last meeting was indeed strange and strained.[1] Stravinsky was at the Gare du Nord on his way to London when he suddenly realised that Diaghilev, Kochno and Markevich were travelling by the same train. 'Diaghilev, seeing that he could not avoid me, addressed me with embarrassed kindness. We went separately to our compartments on the train, and he did not leave his. I never saw him again' (*Exp*).

But at this point it seems best to recall the brighter side of their remarkable twenty years' friendship.

---

[1] This meeting was probably towards the end of June 1929, though in *Expositions* Stravinsky mentions May.

1. The Man

To the end of his life, Diaghilev never lost his belief in the importance of Stravinsky's early ballet scores, particularly *The Rite of Spring*. During the Russian Ballet's last season in London in July 1929, he wrote to a friend:

> Yesterday *The Rite of Spring* proved a tremendous success. At last these fools have got to understanding it. *The Times* says that *The Rite* is to the twentieth century what Beethoven's Ninth was to the nineteenth. At last! Yes, one has to learn to be patient and philosophical, even to rise above the obstacles that puny, narrow-minded men set in the way of whatever seeks to depart from mediocrity. Heavens, all this is as trite as can be – but what's one to do? One can't go on living without some hope of seeing 'in the dawn the rays of tomorrow's sun'.

It seems clear that his devotion to his friend never really wavered; and in the last letter he sent him (7 April 1926)[1] he wrote, 'When in moments of deep disturbance I remember that you are living almost next door in the world, I start to feel better'.

In his grief at Diaghilev's death, Stravinsky must have recalled with sharp pleasure memories of numerous incidents from the early years of their friendship in St. Petersburg – keeping his first business appointment with Diaghilev in the Dominique Restaurant for a talk about his future; visiting Diaghilev's apartment on the Zamiatine Perenlok and feeling disturbed by the perversely large number of mirrors on the walls; meeting Bakst, Benois, Fokine, and the other members of Diaghilev's 'committee' there to discuss ballet plans; going with Diaghilev to the island night clubs on the Neva; and dining with him after a concert, 'in a little sawdust delicatessen, on marinated fish, caviar, Black Sea oysters, and the most delicious mushrooms in the world' (*Exp*). After that came the years of triumph and fame for Diaghilev and his Russian Ballet, and for Stravinsky and his music. This meant that henceforth their relations were bound to be governed partly by business considerations. But even so, there were still moments when they managed to slip away to enjoy themselves together – as, for instance, in pre-war London when they would take an evening off to hear a Gilbert and Sullivan operetta;[2] or Bayreuth when they attended *Parsifal*; or Spain when they spent the Semana Santa of 1921 together in Seville.

Six years after Diaghilev's death, Stravinsky paid formal tribute to him in his *Chronicle*.

> At the beginning of my career he was the first to single me out for encouragement, and he gave me real and valuable assistance. Not only did he like my music and believe in my development, but he did his utmost to make

---

[1] Quoted in *Memories*.
[2] Stravinsky specifically mentions *The Pirates of Penzance*, *Patience* and *Iolanthe* in his *Expositions*.

the public appreciate me. He was genuinely attracted by what I was then writing, and it gave him real pleasure to produce my work, and, indeed, to force it on the more rebellious of my listeners, as, for example, in the case of *The Rite of Spring*. These feelings of his, and the zeal which characterised them, naturally evoked in me a reciprocal sense of gratitude, deep attachment, and admiration for his sensitive comprehension, his ardent enthusiasm and the indomitable fire with which he put things into practice.

But the warmest tribute of all – one paid to Diaghilev during his lifetime and quoted by Stravinsky after his death with approval – was the remark of the painter Constantine Korovine, who said to the impresario one day, 'I thank you, Serge, for being alive'.

6. The French Composer in France
(1929 - 1939)

With the death of Diaghilev, Stravinsky lost one of the few links that still bound him to his native land. He had not seen Russia since the summer of 1914, and he had been resident in Switzerland and France for fifteen years. Although he did not actually become a French citizen until 1934, his allegiance to France was of long standing, and by the end of the 'twenties he had won acclaim as the leading musical figure in the country.

But he was never really accepted as a French composer, even though his neo-classicism seemed to place him in a world apart from that of the Russian nationalists. So long as the Russian Ballet had been based on Paris (or Monte Carlo), his commissions from Diaghilev could be looked on as coming from France. After all, *The Firebird, Petrushka, The Rite of Spring, The Nightingale, Pulcinella, Reynard, Mavra, The Wedding* and *Oedipus Rex* all received their premières in Paris. But after Diaghilev's death and the collapse of the Russian Ballet, it is interesting to see that in the next ten years the only work of his to be commissioned for performance in France was a second ballet score for Ida Rubinstein and her company, viz., *Persephone*, and the United States and Germany showed greater initiative in securing his new works than France. These signs of French apathy were reflected in the tone of certain critical writings too. Whereas in the symposium of essays on his music edited by Merle Armitage and published in New York in 1936 (the first book on his music to appear in America) the contributors seemed to share a sympathetic viewpoint and the symposium had a stimulating effect on the reader, the special number of *La Revue Musicale*, Paris, devoted to his work a few years later (1939) was frequently on the defensive and sometimes almost carping and disparaging in tone.

Stravinsky played the solo part of his *Capriccio* on its first performance at the Salle Pleyel, Paris, on 6 December 1929 with Ansermet conducting. This new work was more gracious and genial if less massive and impetuous than his *Piano Concerto* of 1924, and he scored a real success with it. Once again his services were in considerable demand as executant, and during the next five years he performed it in many of the important towns of Europe.

Meanwhile, another commission had reached him from America. Through his old friend Koussevitzky, who was now the permanent conductor of the Boston Symphony Orchestra, he was asked to supply a symphonic work to commemorate their fiftieth concert season in 1930. He was not anxious to imitate the conventional type of nineteenth century symphony; but just as he had evolved a special symphonic form for the *Symphonies of Wind Instruments* whereby a number of periodic episodes were interlocked in a single movement, so now he wanted to create an original big-scale symphonic work without necessarily conforming to academic convention. His idea was that it should feature extensive contrapuntal development, and in order to increase the means at his disposal he decided to have a chorus as well as an orchestra with the two elements on an equal footing.

For his text he had recourse to the Psalms, choosing extracts from Psalms 39 and 40 and the whole of Psalm 150. It is interesting to find that to begin with he reverted to one of the exiled languages of his heart, and the slow-tempo *Laudate Dominum* in the third movement 'was originally composed to the words of the *Gospodi Pomiluy*' (*Dia*). Only at a later stage did he switch from Slavonic to the Latin of the Vulgate. The greater part of the work was composed 'in a state of religious and musical ebullience' (*Dia*).

The *Symphony of Psalms* was begun early in 1930, but its composition was interrupted by numerous concert tours. During the spring he played his *Capriccio* in Berlin, Leipzig, Bucharest, Prague, and Winterthur, and conducted concerts at Düsseldorf, Brussels and Amsterdam. The new work was finished at Charavines on the shore of Lake Paladru where he and his family were spending the summer. The autumn was filled with a tour of Central Europe that began with Switzerland, continued in Germany and ended in the Netherlands. The first performance of the *Symphony of Psalms* took place on 13 December at the Palais des Beaux-Arts, Brussels, with Ansermet as conductor. (Stravinsky played his *Capriccio* in the same programme.) Koussevitzky conducted the first American performance with the Boston Symphony Orchestra at Boston on 19 December. (The following day Stravinsky played his *Piano Concerto* at a concert devoted to his music and conducted by Robert Siohan at the Théâtre Pigalle, Paris; and on 28 January 1931 he played his *Piano Concerto* at a B.B.C. symphony concert devoted to his music and conducted by Ansermet at the Queen's Hall, London.)

About this time Willy Strecker paid one of his visits to Paris and had a talk with his friend the young violinist, Samuel Dushkin, about the state of contemporary violin music. They both felt sure that if Stravinsky could be persuaded to compose a violin concerto, this would be an important addition to the repertory. A few weeks later Strecker met Stravinsky when he came to Wiesbaden (Strecker's home town) to conduct a concert there and asked him if he would care to write something for the violin, adding that in Dushkin he would find a remarkable executant. In his *Chronicle*, Stravinsky writes: 'I hesitated at first, because I am not a violinist and I was afraid that my slight knowledge of that instrument would not be sufficient to enable me to solve the many problems which would necessarily arise in the course of a major work specially composed for it. But Willy Strecker allayed my doubts by assuring me that Dushkin would place himself entirely at my disposal in order to furnish any technical details which I might require.' As soon as agreement was reached in principle, Strecker telegraphed Dushkin who was on tour in Germany asking him to come to Wiesbaden to meet Stravinsky.

Both musicians approached this meeting with certain reservations. Stravinsky had never seen Dushkin or heard him play. All he knew was that in his early childhood he had been adopted by the American composer Blair Fairchild and had been taught the violin by Léopold Auer, whose playing he remembered well from the period of his youth in St. Petersburg. He was afraid Dushkin might prove to be the sort of virtuoso executant he particularly abhorred.

> I knew that for virtuosi there were temptations and dangers which they were not all capable of overcoming. In order to succeed they are obliged to seek immediate triumphs and to lend themselves to the wishes of the public, the great majority of whom demand sensational effects from the player. This preoccupation naturally influences their taste, their choice of music, and their manner of treating the piece selected (*Chr*).

As for Dushkin, he had always heard that Stravinsky was difficult and could be curt if he did not like someone; and he felt nervous at the prospect of making his acquaintance.

But from the first moment, this meeting, which took place in the warm, friendly atmosphere of the Strecker household in Wiesbaden, was a success. Stravinsky was immediately reassured about Dushkin. He was delighted to find in him, 'besides his remarkable gifts as a born violinist, a musical culture, a delicate understanding, and – in the exercise of his profession – an abnegation that is very rare', and he unreservedly admired his 'beautiful mastery of technique' (*Chr*).

As for Dushkin, he has described this meeting with sensitive understanding:[1]

> Here, among friends, his personal charm was evident at once. It was not long before I realised that he was not only capable of giving tenderness and affection but seemed to be in great need of them himself. In fact, I sensed very soon something tense and anguished about him which made one want to comfort and reassure *him*. The Stravinsky I had heard about and imagined and the Igor Fedorovich I met seemed two different people.

After this auspicious beginning, their friendship prospered.

On his return to Nice, Stravinsky started to compose the first movement of the new *Violin Concerto*; but in February he had to interrupt it in order to go to Paris and London for concerts. In Paris he played his *Capriccio* under Ansermet

---

[1] From 'Working with Stravinsky', by Samuel Dushkin in *Igor Stravinsky* ed. Edwin Corle. New York, 1949.

The French Composer in France (1929 – 1939)

(20 February) and four days later conducted the first performance in France of the *Symphony of Psalms*. (The performance of the new Symphony had been prepared with special care, because the Columbia Gramophone Company had arranged to record it during rehearsals at the Théâtre des Champs-Elysées.) In London, he appeared at the Courtauld-Sargent Concerts at the Queen's Hall on 3 and 4 March, playing his *Capriccio*. He met Dushkin several times during his stay in Paris, and when he returned to Nice after his London visit, the violinist came down to Antibes in order to be near him.

Dushkin has described the nature of their collaboration and explained that his function was 'to advise Stravinsky how his ideas could best be adapted to the exigencies of the violin as a concert display instrument'.[1] At various times

Stravinsky would show him what he had written, and they would discuss together whatever suggestions he might make. A mutual friend once asked Stravinsky, with Diaghilev, Picasso, Massine and others: caricature by Michel Larionov (*c*. 1922) executed on the back of a menu from the Restaurant Au Petit Saint-Benoit, Paris

---

[1] Samuel Dushkin, *op. cit.*

1. The Man

Stravinsky 'How do you find Sam to work with?' He answered: 'When I show Sam a new passage, he is deeply moved, very excited – then a few days later he asks me to make changes'.[1] Sometimes Dushkin would arrange a passage for the violin and play it to him, and Stravinsky would say, 'Yes, that's fine, but it's from another opera'. And once when he was particularly pleased with the way he had arranged a brilliant violinistic passage and tried to insist on the composer keeping it, Stravinsky said: 'You remind me of a salesman at the Galeries Lafayette. You say, "Isn't this brilliant, isn't this exquisite, look at the beautiful colours, everybody's wearing it." I say, "Yes, it is brilliant, it is beautiful, everyone is wearing it – I don't want it." '

At first, Dushkin was astonished to find how slowly the act of composition progressed. He would see Stravinsky at the piano 'intensely concentrated, grunting and struggling to find the notes and chords he [seemed] to be hearing';[2] and when progress was abnormally slow, he would hear the harassed composer talk about the need for faith. He remembered Stravinsky saying, 'You must have faith. When I was younger, and ideas didn't come, I felt desperate and thought everything was finished. But now I have faith, and I know ideas will come. The waiting in anguish is the price one must pay'. And once when they were walking in Stravinsky's garden, the composer confided in him: 'First ideas are very important; they come from God. And if after working and working and working, I return to these ideas, then I know they're good'.[3]

Like Ramuz before him, Dushkin was impressed by Stravinsky's work-table and working habits. He seems to have been particularly struck by the fact that he used a note-book with plain white pages for his first sketches, ruling staves with his special roulette wheel just as and where he needed them 'so that when the page is finished, it looks like a strangely designed drawing, and each page looks different from the preceding page'.[4]

Towards the end of the summer, Stravinsky and his family moved from Nice to the Château de la Vironnière, Voreppe (Isère), a small village near Grenoble. He had originally thought of moving to Paris; but he was so attracted by the beauty of the Isère Valley and by the château and its garden that he decided to settle there instead. Dushkin moved to the same neighbourhood in order to be near by; and while the composer was finishing the fourth and last movement of the *Violin Concerto*, the violinist was practising the first three.

The first performance took place in Berlin at the Philharmonic (23 October). The Berliner Rundfunk Orchestra earned the special condemnation of Hindemith for its bad playing of the new work. The press was divided as usual: some

[1] Quoted by Dushkin in the above-mentioned article.
[2] S. Dushkin, *op. cit.*
[3] Quoted by Dushkin in the above-mentioned article.
[4] S. Dushkin, *op. cit.*

notices were enthusiastic, others were vicious. According to Dushkin,[1] Stravinsky was very angry.

> 'Why are you so upset?' I asked him. 'Hasn't it always been so? Even Voltaire so long ago said of critics, "Le critique est pour l'artiste ce qu'est une mouche sur un cheval de course. Elle le pique mais elle ne l'arrête pas." '[2] He liked that, but as it did not quite calm him, I said, 'No one can please everyone.' Knowing him to be religious, I risked adding, 'Even God doesn't please everyone'. He jumped up and shouted, '*Especially God!*'

Shortly after this, when Stravinsky was invited to write a tribute to Picasso on the occasion of the great 1932 exhibitions of his work in Paris and Zurich, he used the opportunity to score off critics in general. The full text of his tribute is printed in Appendix A.[3] Here it is sufficient to quote: 'If I admire something, I admire it unreservedly; and that is certainly the case with Picasso. I admire him as much for what he is doing and has done as for what he will do in the future. I do not criticise him. Criticism is the job of critics; and one knows only too well what that involves. It's no secret that criticism leads to confusion, the substitution of habit for enthusiasm, and the retardation of the appreciation of contemporary artists. Criticism is a profession for persons of ill-will. . . .'[4] And he followed this up with a quotation, not from Voltaire, but from La Fontaine.

Whatever the critics might say about the *Violin Concerto*, Stravinsky and Dushkin received invitations to play it from all over Europe – including Frankfurt, Cologne, Hanover, Halle, and Darmstadt in Germany, London, Paris, Florence, Milan, Madrid, and various towns in Switzerland, Belgium, Holland and Scandinavia. But this tour made Stravinsky realise that the successful performance of the concerto in any one place depended on the existence of an orchestra of high quality and the feasibility of holding an adequate number of rehearsals. He therefore decided it would be convenient to undertake a recital tour with Dushkin, with a repertory of works for violin and piano, and this would enable them to visit places that did not necessarily support an orchestra.

As the two instruments were to be on an equal footing, he planned a new composition, a kind of sonata for violin and piano in five movements which he called *Duo Concertant*. This was begun at the end of 1931 and finished on 15 July 1932. The recital programme was to be filled up with arrangements of other works. A *Suite Italienne* based on Pergolesi themes used in *Pulcinella* and a *Divertimento* based on Chaikovsky themes used in *The Fairy's Kiss*

---

[1] S. Dushkin, *op. cit.*
[2] 'The critic is for the artist what a fly is on a race-horse. It stings him but doesn't stop him.' (Translation by Dushkin.)
[3] See p.578.
[4] Translation by E. W. W.

would provide contrast; and there would be room for a group of shorter pieces transcribed from some of Stravinsky's earlier works. These transcriptions included an expanded version of *Pastorale*, the Scherzo ('Dance of the Firebird') and 'Lullaby' from *The Firebird*, the 'Russian Dance' from *Petrushka*, and the 'Chinese March' and the 'Nightingale's Songs' from the last two acts of *The Nightingale*. (At a later date, Parasha's air from *Mavra* was added to these transcriptions under the title *Russian Maiden's Song*.) Dushkin's role was to extract an appropriate violin line from the original scores; and Stravinsky then wrote a piano part, which frequently resulted in something widely different from the original composition.

The first performance of the *Duo Concertant* took place in Berlin at the Funkhaus on 28 October 1932. During the autumn and winter, Dushkin and Stravinsky gave violin and piano recitals at Danzig, Paris, Munich, London and Winterthur. In between these dates Stravinsky conducted concerts and/or played his *Capriccio* at Königsberg, Hamburg, Ostrava, Paris, Budapest, Milan, Turin, and Rome. He included in the concert programme of the Rome concert Debussy's *Nuages* and *Fêtes*, which he conducted for the first time; and on this occasion he received a summons to meet Mussolini in his office at the Palazzo Venezia.

As I approached, Mussolini looked up and said: 'Bonjour, Stravinsky, aswy-ez vous' (asseyez-vous) – the words of his French were correct, but the accent was Italian. He was wearing a dark business suit. We chatted briefly about music. He said that he played the violin and I quickly suppressed a remark about Nero. He was quiet and sober, but not excessively polite. . . . (*Exp*).

Afterwards Stravinsky remembered that he had cruel eyes.

The European political situation was darkening. The Fascist dictatorship had been established in Italy for some years; and the meteoric rise of the Nazi party in Germany was causing serious disquiet. In his *Dialogues*, Stravinsky recounts an unpleasant incident that occurred in 1932 to a Jewish friend of his (Eric Schall, the photographer) when he and Vera de Bosset were together in Munich on the occasion of one of his concert tours. This sort of thing was a commonplace in Germany at that time. The free part of the world was beginning to shrink.

Early in 1933 Ida Rubinstein enquired whether he would be prepared to accept another ballet commission. This time she wanted a piece in which there was an important part for herself, and she had chosen a Hymn to Demeter written by André Gide in dramatic verse before the First World War. The role of Persephone particularly appealed to her; but as she did not intend to dance and she was not a trained singer, this meant that she would have to speak and mime her part. At first Stravinsky seems to have been attracted by the idea too; and when he met Gide at Wiesbaden at the beginning of February 1933, the two men rapidly reached agreement. But, later on, the collaboration ran into rough water. Gide was shocked at the way Stravinsky's setting of his words seemed frequently to run counter to the rules of French prosody; and he disliked the idea of his carefully modulated lines having to be subservient to the musical demands of the score. And Stravinsky was intolerant of Gide's disapproval.[1]

It is true that the admixture of melodrama (Persephone) and song (Eumolpus and Chorus), dance (Mercury, Pluto, Demeter, Demophoön; Nymphs, Danaides, Shades, Hours, Friends, Attendants etc.) and mime (Persephone), was a difficult one to fuse together, and the original production was by no means completely successful in the way it tackled the problem; but subsequently Stravinsky seems to have taken an unnecessarily pessimistic view of the work. At the time of its performance he wrote:

> This score, as it is written and as it must remain in the musical archives of our time, forms an indissoluble whole with the tendencies repeatedly asserted in my previous works. It is a sequel to *Oedipus Rex*, the *Symphony of Psalms*, to a whole progression of works whose musical autonomy is in no way affected by the absence of a stage spectacle. *Persephone* is the present manifestation of that tendency.[2]

The phrase 'the musical archives of our time' has a chilly ring about it. It is true that the Ida Rubinstein production of *Persephone* received no more than three performances, and subsequent stage productions were few and far between – Braunschweig (1937), Palermo (1956), Santa Fe (1961), and Covent Garden, London (1961) – but the score is one of the most beautiful things he ever wrote; and it was perverse of him to refer to his use of melodrama as a 'sin',[3] or to suggest (as in his *Dialogues*) that the best way to ensure the work's survival would be for the Gide text to be scrapped and a new libretto written by W. H. Auden. The work is great in its own right.

The composition of *Persephone* occupied him from May 1933 till January 1934. To enable him to be easily available during rehearsals, he and his family moved from Voreppe to Paris for the winter, taking a furnished house in the rue Viet. In March he visited Copenhagen where he played his *Capriccio* for the radio; and this was followed by a brief concert tour of Lithuania and Latvia that he undertook with Dushkin. Back in Paris he played his *Capriccio* at one of Robert Siohan's concerts at the Salle Pleyel, on which occasion the conductor

---

[1] For further details of the Gide/Stravinsky collaboration, see the Register p. 375 *et seq.*

[2] See Appendix A (5).

[3] In his *Conversations*, Stravinsky answers a question of Craft's about his current feelings about the use of music as accompaniment to recitation (i.e., melodrama) with particular reference to *Persephone*, by saying, 'Do not ask. Sins cannot be undone, only forgiven.' But it should be noted that a few years later, with characteristic agility, he had changed his mind and was using serial music to accompany declamation in *A Sermon, A Narrative, and A Prayer* and also in *The Flood*.

was rather disconcerted by a slip of the pianist's memory that occurred in the course of the cadenza.[1]

The first performance of *Persephone* took place at the Opera House, Paris, on 30 April, with the composer conducting. Stravinsky seems to have felt the need for issuing an advance kind of public *apologia* that would clarify his particular way of setting syllables rather than words, his attitude to the vexed question of emotion in music, and his dislike of coruscating orchestral effects. This ended with a splendidly intransigent peroration (another nail in the critics' coffin!):

> Everything truly felt is capable of immense projection. These are not matters of caprice on my part. I am quite sure of the road I am travelling; and there is nothing here to discuss or criticise. There's no point in criticising someone or something that's in a state of functioning. A nose is not manufactured: a nose just is. – Thus, too, my art.

This appeared in *Excelsior* for 29 April: but the editor had exercised his prerogative to make minor changes in the text and certain cuts (including the last two sentences of the above citation); and two days later the paper carried the original uncut text of the manifesto, with an editorial note saying that as a paragraph had been omitted from Stravinsky's article the previous Sunday and as the author felt his full text was definitive and the mere reproduction of the missing paragraph would not give the effect he was aiming at, he had asked for his article to be reprinted in its entirety, and the editor had agreed.[2]

Stravinsky was certainly hurt that Gide never turned up at any of the rehearsals or performances; but he found consolation in the perceptive praise of Paul Valéry, who attended the first performance and wrote immediately afterwards:[3]

> I am only a 'profane listener', but the divine *detachment* of your work touched me. It seems to me that what I have sometimes searched for in the ways of poetry, you pursue and join in your art. The point is, to attain purity through the will. You expressed it marvellously well in the article yesterday which I immensely enjoyed. LONG LIVE YOUR NOSE!

A few weeks later Stravinsky had an appendectomy. His elder son, Theodore, had just had a burst appendix followed by an emergency operation; and he decided to have his own appendix removed, however unlikely the danger of peritonitis might be in his case. Not content with this, however, he forced similar operations on his other children, on Vera de Bosset, and on several of his friends.

---

[1] See Robert Siohan's *Stravinsky*. Paris, 1959.
[2] Both texts are given in Appendix A (5).
[3] From a letter dated 2 May 1934 printed in Stravinsky's *Memories*.

The French Composer in France (1929 – 1939)

On 10 June 1934 he at last became a French citizen. It might have been thought that this important change in status would consolidate the French phase in his life; but in reality it marked the beginning of its end. It was perhaps a sign of his desire to be recognised by his compatriots that in 1935 he reacted to the promptings of various friends (including Valéry) by seeking election to Paul Dukas's seat in the Institut de France after that composer's death; and it was perhaps equally significant that he did not succeed in winning the suffrages of the elderly voters and lost the election to Florent Schmitt.

His naturalisation brought him at least one concrete advantage. It cleared up the position of his author's rights and extended them retrospectively for three years so that all his compositions from 1931 onwards became protected in the United States. (Everything he had composed before that date remained unprotected there, because the United States and the U.S.S.R. had failed to sign the Berne Copyright Convention.)

Towards the end of 1934, he and his family left Voreppe for Paris and settled at 125 rue Faubourg St. Honoré. About this time he decided to write a book of memoirs about himself and his music, which would give him a chance to expand some of the arguments he had already put forward in articles like the 'Avertissement' on neo-classicism and the *Persephone* manifesto [1] and to correct the inaccuracies that had marred so many of his published interviews. The *Chroniques de ma Vie* were written in French with the help of Walter Nouvel. Although they provide a useful record of his life and work until his fifty-second year they are rather poker-faced in manner, and a lot is left unsaid. For instance, referring to *The Rite of Spring* he wrote:

> In reading what I have written about *The Rite*, the reader will perhaps be astonished to notice how little I have said about the music. The omission is deliberate. It is impossible, after the lapse of twenty years, to recall what were the feelings which animated me in composing it.

But when one approaches his latest composition, *Persephone*, and its production at the Paris Opera House, one finds that a similar ban is still in operation – 'But it is all too recent for me to discuss it with the necessary detachment' (*Chr*). There's no doubt that his later volumes of conversations with Robert Craft are more relaxed, more outspoken, more characteristic. In *Expositions* he has said that he preferred the conversational convention because it resulted in books which had the merit that he could jump from one subject to another in them 'without losing time from composition to write a "book".'

The *Chronicle* was published in Paris in two volumes in 1935 and 1936. At the end of the first volume he referred to France as 'ce pays qui devint ma seconde patrie'; and the second volume was devoted entirely to the period of his residence in France.

---

[1] See Appendix A (3) and (5).

1. The Man

1935 was the year of his second American tour, and the concerts at which he appeared were even more successful than those of 1925. The fact that he was able to consolidate his reputation as an authoritative conductor of his own music had a good effect on his publicity generally and eased the way for a number of commissions that were to come to him from the United States during the next few years. During this visit he also gave a number of violin and piano recitals with Dushkin, including one at Denver, Colorado, on 4

Stravinsky, 1935.
Photograph by Edward Weston

March 1935, at which he made his first public speech in English. His manuscript notes for this are extant and run as follows:—

Ladies and gentelmen,

Pleas permit me to express to you my satisfaction and my gratitude for the interest which you, the artistic elite of Denver, have shown towards my art.

S. D. and I have united our efforts in this limited but condesedand (*sic*) and powerful form of duos for v. & p., in order to serve the essence itself of my music, and we are happy to defend before an enlightened public a cause wich is dear to us.

His sons, Theodore and Soulima, were now twenty-eight and twenty-five years old respectively. Theodore was an artist of distinction whose designs had already been featured in the published scores of *Oedipus Rex*, the *Duo Concertant*, and *Persephone*. He had had exhibitions of his work in Paris and Geneva; and his portrait studies, particularly of his father, were becoming quite well known. Soulima was a promising pianist, who had been a pupil of Nadia Boulanger. He made his début in his father's *Capriccio* at a festival concert in Barcelona which his father conducted in November 1933. A year later he played the *Capriccio* and the *Piano Concerto* under his father's direction at a concert of the Orchestre Symphonique in Paris. The time had come when in any case Stravinsky needed a new piece of virtuosity to exploit after the *Piano Concerto* and the *Capriccio*; and the idea occurred to him – why not write a Double Concerto which could be played by himself and his son? At the same time, remembering the line of argument that had led to the composition of the *Duo Concertant*, he decided to dispense with the services of an orchestra and the new composition became a *Concerto for Two Solo Pianos*. It was launched at a recital given by the Université des Annales at the Salle Gaveau, Paris, on 21 November 1935; and on that occasion Stravinsky introduced the new work with a fifteen-minute talk.[1] Subsequently, he and Soulima toured the Concerto in Europe and South America (1936).

During these years, Theodore had plenty of opportunities to observe his father's habits of composition, and *Le Message d'Igor Strawinsky* includes an interesting description of his working schedule.

He finds the morning the most suitable time for composition. Complete silence is essential to him. After rising early, he usually shuts himself immediately after breakfast in the part of the house that serves both as studio and office. He composes invariably at the piano, because, having no confidence in abstractions as such, he needs direct contact with the element of sound and wishes, depite his musical experience and memory, to subject every chord, every interval, every phrase, to a fresh test. He works slowly – '*cent fois sur le métier remettant son ouvrage*' – and rarely composes more than two or three pages a day, sometimes even less. This is how his mornings are spent. A part of the afternoon is devoted to correspondence. Often he complains of the amount of time this takes, particularly when he is planning a concert tour. The evenings – sometimes until quite a late hour – are generally spent in proof-reading or orchestration. Then, despite his concentration on these tasks, it is not essential for him to be on his own. At such times he has an extraordinary faculty of dividing his attention; and while working he enjoys listening to someone reading aloud and

---

[1] See Appendix A(6).

follows with close attention, only occasionally asking for a short interruption when a particularly knotty problem calls for his special attention.[1]

During the winter of 1935/36, the Ecole Normale de Musique, Paris, arranged a composition course under the joint direction of Nadia Boulanger and Stravinsky. There were about ten students including Dinu Lipatti, Maurice Perrin and Léo Préger. The course consisted of two classes a week: one devoted to the analysis and criticism of the students' compositions, the other to a study of works by the great masters. Stravinsky came to the second of these classes about once a month; and when he did, it was his own compositions, particularly recent scores like *Persephone* and the *Concerto for Two Solo Pianos*, that came up for discussion.

Nadia Boulanger would sit at the piano and play a reduction. . . . She would stop at a certain passage, point out subtle harmonic relations, throw light on some surprising modulation, try to explain why it sounded so well, and then turn towards Stravinsky as if for confirmation, and ask him if he had anything to add. But he nearly always confined himself to saying: 'Mais c'est de la musique tonâle!'[2]

The relationship of the different parts of his compositions had always been governed by tonal considerations: so tonality retained the prestige of a *primum mobile*.

In 1936 he entered into negotiations with Lincoln Kirstein and Edward Warburg to write a ballet score on a subject of his own choice for the recently formed American Ballet. The action, which was worked out in collaboration with M. Malaieff, a friend of his son Theodore's, concerns three deals of straight poker, played literally according to Hoyle. *Jeu de Cartes* was the title Stravinsky gave the ballet, and according to the published score, *A Card Game* should be the English title; but in America the ballet is usually referred to by the more idiomatic title of *The Card Party*. The score was finished and dispatched to New York in November 1936. Balanchine started to work on the choreography at once, and the first two deals were ready when Stravinsky reached New York early in the New Year (his third North American visit). An entertaining description of the rehearsals has been given by Lincoln Kirstein,[3] who found that Stravinsky as a man had about him 'the slightly disconcerting concentration of a research professor or a newspaper editor, the serious preoccupation of a man who has so many interrelated activities to keep

---

[1] Theodore Strawinsky, *op. cit.* (English translation by E. W. W.). In his article 'A Personal Preface' (*The Score*, June 1957) Craft recalls how while Stravinsky was engaged in orchestrating the last act of *The Rake's Progress*, he read him Mme. Calderon la Barca's *Life in Mexico*.

[2] Maurice Perrin, 'Stravinsky in a Composition Class'. *Feuilles Musicales*. December 1951. (Also *The Score*, June 1957.)

[3] In 'Working with Strawinsky', *Modern Music* Vol. XIV no. 3, quoted in the Register, p. 397.

straight and in smooth running order that he finds it necessary to employ a laconic, if fatherly and final politeness'.

The Card Party was given its first performance at the Metropolitan Opera House, New York, on 27 April 1937 with the composer conducting. It was accompanied by a revival of *Apollo* with the original Balanchine choreography, and a new choreographic version of *The Fairy's Kiss* made also by Balanchine. It was not only a 'Stravinsky evening' but also a 'Balanchine evening'. This ballet partnership, between composer and choreographer, was gradually assuming considerable importance.

That spring Stravinsky went as far afield as Hollywood, where he met (among other people) Charlie Chaplin. He also visited Washington D.C., where Mr. and Mrs. Robert Woods Bliss showed him round their beautiful house and gardens at Dumbarton Oaks and invited him to compose a concerto grosso to celebrate their thirtieth wedding anniversary the following year.

It was in the course of this American visit that a medical examination in New York revealed tubercular bacilli in his sputum and a lesion in his left lung. His wife and two daughters were already patients in a sanatorium at Sancellmoz; but although on his return to Paris he was ordered to join them, he paid only a short visit to the Château de Montoux, near Annemasse, in order to be near them.

It was at this time, when he was starting to compose the 'Dumbarton Oaks' *Concerto*, that Charles-Albert Cingria, who had been a close friend during the years of his Vaudois exile and whose book on Petrarch had played some part in inspiring him when he was composing the *Duo Concertant*, came over from Geneva and reminded him that their mutual friend C. F. Ramuz would celebrate his sixtieth birthday on 24 September 1938. Since Stravinsky's departure from Switzerland in 1920, the two former collaborators had seen comparatively little of each other. Ramuz had occasionally called on Stravinsky when he visited Paris in the 'twenties, and Stravinsky had occasionally met him in Lausanne when one of his concert tours took him to that part of Switzerland. Now Cingria provided a set of verses (to be spoken) as a setting for a lyric of three stanzas[1] (to be sung). Stravinsky set the lyric for solo voice unaccompanied; and the three-page manuscript of this little work entitled *Petit Ramusianum harmonique* was presented to Ramuz on his birthday and published the same year in *Hommage à C.-F. Ramuz*.[2]

When the 'Dumbarton Oaks' Concerto was finished early in 1938, Stravinsky was not sufficiently well to leave Paris to go to Washington to conduct its first performance; but about this time he received two other commissions from America. These came at a fortunate moment, for not only his health but also his fortune was at a low ebb. Mrs. Bliss commissioned him (for a fee of $2,500)

---

[1] It is not clear whether the words of this lyric were written by Cingria or Stravinsky.
[2] V. Porchet & Cie., Lausanne, 1938.

to compose a symphony to celebrate the fiftieth concert season of the Chicago Symphony Orchestra in 1940/41; and Edward W. Forbes, the Chairman of Harvard University's Charles Eliot Norton Professorship Committee, approached him through Nadia Boulanger and offered him the chair of poetry[1] for 1939/40. The Harvard proposal was that he should live in Cambridge or Boston from October 1939 to May 1940 with two months of vacation for his concert engagements. He would be expected to deliver six public lectures on music; and in recognition of his standing in the musical world, he was accorded the privilege of giving these lectures in French. In the event he found it possible to accept both commissions.

He started to compose the *Symphony in C* in the autumn of 1938 in his Rue St. Honoré flat in Paris. This was the autumn of Munich. Although he has left no commentary on the gloomy political outlook at that moment, he considered that the state of art reflected a general crisis. In an interview with Serge Moreux, which was broadcast on 24 December 1938, he said: 'It is hardly astonishing that the critics have lost their sense of direction, for the crisis is certainly more wide-spread than is at present realised. The state of mankind is deeply affected: knowledge of values and feeling for relationships are submerged. This is extremely serious, for it leads us to transgress the fundamental laws of human equilibrium.'[2]

In his own case, while prospects might look bright on the American horizon, the European picture was getting more sinister all the time. Under the Stalinist régime it seemed as if his ties with his Russian homeland were severed for ever. Under the Nazi régime his music had become unacceptable in Germany. He was scurrilously attacked in the Düsseldorf Exhibition of *Entartete Musik* in May 1938; but the protest of the French Ambassador in Berlin (M. François-Poncet) was without effect. His visits to England were far less frequent than in the past. In the five years 1935/39 he came only twice – on 27 March 1936 to Bournemouth to conduct a special concert devoted to his compositions (including the *Capriccio* with the solo part played by his son Soulima), and to London for two performances of *The Card Party* at one of the Courtauld-Sargent concert series at the Queen's Hall (18 and 19 October 1937). Italy he still visited regularly – Rome in 1936; Positano in 1937, on which occasion he made an excursion to Paestum with Hindemith; a tour of Rome and other Italian towns in 1938; and a short visit in 1939, when he conducted *Persephone* and *Petrushka* at the Maggio Musicale in Florence and *The Card Party* at the Scala, Milan. But the days of his big European tours seemed to be over; and France showed little interest in his current work.

Meanwhile, ill-health had started to take its toll of his family. In the spring

---

[1] Among the other distinguished persons who had held this chair was T. S. Eliot, who lectured on *The Use of Poetry and the Use of Criticism* in 1932/33. Stravinsky was the first representative of music to be elected to it. The fee he received was $10,000.

[2] See Appendix A (7). Translation by E. W. W.

of 1937, just after the New York première of *The Card Party*, he received news of the death of his sister-in-law, Ludmila Beliankin. The following year an autumn concert tour of Italy was interrupted by the death of his eldest daughter Ludmila, on 30 November aged thirty. In 1939 his wife died on March 2nd aged fifty-seven; and a few months later (7 June) his mother died aged eighty-five. After his wife's death he moved to Sancellmoz himself and spent five months in the sanatorium. He wrote the second movement of the *Symphony in C* there and also worked on his Charles Eliot Norton lectures. He discussed their substance with his friend Pierre Souvchinsky, who helped him to draft them in Russian; and later he revised them with Roland-Manuel, who helped him to rewrite them in French.

In September 1939, shortly after the outbreak of the war, he embarked on the S.S. *Manhattan* for New York – on his fourth and what was to prove his longest visit to North America.

7. The French Composer in America (1939 - 1945)

It is always risky to try to assess a composer's reputation at any particular moment. There is the account of what the critics may have said in their daily or weekly or monthly reviews, but very little record of the reaction of the intelligent and sensitive members of the public. Nevertheless it is approximately true to suggest that Stravinsky's reputation reached its nadir in the years immediately preceding the second World War. He himself was conscious of this trend when he wrote in the final pages of his *Chronicle* (1935):

> At the beginning of my career as a composer I was a good deal spoiled by the public. . . . But I have a very distinct feeling that in the course of the last fifteen years[1] my written work has estranged me from the great mass of my listeners. . . . Liking the music of *The Firebird*, *Petrushka*, *The Rite of Spring* and *The Wedding*, and being accustomed to the language of those works, they are astonished to hear me speaking in another idiom. They cannot and will not follow me in the progress of my musical thought. What moves and delights me leaves them indifferent, and what still continues to interest them holds no further attraction for me.

Many of the critics (especially in England) stigmatised much of his neo-classical music as 'the artificial product of a cock-eyed esthetic',[2] and considered that almost the only qualities of his instrumentation deserving of notice were its aridity and brittleness. It is refreshing to find that occasionally some members of the audience had other views. Benjamin Britten remembered being taken as a youth by his master, Frank Bridge, to hear the *Symphony of Psalms* on its first performance in London, 'and when everyone around was appalled and saying how sad about Stravinsky, Bridge was insisting that it was a master-piece'.[3] Nevertheless, Stravinsky's new works, though listened to with a show of politeness, were usually shelved by concert promoters as soon as seemed decent.

At the outbreak of the Second World War, Stravinsky had his Harvard lectures on the *Poetics of Music* (written in French with the help of Roland-Manuel) fully drafted; but the *Symphony in C* for the Chicago Symphony

---

[1] I.e., during the period of his residence in France.
[2] 'Enigmatic Stravinsky'. *The Times*, 4 April 1952.
[3] 'Britten Looking Back'. *The Sunday Telegraph*, 17 November 1963.

Orchestra was only half composed. According to his publisher, Gabriel Paichadze of the Edition Russe de Musique,[1] he was 'perplexed and jittery' at this moment. 'He could neither eat nor sleep, he could not work . . . he got angry, nervous and irritable. All he wanted was to get out as quickly as possible, out of Paris, out of Europe, into America where life was still orderly.'[2]

He landed in New York on 30 September and immediately went to Cambridge, Massachusetts, where he lived for just over two months in Gerry's Landing, the home of Edward Forbes, 'a gentle and cultivated man who looked exactly like his grandfather, Ralph Waldo Emerson' (*Exp*). The lectures were delivered to large audiences in Harvard's New Lecture Hall; and for the benefit of those whose French was limited, a concise synopsis of each one was prepared in English and distributed. Two years later the Harvard University Press published the French text under the title *Poétique Musicale*; and an English translation by Arthur Knodel and Ingolf Dahl followed in 1947.

As Darius Milhaud said in his Preface to these published lectures, 'The *Poetics of Music* brings to light the indissoluble relationship between the two aspects of the Stravinskyan temperament: that is, his music and his philosophy'. The six lectures were each given titles: 1. *Getting Acquainted*, 2. *The Phenomenon of Music*, 3. *The Composition of Music*, 4. *Musical Typology*, 5. *The Avatars of Russian Music*, 6. *The Performance of Music*, followed by an *Epilogue*. Many of the subjects he dealt with had already been touched on in his *Chronicle*; but the lecture form gave him a chance of expounding his views and developing them at greater length. He did not have much to say about his own music; but he commented at some length on Weber, Beethoven, Bellini, Wagner, Verdi, and various Russian composers, and his remarks on Soviet music in particular were so scathing that when the French text of *Poétique Musicale* was reprinted in Paris in 1945, his French publishers judged it expedient to omit (without explanation) the whole of the fifth lecture and to expunge any reference to it elsewhere.

In addition to delivering these lectures, he gave a small group of the more talented Harvard students of composition informal talks about music. 'This course did not comprise *instruction* in composition. Stravinsky merely criticised the works of the young composers or would-be composers. Always outspoken as to the faults and errors in counterpoint and style, he never hesitated to point out passages that merited recognition and revealed the presence of real invention or imagination.'[3] As had been the case with the course he took part in at the Ecole Normale de Musique, Paris, in the winter of 1935/36, much of the discussion centred round his own works, and he would frequently play

---

[1] The last of Stravinsky's compositions to be published by the Edition Russe de Musique was *Persephone*.
[2] Nicolas Nabokov, *Old Friends and New Music*. London, Hamish Hamilton, 1951.
[3] Alexis Kall, 'Stravinsky in the Chair of Poetry'. The *Musical Quarterly*, July, 1940.

1. The Man

on the piano one of his recent scores, like *The Card Party* or the 'Dumbarton Oaks' Concerto, analysing it for the benefit of the students.

In December 1939 he went to San Francisco and Los Angeles to direct two concerts, returning to New York in time to meet Vera de Bosset, who was sailing from Genoa on the *Rex*. She arrived on 13 January; and on March 9th they were married in Bedford, Massachusetts, at the house of Dr. Taracuzio, a Russian who was a professor at Harvard. When the Charles Eliot Norton lectures ended in May, the recently married couple left Boston by boat for New York, and then went on to Los Angeles by train. For some years Stravinsky had thought that if at any time he was forced to move, the climate of Los Angeles would suit him best for reasons of health. Now that he had decided to begin a new life and to live it in America, the die was cast – Los Angeles it would be.[1] In August of that summer, the couple took the formal step of entering the United States from Mexico on the Russian quota and immediately applied for naturalization papers.

When this news reached Europe, a number of his French and Swiss friends seem to have been hurt that he should have decided to surrender his recently acquired French nationality; and in his monograph on Stravinsky,[2] Alexander Tansman, the Polish composer, goes to considerable trouble to defend him.

When Stravinsky definitely decided to settle in the United States, he found a peaceful refuge there, together with conditions of tranquility and security that were vital to him as a composer, and an atmosphere of neutrality which did not perpetually interrupt his artistic schedule and his need to concentrate.

About his love of France and his grief for her war-time reverses there was never any doubt. But what he was determined to avoid at all costs, if he could, was disorder. As soon as he found that in the United States he could work in peace and earn a respectable income, he became relaxed; and his wife saw to it that in Los Angeles he had a comfortable and happy home to live in.

During the war years in Hollywood, the two of them had a small circle of friends, mainly expatriates like themselves, with whom they were on close and familiar terms, including Eugene Berman (the painter), Adolph Bolm, Nadia Boulanger, Aaron Sapiro (Stravinsky's lawyer), Aldous Huxley (the English man-of-letters), Vladimir Sokoloff (the Russian actor), Alexander Tansman, and Franz Werfel (the Austrian novelist and dramatist). Tansman recalled some of their marathon conversations in the following terms:[3]

Frequently I talked with him till late in the night; and our discussions ranged widely over many varied subjects from the latest political scandal to

---

[1] At 124 South Swall Drive, Beverley Hills, May-November 1940; Château Marmont, Hollywood, March-April 1941; and North Wetherly Drive, Hollywood, after that.
[2] Alexander Tansman, *Igor Stravinsky*. Paris, 1948. (Translation E. W. W.)
[3] Alexander Tansman, *op. cit.* (Translation E. W. W.)

116

the Epistles of St. Paul, by way of the esthetic of Bach's music, the style of Gide, the relationship between Spinoza and Bergson, Spanish mysticism as revealed in Spanish art, and so on.

In a letter written to a cousin in Moscow some years later,[1] his wife recalled this period of their life and expressed her agreement with Thomas Mann who in his companion book to *Dr. Faustus* had claimed that 'Hollywood during the war was a more intellectually stimulating and cosmopolitan city than Paris or Munich had ever been'. She added, 'The ferment of composers, writers, scientists, artists, actors, philosophers and phonies did exist and we often attended the lectures, exhibitions, concerts, performances, social gatherings of these people ourselves'.

A striking account of the Stravinsky household as seen by the Huxleys after the war is given in a letter dated 13 May 1951 that Maria wrote to her son Matthew.[2]

> Vera Stravinsky rang up . . . they could not bear going to another cinema, could they visit us? So I said yes the programme would be good but not the refreshments and they came at 9.
>
> We are very fond of them, Stravinsky still looks like father and is very sweet really; always the same programme. Stravinsky, Bob Craft – almost an adopted son of theirs, 26 and very clever, knows everything, terribly nervous and not a pansy – and Aldous stays in the music room and Vera and I stay around somewhere else. . . . They play music and we chat. . . . Last night Stravinsky arrived in an enchanting costume . . . narrow effect in little blue jeans, and a blue jean zipper jacket open on a deep red wine jersey and silk scarf tied with pin. He looked enchanting and was really pleased with himself. I must not forget the always white socks and sandals. I do not know what he makes me think of, a voltigeur in the circus, a leprechaun with the little elegant legs or what? a cyclist? And Aldous *will* turn the heat off when I am gone and poor little Stravinsky shivers and dares not ask and Aldous notices nothing. So finally he came to sit on my bed, and Vera inside the open window in a decollete dress under a lace shawl and velvet bows in her hair looked immense next to the little shivering elfish man.

When Stravinsky came to America in the autumn of 1939, he had brought with him the first two movements of his *Symphony in C*. The third was composed during the period of his Harvard lectures, and the fourth finished in Hollywood in the summer of 1940. The first performance of the complete Symphony was given in Chicago by the Chicago Symphony Orchestra on 7 November 1940 with the composer conducting.

---

[1] Letter from Vera Stravinsky to Vladimir Petrov dated Hollywood, 10 December 1962.
[2] This is quoted in the second volume of Sybille Bedford's biography of Aldous Huxley, London, Chatto and Windus, 1976.

1. The Man

Just over three years later he was to return to Chicago to deliver the William Vaughan Moody Lecture at the University of Chicago (20 January 1944).[1] This was one of a series of composers' concerts presented at the University. He chose as his theme 'Composing, Performing, Listening'; and the programme at the accompanying concert the following evening consisted of the *Duo Concertant*, the *Concerto for Two Pianos*, and the suite from *The Soldier's Tale*. The composer was both pianist and conductor.

The *Symphony in C* had been the sort of commission that suited him ideally, and it resulted in the composition of his greatest symphonic work to date: but not all the other commissions he received in America would prove so attractive. Some years later when Robert Craft asked him a question about patronage, he replied: 'The trick, of course, is to choose one's commission, to compose what one wants to compose and to get it commissioned afterwards' (*Mem*). Carlos Chavez tells the story of how a famous violinist 'wished to enlarge his repertory, but felt discouraged on viewing the recent concerti for his instrument. "Of course," he explained, "I wanted something that would have the attractiveness of the *best* Stravinsky. So I told him I thought that in the literature for the violin there ought to be a work corresponding to the admirable music of *The Firebird*, *Petrushka*, and *The Rite of Spring*. . . . Well, Stravinsky did not finally receive my commission, since he answered drily that he was not interested in decadent music".'[2] Shortly after the war, when Stravinsky was considering the possibility of writing a full-scale opera, a certain unnamed person[3] would have commissioned *The Rake's Progress*, had he agreed to the condition that this person should 'sit in judgment' (*Mem*) while Stravinsky played his music to him at the piano.

The fact that he was living in Hollywood meant that sooner or later he was bound to be approached with the suggestion that he should write music for films. Before the war there had been several occasions on which attempts had been made to use some of his existing music for this purpose. The 1930 orchestral version of *Three Little Songs* (recollections of his childhood) was intended for a French film that was never released. In the mid-thirties, Lotte Reiniger, the silhouette film artist, had planned to use part of the *Pulcinella* concert suite as basis for a trick film to be called *The Dream Circus*; but this project never materialised. In *Expositions*, Stravinsky has given the following account of the way *The Rite of Spring* was pressed into service to accompany the prehistoric section of Walt Disney's colour trick film, *Fantasia*:

In 1938 I received a request from the Disney office in America for permission to use *Le Sacre* in a cartoon film. The request was accompanied by a

---

[1] In *Expositions* Stravinsky recalls that one of the persons who attended this lecture was his friend Jacques Maritain.

[2] Carlos Chavez, 'Perpetual Renewal' from *Stravinsky in the Theatre*, edited by Minna Lederman. London, 1951.

[3] Stravinsky describes him as 'a scion of grocery stores and sciolist of "modern art" ' (*Mem*).

gentle warning that if permission were withheld the music would be used anyway. (*Le Sacre*, being 'Russian', was not copyrighted in the United States.) The owners of the film wished to show it abroad, however (*i.e.* in Berne copyright countries), and they therefore offered me $5,000, a sum I was obliged to accept. . . I saw the film with George Balanchine in a Hollywood studio at Christmas time 1939. I remember someone offering me a score and, when I said I had my own, the someone saying, 'But it is all changed'. It was indeed . . .

Now he began to receive his share of the fatuous and occasionally immoral offers that the film world seems to delight in making. In his *Memories*, he recalls how he was even offered $100,000 'to pad a film with music', and when he refused, was told he could receive the same fee if he were willing to allow someone else to compose the music in his name.

A number of more reasonable film projects, but all of them abortive, belong to the years 1942/44. At one moment he intended to write music for a film about the Nazi invasion of Norway: but the project fell through, and the salvaged music was turned into the *Four Norwegian Moods* (1942). Another war film with a Russian setting was to have a score written by him: this project also collapsed, and the salvaged music became the *Scherzo à la Russe* (1944) and was handed over to Paul Whiteman and his Band. Orson Welles urged him to compose music for a film version of *Jane Eyre*, and Stravinsky went as far as writing a piece 'for one of the hunting scenes' (*Exp*); but no contract was ever signed, and ultimately this music was used as the middle movement of *Ode* (1943). Werfel wanted him to write music for his film *The Song of Bernadette*; but here too the contract was unacceptable, and the music written for the 'Apparition of the Virgin' scene became the second movement of the *Symphony in Three Movements* (1945). It should be added that parts of the other movements of this Symphony appear to have been linked in Stravinsky's mind 'with a concrete impression, very often cinematographic in origin, of the war' (*Dia*).

Outside the film world, there were certain slightly unusual commissions that did not prove abortive.

Early in 1942 he was approached by Ringling Brothers of the Barnum and Bailey Circus and asked to write the music for a polka to be danced by a troupe of young elephants in ballet tutus. Although the whole thing sounded like a stunt, the resulting *Circus Polka* became a very popular act and was performed 425 times.

Two years later, a strange invitation reached him from Nathaniel Shilkret, the music publisher, who wanted to get a group of composers to produce a composite work based on the early chapters of the Book of Genesis. Shilkret himself assumed responsibility for the episode of *The Creation*; and the following commissions were placed by him and accepted:

119

Stravinsky and his mother at Talloires, 1929

The French Composer in America (1939–1945)

Prelude	Arnold Schoenberg
The Fall of Man	Alexander Tansman
Cain and Abel	Darius Milhaud
The Flood	Mario Castelnuovo-Tedesco
The Covenant	Ernst Toch
Babel	Igor Stravinsky

Other sections were to have been written by Béla Bartok, Paul Hindemith, and Serge Prokofiev. The cycle of the seven movements actually completed was performed in Los Angeles in October 1945; but like most composite works it proved to have no independent life of its own, though subsequently some of its individual movements, particularly *Babel* and the *Prelude* have been presented singly.

About this time Stravinsky was so impressed by the jazz musician Woody Herman that he agreed to write a special composition for him and his band. He took great pains to familiarise himself with the special technique of jazz; and the result was the *Ebony Concerto* (1945).

Between these slightly off-beat commissions, there were still examples of the other type of commission – where he was able to choose the sort of composition he wanted to write and arrange to have it commissioned.

Before leaving Europe, his last work for the theatre had been *The Card Party* (produced by the American Ballet in 1937 and revived by the Ballet Russe de Monte Carlo in New York in 1940). In 1941 he made a reduced orchestral version of the Bluebird *pas de deux* from Chaikovsky's *The Sleeping Beauty* for the Ballet Theatre in New York. Shortly after this, he was commissioned by the Werner Janssen Orchestra of Los Angeles to write a work for concert performance. Stravinsky cast it in the form of a themeless ballet entitling it *Danses Concertantes* and calling the different movements March, Theme with Variations, Pas de Deux, and March (reprise). When the time came, it proved perfectly feasible to use the music as a ballet score. Balanchine provided an attractive sequence of plotless dances for the Ballet Russe de Monte Carlo (New York, 1944), and the designs by Eugene Berman were particularly admired.

Stravinsky must have felt pleased once more to have a stake in the theatre world; and early in 1944 another ballet commission came his way. By this time ballet was beginning to become popular in the American theatre; and Billy Rose decided that his forthcoming revue *The Seven Lively Arts* should contain an original ballet. Stravinsky was approached; and when he heard that the choreography would be in the hands of Anton Dolin, with Alicia Markova as the principal dancer, he accepted the commission. As he composed the orchestral score of *Scènes de Ballet* page by page, a piano reduction was made by Ingolf Dahl, which was used for rehearsal purposes. Billy Rose seems to have liked the music in this version, but was upset by Stravinsky's light *concertante* style of orchestration. After the Philadelphia preview, an attempt

1. The Man

was made to persuade him to allow the orchestration to be touched up by a professional 'orchestrator' called Robert Russell Bennett; but naturally he refused, and by the time the revue reached Broadway, a number of cuts had been made in the score.[1]

A commission from the Serge Koussevitzky Music Foundation, which had been set up in memory of the conductor's first wife Natalie, belongs to the previous year. Stravinsky wrote an elegiacal chant in three parts entitled *Ode*; and this was performed by the Boston Symphony Orchestra on 8 October 1943 with Koussevitzky himself conducting. The performance was disastrous. One of the trumpet players failed to transpose his part in the third movement (Epitaph); and considerable confusion was caused by a copyist's error whereby two systems of score on the final page had been copied as one.

About this time, he was contemplating the possibility of writing another piano concerto, or a concerto for orchestra with a *concertante* part for piano; and sketches for such a work were in existence as early as 1942. When invited by the New York Philharmonic Symphony Society to provide them with a symphony, he found this piano concerto material could be incorporated in the first movement of the new symphony, while the music originally intended for the film of *The Song of Bernadette* would fit the second movement. The atmosphere of stress and strain generated by the war is very noticeable in the last movement; and the completed *Symphony in Three Movements* made a powerful impression when it was first performed by the New York Philharmonic Orchestra on 24 January 1946.

Between the *Symphony in C* and the *Symphony in Three Movements* lay five years of deep anxiety. It is true that at first the United States were not directly involved in the War; but in the summer of 1940 as western Europe was overrun by the Nazi hordes, there was little consolation to be found in neutrality. After Japan's lightning attack on Pearl Harbour, Hawaii, on 7 December 1941, America became a direct participant in the struggle. But this commitment was a new cause of anxiety to Stravinsky. Nicolas Nabokov remembers a conversation he had with a mutual friend shortly after Pearl Harbour.

> On his way back to Hollywood after a tour in the East, he had had dinner with a few friends. During dinner the conversation had apparently been of such a concentrated gloom that everyone was overawed. As he was leaving, Stravinsky took this friend aside on the platform at Grand Central Station and asked him in a low, halting whisper: 'Tell me, quite unequivocally, will there be a revolution in America, or not?' The man squirmed, wavered and answered: 'How can I know?...Maybe, maybe not...' 'But where will I go?' said Stravinsky in an appalled and indignant tone.[2]

[1] See p. 420.
[2] Nicolas Nabokov, *Old Friends and New Music*.

Fortunately, there were to be no further displacements for the egocentric composer; and when in August 1944 news of the liberation of Paris came through, the sense of exultation can be felt in the music he was composing (the Apothéose of *Scènes de Ballet*), and the triumphant cry 'Paris n'est plus aux allemands' was inscribed at the end of the ballet score.

The war in Europe ended on 8 May 1945 – in the Far East on 10 August. And on 28 December 1945, Stravinsky changed his nationality for the second time and became an American citizen.

8. The American Composer at Home and Abroad (1945 - 1952)

On the same day that Stravinsky became an American citizen, Ralph Hawkes of the British music publishing house of Boosey and Hawkes, met him in Beverley Hills, 'in the incongruous but unavoidable setting of an hotel dining room complete with dance band and cabaret'[1] and learned from him details of his recent works. These included not only the *Symphony in Three Movements*, the *Ebony Concerto*, and the first movements of his forthcoming *Mass*, but also a revised version of the ballet suite of *The Firebird* for reduced orchestra with double woodwind and other instruments to match.[2] His future plans included the composition of a concerto for string orchestra for Paul Sacher and the Basler Kammerorchester (his first European commission for over twelve years) and the rescoring of *Petrushka* and *The Rite of Spring* for reduced orchestras. (He had already prepared a revised version of the 'Danse Sacrale' in 1943.)

At that time Ralph Hawkes was at the head of the New York branch of Boosey and Hawkes, and he forthwith arranged for his firm to publish all Stravinsky's new works from the *Concerto in D* for string orchestra onwards. At the same time Boosey and Hawkes took over all the works formerly published by the Edition Russe de Musique, which ranged from *Petrushka* (1911) to *Persephone* (1934), a matter of some two dozen different titles, not counting arrangements and transcriptions. This deal allowed Stravinsky to make new versions of his earlier scores where he wanted to use his newly acquired American nationality to safeguard his copyright position, to revise his music where he thought revision necessary, and to correct the numerous mistakes that had occurred in the printing of the Edition Russe de Musique works, especially during the mid-'twenties.

In the event, no revision was made to *The Rite of Spring*; but *Petrushka* was rescored for smaller orchestra, and this led to a review of its orchestral textures and patterns. The new *Petrushka* is the music of the composer of 1910 presented by the orchestrator of 1946; and it may not be to everyone's taste. There is a dichotomy here, for the composer of 28 did not orchestrate like the man of 64, nor could the orchestrator of 64 have composed like the man of 28.

---

[1] Ralph Hawkes, 'American Diary'. *Tempo*, March 1946.
[2] This was the *third* ballet suite. See the Register of Compositions, p. 190.

Radical changes were also made when he revised the *Symphonies of Wind Instruments* in 1947. The altered composition of the orchestra (e.g., the substitution of an ordinary flute for an alto flute) meant that certain passages had to be rewritten. Otherwise, the alterations mainly affected dynamics, accentuation, notation, phrasing and punctuation.

Less radical changes were made in the revised versions of *Apollo Musagetes* (1947), *Oedipus Rex* and the *Symphony of Psalms* (1948), the *Pulcinella* suite, the *Divertimento*, the *Capriccio*, and *Persephone* (1949), the *Concerto for Piano* and *The Fairy's Kiss* (1950), the *Octet* (1952), and *The Nightingale* (1962).

Two works belonging to other publishers were also subjected to extensive revision. In 1952 the original string quartet version of the *Concertino* (published by Wilhelm Hansen) was arranged for a chamber ensemble of twelve instrumentalists; and in 1954 the four *a cappella* Russian Peasant Songs (published by J. & W. Chester under the title *Saucers*) had an accompaniment for four horns added.

Certain transcriptions of earlier works belong to this period too. Immediately after the composition of his *Three Songs from William Shakespeare*, he transcribed the piano accompaniments to the *Two Poems of Balmont* and to four of the songs from his Russian period in the second decade of the century for various small chamber groups (1954); and in 1962 the little piano pieces called *The Five Fingers* were transcribed for fifteen instruments under the title *Eight Instrumental Miniatures*.[1]

The first new work he completed after his naturalisation was the *Concerto in D* for string orchestra, which received its first performance at Basel on 27 January 1947. Its idiom was recognisably close to that of the pre-war concertos (e.g., the 'Dumbarton Oaks' *Concerto*); and at first it did not seem as if his music had made any particular advances during the war. But with his next work a definite change was perceptible.

This was a new ballet score commissioned by Lincoln Kirstein for the Ballet Society. The subject chosen was the classical legend of Orpheus; and Balanchine was the choreographer. Unlike *The Card Party*, *Orpheus* was a work of close co-operation between composer and choreographer throughout, and each scene was carefully planned and timed. At the time he was working on the score, Stravinsky made a close study of the music of Claudio Monteverdi and one or two of his contemporaries; but though it is true that the modal character of some of the music in *Orpheus* gives the score a seventeenth-century flavour, it is really from the greater insistence on polyphony and counterpoint that the music derives its new sound and feeling. This change in orientation was to be even more marked in his next composition, the *Mass*.

---

[1] All these revised versions and transcriptions are noticed in the Register of Compositions.

1. The Man

A vivacious and exhilarating account of life with Stravinsky and his household during Christmas 1947 in Hollywood was written by Nicolas Nabokov,[1] who spent a short holiday with them at this period. In particular, he mentions a session in Stravinsky's study on the day of his arrival.

He sat down at the piano, carefully wiped his glasses with a Sight Saver, and opened the orchestra score of *Orpheus*. A moment later we were both absorbed in it. I stood behind him and watched his short, nervous fingers scour the keyboard, searching and finding the correct intervals, the widely spaced chords, and the characteristically Stravinskian broad melodic leaps. His neck, his head, his whole body accentuated the ingenious rhythmical design of the music by spasm-like bobs and jerks. He grunted, he hummed, and occasionally stopped to make an aside. 'See the fugue here,' he would say, pointing to the beginning of the Epilogue. 'Two horns are working it out, while a trumpet and a violin in unison sing a long-drawn-out melody, a kind of *cantus firmus*. Doesn't this melody sound to you like a medieval vielle [a viol]? Listen. . . .' And his fingers would start fidgeting again on the keyboard. Then, coming to a passage in the Epilogue where a harp solo interrupts the slow progress of the fugue, he would stop and say, 'Here, you see, I cut off the fugue with a pair of scissors.' He clipped the air with his fingers. 'I introduced this short harp phrase, like two bars of an accompaniment. Then the horns go on with their fugue as if nothing had happened. I repeat it at regular intervals, here and here again.' Stravinsky added, with his habitual grin, 'You can eliminate these harp-solo interruptions, paste the parts of the fugue together, and it will be one whole piece'.

Nabokov's description of Stravinsky's study in Los Angeles is as vivid in its way as Ramuz's description of the 'blue room' at Morges.[2]

An extraordinary room, perhaps the best planned and organised workroom I have seen in my life. In a space which is not larger than some twenty-five by forty feet stand two pianos (one grand, one upright) and two desks (a small elegant writing desk and a draughtsman's table). In two cupboards with glass shelves are books, scores, and sheet music, arranged in alphabetical order. Between the two pianos, the cupboards and desks, are scattered a few small tables (one of which is a kind of 'smoker's delight': it exhibits all sorts of cigarette boxes, lighters, holders, fluids, flints, and pipe cleaners), five or six comfortable chairs, and the couch Stravinsky uses for his afternoon naps. (I saw him on it the next day, lying on his back, with an expression of contained anger on his face, snoring gently and methodically.) Besides the pianos and the furniture there are hundreds of gadgets, photo-

---

[1] Published in *Old Friends and New Music*.
[2] See p. 57.

graphs, trinkets, and implements of every kind in and on the desks and tables and tacked on the back of the cupboards. I believe Stravinsky has in his study all the instruments needed for writing, copying, drawing, pasting, cutting, clipping, filing, sharpening, and gluing that the combined effects of a stationery and hardware store can furnish.[1]

Nabokov's account of Christmas with the Stravinskys gives the impression of a gay and contented household, and of a composer at the height of his creative powers.

At the moment of his visit, the score of *Orpheus* was ready, but the ballet had not yet been produced. Stravinsky was also trying to complete the *Mass*, on which he had been working intermittently since 1942. This was one of his few uncommissioned works, and its composition was an act of natural piety. The score of the *Mass* is dated March 1948. The first performance of *Orpheus* was given by the Ballet Society in New York the following month, and it proved a 'smash hit'. The first performance of the *Mass* was given at the Teatro alla Scala, Milan, on 27 October 1948, with Ansermet conducting.

Meanwhile, Stravinsky had reached an important decision – that he would compose a full-length opera in English. This was something he had wanted to do ever since his arrival in the United States; and his relations with his new publishers were such that although the opera was not directly commissioned by any specific person or institution, he felt he would be justified in devoting three years of his composing life to it. The new work was intended to be, not only his first opera in English, but also his first full-length work for the stage, for hitherto he had made a virtue of brevity, and none of his operas or ballets had played for more than an hour.

A subject had already occurred to him. In the course of a visit to the Chicago Art Institute in 1947, he had been impressed by Hogarth's prints depicting *The Rake's Progress*[2] and by the possibility of using this sequence of moral tableaux as the basis of an opera libretto. Wishing to obtain the services of a good librettist, he consulted his friend and neighbour, Aldous Huxley, who recommended W. H. Auden. At that moment Auden's reputation as a poet, particularly a lyricist and ballad-writer, stood high, but his experience of the theatre was limited. Three of his verse plays had been successful in the London *avant garde* theatre of the 'thirties, but in these he had had the benefit of the collaboration of Christopher Isherwood; and when he came to write the

---

[1] Nicolas Nabokov, *op cit.*

[2] What Stravinsky saw in Chicago was not the set of original paintings, which are in the Sir John Soane Museum, Lincolns Inn Fields, London, and may not be removed thence except by Act of Parliament, but a set of the engravings in which the tableaux appear in reverse.

1. The Man

libretto for Benjamin Britten's first opera, *Paul Bunyan* (1941),[1] on his own, the result was described by Virgil Thomson in the *New York Herald Tribune* as 'a flop'. But Auden was also a knowledgeable and enthusiastic opera fan; and this was a quality that was likely to stand him in good stead.

When he was invited by Stravinsky to visit him in Hollywood in November 1947, the meeting proved a great success. The two men got on well together. Stravinsky professed great admiration for Auden's technical proficiency as a poet; and Auden had already written in a letter, 'I need hardly say that the chance of working with you is the greatest honour of my life'.[2] The poet saw at once what was required in the way of a libretto; and within the space of ten days, the two men evolved an outline scenario. This was subsequently published as an appendix to Stravinsky's *Memories*; and it is interesting to find how little it was subsequently modified. Shortly after his return to New York, Auden invited his friend Chester Kallman to collaborate with him on the libretto. The first act was dispatched to Stravinsky by post in January 1948, the second act following at the end of the month; and the third was handed over to him in Washington D.C. at the end of March.

The composition of the music started that summer, and Stravinsky devoted roughly a year to each of the acts. When the third act was completed in the winter of 1951, a brief epilogue was added in the form of a vaudeville quintet, and the score was dated 7 April 1951.

Great interest was aroused by the news that Stravinsky was writing a full-length opera in English; and many of the big opera houses, including the Metropolitan Opera House, New York, and the Royal Opera House, Covent Garden, were anxious to obtain the first performance rights, if possible. But from the beginning the composer had conceived *The Rake's Progress* as a chamber opera, with small orchestra, small chorus, and a limited number of soloists – like *Così fan tutte* – and it seemed more appropriate that it should be launched in a less grandiose setting. In the end it was decided that the first performance should be given in Venice at the Teatro la Fenice during the 14th International Festival of Contemporary Music organised by Ferdinando Ballo. As the Fenice had no resident company of its own, arrangements were made for the Teatro alla Scala, Milan, to supply the chorus and orchestra, while the chief roles were cast from the best available singers. Stravinsky himself agreed to conduct.

Stravinsky and his wife came over to Europe in the summer; and the first rehearsals took place at the Scala, Milan, towards the end of August. Later, the orchestra, chorus and cast moved over to Venice in three specially reserved

---

[1] Described by its authors as a choral operetta, with many small parts rather than a few star roles.

[2] Quoted from a letter to Stravinsky dated 12 October 1947, printed in *Memories*.

railway carriages. The première at the Fenice on 11 September 1951 was a dazzling occasion.

As the *Rake* progressed, it became apparent that Stravinsky had achieved a greater breadth than ever before. The short, tightly corseted movements so characteristic of him had given way to arias and scenas of great lyrical freedom and expansiveness. In spite of the amazing interest and detail of the orchestra, it was a singer's opera, and of a fertility of melodic invention long absent from opera. During the intermissions the people who can't hear music discussed such urgent matters as whether the *Rake* had or lacked what Coleridge, translating Schelling, called 'organic form'. One also heard the expected comments about Stravinsky's right to use the old operatic conventions and formulae – by people who had not yet learned the wisdom of Ezra Pound's remark 'beauty is a brief gasp between one cliché and another' – but the majority of the audience would have conceded him anything or followed him anywhere.[1]

Stravinsky did not have time to write and issue a manifesto or statement about *The Rake's Progress* before the Venice production. Instead, on the evening of his arrival in Milan, he consented to be interviewed by Emilia Zanetti and, in answering her questions, made it abundantly clear that he was still irrevocably opposed to the idea of music drama, which he considered to suffer from total absence of form – 'On doit toujours se borner, se donner des limites' – and ended by confessing his veneration of Monteverdi and his partiality for Donizetti's *L'Elisir d'Amore*. He also gave generous praise to Auden and Kallman for their share in the collaboration, saying that, in his view, their libretto was as good as, if not better than, da Ponte's *Don Giovanni*;[2] and this compliment was later returned by Auden when he published as the final section of *The Dyer's Hand* (1963) a homage to Stravinsky containing his (i.e., Auden's) major essays on music and opera.

Although it was not apparent at the time, *The Rake's Progress* was the peroration to the splendid series of neo-classical works he had been turning out since *Mavra*. It is true that on returning to America he set about to compose a *Cantata*, which could in some ways be looked on as a parergon to *The Rake*. As he wanted to pursue the problems of setting English words to music, he took as his text four early English anonymous lyrics that he found in the anthology *Poets of the English Language* edited by W. H. Auden and Norman

---

[1] Robert Craft, '*The Rake's Progress* in Venice'. Printed in the programme for the production by the Boston University Opera Workshop at the Esquire Theatre, Boston (17 and 18 May 1953).
[2] From '*Strawinsky ha detto*' in *Guida a 'The Rake's Progress'*. XIV Festival Internazionale di Musica Contemporanea, Venice, 1951.

Holmes Pearson; and of the various movements into which this *Cantata* is divided, the setting of *Westron Wind* as a duet for soprano and tenor is close in style to that of an operatic number. But the key movement in the *Cantata* is the second Ricercar 'Tomorrow shall be my dancing day', an elaborate canonic composition, using retrograde motion, inversion and retrograde inversion. This was written just after Robert Craft had introduced him to the music of Anton Webern; and from that moment dated his growing interest in serial music.

9. The American Serialist

In the summer of 1947, the twenty-three year old Robert Craft wrote from New York to Stravinsky, whose music he enthusiastically admired, asking if he might borrow a copy of the score of the *Symphonies of Wind Instruments*, which was at that moment completely unobtainable. He wanted to include this work in one of the programmes of the Chamber Art Society, New York, whose concerts he was conducting. Stravinsky sent a friendly reply, explaining that he had just finished making a new version of the *Symphonies of Wind Instruments* and adding that he would like to conduct it himself at one of the Society's concerts. While Craft was delighted by the idea of the composer's participation, he was embarrassed by the difficulty of finding the money to pay his fee, which could hardly have been less than $1,000: but suddenly Stravinsky made a most generous offer – he was prepared to conduct the *Symphonies of Wind Instruments* and the *Danses Concertantes* without fee, leaving Craft himself to conduct the *Symphony in C* and the *Capriccio*. Craft accordingly travelled to Washington D.C., at the end of March 1948 to meet Stravinsky and confer with him about details; and the two men were introduced to each other by W. H. Auden, who had come over to Washington as well, in order to hand over the completed libretto of *The Rake's Progress*.

The meeting was a success; and Craft forthwith received an invitation to Hollywood, to stay in Stravinsky's house and carry out certain tasks for him. He accepted; the friendship prospered; and in a short time he had become accepted as a *famulus* in the household at North Wetherly Drive.

His first job was to sort a large batch of manuscripts that had just arrived from Paris; and the catalogue he then compiled is a basic document of its kind.[1] Interest in the manuscripts of Stravinsky and other contemporary composers was fanned by an auction sale that took place in Zurich on 17 November 1948; and on that occasion four important manuscripts of Stravinsky's – the instrumental score of *Les Noces* (without chorus or soloists); the piano reduction (two hands) of *Apollon-Musagète*; the full orchestral score of *Perséphone*; and the full orchestral score of the 1947 version of *Pétrouchka* – were sold and fetched good prices.

Craft was also required to help with *The Rake's Progress*, particularly in connection with the pronunciation and accentuation of the English words; and the composer undoubtedly found it useful to have someone at hand who was familiar with English idiomatic usage.

---

[1] This was the first draft of the catalogue printed in Appendix C.

1. The Man

In June 1948, in the course of a concert tour to Colorado, Stravinsky let Craft hear the first music sketches for *The Rake*; and back in Hollywood, he played him the three last movements of his *Mass* (i.e., the *Credo*, *Sanctus*, and *Agnus Dei*). Craft has described the scene as follows:[1]

> Though I have been similarly privileged a hundred times since with other preview auditions of new Stravinsky music, the impression of that first performance of his at the piano is the most memorable. The pages were unbound; the last ones were still ink-wet, in fact, and had to be held or clipped to a music rack above the keyboard. Stravinsky, as soon as he started to play, was aroused to a state of great excitement. The performance was anything but smooth. I was supposed to play treble parts, or vocal parts in treble octaves, but was unable to keep from getting ahead. Stravinsky sang the solo parts one, two, and even three octaves below notation in a deep and tremulous non-voice. He also sang during the purely instrumental music, or groaned with impatience at his incapacity to realise the full score at the piano.

In September 1949, Craft returned to New York to direct the new concert season of the Chamber Art Society; but the programmes were so *avant garde* – Monteverdi, Bach and Mozart were the only old masters featured, and the new masters included Schoenberg, Webern, Berg, and Bartók as well as Stravinsky – that it was hardly surprising that ultimately the enterprise collapsed. But not before he had presented another all-Stravinsky programme consisting of *Persephone*, *Zvezdoliki*, the *Four Studies for Orchestra*, and the ballet version of *Pulcinella*. This concert had the bad luck to lose its general rehearsal, as the Carnegie Hall had been unexpectedly commandeered by Toscanini that day for a recording session. Craft then returned to Hollywood, where he undertook a part-time job as a kind of musical amanuensis to Stravinsky and also started to play an active part in the 'Evenings-on-the-Roof' concerts in Los Angeles. Stravinsky had been associated with these concerts since his arrival at Hollywood – he said they reminded him of the old St. Petersburg series of 'Evenings of Contemporary Music' – and through them he heard many masterpieces of Renaissance and Baroque music as well as the works of contemporary composers like Webern, Boulez, and Stockhausen. Later he was to write and arrange works of his own for performance at these concerts, such as the *Preludium* and *Tango* (new version) and the *Three Songs from William Shakespeare* (1953). The organisation became defunct in June 1954; and subsequent works like *In Memoriam Dylan Thomas* (1954), the version of the *Balmont Songs* with instrumental accompaniment, the revised version of the *Four Russian Peasant Songs* with four horns, the *Four Songs for voice, flute,*

---

[1] Robert Craft, 'A Personal Preface'. *The Score*, June 1957.

harp and guitar, and the *Elegy for J.F.K.* were presented through its successor, the 'Monday-Evening-Concerts'.

Craft had always been interested in the music of Schoenberg, Webern, and Berg as well as that of Stravinsky. When the Chamber Art Society had included *Pierrot Lunaire*, the *Serenade*, and the *Suite* (op. 29) in its programmes, Schoenberg had sent him letters of encouragement. But now that he was living in Hollywood, only ten miles from Brentwood Park, he found that in some ways he was no nearer to Schoenberg than he had been in New York. Stravinsky and Schoenberg were kept separate and isolated by their friends and admirers and disciples.

> Musicians came from all over the world to visit them, not mentioning to one composer their meetings with the other one. That the two men lived so near each other for eleven years and never met is humanly regrettable. Whether it was too late for a musical exchange (it wasn't) is no matter; the important thing is that both composers would have been pleased. We know that Schoenberg had wanted to defend Stravinsky against a Schoenberg disciple; we knew then that Stravinsky was genuinely distressed by the monstrous universal neglect of Schoenberg.[1]

It is likely that Craft proved an able and powerful advocate of serial music; but Stravinsky would not have become a convert, except through conviction. Two factors may have been crucial at that moment. First, *The Rake's Progress* was the largest work he had ever written, and after its completion he may have felt that for the time being he had exhausted that particular neo-classical vein and needed a new orientation. Second, Schoenberg's death in the summer of 1951 (a few weeks before the première of *The Rake's Progress*) meant that the three chief Viennese serialists – Berg, Webern, and Schoenberg – were now all dead: so their contributions to serialism could at last be viewed in a historical perspective. It must be remembered that although at that time Stravinsky had been exposed to a considerable amount of serial music, he was not really familiar with a single example of it.[2] In January and February 1952, he had the opportunity of getting to know Webern's Quartet op. 22 quite well; and a little later he began to make closer acquaintance with some of Schoenberg's works too. But how cautious was his approach to this music can be seen from an interview dating from May 1952. Questioned in Paris about serialism at the time of the Festival of '*L'Oeuvre du XXe Siècle*', he replied:

> Serialism? Personally I find quite enough to do with seven notes of the scale. Nevertheless, the serial composers are the only ones with a discipline that I respect. Whatever else serial music may be, it is certainly pure music.

---

1 Robert Craft, *op. cit.*
2 Robert Craft, *op. cit.*

Only, the serialists are prisoners of the figure twelve, while I feel greater freedom with the figure seven.[1]

But when the time came for him to take the plunge, it was Webern rather than Berg or Schoenberg that he chose as guide and sponsor. As Craft has written:[2]

In the years between 1952 and 1955 no composer can have lived in closer contact with the music of Webern. Stravinsky was familiar with the sound of the Webern *Cantatas* and of the instrumental songs at a time when some of these works had not yet been performed in Europe. The challenge of Webern has been the strongest in his entire life. It has gradually brought him to the belief that serial technique is a possible means of musical composition.

In June 1955, Stravinsky paid tribute to Webern in the following words:[3]

The 15th of September 1945, the day of Anton Webern's death, should be a day of mourning for any receptive musician. We must hail not only this great composer but also a real hero. Doomed to a total failure in a deaf world of ignorance and indifference he inexorably kept on cutting out his diamonds, his dazzling diamonds, the mines of which he had such a perfect knowledge [*sic*].

Despite his whole-hearted allegiance to Webern, his own approach to serialism was a gradual one. He was clearly not going to allow himself to be rushed into a snap decision; and between 1952 and 1957 his serial essays were cautious experiments carried out within a framework of tonal music. This is particularly true of the *Three Songs from William Shakespeare*, the *Canticum Sacrum* (1955) and *Agon* (1953–57). Not until *Threni* (1957–58) and the *Movements* for piano and orchestra (1958–59), does one encounter completely serial works.

Just as many of his earlier followers had jumped off the bandwaggon when *Mavra* and the following compositions of the 'twenties had signalled a radical change of direction from his early style to neoclassicism, so many of his later followers fell away when he accepted serialism as a legitimate method of composition. Among them was his old friend and colleague, Ernest Ansermet, who in his book *Les Fondements de la Musique dans la Conscience humaine*[4] denounced serialism in general and Stravinsky's later works in particular. When the two men met round about 1960, the subject came up for discussion; and Ansermet told Stravinsky he would give him a simple example of why he objected to serialism and its horizontal and vertical organisation. 'Suppose you are the producer of a play which has the important line *Morituri te*

---

[1] 'Rencontre avec Stravinsky'. *Preuves*, May 1952.
[2] Robert Craft, *op. cit.*
[3] Published in *Die Reihe*.
[4] Published by Editions de la Baconnière, Neuchâtel, 1961.

salutant,' he said, 'and suppose you cast a separate player for each of these eight syllables. You then reverse the order of the syllables and alter it perhaps in other ways too, ending up with a shout in which all eight syllables are synchronised. Would you understand what this was supposed to mean?' 'No,' replied Stravinsky, 'I would not necessarily understand it; but it might make an interesting effect.'

One of the results of Stravinsky's serialism was to produce a greater intensity of musical texture in his compositions. The specific gravity of major works like *Threni* and *Movements*, and even of a minor work like *Epitaphium* (1959), is several times denser than that of comparable works of his in the neo-classical idiom. Not only does this result from a greater effort on the part of the composer, but it also calls for greater concentration on the part of the listener. As Stravinsky said in his *Conversations*: 'I know that portions of *Agon* contain three times as much music for the same clock length as some other pieces of mine. Naturally a new demand for greater in-depth listening changes time perspective.' But his new audience had still to be wooed and won. In 1962 he calculated that whereas a new recording of *The Firebird* could count on sales of 30,000 – 50,000 sets in the United States, his latest works, like *Movements*, *A Sermon etc.*, and *The Flood*, were lucky if they sold 3,000 –5,000 records (*Exp*).

Patrons and commissioners were still forthcoming, even though they must have realised that what they were buying was likely to pass through a period of comparative unpopularity and might not give them much musical pleasure at the time. The first batch of works after *The Rake's Progress* were all written for American patrons – the *Cantata* for the Los Angeles Chamber Symphony Society, the *Septet* for the Dumbarton Oaks Research Library and Collection, the *Three Songs from William Shakespeare* for the 'Evenings-on-the-Roof' concerts, Los Angeles – and *Agon*, which was commissioned by Lincoln Kirstein for the New York City Ballet, belongs to this group too, because its composition was started as early as December 1953.

The world-wide success of *The Rake's Progress* meant that sooner or later Stravinsky was bound to be asked to write another opera; and in 1953 Boston University, which had just been responsible for the first American production of *The Rake*, offered to commission a new opera from him with Dylan Thomas as librettist. Stravinsky had already heard Auden speak favourably of Thomas as a poet; and his wife had attended a poetry reading of Thomas's at Urbana. When the two men met in Boston on 22 May, they discovered an instant liking for each other, and in a single session at the Copley-Plaza Hotel the foundations were laid for what seemed likely to be an exciting collaboration and a lasting friendship. At that moment Thomas, who had just directed the first public readings of the incomplete version of *Under Milk Wood*, was on the point of returning to Wales, but he intended to come back to America in the autumn if possible: so Stravinsky invited him to visit Hollywood then and to stay at his house as Auden had done six years previously. As there was no guest room at North Wetherly Drive, Auden had had to doss down on a sofa; but now Stravinsky decided to build an extension from the dining room specially to accommodate his new librettist. During the next few months, difficulties arose with Boston University over the proposed commission; but Stravinsky was still anxious to go ahead and began to explore other sources of financial support. Thomas arrived in New York on 19 October and was expected to reach Hollywood early in November. Stravinsky was awaiting news of his arrival; but the telegram when it came announced, not his arrival, but his death on 9 November. Stravinsky was deeply moved. The opera project lapsed; and in its place he composed a brief but most impressive elegy *In Memoriam Dylan Thomas*, in which Thomas's poem 'Do not go gentle into that good night' set for tenor and string quartet was framed by dirge canons for a quartet of trombones. The world première was given at one of the 'Monday-Evening-Concerts' at Los Angeles on 20 September 1954 with Robert Craft conducting; the first European performance took place in Rome later that autumn.

Stravinsky had always been fond of Italy, and after the Venetian première of *The Rake's Progress* he began to renew his visitations. He was in Rome in the spring of 1954 when the first Italian performance of Hans Werner Henze's *Boulevard Solitude* was given at the Opera House and happened to be an eye- and ear-witness of the scandal that opera provoked. As Henze's music was published by his former publishers, Schott's, he sent to the hotel where Willi Strecker was staying the following brief but reassuring testimonial:

'Trotz der unverständlichen Haltung eines Teiles des Publikums fand ich die Aufführung von H. Henzes Boulevard Solitude sehr eindrucksvoll und voller Talent.[1]

I. Stravinsky
Rome, den 12 April/54

It is true that in his *Dialogues* Stravinsky suggests that he was 'induced' by Willi Strecker 'to sign a squib' recommending Henze's work; but the above draft as reproduced in facsimile[2] is completely in the composer's handwriting.

He was also in Italy the following autumn, when he visited Venice and discussed with Alessandro Piovesan, the artistic director of the International Festival of Contemporary Music, the possibility of writing a special work for one of the Festivals. The outcome was the *Canticum Sacrum ad Honorem Sancti Marci Nominis*, a cantata dedicated to the City of Venice and in praise of its Patron Saint, which was performed for the first time in the Cathedral of St. Mark's as part of the 19th International Festival (13 September 1956). 'The *Canticum* is wholly Stravinsky's conception,' says Robert Craft:[3] 'subject,

---

[1] 'Despite the incomprehensible behaviour of part of the audience, I found the performance of Henze's *Boulevard Solitude* very impressive and full of talent.' (Translation by E. W. W.)
[2] In the Bayerischer Rundfunk programmes for July, August and September 1955.
[3] In 'A Concert for Saint Mark'. *The Score*, December 1956.

selection and form of the texts, the performing ensembles.' Its five movements are cyclic in the sense that the last is the first in retrograde motion. Both of these flanking movements, which deal with the command to preach the Gospel and its fulfilment, are written in a diatonic idiom with strong tonal implications, and this emphasises the distance that has to be covered by the time the music reaches the full serial disclosure of the middle movement. This journey of discovery makes Stravinsky's serialism appear like an adventure of the spirit; but remarkably little understanding of the issues involved was shown by the audience at the première.

As the new work lasted for only seventeen minutes, Stravinsky had originally intended to include in the programme a recomposed work by Carlo Gesualdo di Venosa; but the Venetians refused to admit the music of a Neapolitan composer in St. Mark's Cathedral, so he dropped the idea for the time being and made an instrumental arrangement instead, of J. S. Bach's canonic variations on the Christmas Hymn *Von Himmel hoch da komm ich her*. This was dedicated to Robert Craft; and its first performance took place earlier that summer at the Ojai Festival, California, with which Robert Craft had been associated for several years.

After the première of the *Canticum Sacrum*, he carried out a short European tour, but was taken ill in Berlin when conducting a performance of the *Symphony in C* on 2 October 1956. 'Near the end of the first movement I felt an eclipsing pain and was aware only of an enveloping blackness. Orchestra members said later that I failed to beat the final chords of the movement and did not begin the second movement until after an unconscionable pause, but I did continue and somehow, raggedly no doubt, brought the piece all the way through. In the dressing room afterward, I was unable to write my name, and I had partial loss of speech.'[1] This was a cerebral thrombosis from which he made an excellent recovery, though when he came over to London at the beginning of December, he was still not well enough to appear in public. A B.B.C. concert that he had been billed to conduct (with a programme including the *Symphony of Psalms* and the *Symphony in C*) was taken over by Sir Malcolm Sargent, and Robert Craft conducted the first English performances of the *Canticum Sacrum* and the Bach Variations on *Vom Himmel hoch* at St. Martin-in-the-Fields (11 December 1956).

The controversy aroused by the *Canticum Sacrum* did not discourage the commissioning of a further work for Venice. This time it was the Norddeutscher Rundfunk of Hamburg that became the patron of *Threni*[2] and whose orchestra and chorus helped to perform it for the first time in the Sala della Scuola Grande di San Rocco on 23 September 1958 during the 21st Inter-

---

[1] From a sleeve-note for the *Symphony in C* written by Stravinsky and dated 12 December 1963.
[2] A circumstantial account of the negotiations with Rolf Liebermann over the commission fee is given by Nicolas Nabokov in *Igor Strawinsky*, 1964.

1. The Man

national Festival. Unfortunately Piovesan died shortly before the festival opened: so at Stravinsky's special request the first performance of *Threni* was dedicated to his memory.

Meanwhile, the composition of *Agon* for the New York City Ballet, which had been interrupted by *In Memoriam Dylan Thomas* and the *Canticum Sacrum*, was renewed in 1956, and the new ballet score was ready for a first concert performance on 17 June 1957 when it was conducted by Robert Craft as part of a Los Angeles festival programme to commemorate Stravinsky's seventy-fifth birthday. The first stage production followed about six months later in New York. Whereas in the *Canticum Sacrum* serialism was explored primarily through vocal and choral channels, in *Agon* the serial adventure is expressed in instrumental and choreographic terms; and like the earlier work, it is framed in diatonic movements of strong tonality. (The ballet score opens and closes in an emphatic and unmistakeable C major.)

In 1957 many special concerts of his music were given in various countries to celebrate his seventy-fifth birthday; and of these one of the most outstanding was the programme presented by the Institute of Contemporary Arts at the Royal Festival Hall, London, on 17 June with Manuel Rosenthal conducting *Zvezdoliki, Persephone*, and *The Rite of Spring*. Later that summer Stravinsky visited England to attend the special festival of his music (10–24 August) that was incorporated in the programme of the Summer School of Music at Dartington Hall (Director of Music: William Glock) and greatly enjoyed himself in the relaxed and friendly atmosphere of this gathering of students. His publishers produced a complete catalogue of his published works to date, running to eighty-six different compositions. In the autumn he was the guest of Prince Max Egon zu Fürstenberg at the Donaueschingen Festival and returned there the following year. When the Prince died in April 1959, Stravinsky wrote a moving *Epitaphium* in his memory which was performed at the 1959 Festival.

At the beginning of 1957, two projects in which he was particularly interested came to fruition. His wife Vera de Bosset held an exhibition of her paintings in New York; and the catalogue carried an introduction by Aldous Huxley, which the proud husband later reproduced in his *Dialogues*. And Robert Craft completed an enterprise on which he had been working for some years – a recording by Columbia of the complete works of Webern directed by Craft himself on four LP's.

The publication of the Webern records left Craft free to consider other jobs; and at this point he had a bright idea in connection with Stravinsky's forthcoming seventy-fifth birthday and its attendant publicity. Instead of leaving it to the press to interview the composer and write up reports that were often rather inaccurate and misleading, he would interview Stravinsky himself and make certain the resulting article had the composer's approval. He did so: and *Answers to 35 Questions* duly appeared in various periodicals. When this particular formula was found to work satisfactorily, the two authors became more ambitious. Other questions were devised, other answers given, the conversations being recorded in the logbooks of concert tours as Stravinsky was 'more inclined to talk about himself and his work while abroad performing music than when at home composing it'.[1] He particularly enjoyed the free and easy conversational form, as it did not tie him down to any fixed scheme, but allowed his thoughts liberty to roam wherever they would and enabled him to break off the argument whenever he wanted to. It also gave him a chance to correct tendentious reports that had appeared elsewhere and to publish some of the interesting material he had collected over the past fifty years, particularly letters from correspondents like Diaghilev, Benois, Debussy, Ravel, Gide, Auden and Dylan Thomas. The first volume of these *Conversations* was issued in 1959; and three other volumes followed during the next four years. It is entirely due to Craft's initiative that these scintillating views and reminiscences came to be recorded.

Craft's growing expertise as a conductor made it possible for him to work increasingly closely with Stravinsky as a musical assistant.[2] In the case of concert engagements, he could help by taking rehearsals, and in a concert where Stravinsky did not undertake the whole of the conducting, he could take charge of the remaining items. This led to a recrudescence of touring on a world-wide scale; and Craft's diaries (as reprinted in *Dialogues*) show that during the three years 1959–61 they visited the following places among others:

1959	*March*	Honolulu	1961	*April*	Mexico
		Manila		*September*	Helsinki
	April	Hong Kong			Stockholm
		Tokyo			Berlin
		Kyoto		*October*	Zurich
	September	London			London
				November	Cairo
					New Zealand
1960	*August*	Mexico			Sydney
		Peru			Melbourne
		Chile			Tahiti
		Argentine		*December*	Mexico

All this travelling was fitted in without serious dislocation to his composition schedule. In a letter written to a cousin living in Moscow, his wife has given a vivid account of the appearance of his Hollywood studio at this period.[3]

He composes at a small upright piano that has been muted and dampened

---

[1] Robert Craft. From the Introduction to *A Diary* in the American edition of *Dialogues and a Diary*.
[2] As God says to Noah in the German text of *The Flood*, 'Ich geb' dir Kraft . . .'
[3] Letter to Vladimir Petrov, dated 10 December 1962.

Dec 28/57

Dearest Miranda; how to thank you for this cat, which is, indeed, very nervous

but in spite of it send you with its master all best for the coming New 1958 year Love and Kisses from Igor Stravinsky who is happy to see you soon in Houston

A page from a letter to Miranda Massaco, containing a doodle of a cat

with felt. Nevertheless, and though the room is sound-proofed and the door tightly closed, little noises as though from mice on the keyboard penetrate to the next room. A plywood drawing board is fixed to the music rack and to it are clipped quarto-sized strips of manilla paper. These are used for the pencil-sketch manuscript. A few smaller sheets of paper are thumbtacked around this central manuscript like satellites. They are the navigation charts of serial orders, the calculations of permutations, the transposition of tables – 'Here the twelfth note becomes the second note . . .' and so forth. To the side of the piano is a kind of surgeon's operating table, the tools, in this case, being coloured pencils, gums, stopwatches, electrical pencil sharpeners (they sound unpleasantly like lawnmowers), electric metronomes, styluses – with which Igor draws the staves and of which he is the patented inventor.

He also found time still to produce occasional drawings; and a powerful though slightly saturnine self-portrait is dated 19 March 1962. For a number of years he had enjoyed making rough portrait sketches of some of his friends, including Ramuz (dated 29 June 1917), Picasso (two versions, the earliest dating from 1920), Diaghilev (October 1921), Bakst (1921), Tansman (1942), and Craft (1949). These drawings reveal a flair for catching a likeness; and, the doodle of a cat in a letter to Miranda Massaco, dated 28 December 1957, shows a spirited sense of what may be called 'Jellicle' humour.[1]

Plans to celebrate his eightieth birthday in 1962 proceeded on a much more extensive scale than the seventy-fifth birthday commemoration in 1957.

Three new works received their first performance in 1962, and one older work was recomposed. A few years previously, Paul Sacher had commissioned a new cantata for the Basler Kammerorchester, and the resulting work, *A Sermon, A Narrative and a Prayer*, though finished early in 1961, was not performed until 23 February 1962 in Basel. A television commission led to the composition of *The Flood* to a text compiled by Craft mainly from the Book of Genesis and the York and Chester Cycles of Mystery Plays. This was first styled 'a Biblical Allegory' and later 'a musical play'; and its first performance was telecast by CBS Television Network in the United States on 14 June just before the actual birthday. There was also a short *a cappella* anthem that Stravinsky wrote early in January to an extract from the *Four Quartets* by T. S. Eliot, 'The dove descending breaks the air' dedicated to the poet, and which Craft conducted on 19 February at one of the Monday-Evening-Concerts at Los Angeles. About the same time Stravinsky recomposed his earlier set of easy piano pieces called *The Five Fingers* (1921) and instrumented them for a small ensemble of fifteen players. Under their new title *Eight Instrumental Miniatures*, they received their first performance in Toronto (29 April) with the composer conducting the C.B.C. Symphony Orchestra.

By now honours were descending on him thick and fast. In 1954 he had been presented with the Gold Medal of the Royal Philharmonic Society, London, by Sir Arthur Bliss, the Master of the Queen's Musick, at a concert (on 27 May) at which he conducted the Royal Philharmonic Orchestra in his *Divertimento*, *Scènes de Ballet*, *Orpheus* and a shortened version of the *Petrushka* concert suite. The Jan Sibelius Gold Medal (granted by the Cultural Foundation in Finland) followed two years later. In 1957 he was elected a Fellow of the

---

[1] See *Old Possum's Book of Practical Cats* by T. S. Eliot.

1. The Man

Stravinsky at 24 Russell Square, London (the former offices of Faber and Faber), 1958 with Epstein's bust of T. S. Eliot in the background

Stravinsky rehearsing *The Soldier's Tale*, Zurich, 1961

American Academy of Arts and Letters. In October 1962 Pope John XXIII conferred on him the honour of Knight Commander of St. Sylvester with Star; and he was invested with the insignia of this order in the Cathedral of Santa Fe, New Mexico, at a concert of sacred music (18 August 1963) in the course of which he conducted his *Mass*. In 1963 he was awarded the Wihuri-Sibelius prize[1] of 80,000 Finmark by Wihuri's Foundation for International Prizes; but as he was unable to travel to Helsinki that October, it was received on his behalf by the United States Ambassador. A year later the Mayor of Jerusalem presented him with the golden emblem of Jerusalem on the occasion of the first performance of *Abraham and Isaac*. But perhaps the most signal tribute of all was the dinner party given in his honour at the White House by the President and Mrs. Kennedy on 18 January 1962, just two days after he had received the State Department's medal.

The Stravinskys were welcomed at the front porch of the White House by the President and his wife. The other guests at the party included Leonard Bernstein, Nicolas Nabokov, Goddard Lieberson, Max Freedman, Marshall Field, Arthur Schlesinger, Pierre Salinger, and their wives; and also Lee Radziwill and Helen Chavchavadze. Near the end of the dinner the President

---

[1] The Wihuri-Sibelius Prize was awarded to Jean Sibelius in 1953, Paul Hindemith in 1955, Dmitri Shostakovich in 1958, Stravinsky in 1963, and Benjamin Britten in 1965.

toasted the composer in champagne; and Craft, who was in the composer's party, reported the Presidential speech as follows:

'We have been honoured to have had two great artists' – I am wondering if I.S. realises that Casals is meant by the other – 'here with us in the last months. As a student in Paris, my wife wrote an essay on Baudelaire, Oscar Wilde, and Diaghilev.' (I.S. later: 'I was afraid he was about to say his wife had made a study of homosexuality.') 'I understand that you, Mr. Stravinsky, were a friend of Diaghilev. And I was told that rocks and tomatoes were thrown at you in your youth.' The President's speech is based on V's briefing during dinner, and the story of the *Sacre* première amazed him and even made him laugh aloud. Rocks and tomatoes, I explain later – I.S. has understood the phrase literally – is an American interpretation; they are thrown at baseball umpires. But the speech is short and – because an American President is honouring a great *creative* artist, and that is so absolutely unheard of in American history – it is moving.[1]

It was certainly an occasion that did credit to the imagination of a great President as well as conferring honour on a great composer.

---

[1] Robert Craft. From *A Diary* in the American edition of *Dialogues and a Diary*.

10. The Return of the Native (1962)

When Nicolas Nabokov spent the Christmas of 1947 with the Stravinskys in Hollywood, he was impressed by the thoroughness of the break between the composer and his native land. 'For Stravinsky,' he wrote,[1] 'Russia is a language, which he uses with superb, gourmand-like dexterity; it is a few books; Glinka and Chaikovsky. The rest either leaves him indifferent or arouses his anger, contempt, and violent dislike.' This was particularly true of the way Stravinsky had referred to the recent course of Russian history and culture in 'The Avatars of Russian Music', the fifth of his Harvard lectures on *Poetics of Music*. His peroration to this lecture is quite intransigent:

> Without doubt the Russian people are among those most gifted for music. Unfortunately, though the Russian may know how to reason, cogitation and speculation are hardly his strong points. Now, without a speculative system, and lacking a well-defined order in cogitation, music has no value, or even existence, as art. If the reeling of Russia through the course of history disorients me to the point of making my head swim, the perspectives of Russian musical art disconcert me no less. For art presupposes a culture, an upbringing, an integral stability of the intellect, and Russia of today has never been more completely devoid of these.

This distrust of Russia persisted until his late seventies. In his *Conversations*, referring to the fact that he was frequently being asked if he would consent to conduct in the Soviet Union, he explained that 'for purely musical reasons' he could not and pointed out that the Soviet orchestras were not familiar with the style of his music, nor with that of Berg, Webern and Schoenberg, and such difficulties were not to be overcome in the course of a few rehearsals.

These passages were written at a time when his music was subject to particularly virulent attacks in Russia. As Boris Schwarz has pointed out in an article on the vicissitudes of Stravinsky in Russian musical criticism,[2] 'Soviet evaluations of Stravinsky range from whole-hearted approval in the 1920's to rigid rejection in the 1940's and 1950's.' In 1948 Tikhon Khrennikov, the general secretary of the composers' Union, had referred to him as an apostle

---

[1] In *Old Friends and New Music*. London, 1951.
[2] Boris Schwarz, 'Stravinsky in Soviet Russian Criticism', printed in *Stravinsky: a new appraisal of his work* (ed. Paul Henry Lang).

of reaction in bourgeois music; and his name had been used as a stick to castigate Shostakovich with. When the latter's 9th Symphony was attacked on the grounds of deviationism, he was accused of showing 'the unwholesome influence of Igor Stravinsky – an artist without a fatherland and without confidence in advanced ideas'.[1] But after Stalin's death the climate began to change; and when Khrennikov was attending an international music festival at the University of California and Los Angeles in June 1961, accompanied by Kara Karayev the composer, Igor Bozrodny the violinist, and Boris Yarustovsky the music critic, he brought an official invitation with him that Stravinsky should return to the Soviet Union to conduct a concert of his own music on the occasion of his eightieth birthday. At first the composer proved elusive; but ultimately the delegation ran him to earth in the green room of a hall where he had just conducted a concert, and the invitation was delivered in person. If there was no immediate acceptance, there was no immediate refusal. Stravinsky had always had the courage of his convictions; but at the same time he had the courage to change his convictions if convinced such a change was necessary.

During the next few months, while some of his friends counselled him not to undertake the journey, others felt that, particularly in view of the increasingly liberal policy being followed in the U.S.S.R., he should accept this invitation. At the same time it appeared that his music was gradually returning to favour in Russia. On 18 January 1962 – the very evening when Stravinsky and his wife were being entertained at the White House, Washington – *Petrushka* was revived with considerable acclaim in Moscow at the Kremlin Palace of Congresses; and about the same time the Moscow Philharmonic gave a remarkably successful performance of the *Symphonies of Wind Instruments*.

In the end, Stravinsky accepted and let it be known that the main motive for his so doing was his wish to help the younger musicians in the Soviet Union. 'Nostalgia has no part in my proposed visit to Russia,' he was reported as saying. 'My wish to go there is due primarily to the evidence I have received of a genuine desire or need for me by the younger generation of Russian musicians. No artist's name has been more abused in the Soviet Union than mine, but one cannot achieve the future we must achieve with the Russians by nursing a grudge.'[2] And when he was in Russia, he followed this up by sending a special message to the young Russian readers of *Komsomolskaja Pravda*, urging increased attention to the teaching of music in schools and a tolerant attitude towards musical appreciation.[3]

The Russian visit in 1962 came at the end of an extensive tour, which took him to Toronto in April; Paris, Brazzaville, and Johannesburg in May; Rome

---

[1] *Culture and Life*, 1 October 1946.
[2] In *Newsweek*, 21 May 1962.
[3] See Appendix A (9).

and Hamburg[1] in June; and Israel in August. On 21 September a TU-104, bound for Moscow from Paris, landed at the Sheremetievo Airport; and as the hatch opened, Stravinsky came forward, wearing dark glasses and leaning on his malacca cane, and bowed deeply at the head of the landing stairs. After an absence of forty-eight years, the wanderer had returned to his native country. It was a solemn moment.

The reception committee included Khrennikov and Karayev; also the remarkable pianist, Professor Maria Yudina, who throughout her long career of teaching and performing had always preserved an irrepressible enthusiasm for Stravinsky's music; Xenia Yurievna, his niece, who had come over from Leningrad where she was living at 72 Ulitsa Glinka, nearly next door to the old Stravinsky family apartment on the Krukov Canal; and with her the daughter of the poet Balmont. In fact, it was a muster of old names and new.

When the greetings were over, Stravinsky and his wife, together with Robert Craft, were driven to the National Hotel, which was to be their headquarters for the next fortnight.

Rehearsals with the Russian National Orchestra started the following day. Curiously enough, this was the first time in Stravinsky's career that he had worked with and conducted a Russian orchestra. 'Our only significant criticisms,' says Craft in his Diary, 'are that no one is attentive to tuning . . . and that the harp is thick, honeyed, and weak in volume: two players share the part in *Orpheus*, but it is less penetrating than ever before. The bass drum is another, but satisfying oddity. It is open on one side – sawed in two, in fact. The *secco* articulation from the single head makes the beginning of the *Danse de la terre* (in *The Rite of Spring*) sound like a stampede. I.S. thinks the bassoon timbre different, too. "The *fagotti* at the end of the *Evocation des Ancêtres* sound, for the first time, like the *cinq vieillards* I had imagined." '

Between rehearsals there was a continuous round of sightseeing and entertainment, including a tour of St. Basil's and the Kremlin, the Sparrow Hills and the Novodevichy Monastery, and visits to *Boris Godunov* at the Bolshoi (23 September) and Lermontov's *Masquerade* at the Maly Theatre the following evening.

On Tuesday 25 September the Stravinsky party attended a performance of *Petrushka*, *Orpheus*, and *The Firebird* given by the ballet company of the Leningrad Maly Opera Theatre at the Kremlin Palace of Congresses. According to Craft, the music and staging of these ballets were at times hardly recognisable, but *The Firebird* was 'the best-performed and the best-received' of the three. N. Krushchev was present on this occasion, together with G. Voronov, F. Kozlov, A. Kosygin, D. Polyansky, and M. Suslov.

---

[1] His eightieth birthday was celebrated in Hamburg, where three of his ballets with choreography by Balanchine – *Apollo Musagetes*, *Orpheus*, and *Agon* – were mounted by the Hamburg Opera for a week's run at the end of June.

1. The Man

The first Moscow concert was held the following evening (26 September) at the Chaikovsky Hall; and the programme included *Ode* and *Orpheus* conducted by the composer and *The Rite of Spring* conducted by Robert Craft. As an encore Stravinsky conducted his wind arrangement of *The Song of the Volga Boatmen*; but this (says Craft)[1] 'diminishes the ovation somewhat and dampens the mood, partly because the audience has waited in vain for the strings to play on the second time around, but also, I think, because it is a reference to the wrong Russia and the wrong past'. Nevertheless, the concert was a most moving experience; and when in response to the continuing applause Stravinsky made his final appearance on the platform wearing his overcoat, he told the audience, 'You see a very happy man'.

On 27 September the sight-seeing continued with a visit to the Yusopov estate at Archangelskoye; and in the evening the Stravinsky party went to a performance of Prokofiev's opera *War and Peace*. The following day they visited the Scriabin Museum in the Arbal district; and in the evening the second Stravinsky concert took place with the same programme as on the 26th. During the interval Stravinsky complained of nausea; and Craft sent for a doctor who found his pulse weak and refused to sanction any more conducting. This infuriated Stravinsky, who, after drinking a brandy and a coffee, returned to the platform and finished the concert in style. 'The Soviet medics,' wrote Craft,[2] 'are dumbfounded at the extent of I.S.'s private pharmacy, and incredulous at the – true – story that he has swallowed ten drops of an opium paregoric before the concert and washed it down with two tumblers of whisky.'

The news of this indisposition was seized on by the press, and slightly alarming reports appeared all over the world; but two days later Stravinsky seemed to be back to normal, for on 1 October he attended a lunch at the American Embassy and an evening reception given by Yekaterina Furtseva, the Soviet Minister of Culture, together with some of the leading Soviet composers including Shostakovich, Khachaturian, Khrennikov, and Karayev. According to Craft,[3] this was 'the most extraordinary event of the trip', a kind of party of Dostoievskian intensity, during which good fare and congenial company led to an orgy of self-confession.

> Each musician proposes a toast that is, in effect, an invitation to return to the fold. And each speaker begins by baring his soul, confessing to some guilt, and some shortcoming of his own, some misunderstanding of I.S., some prejudice or lack of sympathy . . . I.S.'s human qualities are lauded – they are Russian qualities, after all – and the man . . . well, all who have met the man have seen how truly *genuine* he is. No one says a word about the composer, and only Shostakovich toasts future works by him . . . (*Dia*).

---

[1] In his Diary, printed in the American edition of *Dialogues and a Diary*.
[2] R. Craft, *op. cit.*
[3] R. Craft, *op. cit.*

The Return of the Native (1962)

To his surprise, Craft found Stravinsky responding whole-heartedly to the congenial Russian atmosphere of this company and revealing more completely the underlying Russian-ness of his character than at any time since their first meeting in 1947; and he quotes the following extracts from his speech:

'The smell of the Russian earth is different; and such things are impossible to forget. . . . A man has one birthplace, one fatherland, one country – he *can* have only one country – and the place of his birth is the most important factor in his life. I regret that circumstances separated me from my fatherland, that I did not bring my works to birth there and, above all, that I was not there to help the new Soviet Union create its new music. But I did not leave Russia only by my own will, even though I admit I disliked much in my Russia and in Russia generally – but the right to criticise Russia is mine, because Russia is mine and because I love it. I do not give any foreigner that right' (*Dia*).

And this was spoken in his deep bass voice, with a slight American accent or intonation suffusing the pronunciation of his native Russian.

His third concert in Moscow took place the following day (2 October) with Kiril Kondrashin's orchestra; and the programme included the *Capriccio*, conducted by Craft, with Tatiana Nikolayeva as pianist.

On Thursday 4 October, the Stravinsky party flew to Leningrad for a visit which followed the same sort of pattern as in Moscow. Craft noted that the Leningrad reception committee was 'smaller, older, poorer than the Muscovite'. It included a nephew of Diaghilev, a daughter of the Latvian painter M. K. Ciurlionis,[1] relatives of Stepan Mitusov, the daughter of Balmont who had already turned up in Moscow a fortnight earlier, and 'one pale elderly gentleman' who burst into tears immediately after greeting Stravinsky. This was Vladimir Rimsky-Korsakov; and Stravinsky had failed to recognise him, apparently because he called him 'Igor Fedorovich' instead of the nickname 'Guima' which the Rimsky-Korsakov family had always used in the old days. Vladimir had been his best man in 1906; and now he was living in the same apartment on the English Prospekt as that in which Stravinsky had written *The Firebird* over half a century ago.

The party was driven to the Yevropaisky Hotel, which was to be their headquarters for the next five days; and in the evening they attended a performance of Tolstoy's *The Living Dead* at the Alexandrinka.

Two days later Stravinsky attended two functions at the Composers'

---

[1] In a footnote to the English edition of *Expositions* (which is not to be found in the American edition), Stravinsky refers to his early admiration for this painter's work and mentions that in 1908 he bought one of his pictures, which showed 'a row of pyramids, of a pale, nacreous tint, in flight toward a horizon, but in *crescendo*, not in the *diminuendo* of orthodox perspective'. This painting, like most of the others in Stravinsky's pre-war collection, was left behind in Ustilug in 1914.

Union: a concert at which his *Octet* and *Septet* were performed for the first time in the Soviet Union, and the opening of an exhibition of Stravinskyana. On this occasion the student instrumentalists were joined by Maria Yudina as the pianist in the *Septet*; and it was she who had organised the exhibition. The same evening the Leningrad Radio broadcast *The Soldier's Tale*; and during the next few days there were recorded concerts of several of his recent works including *The Flood*.

The first Leningrad concert was held on 8 October. The following extract is taken from Craft's Diary:

> I.S. tells the audience that he attended his first concert in this hall, and: 'Sixty-nine years ago I sat with my mother in that corner' – he points to it 'at a concert conducted by Napravnik to mourn the death of Chaikovsky. Now I am conducting in the same hall. I am very happy.' This moving little speech is even more of a success than the music, which was, as I.S. quips, 'half Chaikovsky' (*The Fairy's Kiss*) 'and half Rimsky-Korsakov' (the *Fireworks* and *The Firebird*) (*Dia*).

This programme was repeated the following evening.

These Leningrad concerts (like the previous ones in Moscow) were filled to capacity; but the enthusiasm generated by Stravinsky's visit was by no means confined to the concert audiences. There were also meetings with Leningrad composers and students which went a long way towards fulfilling his original wish that his return to Russia might be helpful to the younger generation. On 5 October he attended a reception at Monferrand House, the headquarters of the Leningrad Composers' Union, at which about thirty musicians, including Dmitri Tolstoy, the son of the writer Alexei Tolstoy, took part in a discussion on the twelve-tone system; and three days later he gave an informal talk after one of his orchestral rehearsals to a group of young musicians on the seriation principle and answered questions such as 'Doesn't it constrain inspiration?' and 'Isn't it a new dogmatism?' Khrennikov, who earlier that year had told Soviet composers in congress that there was no place in the broad stream of Soviet music for those who composed twelve-tone or serial works, presided over this meeting and 'took in good heart the applause that followed Stravinsky's earnest appeal to him to consider serialism seriously'.[1] It was interesting to find that the symbol for the current phase of intellectual growth among many of the Russians, particularly of the younger generation, was not so much the thaw that occurs after the ice-bound winter, as the appearance of the *podsherstok* or young under-hair on animals to replace the old hair that has fallen out.[2] This seemed to augur well for the future.

The round of sight-seeing included visits to the Hermitage and the Pushkin

---

[1] Ralph Parker, 'Stravinsky in Russia'. *New Statesman*, 2 November 1962.
[2] See Ralph Parker, *op. cit.*

Museum, and trips outside Leningrad to Peterhof (renamed Petrodvorets), his birthplace Oranienbaum (renamed Lomonosov), and Tsarkoe-Seloe (renamed Pushkin). On Sunday evening 7 October the Stravinsky party went to the Maryinsky Theatre (renamed the Kirov Theatre), the walls of which carried posters announcing the forthcoming visit of the New York City Ballet bringing a repertory of ballets that included *Agon*. Stravinsky had wanted to hear a performance of Rimsky-Korsakov's *Kitezh* that evening; but, instead, *Lohengrin* was revived for the first time since the German invasion of Russia. This choice of opera gave the visitors scant pleasure.

Earlier that day there had been a family dinner party at Xenia Yurievna's apartment on the Ulitsa Glinka. Craft was most impressed by her collection of Stravinskyana, which contained numerous ancestral portraits of one kind or another, including 'a daguerreotype of Ignatievich, I.S.'s great-grandfather, a mutton-whiskered old tom-cat aged 110. (Ignatievich died aged 111 as a result of a fall suffered while climbing over the fence on his way to a forbidden outing: the doctor had ordered him to stay home, and the family had locked the gate.)' (*Dia*). There were photographic studies of Stravinsky's father in some of his operatic roles, including Holofernes and Sparafucile, and family groups many of which had been taken in Ustilug and Pechisky. 'But the most striking photograph shows I.S. writing down the music of an itinerant and blind old concertina-player' (*Dia*). Craft also saw a small landscape in oils painted by Stravinsky in 1900.

As a young man Stravinsky had been happier in Ustilug than anywhere else in Russia; but in response to Craft's enquiries, it appeared that little or nothing was known of the fate of his country house there. According to Xenia Yurievna, Stravinsky's Beliankin cousins had moved his possessions from Ustilug to a warehouse in Poltava in 1941. But after that they seemed to have disappeared – with one curious exception. Shortly after his arrival in Moscow, the conductor Rozhdestvensky presented him with a copy of the cover of the second book of Debussy's *Préludes*, which he had picked up for a few kopecks in a Moscow bookstall, and which contained the following holograph inscription: After the printed words 'pour piano', Debussy had written 'et pour amuser mon ami Igor Stravinsky, juin 1913'. This was undoubtedly a relic – perhaps the only one extant – from Stravinsky's library in Ustilug.

After the concert on 9 October, Stravinsky and his wife, together with Robert Craft, caught the midnight train for Moscow. 'As we pull out of the station,' wrote Craft in his Diary, 'Diaghilev, Tolstoy, Rimsky-Korsakov, Balmont run alongside for a moment, like another era trying to catch up.'

Back in Moscow, there was a farewell banquet at the Metropole Hotel; and then on Thursday 11 October at noon there came a summons from the Kremlin – Krushchev was prepared to receive them at 1.30 p.m.

When they arrived, they found Krushchev, who had just returned from a twelve-day visit to Turkestan and the Aral Sea region, bubbling over with his impressions. Later on, Stravinsky and his wife told him how beautiful they had found Moscow on this visit; and he replied: 'Yes, not long ago I drove around really looking at it and I was impressed myself, but for eight hundred years it was a pigsty'. He then repeated Khrennikov's invitation that Stravinsky and his wife, together with Robert Craft, should return to the Soviet Union in the near future to stay in a *dacha* in the Crimea; and presently the forty-minute interview was over.

A few hours later the Stravinsky party left the Sheremetievo Airport for Paris.

After recording the Dostoievskyan dinner-party at the Metropole Hotel, Moscow, on 1 October and meditating on the effects of Stravinsky's exile, Craft wrote in his Diary: 'I am certain that to be recognised and acclaimed as a Russian in Russia, and to be performed there, has meant more to him than anything else in the years I have known him.' His decision to return to his native country had indeed been fully vindicated by the genuine warmth of his reception there.

11. Coda (1962-1971)

When Stravinsky entered his ninth decade, he was still remarkably vigorous for his years, and the stream of his compositions showed no signs of drying up. *Abraham and Isaac*, a sacred ballad for baritone and chamber orchestra written to a Hebrew text, was commissioned by the Israel Festival Committee and completed in good time for the 1964 Israel Festival despite the distractions of intensive touring that continued unabated after his return from the Soviet Union. His subsequent compositions seemed to become increasingly involved in the deaths of friends and the idea of death. When President John F. Kennedy was assassinated on 22 November 1963, he decided to compose a quiet intimate tribute. At his request W. H. Auden wrote a brief lyric of four stanzas, each a 'free' *haiku*; and Stravinsky set this *Elegy for J.F.K.* for baritone and three clarinets. On the same day as Kennedy's assassination occurred the death of Aldous Huxley. Stravinsky had already started to compose a set of *Variations* for orchestra, and these he now decided to dedicate to his friend's memory. The death of T. S. Eliot in London on 4 January 1965 inspired him to write an *Introitus* for male voices and small chamber orchestra; and this served as a kind of 'lead-in' to his final major work, the *Requiem Canticles* of 1965/66, which was commissioned through Princeton University and dedicated to the memory of Helen Buchanan Seeger. According to Robert Craft,[1] its sketchbook was

a necrology of friends who died during its composition. The composer once referred to these pasted-in obituaries as a 'practical commentary'. Each movement seems to relate to an individual death.

It should not be thought that the important works of this final period are only the longer ones such as *Abraham and Isaac, Variations*, and the *Requiem Canticles*. Equally powerful in their microcosmic way are miniatures like the *Elegy for J.F.K.* and the *Fanfare for a New Theatre* (1964) dedicated to Lincoln Kirstein and George Balanchine.

Stravinsky continued to carry out touring and conducting engagements with amazing vigour and tenacity for an octogenarian, as can be seen from the following list of places outside the United States visited after his 1962 trip to Russia.

---

[1] From Robert Craft's Afterword to Arnold Newman's photographic album *Bravo Stravinsky!*

1. The Man

1962		1965	
October	Paris	*May*	Copenhagen
	Rome		Paris
	Caracas		Vevey
November	Toronto		Basle
1963			Warsaw
April	Toronto	*June*	Rome
	Hamburg	*July*	Vancouver
May	Budapest	*September*	Hamburg
	Zagreb		London
	Paris	*December*	Toronto
	London	1966	
June	Dublin	*May*	Paris
	Hamburg		Athens
	Stockholm		Lisbon
	Milan	*November*	Honolulu
July	Rio de Janeiro	1967	
November	Rome	*May*	Toronto
	Palermo	1968	
1964		*September*	Zurich
January	Toronto	*October*	Paris
June	London	1970	
	Oxford	*June–August*	Evian
August	Paris		
	Jerusalem		
September	Paris		
	Berlin		

But by 1966 the pace was beginning to tell. In January 1967 he conducted his last recording session (in New York); in May of the same year his last public concert (in Toronto). And then his health began to fail. A great part of the autumn of 1967 was spent in hospital in Hollywood as the result of a bleeding ulcer and a series of thromboses; and all this put a tremendous strain on his devoted wife Vera and his friend and companion Robert Craft. In his diary entry for 5 November 1967,[1] Robert Craft described an afternoon spent with the invalid in the hospital.

Returning to the hospital in the afternoon, I spoon-feed him and hold his bad hand: he says the warmth diminishes the pain. A naturally affectionate, but also a deeply lonely man, feeling now pours out of him. And not a little of it pours into me. For we are very close now, as we were in our first years

---

[1] This diary entry is quoted from Robert Craft's *Stravinsky: The Chronicle of a Friendship*, 1972.

together. . . . This directness of feeling, which in other circumstances each of us would be the first to flee, makes it difficult to control my not heretofore, suffusion-prone eyes, an absurd propensity that I try to excuse by arguing that death is different in I.S.'s case because he can still create: witness the sketches on his piano, and his talk even now about his musical ideas. . . . Yet this is not the principal reason why I cannot bear that the light of this most intensely alive human being I have ever known be extinguished. . . . My uppermost feelings are simply those of love for a best friend and admiration for the fantastic fight and will and courage of an old man.

By 1968 he had recovered sufficiently to be able to resume a certain amount of touring within the United States; and the new formula used on these 'official' occasions was that he would be 'in attendance' at the concert at which his music was to be performed, usually with Craft as conductor.

Although Stravinsky's various attempts to start composing again came to nothing, he managed to work on one or two arrangements of other composers' works. In a single afternoon (15 May 1968) in San Francisco he arranged the piano part of two songs by Hugo Wolf for small chamber orchestra. He considered Wolf 'had a marvellous ear and a marvellous sense of invention, but very little technique'. But the main reason for this particular adaptation (according to Robert Craft)[2] was that he wanted to say something about death and felt he could not compose anything of his own. These two songs were ultimately published and performed in their new guise: but he was not so fortunate with a set of Bach transcriptions he was working on the following year. Craft's laconic, but revealing diary entry for 2 October 1969 runs as follows:

Berlin. At my dress rehearsal this morning, I decide, together with Nicolas Nabokov, not to play I.S.'s new Bach transcriptions, too little if anything of I.S. being discernible in them as they stand now, virtually unedited.

As the ability to compose and conduct died away, Craft did his best to encourage other activities likely to interest him. For instance they listened together to a lot of recorded music, and Stravinsky derived particular pleasure from Beethoven. In view of his earlier attitude of suspicion towards that composer, it is moving to find him writing so perceptively about his music in his last book *Themes and Conclusions*. Indeed, in the Foreword to that volume dated 1 March 1971, he wrote:

It is almost five years now since I have completed an original composition, a time during which I have had to transform myself from a composer to a listener. The vacuum which this left has not been filled, but I have been

[2] See Craft's diary entry for 15 July 1967.

able to live with it, thanks, in the largest measure, to the music of Beethoven.

During these declining years, Stravinsky and Craft managed to continue the collaboration they had opened up in 1959 with the first of their so-called 'conversation' books. As can be seen from the details given in the Bibliography, the first four volumes in the series were published between 1959 and 1963. *Themes and Episodes* followed in 1966 and *Retrospectives and Conclusions* in 1969, both of them containing substantial chunks of Craft's diaries as well as numerous other items. These two volumes were published in the United States. In Great Britain a single volume was issued, *Themes and Conclusions* (1972), which omitted Craft's diary entries, but included all the other items in the two American volumes, plus a certain amount of later material. Clearly, as the years went by, the influence of Craft in this collaboration became of increasing importance. He suggested subjects and ways of treating them and did his best to ease the actual drudgery of writing; but although the main share in the actual drafting may have been his, Stravinsky still exercised control over what was printed and published under their joint names and accepted his share of responsibility.

The fact that Craft was now in such close contact with Stravinsky did not necessarily endear him to all the musician's friends and relations. There is a revealing passage in his diary entry for 24 May 1969 about the critical attitude of an old acquaintance of Stravinsky's (there referred to as X), which should be considered in the light of the fact that Stravinsky had just fallen ill and been taken to hospital in New York, and at the same time he and his wife had decided to give up their house in Hollywood and move to a hotel in New York.

> Like other acquaintances of I.S. of other eras, X is very free in advising me about what is best for him, exactly what he needs, where he should go, what he should do, what my own attitude should be. . . . Return to Hollywood, says X, leaving I.S.'s own feelings out of consideration . . . and unable to imagine the sheer physical impossibility of life there now for both I.S. and V., neither of whom can manage the stairs any more, let alone look after the house. But I myself am unable now, or unwilling, to sympathise with the point of view of people like X. I do not doubt that I have been guilty of mistakes and misjudgments in trying to take care of I.S. But I have given all of myself to him and to the job, at least, and if I hadn't a great deal more might have gone wrong and his musical life would have come to an end. . . . The responsibility for every decision has been mine, furthermore, with no help from the X's, or, for that matter, from anyone in I.S.'s own family except V.

The move to Essex House, New York, took place in the autumn of 1969; and this ushered in an unfortunate period of strained relations with some of his children. For many years his eldest son, Theodore, the artist, had been living in Geneva. His second son, Soulima, had abandoned his career as a concert pianist and was working in the Music Department of the University of Illinois. His surviving daughter, Milène, had married André Marion, a Frenchman who worked for a travel agency in Hollywood. For some years Marion had been helping Stravinsky as his accountant and business manager, and he was also in close touch with Stravinsky's then lawyer, William Montapert. Sometime in 1969 Stravinsky decided to make a gift of some citrus groves in Arizona to his three children. The intention was that this would be handed over to them in equal parts: but for some reason or other, months after the various papers had been signed, the Stravinskys discovered that in fact the gift had not got beyond the Marions. In due course this was straightened out: but confidence had been shaken, and Stravinsky lost no time in transferring the power of attorney he had given William Montapert from Montapert to Arnold Weissberger. An important part of the removal from Hollywood to New York was the transfer of Stravinsky's valuable collection of his own manuscript scores. Some difficulty occurred over this, due possibly to misunderstandings; and in the end Stravinsky decided to bring a suit for

Stravinsky aged 88, at Evian les Bains in the summer of 1970. Photograph by Lord Snowdon

recovery of these manuscripts. This was successful as far as the manuscripts were concerned; but it also succeeded in widening the rift between the father and his children.

A bad attack of pneumonia in April 1970 led to a further period of hospitalisation; but once again he made a remarkable recovery, and by June he and his wife, together with Robert Craft, had flown over to Europe to spend the summer at Evian on the French side of Lake Geneva. While staying there, the Stravinsky party received a number of visitors including two of his relations – Theodore, his eldest son, from neighbouring Geneva, and Xenia, his niece, Yury's daughter, from Leningrad – but not his other son, Soulima, though apparently he and his family were spending the summer only about 150 miles away.

Xenia had apparently been empowered to sound out her uncle about the possibility of returning to settle in the U.S.S.R. And a few months later Khrennikov telephoned the Stravinskys in New York from Moscow to invite them to spend the summer in the U.S.S.R. But neither invitation was followed up.

Back in New York, Stravinsky got through the first part of the winter reasonably well, but in mid-March he succumbed to an attack of pulmonary edema, which brought him back to the same room in the same hospital as the previous year. Robert Craft has described the scene (diary entry for 18 March 1971):

> He is processed like a product on an assembly line, the chest clamped with cathodes, the trachea scoured by a vaccum cleaner, the nostrils invaded with plastic oxygen tubes, the right inner elbow embrocated to expose a vein that a Draculess then punctures to draw a remarkably copious 'specimen'. The left arm, meanwhile, is strangled by a sphygmomanometric pump, implanted with a tube for intravenous feeding (a rivulet of diuretics to flush the fluid from the lung), and bandaged to an ironing-board splint. Last and worse, he is catheterised, the deed done by the head of the Urology Department who, apologising for the discomfort, says afterward, 'Maestro, I hope we are still friends'. But the maestro angrily demolishes any assumption that they ever were.

On being discharged from hospital on 30 March, he returned, not to Essex House, but to an apartment on Fifth Avenue with a view of Central Park that his wife had just acquired. Three days later there is the following entry in Craft's diary:

> I.S. is obliged to write a short note in Russian, which he does, but signs his name in Latin letters. V. asks him to do the signature over in Russian, whereupon he takes the pen and, aware that she is watching him, writes, not his name, but 'Oh, how I love you!'

Coda (1962–1971)

Early in the morning of Tuesday 6 April 1971 he died.

The funeral service was held in Venice on 15 April; and he was buried on the Island of San Michele, near the last resting place of his friend, Serge Diaghilev. At a later date a memorial sculpture by Giacomo Manzù was erected to mark his grave.

Part Two

REGISTER OF WORKS

CONTENTS

INTRODUCTION

2. Register of Works

2. Register of Works

2. Register of Works

2. Register of Works

2. Register of Works

2. Register of Works

2. Register of Works

2. Register of Works

2. Register of Works

INTRODUCTION

In compiling this Register, it has been found convenient to adhere to certain lines of procedure.

Titles

Where a generic title is concerned, e.g. symphony or concerto, it is generally given in English alone. Specific and descriptive titles are given in Russian and/or French and/or English and/or any other language as seemed appropriate to the nature of the work and the nationality of the composer at the moment of composition. In some places the spelling of the Russian titles has been modified to conform with contemporary practice.

Instrumentation

The composition of the orchestra is usually given in accordance with the recognised woodwind / brass / percussion / keyboard instruments / strings formula. An attempt has been made to be precise over the different instruments of percussion employed. Alternative instruments are not always specified.

Date of Composition

The place and the commencing and terminal dates of composition have been given where these are known. There are sometimes different dates for short scores and full scores.

Dates of First Performances

It is sometimes difficult to establish the correct dates for the St. Petersburg first performances of Stravinsky's early works. Public performances were frequently preceded by private performances; and it is not always clear whether a proper adjustment has been made to reconcile the Gregorian and Julian Calendars.

Publication

The name of the original publisher is given; and when subsequently a different publishing-house has taken the work over, this is noticed too. Particulars are not usually given of publishers acting as agents for the original publishers in foreign countries. Dates of publication are given where known.

Duration

The time lengths are approximate.

2. Register of Works

Location of Manuscripts

Details of the location of manuscripts are given where known. 'MS comp' means that one or more manuscripts are in the possession of the composer, as set out in *A Catalogue of Manuscripts* (1904–1952) *in Stravinsky's possession* compiled by Robert Craft and printed in Appendix C. The numeration is given in square brackets e.g. [C 1], [C 10], etc.

Transcriptions &c.

Details of transcriptions and different instrumentations are included so long as they have been made by Stravinsky himself. (The same is true of piano reductions and vocal scores.) The only exception to this rule has been the admission of the two-piano transcription of the *Study for Pianola* made by Stravinsky's son, Soulima, in 1951; and the reason for this is that this transcription seems to be the nearest one can get to the original score, which was never published except as a pianola roll. Transcriptions and instrumentations are placed at the end of the entry for the work concerned. Where more than one original composition has been drawn on to form a new work (as is the case with the two *Suites for small orchestra*, the *Four Studies for orchestra*, and the *Four Songs for voice, flute, harp and guitar*) the new work is entered as an appendage to the last of the original compositions to be laid under contribution – e.g., the *Suites for small orchestra* are to be found under no. 27 *Five Easy Pieces for piano duet*, the *Four Studies for orchestra* under no. 33 *Study for Pianola*, and the *Four Songs for voice, flute, harp and guitar* under no. 38 *Four Russian Songs*.

Theatre Productions

Where a work was written for the theatre, brief details are usually given of its first stage production and of any subsequent productions that seem worthy of special attention. There are also references to stage productions of works not originally intended for the stage. Fuller details of ballet productions will be found in *Stravinsky and the Dance* published by the New York Public Library in 1962.

A. Original Compositions

1. TARANTELLA

For piano. Dedicated to A. Kudnev. Dated 14 October 1898 (O.S.). Unpublished. Manuscript in the State Public Library, Leningrad.

2. STORM CLOUD

Romance for voice and piano, set to the words of A. S. Pushkin. 25 January 1902 (O.S.). Unpublished. Manuscript in the Central State Literature and Art Archives, Moscow.

3. SCHERZO

For piano. Dedicated to Nicolas Richter – 'témoignage d'un profond respect de la part de l'auteur'. 1902. Published by Faber Music, 1973. Manuscript in the State Public Library, Leningrad.

4. SONATA IN F SHARP MINOR

For piano. Composed at St. Petersburg and Samara, 1903/04. Dedicated to Nicolas Richter. I. *Allegro*; II. *Scherzo*; III. *Andante*; IV. *Finale*. Published by Faber Music, 1973. Privately performed by Nicolas Richter to the Rimsky-Korsakov circle on 9 February 1905 (O.S.). Publicly performed (also by Richter) at one of the evenings of Contemporary Music, St. Petersburg. According to Schaeffner, the manuscript was given to Richter. It is now in the State Public Library, Leningrad.

Stravinsky admitted (*Chr*) that in this early composition he was 'constantly confronted by many difficulties, especially in matters of form' and that he accordingly went to seek Rimsky-Korsakov's advice at the end of the summer of 1903. During the fortnight he spent with him in the country, he composed the first part of a sonatina under Rimsky-Korsakov's supervision. To the end of his life he thought this piano sonata had been lost – 'fortunately lost' as he wrote in his *Memories* – and when he visited the U.S.S.R. in 1962, apparently no one informed him that for some years the manuscript had been in the safe keeping of the State Public Library, Leningrad.

5. CANTATA

For the 60th birthday of N. A. Rimsky-Korsakov: for mixed choir and piano. Composed in 1904. First performance, 6 March 1904 (O.S.) in the apartment of Rimsky-Korsakov. The choir was made up of S. N., N. N., and V. N. Rimsky-Korsakov, A. V. Ossovsky, S. S. Mitusov, and I. I. Lapshin. Unpublished. Manuscript lost.

6. THE MUSHROOMS GOING TO WAR

Song for bass and piano. Composed in 1904. Unpublished. The manuscript is in the composer's collection [C 1].

7. CONDUCTOR AND TARANTULA

Song for voice and piano, set to the words of Kosma Prutkov. Composed in 1906. First performance, 6 March 1906 (O.S.) in the apartment of Rimsky-Korsakov. Unpublished. Manuscript lost.

8. ФАВНЬ И ПАСТУШКА – FAUNE ET BERGÈRE – FAUN AND SHEPHERDESS (op. 2)

Song suite for mezzo-soprano and orchestra (3.2.2.2 – 4.2.3.1 – percussion, timp. – string 5tet). Words by A. Pushkin; French translation by A. Komaroff; German by Heinrich Möller. Composed at Imatra and St. Petersburg, 1906; the instrumentation completed in 1907. Reduction for voice and piano by the composer. Dedicated to his wife, Ekaterina Grabrielovna Stravinsky. Published by Belaiev, Leipzig, 1908[1] (later by Boosey & Hawkes). Duration, *c.* 10 minutes.

  1. 'Пастушка' – 'Shepherdess.' *Andantino*
  2. 'Фавнъ' – 'Faun.' *Moderato/Allegro moderato*
  3. 'Рѣка' – 'Torrent.' *Andante/Allegro*

First private performance by the St. Petersburg Court Orchestra, conducted by H. Wahrlich, 27 April 1907 (*Chr*). First public performance, Belaiev's Season of Russian Symphony Concerts, St. Petersburg, conducted by Felix Blumenfeld, 16 February 1908.

Stravinsky's own comment on this song cycle was: 'The *Faun* sounds like Wagner in places, like Chaikovsky's *Romeo and Juliet* in other places (but never like Rimsky-Korsakov, which must have troubled that master), and like Stravinsky not at all, or only through thickly bespectacled hindsight' (*Con*). He has also said that Rimsky-Korsakov found the first song strange and the use of whole-tone progressions suspiciously Debussy-ist (*Mem*). The last five

---

[1] The piano reduction was published in 1908, the full score in 1913.

bars of the third song clearly foreshadow the coda to the Finale of *The Firebird*. Both works end in the key of B major with an octave B held by the strings playing tremolo, while the inner parts move towards a final resolution on the major triad.

9. SYMPHONY IN E FLAT[1] (op. 1)

For orchestra (3.2.3.2 – 4.3.3.1 – percussion – string 5tet) – composed at Ustilug 1905/7 – dedicated to 'my dear teacher N. A. Rimsky-Korsakov'. The MS was presented to Rimsky-Korsakov and is presumably still with the family (*Mem*).

    I.   *Allegro Moderato*
    II. Scherzo. *Allegretto*
    III. *Largo*
    IV. Finale. *Allegro molto*

Published by Jurgenson, Moscow (1914). Subsequently, like all the items in the Jurgenson catalogue, it was taken over by the Musical Section of the State Publishing House, Moscow. First private performance by the St. Petersburg Court Orchestra, conducted by H. Wahrlich, 27 April 1907 (*Chr*). First public performance, Belaiev's Season of Russian Symphony Concerts, St. Petersburg, conducted by Felix Blumenfeld, 22 January 1908. Duration: *c.* 30 minutes.

As Stravinsky himself said (*Con*), this Symphony may lack personality, but at least it demonstrates definite technical ability. It was written under the close supervision of Rimsky-Korsakov (*Chr*). As soon as one part of a movement was finished Stravinsky would show it to Rimsky-Korsakov: so the whole composition, including its instrumentation, was under his control. There are traces of the influence of Chaikovsky, Wagner and Rimsky-Korsakov himself in the score; but it owes most to the example set by Glazunov as a symphonic composer. In his *Chronicle*, Stravinsky admits that as a young man he greatly admired Glazunov for the perfection of his form, the purity of his counterpoint and the ease and assurance of his writing. At the age of fifteen he even went so far as to transcribe one of Glazunov's string quartets for piano. But admiration soon changed to dislike. In his *Memories*, he called him one of the most disagreeable men he had ever met and said that the only bad omen at the first (private) performance of his Symphony was that Glazunov, who was present, came to him afterwards saying, 'very nice, very nice'. Subsequently, in a letter to *The Observer* reprinted in his *Dialogues*, he modified this recollection and recalled that Glazunov passed him in the aisle after the performance and commented 'Rather heavy instrumentation for such music'.

---

[1] On the title page, this score is designated as '*Symphonie No. I Es dur pour grand orchestre*'.

Original Compositions

The first movement is an academic exercise in the writing of a sonata allegro. A certain monotony ensues from the way the opening limb of the main theme is plugged by repetition, imitation, and modulation. In the Scherzo, the climate of the Symphony changes. The movement is gay, busy and eager, and gives the impression that the young composer has found something he is anxious to say. An episode marked *pochissimo meno mosso* introduces a Russian folk song which is very similar to the one Stravinsky subsequently used as the first theme of the 'Dance of the Nursemaids' in *Petrushka*. (This Scherzo used occasionally to be extracted from the Symphony and played on its own as an interlude at performances of the Russian Ballet.) The last movement contains another interesting quotation. Towards the end of an episode in G sharp minor, the key modulates to B major and a kind of folk tune is given to the woodwind. In the score the first line of a nonsense rhyme is printed under the notes – 'Tchitcher Yatcher'. Words and tune are identical with the third of the *Three Little Songs* (*Recollections of my Childhood*) written in 1913. This was probably one of the themes Stravinsky used as a basis for improvisation in his early years; and in the song it accompanies words that poke fun at an old usher who used to force pupils to attend certain concerts as part of the school curriculum. Its insertion in the Symphony may be regarded as a kind of private joke.

Revised Version

After its first performance, Stravinsky revised the work slightly, and it was heard in this form when conducted by Ansermet at Montreux (2 April 1914) and by Stravinsky himself in Paris (16 November 1928) and Chicago (22 January 1935).

10. PASTORALE

Song without words for soprano and piano. Composed at Ustilug, 1907. Dedicated to Nadezhda Rimsky-Korsakov. Published by Jurgenson, 1910; (later by Chester and by Schott's). Performed at the same time as the *Two Melodies* (op. 6) at one of the St. Petersburg Evenings of Contemporary Music in the winter of 1908.[1] Duration: c. 4 minutes.

A cool, beautifully poised vocal line set above an accompaniment that has a bass accompaniment in the left hand like a drone and a charming legato counter theme in the treble distinguished by a gruppetto of five hemidemisemiquavers that comes on a strong beat at the beginning of almost every phrase.

---

[1] This had been preceded by a private performance by Stravinsky and Maximilian Steinberg at one of Rimsky-Korsakov's weekly gatherings on 31 October 1907. (See V. Yastrebtzev's *Recollections of Rimsky-Korsakov*, Vol. II. Moscow, 1962.)

2. Register of Works

Instrumentation

For soprano, oboe, cor anglais, clarinet and bassoon made at Biarritz, December 1923. Published by Schott's.

Transcriptions

   (i) for violin and piano by I. Stravinsky and S. Dushkin (lengthened version). 1933. Schott's. Duration: *c.* 6 minutes.
   (ii) for violin, oboe, English horn, clarinet and bassoon (lengthened version). 1933. Schott's.

11. TWO MELODIES (op. 6)

For mezzo-soprano and piano. Words by S. Gorodetzky. (German translation by S. Gorodetzky; French by M. D. Calvocoressi; English by M. D. Calvocoressi.) Published by Jurgenson (1912?)

   (1) 'Весна' ('Монастырская') – 'Chanson de printemps' ('La Novice') – 'Spring' ('The Cloister'). Composed at Ustilug, December1907. Dedicated to Elizabeth Theodorovna Petrenko.
   (2) 'Росянка' ('Хлыстовская') – 'La rosée sainte' ('Chant mystique des Vieux-Croyants Flagellants') – 'A song of the Dew' ('Mystic Song of the Ancient Russian Flagellants'). Composed at Ustilug, 1908. Dedicated to Serge Gorodetzky.

First performed by Elizabeth Petrenko (with the composer at the piano) at one of the St. Petersburg Evenings of Contemporary Music in the winter of 1908. Duration: *c.* 8 minutes.

Stravinsky referred to Gorodetzky as 'one of a group of writers who, by their talent and their freshness, were destined to put new life into our somewhat old-fashioned poetry' (*Chr*) – a claim that could hardly be substantiated by the two poems he chose to set, for their most distinctive quality seems to be a faded sentimentality. 'Spring' is the lament of a love-lorn bell-ringer's daughter on the point of entering a cloister. The opening bell-like figure in the piano accompaniment looks forward to the magic carillon passage in *The Firebird*; but Gorodetzky did not altogether approve of it, for Stravinsky relates (*Mem*) that after hearing the songs performed he confided to him that 'the music is very pretty, but it really does not interpret my texts accurately, since I describe a time-to-time ringing of long, slow bells and your music is a kind of jingle bells'. 'The Song of the Dew' describes the activities of a group of virgins collecting dew in the early morning in order to improve their chances of marriage. The setting is rather disjointed. Both songs contain passages of near-recitative or declamation.

Rimsky-Korsakov apparently felt that in these songs Stravinsky inclined too much to 'modernism'. After a private performance of 'Spring' on 25 Dec-

178

ember 1907, he said, 'I keep to my opinion of the *Spring* song. What pleasure can anyone have in composing music to the words of such false Russian folk language? For me, all this "lyrical impressionism" is contemporary decadence. It is full of mist and fog, but meagre in content of ideas'.[1]

12. SCHERZO FANTASTIQUE (op. 3)

For large orchestra (4.3.4.3 – 4.3.0.0. – cymbals, celesta, 3 harps[2] – string 5tet). Composed at Ustilug, June 1907[3] to March 1908. Dedicated to Alexander Siloti.[4] Published by Jurgenson (later by Schott's). First performance Siloti Concerts, 6 February 1909, St. Petersburg, conducted by Alexander Siloti. Duration: *c.* 16 minutes.

This Scherzo was written as a piece of 'pure' symphonic music (*Con*). It was seen in manuscript by Rimsky-Korsakov shortly before his death, and he spoke highly of it to some of his friends. Although it is an early apprentice work, it is effective and promising. Fifty years after its composition, Stravinsky conducted three performances of it and was surprised to find the music did not embarrass him. 'The orchestra "sounds", the music is light,' he wrote (*Con*), 'in a way that is rare in compositions of the period, and there are one or two quite good ideas in it such as the flute and violin music at no. 63 and the chromatic movement of the last page. Of course the phrases are all four plus four plus four, which is monotonous, and, hearing it again, I was sorry that I did not more exploit the alto flute . . . I see now that I did take something from Rimsky's Bumblebee (nos. 49–50 in the score), but the *Scherzo* owes much more to Mendelssohn by way of Chaikovsky than to Rimsky-Korsakov.' Also to Dukas, Wagner (figs. 37–39) and Debussy (figs. 45–46).

The fantastic element in the *Scherzo* is represented by a far deeper exploration of the potentialities of chromaticism than Stravinsky had ventured on before. In fact, the whole of the *Con Moto* part of the *Scherzo* is chromatic, and the only diatonic relief is provided by the central episode (*Moderato assai*) with its rhapsodic theme that recalls Wagner so vividly.

Ballet Adaptation

On 10 January 1917 the *Scherzo Fantastique* was performed as a *ballet blanc* entitled *Les Abeilles* at the Paris Opera House with choreography by Leo Staats. For this purpose a scenario had been devised based on an episode culled from Maeterlinck's *La Vie des Abeilles*. The adaptation was unauthorised by Stravinsky (then living at Morges); and Maeterlinck protested. 'The affair was

---

[1] Quoted by V. Yastrebtzev in his *Recollections of Rimsky-Korsakov.*
[2] Reduced from 3 harps to 2 when a new edition of the score was published in 1930 (*Con*).
[3] He was already corresponding with Rimsky-Korsakov about the project in June and July 1907.
[4] The authority for this dedication is Paul Collaer.

settled,' writes Stravinsky (*Con*), 'and, finally, some bad literature about bees was published on the fly-leaf of my score, to satisfy my publisher, who thought a "story" would help to sell the music.' This preliminary note runs as follows:

> This piece is inspired by an episode in the life of the bees. The first section gives an impression of life and activity in the hive. The central section, a slow movement, depicts sunrise and the nuptial flight of the queen bee, the love fight with her chosen mate, and his death. The third section, a reprise of the first, shows the peaceful activity of the hive continuing. Thus the whole piece becomes for us human beings the fantastic picture of an eternal cycle.

13. FEU D'ARTIFICE – FEUERWERK – FIREWORKS (op. 4)

A fantasy for large orchestra (3.2.3.2 – 6.3.3.1 – timp., triangle, cymbals, big drum, celesta, campanelli, 2 harps – string 5tet).[1] Composed at Ustilug, May and June 1908. Dedicated to Nadia and Maximilian Steinberg. Published by Schott's, 1910. First performance, Siloti Concerts, 6 February 1909.[2] St. Petersburg, conducted by Alexander Siloti. Duration: *c.* 4 minutes.

In his *Chronicle*, Stravinsky describes how on his last visit to Rimsky-Korsakov (in April or May 1908) he told him about this orchestral fantasy that he proposed to write. 'He seemed interested, and told me to send it to him as soon as it was ready ... I finished it in six weeks and sent it off to the country place where he was spending the summer. A few days later a telegram informed me of his death, and shortly afterwards my registered packet was returned to me: "Not delivered on account of death of addressee".'

This short piece – virtually another fantastic scherzo – is remarkable for its compact, explosive force. A chromatic whirling semiquaver figure marked *Con fuoco* accompanies a simple diatonic theme. This is at first presented fragmentarily by the brass, trumpets echoing the horns bar by bar, leading to the first full statement of the four-bar-long theme in canon. A fortissimo restatement in the form of a fugato (fig. 7) contains six different entries of one limb of the theme in the course of only three bars. The whirling movement is interrupted by two interlocked episodes – one (*Lento*) where a poignant phrase for English horn solo is marked *lamentoso*; and the other (*Allegretto*) where a fluent arpeggiated figure for woodwind accompanies a *cantabile* theme. The return of the *tempo primo*, marked by a series of instrumental explosions, leads to the reappearance of the original theme at first in retrograde motion and then (without pause) in its direct form.

---

[1] The score specifies 16 first violins, 14 second violins, 12 violas, 10 cellos, and 8 double-basses.
[2] The date 17 June 1908 first given in *Igor Stravinsky* (ed. Edwin Corle), New York, 1949, would seem to be incorrect.

Original Compositions

Ex.1

(*N.B. The ringed note is an altered note*)

In *Fireworks* Stravinsky broke away from the four-plus-four-plus-four-plus-four barring that had given his previous works a stamp of monotony, and for the first time achieved a satisfactory degree of asymmetry.

Glazunov was present at the first performance on 17 June 1908 and, according to Stravinsky,[1] made the comment 'Kein Talent, nur Dissonanz'. Pierre Suvchinsky, who was also present, remembered there were cries of 'Author!' after its performance, and Stravinsky appeared on stage walking very rapidly and holding his fur hat in his hand. Diaghilev also attended this performance and was so favourably impressed that he decided to invite Stravinsky to work for his Russian Ballet Company.

Stage Adaptations

In 1917 the Russian Ballet presented in Rome a version of *Fireworks* for which Diaghilev had commissioned the Italian futurist painter Giacomo Balla to prepare special scenery and lighting effects. There was no dancing in the ordinary sense. Balla's décor was composed of various geometrical structures made of transparent materials lit from within.

In 1957 Alan Carter used the music, together with the scores of the *Circus Polka*, *Ode*, and the *Ebony Concerto*, as the basis for a ballet called *Feuilleton*, which was produced at the Bayerische Staatsoper, Munich.

14. FUNERAL DIRGE – CHANT FUNEBRE (op. 5)

For wind instruments in memory of Rimsky-Korsakov. Composed at Ustilug in the summer of 1908. First performance, Belaiev's season of Russian Symphony Concerts, autumn of 1908, St. Petersburg, with Felix Blumenfeld conducting. Unpublished. MS lost.

In his *Chronicle* Stravinsky writes: 'The score of this work unfortunately disappeared in Russia during the Revolution. . . . I can no longer remember the music, but I can remember the idea at the root of its conception, which was that all the solo instruments of the orchestra filed past the tomb of the master in succession, each laying down its own melody as its wreath against a deep background of *tremolo* murmurings simulating the vibrations of bass voices

---

[1] See letter from Stravinsky to *The Observer*, reprinted in *Dialogues and a Diary*.

181

singing in chorus.' In *Memories* he says: 'I remember the piece as the best of my works before the *Firebird*, and the most advanced in chromatic harmony.'

15. FOUR STUDIES (op. 7)

For piano. Composed at Ustilug, June and July 1908. Published by Jurgenson, 1910. (Later by Anton J. Benjamin, Hamburg.)

  (1) *Con Moto* (C minor) Dedicated to E. Mitusov
  (2) *Allegro brillante* (D major) to Nicolas Richter
  (3) *Andantino* (E minor) to Andrey Rimsky-Korsakov
  (4) *Vivo* (F sharp major) to Vladimir Rimsky-Korsakov

First performed by Stravinsky in 1908 (*Exp*).

In these Studies, Stravinsky pursues his chromatic researches through a series of extended suspensions that occasionally call to mind the harmonic methods of Scriabin. The first two Studies show a preoccupation with the combination of quintuplets with duplets, triplets and even sextuplets, which results in a somewhat blurred outline and a lack of metric definition. By way of contrast, the fourth Study has a powerful legato semiquaver movement accompanied by a staccato quaver bass – in the central episode the roles of the right and left hands are reversed – and the music flows without break from the first to the final bar.

16. ЖАРЪ - ПТИЦА – L'OISEAU DE FEU – THE FIREBIRD

Fairy story ballet in two scenes,[1] composed after the Russian national fairy story by M. Fokine (4.4.4.4. – 4.3.3.1 – triangolo, tamburo, piatti, gr. cassa, tamtam, timp., campanelli, xylophone, celesta, piano, 3 harps – string 5tet.[2] Stage band: 3 trumpets, 2 tenor tubas, 2 bass tubas). Composed at St. Petersburg, November 1909 to 18 May 1910. Dedicated to 'my dear friend Andrey Rimsky-Korsakov'. Published by Jurgenson 1910 (later by Schott's). Piano reduction by the composer. First performance, Russian Ballet, Opera House, Paris, 25 June 1910, conducted by Gabriel Pierné. Duration: *c.* 45 minutes.

  (i) Introduction
  (ii) *Scene One:* 'Kashchei's Enchanted Garden'
  (iii) 'Appearance of the Firebird pursued by Ivan Tsarevich'
  (iv) 'Dance of the Firebird'

[1] In the French translation of the subtitles of Stravinsky's early ballets (*The Firebird, Petrushka*, and *The Rite of Spring*) the Russian word КАРТИНА is given as *tableau*. The English word 'tableau' has been avoided in translation, as it has a static connotation that is quite at variance with the stage content of these scenes.
[2] The score specifies 16 first violins, 16 second violins, 14 violas, 8 cellos, 8 double-basses.

     (v) 'Ivan Tsarevich Captures the Firebird'
    (vi) 'Supplication of the Firebird'
  (vii) 'Appearance of Thirteen Enchanted Princesses'
 (viii) 'The Princesses' Game with the Golden Apples (Scherzo)'
   (ix) 'Sudden Appearance of Ivan Tsarevich'
    (x) 'The Princesses' Khorovod (Round Dance)'
   (xi) 'Daybreak'
  (xii) 'Magic Carillon; Appearance of Kashchei's Guardian Monsters; Capture of Ivan Tsarevich'
 (xiii) 'Arrival of Kashchei the Immortal; His Dialogue with Ivan Tsarevich; Intercession of the Princesses'
 (xiv) 'Appearance of the Firebird'
  (xv) 'Dance of Kashchei's Retinue under the Firebird's Spell'
 (xvi) 'Infernal Dance of all Kashchei's Subjects'
(xvii) 'Lullaby (Firebird)'
(xviii) 'Kashchei's Death'
 (xix) *Scene Two:* 'Disappearance of the Palace and Dissolution of Kashchei's Enchantments; Animation of the Petrified Warriors; General Thanksgiving'

The manuscript of the ballet score was purchased by Jean Bartholoni from the composer and presented by him to the Conservatoire de Musique, Geneva, in 1920.

Composition

The idea of adding to the Russian Ballet repertory a new story ballet based on the legend of the Firebird had been discussed by Diaghilev and his entourage in the early part of 1909; and after the success of his season in Paris that summer he decided to go ahead. The scenario was worked out by Fokine who was to be responsible for the choreography; but the choice of a composer was not an easy one to make. Alexandre Benois seems to have favoured Nicolas Cherepnine; but Diaghilev wanted his old professor of harmony, A. K. Liadov. On investigation, however, it appeared unlikely that Liadov would be able to deliver the score on time: so Diaghilev decided to turn to Stravinsky, who had already instrumented two of the numbers of *Les Sylphides* for the 1909 Paris production of that ballet. Stravinsky was flattered by the invitation and made it clear he was quite prepared to drop his opera *The Nightingale*, of which he had just completed the first act, in order to tackle the new score. Although Diaghilev was unable to place the definite commission before December,[1] Stravinsky made an early start at the beginning of November when he moved to a *dacha* belonging to the Rimsky-Korsakov family about 70 miles south-east

---

[1] The commission fee was 1,000 roubles (*Con*).

of St. Petersburg. There the opening bars of the Introduction were written (*Exp*). Returning to St. Petersburg in December, he worked quickly, and the composition was finished by March. The orchestral score was ready a month later and was mailed to Paris by mid-April. After final retouches, it was dated 18 May 1910.

It can now be seen that the subject of *The Firebird* called for the sort of descriptive music that Stravinsky did not really want to write. Nevertheless, he flung himself into the task with ardour, anxious to show that the trust in him was not misplaced, and was successful, not only in turning out some scintillating dance numbers, but also in evolving a curiously naïve but effective type of dumb recitative to fit the numerous passages of mime. In his *Memoirs*, Fokine recalled how Stravinsky brought him 'a beautiful Russian melody' for the entrance of Ivan Tsarevich, and how he (Fokine) suggested 'not presenting the complete melody all at once, but just a hint of it, by means of separate notes [*sic*], at the moments when Ivan appears at the wall, when he observes the wonders of the enchanted garden, and when he leaps over the wall'.[1] There is no doubt that Stravinsky had studied the scenario so closely with Fokine that he knew exactly what the choreographic requirements were; and Fokine created the choreography section by section as the music was handed to him (*Chr*).

The French critic, R. Brussel, who visited St. Petersburg that winter, has described[2] how Diaghilev invited him to come and hear Stravinsky play through his score. 'At the appointed hour, we all met in the little ground-floor room on Zamiatin Perenlok, which saw the beginnings of so many magnificent productions. The composer, young, slim, and uncommunicative, with vague meditative eyes, and lips set firm in an energetic looking face, was at the piano. But the moment he began to play, the modest and dimly lit dwelling glowed with a dazzling radiance. By the end of the first scene, I was conquered: by by the last, I was lost in admiration. The manuscript on the music-rest, scored over with fine pencillings, revealed a masterpiece.'

Stravinsky attended every rehearsal with the Russian Ballet in St. Petersburg; and Karsavina, who had been cast for the title role in the new ballet in the place of Pavlova who had refused to undertake the part because she thought the music so complicated and meaningless, has paid a moving tribute to his kindness and patience on those occasions. 'Often he came early to the theatre before a rehearsal began in order to play for me, over and over again, some specially difficult passage. I felt grateful, not only for the help he gave me, but for the manner in which he gave it. For there was no impatience in him with my slow understanding; no condescension of a master of his craft towards the slender equipment of my musical education. It was interesting to watch him at

---

[1] *Fokine: Memoirs of a Ballet Master*, translated by Vitale Fokine. London, Constable, 1961.
[2] Quoted by Serge Lifar in *Serge Diaghilev: an intimate biography*. Putnam, London, 1940.

the piano. His body seemed to vibrate with his own rhythm; punctuating staccatos with his head, he made the pattern of his music forcibly clear to me, more so than the counting of bars would have done.'[1]

When the company left for Paris early in the spring, he stayed behind in order to enjoy a short holiday in the country at Ustilug. But he joined them in time for the final rehearsals at the end of May. 'The first *Firebird*! I stood in the dark of the Opéra through eight orchestra rehearsals conducted by Pierné. The stage and the whole theatre glittered at the *première* and that is all I remember' (*Con*).

Synopsis

The story of the ballet deals with two types of magic beings: the glittering Firebird who plays the part of a good fairy, and the green-taloned ogre, Kashchei, the embodiment of evil. Woe betide the human beings that stray into his enchanted domains! The maidens are held captive, the men turned to stone. Kashchei himself is immortal – but only so long as his soul, which is preserved in a casket in the form of an egg, remains intact.

The plot shows how a young Prince, Ivan Tsarevich, wanders into Kashchei's magic garden at night in pursuit of the Firebird, whom he finds fluttering round a tree bearing golden apples. He captures it and exacts a feather as forfeit before agreeing to let it go. He then meets a group of thirteen maidens and falls in love with one of them, only to find that she and the other twelve maidens are princesses under the spell of Kashchei. When dawn comes and the princesses have to return to Kashchei's palace, he breaks open the gates to follow them inside; but he is captured by Kashchei's guardian monsters and is about to suffer the usual penalty of petrifaction, when he remembers the magic feather. He waves it; and at his summons the Firebird reappears and reveals to him the secret of Kashchei's immortality. Opening the casket, Ivan smashes the vital egg, and the ogre immediately expires. His enchantments dissolve, all the captives are freed, and Ivan and his Tsarevna are betrothed with due solemnity.

Treatment and Music

According to Benois,[2] Diaghilev's collaborators were anxious to create a ballet by transforming material derived from ancient Russian legends and fairy tales for children into a subtler, more significant kind of fable intended to appeal to adult audiences; and at one time Stravinsky seems to have adopted this standpoint, for Edwin Evans[3] quotes him as saying: 'Russian legends have as heroes characters that are simple, naïve, sometimes even frankly stupid, devoid of all malice, and it is they who are always victorious over characters

---

[1] From a 'Recollection of Stravinsky' by Tamara Karsavina. *Tempo*, Summer 1948.

[2] *Reminiscences of the Russian Ballet*. Putnam, London, 1941.

[3] *Stravinsky: 'The Fire-Bird' and 'Petrushka'*. Oxford University Press, 1933.

that are clever, artful, complex, cruel and powerful.' Ivan Tsarevich overcomes Kaschei 'because he yielded to pity, a wholly Christian notion which dominates the imagination and the ideas of the Russian people. Through pity he acquired power to free the world from the wickedness of Kashchei'. This is all very well in theory; but the ballet is so constructed that Ivan Tsarevich hardly emerges as more than a passive onlooker despite the fact that he is present on the stage from the beginning to the end, whereas Kashchei is a much more positive character, though he has comparatively little time in which to reveal his qualities.

The composition of *The Firebird* posed an interesting problem – how to differentiate in musical terms between the natural and supernatural elements in the action. The clue to Stravinsky's solution is to be found in Rimsky-Korsakov's *The Golden Cockerel*, which though finished in 1907 was not publicly performed, because of censorship difficulties, until 1910. There the human element was associated with diatonic themes and the magical element with chromatic arabesques of an oriental character. Stravinsky took this hint. The music for Ivan Tsarevich, the Princesses, and the hymn of thanksgiving in the finale is all strongly diatonic in character – the two Khorovod themes are folk melodies (*Mem*), the first being *In the Garden* from the Government of Novgorod,[1] and the theme of the finale is based on *By the Gate*[2] whereas all the magical element, including the music for the Firebird and Kashchei, is conjured out of one chromatic interval, the augmented fourth.

The opening bar of the Introduction shows how sometimes a major third and sometimes a minor third is fitted into this interval of an augmented fourth (or diminished fifth).

Ex.2

The major and minor thirds (as marked) become associated, when developed in sequence, with Kashchei and his enchantments. In the 10th and 11th bars of the Introduction, alternating major and minor thirds rise through two octaves –

Ex.3

[1] No. 79 in Rimsky-Korsakov's *100 Russian National Songs* (op. 24) published in 1876.
[2] No. 21 in Rimsky-Korsakov's 1876 Collection.

until the two final major thirds are expanded into a chordal trill –

Ex.4

which on examination turns out to be the precursor of the C major/F sharp major polytonal combination that was subsequently to become the basic motive of *Petrushka*.

For the Firebird itself, the first four notes of the opening figure in the first bar of the Introduction form a germinal pattern, together with the reversal of the motive and both inversions.

Ex. 5

The use of this chromatic figuration gives the music associated with the Firebird a kind of iridescent sheen. Sometimes the result can be a little debilitating in a quasi-oriental way, as in the 'Supplication of the Firebird':

Ex. 6

– or touchingly expressive, as in the oboe/cello solo in the 'Lullaby':

Ex.7

187

But the germinal motive is subjected to so many ingenious permutations and developments, and is used with such economy and logic that the score is welded into a remarkably homogeneous whole.

The rhythmic aspect is also remarkable – particularly the subtle use of syncopation in the bass of the Firebird's Dance to suggest its fluttering and pecking movements, the strange mathematical pattern of the magic carillon with its spreading ripples of sound, and the magnificent dynamic urge of the 'Infernal Dance' with its insistence on a constantly sustained, undeviating beat. It should be noted, however, that the syncopations and other rhythmic ingenuities are all carried out within the framework of regular barring, and most of the phrasing is four-bar square. The Finale provides a welcome change, when the notes of its 6/4 theme are equalised to form a 7/4 passage.[1]

The orchestra Stravinsky wrote for was large – 'wastefully large', as he says in his *Expositions* – but it enabled him to indulge in every type of orchestral effect, and the instrumentation is particularly brilliant. In this score he showed himself to be at least the equal of his old master. It is true that he borrowed some of his effects, e.g., the horn and trombone glissandi,[2] from Rimsky-Korsakov; but completely original was 'the natural-harmonic string glissando near the beginning, which the bass chord touches off like a Catherine-wheel. I was delighted to have discovered this, and I remember my excitement in demonstrating it to Rimsky's violinist and 'cellist sons. I remember, too, Richard Strauss's astonishment when he heard it two years later in Berlin' (*Exp*). (It should be noted that in the ballet score and the 1919 suite the 1st violins are directed to tune their E string down to D, whereas in the 1945 Suite they are directed to play the passage on the open D string.)

The Firebird is the first work of Stravinsky's artistic maturity. Successful though the music is from the descriptive point of view, it suffers occasionally from an excess of expressiveness. The piano reduction, which was engraved shortly before the full score, contains some rather flamboyant directions – *passionato, con tenerezza, timidamente, lamentoso* etc. These are deleted in the full score, while others are changed, e.g., *Con maligna giola* becoming *Poco meno mosso*, and *Sostenuto mystico* becoming *Adagio*. Such effusiveness must have become increasingly embarrassing to Stravinsky as time went on; but on

---

[1] Fig. 203 of the full score, and fig. 202 of the piano reduction. (The full score has an extra figure between figs. 195 and 196 of the piano reduction.)

[2] Some of these – e.g., the trombone glissandi in the 'Infernal Dance' and the horn glissandi of harmonics in the Finale – appear for the first time in the 1919 Suite. In this connection it should be mentioned that Ernest Ansermet maintains that the following trumpet passage is missing just before fig. 14 of the 'Infernal Dance' in the 1919 Suite, either because Stravinsky forgot to insert it in the MS full score or because its omission was not noticed in the proofs:

various occasions he did his best to adjust matters by producing shorter suites for concert performance. Yet from the first the public was attracted by the romantic element in the ballet's subject matter and musical idiom, and *The Firebird* has been his most popular work, though certainly one of his least characteristic ones, for over half a century.

Concert Suites[1]

1 (a). The first concert suite, called 'suite tirée du conte dansé "L'oiseau de feu" ' on the title-page and sometimes referred to as a symphonic suite, was made in 1911 and published by Jurgenson (1912). The orchestration is more or less the same as in the ballet score.[2] In fact, the score is printed from the same plates as the ballet score, occasionally with slight modifications to provide suitable endings for the movements. Duration: *c*. 21 minutes.

    I. Introduction – 'Kashchei's Enchanted Garden' – 'Dance of the Firebird' (i.e., the whole of nos. i, ii, iii and iv, with the exception of figs. 3, 4, 5, 6 and the first four bars of 7)[3]
    II. 'Supplication of the Firebird' (no. vi as far as fig. 41 where two bars are added to make a close)
    III. 'The Princesses' Game with the Golden Apples' (no. viii with seven bars added to make a close)
    IV. 'The Princesses' Khorovod' (no. x)
    V. Infernal Dance of all Kashchei's Subjects' (no. xvi)

1 (b). Berceuse. This number was published separately with reduced wind by Jurgenson (1912).

2. The second concert suite was made at Morges in 1919 for smaller orchestra (2.2.2.2. – 4.2.3.1. – percussion, timpani, xylophone, harp, piano – string 5tet). Published by J. & W. Chester. Duration: *c*. 26 minutes. Some MS sketches are in the composer's collection, [C 4] and [C 31].

    I. Introduction – 'The Firebird and its Dance' – 'Variation of the Firebird' (no. i followed by three bars of no. ii; 15 bars extracted from no. iii; no. iv minus the last five and a half bars)
    II. 'The Princesses' Khorovod (Round)' (no. x)

---

[1] There is a thorough examination of the different concert suites in Arthur Dennington's article 'The Three Orchestrations of Stravinsky's "Firebird" ' in *The Chesterian*, winter 1960.
[2] The MS ballet score in the Conservatoire, Geneva, has pencil markings showing the cuts to be made to produce this suite, which does not include the stage band or the tam-tam, and which has 6 double-basses instead of 8.
[3] The small Roman numerals refer to the numbering of the different movements of the ballet score as given above. The figure references are to those of the ballet score.

2. Register of Works

    III. 'Infernal Dance of King Kashchei' (no. xvi)[1]
    IV. 'Lullaby' (no. xvii plus four extra bars added as coda to the 'Lullaby' followed by six bars from the introductory *sostenuto* to the Finale no. xix)
    V. Finale (no. xix minus the introductory *sostenuto*)

3. The third suite (called a 'ballet suite') was made in 1945. It is written for the same reduced orchestra as the second concert suite. Published by Leeds Music Corporation. Duration: *c*. 28 minutes. Some MS material is in the composer's collection [C 92].

    *I. Introduction – 'Prelude and Dance of the Firebird' – 'Variations (Firebird)'
    II. 'Pantomime I.' (Bars 5 – 8 after fig. 20 followed by figs. 27 and 28)
    III. 'Pas de deux: Firebird and Ivan Tsarevich' (no. vi as far as fig. 41)
    IV. 'Pantomime II.' (Fig. 41 followed by figs. 53 and 54 minus the *quasi recitativo* bar two bars after fig. 54)
    V. 'Scherzo: Dance of the Princesses' (no. viii)
    VI. 'Pantomime III.' (no. ix)
    *VII. 'Rondo (Khorovod)'
    *VIII. 'Infernal Dance'
    *IX. 'Lullaby (Firebird)'
    *X. 'Final Hymn'

The numbers marked with * are substantially the same as those in the second suite, but the instrumentation has been slightly revised. A snare-drum has been added to the percussion; and an interesting feature is the way the chords for trumpets and trombones in the 7/4 section of the finale have been altered from crotchets to staccato quavers with a quaver rest between each.

Ballet Productions

The original ballet production by the Russian Ballet (Opera House, Paris, 25 June 1910) had choreography by M. Fokine. The scenery was executed after designs by Alexandre Golovine. The costumes were also by Golovine, with the exception of those of the Firebird and the Tsarevna which were by Leon Bakst. The title role was danced by Karsavina, the Tsarevna by Fokina, Ivan Tsarevich by Fokine and Kashchei by Bulgakov. About 1922 the original scenery was badly damaged and the ballet was removed from the Russian Ballet's repertory. Subsequently it was redesigned by Natalie Goncharova,

---

[1] The eight-bar bridge passage between the 'Infernal Dance' and the 'Lullaby' was an afterthought and was added in 1924 on a loose leaf after the first edition of the full score had been published.

190

and the first performance of the new production with her settings and costumes was given by the Russian Ballet at the Lyceum Theatre, London, on 25 November 1926. It was revived by the Royal Ballet at the Empire Theatre, Edinburgh, on 23 August 1954, also with the Goncharova designs.

The third suite was used as basis for a new ballet produced by the New York City Ballet with choreography by Balanchine in 1950.

There have been numerous other productions of the ballet in Europe and America, only a few of which have reproduced the original Fokine choreography.[1]

Transcriptions

(a) *Prélude et Ronde des Princesses* for violin and piano (1929). Dedicated to Paul Kochanski. Schott's.

(b) *Berceuse* for violin and piano (1929). Dedicated to Paul Kochanski. Schott's.

(c) *Berceuse:* new transcription for violin and piano by I. Stravinsky and S. Dushkin (1933). Schott's.

It appears that Dushkin made an earlier transcription of the *Berceuse* – probably about 1931. When he played it to Stravinsky he thought the composer looked unhappy and he was slightly hurt. 'Don't you like it?' he asked. 'It sounds like Kreisler's arrangement of Rimsky-Korsakov's *Chant Hindou*,' Stravinsky said. When Dushkin replied 'Well, it *is* rather Oriental, isn't it?' Stravinsky lowered his head and said sadly, 'Yes, I'm afraid that's the trouble with it'.[2]

(d) *Scherzo* for violin and piano by I. Stravinsky and S. Dushkin (1933). Schott's. MS Comp. [C 60].

(e) 'Summer Moon' (Leeds Concert Songs). Lyric by John Klenner; music by I. Stravinsky. Published by Leeds Music Corporation 1946. There are two versions of the lyric of this slow foxtrot song. The first starts:

> *Summer Moon, you bring the end of my love story;*
> *All too soon my love and I are apart.*
> *Summer Moon, why shine in Indian Summer glory?*
> *Summer Moon, while I'm alone with my heart?*

The second version starts:

> *Summer Moon, our one last rendez-vous we're keeping;*
> *All too soon my love and I are apart.*
> *Summer Moon, the mist of autumn time comes creeping*
> *All too soon I'm so alone with my heart.*

---

[1] For full list of these productions, consult *Stravinsky and the Dance*. New York, 1962.
[2] 'Working with Stravinsky' by Samuel Dushkin, contributed to *Stravinsky*, a Merle Armitage Book, edited by Edwin Corle, New York, 1949.

The tune is a variant of the first theme of the 'Princesses' Khorovod' (no. x), the well known Russian folksong, *In the Garden.*

Stravinsky's part in this adaptation seems to have been minimal. Originally the publishers announced that 'Summer Moon' had been 'adapted by Igor Stravinsky from his own *Firebird* Ballet Suite'; but subsequently they changed the form of the announcement to 'adapted from the *Firebird* suite of Igor Stravinsky'. In a version dated 1948 the arranger's name is given as Lou Singer.

16 (A). CANON (ON A RUSSIAN POPULAR TUNE)

For orchestra (3.3.3.3. – 4.3.3.1. – timp., bass drum, piano, harp – string 5tet). Composed in 1965. Published by Boosey & Hawkes, 1973. First performance, C. B. C., Toronto, 16 December 1965, conducted by Robert Craft. Duration: *c.* fifty seconds.

In this ingenious opusculum (described as a Canon for Concert Introduction or Encore) the theme of the finale of *The Firebird* was worked into a brief canon for full orchestra. The direction is *fortissimo e moderato*, the key C major, and the time signature oscillates between 2/4 and 3/4. Flutes, oboe and cor anglais maintain a high G ostinato, while the main theme in crotchets is given to clarinets, piano (right hand), harp (right hand), violins and violas, starting on G. There are two augmented canons: one starting on G for horns, and the other starting on D for trumpets. A canon by inversion is given to bass clarinet, bassoons, trombones, piano (left hand), cellos and double-basses starting on D; and there is an augmented canon by inversion starting on C for timpani and harp (left hand).

17. TWO POEMS OF VERLAINE (op. 9)[1]

For baritone and piano. Composed at La Baule, July 1910. Dedicated 'to my brother Gury Stravinsky'. French words by Paul Verlaine (Russian translation by S. Mitusov; English by M. D. Calvocoressi; German by M. D. Calvocoressi). Published by Jurgenson, 1911 (later by Boosey and Hawkes).

    (1) 'Un grand sommeil noir . . .' (from *Sagesse*)
    (2) 'La lune blanche . . .' (from *La Bonne Chanson*)

These songs were composed for Stravinsky's brother Gury; and he always grieved that his brother 'did not live to sing them professionally' (*Mem*). They marked the first occasion on which Stravinsky set a French text; and another

---

[1] Stravinsky's use of opus numbers to distinguish his works ceases with these two songs. It is not known whether opus 8 was reserved for *Pastorale, The Nightingale* or *The Firebird*.

Original Compositions

such occasion would not arise until he composed *Persephone* to André Gide's poem in 1934. Certain French critics have found these settings unacceptable. Robert Siohan considers their character as music to be at variance with the true nature of Verlaine's poetic thought, and goes so far as to suggest that the ideal way to appreciate them is for the listener to hear them sung in Mitusov's Russian translation, provided he is ignorant of that language.[1] This is a rather severe judgment on two very innocuous songs.

It is somewhat surprising to find both songs are in the key of B flat minor, and both are comparatively slow in tempo: so they lack elements of contrast. The opening accompaniment to 'Un grand sommeil noir' consists of alternating fifths and thirds doubled at the octave and is close in feeling to the Debussy-like introduction to *The Nightingale*. An occasional chord of the 13th reminds one of Ravel; and a splash of the whole-tone scale (in 'La lune blanche') confirms the French atmosphere that pervades the two songs. There is an interesting polytonal passage in the accompaniment to 'La lune blanche' (last bar but four) where a sequence of minor common chords whose roots descend by whole-tone intervals in the right hand is accompanied by a sequence of chords of the minor seventh whose roots rise by major thirds in the left. There are two passages in the same song where the piano accompaniment spreads out into three, four and even five parts and the texture becomes rather too thick for clarity. It is not surprising therefore to find that later on Stravinsky decided to instrument these songs.

Instrumentation

For baritone and orchestra (2.0.2.0. – 2.0.0.0. – string 5tet) made in 1951. Published by Boosey and Hawkes, 1953. According to Stravinsky (*Exp*) these songs were already 'partially orchestrated' at La Baule in the summer of 1910; and a manuscript orchestral version of 'Un grand sommeil noir' exists in the composer's collection dated Salvan 27 July 1914 [C 7]. Other manuscript material appertaining to the 1951 instrumentation is also in his collection [C 97].

18. ПЕТРУШКА – PÉTROUCHKA – PETRUSHKA

Burlesque in four scenes by Igor Stravinsky and Alexandre Benois (4.4.4.4 – 4.4.3.1. – Percussion, timpani, xylophone, celesta, piano, 2 harps – string 5tet). Composed at Lausanne / Clarens / Beaulieu / Rome, August, 1910 to 26 May 1911. Dedicated to Alexandre Benois. Published by Edition Russe de Musique 1912, (later by Boosey and Hawkes). Reduction for piano duet by the composer. First performance, Russian Ballet, Théâtre du Châtelet, Paris, 13 June 1911, conducted by Pierre Monteux. Duration: *c.* 43 minutes.

[1] *Stravinsky* by R. Siohan. Paris, Editions du Seuil, 1959.

193

2. Register of Works

Scene I.   'The Shrove-tide Fair' – leading to the 'Legerdemain scene' and the 'Russian Dance'

Scene II.   'In Petrushka's Cell'

Scene III. 'In the Blackamoor's Cell' – including the 'Dance of the Ballerina' and the 'Valse (for the Ballerina and Blackamoor)'

Scene IV. 'The Shrove-tide Fair' (evening) – including the 'Wet-Nurses' Dance', the 'Dance of the Coachmen', and the 'Masqueraders' Scene'

The manuscript of the full score, dated 13/26 May 1911, is with Boosey and Hawkes, New York.

Composition

The composition of *Petrushka* is very fully documented. In his *Chronicle* Stravinsky relates how after *The Firebird* he wanted to refresh himself by composing 'an orchestral piece in which the piano would play the most important part – a sort of *Konzertstück*'. He continues: 'In composing the music, I had in my mind a distinct picture of a puppet, suddenly endowed with life, exasperating the patience of the orchestra with diabolical cascades of *arpeggi*. The orchestra in turn retaliates with menacing trumpet-blasts. The outcome is a terrific noise which reaches its climax and ends in the sorrowful and querulous collapse of the poor puppet.' Having finished this movement, he cast round for a suitable title – something that would express both the character of his music and the personality of the puppet. He turned over this problem during his lakeside walks. 'One day,' he continues, 'I leapt for joy. I had indeed found my title – *Petrushka*, the immortal and unhappy hero of every fair in all countries.'

Towards the end of the summer Diaghilev called on Stravinsky at Lausanne, expecting to find his friend had started on the sketches for *The Rite of Spring*, and was much astonished to be confronted with a substantial instalment of a completely different work, and one that appeared to be intended for concert, not stage performance. When Stravinsky played him the first two movements – the first one called 'Petrushka's Cry' and the second the 'Russian Dance' – he immediately perceived the dramatic possibilities of the subject and started to persuade Stravinsky to alter the course of the work and expand it into a ballet[1] by developing the theme of the puppet's sufferings. Together they agreed on the scene of action – the Shrovetide Fair in St. Petersburg, 'with its crowd, its booths, the little traditional theatre, the character of the magician, with all his tricks; and the coming to life of the dolls – Petrushka, his rival, and the dancer – and their love tragedy, which ends with Petrushka's death'.

---

[1] The commission fee was 1,000 roubles (*Exp*).

Original Compositions

It was at this point that Diaghilev suggested the stage action and design should be worked out in detail with Alexandre Benois, who from his youth had been a devotee of the Russian puppet theatre. Stravinsky agreed; and Diaghilev wrote to Benois, who was at that moment in St. Petersburg, explaining the position and adding 'Who else but you could help us in this problem?' Benois, despite the fact that he had recently quarrelled with Diaghilev over the attribution of the ballet of *Sheherazade*, found the invitation too tempting to refuse; and when Diaghilev returned to St. Petersburg in the autumn, the two men had several conferences together at Diaghilev's apartment. Not much progress could be made, however, until they were joined by the composer. Stravinsky, who had moved from Clarens to Beaulieu in November, arrived late in December on a brief visit to his mother in St. Petersburg, bringing with him the music for the first two scenes of the ballet and the beginning of the third. Benois was delighted by what he heard; and when Stravinsky returned to the South of France, the collaboration continued by correspondence, until Benois joined Stravinsky and Diaghilev at Monte Carlo in the spring of 1911.

The movement originally entitled 'Petrushka's Cry' had become the second scene of the ballet; the 'Russian Dance' had been fitted into the end of the first scene; the third scene had been composed and the fourth begun, when Stravinsky fell ill in February from nicotine poisoning. This meant that the last part of the ballet was not finished until May, when the Russian Ballet was performing at the Costanzi Theatre in Rome. Benois writes:[1] 'The finale did not come to Stravinsky at once, and he had to search and use different combinations for it. He finished composing the music only a few weeks before the performance. We were staying at the same hotel in Rome [the Albergo d'Italia] for nearly a month, and every morning I used to hear from my room a confused tangle of sounds, interrupted from time to time by long pauses. This was the maturing of the last bars of the fourth scene.'

Synopsis

In the published score of the ballet, which is dedicated to Benois, the names of Stravinsky and Benois appear as joint authors of the scenario. If one attempted to allocate their respective shares in this collaboration, it would probably be fairly accurate to say that the characters of the puppets and the idea of using the St. Petersburg Shrove-tide Fair as a setting were due to Stravinsky, while Benois was responsible for all the 'public' at the Fair, with the exception of the *riageni*, or masked revellers, who were suggested by Stravinsky. Benois looked on the members of the crowd as real live individuals and insisted they should be treated accordingly.

The 1911 score is prefaced by an outline synopsis and a general note, each printed in Russian and French. The revised 1947 version reprints both texts,

---

[1] *Reminiscences of the Russian Ballet*. London, Putnam, 1941.

in French and English. (The English translation is not completely reliable.)
The following outline scenario is based on a conflation of these two notes:

Scene I. (*The Admiralty Square, St. Petersburg, during the 1830's. It is a sunny winter's day, and the scene shows a corner of the Shrove-tide Fair. In the background, a glimpse of roundabouts, swings and a helter-skelter. On the left, a booth with a balcony for the 'Died' (the compère of the fair). Beneath it, a table with a large samovar. In the centre, the Showman's little theatre. On the right, sweetmeat stalls and a peepshow.*) Crowds of people are strolling about the scene – common people, gentlefolk, a group of drunkards arm-in-arm, children clustering round the peepshow, women round the stalls. A street musician appears with a hurdy-gurdy. He is accompanied by a dancer. Just as she starts to dance, a man with a musical box and another dancer turn up on the opposite side of the stage. After performing simultaneously for a short while, the rivals give up the struggle and retire. Suddenly the Showman comes out through the curtains of the little theatre. The curtains are drawn back to reveal three puppets on their stands – Petrushka, the Ballerina and the Blackamoor. He charms them into life with his flute, and they begin to dance – at first jigging on their hooks in the little theatre, but then, to the general astonishment, stepping down from the theatre and dancing among the public in the open.

Scene II. (*Petrushka's Cell. The cardboard walls are painted black, with stars and a crescent moon upon them. Devils painted on a gold ground decorate the panels of the folding doors that lead into the Ballerina's Cell. On one of the walls is a portrait of the Showman scowling.*) While the Showman's magic has imbued all three puppets with human feelings and emotions, it is Petrushka who feels and suffers most. Bitterly conscious of his ugliness and grotesque appearance, he feels himself to be an outsider, and he resents the way he is completely dependent on his cruel master. He tries to console himself by falling in love with the Ballerina. She visits him in his cell, and for a moment he believes he has succeeded in winning her. But she is frightened by his uncouth antics and flees. In his despair, he curses the Showman and hurls himself at his portrait, but succeeds only in tearing a hole through the cardboard wall of his cell.

Scene III. (*The Blackamoor's Cell. The wall-paper is patterned with green palm-trees and fantastic fruits on a red ground. On the right, a door leading into the Ballerina's cell.*) The Blackamoor, clad in a magnificent costume, is lying on a divan, playing with a coconut. Though he is brutal and stupid, the Ballerina finds him most attractive and successfully uses her wiles to captivate him. Their love-scene is interrupted by the sudden arrival of Petrushka, furiously jealous. He is thrown out by the Blackamoor.

Scene IV. (*The Fair, as in Scene I.*) It is evening, and the festivities have reached their height. A group of wet-nurses dance together. A peasant playing a pipe crosses the stage leading a performing bear. A bibulous merchant, accompanied by two gypsies, scatters handfuls of banknotes among the crowd. A group of coachmen strike up a dance and are joined by the nurses. Finally a number of masqueraders – including devil, goat and pig – rush on to the scene while Bengal flares are let off in the wings.

At this moment there is a commotion in the Showman's theatre. The rivalry between the puppets has taken a fatal turn. Petrushka rushes out from behind the curtain, pursued by the Blackamoor whom the Ballerina tries to restrain. The Blackamoor strikes down Petrushka with his scimitar. It begins to snow; and Petrushka dies, surrounded by the astonished crowd. (In the commotion the Blackamoor and Ballerina have disappeared.) The Showman is fetched, and he reassures the bystanders that Petrushka is nothing more than a puppet with a wooden head and a body stuffed with sawdust. The crowd disperses as the night grows darker, and the Showman is left behind. But as he starts to drag the puppet off the stage, he is startled to see Petrushka's ghost appear on the roof of the little theatre, jeering and mocking at everyone whom the Showman has fooled.

Treatment

The choreography of the ballet was entrusted to Fokine. The fact that Benois insisted that the appearance and movements of the members of the crowd in the Fair scenes should be treated realistically, as distinct from the few set dance numbers for the wet-nurses, coachmen and so on, posited a problem that Fokine was not altogether successful in solving, though he incorporated certain popular dances in his choreography, in particular the *kazachok* (kicking dance) and the *presiatka* (heel dance). Benois, in his desire to see a more or less literal reconstruction of the old *balagani* that had been the delight of his childhood, decided that the presence of various different types at the Fair would give the illusion of life. There were to be people of good society with elegant manners, military men like real soldiers and officers of the time of Nicholas I, street-hawkers who seemed to be really offering their wares, and peasants looking like real *muzhiks* and *babas*. This admixture of realistic acting with the conventions of ballet dancing was bound to prove awkward and clottish in the long run. As Stravinsky says when referring to Fokine's choreography (*Chr*): 'It was a pity that the movements of the crowd had been neglected. I mean that they were left to the arbitrary improvisation of the performers instead of being choreographically regulated in accordance with the clearly defined exigencies of the music. I regret it all the more because the *danses d'ensemble* of the coachmen, nurses and maskers, and the solo dances, must be regarded as Fokine's finest creations.'

There were other respects in which the ballet fell short of Stravinsky's intentions. He had conceived the Showman 'as a character out of Hoffman, a lackey in a tightly modelled blue *frac* with gold stars' (*Mem*) instead of a kind of Russian Metropolitan, and the flute music that accompanies his legerdemain was accordingly written as a Weber-like cadenza. He had thought of the Blackamoor 'as a kind of Wilhelm Busch caricature and not as the merely mechanical comic-relief character he is usually made out to be', and the music at the beginning of the Third Scene was intended to show him mono-tonously padding up and down the sides of his cell like a caged tiger and occasionally interrupting his pacing with an outburst of vicious snarling. The coconut episode is an interpolation made by Benois at Fokine's request and has the disadvantage that where the slow dance theme is resumed after the snarling episode[1] it accompanies a choreographic passage where the Blacka-moor prostrates himself before the coconut and worships it, thereby giving the music a quasi-religious significance which is at variance with Stravinsky's intention. And at the end of the ballet, Fokine's choreography was ambiguous at the most important moment. Petrushka's ghost, as Stravinsky conceived the story (*Mem*), 'is the real Petrushka, and his appearance at the end makes the Petrushka of the preceding play a mere doll. His gesture is not one of triumph or protest, as is so often said, but a nose-thumbing addressed to the audience. The significance of this gesture is not and never was clear in Fokine's staging.'

Nevertheless, with all its imperfections, the ballet as originally conceived by Stravinsky and worked out in collaboration with Benois and Fokine created such an indelible impression on its first performance and has become so well known and well loved that one cannot imagine any drastic changes or revisions ever being desirable.

Music

The musical idea that dominated the first movement of the original *Konzert-stück*[2] was the bitonal effect and implications of the superimposed common chords of C major and F sharp major. This is first heard in the form of a slow expressive arpeggio played by two clarinets:

Ex.8

---

[1] Fig. 68 in the 1911 score; fig. 132 in the revised 1947 version.
[2] Now Scene II of the ballet.

This combination with all its clashes and ambiguities provides the clue to the two conflicting elements in Petrushka's character – the puppet and the human. It is true that the six notes of these superimposed triads are part of the scale of eight different notes (minor seconds alternating with major seconds) that Olivier Messiaen calls 'the second mode of limited transpositions';[1]

Ex.9

but in view of Stravinsky's well known habit of composing at the piano and the fact that in this score the piano was originally intended to play a concertante role, the combination of a black note chord with a white note chord clearly resulted from the composer's preoccupation with bitonality. The exploitation of this device accompanies Petrushka in all his quirks and paroxysms.[2]

For the general bustle and disorder of the crowd in the Fair Scenes, he took an accordion motif, which in its simplest form (of alternating fifths and thirds) recalled the device he had already used in the introduction to *The Nightingale* and in the song 'Un grand sommeil noir'. Here, however, it was entirely diatonic in character, producing a drone effect of D minor in Scene One and D major in Scene Four, where the alternating chords are expanded and filled out. This provided a background for numerous episodes of a popular character, and Stravinsky had no hesitation in using folk-song material when it suited his purpose.[3]

When the curtain rises at the beginning of the ballet, there is heard what Stravinsky has called 'a half-pagan, half-liturgical' theme – an Easter Song known as the 'Song of the Volochebniki' from the province of Smolensk[4] – and this reappears later in Scene Four. The second theme in the 'Russian Dance'[5] is a 'Song for St. John's Eve', which was taken down in 1886 in the village of Bashevskaia in the county of Totemsk.[6] The first theme of the 'Nursemaids' Dance' is a well known dance song,[7] for which there exist two different sets of words. It was used as early as 1858 by Balakirev in his *Overture on Three Russian Themes*; and under the title *Down the Petersky* it became a very

---

[1] *Technique de mon langage musical.* Leduc, Paris, 1944.
[2] A useful analysis of the score is given by Edwin Evans, *op. cit.*
[3] The best study of Stravinsky's borrowings is Frederick W. Sternfeld's article *Some Russian Folk Songs in Stravinsky's Petrouchka* which appeared in the March 1945 issue of *Notes* published by the Music Library Association, Washington D.C.
[4] Taken from Rimsky-Korsakov's Collection of 100 Russian Folk Songs, 1876.
[5] Fig. 41 in the original score; fig. 76 in the revised 1947 version.
[6] From the Collection of Istourine & Diutsch published in 1894.
[4] From Rimsky-Korsakov's Collection of 40 Russian Folk Songs, 1882.

2. Register of Works

popular item in Shaliapine's repertory. The second theme of the Wet-Nurses' Dance is a love song ('Akh vy sieni, moi sieni');[1] and the tune accompanying the 'Dance of the Coachmen' is headed 'Street Song (County of Tombosk)' by its editors[2] and is a variant of a more popular tune known as 'Umorilas'. Nicolas Nabokov is quoted[3] as having said that both the main theme of the 'Russian Dance' and the theme of the 'Gypsy Dance' in the Fourth Scene are derived from Russian folk songs as yet unidentified.

In addition, Stravinsky used a popular Russian *chanson* for the hurdy-gurdy tune in Scene One,[4] and this was supplied (at his request) by Andrey Rimsky-Korsakov (*Exp*). The second hurdy-gurdy tune[5] is the well known music-hall ditty 'Elle avait un' jambe en bois'. Stravinsky relates (*Mem*) how this tune was played by a hurdy-gurdy every afternoon beneath the window of the room in the hotel at Beaulieu where he was staying at the time; and since it struck him as a good tune for the scene he was then composing, he wrote it in.[6] (The date of this particular episode is fixed by the fact that at about the same time he received news of Tolstoy's death at Astapovo on 20 November 1910.)

There are also two borrowings from Joseph Lanner. The first theme of the Waltz in Scene Three (see Ex. 59a) comes from the *Steyrische Tänze* (op. 165) and the second theme from *Die Schönbrunner* (op. 200).

The use of this material helped to set the popular atmosphere of the Fair Scenes without in any way detracting from the originality of the score. In particular, the burlesque elements show an almost inexhaustible fertility of imagination. The Russian Dance is as inevitable in its regular pulse as a piece of clockwork machinery and as resilient as a spring. The whole of the Second Scene is a brilliant mosaic of pithy episodes, each one perfectly characterised, carefully contrasted, and fitting neatly into place. Petrushka's death Scene, with its brief ejaculatory phrases, is an epitome of all that has gone before. Although the beat usually remains constant in the various dance numbers, the time signatures display considerable irregularity, and the grouping of the metres is very varied. The old symmetrical four-square formula hardly appears at all, except where folk songs or popular music are quoted. The orchestration is brilliant, but restrained. There is no filling in for the sake of filling in. The only weakness of the original score is the casual way in which the piano, which played a predominant role in the original conception of the

---

[1] Included in Swerkoff's Collection of 50 Russian Songs for Voice and Piano.
[2] From Chaikovsky's Collection of 65 Russian Folk Songs for voice & piano, edited by N. Prokunin, 1898.
[3] See Frederick W. Sternfeld, *op. cit.*
[4] Fully stated at fig. 15 in the 1911 score and fig. 26 in the revised 1947 version.
[5] Fig. 13 in the 1911 score; and fig. 23 in the revised 1947 version.
[6] Later he discovered it was still copyright, and an arrangement was accordingly made to pay Mr. Emile Spencer, its composer, a suitable royalty every time *Petrushka* was performed. There is an account of the origin of this song, 'Simple histoire d'une collaboration' by Jose Bruyr, in *La Revue Musicale*, May–June 1939.

Konzertstück and which is indissolubly linked with the portrayal of Petrushka's character in the Russian Dance and throughout the scene in Petrushka's cell fades out in the rest of the ballet. It even has no comment to make when Petrushka dies in the falling snow. (This deficiency was remedied in the revised 1947 version of the score.)

Ballet Productions

The original ballet production by the Russian Ballet (Théâtre du Châtelet, Paris, 13 June 1911) had choreography by M. Fokine. The scenery and costumes were by Alexandre Benois.[1] Conductor, Pierre Monteux. The title role was danced by Vaslav Nijinsky, the Ballerina by Tamara Karsavina, the Blackamoor by Orlov, and the Showman by Enrico Cecchetti. It was revived by the Royal Ballet at Covent Garden on 26 March 1957.

There have been numerous other productions of the ballet in Europe and America, only a few of which have reproduced the Fokine choreography.[2]

Revised Version (1947)

In 1946 Stravinsky revised the score for smaller orchestra (3.3.3.3 – 4.3.3.1 – percussion, timpani, xylophone, celesta, harp, piano – string 5tet). This score, which is dated Hollywood, October, 1946, was published the following year and is usually referred to as the revised 1947 version. The manuscript score, on the title page of which Stravinsky had written 'This manuscript belongs to me/ Igor Stravinsky/1946', was sold in a sale at Zurich in 1948 and acquired by Louis Koch for his collection.[3] Other MS material is in the composer's collection [C 88].

The music is substantially the same; but the instrumentation has been radically altered and simplified. There are numerous changes in time signatures, barring, performing instructions, metronome markings etc. A nine-bar ending for concert performance has been added at the end of the 'Masqueraders' Scene'.[4] Closer attention is paid to figuration and to the part played by each individual instrument. (Reference has already been made to the way the piano part has been extended in Scenes Three and Four.) Figures that were harmonic in origin have now been laid out afresh on contrapuntal lines.

Whereas the original version was written by a composer who was thinking primarily in terms of a ballet score, the 1947 version seems to have been made by a composer thinking in terms of concert performance. For instance, the accompaniment to the Wet-Nurses' Dance has been revised,[5] the legato

[1] The bear was designed by Valentine Serov (*Exp*).
[2] For a full list of these productions, consult *Stravinsky and the Dance*. New York, 1962.
[3] See Georg Kinsky, *Manuscripte, Briefe, Documente, von Scarlatti bis Stravinsky: Katalog der Musikautographen-Sammlung Louis Koch*. Hoffmannsche Buchdruckerei, Stuttgart, 1953.
[4] One bar before fig. 251 in the revised 1947 version (or fig. 125 in the 1911 score).
[5] Fig. 90 in the original score; fig. 170 in the 1947 version.

1911 *Version*	1947 *Version*

4 bars before fig. 10
  Meno mosso ♩=100
	Fig. 18
	  Meno mosso ♩=88

Fig. 12
  ditto
	Fig. 22
	  ditto

Fig. 31
  cadenza ad lib.
	Fig. 60
	  cadenza – poco più mosso ♩=60

Fig. 51
  Furioso ♩=108
	Fig. 100
	  [♩=76]

Fig. 52
  Adagietto ♪=54
	Fig. 102
	  Andantino ♪=80

Fig. 53
  ♪=84
	Fig. 103
	  [♪=80]

2 bars before fig. 56
  Meno mosso ♩=72
	2 bars before fig. 108
	  Meno mosso ♪=72

5 bars before fig. 63
  Feroce stringendo ♩=144
	Fig. 120
	  L'istesso tempo ♩=126

Fig. 63
  ♩=112
	Fig. 121
	  [♩=126]

Fig. 67
  Tempo del principio ♩=144
	Fig. 130
	  Con furore ♩=138

Fig. 74
  Stringendo ♩=144
	Fig. 148
	  Con furore ♩=138

Fig. 76
  Vivace ♩=80
	Fig. 151
	  Vivo ♩=160

Fig. 82
  Con moto ♩.=84
	Fig. 161
	  Tempo giusto ♩.=63

Fig. 90
  Allegretto ♩=69
	Fig. 170
	  Allegretto ♩=116–120

Fig. 101
  Tempo del principio ♩.=84
	Fig. 192
	  [♩.=69]

Fig. 103
  Più mosso ♩=126
	Fig. 199
	  Più mosso ♩=138

3 bars before fig. 105
  Tempo I ♩.=84
	Fig. 205
	  Tempo I ♩.=69

Fig. 118
  [♩=112]
	Fig. 237
	  Tempo giusto ♩=132

4 bars before fig. 131
  Lento ♩=48
	Fig. 262
	  L'istesso tempo ♩=50

Fig. 131
  ♩=72
	Fig. 263
	  [♩=50]

phrases for the four bassoons of the original being replaced by staccato figuration for two clarinets and two bassoons reinforced by a new figure (also staccato) for three trumpets. This change particularly incensed Ernest Ansermet, a devoted advocate of the original version. 'What has this staccato passage to do with the soft flesh and typical movements of the nurses?' he asks.[1] '... Stravinsky seems to want to forget that his music – or at least this passage – was originally derived from a definite subject.'

There is no doubt that the Stravinsky of 1946, however skilful an orchestrator he might be, could not approach the music in the same spirit as the Stravinsky of 1910. The later version stems from the different viewpoint of an older, more experienced man; and some people may legitimately prefer the original.

The table opposite gives the major changes in metronome markings.

Concert Suite

There is no special suite for concert performance. In the concert hall the ballet score is usually performed complete. When a shorter version is preferred, one can start with the 'Legerdemain Scene' in Scene One followed by the 'Russian Dance' and Scenes Two and Four. In order to shorten the final movement, Stravinsky occasionally authorised the use of the special nine-bar concert ending after the 'Masqueraders' Scene' mentioned above.

Transcriptions

Three Movements for Piano Solo (Anglet, 1921).[2] Dedicated to Artur Rubinstein. Edition Russe de Musique (later Boosey and Hawkes). 1. 'Russian Dance.' 2. 'In Petrushka's Cell.' 3. 'The Shrove-tide Fair.'[3] Rubinstein paid Stravinsky 'the generous sum of 5,000 francs' for this arrangement (*Exp*). Manuscript material in the composer's collection [C 38].

Russian Dance for violin and piano by I. Stravinsky and S. Dushkin (Voreppe 17 April 1932). Edition Russe de Musique (later Boosey and Hawkes). MS comp. [C 60].

19. TWO POEMS OF BALMONT

For high voice and piano. Composed at Ustilug 1911. Russian words by K. Balmont (French translation by M. D. Calvocoressi; English by Robert Craft; German by Berthold Feiwel). Published by Edition Russe de Musique 1912 (later by Boosey & Hawkes). Duration: *c.* 2½ minutes.

---

[1] In *Les Fondements de la Musique dans la Conscience Humaine*. Neuchâtel, 1961.
[2] For Stravinsky's views on this transcription, see Appendix A(6).
[3] This movement includes the whole of the fourth scene of the ballet up to the end of the 'Masqueraders' Scene together with the concert ending published in the revised 1947 version.

(1) 'Незабудочка – Цвѣточекъ' – 'The Flower.' Dedicated 'to my Mother'
(2) 'Голубь' – 'The Dove.' 'To my sister-in-law Ludmila Beliankin.'

Manuscript with Boosey & Hawkes, London.

Although only a year separates them, these songs show a considerable advance on the *Two Poems of Verlaine*. Gone is the dependence on a shifting web of harmonies related closely to the current French idiom. Each lyric is quite short (consisting of three quatrains); and the vocal line is broken down into brief episodes, within which the voice is confined to a limited series of notes in varying combinations. (See Ex. 68.) Perhaps the most striking example occurs in bars 13 and 14 of 'The Dove' where two isolated phrases explore two intervals of a second – E natural / F sharp, and D sharp / F natural. The vocal phrases belong to widely varying modes. Some of them (like the *Più Mosso* section in 'The Flower') are strongly diatonic, almost in the manner of a folksong; others (see particularly the vocal phrase in the 5th and 6th bars of 'The Flower') are closely related to the second mode of limited transpositions, which probably resulted from Stravinsky's recent preoccupation with certain aspects of bitonality in *Petrushka*.[1] Tonal allegiance is uncertain. Neither song carries a key signature; both songs are contrasted in tempo, 'The Flower' being comparatively slow, with the vocal part marked *dolcissimo,* and 'The Dove' rather quicker.

Instrumentation

For high voice and chamber orchestra (2 fl, 2 cl, piano, 2 vl, 1 vla, 1 vc) 1954. Published by Boosey & Hawkes.

20. ЗВѢЗДОЛИКІЙ (ZVEZDOLIKI) – LE ROI DES ÉTOILES

Cantata for male voice choir (tenors and basses) and orchestra (4.4.4.4 – 8.3.3.1 – percussion, timpani, celesta, two harps – string 5tet). Russian words by K. Balmont (French translation by M. D. Calvocoressi). Composed at Ustilug 1911/12. Dedicated to Claude Debussy. Published by Jurgenson (1913). Vocal score by the composer. Duration: *c.* 6 minutes. First performance, Institut Nationale de Radio-diffusion Belge, Brussels, 19 April 1939, conducted by Franz André. The manuscript score was presented by Stravinsky to Debussy.[2]

In contrast to the two simple and graceful lyrics by Balmont that Stravinsky had just set as songs, *Zvezdoliki* (to be literally translated 'Starface' or 'The Starface One') is a visionary poem of apocalyptic imagery and symbolism. Nearly half a century later, Stravinsky said (*Mem*) that while it may be obscure as poetry and as mysticism, 'its words are good, and words were what I needed,

---

[1] See p. 198 above.
[2] According to André Schaeffner, it was sold by Debussy's heirs to a music dealer after his death, since when all trace of it has been lost.

not meanings' – namely, a text that would be a pretext for a male voice cantata accompanied by a very large orchestra.

He divided his tenors and basses into two groups each, and nearly the whole of the text is set to chords in four-part harmony, with the exception of a few unison phrases. There are several instances – and this is unusual in view of his love of syllabic setting – where the same chord is repeated for successive syllables, thereby stressing the declamatory nature of the text. The parts move at no great distance from each other, and the chords generally consist of a major triad in one or other of its inversions with an added note of the 7th or 9th or 11th or 13th. For instance, the second chord used in the opening choral phrase consists of the A minor triad with a diminished 11th added (see Ex. 10), which means that its enharmonic effect is as if the major third was sounding simultaneously with the minor third[1] and results in a certain degree of friction and blurring – a kind of aural halo.

Ex.10

From the beginning it was realised that there would be difficulties of intonation, and this led to the extraordinary conclusion that the work was unperformable. Debussy himself said of the music[2] 'It is probably Plato's "harmony of the eternal spheres" . . . and except on Sirius or Aldebaran, I do not foresee performances of this "cantata for planets". As for our more modest Earth, a performance would be lost in the abyss.' In fact, the work had to wait over a quarter of a century before being heard.[3]

Although the accompaniment is laid out for a vast orchestra, there is only one passage (marked *Maestoso e tranquillo*)[4] where the full complement of woodwind and brass is employed together, and at this point the strings are silent. Elsewhere the string sections are divided into two, three or even four

---

[1] This device is used even more extensively in the 'Mystical Circles' movements of the *Rite of Spring* (fig. 91 *et seq.*).

[2] Letter to Stravinsky dated 18 August 1913, printed in *Mem.*

[3] In a letter from Maurice Ravel to Mme. Hélène Casella (dated 2 April 1913) there is a suggestion that Ravel was trying to arrange a performance of the work in Paris during the 1913/14 season of the Société Musicale Indépendante. There is also a fragmentary MS note in Stravinsky's handwriting (in pencil) on a copy of the score he sent to Edwin Evans (now in the Central Music Library, London), from which it appears he was trying to interest Sir Thomas Beecham in it, probably about the same time.

[4] At the same point the choral entry is marked 'Maestoso!'

groups. They play with mutes throughout; and there are frequent tremolo passages *sul tasto* or *sul ponticello*. Although Stravinsky naturally shows concern that the low-pitched chorus shall be audible – and this means that at orchestral climaxes the chorus generally sings in unison and when it passes into four-part harmony the orchestral texture is lightened – the layout of the score gives plenty of scope for bitonal movement between the chorus and the orchestra and some quite complicated chords result. For instance, the final chord in the last bar consists of the orchestra (strings only) playing a chord of C major with the addition of the (minor) 7th and 9th while the chorus sings a G major triad with added 7th, the only notes common to both chords being G and D. It will be seen that this agglomeration of notes contains the chord of G with both its major and minor thirds sounding.

Ex. 11

The movement of this cantata is rather sluggish. For the most part, the time signature is a slow 6/4. There are no metrical surprises.

In performance, the achievement seems disproportionate to the means employed; but perhaps that is part of the transcendental effect aimed at.

The printed score includes a setting of the title *Zvezdoliki* for six-part male voice choir unaccompanied. Unlike the settings of Hebrew letters in *Threni*, this is not intended for performance; nor is it a quotation from the score. It should be regarded as a musical motto. (See Ex. 12.)

Although *Zvezdoliki* was published by Jurgenson shortly before the outbreak of the First World War, few copies of the full score appear to have survived;

Ex. 12

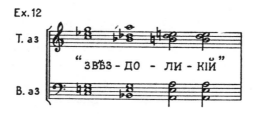

and as has already been mentioned, all trace of the original manuscript was lost shortly after Debussy's death and the sale of his effects. Early in 1939 a copy of the full score turned up at a public sale in Brussels. It was bought by the library of the Conservatoire; and after Paul Collaer, who was then head of the Flemish Radio, had obtained permission from the publishers, the orchestral material was copied for the Institut National de Radio-diffusion Belge.[1] Collaer arranged for the first performance of *Zvezdoliki* to be given on 19 April 1939 at a public concert which was broadcast. The conductor was Franz André.

21. ВЕСНА СВЯЩЕННАЯ – LE SACRE DU PRINTEMPS – THE RITE OF SPRING[2]

Scenes of pagan Russia in two parts by Igor Stravinsky and Nicolas Roerich (5.5.5.5 – 8.5.3.2 – percussion,[3] timpani – string 5tet). Composed at Ustilug/Clarens, 1911/13. Dedicated to Nicolas Roerich. Published by Edition Russe de Musique (later by Boosey & Hawkes). Reduction for piano duet by the composer.[4] First performance, Russian Ballet, Théâtre des Champs-Elysées, Paris 29 May 1913, conducted by Pierre Monteux. Duration *c*. 34 minutes.

Part One: The Adoration of the Earth

Introduction
'Auguries of Spring (Dances of the Young Girls)'
'Mock Abduction'
'Spring Khorovod (Round Dance)'
'Games of the Rival Clans'
'Procession of the Wise Elder'
'Adoration of the Earth (the Wise Elder)'
'Dance of the Earth'

Part Two: The Sacrifice

Introduction[5]
'Mystical Circles of the Young Girls'
'Glorification of the Chosen Victim'
'The Summoning of the Ancients'
'Ritual of the Ancients'
'Sacrificial Dance (the Chosen Victim)'

---

[1] See 'A propos d'une première audition d'Igor Stravinsky' by Darius Milhaud in *La Revue Musicale*, May–June 1939.
[2] The Russian title can be literally translated 'Sacred Spring' or 'Holy Spring'. The French title *Le Sacre du Printemps* was due to Bakst. According to Stravinsky (*Exp*), in English 'The Coronation of Spring' is nearer his original meaning than 'The Rite of Spring'.
[3] The very important percussion section includes big drum, tamtam, triangle, tambour de basque, guero rape, and antique cymbals in A flat and B flat. Two players are specified for the five timpani.
[4] The full score was published in 1921; the piano duet version in 1913.
[5] According to Edwin Evans, who heard part of the piano reduction when Stravinsky visited London in the summer of 1912, this introduction was originally entitled 'Pagan Night'.

2. Register of Works

The manuscript of the full score, which was with Boosey & Hawkes, New York, was handed back to the composer on his 80th birthday. Rough sketches for the whole work,[1] together with the working manuscript of the full score of Part One, are in the collection of M. André Meyer, Paris. Another manuscript is in the collection of M. Théodore Stravinsky. A few sketches are in the composer's collection [C 3] and [C 4].

Composition

The initial impulse that led to the creation of *The Rite of Spring* was derived from a fleeting vision that Stravinsky had in St. Petersburg during the spring of 1910 when he was finishing the last pages of *The Firebird*. This came to him unexpectedly, as his mind was then preoccupied with completely different things. In his *Chronicle* he states: 'I saw in imagination a solemn pagan rite: wise elders, seated in a circle, watching a young girl dance herself to death. They were sacrificing her to propitiate the god of spring.' At this stage the vision was not accompanied by any concrete musical ideas. Before leaving St. Petersburg he described his dream to his friend, Nicolas Roerich, who he thought would be interested in it from the archaeological point of view; and on reaching Paris he also mentioned it to Diaghilev, who immediately saw its balletic potentialities. He seems to have expected Stravinsky to start its composition right away and was accordingly rather startled when visiting him later that summer in Switzerland to be confronted by sketches for a new *Konzertstück* for piano and orchestra instead of the promised pagan rite symphony (then called *Great Sacrifice*).

It was not until the following summer when *Petrushka* had been successfully launched that Stravinsky had time to sketch out the new work. Roerich, whom he had chosen as his collaborator, was not only a painter of considerable talent – he had designed the Polovtsian Dances from *Prince Igor* for the Russian Ballet – but also an archaeologist who had travelled extensively, becoming one of the greatest authorities on the ancient Slavs. According to Konstantin Yuon,[2] 'folklore, the link between mythology, geology and the seismic and cosmic forces of nature always stirred his imagination'; and it was certainly appropriate that he should help Stravinsky with the scenario of this new ballet. The original scenario seems to have been drafted by Stravinsky in 1910, and a second version worked out with Fokine that summer. In July 1911 Roerich was staying with Princèss Tenisheva at Talashkino, her country estate near Smolensk; and Stravinsky was invited to join them. He left Ustilug for Brest Litovsk, but discovering that he would have to wait two days there for the next train to Smolensk he bribed the conductor of a goods train to let him ride

---

[1] These rough sketches are in a blank book, which also contains fragments of the *Japanese Lyrics* and the *Pribaoutki*, a few bars of *The Nightingale*, and parts of an unidentified work for piano, violin and cello.

[2] Konstantin Yuon, *A Fine Artist*. 'Culture and Life' No. 8, Moscow, 1958.

in the cattle truck, where he found himself alone with a bull (*Exp*). As soon as he arrived in Talashkino he set to work with Roerich, and in a few days' time a revised scenario was worked out and the titles and order of the different episodes agreed. Roerich also sketched the backcloths and designed a number of costumes for the dancers after real costumes in the Princess's collection of Russian ethnic art.

Sometime later, but before the first performance of the ballet, Roerich sent Diaghilev the following description of the action:

'In the ballet of *The Rite of Spring* as conceived by myself and Stravinsky, my object is to present a number of scenes of earthly joy and celestial triumph as understood by the Slavs . . . My intention is that the first set should transport us to the foot of a sacred hill, in a lush plain, where Slavonic tribes are gathered together to celebrate the spring rites. In this scene there is an old witch, who predicts the future, a marriage by capture, round dances. Then comes the most solemn moment. The wise elder is brought from the village to imprint his sacred kiss on the new-flowering earth. During this rite the crowd is seized with a mystic terror . . . After this uprush of terrestrial joy, the second scene sets a celestial mystery before us. Young virgins dance in circles on the sacred hill amid enchanted rocks; then they choose the victim they intend to honour. In a moment she will dance her last dance before the ancients clad in bearskins to show that the bear was man's ancestor. Then the greybeards dedicate the victim to the god Yarilo.'[1]

On his return to Ustilug Stravinsky started to compose the 'Auguries of Spring' movement of Part One and had reached the 'Spring Khorovod' by the time he left Ustilug for Clarens in the autumn of 1911. The pastoral introduction to Part One was added before Christmas after the rest of Part One had been completed and by the following spring he had reached the 'Glorification of the Chosen Victim'. At this point his rate of progress slowed up, for Diaghilev decided to postpone the production of *The Rite* from 1912 to 1913. He continued working on the score when he returned to Ustilug and Clarens after visiting Paris and London in the summer of 1912, and the 'Sacrificial Dance' was completed on 17 November. 'I remember the day well,' he writes in *Expositions*, 'as I was suffering from a raging toothache, which I then went to treat in Vevey.' The Introduction to Part Two was the last movement to be written. The full score is dated 8 March 1913; but eleven bars were added to the Introduction to Part Two (figs. 86 and 87) on 29 March.

There have been many attempts to explain the motive force behind *The Rite of Spring* – including an article in *Montjoie* (29 May 1913) signed by Stravinsky but later disowned by him, which was based on an interview he gave to Ricciotto

---

[1] From a letter quoted in *Serge Diaghilev* by Serge Lifar, London, 1940.

Canuedo. It has been said that in his score Stravinsky wanted to express the rebirth of nature after the suspension of winter, the victory of the sun with its renewal of light and heat, and the regeneration of human life through the sacrifice of the individual, and at the same time to emphasise the mental awe that is aroused by the great natural forces of creation and the vague yet profound disquiet that accompanies the approach of adolescence. With his usual flair for producing a pregnant apothegm, Jean Cocteau called it 'the georgics of prehistory'. The truth is that *The Rite* was born of one of the strongest emotions in Stravinsky's life. When many years later Robert Craft asked him what he had loved most in Russia, he replied: 'The violent Russian spring that seemed to begin in an hour and was like the whole earth cracking. That was the most wonderful event of every year of my childhood' (*Mem*).

Music

Although in this score Stravinsky was casting his imagination back to an early, almost prehistoric period, he made no conscious use of Russian folk song, with the exception of the opening bassoon melody at the beginning of the Introduction to Part One, which he borrowed from a collection of Lithuanian folk music.[1] Nevertheless, the melos of *The Rite* (like that of many of his succeeding so-called 'Russian' works) sounds folklike in character and shows that in the act of composition he was able 'to tap some unconscious "folk" memory' (*Mem*). His themes are simple and diatonic, often containing no more than four different notes. Generally speaking, he develops them by repeating and rearranging the notes and altering their time values so as to avoid the minimum literal repetition or imitation needed to achieve formal symmetry. This means that the patterns of his melos are irregular; they are continually shifting, changing and being renewed. So restless a method of thematic exposition was certainly calculated to exasperate listeners who had been nurtured on the regular formal music of the eighteenth and nineteenth centuries.

The restricted range of this thematic material gives little scope for contrapuntal development; but occasionally a simple phrase is treated in canon,[2] or two or more themes overlap or are simultaneously deployed.[3]

Harmonically, the score carries on from the point where *Zvezdoliki* left off. Most of the harmony in *The Rite* radiates from an aggregation of notes formed by the superimposition of two chords with their roots a semitone apart. One of these sometimes carries a minor seventh. For instance, the repeated chord at the opening of the 'Auguries of Spring' movement (which was the first part of

---

[1] Anton Juszkiewicz, *Litauische Volks-Weisen*. Cracow, 1900. (No. 157.)
[2] Fig. 21.
[3] Fig. 11.

the score to be composed) consists of the chord of E major (or F flat major) and the chord of E flat major with the minor seventh added.[1]

Ex. 13a

In view of Stravinsky's well known habit of composing at the piano, it seems likely that it came into existence as a bitonal aggregation of two separate chords that conveniently fitted his two hands. But it can also be explained as an inversion of the chord of the 13th, viz.

Ex. 13b

This explanation also fits the strange *ppp* chord in the 'Adoration of the Earth' movement, which precedes the frenzied 'Dance of the Earth'. (The chord is here given in the layout and notation Stravinsky himself uses in the reduction for piano duet.)

Ex. 14

Ernest Ansermet says this chord represents 'the maximum harmonic tension that musical conscience can express'[2] (though it might possibly be maintained

---

[1] Fig. 13.
[2] In *Les Fondements de la Musique dans la Conscience Humaine*.

that serial harmony is capable of greater tension). It could also be looked on as an aggregation of the following triads:

Ex.15

It will be seen that the constituent chords in these polytonal aggregations are sometimes major (with a rising connotation) as in the 'Auguries of Spring' movement already quoted, and sometimes minor (with a falling connotation) as in the opening of the Introduction to Part Two:

Ex.16

This major/minor ambivalence is a characteristic of the score. Occasionally a tune seems unable to decide whether it is in the major or the minor;[1] and there are cases where an *ostinato* accompaniment or a harmonised passage includes both major and minor thirds simultaneously.[2]

The metrical aspect of the score is of special interest. Either Stravinsky chooses a regular metrical pattern and tries to upset it by violently syncopated accents, as is the case with the 'Auguries of Spring' movement (a regular 2/4) and the 'Dance of the Earth' (a regular 3/4); or he allows his metre to follow the break-up of the melos, in which case it falls into irregular patterns calling for innumerable changes of time signature, as is the case with movements like the 'Glorification of the Chosen Victim', the 'Summoning of the Elders', and the 'Sacrificial Dance'. At first sight these time changes may appear bewildering; but if any homogeneous passage is examined, it will be found that the

---

[1] See the oboe solo at fig. 5 of the Introduction to Part One.
[2] See the bassoon/horn *ostinato* at fig. 10 and 11 of the Introduction to Part One, and the harmonisation of the tune in the 'Mystical Circles' movement of Part Two (fig. 91 *et seq.*).

composer has merely utilised every possible device of compound metre, which means no more than the combination of twos and threes in various irregular groupings.

The 'Sacrificial Dance' provides a good example. It is perhaps significant that when this movement was first composed, Stravinsky could play it, but did not know (at least to begin with) how to write it down (*Exp*). In the original score, the time signatures of the opening bars are as follows:

3/16   5/16   3/16   4/16   5/16   3/16   4/16

Some years later they were altered as follows:

3/16   2/16   3/16   3/16   2/8   2/16   3/16   3/16   2/8

In the 1943 revision, the note values were augmented for greater ease of reading, and certain bars were changed to prevent the barring from coinciding with the phrasing:

3/8   3/8   2/8   3/8   2/4   3/8   2/8   3/8   2/4

Reduced to its simplest statement the metre of this passage is

3 + 2 + 3 + 3 + 2 + 2 + 2 + 3 + 3 + 2 + 2   or
3 + 3 + 2 + 3 + 2 + 2 + 3 + 2 + 3 + 2 + 2

The metrical framework of the score is often underlined by *ostinato* accompaniments, which show much variety of structure. Some are fully developed at their first appearance; others are built up as they go along. In the 'Sacrificial Dance' there is a complex *ostinato*, mainly for percussion, which is virtually a counter-subject in itself and fills a 5/4 bar.[1] The time signature of the main subject oscillates between 5/4, 4/4 and 3/4. At first, the *ostinato* has its final limbs lopped off to make it fit the bars; but later it persists in its uncut 5/4 shape and marches relentlessly across the bar lines.

A tremendous internal tension is set up in the score between the simplicity of the thematic material and the discordant complexity of the harmonic texture. This is exacerbated by the instrumentation, highly sophisticated means being employed to get a deliberately primitive effect. Percussion is raised to the importance of a fourth orchestral department. The orchestra is the largest that Stravinsky ever wrote for. (This was mainly due to the fact that Diaghilev promised him that for the 1913 season of the Russian Ballet the theatre orchestra would be greatly enlarged (*Exp*). Otherwise it is possible he might have laid out his score on more moderate lines.) But the volume of sound that assaults the ear, though big and occasionally overwhelming, never escapes control. Almost the sole moments of respite are provided by the quiet introductions to the two parts with their impressionist writing. The composer

---

[1] Fig. 174 *et seq.*

himself has said (*Exp*) that the idea behind the first introduction was that it 'should represent the awakening of nature, the scratching, gnawing, wiggling of birds and beasts.'

Ballet Productions

Stravinsky worked smoothly and expeditiously with Roerich in drawing up the senario of *The Rite of Spring*; but the creation of the choreography for the ballet proved to be a difficult and exasperating task. Diaghilev had decided to entrust the choreography to Nijinsky, who though one of the greatest dancers of all time had so far shown little aptitude as a choreographer. His first ballet, a setting of Debussy's *L'Après-Midi d'un Faune* (produced at the Théâtre du Châtelet, Paris, on 29 May 1912) had led to protests from the audience owing to his naïve introduction of a representation of the sexual act just before the curtain fell.[1] For *The Rite* he demanded a large number of rehearsals – it is said there were no fewer than 120 – and great difficulty was caused by his insistence on metrical synchronisation between the dance steps and the music. This led to an orgy of counting; and the rehearsals, which were disliked by the dancers, were generally referred to as 'arithmetic classes'. Stravinsky, who was alarmed by Nijinsky's ignorance of the rudiments of music, had little confidence in this method of working. ' "I will count to forty while you play", Nijinsky would say to me, "and we will see where we come out". He could not understand that though we might at some point come out together, this did not necessarily mean we had been together on the way' (*Exp*).

It is now theatrical history that the first performance by the Russian Ballet (Théâtre des Champs-Elysées, Paris, 29 May 1913) created a scandal of the first magnitude. This was unexpected, for the dress rehearsal had gone off without incident. But on the first night laughter broke out and mild protests could be heard during the orchestral introduction; and as soon as the curtain rose on a group of knock-kneed, long-braided maidens[2] jumping up and down, the storm broke. In his *Expositions*, Stravinsky recalls hearing cries of 'ta gueule' from behind him, and Florent Schmitt shouting 'Taisez-vous garces du seizième'. He then left the auditorium in a furious temper and went back stage.

The scandalous scene in the theatre has been described by various eye-witnesses.

According to Carl van Vechten, 'a certain part of the audience was thrilled by what it considered to be a blasphemous attempt to destroy music as an art, and, swept away with wrath, began, very soon after the rise of the curtain, to make cat-calls and to offer audible suggestions as to how the performance should proceed. The orchestra played unheard, except occasionally when a slight lull occurred. The young man seated behind me in the box stood up

---

[1] 'This ballet's famous representation of the act of love, and its exhibition of sexual organs, was entirely Diaghilev's idea' (*Mem*)'

[2] 'Lolitas' Stravinsky calls them in his *Expositions*.

during the course of the ballet to enable himself to see more clearly. The intense excitement under which he was labouring betrayed itself presently when he began to beat rhythmically on top of my head with his fists. My emotion was so great that I did not feel the blows for some time'.

According to Romola Pulsky (later Nijinsky's wife) who was in the auditorium during the first part of the ballet, 'One beautifully dressed lady in an orchestra box stood up and slapped the face of a young man who was hissing in the next box. Her escort arose, and cards were exchanged between the men'.

Jean Cocteau saw the old Comtesse de Pourtalès stand up in her box with her face aflame and her tiara awry and heard her cry out, as she brandished her fan, 'This is the first time in sixty years that anyone has dared to make fun of me!'

Towards the end of the ballet, just before the beginning of the 'Sacrificial Dance', as the hitherto motionless figure of the Chosen Victim was seen to be seized by growing paroxysms of trembling, Marie Rambert heard the gallery call out, 'Un docteur ... un dentiste ... deux docteurs ...' and so on.

Meanwhile, there was a scene of a great confusion back stage. Diaghilev kept ordering the electricians to turn the houselights on or off, hoping in that way to quieten the audience (*Chr*). Nijinsky, with Stravinsky behind him, stood on a chair in the wings, beating out the rhythm with his fists and 'shouting numbers to the dancers, like a coxswain' (*Exp*). At the end of the performance everyone was completely exhausted.

The role of the Chosen Victim was danced by Marie Piltz, and the Wise Elder by Varontsov. The orchestra was conducted by Pierre Monteux. There were three performances of the ballet during the Paris season and three in London later that summer. After that, the Nijinsky version was never seen again.

One of the few objective assessments of Nijinsky's choreography has been given by Cyril E. Beaumont, who saw the ballet danced in London. He mentions Nijinsky's insistence on 'slow, uncouth movements in which the dancers were so seemingly obsessed by the earth that they appeared unable to stand upright . . . The feet were turned inwards and movements made inwards in complete opposition to the traditions of classical ballet. There was also a kind of counterpoint in mass movement, in that now and again one group of dancers danced heavily in opposition to another group which danced lightly. The movements generally were symbolic rather than emotional.'[1]

After the First World War, Diaghilev decided to revive *The Rite of Spring* and invited Leonide Massine to prepare a completely new choreographic version.[2] The action was stripped of its historical and archaeological pretensions, and the ballet was danced before a single backcloth (Roerich's original

---

[1] Cyril W. Beaumont, *Complete Book of Ballets*. London, 1937.
[2] Stravinsky wrote an article on this new interpretation by Massine, which was printed in *Comoedia Illustré*. Paris, 11 December 1920.

design for Part II). The first performance of this version was given at the Théâtre des Champs-Elysées, Paris, on 15 December 1920, with Ernest Ansermet as conductor. The role of the Chosen Victim was danced by Lydia Sokolova.

Since then there have been about half a dozen other ballet productions,[1] including a version with choreography by Kenneth Macmillan and décor by Sydney Nolan mounted at Covent Garden on 3 May 1962; but the work is more popular and seems to make a greater impact in the concert hall than on the stage.

Its triumphant rehabilitation as one of the most important works in the symphonic repertory of the twentieth century dates from its first concert performances – in Moscow (February 1914; conductor, S. Kussevitzky), Paris (Casino de Paris, April 1914; conductor, Monteux), and London (Queen's Hall, 7 June 1921; conductor, Eugene Goossens).[2]

Film Production

In 1938 Stravinsky was approached by the Walt Disney office and asked for permission to use the score of *The Rite of Spring* to accompany the prehistoric section in the forthcoming cartoon colour film *Fantasia*. Although consent was given, it was clearly a case of *force majeure*, for 'the request was accompanied by a gentle warning that if permission were withheld the music would be used anyway. (*Le Sacre*, being "Russian", was not copyrighted in the United States.)' (*Exp*).

For Disney's purposes, the order of some of the movements was changed and a few cuts made. The instrumentation was tinkered with, e.g., the horn glissandi in 'The Dance of the Earth' were transposed an octave higher (*Exp*). The original scenario was completely abandoned, and in its place Disney substituted a sketch of the prehistoric period of the world when life was just beginning to emerge from the protozoic slime. The earth was shown in spasmodic travail, quaking and spouting volcanoes, while the clumsy animals of that period – dinosaurs, dinotheres, pterodactyls and the like – agonised as they fought each other savagely and tried in vain to adapt themselves to the violent climatic fluctuations that led to their inevitable extinction.

Although this treatment did violence to Stravinsky's original conception and the score was somewhat maltreated, *Fantasia* on its release in 1941 proved

---

[1] The strangest of all – and one that comes outside the scope of this monograph because not a single note of Stravinsky's music was used – was *Le Sacre du Printemps*, a dance mime devised by Sebastian Voirol to accompany a poem he had specially written for the occasion. This version was produced by Mme. Lara for the 'Art et Liberté' Company at the Théâtre des Champs-Elysées, Paris, on 3 June 1917 with scenery and costumes by Martine. The complete text is not available; but brief quotations were included by André Coeuroy in his article 'Stravinsky et Nos Poètes'(*Revue Musicale*, Dec. 1923).

[2] For an account of the Paris concert, see Stravinsky's *Expositions and Developments*. Eugene Goossens wrote at length about the London concert in his *Overture and Beginners*. (London, 1951.)

Original Compositions

a very popular film and did much to familiarise an enormous public with his music.

Changes in the Score

The full ballet score is used for all concert performances, and no separate concert suite has ever been made.

The original score was published by Edition Russe de Musique in 1921. It contains a few printer's errors, but not very many considering the complexity of the instrumentation. Shortly after publication – probably as a result of the revival of the ballet in 1920/21 – a few revisions were carried out. These included the addition of a part for two piccolo flutes at figure 53, revised parts for the timpani in the opening bars of 'Games of the Rival Clans' (fig. 57) and at the two subsequent restatements of this timpani theme, and a rewritten passage for the two bassoons, eight horns[1], two tubas and timpani four bars before fig. 59. In the 'Glorification of the Chosen Victim' movement, all the brass instruments were instructed to play *ouvert*, the frequent directions of *sord.* and *bouché* in the original being removed. Similarly, a move towards simplicity was made in the final section of the 'Sacrificial Dance', where all the alternating *pizzicato* and *arco* directions were suppressed, and the strings were instructed to play *arco* only from fig. 186 to the end.

At a later date (as mentioned above), Stravinsky revised the barring in the 'Glorification of the Chosen Victim' and the 'Sacrificial Dance' movements.

In 1943 he decided to embark on a rescoring of the 'Sacrificial Dance' for a performance (unrealised) by the Boston Symphony Orchestra. Instead of the semi-quaver, he adopted the quaver as the unit of measure[2] in an attempt to facilitate performance. Of this version he wrote (*Exp*): 'The instrumentation has been changed too – improved, I think – in many ways. The music of the second horn group, for example, is considerably amended – I was never satisfied with the horn parts – and the muted horn note following the five-note trombone solo is given to the much stronger bass trumpet in this version.' The string parts were also radically rewritten and the final chord changed to 'an aggregation of distinctly-voiced pitches'.[3] This rescoring went no further than the 'Sacrificial Dance', which was separately published by Associated Music Publishers Inc. in the United States in 1945. (The manuscript orchestral score of this version is in the collection of Nadia Boulanger; and some manuscript sketches are in the composer's collection.) [C 78].

A four-handed piano reduction was made by Stravinsky himself, probably

---

[1] Unfortunately, when these revisions were incorporated in the published score, the parts for the 6th and 8th horns were erroneously given a treble instead of a bass clef.
[2] Curiously enough, the metronome direction is wrongly given as $\quarternote = 126$ (which is literally the same as in the original version); but as all note values have been doubled, it should be $\halfnote = 126$ or $\quarternote = 252$.
[3] The final chord consists of the same notes; but in the 1943 version the notes are divided between all eight horns (instead of only four horns) and all the strings (instead of only the cellos and double basses) as well as the three trombones and two tubas.

217

as and when the work was being composed in 1911 and 1912 and before the orchestration was completed. There are a few minor discrepancies between this and the full orchestral score. For instance the bar before figure 44, which is a 2/4 bar in the piano reduction, appears as a 3/4 bar in the orchestral score; and the bass *ostinato* is maintained unchanged from figure 62 to 64 in the orchestral score, whereas in the piano reduction it moves up a tone at the great trill in the 6/4 bar six bars before figure 64. It seems likely that in the case of such discrepancies, the orchestral score represents Stravinsky's second thoughts.

22. TROIS POÉSIES DE LA LYRIQUE JAPONAISE – THREE JAPANESE LYRICS

For soprano and piano – also soprano and chamber orchestra (2 fl, 2 cl, piano, 2 vl, 1 vla, 1 vc). Russian words by A. Brandta, French by Maurice Delage, English by Robert Burness, German by Ernst Roth. Published by Edition Russe de Musique in both the piano and orchestral versions 1913 (later by Boosey & Hawkes). Duration: *c.* 3½ minutes.

1. 'Akahito'. Dedicated to Maurice Delage. Composed at Ustilug. The piano version is dated 6/19 October 1912; the orchestral version, Clarens 16/29 December 1912.

2. 'Mazatsumi'. Dedicated to Florent Schmitt. Composed at Clarens. The piano version is dated 5/18 December 1912; the orchestral version 8/21 December 1912.

3. 'Tsaraiuki'. Dedicated to Maurice Ravel. Composed at Clarens. Both the piano and the orchestral versions are dated 9/22 January 1913.

Manuscripts of both the piano and the orchestral versions with Boosey and Hawkes, London. Some manuscript material is in the composer's collection [C 4] and also in the collection of M. André Meyer, Paris.

From a letter of Ravel's (reprinted in Stravinsky's *Conversations*) it appears that the first performance of these Japanese Lyrics took place in Paris on 14 January 1914 at a concert of the Société Musicale Indépendante which also included Ravel's *Trois Poèmes de Mallarmé*.

Stravinsky must have found it a great relief during the latter stages of the composition of *The Rite of Spring* to work on this set of miniature songs. From the dating of the manuscripts, it looks as if the idea of accompanying them with a small chamber ensemble came to him only after composing 'Mazatsumi' for voice and piano.

In the summer of 1912 he had read a little anthology of Japanese lyrics, some of them hai-kais. 'The impression which they made on me was exactly like that made by Japanese paintings and engravings. The graphic solution of problems of perspective and space shown by their art incited me to find something analagous in music' (*Chr*). He chose three little lyrics about the coming of the Japanese spring – the longest has no more than forty syllables. In setting them, he was unable to lengthen the vocal line by repeating words or phrases, as that would have destroyed the pure line of the verse: so each syllable had to be presented clearly and given its precise value. In fact, every syllable of each of the three lyrics is set to equal quavers, with the exception of a fractional lengthening of the last syllable but two in 'Akahito', an effect of slight acceleration in the last phrase of 'Mazatsumi', and two brief phrases set to equal crotchets also in 'Mazatsumi'. The vocal line proceeds in a series of cool calculated phrases of irregular length, separated by pauses also of irregular length. This broken outline has all the freshness and vigour of a spontaneous sketch. The great force of these songs lies in their terseness and understatement.

The chamber orchestra accompaniment is also mainly linear.

In 'Akahito', the opening ostinato phrase for flute and clarinet recalls the tranquil clarinet theme that frames the Spring Khorovod in *The Rite of Spring*. As the snow begins to fall, there are pointilliste touches from the wind instruments and the strings (harmonics and pizzicato).

'Mazatsumi' is more extended than the other two and has a sixteen-bar introduction for the orchestra, with a flutter-tongue scale for the flute, sudden arpeggi for the piano and flute, burblings for the clarinet, harmonic glissandi for the viola, and occasional trills for clarinet and violin. This miniature tone poem is extraordinarily evocative of a spring thaw. Some of the musical material is prophetic of the idiom Stravinsky was to use in Act II of *The Nightingale*.

The interval of the seventh (and occasionally the ninth) is prominent in the accompaniment to 'Tsaraiuki'. The little 6-bar instrumental coda is particularly sensitive and beautiful.

The tonality of the songs is vague, and even evanescent. 'Akahito' has a key signature of four flats and seems to imply an A flat major/minor tonality. The other two songs have no key signatures. The arpeggi in 'Mazatsumi' are generally made up of bitonal constituents, and the vocal line seems to revolve round A major/minor. In 'Tsaraiuki' the voice modulates from what may be A sharp minor to C flat major/minor. Here the lack of agreement between voice and accompaniment produces an almost atonal effect and has even led some critics to think they can detect the influence of Schoenberg. But the song is really the precursor of the attenutated, almost abstract idiom that Stravinsky was about to exploit in Act III of *The Nightingale*.

A fourth song is referred to in a letter Ravel wrote to Mme. Hélène Casella from the Hôtel des Crêtes, Clarens (on 2 April 1913), suggesting the following programme for one of the Société Musicale Indépendante concerts in Paris:

   (a) *Pierrot Lunaire* (21 numbers, 40 minutes)   Schoenberg
   (b) *Mélodies Japonaises* (4 numbers, 10 minutes)   Stravinsky
   (c) 2 *Poésies de S. Mallarmé*   Ravel

Nothing further is known of this fourth Japanese lyric; and in the event the proposal to perform *Pierrot Lunaire* at this concert was dropped.

2. Register of Works

23. ТРИ ПѢСЕНКИ (ИЗЪ ВОСПОМИНАНІЙ ЮНОШЕСКИХЪ ГОДОВЪ) – THREE LITTLE SONGS ('Recollections of my Childhood')

For voice and piano. Composed about 1906: definitive version, Clarens, October–November 1913. Russian popular texts; French translation by C. F. Ramuz, English by Robert Burness. Published by Edition Russe de Musique 1914 (later by Boosey & Hawkes). Duration: *c.* 1 minute 30 seconds.

1. 'Сороченька' – 'La Petite Pie' – 'The Magpie'. Dedicated to his son Sviatoslav Soulima. (Dated 6/19 October 1913.)
2. 'Ворона' – 'Le Corbeau' – 'The Rook'.[1] To his daughter Ludmila.
3. 'Чичеръ Ячеръ' – 'Tchitcher-Iatcher' – 'The Jackdaw'. To his son Theodore. (Dated October–November 1913.)

Manuscript with Boosey & Hawkes, London. Some manuscript material is in the composer's collection [C 4].

These little songs are based on melodies that Stravinsky had invented and used as themes for improvisation to amuse his companions in early years (*Chr*). According to *Expositions*, an early version existed about 1906, for he remembered playing them over to Rimsky-Korsakov, and (as has already been pointed out) there is a reference to 'The Jackdaw' in the last movement of the *Symphony in E flat*. The words are based on Russian popular texts, and 'the third song uses pure onomatopoeic nonsense words' (*Exp*). The piano accompaniment clearly dates from 1913, for it contains numerous references to procedures that Stravinsky had just developed in *The Rite of Spring*, e.g., the use of acciaccaturas in 'The Magpie',[2] and the appearance of a dissonant chord sequence driving against the main theme in 'The Jackdaw'.[3]

These gay little songs are the forerunners of several groups of songs that Stravinsky was to compose to Russian popular texts during the next five or six years; but it should be noted that the phrases of the vocal line are still being presented in a symmetrical form.

Instrumentation

The *Three Little Songs* were orchestrated for voice and small orchestra (2.2.2.2 – 0.0.0.0 – string quartet[4]) at Nice in 1929 and 1930.[5] ('The Magpie' is dated 25–26 December 1929; 'The Rook' 29 December 1929; 'The Jackdaw', 4 January 1930.) 'The Magpie' has been lengthened from 15 to 51 bars, 'The

---

[1] A MS draft of this song showing a variant accompaniment for piano is reproduced in Alexandre Tansman's *Igor Stravinsky*. Paris, 1948.

[2] See the flutes and oboes at fig. 21 in *The Rite of Spring*.

[3] Compare this with the middle section of the 'Spring Khorovod' in *The Rite of Spring*.

[4] That is – for full strings without double-basses.

[5] 1933 is the date given in Stravinsky's *Chronicle* and *Expositions*. (In the English translation of the *Chronicle* it is misprinted 1923.) The orchestral score of the complete suite was probably written in 1933.

Rook' from 40 to 59 bars, and 'The Jackdaw' from 18 to 29 bars – and the songs become a suite by the addition of brief instrumental introductions. The introduction to 'The Rook' contains a modulatory passage (four bars long) from E flat major (the key of the preceding song) to F Major marked 'jonction' in the manuscript. 'The Jackdaw' has been transposed from E major to E flat major so as to fit into this scheme. Stravinsky has started to tease the symmetry of the vocal line by introducing asymmetric pauses between some of the phrases. The orchestration has lively touches of onomatopoeia – especially a hoarse bar for clarinets and bassoons that appears twice in the introduction to 'The Jackdaw'.

This orchestral version was intended for a French film that was never released (*Exp*). Duration: *c.* 3 minutes. Published by Edition Russe de Musique 1934 (later Boosey & Hawkes). Manuscript with Boosey and Hawkes. Other manuscript material is in the composer's collection [C 53].

24. СОЛОВЕЙ – LE ROSSIGNOL – THE NIGHTINGALE – DIE NACHTIGALL

A musical fairy tale[1] in three acts by I. Stravinsky and S. Mitusov after the story by Hans Andersen. French translation by M. D. Calvocoressi; English translations (1) by Basil T. Timotheieff and Charles C. Hayne,[2] and (2) by Robert Craft; German translations (1) by Liesbeth Weinhold and (2) by A. Elukhen and B. Feiwel. (3.3.3.3 – 4.4.3.1 – timpani, percussion,[3] piano, celesta, optional parts for guitar and mandoline – string 5tet.) Act I composed at Ustilug, 1908 to the summer of 1909; Acts II and III, Clarens 1913/Leysin 1914. The printed score bears no dedication; but according to Paul Collaer,[4] the opera was dedicated to S. Mitusov. Published by Edition Russe de Musique, 1923 (later Boosey & Hawkes). Vocal score by the composer. First performance, Russian Ballet, Opera House, Paris, 26 May 1914, conducted by Pierre Monteux. Duration: *c.* 45 minutes. The manuscript of the full score is with Boosey & Hawkes, New York, and the manuscript of the vocal score (dated Leysin, Grand Hotel, 14/27 March 1914) with Boosey & Hawkes, London. Other manuscript material is in the composer's collection [C 2] and [C 4].

Libretto and Synopsis

The conception of *The Nightingale* dates back to the period when Stravinsky was still working under Rimsky-Korsakov. The choice of a story by Hans

---

[1] The French description is 'conte lyrique'.
[2] This was the translation made (and published) for the 1914 production of the opera at Drury Lane, London. In this libretto it is erroneously stated that the part of the Nightingale is sung by a *tenor*!
[3] The percussion section includes cymbals, antique cymbals, triangle, side drum, big drum, two sets of campanelli, tambourin and tam-tam.
[4] *Stravinsky*. Brussels, 1930.

2. Register of Works

Andersen as basis for the opera he was planning was made in an endeavour to recapture the lost beauty of the fairy-tale world he had entered as a boy (*Exp*). The libretto, as drafted by him and his friend Stepan Mitusov, is divided into three acts:

Act I.   'The Edge of a Wood by the Seashore.'
Act II. 'The Throne Room in the Emperor of China's Porcelain Palace.'
Act III. 'A Hall in the Palace containing the Emperor's Bedchamber.'

The whole opera is so brief – it plays for only three quarters of an hour – that it would seem more sensible to look on it as a one-acter divided into three scenes.

After an orchestral introduction, the curtain rises on the first act showing the edge of a wood by the seashore just before dawn, with a fisherman in his boat who sings of the regular nightly visitations of the Nightingale and the beauty of its exquisite song. Presently the Nightingale is heard; but its song is interrupted by the arrival of a group of Palace officials – Chamberlain, Bonze, Kitchen-maid and courtiers – who bring it an invitation from the Emperor to sing to him in his palace. At first they are misled by various noises – the lowing of a heifer, the croaking of frogs – but at last the Nightingale is heard again. The bird makes it clear it prefers to sing in the open air: nevertheless, it is prepared to accept the Emperor's invitation and settles on the Kitchen-maid's hand accordingly. As the party returns to the palace bearing the Nightingale in triumph, the fisherman resumes his song.

The second act opens with a 'Draughts' Entracte sung and danced by the chorus in front of net curtains, which part to reveal the interior of the Emperor's Palace of Porcelain lit by thousands of torches and lanterns and decorated with tinkling flowers for a fête. There is a procession, in the course of which the Emperor is carried in, seated in his baldaquin. The Nightingale sings, and the Emperor is moved to tears. Suddenly three Japanese envoys arrive with a gift for the Emperor from the Emperor of Japan – a large mechanical nightingale. This artificial toy is wound up and while it is in action, the real Nightingale slips out of the Throne-Room without being noticed. The Emperor stops the mechanical nightingale and is about to ask the real Nightingale to resume its song, when he realises it has disappeared and is so displeased that he banishes it from his empire. As the curtain falls, the fisherman is heard off-stage, singing of the approach of death.

After a short orchestral introduction, the curtain rises on a hall in the palace where the Emperor lies ill in his bedchamber. Death, wearing the Emperor's crown and holding his sword and banner, is seated by his bedside, accompanied by a chorus of lurking spectres who represent the Emperor's good and bad deeds. The Nightingale returns and by its singing redeems the banner, the sword and the crown. Death and the spectres depart; the courtiers enter the antichamber; and the Emperor, now fully restored to health, confronts them in the full splendour of his ceremonial robes. The courtiers prostrate themselves; the curtain falls; and the voice of the fisherman is heard once more off-stage singing of sunrise and birdsong.

Composition and Treatment

The composition of *The Nightingale* had a chequered history. The idea of the opera was discussed, and the libretto worked out, in 1908; and Rimsky-Korsakov heard and approved the preliminary musical sketches of Act I (*Chr*). The orchestration of the first act was finished by the end of the summer of 1909; but at this point the continuation of the opera was interrupted by the commissioning of *The Firebird* and Stravinsky's subsequent work for the Russian Ballet.

Towards the end of the summer of 1913, he received from the newly founded Free Theatre of Moscow a request to complete *The Nightingale* for a payment of 10,000 roubles (*Con*). Though tempted by so large a fee, he was dubious whether to accept or not, as the first act had been completed more than four years previously, and since then his musical language had developed almost beyond recognition. Fearing the subsequent acts were bound to be in a completely different style, he suggested to the directors that they should present Act I by itself as an independent lyrical scene; but they refused, and in the end he agreed to complete the opera as they wished. In his *Chronicle* he wrote: 'As there is no action until the second act, I told myself it would be not unreasonable if the music of the Prologue [i.e., Act I] bore a somewhat different character from that of the rest. And, indeed, the forest with its nightingale, the pure soul of the child who falls in love with its song – all this gentle poetry of Hans Andersen's could not be expressed in the same way as the baroque luxury of the Chinese court, with its bizarre etiquette, its palace fêtes, its thousands of little bells and lanterns, and the grotesque humming of the mechanical Japanese nightingale ... In short, all this exotic fantasy, obviously demanded a different musical idiom.' Having decided to proceed with the composition, he paid a brief visit to Mitusov in Warsaw on his way from Russia to Switzerland at the beginning of the autumn so that they could agree on the final adjustments to the libretto; and the score of Acts II and III was written at Clarens in the autumn of 1913 and Leysin in the winter of 1914.

Before the opera could be completed, however, its destination changed. By the beginning of 1914, the Moscow Free Theatre enterprise collapsed; and on hearing this news, Diaghilev hastened to Leysin in January 1914 in order to negotiate with Stravinsky for permission to produce the opera during his forthcoming Russian Ballet Seasons in Paris and London. This right appears to have been granted without further fee (*Con*).

It is interesting to see how Stravinsky and Mitusov managed to incorporate a number of Andersen's fantastic touches in their libretto, such as the pompous priest's invariable answer of 'Tsing-Pe!'[1] to any question, and the episode where the ladies of the court try to imitate the nightingale's song by gargling with water. The following passage from Andersen's story was taken as a cue for the setting of Act II and for the 'Draughts' interlude with which it opens: 'The palace was festively adorned. The walls and the flooring, which were of porcelain, gleamed in the rays of thousands of golden lamps. The most glorious flowers, which could ring clearly, had been placed in the passages. There was a running to and from and a thorough draught.' But it is curious that Stravinsky made no use of Andersen's statement that the Emperor insisted on the real bird and the artificial bird singing a duet together, which 'did not turn out very well, because the real nightingale sang in her own way, while the other bird's song was purely mechanical'.

The action posed a fascinating but awkward problem – how to treat the Nightingale itself and its song. Once Stravinsky had decided to cast the bird as a coloratura soprano, a further decision had to be taken – what to do with the singer? Quite early on, it was agreed that the singer must be in the orchestra pit; and this meant there would be no character on the stage to represent the nightingale, only a tiny, almost invisible bird for a small part of the action.

The idea of getting the singers off the stage was one that certainly appealed to Diaghilev. For the 1914 summer season of the Russian Ballet in Paris and London, he had already decided to mount Rimsky-Korsakov's *The Golden Cockerel* with a double cast of singers and dancers:[2] so he was doubtless pleased when it proved feasible to put the singer for the fisherman's role in the orchestra pit as well, leaving a silent figure on the stage to mime the part. At one point he seems to have been opposed even to the idea of the chorus of spectres appearing on the stage in the last act.[3] But though these moves helped to keep the stage clear for the various spectacular processions and passages of dancing, they did little to help put the opera over. The remoteness of the Nightingale's voice certainly has a romantic, slightly unworldly quality in the theatre; but so long as the singer's face is invisible, the words are difficult to capture, and this is a serious loss, particularly in the last act where the intimate dialogue between Death, the Nightingale and the Emperor has a line of argument that needs careful following.

However, the action of the opera at least allows the Nightingale to be fully established as a musical character from quite early on in Act I, whereas the other main character, the Emperor, has a rather thin time. It is true that his initial appearance in Act II is led up to by a magnificent outburst of ceremonial elaboration (the 'Chinese March'); but after that, his vocal contribution is

---

[1] The 'Tsing' is usually accompanied by the cymbals and the 'Pe' by the big drum.
[2] In the event, the singers were not placed in the orchestra pit, but were ranged in tiers on either side of the stage.
[3] See Benois's letter to Stravinsky dated 14–17 February 1914, printed in *Memories and Commentaries*.

extremely brief. His illness in the third act is treated with considerable sensitivity; but his sudden cure seems to be inadequately prepared and the final greeting to his astonished courtiers is a dramatic and musical anticlimax.

It seems likely that from an early stage Stravinsky was conscious of these (and maybe other) shortcomings in his opera. In London early in 1913 he had already expressed his doubts about opera as an art form. Speaking to a press reporter[1], he said: 'I dislike opera. Music can be married to gesture or to words—not to both without bigamy. That is why the artistic basis of opera is wrong and why Wagner sounds at his best in the concert-room. In any case opera is in a backwater. What operas have been written since *Parsifal*? Only two that count—*Elektra* and Debussy's *Pelléas*.' Nearly forty years later, when he had written *The Rake's Progress*, he found *The Nightingale* more remote 'than the English operas of three centuries ago or than the Italian-Mozartian opera which has been so neglected and misunderstood by the world of musical dramatists';[2] and in 1959, after conducting *The Nightingale* in Los Angeles, he considered that, while the first act was 'at least operatic', the later acts were 'a kind of opera-pageant ballet' (*Mem*). His final comment was: 'Perhaps *The Nightingale* only proves that I was right to compose ballets since I was not yet ready for an opera' (*Exp*).

But it is only fair to remember that from the beginning of their collaboration, Stravinsky and Mitusov looked on *The Nightingale* as a story and not a drama; and one wishes that when planning the action they could have devised some form of commentary (perhaps as C. F. Ramuz did for *The Soldier's Tale*) that would have allowed the narrative element to emerge more clearly.

Music

The first act of *The Nightingale* precedes *The Firebird* by a year. In his *Memories* Stravinsky recalls an entry in a diary he kept during 1908, in which he had written 'Why should I be following Debussy so closely, when the real originator of this operatic style was Mussorgsky?' The debt to Debussy's *Nuages* is particularly noticeable in the Introduction, with its slowly oscillating fifths and thirds; and a common origin for this figure can be found in one of the songs in Mussorgsky's *Without Sunlight* cycle. The optional humming passage for the chorus at figure 5 is reminiscent of Debussy's *Sirènes*. The slightly debilitating chromaticism associated with the Nightingale's first outbursts of song shows an awareness of Scriabin and his current harmonic explorations; but a firmer control and a more original line of musical treatment are apparent as soon as the mixed group of courtiers enters.

Stravinsky's musical idiom had changed considerably when in 1913 he sat down to write the second act, and the 'Draughts' entracte opens with a whoosh

---

[1] From *The Daily Mail*, 13 February 1913.
[2] From the Programme Note for the Boston University Opera Workshop's production of *The Rake's Progress*, 17 and 18 May 1953.

of sound that in later years he was to liken to the tintinnabulation of the St. Petersburg telephone in the first decade of the century (*Exp*). The artificial ceremony of the Chinese Court seemed to call for a bizarre form of musical *chinoiserie*: so in the 'Draughts' interlude, the 'Chinese March' and the 'Solemn Procession' at the end of the opera he adopted the Chinese pentatonic scale, usually but not invariably in its black-note form. The pentatonic themes are generally underlined by parallel pentatonic strands moving six degrees of the pentatonic scale lower and thereby producing ninths or tenths. There are also occasions when a 'shadow' scale is used for underlining. This is an artificial scale created by taking the five notes of the Chinese pentatonic scale, e.g., F sharp, G sharp, A sharp, C sharp, D sharp, and adding notes that are alternately a major 7th or a minor 7th lower, thereby producing an artificial pentatonic scale of G, A sharp, B, D sharp, E. The tonal implications of the Chinese black-note pentatonic scale are F sharp major and/or D sharp minor; those of the shadow scale are E minor and/or D sharp major.

Ex.17

etc.

The bitonal potentialities of this material are exploited, frequently over a kind of ostinato bass built up of moving or superimposed fifths. When the Nightingale bursts into song, it is found to have progressed from the *Lakmé*-like vocalises of the first act to freer chromatic *melismata* built round a number of major and minor thirds.

In the third act, the *chinoiserie* style is almost wholly abandoned (except for the final 'Solemn Procession') in favour of a more developed chromatic style, moving further away from tonality without ever becoming actually atonal. Certain passages are of an intense simplicity. For instance, the theme of the opening chorus of spectres is constructed out of only three notes contained within the compass of a minor third. Similarly, there is an exquisite little two-bar theme, which appears first – *dolcissimo pianissimo* – as an instrumental interlude[1] before Death's first vocal intervention and is later taken over by the Nightingale when it sings to Death of his garden, the churchyard, 'where the white roses grow, where the alder blossom smells sweet, and where the fresh grass is moistened by the tears of survivors'.[2] This consists of four notes

---

[1] 4 bars before fig. 118 (solo viola accompanied by piano).
[2] 4 bars before fig. 124, fig. 124 *bis*, and fig. 125. (Solo viola or flute accompanied by clarinet, with the optional addition of mandoline accompanied by guitar.) The quotation is from Hans Andersen's story.

within the compass of a major third and is accompanied by alternately rising and falling *arpeggi* built round a framework of fourths.

Ex.18

Both these little themes are static and are not developed in any way. These and one or two other brief passages represent the most serene and spiritual point reached by Stravinsky before the codas of *The Wedding* and the *Symphonies of Wind Instruments* and the 'Apotheosis' in *Apollo Musagetes*.

The orchestration does everything within its power to underline the bizarre nature of the action; but the score contains no metrical innovations. While the maintenance of an unswerving metrical pulse is a feature of the ceremonial music (i.e. the 'Draughts' interlude, the 'Chinese March' and the final 'Solemn Procession') and of the 'Song of the Mechanical Nightingale', the intimate lyrical passages (particularly the trio between the Emperor, Death and the Nightingale in Act III) have much more elasticity, and the voices are allowed a considerable measure of freedom. Syncopation is almost entirely absent; changes of time signature are not especially frequent; the melodic line tends to fall into regular phrases, four bars by four; and the result is to bring *The Nightingale* much closer to *The Firebird* and *Petrushka* than *The Rite of Spring*.

The idiom of Acts II and III is certainly more original and mature than that of Act I, and the difference between the two parts must have disconcerted some of the early listeners; but with the passage of time this gap has narrowed and the variations in style now seem to be much less of a flaw than they at first appeared. It is the nature of the work that it is built up out of contrasted musical styles, and its weaknesses are to be found, not in stylistic disparities, but in the imperfect fusion of the operatic, balletic and narrative elements.

Production

When *The Nightingale* was originally commissioned by the Free Theatre of Moscow, Alexandre Benois, who was then working for the Moscow Arts Theatre, was approached to see if he would act as designer. In his *Memories*, Stravinsky has published the correspondence that passed between Benois and himself, from which it is clear that Benois found difficulty in acceding to the request owing to the fact that the two theatres were rivals. But as soon as the

Free Theatre enterprise collapsed and the new opera passed into Diaghilev's hands, Benois felt free to accept, and his letters from Moscow and St. Petersburg during the first three months of 1914 show how absorbed he was in his task. The only difficulty was that he had nothing more than the libretto on which to base his designs, for the score was not available until the spring.

Although Diaghilev had persuaded Sir Joseph Beecham, who was responsible for the London season of the Russian Ballet at Drury Lane that summer, to meet the expenses of this new opera production, he managed to reserve the first performance for his Paris season.[1] It was given there at the Opera House on 26 May 1914. The choreography was entrusted to Boris Romanov, and the stage production was by Alexander Sanin. Pierre Monteux conducted; and the opera was sung in Russian. The first of four London performances was given at Drury Lane on 18 June with Emile Cooper as conductor.

Stravinsky considered that scenically *The Nightingale* was the most beautiful of all his early works for Diaghilev (*Mem*). Benois himself was delighted by the stage spectacle, and particularly with the Chinese March. 'As the procession appeared from the wings, each link made two rounds of the stage and sank down on the floor within the space lit up with lanterns, thus forming a gorgeous and motley carpet of living flowers who emphasised by their movements the principal points of the action. In the light of the huge blue lanterns the fantastic costumes stood out vividly against the background of white and blue china columns, and when the Emperor, sparkling with gold and jewels, stepped forward from under his gigantic umbrella and the crowd fell down to worship him, the effect was so great that for the first time in my life I felt genuinely moved by my own creation.'[2]

Unfortunately the greater part of the settings and costumes perished in the Drury Lane store during the First World War.

Revised Version (1962)

The revised version published by Boosey & Hawkes in 1962 contains, as well as the original Russian text and the French translation by M. D. Calvocoressi, a new English translation by Robert Craft and a new German translation by A. Elukhen and B. Feiwel. A comparison with the original version shows that the alterations in the score are minimal. Perhaps the most important is the suppression of a bar before fig. 133 so that the last note of the Emperor's greeting at the end of the 'Funeral March' in Act III coincides with the first bar of the reprise of the fisherman's song.[3] As will be seen from the following comparative table, there are a few changes in dynamic markings, the main effect of which is to adopt slightly faster tempi than those specified in the

---

[1] Alexandre Benois, *Reminiscences of the Russian Ballet*.
[2] A. Benois, *op. cit.*
[3] This modification appears also in *The Song of the Nightingale*.

original version. In particular, the fisherman's song is speeded up in Acts I and II, reverting to nearly its original tempo at the end of Act III – a change that helps the opera's forward flow.

Original Version (1914)	Revised Version (1962)
Act I Figs. 8, 13, 48: *Larghetto* ♪=60	*Larghetto* ♪=80
Act II Fig. 63: *Lento* ♩=48 Fig. 95: ♩=52 circa Fig. 99: *Larghetto* ♪=56[1]	*Lento* ♩=56 ♪=108 *Larghetto* ♪=80
Act III Fig. 101: *Molto ritmico* ♪=120 Fig. 108: *Lento* ♪=60 Fig. 110: ♩=63 Fig. 115: *L'istesso tempo* ♫=96 Fig. 116: *Lento* ♩=56–54 Fig. 133: ♪=54	*Con moto* ♪=120 *Lento* ♪=72 ♩=60 ♫=96 *Lento* ♩=60 ♪=54 (*più largo che sopra*)

24 (A). CHANT DU ROSSIGNOL – ПѢСНЯ СОЛОВЬЯ – THE SONG OF THE NIGHTINGALE

Symphonic poem in three parts for orchestra (2.2.2.2 – 4.3.3.1 – percussion timpani, celesta, piano, two harps – string quintet). Completed at Morges on 4 April 1917. Published by Edition Russe de Musique, 1921 (later by Boosey & Hawkes). Piano reduction by the composer. First performance: Orchestre de la Suisse Romande, Geneva, 6 December 1919, conducted by Ernest Ansermet. Duration: *c.* 20 minutes. MS. comp. [C 19]. A notebook containing 'Fragments spécialement composés' for this 'poème chorégraphique' (the 'première apparition du rossignol' being dated 1 Dec. 1916) passed through the hands of an American dealer in 1967.

1. 'The Fête in the Emperor of China's Palace'
2. 'The Two Nightingales'
3. 'Illness and Recovery of the Emperor of China'

At the end of 1916 Diaghilev visited Stravinsky at Morges with the proposal that he should mount *The Nightingale* in ballet form. Stravinsky put up a counter-proposal. 'I had been thinking of making a symphonic poem for orchestra by combining the music of Acts II and III of *The Nightingale*, which

---

[1] In the vocal score this is misprinted ♩ = 56.

were homogeneous, and I told Diaghilev I would place that at his disposal if he cared to make a ballet of it. He warmly welcomed the suggestion, and I adapted a scenario from Andersen's fairy story to serve the purpose' (*Chr*). This scenario, which consists mainly of quotations from Andersen, is prefixed by the piano reduction of the score and runs as follows:

1. *The Fête in the Emperor of China's Palace.* In honour of the Nightingale that sang so sweetly 'the palace was festively adorned. The walls and the flooring, which were of porcelain, gleamed in the rays of thousands of golden lamps. The most glorious flowers, which could ring clearly, had been placed in the passages. There was a running to and fro, and a thorough draught, so that all the bells rang loudly. . . .' The Nightingale is placed on a golden perch; and a CHINESE MARCH signals the entrance of the Emperor.

2. *The Two Nightingales.* 'The Nightingale sang so gloriously that the tears came into the Emperor's eyes. . . . The lackeys and chambermaids reported that they were satisfied too; and that was saying a good deal, for they are the most difficult to please. . . .' Envoys arrive from the Emperor of Japan with the gift of a mechanical nightingale. 'So soon as the artificial bird was wound up, he could sing a piece, and then his tail moved up and down, and shone with silver and gold. . . . He had just as much success as the real one, and then it was much handsomer to look at. . . . But where was the living Nightingale? No one had noticed that it had flown away out of the open window. . . .' The fisherman is heard out-of-doors, singing for joy because his friend has returned.

3. *Illness and Recovery of the Emperor of China.* 'The poor Emperor could scarcely breathe. He opened his eyes and saw that it was Death who sat upon his chest, and had put on his golden crown, and held in one hand the Emperor's sword, and in the other his beautiful banner. And all around, from among the folds of the splendid velvet curtains, strange heads peered forth . . . these were all the Emperor's bad and good deeds. . . . They told him so much that the perspiration ran from his forehead.' The mechanical bird refused to sing. Then the little live Nightingale was heard singing outside the window. 'And as it sang the spectres grew paler and paler. . . . Even Death listened and said, "Go on, little Nightingale, go on!" . . . And Death gave up each of its treasures for a song . . . and floated out at the window in the form of a cold white mist. . . . The Emperor fell into a sweet slumber. The sun shone upon him through the window when he awoke refreshed and restored.'

FUNERAL MARCH. 'The courtiers came in to look at their dead Emperor, and – yes, there they stood astounded, and the Emperor said "Good morning!" ' Meanwhile, the friendly Nightingale has flown back to the fisherman who is heard singing his song once more.

For this symphonic poem, not only was all the music of Act I omitted, but substantial cuts were made in the music of Acts II and III.

Original Compositions

In Part I of *The Song of the Nightingale*, the 'Draughts' entracte is taken over almost *in toto* from the opera; but the Kitchenmaid's short piece of declamation[1] is cut, and in its place a new passage for the Nightingale (15 bars Andantino 3/8) is inserted with flute trills and arabesques. The 'Draughts' interlude music is then resumed for 9 bars as in the opera; and after a slightly shortened bridge passage the 'Chinese March' follows intact.

From here onwards the rehandling of the operatic material is more marked. The 'Nightingale's Song' in Part 2 is based on the air that the Nightingale sings at this point in the opera; but then a preliminary statement of the Nightingale's song to Death from the third act of the opera is inserted. This leads to a more or less identical repeat of a substantial portion (65 bars) of the 'Draughts' interlude, which is interrupted by the entry of the Japanese envoys (transposed a major third higher than in the opera) and the scene where the Mechanical Nightingale plays (in its original key). A few bars of the opera score are cut; and then the remainder of Part 2 of the symphonic poem is identical with the end of Act II of the opera, including the fisherman's song, which here makes its first appearance.[2]

The third part opens with the orchestral introduction to Act III of the opera intact: but the chorus of spectres is omitted, and the material that follows (mainly connected with the Nightingale) is rehandled and cross-cut with four separate statements of the Nightingale's song to Death. It is difficult to talk of keys in connection with this almost atonal theme: but if it is agreed that the theme comes to rest on a major third, (see Ex. 18), then it can be suggested that these four statements are in the keys of D, E flat, E (natural) and G, in contrast to the opera where the theme appears only in G. The 'Funeral March' and the final repeat of the fisherman's song are as in the opera, but with certain important transpositions – the key of the March is raised a semitone (from B to C), the Emperor's greeting to his courtiers (here entrusted to harps and timpani) is also raised a semitone, but by an unexpected modulatory twist the final reprise of the fisherman's song which follows immediately is played in A flat major instead of the C major of the opera.

The fact that in the symphonic poem the voice of the Nightingale is replaced by solo flute and solo violin means that the restricted range of the vocal line can be considerably extended, and this leads to a readjustment of the whole score, the orchestration of which is lightened in texture to enable not only solo instruments, but also groups of instruments, to be treated on *concertante* lines. The repetition of certain material and the transposition of keys are intended to strengthen the symphonic nature of the new arrangement. But it must be admitted that the initial inspiration that led to the composition of the

---

[1] Fig. 63 in the opera.
[2] Some ballet performances of *The Song of the Nightingale* include a preliminary statement of the fisherman's song right at the beginning of the score.

original work was not really symphonic in intention, and it is perhaps sufficient to look on *The Song of the Nightingale* as a pleasant orchestral reminder of some of the lyrical delights that are to be found in the opera.

Ballet Productions

As soon as Diaghilev knew that Stravinsky was willing to make a symphonic suite from his opera score, he commissioned a young Futurist painter, Fortunato Depero, then living in Rome, to design the new ballet. Depero planned 'a fantastic garden scene of huge plastic flowers'; and for costumes there were to be 'geometrical Chinese masks, cylindrical sleeves and heads in compartments'.[1] This was in 1917. In the event, the production of the ballet was delayed until 1920; and by then Depero's work could no longer be used, for his landlady in Rome had 'dismantled the set, selling the pieces for the back rent the artist owed her'. The new designer was Henri Matisse; the choreographer Leonide Massine. The first performance of *The Song of the Nightingale* in ballet form was given by the Russian Ballet at the Opera House, Paris, on 2 February 1920 with Ansermet conducting. Five years later a new choreographic version was made for the Russian Ballet by George Balanchine.

Transcriptions

Songs of the Nightingale and Chinese March for violin and piano by I. Stravinsky and S. Dushkin (Voreppe, 1932). Edition Russe de Musique (later Boosey & Hawkes). MS comp. [C 60].

25. THREE PIECES FOR STRING QUARTET

For two violins, viola and cello. Composed at Salvan, 1914. Dedicated to Ernest Ansermet. Edited by F. H. Schneider.[2] Published by Edition Russe de Musique, 1922 (later by Boosey & Hawkes). First performance, Flonzaley Quartet, Chicago, 8 November 1915. Duration: *c.* 8 minutes. MS comp. [C 8].

    (i) M.M. ♩=126
   (ii) M.M. ♩= 76
  (iii) M.M. ♩= 40

When these little pieces were first published in 1922, they had no titles, and bore no general directions of mood or tempo (apart from the metronome markings). This made it appear as if Stravinsky wanted them to be treated as abstract music; but the content of each individual piece was slight, and the

---

[1] See *Stravinsky and the Dance*. New York, 1962.
[2] This is the first example of Stravinsky's post-war attempt to protect his music in America by resorting to the stratagem of appointing an American editor.

three of them seemed hardly to form a coherent whole. Also, the writing for string quartet was not very reassuring; and although it called for virtuosity on the part of the four players, there were moments when it looked as if the composer was aiming at effects that were beyond the natural capacity of a string quartet. For instance, the fragmentation of the second piece made it necessary to pepper the score with unusual directions to the players: 'excessivement court et sec' . . . 'donnez une sonorité très fine et douce' . . . 'donnez un son étranglé' . . . and (to the second violin and viola players) 'renversez vite l'instrument (tenez-le comme on tient un violoncelle) afin de pouvoir exécuter ce pizzicato qui équivaut à l'arpège renversé'

Academic critics were appalled. After quoting four bars of the second piece in *The New Music* (1924), George Dyson exclaimed, 'If this type of passage has any proper place in the art of the string quartet, then the end is near'.

But an essential piece of information was lacking, for these were really contrasting studies in popular, fantastic and liturgical moods. When the *Three Pieces* were played from the manuscript by the Flonzaley Quartet, under the title, 'Grotesques', at the Aeolian Hall, New York, on 30 November 1915, they were introduced by Daniel Gregory Mason who made this point clear; and Amy Lowell who heard them performed wrote a poem,[1] in which she attempted to 'reproduce the sound and movement of the music as far as is possible in another medium'. Here are three extracts:

First Movement

> . . .
> *Bang! Bump! Tong!*
> *Petticoats,*
> *Stockings,*
> *Sabots,*
> *Delirium flapping its thigh-bones;*
> *Red, blue, yellow,*
> *Drunkenness steaming in colours;*
> *Red, yellow, blue,*
> *Colours and flesh weaving together,*
> *In and out with the dance,*
> *Coarse stuffs and hot flesh weaving together.*
> . . .

---

[1] Printed in *Some Imagist Poets, 1916*. London, Constable, 1916.

Second Movement

> *Pale violin music whiffs across the moon,*
> *A pale smoke of violin music blows over the moon,*
> *Cherry petals fall and flutter,*
> *And the white Pierrot,*
> *Wreathed in the smoke of the violins,*
> *Splashed with cherry petals falling, falling,*
> *Claws a grave for himself in the fresh earth*
> *With his finger-nails.*

Third Movement

> *An organ growls in the heavy roof-groins of a church,*
> *It wheezes and coughs.*
> *The nave is blue with incense,*
> *Writhing, twisting,*
> *Snaking over the heads of the chanting priests.*
>   Requiem aeternam dona ei, Domine . . .

When in 1928 Stravinsky decided to include these *Three Pieces* in his *Four Studies for orchestra*, they were given titles – 1. 'Dance', 2. 'Eccentric', 3. 'Canticle'. The 'Dance', with its melody confined to four notes within the compass of a fourth, is now seen to be a precursor of the long series of popular Russian tunes that Stravinsky poured out in profusion during the four years 1914–1917. 'Eccentric' turns out to have been inspired by a performance of Little Tich that Stravinsky saw in London in the summer of 1914, 'and the jerky, spastic movement, the ups and downs, the rhythm – even the mood or joke of the music – was suggested by the art of the great clown' (*Mem*). Stravinsky himself thought very highly of the 'Canticle' – 'the last 20 bars are some of my best music of that time' (*Exp*).

As time went on, much of the material originally contained in the *Three Pieces for String Quartet* proved germinal. The little four-note theme of the 'Dance' (Ex. 19) became the spring-board from which the composer launched himself into the more extended main theme of the last movement of the *Symphony in C* (Ex. 20).

Ex.19

Ex.20
Tempo giusto

f e staccato

etc.

Original Compositions

In 'Eccentric' there is a little phrase marked 'sur la touche' for the strings (Ex. 21) which was later transformed into the subject of the instrumental fugue in the second movement of the *Symphony of Psalms* (Ex. 22).

The refrain of the 'Canticle' with its initial triplet figure (Ex. 23) is more fully worked out in the coda of the *Symphonies of Wind Instruments* (Ex. 24).

For details of the orchestral version of these three pieces, see *Four Studies for Orchestra* no. 33 (A).

Ballet Production

These *Three Pieces for String Quartet,* together with the *Concertino* (no. 42), formed the basis of a ballet entitled *The Antagonists,* which was produced by the American Dance Festival at New London, Connecticut, in 1955 with choreography by Ruth Currier.

235

2. Register of Works

26. PRIBAOUTKI – CHANSONS PLAISANTES

Song games for voice,[1] flute, oboe (=cor anglais), clarinet, bassoon, violin, viola, cello, double-bass. Russian popular texts; French translation by C. F. Ramuz, German by R. St. Hoffmann. Composed at Salvan, 1914. Dedicated 'à ma femme'. Published by Ad. Henn, Geneva 1917 (later by J. & W. Chester). Reduction for voice and piano by the composer. Duration: *c.* 5 minutes.

1. 'Корнило' – 'L'Oncle Armand' – 'Onkel Peter' – 'Kornillo'
2. 'Наташка' – 'Le Four' – 'Marianne' – 'Natashka'
3. 'Полковникъ' – 'Le Colonel' – 'Der Oberst' – 'The Colonel'
4. 'Старецъ и Заяцъ' – 'Le Vieux et le Lièvre' – 'Der Greis und der Hase' – 'The Old Man and the Hare'

First performance, Paris, Salle Gaveau, May 1919. MS comp. [C 9].

What *pribaoutki* are can best be described in Stravinsky's own words. 'The word *pribaoutki* denotes a form of popular Russian verse, to which the nearest English parallel is the limerick. It means "a telling", *"pri"* being the Latin *"pre"* and *"baout"* deriving from the Old Russian infinitive "to say". *Pribaoutki* are always short – not more than four lines usually. According to popular tradition they derive from a type of game in which someone says a word, which someone else then adds to, and which third and fourth persons develop, and so on, with utmost speed.'[2] The texts used in these songs are probably derived from the Afanasiev collection of Russian stories or the Kireievsky collection of Russian popular poems – 'these two great argosies of the Russian language and spirit' as Stravinsky calls them (*Exp*).

In setting these Russian jingles, Stravinsky made a discovery that particularly pleased him. 'One important characteristic of Russian popular verse is that the accents of the spoken verse are ignored when the verse is sung. The recognition of the musical possibilities inherent in this fact was one of the most rejoicing discoveries of my life' (*Exp*). While this confirmed his determination to use the syllable as his unit in setting literary texts, it becomes particularly difficult to reproduce the specifically Russian effect of these *pribaoutki* settings in translation.[3]

As in the first of the *Three Pieces for String Quartet*, the limbs of the vocal melody are usually restricted to repetitions of a limited number of notes contained within a compact compass and repeated in slightly varying patterns.

---

[1] According to Stravinsky (*Exp*), these songs should be sung only by a man's voice. He composed them with his brother Gury's baritone in mind.

[2] Another definition of *pribaoutki* is given by Stravinsky in his *Conversations*: 'a kind of droll song, sometimes to nonsense syllables, sometimes in part spoken'. It is worth noting that these songs had a strong seminal effect on Edith Sitwell's early poetry. (See *Taken Care Of*, 1965.)

[3] Stravinsky has said (*Con*) that he prefers to hear his Russian vocal music sung in Russian or not at all.

Occasionally a special vocal inflexion leads to a high note which generally drops a seventh to regain its normal level. Although the tunes sound authentically popular, they are original compositions and contain no conscious borrowing of folk material. This is true not only of the *Pribaoutki*, but also of the *Cat's Cradle Songs*, *Reynard*, the 'Saucers' and the *Four Russian Songs*. As Stravinsky says in his *Memories*, 'if any of these pieces *sounds* like aboriginal folk music, it may be because my powers of fabrication were able to tap some unconscious "folk" memory'.

While the vocal line is fundamentally diatonic, the instrumental accompaniment adds a number of piquant chromatic touches, sometimes with polytonal implications. There are also several onomatopoeic effects, such as the delicious cadenza for oboe and clarinet at the end of the first song, which sounds like the gurgle of an emptying bottle.

27. VALSE DES FLEURS

For two pianos. Composed Clarens 30 August 1914. Unpublished. Performed in New York at a concert organised by Robert Craft in 1949. The manuscript was formerly in the composer's collection, but seems to have been mislaid after the 1949 concert [C 6].

28. THREE EASY PIECES

For piano duet (easy left hand). Composed at Clarens, 1914–15. Published by Ad. Henn, Geneva 1917 (later by J. & W. Chester). Duration: *c.* 3 minutes. First performance by José Iturbi and the composer, Lausanne, 8 November 1919. MS comp. [C 10].

1. *March*　Dedicated to Alfredo Casella
2. *Waltz*　To Erik Satie
3. *Polka*　To Serge Diaghilev

Here Stravinsky has moved out of the world of Russian popular music that he had begun to explore in *Pribaoutki* and is exploiting a more international type of light music – just as in *Petrushka* he had turned from the popular music of the fairground to the light music accompanying the scene between the Ballerina and the Blackamoor. This new line of development was ultimately to lead to *The Soldier's Tale*.

In these three pieces, the left hand part has been made as easy as possible, each piece having a simple accompanying figure which is used as an unchanging ostinato. In contrast, the right hand part is fully extended.

When Stravinsky visited Rome in February 1915, he took these pieces with him, and during his stay invited Diaghilev to play them with him. 'On reaching the Polka I told him that in composing it I had thought of him as a circus ring-master in evening dress and top-hat, cracking his whip and urging on a rider on horseback. At first he was put out, not quite knowing whether he ought to be offended or not; but we had a good laugh over it together in the end' (*Chr*). (A slightly different account is given by Stravinsky in his *Dialogues*, where he says the Polka was composed first and played to Diaghilev and Casella in a hotel room in Milan, the March was written after his return to Morges, and the Waltz followed later.)

It was during this visit that Stravinsky tried to find a new publisher for his music. The outbreak of the First World War had cut him off from the Berlin headquarters of the Edition Russe de Musique: so he asked Casella to introduce him to Tito Ricordi. When the introduction was carried out, Stravinsky offered the Italian firm the *Three Easy Pieces* for piano duet; but Ricordi took fright at his conditions, and the deal did not go through.[1] The duets had to wait for publication until 1917, when they were brought out by Ad. Henn of Geneva.

Transcriptions

In 1915 Stravinsky transcribed the 'Polka' for cimbalom solo (for the repertory of Aladar Racz), transposing it a tone lower because the range of the instrument did not include the high F sharp in the penultimate bar. This arrangement is unpublished; but Stravinsky's manuscript was reproduced to illustrate an article by Mm. Yvonne Racz-Barblan in *Feuilles Musicales*.[2]

In his *Dialogues*, Stravinsky refers to what may or may not have been the same transcription of the Polka as being 'for cimbalom and small ensemble'.

The manuscript of a version of the 'March' for twelve instruments dated 25 March 1915 is in the composer's collection [C 10]. This is unpublished. He says that he also made a version of the 'Waltz' for seven instruments (*Dia*).

About six years later, the Three Pieces were orchestrated to form part of *Suite no. 2*. For details see the entry under *Five Easy Pieces for piano duet*, nos. 32 (A) and 32 (B).

29. SOUVENIR D'UNE MARCHE BOCHE

For piano. Dated Morges, 1 September 1915. The manuscript of this work was printed in facsimile in *The Book of the Homeless* (*Le Livre des Sans-Foyer*), edited by Edith Wharton, published in London by Macmillan & Co. Ltd. in 1916, and sold for the benefit of the Belgian orphans.

Thirty-seven bars of a brash sort of march in C major are followed by a jaunty trio, sixteen bars long, in F major. The C major march is then repeated *da capo al fine*. A work of small importance.

---

[1] Alfredo Casella, *Stravinski*. (Nuova edizione) 'La Scuola', Brescia, 1951.
[2] See Pierre Meyland, *Une amitié célèbre*. Editions du Cervin, Lausanne, 1961. Also the article by Mme. Yvonne Racz-Barblan in *Feuilles Musicales*, Lausanne. March–April 1962.

The manuscript is in the Library of Congress, Washington, D.C. A copy, but not in Stravinsky's hand, though signed and dated by him, is in the composer's collection [C 13].

30. CAT'S CRADLE SONGS – BERCEUSES DU CHAT – KATZEN-LIEDER

For contralto and three clarinets (piccolo clarinet in E flat = clarinet in E flat; clarinet in A = clarinet in B flat; bass clarinet in B flat = clarinet in A). Russian popular texts; French translation by C. F. Ramuz, German by R. St. Hoffmann. Composed at Clarens, Château d'Oex and Morges, 1915–16.[1] Dedicated to Natalie Gontcharova and Michel Larionov. Published by Ad. Henn, Geneva, 1917 (later by J. & W. Chester). Reduction for voice and piano by the composer. Duration: *c.* 5 minutes.

1. 'Спи Котъ' – 'Sur le Poêle' – 'Hinterm Herd'
2. 'Котъ На Печи' – 'Interieur' – 'Katzenidylle'
3. 'Бай-Бай' – 'Dodo' – 'Wiegenlied'
4. 'У Кота Кота' – 'Ce qu'il a le Chat' – 'Was Gehört der Katz?'

The manuscripts of two of these berceuses are in the collection of M. André Meyer, Paris. Other manuscript material is in the composer's collection [C 14].

These songs are further essays in the popular Russian idiom already used in *Pribaoutki*; but here the utterance is even terser and more epigrammatic. The accompaniments show masterly skill in exploiting the various registers and timbres of the clarinet. Its lithe and sinewy arabesques form a most appropriate commentary on a domestic corner of the animal world.

31. БАЙКА – RENARD – REYNARD

A burlesque story about the fox, the cock, the cat and the goat,[2] to be sung and played on the stage. Text adapted by I. Stravinsky from Russian popular tales; French translation by C. F. Ramuz, German by Rupert Koller, English by Rollo M. Myers. (1.1.1.1 – 2.1.0.0 – percussion, timpani, cimbalom – solo string 5tet – 2 solo tenors and 2 solo basses). Begun at Château d'Oex, spring 1915, and finished at Morges, 1916.[3] Dedicated to Princess Edmond de Polignac. Published by Ad. Henn, Geneva, 1917 (later by J. & W. Chester).

---

[1] The sketch for the first song is dated Morges 11 September 1915. (See the facsimile reproduction in *Stravinsky* by Frank Onnen, The Continental Book Company, Stockholm, 1948.) According to the Catalogue of the *Collection Musicale André Meyer* (Abbéville), the others are dated 18.5.1915, summer 1915 and 2 November.

[2] The Russian text has 'ram' instead of 'goat'; but Stravinsky seems to have accepted the change of animal made by Ramuz in the French translation.

[3] The manuscript vocal score is signed and dated (in Russian) 'Morges, 1 August 1916 at noon, sky without clouds'.

2. Register of Works

Vocal score by the composer. First performance, Russian Ballet, Opera House, Paris, 18 May 1922. Duration: *c*. 20 minutes. The following note is prefixed to the score:

> *Reynard* is to be played by clowns, dancers or acrobats, preferably on a trestle stage with the orchestra placed behind. If produced in a theatre, it should be played in front of the curtain. The players remain all the time on the stage. They enter together to the accompaniment of the little introductory march, and their exeunt is managed in the same way. The roles are dumb. The singers (two tenors and two basses) are in the orchestra.

MS comp. [C 15], [C 16] and [C 69].

Synopsis and Composition

Stravinsky's interest in the animal world now moved from birds and cats to the denizens of the farmyard. From Afanasiev's collection of Russian stories, he chose one or two episodes relating to the exploits of Reynard the Fox, from which he fashioned his own libretto. He was determined to avoid the trap he had fallen into when setting Andersen's fairy tale of *The Nightingale*: so from the beginning he made it clear that this was no opera, but a kind of chamber cantata accompanying stage action in mime. This meant that the four men's voices (two tenors and two basses) are not to be directly identified with any of the stage characters (Reynard, Cock, Cat and Goat) even when they appear to be singing in character; and this left him free to use them as soloists, or as a vocal duet, or trio, or quartet, as seemed musically desirable.

The libretto in its final form may be summarised as follows:

> The Cock is seen strutting up and down on his perch. Reynard enters disguised as a nun and begs him to come down in order to confess his sins, particularly in view of the fact that he has a harem of forty wives or more. Although the Cock penetrates Reynard's disguise, he allows himself to be persuaded and leaps. (*Salto mortale*.) Reynard captures him at once and tucks his head under his arm. The Cock is appalled at his predicament and calls on his friends, the Cat and the Goat, for help. They appear on the scene, and after they've driven Reynard off, all three of them dance together.
>
> The Cat and Goat go off, and the Cock gets back on his perch. Reynard re-enters and, dropping his disguise as a nun, tries to wheedle the Cock down from his perch again by promising him a barn full of corn. For the second time the silly Cock succumbs to Reynard's blandishments and leaps. (*Salto mortale*.) Reynard captures him and tucks his head under his arm. The Cock calls on the Cat and Goat to save him, but there is no reply, and Reynard starts to pluck him. In his extremity, the Cock prays to the Almighty to protect his family, and at the moment he faints the Cat and Goat reappear, singing a *pribaoutka* which they accompany on the *guzla*. Reynard peeps

out of his lair, and when they see him they threaten him with a big knife. They then proceed to drag him out of his lair by his tail and strangle him to the accompaniment of excruciating howls from the four singers in the orchestra. The three animals wind up with a merry dance, at the end of which the singers stop singing and announce that the play is over, adding (in the spirit of the old mummers' *quête*)

If you've enjoyed the tale of the Fox,
Drop your pennies in the box!

The first draft of the libretto was ready early in 1915, and Stravinsky started to compose the music with the 'plink . . . plink . . .' *pribaoutka* for the Cat and Goat where they are supposed to be accompanying themselves on the *guzla*.[1] This was written at Château d'Oex in the spring. Realising, however, that his original text was too short, he lengthened it by repeating the *salto mortale* episode and allowing the Cock to succumb twice instead of once to Reynard's wiles. The rest of the music was written at Morges.

On 29 December 1915 Stravinsky was in Paris to conduct *The Firebird* at a special gala performance given by the Russian Ballet at the Opera House to raise funds for the Red Cross. Three days later Diaghilev and his company sailed for New York, leaving Stravinsky behind. He took advantage of this opportunity to call on his friend the Princess Edmond de Polignac.[2] In her *Memoirs* the Princess wrote: 'My intention at that time was to ask different composers to write short works for me for small orchestra of about twenty performers. I had the impression that, after Richard Wagner and Richard Strauss, the days of big orchestras were over, and that it would be delightful to return to a small orchestra of well chosen players and instrument.' She offered Stravinsky a commission fee of 2,500 Swiss francs for *Reynard*, which he was delighted to accept, for the war had cut him off from the income derived from his Russian estate, and there were no royalties coming in from the Russian Ballet or his publishers.

The Princess's commission determined the choice of a small chamber ensemble, though Stravinsky points out that he could have used a larger orchestra had he wished (*Exp*). The March with which the action opens and closes was the last part of the score to be written.

Music

The *guzla* which is supposed to accompany the 'plink . . . plink . . .' *pribaoutka* set Stravinsky a problem to solve. As he says, 'the *guzla* is a museum piece now, and it was rare even in my childhood in St. Petersburg. A kind of

---

[1] Fig. 62.
[2] This visit must have been in January 1916 and not April 1915 as stated in Stravinsky's *Expositions*.

goat-string balalaika, it is strapped over the player's head like the tray of a cigarette girl in a night club. The sound produced is deliciously live and bright' (*Exp*). He needed to find a substitute instrument, and here he had a stroke of good luck.

Sometime in 1915, Ernest Ansermet had taken him to hear Aladar Racz play the Hungarian cimbalom at Maxim's Bar, Geneva. Racz has vividly described this meeting.[1] 'Ansermet asked me if I could play a solo; but I answered that that was virtually impossible because of the noise. Ansermet then asked the proprietor to call for silence, and I played a Serbian *kolo*, at which Ansermet's companion rushed forward to the cimbalom. He was wearing a monocle, a red tie, a green waistcoat and a tight jacket. It was Igor Stravinsky. He struggled with his sleeve in order to shoot out his cuff, on which he wanted to note down the music. As a young man I was rather too sure of myself; and I looked him up and down thinking "You won't be able to take down what I'm playing!" And indeed he soon stopped taking notes.'

Stravinsky was fascinated by the trapezoid shape of the cimbalom, its full rich timbre, and the special stick technique used in playing it. He immediately decided to buy an instrument for himself: so he called on Racz early one morning, and together they went to visit an old Hungarian gipsy who had one for sale. According to Racz's wife,[2] 'Stravinsky tried to produce new sounds by striking the strings on the wrong side of the bridge; but the old gipsy stopped him at once, snatching the sticks from his hands and explaining that that was not the way to play the instrument. He was obviously afraid that his customer would not buy it if he were dissatisfied by its sonority; and he naturally couldn't understand that Stravinsky particularly wanted to use it to produce unnatural sounds – something that might possibly imitate the cries of animals.'

Clearly the cimbalom was just the right sort of instrument to imitate the *guzla* in the 'plink . . . plink . . .' *pribaoutka*, and this meant that it ought also to play an important part in the rest of the score. When it came to the point, *Reynard* was actually composed on the cimbalom, whereas hitherto Stravinsky had always used the piano as his medium for composition (*Exp*).

This had a definite effect on the style of the work. The timbre of the cimbalom gives a rich, raucous tang to the sound of the chamber orchestra; and its special technique, with its fast-moving, far-ranging scales and *arpeggi*, and its ability to repeat notes or to trill with considerable rapidity, is exploited with virtuosity. The flourish with which it greets each of Reynard's entries might almost be taken as a motto for the whole work, viz.:

---

[1] From a radio broadcast of 1956 quoted in his wife's article 'Igor Stravinsky vu par le cymbaliste Aladar Racz' printed in *Feuilles Musicales*. Lausanne, March–April 1962. See also Pierre Meylan's study, *Une amitié célèbre*. Lausanne, 1961. Translation by E. W. W.
[2] In the article already referred to.

Ex. 25

The cimbalom part is certainly of *concertante* importance[1] and in view of this, it is not surprising to find that Stravinsky frequently consulted Racz during its composition, usually by sending him postcards on which he had written a few bars of the cimbalom part with a metronome indication, and asking if these passages were playable.[2] It should be noticed that the score makes special provision for a cimbalom without a low D, in which case certain out-of-range passages are to be shared between the cello and/or double bass and/or timpani.

It is interesting to find that, apart from the writing for cimbalom, the composer's main concern in dealing with this chamber ensemble was directed to the wind and brass rather than the strings. The latter help to point the way the music is stressed and articulated and frequently offer accompanying figures; but the brass and particularly the woodwind are as busy as the voices in proliferating melodies and counter-melodies.

The vocal writing recalls that of *Pribaoutki* and the *Cat's Cradle Songs* – with one important exception. Whereas in the earlier songs each melodic limb was usually confined within a fairly narrow compass, in *Reynard* Stravinsky does not hesitate to use wide intervals – leaps of a sixth, seventh, octave, ninth, tenth and even a double octave (with some of the high notes falsetto) are quite common – and these help to emphasise the overweening assurance of the Cock and the wheedling astuteness of Reynard. The melos is based on a variety of modes; and as the different melodies follow each other closely or combine together, the texture becomes increasingly polymodal.

Passages with block harmonies appear at climaxes, particularly where the captured Cock calls on the Cat and Goat to deliver him.[3] Such passages are a foretaste of *The Wedding*. And there is a particularly interesting anticipation of the *Symphonies of Wind Instruments* in two bars of the 'plink . . . plink . . .' *pribaoutka*.[4]

The metre is more varied than in the *Pribaoutki* and *Cat's Cradle Songs*, but much less complex than in *The Rite of Spring*. There are some examples of compound metres, e.g. the 7/8 stringendo when Reynard captures the Cock,[5]

---

[1] It should be mentioned that about 1954 Stravinsky authorised the performance of a version of *Reynard* at the 'Evenings on the Roof' concerts at Los Angeles with piano replacing cimbalom.
[2] Pierre Meylan, *op. cit.*
[3] Figs. 22 and 55.
[4] See the third and fourth bar after fig. 67.
[5] Figs. 20 and 53.

and a brief but interesting passage with a cumulative ostinato in the bassoon –
a basic figure of six quavers, with two quavers added at each repetition, making
a pattern of 6 + 8 + 10 + 12.[1]

It is fascinating to see how Stravinsky has achieved a satisfactory form for
this work, while using musical material which by its very nature is short and
terse, and which is usually not subjected to development. The one exception is
perhaps the *grazioso* passage[2] after the first intervention by the Cock and
Goat, where the main theme is developed by oboe, bassoon and trumpet and
brought to a fugato climax. The repetition of Reynard's attempt to seduce the
Cock allows some of the material to be repeated (in its original key), and this
helps to give the score a certain degree of formal symmetry.

Reynard may not be one of Stravinsky's most popular works, but it is
indubitably one of his most original creations.

Production

Although (as has been mentioned above) *Reynard* was commissioned in
1916 by the Princess Edmond de Polignac, there was no particular plan for its
production at that time.

A few years after the war, Diaghilev expressed interest in it, and it was
produced by the Russian Ballet at the Opera House, Paris, on 18 May 1922.
The décor and costumes were by Michel Larionov, and the choreography by
Nijinska (who also danced the title role). The orchestra was conducted by
Ansermet. Stravinsky has placed it on record that this production gave him
the greatest satisfaction, both musically and scenically (*Chr*). But Diaghilev
had made a miscalculation in mounting it within the enormous framework
of the Paris Opera House. So intimate a work needed to be heard and seen in
smaller-scale surroundings if it was to prove effective.

At the same time it must be admitted that it is a difficult piece for any ballet
company to keep in its repertory. It is short; and each performance demands
careful preparation and presentation. Perhaps in the course of time it will be
found to be ideal for television.

32. FIVE EASY PIECES

For piano duet (easy right hand). Composed at Morges, 1916/17. Dedicated
'à Madame Eugenia Errazuriz – hommage très respecteux'. Published by Ad.
Henn, Geneva, 1917 (later by J. & W. Chester). Duration: *c.* 9 minutes. First
performance by José Iturbi and the composer, Lausanne, 8 November 1919.
MS comp. [C 18] and [C 68].

---

[1] Fig. 72.
[2] Figs. 29–38. The 'grazioso' direction is missing from the vocal score.

1. *Andante*
2. *Española*
3. *Balalaika*
4. *Napolitana*
5. *Galop*

By 1916 Stravinsky's elder children, Theodore and Mika, had made sufficient progress in their musical studies for him to wish to write them a set of piano duets with easy right hand. They were given easy melodies to play, frequently doubled at the octave. Simple keys were chosen so as to avoid accidentals as far as possible; and any complicated passage-work was put into the bass. For instance, the left-hand accompaniment to *Española* is quite thickly written and tricky to play, and it takes a good pianist not to overweight the light, slowly moving melody in the treble.

The *Española* was written after his trip to Spain in 1916; the *Napolitana* after his visit to Naples the following year. The *Balalaika*[1] and the *Galop* followed; and the last number to be written was the *Andante* prelude. This *Andante* is in serious vein; but the remaining four numbers are distinguished by high spirits, occasional distortions and a marked tendency towards satire.

Orchestration

The *Eight Piano Duets* (nos. 28 and 32) were orchestrated at various times between 1917 and 1925 to form two Suites, as follows:

(A) SUITE No. 1 for small orchestra (2.1.2.2 – 1.1.1.1 – bass drum – string 5tet). Instrumented between 1917 and 1925. The full score is dated 31 December 1925. Published by J. & W. Chester. Duration: *c*. 5 minutes. MS comp. [C 46].

1. *Andante* (transposed up a whole tone)
2. *Napolitana*
3. *Española*
4. *Balalaika*

(B) SUITE (No. 2) for small orchestra (2.1.2.2 – 1.2.[2]1.1 – percussion, piano[3] – string 5tet). Instrumented in 1921. Published by J. & W. Chester. Duration: *c*. 7 minutes. The MS is with J. & W. Chester.

1. *March*
2. *Waltz* (transposed from C to D)
3. *Polka*
4. *Galop*

[1] In his *Memories*, Stravinsky points out that the melody in the *Balalaika* is his own original composition, and in his *Dialogues* he says this number is his favourite.
[2] The second trumpet (in A) appears only in the *Galop*.
[3] The piano appears only in the *March* and the *Galop*.

2. Register of Works

The second Suite (which preceded the first in point of time) was written in 1921 at the request of a Paris music-hall which wanted incidental music for a little sketch.[1] In his *Chronicle* he wrote: 'Although my orchestra was more than modest, the composition as I wrote it was given only at the first few performances. When I went to see the sketch again a month later, I found that there was but little left of what I had written. Everything was completely muddled; some instruments were lacking or had been replaced by others, and the music itself as executed by this pitiful band had become unrecognisable. It was a good lesson. . . .'

In later years the score of these two suites was used for various ballets, including *Petite Suite* with choreography by José Limon (New York, Stadium Concerts, 1936); *Capricci alla Stravinsky* with choreography by Aurel Milloss (Rome, Teatro delle Arte, 1943); *Afterthoughts* with choreography by Jerome Robbins (New York, American-Russian Friendship Society, 1946); *Les Baladins* with choreography by Michel Descombey (Paris, Opéra Comique, 1958).

33. TROIS HISTOIRES POUR ENFANTS – THREE TALES FOR CHILDREN

For voice and piano. Words from Russian popular texts: French translation by C. F. Ramuz. Dedication 'Pour mon fils cadet'. Published by J. & W. Chester, 1920. Duration: *c.* 2 minutes.

1. 'Тилимъ-бомъ' – 'Tilimbom'. Composed at Morges, 22 May 1917
2. 'Гуси, Лебеди . . .' – 'Les canards, les cygnes, les oies . . .' Morges, 21 June (?) 1917
3. 'Пѣсенка Медвѣдя' – 'Chanson de l'ours'. Morges, 30 December 1915 (o.s.)

MSS with J. & W. Chester. MSS of 'Tilimbom' and 'L'Ours' with the composer [C 12], [C 16] and [C 22].

In these three songs Stravinsky continues his exploration of the animal world: cat, goat and cock in 'Tilimbom'; ducks, swans, geese and fleas in the second song; and a bear in the third. In 'Tilimbom', where a fire breaks out in the farmyard, the contrasted bell-like chimes in the accompaniment are splendidly suited to their different pianistic registers and the fire alarm rings out tocsin clear over an ostinato bass (see Ex. 30). In the second song, there is an effective contrast in the voice between the main part of each line which is set to bustling quaver phrases with an occasional semiquaver division, while the feminine line-endings are treated in augmentation and set to crotchets.

The 'Bear's Song' is a nursery rhyme that comes in the middle of a story by Afanasiev about an old woodcutter and his wife. The woodcutter has chopped

[1] In the MS score there are indications that a man or a woman in this sketch sang several phrases in the Polka.

off one of the bear's paws and the wife is about to cook it. The bear makes himself a birch paw, pursues the woodcutter into his hut and chases the woodcutter and his wife round the room, until he finally corners them and eats them. The vocal part is confined to the first five notes of the scale of C major repeated above an ostinato of two notes only, A flat followed by D flat, sounding like the bear's lumbering footsteps.[1]

Instrumentations

'Tilimbom' for voice and orchestra (3.2.2.0 – 2.1.0.0 – timpani– string 5tet). In this version, written at Biarritz in December 1923, the song is lengthened from its original 36 bars to 64. Published by J. & W. Chester. MS with J. & W. Chester.

In 1954 the first two songs were re-instrumented for flute, harp and guitar and form part of *Four Songs*, cf. no. 43 (A).

THE SONG OF THE NIGHTINGALE

Symphonic Poem for orchestra, 1917 – see no. 24 (A).

34. VALSE POUR LES ENFANTS – A WALTZ FOR CHILDREN

For piano. Composed at Morges about 1917. Published in *Le Figaro*,[2] 21 May 1922. MS comp. [C 17].

This rather charming little waltz (56 bars long) can be looked on as a forerunner of the pieces in *The Five Fingers*. The bass is a two-bar ostinato using only five notes; but the tune in the treble ranges more widely, covering thirteen notes within the compass of an eleventh. (See p. 248.)

35. ПОДБЛЮДНЫЯ – FOUR RUSSIAN PEASANT SONGS ('SAUCERS')

For female voices unaccompanied. Words after Afanasiev's collection of Russian popular texts. First performance, Geneva, 1917 (conducted by Vassily Kibalchich). Duration: *c*. 3 minutes. MS comp. [C 14] and [C 16].

1. 'У Спаса въ Чигисахъ' – 'On Saints' Days in Chigisakh'. Morges, 22 October 1916. (4-part chorus)

---

[1] Like the *Pribaoutki*, this song also influenced some of Edith Sitwell's early poems. See particularly 'Dark Song' in *Bucolic Comedies* and Malinn's Song in section XIV of *The Sleeping Beauty*.

[2] There it is described (in a facsimile of Stravinsky's own handwriting) as 'Une valse pour les petits lecteurs du "Figaro"'. The suggestion in the newspaper heading that the waltz was 'improvisée' is incorrect.

VALSE POUR LES ENFANTS

Improvisée au *Figaro* par

IGOR STRAWINSKY

COLLECTION PARTICULIÈRE DU *FIGARO*

Igor Strawinsky

Mai 1922

'Valse pour les Enfants' – copy of the first (and so far only) publication of this work in *Le Figaro*, 21 May 1922

Original Compositions

2. 'Овсень' – 'Ovsen'.[1] Morges, 1917. (2-part chorus)
3. 'Щука' – 'The Pike'.[2] Salvan, 1914. (3 solo voices and 4-part chorus)
4. 'Пузище' – 'Master Portly'.[3] 1915 (1 solo voice and 4-part chorus)

Publication

Although J. & W. Chester's contract with the composer for this work is dated December 1919, publication by that firm was delayed until 1932, when the songs appeared with Russian, French and English texts. The German rights were handled by Schott's, whose edition (with Russian and German texts) preceded the Chester edition and appeared about 1930, just before the publication of the *Violin Concerto*.

Genesis

In *Expositions*, Stravinsky explains that 'choruses of this sort were sung by the peasants while fortune-tellers read their fingerprints on the smoke-blackened bottoms of saucers' and suggests that the title 'Saucer-readings' or 'Saucer-riddles' might be closer in meaning to the Russian original. Judging from the place-names mentioned, e.g., Chigisakh and Bielaozero, he assumes the texts (which are taken from Afanasiev) to be North Russian in origin, adding: 'Probably they are from the neighbourhood of Pskov, but whether saucer sorcery was peculiar to that part of Russia, I am unable to say.'

These *a cappella* choruses for women's voices are diverting examples of Stravinsky's Russian popular idiom, very close in style to parts of *The Wedding*. Sometimes the verse sections are separated by gay choral refrains, which in the cases of nos. 1 and 3 are no more than brief, repeated cries, and this gives an element of dynamic contrast and relief.

New Version (1954)

For equal voices with accompaniment of four horns. Composed 1954. Published by J. & W. Chester with English words, 1958. (No translator's name given.) First performance, 'Monday Evening Concerts', Los Angeles, conducted by Robert Craft, 11 October 1954. Duration: *c*. 3 minutes 40 seconds.

In this new version, the choral part has been left almost intact, though the barring is frequently changed – presumably for greater ease in conducting. The first song now has a *da capo* repeat, and the second song has been transposed a major third higher. Each song is preluded by an upward flourish for two horns, the second horn following in close canonic imitation of the first; and this feature is used as a *ritornello* in the third song. The style of writing

---

[1] A beneficent solar deity honoured in Russian mythology.
[2] The text describes a mighty pike which has swum the length of the old waterway from the White Sea through Lake Ladoga to Novgorod, a distance of several hundred miles.
[3] Master Portly is a sack like a large belly containing seeds, which are scattered over a turnip field and turn out to be lice and fleas.

recalls the trumpet fanfares in the opening and closing movements of *Agon*, which were being composed about the same time.

Apart from these preludial flourishes, the horns accompany the voices, sometimes by canonic imitation, sometimes by adding one or two parts to a passage where the voices are already singing in two parts. In the third song, the third solo voice part (low alto) is transferred to one of the horns and a second horn part added, producing a passage in four-part harmony (two vocal parts and two horns). The horns are rarely in unison with the voices, except during the forte choral refrains. A sprightly instrumental coda has been added to no. 1.[1]

36. CANONS FOR TWO HORNS

This work (written in 1917) is unpublished. According to Robert Craft,[2] Stravinsky's daughter Ludmilla 'was once in grave danger from an appendix and was saved by a Swiss doctor who would take no payment from Stravinsky but music. The doctor was a horn player and Stravinsky sent him a set of canons for two horns, which one may hope still exists with the family of Dr. Roux, somewhere in the neighbourhood of Geneva'.

37. СВАДЕБКА – LES NOCES – THE WEDDING[3]

Russian choreographic scenes[4] with song and music. Written for four part chorus (SATB) with four soloists (soprano, mezzo-soprano, tenor, bass) and an orchestra consisting of 4 pianos, xylophone, timpani, 2 crotales and a bell, together with 2 side drums (with and without snare), 2 drums (with and without snare), tambourine, bass drum, cymbals and triangle. Words adapted by I. Stravinsky from Russian popular texts collected by Afanasiev and Kireievsky; French translation by C. F. Ramuz; English translation by D. Millar Craig. Begun at Clarens in 1914, and the short score finished at Morges on 4 April 1917. After various attempts at different instrumentations had been discarded, the form of the final and definitive instrumentation was decided on at Garches in 1921, and the work was carried out at Biarritz the following year and finished at Monaco on 6 April 1923. Dedicated to Serge de Diaghilev. Vocal score by the composer; published by J. & W. Chester, 1922.[5] Duration:

---

[1] In the third song, a *da capo* repeat from the last bar but two, although not marked in the score, is in fact made in the recording conducted by Stravinsky himself on Philips AO1493L.
[2] 'A Personal Preface'. *The Score*, June 1957.
[3] In *Expositions* Stravinsky says that 'Little Wedding' would be the best equivalent of the Russian title, if 'little' could be made to mean not 'small' but 'peasant'.
[4] In the programme of the first London production (1926), the ballet was subtitled 'Village Wedding Customs'.
[5] The full score was published by J. & W. Chester a year or two later.

c. 35 minutes. First performance, Russian Ballet, Théâtre de la Gaieté Lyrique, Paris, 13 June 1923, conducted by Ernest Ansermet.

This cantata is constructed in two parts as follows, and the different scenes follow each other without pause.

Part One

    Scene 1: 'At the Bride's House' ('The Tresses')
    Scene 2: 'At the Bridegroom's House'
    Scene 3: 'The Bride's Departure'

Part Two

    Scene 4: 'The Wedding Feast' ('The Red Table')

About half a dozen pages of some of the MS sketches were presented by Stravinsky to Lord Berners in an illuminated folder. The bulk of the remaining sketches, including the full orchestral score of the 1917 version, were sold to Werner Reinhart for 5,000 Swiss francs and are now in the Stiftung Rychenberg, Winterthur. The MS of the final score is with J. & W. Chester Ltd. Other MS material is in the composer's collection [C 42].

Composition and Instrumentation

According to Stravinsky the idea of writing a dance cantata based on the subject of a Russian peasant wedding occurred to him as early as 1912 (*Exp*). At that time he was completely immersed in *The Rite of Spring*, and it wasn't until 1914 that the work began to take definite shape in his mind. After visiting London for the first performance of *The Nightingale* that June,[1] he decided he would have to return to Russia to collect the necessary material for the libretto: so, taking train from Switzerland (where he and his family had just settled at Salvan in the Valais), he journeyed to Ustilug in July and went on to Kiev where he found a copy of Kireievsky's great collection of Russian Popular Poems.[2] He also brought back with him Sakharov's Collection and Dal's Dictionary of Russian Phrases, which had been in his father's library. The Kireievsky collection included an extensive group of wedding songs, which he drew on for his text. As he says, *The Wedding* 'is a suite of typical wedding episodes told through quotations of typical talk. . . . As a collection of clichés and quotations of typical wedding sayings it might be compared to one of those scenes in *Ulysses* in which the reader seems to be overhearing scraps of conversation without the connecting thread of discourse' (*Exp*). (By 'discourse' in this connotation he seems to mean 'description'.) Most of these conversational tags and scraps seem to be based on folk material; but in his *Conversations*, Stravinsky recalls that when Kireievsky was compiling this collection,

---

[1] See p. 49.
[2] *Sobranniye Piesni.* 10 vols. Moscow, 1868–74.

he asked Pushkin to show him his collection of folk verse, 'and Pushkin sent him some verses with a note reading: "Some of these are my own verses; can you tell the difference?" Kireievsky could not, and took them all for his book' – so (suggests Stravinsky) perhaps there is a line or two of Pushkin's in the libretto of *The Wedding*.

The two-part layout of the libretto means that in Part One there are substantial elements of ritualistic lamentation (e.g., the bride lamenting the loss of her virginity, and the mothers of the bride and bridegroom lamenting the loss of their children) and of ritualistic prayer (e.g., the bridegroom imploring his parents' blessing, and the chorus of friends calling on God, the Virgin Mary and the saints, particularly Cosmos, Damien and Luka, to bless the marriage), while Part Two contains the slightly coarse and tipsy fun of the guests at the wedding feast, followed by the bedding of the bride and groom. All this produces the impression of a typical Russian peasant wedding of the early nineteenth century.

Although various characters emerge from the libretto – the bride Nastasia and her groom Fetis, their parents, the *svat*, the marriage-broker, the best man, bridesmaids, friends etc. – Stravinsky follows the usage he established in *Reynard* of refusing to identify any particular character with any particular singer. For instance, the bridegroom's words are frequently sung by a tenor; but at the end of the cantata his final apostrophe to his bride –

> *Dear Heart, dear Wife, my own,*
> *Dearest treasure, my sweet, my honey,*
> *Fairest flower, let us live in happiness*
> *So that all men may envy us. –*

is entrusted to a bass. And the stichomythia passage in the Wedding Feast –[1]

> *Hear the Bridegroom saying –*
> *'I would sleep now,'*
> *And the Bride replying –*
> *'Take me with you'.*
> *Hear the Bridegroom saying –*
> *'Is the bed narrow?'*
> *And the Bride replying –*
> *'Not too narrow.' etc. –*

is set antiphonally for chorus (sopranos and altos) and a trio of soloists (soprano, mezzo-soprano and tenor) who speak for both bride and groom.

Not only did Stravinsky string together these various scraps and tags of popular verse to form a connected libretto, but he also arranged the dialogue – particularly in the second part – so that occasionally there is an overlap, two

---

[1] Fig. 114.

252

or more different strands of conversation being deployed simultaneously in a kind of verbal counterpoint.

The composition of the music was begun at Clarens in the late summer or autumn of 1914. The following winter he and his family spent about two months at the Château d'Oex. They were quartered in a hotel where Stravinsky found it impossible to compose. In his *Chronicle* he writes: 'I was anxious, therefore, to find a piano in some place where I could work in peace. . . . A music dealer of whom I made my first enquiries provided me with a sort of lumber-room, full of empty *Chocolat Suchard* packing-cases, which opened on to a chicken-run. It contained a little upright piano, quite new and out of tune. The cold in this room, which was devoid of any heating apparatus, was so acute that the piano strings had succumbed to it. For two days I tried to work there in overcoat, fur cap, and snow-boots, with a rug over my knees. But I could not go on like that. Finally I found in the village a spacious and comfortable room in a house belonging to lower middle-class folk who were out all day. I had a piano installed there, and at last could devote myself to my work.' By the time Diaghilev and his entourage came to Switzerland from Rome in the spring of 1915 and settled at Bellerive, Ouchy, the first two scenes of *The Wedding* were ready in short score; and when Stravinsky played them over for the first time, the impresario was so moved that he burst into tears, saying this would certainly prove to be 'the most beautiful and the most purely Russian creation' of the Russian Ballet (*Exp*). For his part, Stravinsky was so touched by this spontaneous outburst of enthusiasm that he decided to dedicate the score to his friend. But further progress was delayed by work on *Reynard*; and it wasn't until the beginning of 1917, when Stravinsky and his family had moved from the Villa Rogie Vue to the Villa Bornand in Morges, that intensive work on the score was resumed. C. F. Ramuz, who was already working on the French translation of the text, has described[1] how Stravinsky turned one of the attic rooms into a studio, reached by a half-hidden wooden staircase well barricaded by doors, and how of a summer afternoon the sound of the composer at his piano and percussion instruments could be heard in the little square outside, where two or three women were usually to be found on a bench, knitting in the shade of the trees. These would raise their heads for a moment in bewilderment, and then with an indulgent 'C'est le monsieur russe!' resume their knitting.

The short score was finished by April 1917.

From the outset, the work had been conceived as a cantata: so the writing for voices took precedence. The singing starts without instrumental preliminary at the beginning of Part One and continues unbroken until the end of Part Two, when there is a brief instrumental coda 21 bars long. There are no instrumental interludes or ritornelli.

---

[1] In *Souvenirs sur Igor Stravinsky*. Editions Mermod, Lausanne, 1929.

2. Register of Works

The instrumentation of *The Wedding* posed a problem that Stravinsky found difficult to solve. To begin with, he scored the first scene for a monster orchestra. According to André Schaeffner,[1] his idea was 'to establish two categories of sound: *wind* (including voices) and *percussion*: the first would be provided by the choir, woodwind and brass, the second by two string orchestras, the one playing pizzicato and the other with the bow. Only a few pages were written of a score needing about 150 players for performance, which made the work virtually unplayable'. The next stage was a decision 'to divide the various instrumental elements – strings, woodwinds, brass, percussion, keyboard (cimbalom, harpsichord, piano) – into groups and to keep these groups separate on the stage' (*Exp*). This orchestral version was virtually complete by the autumn of 1917; but he then thought of what seemed to be a simpler solution, consisting of 'an electrically driven mechanical piano and harmonium, an *ensemble* of percussion instruments and two Hungarian cimbaloms' (*Chr*). This orchestra included two keyed bugles or flugelhorns[2] as well (*Exp*). But although the first two scenes were instrumented on these lines in 1919, the difficulties of being able to find two good cimbalom players whenever the work was to be performed and of synchronising the mechanical elements with the singers and the non-mechanical instrumentalists proved too great, and this project too had to be abandoned.

In 1921, when he was staying with Gabrielle Chanel at Garches, he at last found the definitive solution – the vocal part was to be accompanied by an orchestra of·percussion divided into instruments with and without definite pitch, viz., four (non-mechanical) pianos, xylophone, timpani, two crotales (tuned to B natural and C sharp) and a bell, as opposed to two side drums (with and without snare), two drums (with and without snare), tambourine, bass drum, cymbals and triangle. The greater part of the instrumentation was carried out at Biarritz in 1922, and the orchestral score was completed at Monaco on 6 April 1923.

Music

The melos of the vocal writing in *The Wedding* is modal and mainly non-chromatic, and the musical metres closely follow the varied and often irregular pattern of the verbal metres of the Russian popular texts. The idiom is a development of the vocal style of writing Stravinsky had already established in the third number of *Saucers*, and some of the *Pribaoutki, Cat's Cradle Songs* and *Tales for Children*.

The melodic material is all original, with the exception of two, possibly three tunes. In the second scene of Part One the bridegroom's request for a blessing –

---

[1] *Strawinsky*. Les Editions Reider, Paris, 1931. Translation by E. W. W.
[2] In his *Conversations* Stravinsky says that hearing Shorty Roger's trumpet playing in Los Angeles in 1957 reminded him of the keyed bugles he wanted to write for in *The Wedding* and influenced him in choosing that instrument for the orchestra in *Threni*.

> *Bless me, my father, my mother,*
> *Bless your child who proudly goes*
> *Against the strong wall of stone*
> *To break it. –*

sung as an unaccompanied duet by two bass voices,[1] is (according to Schaeffner)[2] a slightly altered liturgical theme taken from a collection of chants for the Octave services. The theme in the Wedding Feast that makes its first appearance when the bride sings 'I have donn'd a golden belt'[3] is a workers' melody, a proletarian song, and was given Stravinsky by his friend Stepan Mitusov as early as 1906 or 1907 (*Mem*). Another theme in the same scene, a staccato syncopated interjection from the hiccuping bass – 'I have lost the golden ring with precious stones'[4] – is a reminiscence of the drunken singing of two Vaudois revellers who were in the same compartment with Stravinsky when he was returning from Château d'Oex to Clarens in the Montreux-Bernese Oberland train at the end of January 1915. It is typical of his method of composition that the 'Tresses' theme with which the cantata opens

Ex. 26

Sop. Solo

should be altered to fit the characteristic syncopations of the 'Drunk' theme, thereby becoming the main subject of the last section of Part Two.[5]

The greater part of the original melodic material in *The Wedding* is developed from a single 'cell', the interval of a fourth divided into a major second and minor third.

Ex. 27a

(The 'cell' (a) with its reversal (b) is given here at the same pitch as the 'Tresses' theme at the opening of the cantata.) All the following permutations of this three-note theme are also to be found in various parts of the score:

---

[1] Fig. 50.
[2] André Schaeffner, *op. cit.*
[3] Two bars after fig. 110. There are subsequent appearances at figs. 120, 124, 130–2, and in the orchestral accompaniment at fig. 125.
[4] Figs. 91, 127 & 129. As Pierre Meylan says (*op. cit*), this is the only musical contribution made by the Canton de Vaud to *The Wedding*. But it is an important one!
[5] It appears in the vocal parts at fig. 114, five bars after fig. 121, and figs. 122 and 133, and in the orchestra at figs. 93, 115, 116, 126, and from six bars before 135 fig. to the end of the work.

Ex.27 b

The 'cell' also appears with the positions of the major second and minor third reversed.

Ex.27 c

The pervasive nature of this 'cell' means that a great part of the melodic material is in the dorian or aeolian mode, according to whether the scale is made up of two conjunctive or disjunctive fourths.

The lamentations of the bridegroom's two parents in scene 2[1] –

> *Last night Pamfilievitch*
> *Sat within his house*
> *Brushing his fair locks.*
> *Now to whom will these curls belong? –*

and of the bride and bridegroom's mothers in scene 3[2] –

> *My own dear one, child of mine,*
> *Do not leave me, little one –*

are substantially the same theme. This appears in an extended form in scene 3, where after the long opening wail on two notes a semitone apart, the voice moves into a slow undulating phrase like a gentle benison.

Ex.28

---

[1] Fig. 35 *et seq.*
[2] Fig. 82 *et seq.*

Original Compositions

This is based on a hybrid scale where the presence of an augmented second produces a quasi-oriental flavour:

Ex.29

(The E is bracketed because it appears in the accompaniment, but not in the sung melody.)

It must not be thought that the themes of *The Wedding* are as short as the three-note 'cell' given above.[1] A few are brief and are repeated in varying patterns, often after an intensive climax or at a change of scene; others are fluent and fill out a phrase or sentence. Themes frequently combine and interlock in skilful counterpoint – especially in Part Two – and sometimes they are subject to a simple process of development by means of modulation. The presence of the minor third in the 'cell' motif provides a cue for the re-exposition of material at that interval;[2] and the presence of the major second leads to the bitonal use of superimposed chords with their roots a major second apart.[3]

So long as the syllables of the Russian text are set more or less evenly in accordance with Stravinsky's preferred method, irregular musical metres prevail; but as soon as the comic element comes to the fore in the 'Wedding Feast', the need for syncopation arises, and this presupposes the existence of regular metres. The beat is constant; and the whole work is carefully geared to two metronome rates of 80 or 120 to the minute.[4]

The orchestra has a subservient role to play. Its prime duty is to accompany the voices. The instruments with definite pitch underline and support the vocal part, sometimes moving in parallel strands, sometimes producing block harmonies, sometimes weaving a contrasting counterpoint, sometimes merely building up an accompanying ostinato. The instruments without definite pitch emphasise and accentuate the metrical skeleton. But at the end it is the orchestra that brings the work to a glorious conclusion.

The choral climax of the 'Wedding Feast' is marked by the chiming of a fortissimo bell chord (4 pianos in unison, 2 crotales, 1 bell). The choir stops

---

[1] The 'budding' of the melodic line from this single 'cell' is analysed in considerable detail by Victor Belaiev in his outline *Igor Stravinsky's 'Les Noces'*. Oxford University Press, London, 1928.
[2] See particularly the lamentation of the two mothers, figs. 83–85.
[3] See the climaxes of Scenes 2 & 3 (C major and D major), Part Two at fig. 94 (C sharp minor and D sharp minor), and the bell chord in the coda (B with C sharp added).
[4] With the exceptions of 11½ bars marked *poco più mosso* (♩ = 112) at fig. 40, and seven bars marked *poco meno mosso* at fig. 103. It should be noted that there is an important change of tempo from ♩ = 120 to ♩ = 80 at fig. 133, which is not marked in some copies of the full score.

singing; and a solo bass voice unaccompanied is heard chanting the opening modal theme of the cantata in its syncopated form – '*Dear Heart, dear Wife . . .*' The time signature is 3/4, and the singer's phrases are punctuated by the tolling of the bell chord on every eighth beat. The voice dies away – '*. . . so that all men may envy us*' – and the syncopated theme is taken over by the four pianos. The tolling of the bell chord continues on every eighth beat (with the exception of one chime which is three beats late);[1] and as the chorus and then the solo voice cease singing, and the main theme dies away on the pianos, pools of silence come flooding in between the measured chimes of the bell chord, and the ripples of the music pass away to the limitless horizon in a miraculously radiant close.

Production

There is no scenario to *The Wedding*, nor is there even any printed instruction about the staging and performance as was the case with *Reynard*; but the score, in addition to identifying various characters, carries a few stage directions, which deserve attention since they presumably embody some of Stravinsky's wishes for the staging of the work.

In Part One the rise of the curtain is marked at the eleventh bar. At the beginning of the coda to the third scene, there is the direction: '*Departure of the bride; everyone leaves the stage, accompanying her. The mothers of the bride and groom enter from opposite sides of the stage.*' Then, after their lamentation, '*Both mothers go out. The stage is empty.*'

In Part Two ('The Wedding Feast'), the point is marked where '*the bride's mother leads her daughter to her son-in-law*'. Half-way through the scene, '*One of the friends chooses a man and his wife from among the guests and sends them to warm the bed for the bridal pair.*' A little later, '*The bride and groom embrace.*' Near the end of the scene, '*The couple who have been warming the bed come out of the bedroom. After Fetis and Nastasia have been escorted to the bedroom and put to bed, they are left alone, and the door is closed. The two fathers-in-law and mothers-in-law seat themselves on a bench in front of the door, and all the wedding guests face them.*' And twenty-two bars before the end there is the direction '*The curtain falls slowly during the following music.*'

Stravinsky's original idea was that *The Wedding* should be a kind of *divertissement*. In his *Chronicle* he writes: 'It was not my intention to reproduce the ritual of peasant weddings, and I paid little heed to ethnological considerations. My idea was to compose a sort of scenic ceremony, using as I liked those ritualistic elements so abundantly provided by village customs which had been established for centuries in the celebration of Russian marriages. I took my inspiration from those customs, but reserved to myself the right to use

---

[1] When this discrepancy was pointed out to Stravinsky by Pierre Boulez in the course of a television programme in 1965, the composer agreed this was an error and deleted the extra bar's rest (i.e. the 10th bar after fig. 134). But after reflection, he came to the conclusion that to do so was an error – he had been less than sober at the time! – and accordingly he withdrew the deletion (*Themes and Conclusions*).

them with absolute freedom. . . . I wanted all my instrumental apparatus to be visible side by side with the actors or dancers, making it, so to speak, a participant in the whole theatrical action. For this reason, I wished to place the orchestra on the stage itself, letting the actors move on the space remaining free. The fact that the actors on the stage would wear uniform Russian-style costumes while the musicians would be in evening dress not only did not embarrass me, but, on the contrary, was perfectly in keeping with my idea of a *divertissement* of the masquerade type.'

In the event the Russian Ballet production was a compromise. Apart from the dancers, only the four pianos were on the stage, the rest of the instrumentalists and singers being in the orchestra pit. A sober simplified décor and costumes were provided by Natalia Goncharova, her earlier designs in gay peasant colouring having been rejected as unsuitable; and a beautifully austere choreography was devised by Bronislava Nijinska. Ernest Ansermet conducted; and the four pianists were Georges Auric, Edouard Flament, Hélène Léon and Marcelle Meyer. The first performance at the Théâtre de la Gaieté Lyrique, Paris, on 13 June 1923 was preceded by a private audition in concert form at the house of the Princess Edmond de Polignac.

In his *Chronicle* Stravinsky professed considerable dissatisfaction with Diaghilev's staging of the work, though he had words of praise for the décor and seemed not to dislike the choreography. In his *Memories* he is more explicit and says that Nijinska's choreography for *Reynard* and *The Wedding* pleased him more than any other of his works as presented by the Russian Ballet, and particularly praises 'her conception of *The Wedding* in blocks and masses'. In his *Expositions*, he goes further and says: 'The first staging of *The Wedding* was in general compatible with my conception of the ritualistic and non-personal. . . . The curtain was not used, and the dancers did not leave the stage even during the lamentation of the two mothers, a wailing ritual which presupposes an empty set; the empty set and all other changes of scene, from the bride's to the groom's to the church, are created solely by the music. But though the bride and groom are always present, the guests are able to talk about them as if they were not there – a stylization not unlike Kabuki theatre.'

A fascinating glimpse of Stravinsky at rehearsals of *The Wedding* at Monte Carlo is given by Serge Lifar, who at that time was in the *corps de ballet* of Diaghilev's company, having arrived from Kiev only a few months previously at the age of 17.

> Every rehearsal of *The Wedding* was attended by the composer, Igor Stravinsky, but not by any means as a simple spectator, for nothing could exceed his eager interest. To begin, he would only indicate roughly what was meant, but soon he was angrily gesticulating, and then, thoroughly aroused, would take off his coat, sit down to the piano and, reproducing all the symphonic sonority of the work, begin singing in a kind of ecstatic, but

terrible voice, which carried so much conviction that no one could have thought it comical. Often he would go on in this way till he was completely exhausted. But still, a new life would have been infused into the rehearsal, and the whole company would start dancing for all it was worth. Practice ended, he would put on his coat, raise the collar, and walk off to the bar, a weak and puny little man. And it seemed strange that this all-but-common-place looking mortal (though his individual and striking features distinguished him from all others) had a moment before, been a composer of genius.[1]

The first English performance was given by the Russian Ballet at His Majesty's Theatre, London, on 14 June 1926. Eugene Goossens conducted; and the four pianists were Georges Auric, Francis Poulenc, Vittorio Rieti and Vladimir Dukelsky. Its reception was mixed. The public was puzzled; and the press criticisms were so wilfully obtuse, if not actively hostile, that no less a person than H. G. Wells seemed to think some sort of public protest was called for. He accordingly wrote the following spirited letter (dated 18 June 1926) which was reprinted as a throwaway and handed out with the programmes at the theatre.

I have been very much astonished at the reception of *Les Noces* by several of the leading London critics. There seems to be some undercurrent of artistic politics in the business. I find in several of the criticisms to which I object, sneers at the *élite*, and in one of them a puff of some competing show. Writing as an old-fashioned popular writer, not at all of the highbrow sect, I feel bound to bear my witness on the other side. I do not know of any other ballet so interesting, so amusing, so fresh or nearly so exciting as *Les Noces*. I want to see it again and again, and because I want to do so I protest against this conspiracy of wilful stupidity that may succeed in driving it out of the programme.

How wilful the stupidity is, the efforts of one of our professional guides of taste to consider the four grand pianos on the stage as part of the scene, bear witness.

Another of these guardians of culture treats the amusing plainness of the backcloth, with its single window to indicate one house and its two windows for the other, as imaginative poverty – even he could have thought of a stove and a table; – and they all cling to the suggestion that Stravinsky has tried to make marriage 'attractive' and failed in the attempt. Of course they make jokes about the mothers-in-law; that was unavoidable. It will be an extraordinary loss to the London public if this deliberate dullness of its advisers robs it of *Les Noces*.

That ballet is a rendering in sound and vision of the peasant soul, in its

---

[1] Serge Lifar, *Serge Diaghilev*. Putnam, London, 1940.

gravity, in its deliberate and simple-minded intricacy, in its subtly varied rhythms, in its deep undercurrents of excitement, that will astonish and delight every intelligent man or woman who goes to see it. The silly pretty-pretty tradition of Watteau and Fragonard is flung aside. Instead of fancy dress peasants we have peasants in plain black and white, and the smirking flirtatiousness of Daphnis and Chloe gives place to a richly humourous solemnity. It was an amazing experience to come out from this delightful display with the warp and woof of music and vision still running and inter-weaving in one's mind, and find a little group of critics flushed with resent-ment and ransacking the stores of their minds for cheap trite depreciation of the freshest and strongest thing that they had had a chance to praise for a long time.   (*Signed*) H. G. WELLS

English musical criticism was at a very low ebb in the 1920's, and H. G. Wells's generous and perceptive letter brought a breath of fresh air into a particularly fetid atmosphere.

The Nijinska version of the ballet was revived in New York by the Ballet Russe de Monte Carlo in 1936 and at the Royal Opera House, Covent Garden, by the Royal Ballet on 23 March 1966; and about half a dozen other versions have been produced in Europe and America.

38. STUDY

For pianola. Composed at Morges and Les Diablerets, 1917. Dedicated to Madame Eugenia Errazuriz.[1] Published by the Aeolian Company Ltd., London (Pianola roll T967 B). First performance, the Aeolian Hall, London 13 October 1921. Duration: *c.* 2 minutes 15 seconds. The manuscript was presented to Madame Eugenia Errazuriz. A notebook sketch dated 10 Nov-ember 1917 is in the composer's collection [C 21] and [C 35].

Stravinsky paid his first visit to Spain in the spring of 1916, when he went to Madrid to meet Diaghilev on his return from North America. In his *Chronicle* he mentions how much he enjoyed spending the evenings in Spanish taverns 'listening to the preliminary improvisations of the guitarist and the deep-voiced singer with astonishing breath control singing her long Arab cantilena embellished with *fioriture*'. The following year when the Aeolian Company of London asked him to compose a work expressly for pianola,[2] he produced a *Study* in the Spanish style. 'Many of the musicians who had preceded me in visiting Spain had, on their return, put their impressions on record in works devoted to the music they had heard there – first and foremost Glinka, with his incomparable *Jota Aragonaise* and *A Night in Madrid* – and on my side I

[1] The authority for this dedication and the presentation of the MS is Paul Collaer.
[2] He had originally seen a demonstration of the pianola by the Aeolian Company in London in the summer of 1914. For his other arrangements for player-piano, see Appendix D.

was delighted to conform with this custom. This piece was inspired by the surprising results of the mixture of strains from the mechanical pianos and orchestrinas in the streets and little night taverns of Madrid' (*Chr*).

This *Study* lies midway between the *Española* of the *Five Easy Pieces* and the *Royal March* of *The Soldier's Tale*. The main theme is distinguished by the sort of vocal *fioriture* characteristic of Spanish singing and suffers from the pianola's inability to sustain long legato notes. Much use is made of the triplet cadence which is also characteristic of the Spanish idiom. Every register of the pianola is exploited, and at times the chording is rather thick.

Transcription

For two pianos, entitled *Madrid*. Published by Boosey & Hawkes, 1951. According to the title-page, this transcription was made by Stravinsky's son Soulima from the *Four Studies for Orchestra*: so it is uncertain whether it literally reproduces the original pianola score or not.

Orchestration

Subsequently this *Study* was orchestrated and under the title *Madrid* it formed the fourth of the *Four Studies for Orchestra*, the first three being orchestral versions of the *Three Pieces for String Quartet* (see no. 20).

38 (A). FOUR STUDIES

For orchestra (3.3.4.2 – 4.3.2.1 – timpani, piano, harp – string 5tet). The orchestration of the first three Studies was begun in 1914 and finished at Morges, 1918; the set of four was completed on 2 October 1928. Published by Edition Russe de Musique[1] (later by Boosey & Hawkes). First performance, Berlin, 7 November 1930. Duration: *c.* 12 minutes. MS comp. [C 8], [C 51] and [C 53].

1. *Dance*
2. *Eccentric*
3. *Canticle*
4. *Madrid*

The only changes in the *Three Pieces for String Quartet* in their new orchestral guise are the addition of four bars accompaniment at fig. 6 of *Eccentric* leading up to the flute solo and a rebarring of part of the *Canticle* in a not altogether successful attempt to rationalise some of the triplet groupings. The third and fourth trumpets and the third and fourth trombones are used only in *Madrid*.

The instrumentation helps these four pieces to take on an extra dimension.

[1] This score is chock full of misprints. An informative article by Norman Del Mar clarifying the position appeared in *The Score* (October 1957) under the title 'Confusion and Error'.

The chanter and drone effects of the *Dance* are more clearly underlined. *Eccentric* now sounds like a sequel to the puppet music in *Petrushka*. The *Canticle* glows with the colours of an ikon. The full cubistic intricacy of *Madrid* is revealed without losing the important local colour provided by the timbre of the piano.

39. BERCEUSE

For voice and piano. Russian words by I. Stravinsky; French translation by C. F. Ramuz. Dedicated 'à ma fillette'. Composed at Morges, 10 December 1917. Published by Faber and Faber, London, in *Expositions and Developments*, 1962. Duration *c.* 45 seconds. MS comp. [C 14] and [C 35].

This lullaby for Stravinsky's little daughter Ludmila, known familiarly as Mika or Mitoucha, is mentioned in his *Chronicle* in connection with 'Tilimbom' and the 'Bear's Song' (of the *Three Tales for Children*). It comes from one of the manuscript sketch books, in which he wrote out various little pieces for his children.[1] It is characteristic of the Russian popular idiom he was using at that moment that while the vocal melody is in G major (with a tendency to slip into E Aeolian), the bass has a flattened seventh (F natural), which pulls the tonality towards C.

One of the reasons for Stravinsky's decision not to publish this 'Berceuse' with the *Three Tales for Children* may have been because the notes of this bass are identical with those of the ostinato bass in 'Tilimbom'.

40. DUET FOR TWO BASSOONS

This work was sketched out in 1918, but is unpublished. MS Comp. [C 28].

41. HISTOIRE DU SOLDAT – THE SOLDIER'S TALE

To be read, played and danced, in two parts. French libretto by C. F. Ramuz. English translations by (i) Rosa Newmarch and (ii) Michael Flanders and

---

[1] See 'A Personal Preface', by Robert Craft. *The Score*, June 1957.

2. Register of Works

Kitty Black; German translation, adapted from the French,[1] by Hans Reinhart. Chamber orchestra consisting of 1 clarinet, 1 bassoon, 1 cornet à pistons, 1 trombone, 1 violin, 1 double-bass and 1 percussionist playing two side drums of different size without snare, bass-drum, cymbals, tambourine, triangle. Composed at Morges, 1918. Dedicated to Werner Reinhart. Published by J. & W. Chester, 1924. Piano reduction by the composer. Duration of music *c*. 35 minutes. First performance, Théâtre Municipal de Lausanne, 28 September 1918, conducted by Ernest Ansermet. The manuscript score was given by the composer to Werner Reinhart and is now in the Stiftung Rychenberg, Winterthur. A pencil manuscript of the piano reduction of the Three Dances used by Lumila Pitoëff for rehearsal purposes was in the collection of the late Dr. A. Wilhelm of Basel. Two manuscript notebooks containing musical sketches are in the composer's collection [C24].

Genesis of the Work

Stravinsky and Ramuz first met in Switzerland in the autumn of 1915. At that time Ramuz was living in the hamlet of Treytorrens, and in his monograph on Stravinsky[2] he has described how Ansermet brought over his Russian friend by train one afternoon during the period of the vintage and they met at the station of Epesses. The acquaintance quickly ripened into friendship, and when a few weeks later Ramuz moved to L'Acacia, Cour, Lausanne, a close collaboration started between the two artists. Stravinsky, who at that time was living in the Villa Rogie Vue, Morges, invited Ramuz to translate the Russian text of *Reynard*; and the translation of various groups of Russian songs followed. When Stravinsky moved to the Villa Bornand at the beginning of 1917, there was a concentrated spell of work on the French version of *The Wedding*. The fact that Ramuz knew no Russian meant that to a large extent he had to rely on Stravinsky's literal renderings into French, and this necessitated an unusually close degree of collaboration, during which the two men grew to like and esteem each other. The progress of this friendship has been depicted with great skill in Ramuz's book *Souvenirs sur Igor Stravinsky*.

When the short score of *The Wedding* was finished, the question arose – what next? At that moment both artists were suffering considerably from the effects of the First World War. Stravinsky had been cut off from his family estate in Russia; he was receiving no royalties from his publishers, the Edition Russe de Musique, which had its headquarters in Berlin; stage performances of his music by the Russian Ballet were very infrequent; and there were virtually no concert performances of his music at all. As for Ramuz, the greater part of his income came from sales of his novels in France; and his royalties had been

---

[1] 'Freie Nachdichtung' is the phrase used on the title-page of the German libretto. In his *Expositions*, Stravinsky expressed a preference for the German version.
[2] C. F. Ramuz, *Souvenirs sur Igor Stravinsky*. Lausanne, 1929.

seriously affected. In these circumstances, the two artists thought they would try to solve their difficulties by writing a new work that would be as simple as possible to produce. They would devise something that did not need a large theatre, a large cast or a large orchestra – that could be mounted in any type of hall or theatre, or even in the open air. They would have a kind of mobile theatre unit that could tour Switzerland; and in their innocence they imagined that a small company of players and a small band of instrumentalists would be easy to recruit and inexpensive to maintain.

Ramuz, being a novelist and not a playwright, suggested he should write a story rather than a play and adapt it for stage presentation as a kind of acted narration. It was agreed that Stravinsky's music should be independent of the text and capable of separate performance as a concert suite. When they came to discuss the subject, Stravinsky remembered that in the spring of 1917 he had had the idea of using some of the tales from Afanasiev's Collection that dealt with the cruel period of enforced recruitment for the Russo-Turkish wars under Nicholas I. He had been particularly attracted by one of the stories in which 'the Soldier tricks the Devil into drinking too much vodka. He then gives the Devil a handful of shot to eat, assuring him it is caviar, and the Devil greedily swallows it and dies' (*Exp*). After showing Ramuz the rough synopsis, he introduced him to other episodes from Afanasiev's Collection which featured 'the Soldier who deserts and the wily Devil who infallibly comes to claim his soul' (*Chr*). Ramuz's imagination was fired by this material, and he set to work on the libretto without delay.

From the beginning, the Narrator or Reader was planned to be the main character on the stage. The various episodes of the Soldier and the Devil were to be presented in tableau form: so the Soldier and the Devil would be actors. Sometimes they were to be given spoken dialogue; sometimes they would act in mime. At a later stage, it was agreed that the Narrator himself should occasionally intervene in the action; and according to Stravinsky, Ramuz took this idea from Pitoëff who had himself borrowed it from Pirandello (*Exp*). It was also decided to introduce a suite of dances for a dancer (the Princess) as a *divertissement* towards the end of the Second Part,[1] and that her role should be a silent one. At one point, the King her father was to have appeared as a character in the play;[2] but in the end this role was suppressed, and the dialogue between the King and the Soldier absorbed into the narration.

Although in its origins the story was Russian, the collaborators decided to broaden and humanise their treatment so as to give it an international appeal. In its final form, it is a kind of miniature version of the Faust legend. Here is a brief synopsis:

---

[1] In an early (discarded) version there were to be two dancers at this point: the first for the *Tango*, the second for the *Waltz*, and both of them for the *Ragtime*.
[2] C. F. Ramuz, *Lettres 1900–1918*. Editions Clarefontaine, Lausanne, 1956. See particularly Ramuz's letters to Stravinsky dated 15 and 20 July 1918.

2. Register of Works

Part One, Scene 1 – ('Scène au bord du ruisseau' – 'The Banks of a Stream'.) The Soldier, returning to his native village with a fortnight's leave, is accosted by the Devil disguised as an old man with a butterfly net. The Devil obtains the Soldier's fiddle in exchange for a magic book and invites him to spend three days of his leave with him. The Soldier accepts.

Scene 2 – ('Scène du sac' – 'A crossroads in the open country, showing a frontier post and the village belfry in the distance'.)[1] On reaching his native village, the Soldier finds he has been away not three days but three years. The Devil appears disguised as a cattle merchant and explains that with the help of the magic book the Soldier can make his fortune.

Scene 3 ('Scène du livre' – 'A room'.) By now the Soldier is thoroughly disillusioned by his wealth. The Devil disguised as an old clothes woman[2] calls on him and displays her wares, including a fiddle which he recognises as his. He wants to buy it back, but finding he can get no sound out of it, hurls it into the wings and tears up the book in despair.

Part Two, Scene 4 – ('Scène du jeu de cartes'[3] – 'A room in the palace'.) The Soldier, who has now lost his wealth, comes to a town where the King's daughter is ill and the King has promised her hand in marriage to whoever succeeds in curing her. The Soldier meets the Devil disguised as a virtuoso violinist and plays cards with him. He goes on losing and plying him with

---

[1] This stage direction comes from the German version of the libretto. The French text merely says, 'Le décor représente le clocher du village vu à une certaine distance.' But the frontier post is of special importance, since this is the same scene as Scene 6 where it is vital to know that the Soldier has in fact crossed the frontier and passed into the Devil's power.
[2] The French text says 'Le Diable en vieille marchande à la toilette'. In the course of time, the original conception behind this disguise seems to have become forgotten or misunderstood. According to Stravinsky, 'this old woman is a procuress, and the portraits she produces from her basket are meant to be her gallery-for-hire. This was the original *l'Histoire*, at any rate; the more innocent old woman of subsequent productions deprives the episode of its point' (*Exp*). Stravinsky's remark is borne out by the fact that there are certain important excisions in the text of this scene. At one point the Devil tried to arouse the Soldier's pity:

> Je n'ai pas toujours été dans l'état où vous me voyez. J'ai été belle, monsieur, j'ai été riche, j'ai été fêtée. Les poètes ont chanté mon corps de façon détaillée. On s'est fait sauter la cervelle pour l'amour de moi. J'ai tenu l'empereur de toutes les Allemagnes dans mes bras . . . Le prince héritier son fils, deux grands ducs . . .

Later he offered him a splendid picture:

> Alors ce magnifique tableau d'académie,
> Qui représente au naturel Vénus endormie
> Je n'ai jamais vu de gorge si belle qu'à une jeune Hongroise
> qui est comme moi dans le malheur . . . Cette personne a quatorze ans . . . Si Monsieur veut bien se rendre compte . . .

These lines appear in the 1920 text of *Histoire du Soldat* (Editions des Cahiers vaudois), but not in the 1924 edition of the libretto (J. & W. Chester Ltd., London) or Vol. 9 of Ramuz's *Oeuvres Complètes* (Edition Mermod, Lausanne, 1941).
[3] According to Ramuz, this scene is preceded by 'Scène devant le rideau'.

wine, until the Devil falls unconscious, and he is able to recover his old fiddle.

Scene 5 – ('Scène de la fille guèrie' – 'The Princess's room'.) The invalid Princess is lying on a couch. The Soldier enters and plays his fiddle. The Princess rises and dances a tango, a waltz and a ragtime, at the end of which she falls into the Soldier's arms. During their embrace, the Devil enters dressed as a devil (with forked tail and pointed ears). The Soldier fiddles him into contortions and with the help of the Princess drags his body into the wings.

Scene 6 – ('Scène des limites franchies' – same as Scene 2.) Sometime after their marriage, the Soldier and Princess decide to visit his native village; but as soon as he crosses the frontier, he falls into the power of the Devil, who appears in gorgeous scarlet apparel, and has got hold of the fiddle again. He follows the Devil very slowly, but without resisting.

The libretto carries the following introductory note concerning the staging: *A small stage mounted on a platform. A stool (or barrel) at either side. On one of the stools the Narrator sits in front of a small table on which there are a carafe of white wine and a glass. The orchestra is placed on the opposite side of the stage.*

Music

In order to understand how the music fits the narration and stage action, it must be realised that in each of four out of the six scenes (i.e., Scenes 1, 2, 4 and 5) the curtain is raised and lowered *twice*. In two cases (Scenes 2 and 4) the effect is to reveal first a static tableau followed later by a scene with action.[1]

Part One

(1) 'The Soldier's March (Marching Tunes)' – Narration during the music. A few bars before the end of this number the curtain rises on

Scene 1

The narration continues until the Soldier begins to play his fiddle.

(2) 'Airs by a Stream' – After 28 bars the curtain falls[2] and rises six bars later (on the same scene). The music is followed by the scene between the Soldier and the Devil disguised as a lepidopterist, at the end of which the curtain falls.

---

[1] This arrangement may have been necessitated by the restricted size of the inner stage at the Lausanne Théâtre Municipal, where the work was first produced. According to Stravinsky, this 'was only as large as two armchairs together' (*Exp*).
[2] Fig. 5.

Interlude

Narration

(1) 'The Soldier's March (Marching Tunes)' (repeated) – The narration continues, and towards the end of it the curtain rises on

Scene 2

Tableau: the Devil disguised as a cattle merchant is revealed leaning on his stick. The narration finishes and is followed by

(3) 'Pastorale' Towards the end of this music the curtain falls. As soon as the music has ended, the curtain rises again on the same setting, and the scene between the Soldier and the Devil follows. At the end of the scene the music of

(3) 'Pastorale' is repeated to an empty stage. The curtain falls in the last bar but two.

Interlude

Narration.

(2) 'Airs by a Stream' (repeat).

Narration (concluded).

Scene 3

The curtain rises, and the scene between the Soldier and the Devil disguised as an old clothes woman follows, ending with a shortened version of

(2) 'Airs by a Stream' – The curtain falls in the last bar but two.

Part Two

(1) 'The Soldier's March (Marching Tunes)' – altered version. Narration during the music. Narration continues after the music.

(4) 'Royal March' – After 91 bars[1] the curtain rises on

Scene 4

Tableau: the Devil is revealed disguised as a virtuoso violinist. After another 34 bars[2] the curtain falls, and the music ends 14 bars later. Narration (concluded). The curtain rises on the same setting, and the scene between the Soldier, the Narrator and the Devil follows, at the end of which

(5) 'The Little Concert' starts and the curtain falls. Three quarters of the way through the 'Little Concert',[3] the Narrator shouts out eight lines of couplets. The music ends.

---

[1] i.e. at fig. 14.
[2] i.e. at fig. 19.
[3] At fig. 22.

Scene 5

(6) 'Three Dances': Tango, Waltz, Ragtime – The curtain rises at bar 10 of the Tango. The curtain falls at the end of the *Ragtime*[1] and immediately rises again on the same setting.

(7) 'The Devil's Dance' – At the end of this number, the Devil is dragged offstage, and the Soldier and the Princess fall into each other's arms.

(8) 'The Little Chorale' is played during their embrace.

(9) 'The Devil's Song' (melodrama).

(10) 'The Great Chorale' – The curtain falls during the first bars of this number. The phrases of this chorale are punctuated by eight fermatas (including the final chord). Short sections of narration are intercalated during the fourth, sixth and seventh fermatas. When the chorale has ended, the narration continues. End of narration. The curtain rises on

Scene 6

(11) 'The Devil's Triumphal March' – The curtain falls slowly after the last two chords from the violin;[2] and the percussion is left to carry on until the end, alone.

This schematic analysis shows how carefully the incidental music is dove-tailed into the action, resulting occasionally in passages of melodrama where the Narrator or Devil speaks freely or rhythmically over and through the music. It also shows how during the exposition of the main subject of the play in Part One, only three musical numbers are used, each of them being heard more than once, whereas in Part Two, after the initial repeat of the 'Soldier's March', there are no further repeats, and the music is continuous from the 'Little Concert' to the 'Devil's Triumphal March', with the exception of a brief passage of narration after the 'Great Chorale'. The result is that as the play reaches its climax, the music, which has so far been incidental, and carefully geared to the narration and dramatic action, takes over and imposes its own values and pace on the work as a whole, thereby raising it to a higher power than the mere sum of its parts. And this is the justification for the inclusion of *The Soldier's Tale* in such an authoritative work of reference as Alfred Loewenberg's *Annals of Opera*, even though it is very far from being an opera in the traditional sense of the word, since not a syllable of the text is actually sung.

The eleven musical numbers of the score follow the direction already taken by Stravinsky in his non-Russian works during the previous four years and consolidate the ground already covered. In fact, this music may be looked on as the epitome and summation of the taut, condensed, almost burlesque style

---

[1] A variant arrangement is hinted at in some versions of the text whereby the curtain falls at about fig. 4 in the *Tango*, leaving the Princess to execute her three dances in front of the curtain.
[2] One bar before fig. 17.

2. Register of Works

of the second of the *Three Pieces for String Quartet*, the *Eight Easy Pieces for Piano Duet* and the *Study for Pianola*.

Of the various marches, the 'Soldier's March' struck Ramuz as being rather 'federal' in character in view of the prominent parts played by the cornet à pistons and trombone, while Stravinsky has admitted that in composing it – (the initial phrase for these two instruments was his first thematic idea for *The Soldier's Tale*) – he may have been influenced by the popular French song 'Marietta' (*Exp*). The 'Royal March', which is in the style of a Spanish *pasodoble*, was suggested to him by an incident he had witnessed in Seville during the Holy Week processions of 1916. He was standing in a street with Diaghilev 'and listening with much pleasure to a tiny "bullfight" band consisting of a cornet, a trombone, and a bassoon. They were playing a *pasodoble*, when suddenly a large brass band came thundering down the street in the Overture to *Tannhäuser*. The *pasodoble* was soon drowned out' (*Exp*).

Of the various dances, the *Tango* was then very popular in the dance halls of Western Europe.[1] An even greater novelty was American ragtime. Ansermet had recently returned from an American tour and had brought back a selection of jazz material which Stravinsky studied with interest. As he says in his *Expositions*: 'My knowledge of jazz was derived exclusively from copies of sheet music, and as I had never actually heard any of the music performed, I borrowed its rhythmic style not as played, but as written. I *could* imagine jazz sound, however, or so I liked to think. Jazz meant, in any case, a wholly new sound in my music, and *L'Histoire* marks my final break with the Russian orchestral school in which I had been fostered.'

The two chorales were based closely on the Lutheran chorales of the German Protestant Church. And the traditional tune of the *Dies Irae* seems to have been lurking in his subconscious mind, for during the composition of the score he had a dream in which he saw 'a young gypsy sitting by the edge of the road. She had a child on her lap for whose entertainment she was playing a violin. The motive she kept repeating[2] used the whole bow, or as we say in French, "avec toute la longueur de l'archet". The child was very enthusiastic about the music and applauded it with his little hands' (*Con*). And Stravinsky was especially pleased to be able to remember the motive after awakening. (See Ex. 204.) This dream sequence has an almost Giorgionesque feeling about it, which fits in well with the pastoral quality of some of the scenes in *The Soldier's Tale*.

In view of the emphasis laid on the Soldier's fiddle in the play, it is not surprising to find the violin playing a *concertante* role in the chamber orchestra;

---

[1] In *Souvenirs du Diable* (printed in *Hommage á C. – F. Ramuz*, La Concorde, Lausanne, 1947) Jean Villard-Gilles recalls that in 1918 the dance bands at Montreux 'nous apportaient d'Argentine – don inestimable – l'aphrodisiaque tango!'

[2] This motive is first heard from the cornet followed by the bassoon in the 'Little Concert' (figs. 13–15, 17 and 18) and, later, from the violin in the *Tango* (figs. 4 and 8).

and the composer's new enthusiasm for jazz led to special concentration on percussion too. He had bought a set of instruments from a shop in Lausanne and learnt to play them himself (*Exp*). Throughout the score the percussion is given a part of maximum virtuosity. In the 'Devil's Triumphal March', it starts by underlining the violin theme; but gradually develops a more or less independent existence so that, when the other instruments leave off, it brings the work to a strange and memorable conclusion. It is as if, once the Devil has carried off the Soldier, the spirit of the music should abandon its body, leaving only a skeleton behind.

In his *Chronicle* Stravinsky has set out the reasons that led to his final choice of instruments. 'I knew only too well that I should have to make do with a very small number of instrumentalists. The easiest solution would have been to use a polyphonic instrument like the piano or harmonium. The latter was out of the question, chiefly because of its dynamic poverty due to the complete absence of accents. Although the piano has much more varied polyphonic qualities and offers many particularly dynamic possibilities, I had to avoid it for two reasons: either my score would have seemed like a piano arrangement – and that would have given evidence of a certain lack of financial means, not at all in keeping with our intentions – or I should have had to use it as a solo instrument, exploiting every possibility of its technique. In other words, I should have had to be specially careful about the "pianism" of my score and make it into a vehicle of virtuosity in order to justify my choice. So there was nothing for it but to decide on a group of instruments, which could include the most representative types, in treble and bass, of the different instrumental families: for the strings, violin and double-bass; for the woodwind, clarinet (because it has the biggest compass) and bassoon; for the brass, cornet and trombone; finally, the percussion to be played by a single musician; the whole, of course, under a conductor.' (It is purely fortuitous that Stravinsky's orchestra for *The Soldier's Tale* resembles Satie's for *Le Piège de Méduse* with its clarinet, trumpet, trombone, violin, cello, double-bass, and percussion. Though written in 1913, *Le Piège* was not performed until 1921. There is also a close resemblance with some of the American jazzbands – for instance, the 1916 New Orleans Dixieland jazzband consisted of clarinet, trumpet, trombone, piano and drums – but Stravinsky's first chance of hearing a jazzband did not come until some time after the completion of his score.)

The greater part of the musical material is diatonic and recognisably based on major or minor modes; but occasionally one of the parts gets squeezed into chromatic shape.[1] Only two of the eleven numbers (i.e., the 'Royal March' and the *Ragtime*) bear key signatures; but the tonality of each movement or phrase is usually quite easy to determine. For instance, although the part-writing in the two chorales is bold and full of unusual clashes, each phrase

---

[1] As, for instance, the main theme of the 'Soldier's March' at figs. 10–12.

closes on a common chord, and the tonal and modulatory scheme is perfectly clear. An ambiguous use of both major and minor thirds is frequently found, particularly in the violin part;[1] and this sometimes gives the effect of a 'melodic' minor scale with the leading note in both its normal and flattened position. The cornet and clarinet fanfares add a clash of tonalities; and there are several delicately balanced polytonal passages in the exquisite 'Pastorale'.

Stravinsky makes full use of the devices of prolongation and elision in order to break up the symmetry of the phrasing, and the work is particularly rich in metrical counterpoint. A good example of foreshortening comes in the *Tango*[2] where an accompanying figure of a quaver followed by two semiquavers (2/8) suddenly dashes off into a hurried figure of three equal semiquavers (3/16) for a few bars before resuming its normal gait. In the following example from the 'Little Concert',[3] it can be seen how a theme in an irregular metre is accompanied by at least three different regular metres. (The time signatures of the accompaniment have been altered to make this point clear.)

Ex. 32

An interesting and unusual feature is the way themes are apt to stray from one number to another. For instance, the 'Little Concert', which stands almost at the musical centre of the work, is like a magpie's nest: most of its themes are borrowed from elsewhere, and yet it manages to preserve a distinct form, timbre and character of its own.

But the most remarkable feature of the score is the brilliant handling of the chamber orchestra. The instruments are contrasted with each other and balanced with superb adroitness and audacity. Blend is eschewed; and differences in pitch and timbre and colour are exploited to obtain extradimensional effects. The music is unique in the way it combines linear precision with sonorous perspective.

---

[1] *Cf.* the basic theme of the 'Little Concert'.
[2] Fig. 4.
[3] Fig. 21.

Original Compositions

Production

The 1918 production of *The Soldier's Tale* took place thanks to the generosity of Werner Reinhart of Winterthur. As Stravinsky says, 'he paid for everybody and everything, and finally even commissioned my music' (*Exp*). Ramuz and Stravinsky were responsible for the casting and the preliminary rehearsals; but the final production was in the hands of Georges Pitoëff. René Auberjonois was responsible for the scenery and costumes; and Ansermet conducted a band of picked players drawn mainly from Geneva and Zurich. The cast was as follows:

Narrator:	Elie Gagnebin
The Soldier:	Gabriel Rosset
The Devil (spoken part):	Jean Villard-Gilles
(danced part):	Georges Pitoëff
The Princess (danced part):	Ludmila Pitoëff

Gagnebin, Rosset and Villard-Gilles were students of Lausanne University and had had very little experience of the stage. It is interesting to see from Ramuz's published correspondence[1] that Villard-Gilles (who was then only twenty) found the part of the Devil quite tricky to play. He was able to tackle the action and the dialogue, but was baffled by the dance numbers. The 'Devil's Triumphal Dance' is the climax of the work; and it was essential it should make its full effect. Suddenly, a way out of the difficulty occurred to the two main collaborators. On 5 September 1918 Ramuz wrote to Auberjonois: 'Yesterday evening Stravinsky told me of his intention to dance the last scene. That will be perfect. Please encourage him to do so.' In an undated letter to Stravinsky (possibly written on the same day) Ramuz says: 'And then please dance the final scene yourself. You'll do so with rhythmic vitality and save the day.' This would certainly have been a splendid solution; but in the end, other counsels prevailed, and Georges Pitoëff was persuaded to take over the Devil's dances, leaving Villard-Gilles to tackle the spoken part.

A lively account of the rehearsals is given by Villard-Gilles in his article *Souvenirs du Diable*:[2]

> Stravinsky and Ramuz were in charge of daily rehearsals – the former always in a frenzy of enthusiasm, inventiveness, joy, indignation, headache; leaping on the piano as if it were a dangerous foe that had to be subdued by a bout of fisticuffs, then bounding on to the stage, swallowing glasses of kirsch whose after-effects had to be combated with the aid of aspirin: the latter, calm, attentive, friendly, rather bashful when giving advice, seeing things from our point of view, trying (like us) to find the right answers,

---

[1] *Op. cit.*
[2] Printed in *Hommage à C. F. Ramuz*. (Translation by E. W. W.)

showing an indomitable patience, and following with malicious enjoyment the genial capers of his collaborator. In the presence of these two artists with their complementary temperaments, we felt ourselves imbued with vital intensity and could think of nothing but our work.

The first performance at the Théâtre Municipal, Lausanne, on 28 September 1918 seems to have been a great success. 'The true note was struck then,' says Stravinsky in his *Chronicle*, 'but unfortunately I have never since seen a performance that has satisfied me to the same degree.' But the following performances that had been planned for Geneva and other Swiss towns never took place because of the influenza epidemic that had already started to sweep over Switzerland and the whole of war-exhausted Europe. One after another, musicians, actors and stage-hands succumbed to it, and the tour of *The Soldier's Tale* had to be abandoned.

For some years afterwards the work lay under a cloud. When Stravinsky renewed his links with the Russian Ballet in 1919, he found Diaghilev very hostile to it for the simple reason that it had been planned and carried out without any reference to him. From Ramuz's published correspondence it is clear that early in 1920 he (Ramuz) received a suggestion from Stravinsky that the concert suite should be used as the basis for a ballet to be designed by Picasso; but not unnaturally he was unwilling to allow his share of the work to be jettisoned to make a choreographer's holiday. In his *Memories*, Stravinsky refers to this project, saying that in the early 1920s Diaghilev suddenly decided to stage *The Soldier's Tale*. 'His plan was eccentric. The dancers were to go about wearing advertisements, American side-walk walking-advertisements, "sandwich men", as they are called, or pickets. Massine would eventually have been blamed for the choreography of this undanceable ballet, but it was all Diaghilev's idea.'

Later in 1920 Ramuz published the text of the libretto as one of the *Cahiers vaudois*, and it was now Stravinsky's turn to be peeved, because owing to an oversight on Ramuz's part the publication omitted to make proper acknowledgment of Stravinsky's co-authorship.

In the spring of 1924 three stage performances were given in Paris at the Théâtre des Champs-Elysées. Those of April 24 and 26 were disastrous; that of April 27 was a little better. But the German productions that year (at Berlin and Frankfurt) reached a higher standard, and gradually the reputation of the work began to spread. It was naturally difficult to fit it into the repertory of any ordinary opera or ballet company, as it made such extraordinary demands; but as festival and other special productions occurred, it received more careful treatment and began to be accepted as a masterpiece in a unique form.[1]

[1] According to *Stravinsky & the Dance* (1962) there have been fifteen different productions in the seventeen years 1944–61 as against less than a dozen for the quarter of a century 1918–1943.

Original Compositions

Concert Suite

The concert suite (entitled in French 'Grande Suite') consists of eight numbers as follows:

    I. 'The Soldier's March' (1)[1]
    II. 'The Soldier's Violin' (2)
    III. 'Royal March' (4)
    IV. 'The Little Concert' (5)
    V. 'Three Dances': *Tango, Waltz, Ragtime* (6)
    VI. 'The Devil's Dance' (7)
    VII. 'Chorale' (10)
    VIII. 'The Devil's Triumphal March' (11)

First performance: Wigmore Hall, London 20 July 1920 (under E. Ansermet). Published by J. & W. Chester, 1922.

Transcription

A Suite was arranged for violin, clarinet and piano in the autumn of 1919, consisting of the following numbers:

    I. 'The Soldier's March' (1)
    II. 'The Soldier's Violin' (2)
    III. 'The Little Concert' (5)
    IV. *Tango; Waltz; Ragtime* (6)
    V. 'The Devil's Dance' (7)

Duration: *c*. 25 minutes. Published by J. & W. Chester, 1920. First performance Lausanne, 8 November 1919. MS comp. [C 24]. MS copies of the violin and clarinet parts are with J. & W. Chester.

Reinhart, as well as being an amiable Maecenas, was an amateur clarinettist of some distinction; and Stravinsky made this special transcription for his benefit. One honours the motive, but deplores the principle. The arguments against including the piano among the orchestral instruments in the score of *The Soldier's Tale* have been adequately expounded by Stravinsky himself (as quoted above); and the idea of arranging any part of *The Soldier's Tale* for a chamber music combination other than the definitive seven-man band is thoroughly disagreeable and an error of musical taste.

42. RAG-TIME

For eleven players (Fl – Cl – Cor – Cornet à Pistons – Trb – big drum, caisse claire à corde, caisse claire sans corde, cymbals – cimbalom – 1st Vl – 2nd Vl – Vla – Cb). Composed at Morges, 1918.[2] Dedicated to Madame

---

[1] The Arabic numbers correspond to the numbers in the full score as given above.
[2] Stravinsky finished the summary sketch of this work on 21 March 1918 and the instrumental score at the precise moment the Armistice was signed i.e. 11 a.m. on 11 November 1918.

Eugenia Errazuriz. Published by Editions de la Sirène, Paris, 1919 (later by J. & W. Chester). Piano reduction by the composer. Duration: *c.* 4 minutes 30 seconds. First performance, the Philharmonic Quartet and a small orchestra, Aeolian Hall, London, 27 April 1920 (conducted by Arthur Bliss). MS comp. [C 26] and [C 35].

This is a further essay in the new jazz idiom that Stravinsky had first tried out in the *Ragtime* of *The Soldier's Tale*. The chamber orchestra has been increased from seven players to eleven, with the cimbalom featuring prominently in a kind of *concertante* part. The new piece is about twice the length of the dance in *The Soldier's Tale*; and the peculiar technique of the cimbalom leaves its mark on the texture, which is predominantly linear. The time signature is a constant 4/4 from the first bar to the 178th and last – a most unusual feature in Stravinsky's music of this period – and this regular framework throws into relief the emphasis laid on syncopation.

The basic idea behind this work was to produce a composite portrait of the new type of popular dance music that had just emerged in North America, 'giving it the importance of a concert piece, as in the past composers had done for the minuet, waltz, mazurka and so on' (*Chr*). Though intended primarily for concert performance, it was produced as a dance *divertissement* by Leonide Massine and Lydia Lopokova at the Royal Opera House, Covent Garden, on 3 April 1922. Another choreographic arrangement was made by George Balanchine in 1960 when it was included as a dance duet in the New York City Ballet's production *Jazz Concert*.

The cover to the composer's reduction for piano solo (published in 1919) was decorated with a splendidly bold, endless-line-drawing of two musicians by Picasso.[1]

43. FOUR RUSSIAN SONGS

For voice and piano. Words from Russian popular texts; French translation by C. F. Ramuz. Dedicated to Mme. and M. Maja and Bela Strozzi-Pečić. Published by J. & W. Chester, 1920. Duration: *c.* 4 minutes 45 seconds.

1. 'Селезень (Хороводная)' – 'Canard (Ronde)'. Composed at Morges, 28 December 1918.
2. 'Запѣвная' – 'Chanson pour compter'. Morges, 16 March 1919.
3. 'Подблюдная' – 'Le Moineau est assis. . . .' Morges, 23 October 1919.
4. 'Сектантская' – 'Chant dissident'. Morges, March 1919.

Manuscript with J. & W. Chester. Other manuscript material is in the composer's collection [C 4], [C 29] and [C 35].

---

[1] Two other sketches for this cover by Picasso are reproduced in the English edition of *Memories and Commentaries*. (Only one appears in the American edition.)

Original Compositions

The origin of this group of songs is referred to in Stravinsky's *Chronicle*, where he mentions that during the winter of 1919 he met a Croat singer, Mme. Maja de Strozzi-Pečić, who had a beautiful soprano voice. 'She asked me to write something for her, and I composed *Four Russian Songs* on folk-poems which Ramuz translated for me.'

Interesting though these songs are singly, they seem to form a rather mixed bag, a collection of oddments, rather than a deliberately planned suite or cycle.

The first song is really a companion piece to the animal songs that were collected in the *Three Tales for Children*. The second song is a *pribaoutka*, a nonsense song, a children's counting game. The third song looks as if it had been originally intended to form one of the *a cappella* Russian Peasant Songs called *Saucers*.[1] The verses are separated by a brief refrain ('Glory! glory!') very like the refrains in the first, third and fourth of the *Four Russian Peasant Songs*; and one has the feeling that the vocal layout would be more effective if part of it were sung by a choir instead of a solo voice.

In these first three songs, the melodic line, as is usual with the works of Stravinsky's Russian popular period, is almost entirely diatonic; but in the fourth song there is a significant change of idiom. This song is an extraordinary kind of Russian spiritual, in which the text –

> *Snowstorms, blizzards, wild snowstorms,*
> *Closed are my ways, (closed all my ways to Thy Kingdom).*
> *No path is open to man or horse,*
> *Closed are all paths (closed to man and horse)*
> *To my Father . . .*

Ex.33

---

[1] This is confirmed by the Russian title, which means 'Saucer'.

seems to match the desolate mood of a Russian, cut off at that moment from his native land because of the Bolshevist Revolution, and forced into involuntary exile. These opening lines are set to a chromatic form of lamentation, which, instead of alternating between the customary two notes a semitone apart and occasionally taking in a few wider intervals like a sob (as in *The Wedding*),[1] explores with desperate intensity all the semitones contained within the compass of a diminished fifth. This introduces a new note into Stravinsky's vocal idiom – one that in fact is not heard again until his use of serial procedures in the *Three Songs from William Shakespeare* (1953) and the Song 'Do not go gentle' from *In Memoriam Dylan Thomas* (1954) promotes the chromatic intervals of the scale to new importance and dignity. This unusual passage of lamentation is followed by phrases in the usual Russian diatonic folk style; and the song ends with a kind of religious *Gloria* (as opposed to the lay shouts of 'Glory! glory' in *Saucers*), where for some obscure reason Stravinsky suddenly abandons bar lines altogether, although the passage is clearly written in irregular groups of 2/8, 3/8 and 4/8 bars.

The supposition that these four songs were hurriedly put together from an assortment of sketches is borne out by examination of the piano accompaniment. In the first three songs, it is written in Stravinsky's usual dry staccato, almost martellato style: but in the fourth, a substantial part of the accompaniment was obviously planned with the cimbalom in mind,[2] and the piano accompaniment reads like the piano reduction of a chamber ensemble score, for it also contains passages that are obviously intended for one or more woodwind instruments, including one with an arpeggio arabesque just before the final coda, which is printed in small type on a separate stave and cannot originally have been intended to form part of a piano accompaniment at all.[3]

These four songs carry few indications of expression, though each one has a metronome marking. The dynamic markings are few, and sometimes inadequate and confusing. For instance, in the fourth the accompaniment is marked *piano* in bar one, while there is no marking for the voice except a single *forte* at the beginning of the fifth bar. Later the accompaniment is marked *subito piano* at the beginning of the coda, thereby implying that the previous passage has carried some degree of *forte*, though there is no marking to that effect. Some critics have noticed only the *piano* marking and have decided that the song expresses an exile's extreme sadness, resignation and humility.[4] This is exaggerated. It certainly includes a quiet rapt passage in the

---

[1] *Cf.* Ex. 28 above.
[2] This is confirmed by Stravinsky in his *Expositions and Developments*.
[3] It should be added that a manuscript version of the first three songs with accompaniment for voice, cimbalom and flute exists in the composer's collection [C 29].
[4] 'Alors que Stravinsky semble avoir voulu exprimer par la conjonction chant-piano un état d'âme de tristesse resignée et plaintive, tout le morceau est pianissimo . . .' Pierre Meylan in *Une amitié célèbre*.

final Gloria; but it also has a joyous outburst where the singer describes how his brothers and sisters are gathered together in the Kingdom of God, and the vocal phrase is accompanied or echoed by the same phrase in the piano harmonised with open fifths.

43 (A). FOUR SONGS

For voice, flute, harp and guitar. Phonetic Russian text by the composer; English translation by Robert Craft and Rosa Newmarch. Published by J. & W. Chester, 1955. Duration: *c.* 4 minutes 30 seconds.

1. 'The Drake' (no. 1 of *Four Russian Songs*, instrumented in 1953)
2. 'A Russian Spiritual' (no. 4 of *Four Russian Songs*, instrumented in 1954)
3. 'Geese and Swans'[1] (no. 2 of *Three Tales for Children*, instrumented in 1954)
4. 'Tilimbom' (no. 1 of *Three Tales for Children*, instrumented in 1954)

First performed at one of the 'Monday Evening Concerts', Los Angeles, conducted by Robert Craft, 21 February 1955.

With these Songs an element of confusion enters into the nomenclature of Stravinsky's works. On the title page of the first impression they are called 'Four Songs'; but in the running headline above the first song they appeared as 'Four Russian Songs'. In order to avoid confusion with the *Four Russian Songs* (38) and the *Four Russian Peasant Songs* (30), it is best always to refer to them as the *Four Songs*.

Whatever may have been the virtues of the French translations of the Russian texts of his songs made by C. F. Ramuz between 1915 and 1919, Stravinsky seems to have got tired of them by 1953, for they are suppressed in the *Four Songs*. In a brief introductory note, he explains: 'The sound of the syllables of this old Russian poetry is closely connected with the music I composed to it. To the musician's ear, the right pronunciation of the syllables is much more explicit than the best translation, which is unavoidably different from the sound of the original pattern.'[2] He accordingly worked out a phonetic transcription for English-speaking performers. But he was not altogether logical in his attitude, for while he dropped Ramuz's French translations, he printed new English translations by Robert Craft for nos. 1–3 and reprinted Rosa Newmarch's English translation of no. 4 – all four translations being perfectly singable.

---

[1] The original date of composition is incorrectly given as 1915. (See no. 28.)
[2] In his *Conversations* (1959) he was to write that there were many instances in his Russian vocal music of translation destroying both text and music. 'I am so disturbed by them I prefer to hear those pieces in Russian or not at all.' Yet only a year or two later (c. 1961) he conducted a performance of the *Four Songs* in their English translations which was recorded and issued by Philips (A 01493 L).

There are few musical changes in these songs. The vocal line is taken over almost intact from the previous songs with piano accompaniment. There are no transpositions. Occasionally, a new feature or figure is added to the accompaniment. Particularly effective is the canonic entry for flute at figure 13 in 'Tilimbom'. But the half bar's fermata before the final phrase (also in 'Tilimbom') is a good idea that does not quite come off in performance, for the speed of the song is too great for a pause of only half a second to register clearly. Special care has been given to phrasing and to expression and dynamic markings. Wherever the metre is irregular (as in nos. 1 and 2), the barring has been revised in an attempt to break it down into smaller units and so correct the composer's earlier tendency to use barring as a substitute for phrasing.

The choice of instruments is somewhat strange. It has already been shown that originally the Russian Spiritual must have been intended for a small chamber music ensemble including cimbalom and one or more woodwind instruments. The harp is not really an adequate substitute for the cimbalom, and its timbre sounds somewhat emasculated. It is curious to hear the brash sound of the guitar associated with the harp in this particular context, though the guitar is certainly suited to the gay animal spirits of the other three songs, particularly when it is used to play rapidly repeated chords as in nos. 3 and 4.

44. PIANO-RAG-MUSIC

For piano solo. Composed at Morges, 28 June 1919. Dedicated to Artur Rubinstein. Published by J. & W. Chester, 1920. Duration: *c.* 3 minutes. First performance, José Iturbi, Lausanne, 8 November 1919.[1] One manuscript with J. & W. Chester; another with the composer [C 32]. The latter is signed and dated, 'Morges, 1919, 28 juin à midi', and carries the following pencilled comment: 'Les cloches de l'église sonnaient midi; à 3 heures j'entendais les canons à la frontière qui tonnaient la signature de la paix à Versail.'

According to Stravinsky's *Chronicle*, this piano piece was composed 'with Artur Rubinstein and his strong, agile, clever fingers in mind'. Stravinsky goes on to say: 'It was inspired by the same ideas, and my aim was the same, as in *Rag-Time*, but in this case I stressed the percussion possibilities of the piano. What fascinated me most of all in the work was that the different rhythmic episodes were dictated by the fingers themselves. My own fingers seemed to enjoy it so much that I began to practise the piece; not that I wanted to play it in public . . . but simply for my personal satisfaction.'

---

[1] The *Piano-Rag-Music* was not mentioned in the preliminary publicity for this concert that appeared in the *Gazette de Lausanne* for 5 November 1919. As no records of this concert seem to have survived and there were no press reviews, it is possible (though unlikely) that the *Piano-Rag-Music* did not receive its première until the second concert of the tour at the Zurich Tonhalle on 20 November 1919. (See 'En 1919 Igor Stravinsky donna trois concerts de ses oeuvres à Lausanne, Zurich et Genève' by Pierre Meylan. *Revue Musicale de Suisse Romande*, June 1964.)

Whereas in *Rag-Time* the element of syncopation was related to a tight unvarying metrical scheme, here Stravinsky relaxed his discipline and allowed his sense of improvisation to dictate a work that is almost rhapsodic in form – a turbulent spate of music carrying all sorts of flotsam in its stream. The result is rather incoherent; and the improvisatory nature of the work is, if anything, emphasised by the frequent cessation of barring, which makes it appear as if various passages are to be looked on as cadenzas, despite the composer's obvious dislike of tempo rubato and his insistence on a regular quaver beat. Ostinatos are used; and the melodic line is sometimes reduced to fragments of the chromatic scale. How close this brings the music to *The Soldiers' Tale* can be seen by comparing the following passage with the extract from the 'Little Concert' already quoted above (Ex. 32).

Ex.34

Under the title *The Least Flycatcher*, this music was used by Paul Taylor for a dance solo produced by the Paul Taylor Company in New York in 1961.

45. THREE PIECES FOR CLARINET SOLO

Composed at Morges, 1919. Dedicated to Werner Reinhart. Published by J. & W. Chester, 1920. Duration: *c.* 3 minutes 45 seconds. First performance, Edmond Allegra, Lausanne, 8 November 1919.

    I. *Sempre piano e molto tranquillo* ♩= 52
    II. ♪= 168
    III. ♪= 160

The clarinet in A is prescribed for nos. I and II; the clarinet in B flat for no. III. The manuscript was given by Stravinsky to Werner Reinhart and is now in the Stiftung Rychenberg, Winterthur. The complete sketches are in the composer's collection [C 27].

Stravinsky wrote these *Three Pieces* for and dedicated them to Werner Reinhart as a token of gratitude for the generous way he had financed the first production of *The Soldier's Tale*. Reinhart himself was an amateur clarinettist; and Stravinsky had already shown a predilection for that instrument, particularly in the *Cat's Cradle Songs*.

An extended composition for a solo instrument is always difficult to handle; but Stravinsky seems to have welcomed the challenge. In the Tango of *The Soldier's Tale* he had already come very close to writing a movement for a violin solo (with percussion); but here he was writing for a wind instrument that could not emulate the violin's double-stopping, and there was no accompanying percussion. The last of these *Three Pieces* resembles both the *Tango* and the *Ragtime* of *The Soldier's Tale* in style. The other two pieces are more original. The first exploits the lower range of the instrument in a mood of meditative tranquillity; and the second is written without barlines in an improvisatory vein with fast-flowing arpeggios and arabesques, slightly reminiscent of the ebullient opening of 'Mazatsumi' (in the *Three Japanese Lyrics*), framing a slower, quieter, lower-pitched middle section.

46. PULCINELLA

Ballet with song in one act. Music after Giambattista Pergolesi. (2.2.0.2 – 2.1.1.0 – string 5tet *concertino* (1.1.1.1.1) together with string 5tet *ripieno* (4.4.4.3.3) and soprano, tenor and bass soloists.) Composed at Morges, between 1919 and 20 April 1920. Vocal score by the composer; published by J. & W. Chester, 1920. Full score published by Edition Russe de Musique (later by Boosey & Hawkes). Duration: *c.* 35 minutes. First performance by the Russian Ballet at the Opera House, Paris, 15 May 1920, conducted by Ernest Ansermet. The MS of the vocal score, dated Morges, 11 April 1920, is with J. & W. Chester Ltd. Other manuscripts are in the composer's collection [C 34].

Genesis of the Work – Derivation and Treatment of the Music

It was not easy for Stravinsky to pick up the threads of his artistic career again, even though the war was over. For the five years immediately preceding the outbreak of the war, he had been in close touch with Diaghilev, and four of his major works had been produced by the Russian Ballet. Diaghilev had now managed to reassemble his company of dancers in London. A season at the Coliseum starting on 5 September 1918 ran until 29 March 1919, during which period each variety programme included the performance of a single ballet. After a brief tour to Manchester, the company returned to London to open a season of their own at the Alhambra (30 April to 30 July). Later in the year, a third season was held at the Empire Theatre (29 September to 20 December). At this moment *The Firebird* and *Petrushka* were in the repertory, but not *The Rite of Spring*. Diaghilev was anxious to bring back *The Nightingale*, not as an opera, but in the form of a danced version of the symphonic poem, *The Song of the Nightingale*. Stravinsky, however, was not so keen. He had begun to realise that in the theatre his scores were at the mercy of orchestras that were often little better than scratch groups of instrumentalists playing under inadequate conditions, whereas in the concert hall he could rely on proper conditions of rehearsal and performance by accredited orchestras. He would have been happier if Diaghilev had shown more interest in his latest (wartime) works for the stage viz. *Reynard* and *The Soldier's Tale*: but Diaghilev was absurdly jealous of the reported success of the Swiss production of the latter work and seemed to regard its composition even as a breach of faith (*Chr*). Doubtless he would have been delighted to mount *The Wedding* had it been ready: but Stravinsky had still not discovered how to solve the problem of its instrumentation.

At first Diaghilev must have wondered how he could entice the lost sheep back into the Russian Ballet fold. Then, recalling the recent success of *The Good-Humoured Ladies* danced to Scarlatti's music arranged and orchestrated by Tommasini, he decided to tempt him by offering him the chance of carrying out a similar work of adaptation and rehabilitation for another eighteenth-century composer. Strolling with him one spring afternoon in the Place de la Concorde, Paris, he said: 'Don't protest at what I am about to say. I know you are much taken by your Alpine colleagues, but I have an idea that I think will amuse you more than anything they can propose. I want you to look at some delightful eighteenth century music with the idea of orchestrating it for a ballet' (*Exp*). When he added that the composer he had in mind was Pergolesi, Stravinsky at first thought he must be mad. At that time he knew little of Pergolesi's music except the *Stabat Mater* and *La Serva Padrona*, neither of which interested him in the least.[1] But Diaghilev let it be understood that he had gathered together copies of unknown or little known works, many of them in manuscript, that he had found in various Italian music conservatories and libraries, and also in the British Museum; and Stravinsky agreed to look at this material and give his opinion without prejudice.

Although it is possible that the material Diaghilev handed over contained a small proportion of unknown unpublished work, the music actually chosen by Stravinsky comes entirely from published sources of Pergolesi's music, particularly the Trio Sonatas, various other instrumental works, and three of the operas – two of them, *Lo Frate 'nnamorato* (1734) and *Il Flaminio* (1735), comic operas with librettos written in Neapolitan dialect, and the third *Adriano in Siria* (1734) an *opera seria* composed to Metastasio's text. But the important thing was that, having read the music through, he straightway fell in love with it and agreed to accept Diaghilev's commission.

It was now necessary to agree on a plan of action for the ballet; and at this point Diaghilev produced an old manuscript found at Naples dating from 1700,[2] which contained a number of comic episodes in which the leading part was played by Pulcinella, the traditional hero of the Neapolitan *commedia*

---

[1] This account, based on Stravinsky's own recollections in *Expositions*, is slightly at variance with the earlier account given in his *Chronicle* where he says Diaghilev knew he had an immense liking and admiration for Pergolesi's Neapolitan music, 'So entirely of the people and yet so exotic in its Spanish character'. But in his later *Conversations* he is refreshingly frank and admits that *Pulcinella* is the only work of Pergolesi's that he really likes.

[2] This statement is based on the Note prefixed to the score of *Pulcinella*. A slightly different account is given in *Expositions* where Stravinsky says Diaghilev had found a book of Pulcinella stories in Rome.

dell'arte. The episode chosen as a basis for the ballet was called *The Four Pulcinellas.*

> All the local young girls are in love with Pulcinella; but all the young men to whom they are betrothed are mad with jealousy and plot to kill him. Just when they think they are at the point of success, they borrow costumes resembling that of Pulcinella and present themselves to their sweethearts in disguise. But Pulcinella – cunning fellow! – had arranged to change places with Fourbo, his double, who made a pretence of succumbing to the blows of Pulcinella's enemies. The real Pulcinella now disguises himself as a magician and resuscitates his double. At the very moment when the four young men, thinking they have got rid of their rival, come to claim their sweethearts, Pulcinella appears and arranges marriages for them all. He himself weds Pimpinella, receiving the blessing of Fourbo, who in his turn assumes the magician's guise.

In order to fit this argument – as Stravinsky rightly says (*Exp*), *Pulcinella* is more an *action dansante* than a ballet – he had to choose suitable operatic and chamber music numbers for conversion into dance numbers. At first, he was naïve enough to look for 'rhythmic' rather than 'melodic' numbers, only to discover that in eighteenth century music such a distinction does not really exist. As for the instrumentation, he wanted to use a small orchestra with certain eighteenth century features. The woodwind would exclude clarinets; the strings would be divided into *concertino* and *ripieno* groups; and there would be no percussion. The operatic numbers called for soprano, tenor and bass soloists; and the three singers would form part of the orchestra (as in *Reynard*) and would not be identifiable with any of the characters on the stage. In performance the effect of this device is to hint at a further musical dimension behind the instrumental score and behind the danced action on the stage.

He showed great skill in the selection, arrangement and occasional transposition of the music by Pergolesi that he decided to use.[1] The score is more than a suite of individual numbers – it has a definite entity of its own produced by the careful relation of textures, dynamics, tonalities[2] and instrumental colours. The sequence of the movements and the sources from which they have been taken are as shown in the table on page 247.

Stravinsky took over Pergolesi's melodies and basses virtually unaltered. His own contribution was occasionally to break up the formal symmetry of the eighteenth century music through the elision or lengthening or repetition of phrases, and also to throw out of focus the traditional harmonic scheme by

[1] It is possible that not all the music used is by Pergolesi. See particularly 'Two Centuries of Pergolesi Forgeries and Misattributions' by Frank Walker, and 'Notes on the Instrumental Works attributed to Pergolesi' by C. L. Cudworth in *Music and Letters*, October 1949.
[2] For instance, the transition from F minor to E Major at the end of 'Se tu m'ami' (no. 13) is like a douche of cold water.

Original Compositions

1. *Overture*	Trio Sonata I, 1st movement
2. *Serenata* (tenor solo)	*Il Flaminio* Act I. Aria (Polidoro)
3. *Scherzino*, with *Poco più vivo* leading to	Trio Sonata II, 1st movement
4. *Allegro*	Trio Sonata II, 3rd movement[1]
5. *Andantino*	Trio Sonata VIII, 1st movement
6. *Allegro*	*Lo Frate 'nnamorato*. Overture to Act II
7. *Allegretto* (soprano solo)	*Adriano in Siria*. Act III. Arietta (Aquilio)[2]
8. *Allegro assai*	Trio Sonata III, 3rd movement
9. *Allegro* (*alla breve*) (bass solo)	*Il Flaminio* Act I. Aria (Bastiano)
10. (a) *Largo* (trio)	*Lo Frate 'nnamorato*.
(b) *Allegro* (duet – soprano and tenor)	(a) Act III Aria (Ascanio)
	(b) Act II Canzona (Vannella)
(c) *Presto* (tenor solo)	(c) Overture to Act III
11. *Allegro alla breve*	12th Suite for Strings
12. *Allegro moderato*	Trio Sonata VII, 3rd movement
13. *Andantino* (soprano solo)	Canzona per soprano 'Se tu m'ami'
14. *Allegro*	Eight lessons for the Harpsichord (2nd set), VIIth Sonata[3]
15. *Gavotta con due variazioni*	Eight Lessons for the Harpsichord (1st set), II Sonata
16. *Vivo*	Symphony for Cello and Double-Bass, 3rd movement
17. *Tempo di minué* (trio)	*Lo Frate 'nnamorato*. Act I. Canzona (Don Pietro)
18. *Allegro assai*	Trio Sonata XII, 3rd movement

use of *ostinati* and the prolongation of certain harmonies. While the results are characteristic of Stravinsky's own idiom, they are much gentler and less pungent than anything in his later compositions.

The instrumentation is very varied and skilful. Each movement is scored for a different combination of instruments, with full exploitation of *concertante* groupings, not only between the *concertino* and *ripieno* elements in the strings,

---

[1] *N.B.* the *concertante* solo violin part has been added by Stravinsky.
[2] This arietta is also to be found in the second of the *Quattro Cantate da Camera* collected by Gioacchino Bruno.
[3] This Allegro also appears as a Rondo in the *Suite per clavicembalo*.

but also in the woodwind and brass. Some of the scoring is extremely witty –
e.g., the duet between double-bass and trombone in the *Vivo* (no. 16). In the
absence of percussion, brilliant effects are obtained by using dry instrumental
timbres to point and emphasise the metrical structure.

In all this, no violence is done to the spirit of the original. In his various
writings, Stravinsky speaks of his relationship to Pergolesi and his music in
terms suitable to a love affair. This was no rape, but a seduction, carefully
planned, successfully carried out, and vastly enjoyed – at least by Stravinsky!

The effect on his own style was not immediately apparent. (There is no sign
of Pergolesi's influence in his next two works – the *Concertino* and the *Symphonies of Wind Instruments*.) But, as he says in his *Memories*, his work on
Pulcinella undoubtedly led to a new appreciation of eighteenth-century
classicism on his part and to a new style of composition distinguished by
certain classical features. This was a moment when he had reached a definite
turning-point in his life. After the Bolshevist Revolution, return to Russia
seemed out of the question: so, in order to be nearer the heart of musical affairs,
he decided to leave Switzerland and settle in France. And at the same time he
needed a new set of musical values to replace the old ones. His allegiance to a
Russian popular melos was to be transferred to a new melos based on the
traditional music of Western Europe, particularly Italy. As he says in his
Expositions, '*Pulcinella* was my discovery of the past, the epiphany through
which the whole of my late work became possible. It was a backward look, of
course – the first of many love affairs in that direction – but it was a look in the
mirror, too.'

Productions

It was part of Diaghilev's bait to offer Stravinsky the chance of collaborating
with two of his most brilliant artists. In his *Chronicle* Stravinsky admits, 'the
proposal that I should work with Picasso, who was to do the scenery and
costumes and whose art was particularly near and dear to me, recollections of
our walks together and the impressions of Naples we had shared,[1] the great
pleasure I had experienced from Massine's choreography in *The Good-
Humoured Ladies* – all this combined to overcome my reluctance'.

Although this collaboration was entered on with great good-will on all
sides, it soon ran into difficulties. First of all, Picasso got on the wrong side of
Diaghilev, who wanted *commedia dell'arte* designs and was annoyed when he
was offered 'Offenbach-period costumes with side-whiskered faces instead of
masks' (*Con*). He was apparently so put out that the evening he was shown
these designs concluded with his 'throwing the drawings on the floor, stamping
on them, and slamming the door as he left' (*Con*). Picasso was at first deeply
offended; but after he had recovered his equilibrium, he produced a new setting

---

[1] In the spring of 1917.

showing an eighteenth-century theatre with its lustre, boxes and baroque decorations as a framework for a smaller scene where the *commedia dell'arte* action would take place. Finally the theatrical framework was scrapped and only the Neapolitan scene remained – the entrance to a narrow, moonlit street, with a glimpse of the Bay of Naples and Vesuvius in the background. As for the costumes, they seem to have been more or less last-minute improvisations.[1]

Similar misunderstandings occurred over the choreography. Stravinsky sent the different movements, as he composed them, from Morges to Paris in piano score; and Massine started to work on them straight away. But under the impression that the work was going to be scored for full orchestra (like *Petrushka* and the other earlier ballets) Diaghilev seems to have encouraged Massine to work to a scale that proved completely false when it was realised that Stravinsky had specified a small orchestra of only 33 players. In the early months of 1920, Stravinsky paid frequent visits to Paris to attend rehearsals; and in his *Chronicle* he writes: 'It often happened that when I was shown certain steps and movements that had already been decided upon I saw to my horror that in character and importance they in no wise corresponded to the very modest volume of my little chamber orchestra. They had wanted, and looked for, something quite different from what my score could offer. The choreography had, therefore, to be altered and adapted to the volume of my music, and that caused them no little annoyance, though they realised that there was no other solution.'

Despite these difficulties, the final result was satisfactory. It is true that Picasso's scenery 'filled only a part of the huge stage of the Paris Opéra and it was completely described by its own frame (rather than that of the Opéra)' (*Exp*) – also that the choreography of the Gavotte remained out of scale with its simple setting for wind octet (*Mem*). Nevertheless, Stravinsky considered *Pulcinella* to be 'one of those productions where everything harmonises, where all the elements – subject, music, dancing[2] and artistic setting – form a coherent and homogeneous whole' (*Chr*).

At the first performance at the Paris Opera House on 15 May 1920, Ansermet conducted. Massine himself danced the title role; Karsavina was Pimpinella; and Cecchetti, the company's veteran ballet-master, appeared in the minor part of the Doctor. The ballet was a great success with the public. Critics, however, were divided in their opinion of the music. The academicians and preservationists cried 'Sacrilege!' but the younger generation of musicians was enchanted.

There have been many other productions of *Pulcinella*, mainly in Europe;

---

[1] See *Picasso* by Jean Cocteau as reprinted in *Le Rappel à l'ordre*, Paris, 1926.
[2] A detailed account of the action and choreography is contained in Cyril W. Beaumont's *Complete Book of Ballets*, Putnam, London, 1937.

but none of them has reproduced Massine's choreography. Occasionally the title of the ballet has been changed. This was the case with the version Leon Woizikovsky did for his ballet company in 1935, *Les Deux Polichinelles*, and and also with Todd Bolender's two versions, *Commedia Balletica* for the Ballet Russe de Monte Carlo in 1945 and *Games* for Ballets U.S.A. in 1958.

Concert Suite

The concert suite is arranged for the same small orchestra as the ballet score and consists of eleven movements as follows:

- I. *Sinfonia (Overture)* (1)[1]
- II. *Serenata* (2)
- III.   (a) *Scherzino* (3)
  - (b) *Allegro* (4)
  - (c) *Andantino* (5)
- IV. *Tarantella* (12)
- V. *Toccata* (14)
- VI. *Gavotta con due variazioni* (15)
- VII. *Duetto* (16)
- VIII.   (a) *Minuetto* (17)
  - (b) *Finale* (18)

The vocal parts in nos. II and VIII(a) have been replaced by instruments. The suite was made about 1922; and the first performance was given by the Boston Symphony Orchestra conducted by Pierre Monteux on 22 December 1922. Published by Edition Russe de Musique, 1924 (later by Boosey & Hawkes). Duration: *c.* 22 minutes.

A revised version was made in 1949. Textually this is almost identical with the earlier suite; but metronome markings have been added, and the *Duetto* has been retitled *Vivo*.

Transcriptions

(1) *Suite for violin and piano, after themes, fragments and pieces by Giambattista Pergolesi.* Arranged at Nice in the summer of 1925 and finished on 24 August 1925. Dedicated to Paul Kochanski. Published by Edition Russe de Musique 1926 (later by Boosey & Hawkes). MS comp. [C 48].

- I. *Introductione* (1)
- II. *Serenata* (2)
- III. *Tarantella* (12)
- IV. *Gavotta con due variazioni* (15)
- V. *Minuetto e Finale* (17 and 18)

---

[1] The numbers in brackets refer to the numbers of the ballet score as given above.

(2) *Suite Italienne*: transcription for 'cello and piano by I. Stravinsky and G. Piatigorsky, 1932. Published by Edition Russe de Musique 1934 (later by Boosey & Hawkes). MS comp. [C 61].

    I. *Introductione* (1)
    II. *Serenata* (2)
    III. *Aria* (9)
    IV. *Tarantella* (12)
    V. *Minuetto e Finale* (17 and 18)

(3) *Suite Italienne:* transcription for violin and piano by I. Stravinsky and S. Dushkin. Arranged about 1933. Published by Edition Russe de Musique, 1934 (later by Boosey & Hawkes).

    I. *Introduzione* (1)
    II. *Serenata* (2)
    III. *Tarantella* (12)
    IV. *Gavotta con due variazioni* (15)
    V. *Scherzino* (10.c)[1]
    VI. *Minuetto e Finale* (17 and 18)

47. CONCERTINO

For string quartet. Composed at Carantec and Garches, July, August and September 1920. Dedicated to the Flonzaley Quartet.[2] Published by Wilhelm Hansen 1923. Reduction for piano duet by the composer. Edited and revised by Julia A. Burt, New York. Duration: *c.* 6 minutes. First performance, Flonzaley Quartet, New York, 3 November 1920. The manuscript score dated 24 September 1920 and the manuscript reduction for piano (four hands) are in the Library of Congress, Washington D.C. Other manuscript material is in the composer's collection [C 35].

    This work was suggested by M. Alfred Pochon, Leader of the Flonzaley String Quartet, a group of Vaudois string players. In his *Chronicle* Stravinsky explains: 'M. Pochon wished to introduce a contemporary work into their almost exclusively classical repertoire, and asked me to write them an *ensemble* piece, in form and length of my own choosing, to appear in the programmes of their numerous tours. So it was for them that I composed my *Concertino*, a piece in one single movement, treated in the form of a free sonata *allegro* with a definitely *concertante* part for the first violin.'

    The *Concertino* starts off with an acidulated preliminary flourish, an ascending scale passage in which the scale of C major (1st violin and cello) is

---

[1] *N.B.* – 10 (c) and not 3!
[2] The MS score, finished on 24 September 1920, bears a dedication to André de Caplet.

combined with the scale of B major[1] (viola); and this leads to a passage where the scale material passes over into a phrase of calm and serious character and the strings are given the direction 'Glissez avec tout l'archet'. This is preceded and followed by passages of busy but rather fussy figuration. A return of the acidulated scale flourish (this time B flat major combined with A major) leads to an *Andante* section, which turns out to be a long cadenza for the first violin with double-stopping, accompanied by two pizzicato notes from the cello at the interval of a major 10th, played sometimes at a crotchet's distance and sometimes at a quaver's.

Ex.35

This is the most memorable section of the work. A resumption of the busy figuration leads to a climax with syncopated repeated chords marked *très mordant*; and from this emerges a three-, or maybe four-bar theme like a Russian popular dance tune, but too brief and slight to hold the listener's attention for long. There is a hint of fugato treatment; the syncopated chordal climax returns, followed by a repetition of the acidulated scale flourish (back to C major and B major); and then in a quiet coda the *Andante* movement returns, referring first to the phrase of calm and serious character *Glissez avec tout l'archet* and then to the cadenza, which brings the work to a close with the emotional direction *sospirando* in the last bar.

Ex.36

[1] Not the scale of C sharp major, as erroneously stated in Roman Vlad's *Stravinsky*, Oxford University Press, 1960.

Original Compositions

The first violin part is excellently written throughout, but the remaining part-writing is not particularly interesting, and the work makes a strangely unsatisfying impression as a whole.

According to Casella,[1] despite all the meticulous care put into the preparation of this piece, 'its performance by the Flonzaley Quartet showed an almost complete lack of artistic understanding and resulted in a clamorous failure'. He goes on to recall that one day Onnou, the leader of the Pro Arte Quartet, said to him, 'You have no idea how completely one has to forget Spohr in order to be able to play this sort of music'.

Re-instrumentation

In 1952 Stravinsky arranged the original string quartet version for twelve instruments – flute, oboe, cor anglais, clarinet in A, 2 bassoons, 2 trumpets in B, tenor trombone, bass trombone, violin obligato, cello obligato. Published by Wilhelm Hansen 1953. Duration: *c*. 6 minutes. First performance by the Los Angeles Chamber Symphony Orchestra on 11 November 1952. MS comp. [C 35].

In the programme note for the first performance of the *Concertino* in its new guise, Stravinsky wrote: 'My present intentions towards my earlier work have led me to re-bar it rather extensively, to clarify some of the harmony, and to punctuate and phrase it more clearly.' The violin cadenza remains untouched. Elsewhere the violin and cello parts have been adjusted so that the two instruments frequently form a *concertante* group on their own. The success of this new version confirms one's feeling that the string quartet was not the ideal medium for the original composition.

Ballet Production

The *Concertino*, together with the *Three Pieces for String Quartet* (no. 25), formed the basis of a ballet entitled *The Antagonists*, which was produced by the American Dance Festival at New London, Connecticut, 1955, with choreography by Ruth Currier.

48. SYMPHONIES OF WIND INSTRUMENTS

For 3 flutes, alto flute in G, 2 oboes, cor anglais, clarinet in B flat, alto clarinet in F, 3 bassoons (3 = double bassoon), 4 horns, 2 trumpets in C, trumpet in A, 3 trombones, tuba. Dedicated to the memory of Claude Achille Debussy. Composed at Carantec and Garches, in the summer of 1920 and finished on 20 November 1920. Duration: *c*. 12 minutes. Publication: (i) A piano version of the last section (51 bars[2] long) was published as 'Fragment des *Symphonies*

---

[1] *Strawinski*. Brescia, 1947.
[2] The same section covers 54 bars in the 1926 edition and 61 bars in the revised and rebarred 1947 version.

pour instruments à vent à la mémoire de Claude Achille Debussy' in a music supplement of *La Revue Musicale*, December 1920, entitled 'Tombeau de Claude Debussy', where it appeared as no. VII of a set of ten compositions by different composers with the footnote 'Copyright 1920 by J. & W. Chester & Co.'. (ii) The first publication of the complete work was in 1926 by Edition Russe de Musique in a piano reduction made by Arthur Lourié. The full score was not printed. (iii) The revised version of 1947 (see below) was published by Boosey & Hawkes in 1952. First performance, Queen's Hall, London, 10 June 1921, conducted by S. Koussevitsky. The manuscript full score, which was in the composer's collection [C 36], is now in the Library of Congress, Washington, D.C.

Analytical Note

The *Symphonies of Wind Instruments* are not a symphony in the classical sense. The word symphony is here used in its original, fundamental sense of a 'sounding together' of different instruments, rather than in its later sense as an orchestral composition with a first movement in so-called sonata form.

In the summer of 1920 Stravinsky received a request to contribute to a special musical supplement the *Revue Musicale* was planning to issue as an act of homage to the memory of Debussy who had died on 25 March 1918. The friendship between the two composers dated back to the summer of 1910, when they had met after the first performance of *The Firebird* in Paris, and was based on mutual admiration. This led Stravinsky to dedicate his cantata *Zvezdoliki* to his French friend, and Debussy reciprocated by dedicating the third of his three pieces for two pianos, *En Blanc et Noir*, to Stravinsky. The two composers saw little of each other during the war, and Debussy's death at one of the darkest moments of that struggle caused Stravinsky real grief. When he accepted the *Revue Musicale* commission, he had already (in July 1919) started to draft a work which was originally written for harmonium. He now added (on 20 June 1920) an extended chorale, a processional of solemn, irregular but carefully spaced chords, which moved slowly towards a serene close and formed a coda to the main work. A piano reduction of this composition was published in the Debussy number of the *Revue Musicale*.

Whereas in the final chorale, he extended an idea he had already briefly touched on in the third of the *Three Pieces for String Quartet*, the other sections show a preoccupation with the instrumental development of the Russian popular material already used in many of his vocal compositions, particularly the numerous songs composed during his Swiss exile and *The Wedding*, and also in parts of *The Soldier's Tale*. The new composition can accordingly be looked on as a kind of symphonic summary of some of the musical ideas that had been fermenting in his mind during the previous six years. Having grown rather suspicious of the 'expressive' quality of the strings, he decided to banish them from his score and to concentrate on an orchestra consisting of triple woodwind plus eleven brass instruments, twenty-three players in all.

The *Symphonies of Wind Instruments* are ingeniously constructed out of contrasted musical material, geared (as in *The Wedding*) to three different but closely related speeds. This material, which is predominantly diatonic in character and frequently bitonal in treatment, can be divided into (1) episodes and (2) motives. (For facility of reference, these episodes and motives are here given invented titles.)

(1) *Episodes*

    A. 'Two Russian Popular Melodies' (see Ex. 39):

        (i) on five notes (flute solo accompanied by two flutes)

        (ii) on three notes (bassoon solo accompanied by three flutes – plus oboe, cor anglais and tuba for the recapitulation) N.B. This is the only passage in the whole work that is written in regular metre.

    B. 'Pastorale' (a two-part, freely flowing dialogue between flute and clarinet)

    C. 'Wild Dance' (a quick staccato episode, almost presto)

    D. 'Chorale' (see Ex. 24) (a very slow, legato processional – at first written only for brass; but the woodwind joins in towards the end)

After the exposition of A (i), A (ii) and B, each of these episodes is recapitulated in reverse order, B in a considerably shortened form. The recapitulation of A (i) leads to the exposition of C, and this is followed by a further appearance of C where part of the material is developed and varied rather than recapitulated. The work ends with D, which has no recapitulation. Each exposition or recapitulation is preceded by a prelude (or interlude) which is like a musical mosaic made up of brief references to parts of the various episodes or to the following motives:

(2) *Motives*

(*Z*) The 'Bell' motive, for flutes and clarinets, punctuated by trumpets and trombones[1] with which the work opens, (see Ex. 199) similar in cast of thought to the 'Tresses' opening of *The Wedding*.

(*Y*) A little two-bar motto[2] (sometimes for two oboes and cor anglais; sometimes for cor anglais and two bassoons)

(*X*) A group of quickly chiming chords (for woodwind, sometimes reinforced by horns)

(*W*) A counterpoint triplet phrase in three parts, the upper part being accompanied by a series of rising sixths,[3] which never appears on its own, but is used as a kind of interjection.

The three different speeds to which this musical material is geared are:

$$\text{I. } \; = 72 \qquad \text{II. } \; = 108 \qquad \text{III. } \; = 144$$

It will be seen that the second speed is half as fast again as the first speed; and the third, twice as fast as the first. I. embraces D,[4] *W*, *X*; II. A (i), A (ii),[5] B, *Y*; III. C. In the following schematic representation of the work, all speeds are $\; = 72$, except boxed references which are at $\; = 108$ and circled references which are at $\; = 144$.

Prelude—Z D Z Ⓒ D Y
   Exposition—[A(i) and A(ii)]
Interlude—Z D Y D (with *W* interjected)
   Exposition—[B]
Interlude—Y Z D Y
   Recapitulation (shortened)—[B]
Interlude—Y Z
   Recapitulation—[A(ii)]

---

[1] The instrumental details here given refer to the only published score available i.e., to the 1947 edition.

[2] E.g., two bars before fig. 4 [fig. 6 in the 1947 edition]; fig. 15 [26] etc. (All references in square brackets are to the 1947 edition.)

[3] This first appears in the trombones at fig. 7 [one bar before fig. 12] and is later taken over by other instruments.

[4] In its early publication in the *Revue Musicale*, the metronome marking of the chorale (D) was given as $\; = 100$; and this seems to show that the slower tempo was an afterthought.

[5] In the piano reduction of the 1920 version, no *Più Mosso* is marked at fig. 21 [38], and no *Meno Mosso* at fig. 22 [39]: so the implication was that the A(ii) theme was to be played at the slower speed of $\; = 72$ when recapitulated. This was corrected in the 1947 version.

Original Compositions

Interlude—Z Y
   Recapitulation— $\boxed{\text{A(i)}}$
Interlude— $\boxed{X}$ D $\boxed{X}$ Ⓒ $\boxed{X}$
   Exposition— Ⓒ
*Interlude—*D $\boxed{X}$
   Recapitulation (shortened)— Ⓒ
Interlude— $\boxed{X}$
   Exposition—D

Early Performances

The first performance of the *Symphonies of Wind Instruments* was given by Serge Koussevitzky in London in the course of a series of Russian Festival Concerts he was conducting at the Queen's Hall. The preliminary advertising of the concert on 10 June 1921 gave the following programme without any mention of Stravinsky's new work:

The Isle of Death	Rachmaninov
'The Battle of Kerjenez' (from the opera *The Legend of the Invisible Town Kitesh and the Maiden Fevronia*)	Rimsky-Korsakov
Concerto for Violin	Glazunov
Prometheus	Scriabin

Despite announcements that had been made to the contrary, the *Symphonies of Wind Instruments* were performed at the end of this strangely romantic programme; and in order to make room for the new work, the extract from *Kitesh* seems to have been dropped in favour of the Marches from *The Golden Cockerel* by Rimsky-Korsakov. The following day the notice in *The Times* said: 'Apparently the parts arrived at the eleventh hour; the work was, presumably, rehearsed, it was played, and was received by a large audience with a good deal of applause, in which some hisses mingled. . . . M. Koussevitzky seemed pleased with the performance of his players, so we must suppose that it really did sound more or less as intended.'

Stravinsky, who had arrived in London from Paris on the evening of 7 June just in time to put in an appearance that evening at the concert performance of *The Rite of Spring* conducted by Eugene Goossens at the Queen's Hall, was present at the Koussevitzky concert three days later; but although he stood up in his seat to acknowledge the applause, there were certain aspects of the performance that upset him deeply, and in his *Chronicle* he explains:

> I did not, and indeed I could not, count on any immediate success for this work. It lacks all those elements that infallibly appeal to the ordinary listener, or to which he is accustomed. It is futile to look in it for passionate

impulse or dynamic brilliance. It is an austere ritual which is unfolded in terms of short litanies between different groups of homogeneous instruments. I fully anticipated that the cantilena of the clarinets and flutes frequently taking up their liturgical dialogue and softly chanting it would not prove sufficiently attractive for a public which had so recently shown me its enthusiasm for the 'revolutionary' *Rite of Spring*. This music is not meant to 'please' an audience, nor to arouse its passions. Nevertheless, I had hoped that it would appeal to some of those persons in whom a purely musical receptivity outweighed the desire to satisfy their sentimental cravings. Unfortunately the conditions under which the work was given made that impossible. In the first place, it was badly situated in the programme. This music, composed for a score of wind instruments – an ensemble to which audiences were not accustomed at that time and whose sonority was bound to seem rather disappointing – was placed immediately after the pompous marches from *The Golden Cockerel* with their well-known orchestral brilliance. And this is what happened. As soon as the marches were finished, three quarters of the instrumentalists left their seats, and on the vast stage of the Queen's Hall I saw my twenty players still in their places at the back of the platform at an enormous distance from the conductor. The sight was most peculiar. To see a conductor gesticulating in front of an empty space, with all the more effort because the players he was supposed to be conducting were so far off, was disturbing enough. To control a group of instruments at such a distance is an extremely difficult task. It was particularly so on this occasion because the character of my music needed the most delicate care if it was to reach and win the ear of the public. Both my work and Koussevitzky himself were the victims of these untoward circumstances in which no conductor in the world could have made good.

Much though one sympathises with Stravinsky over this *débâcle*, one cannot help feeling that, quite apart from the choice of the other works in the programme, the grouping (or lack of grouping) of the players was something the conductor and the composer could have seen to in rehearsal.

Some of the other performances of the *Symphonies* in the 1920's seem to have been just as unfortunate. At the time of Stravinsky's American tour in 1925, he was interviewed by S. Roerig,[1] who quoted him as saying: 'A short while ago, I heard so extraordinary a performance of the *Symphonies of Wind Instruments* that I myself could make neither head nor tail of it . . . . In this case, the conductor kept dancing about on the podium, flinging his arms about wildly, particularly during a passage where two solo instruments were playing a delicate pianissimo. The audience naturally thought that something had

---

[1] *Strawinsky über seine Musik* contributed by S. Roerig to *Blätter der Staatsoper und der Städtischen Oper*, Berlin (1927).

gone wrong – otherwise the conductor would not have been making such an extraordinary fuss in order to produce sounds that were the reverse of "noisy".'

Revised Version (1947)

For 3 flutes, 2 oboes, cor anglais, 3 clarinets in B flat, 3 bassoons (3 = double bassoon), 4 horns, 3 trumpets in B flat, 3 trombones, tuba. MS comp. [C 36] and [C 86].

This revised version, though started in 1945, was not published until 1947. The change of instruments led not only to a certain amount of rescoring, but also to a few modifications of the music. For instance, the deletion of the alto flute meant that the flutes could no longer manage the accompaniment to the A (i) tune in consecutive sevenths at fig. 4 [6 and 7]. The modified accompaniment now goes no lower than middle C, and a 3/4 bar has been added at the end of the exposition to smooth the join with A (ii).[1]

A similar modification to the accompaniment (but transposed) has been made at the recapitulation of A (i).[2] Elsewhere a few notes have been changed. For instance, the second bassoon is given a C natural instead of a C flat at fig. [47], two bars before fig. [49], and the second bar after fig. [50].

The mistake (mentioned above) over the tempo of A (ii) at its recapitulation has been corrected. An impossibly short 1/8 bar at the end of one of the phrases of the pastoral episode (B) has been doubled in length.[3] An irrational

---

[1] One bar before fig. [8] in the 1947 version.
[2] Fig. [40].
[3] One bar before fig. [18].

poco rallentando marking one bar before fig. 25 in the 1920 version has been replaced by a fermata.[1] And there are a few changes in note values.

In accordance with Stravinsky's later practice, the work has been rebarred. This means that wherever possible larger irregular units have been broken down into twos and threes. The result is not always an improvement. Ansermet is particularly scathing on this point, calling the revised notation pedantic and complaining that it is not only worse adapted to the cadential structure of the motives, but also less easy to perform.[2]

49. LES CINQ DOIGTS – THE FIVE FINGERS

Eight very easy tunes on five notes for piano. Composed at Garches, the last piece being dated 18 February 1921. Duration: *c.* 8 minutes. Published by J. & W. Chester, 1922. 1. Andantino, 2. Allegro, 3. Allegretto, 4. Larghetto, 5. Moderato, 6. Lento, 7. Vivo, 8. Pesante. MS comp. [C 39].

In his *Chronicle* Stravinsky explains how in these easy little pieces for children 'the five fingers of the right hand, once on the keys, remain in the same position sometimes even for the whole length of the piece, while the left hand, which is accompanying the melody, executes a harmonic or contrapuntal pattern of the utmost simplicity'. In order to emphasise the restricted contour of the melody, the right hand of each piece is prefaced by the appropriate five-note series, e.g.,

Ex. 40

– a foretaste of other more complicated series to be used a third of a century later! Although a piece like the *Allegro* march with its jolly fanfare effects belongs to the same mood as the *Easy Pieces for Piano Duet*, the Italian titles of this set of eight carry on the usage already adopted in the score of *Pulcinella*, and the fourth piece (*Larghetto*) is definitely written in the same style as the *Serenata* movement in the ballet – a 6/8 *alla siciliana*. The only piece that seems to hark back to the Russian popular style of the war years is the rather slow sad dance, no. 6 *Lento*. Most of the other numbers accept the prevailing major/minor mode conventions of the eighteenth and nineteenth centuries, – there are echoes of Fauré in the second and fifth pieces – but apply to them Stravinsky's special processes of elision and overlapping. These inevitably lead to those dominant/tonic superimpositions that were later to form such

---

[1] One bar before fig. [42].
[2] *Les Fondements de la Musique dans la Conscience Humaine.* Neûchatel, 1961.

Original Compositions

a marked characteristic of his neo-classical style. Here they can be seen in all their starkness in the rather clumpy Tango (no. 8 *Pesante*)

Ex.41

It is worth noting that not only do the metres of these eight pieces show great regularity, but there are also repeat marks in nos. 1, 2, 4 and 5, and there could easily have been one in no. 6 as well, had Stravinsky felt inclined. So considerable an element of symmetry is rather novel in his style.

These little pieces represent the first fruits of some of the lessons he had learnt in handling Pergolesi's music in *Pulcinella*.

Instrumentation

In 1961 Stravinsky orchestrated the last piece (no. 8 *Pesante*) for an ensemble of about twelve instruments, including trumpet, trombone, clarinet, oboe, and bassoon, and it was performed by Robert Craft in Mexico City (December 1961). This version was withdrawn by the composer, who recomposed all eight pieces in 1962 for a small ensemble under the title:

49 (A). EIGHT INSTRUMENTAL MINIATURES

For fifteen players.[1] Dedicated to Lawrence Morton. Published by J. & W. Chester, 1963. Duration: *c.* 8 minutes.

I. *Andantino* ♩=76	[1. *Andantino*][2]
II. *Vivace* ♩.=126	[7. *Vivo*]
III. *Lento* ♩=63	[6. *Lento*]
IV. *Allegretto* ♩=126	[3. *Allegretto*]
V. *Moderato alla breve* 𝅗𝅥=84–88	[5. *Moderato*]
VI. *Tempo di Marcia*	[2. *Allegro*]
VII. *Larghetto* ♩.=68–69	[4. *Larghetto*]
VIII. *Tempo di Tango*	[8. *Pesante*]

The first four numbers[3] were first performed at the 'Monday Evening Concerts' Los Angeles, 26 March 1962, conducted by Robert Craft; and the complete

---

[1] 2 fl, 2 ob, 2 cl, 2 fg, 1 horn, 2 violins, 2 violas, 2 cellos.
[2] The references to corresponding movements in *The Five Fingers* are given in square brackets.
[3] Programmed then as 'Four Movements from *Les Cinq Doigts*'.

set of eight was first performed by the C.B.C. Symphony Orchestra conducted by the composer at the Massey Hall, Toronto, on 29 April 1962.

In the process of instrumentation, the original piano pieces were to a certain extent recomposed. Not only was the original material rethought in instrumental terms, which involved (in Stravinsky's own words) 'rhythmic rewriting, phrase regrouping', but it also underwent 'canonic elaboration, new modulation'. As can be seen from the above specification, the movements of the *Eight Instrumental Miniatures* follow in a different order from that of the pieces in *The Five Fingers*. All the movements are in their original keys, with the exceptions of nos. II (A major instead of F major) and VI (B major instead of C major).[1] These changes lead to a more varied key sequence than in the set of piano pieces, viz.

> I. C major, II. A major, III. D major/minor, IV. C major, V. E minor, VI. B major, VII. E minor, VIII. C major.

The ingenious canonic elaboration of the main theme at the reprise should be noticed in no. I. Nos. IV and V have been slightly lengthened.

SUITE [no. 2]

For small orchestra, 1921 – see no. 32 (B).

50. MAVRA

Opera buffa in one act after A. Pushkin's story *The Little House in Kolomna* for soprano, mezzo-soprano, contralto, tenor and orchestra (3.3.3.2 – 4.4.3.1 – Timp. – 1 1st Vl, 1 2nd Vl, 1 Vla, 3 Vc, 3 Cb). Russian verse libretto by Boris Kochno. English translations by (i) Robert Burness and (ii) Robert Craft; French by Jacques Larmanjat; German by A. Elukhen. Composed at Anglet and Biarritz between the end of the summer of 1921 and 9 March 1922. The overture was written a few weeks later at Monte Carlo, Marseilles and Paris. Dedicated to the memory of Pushkin, Glinka and Chaikovsky. Published by Edition Russe de Musique 1925 (later by Boosey & Hawkes). Vocal score by the composer. Edited by Albert Spalding, New York. Duration: *c.* 25 minutes. First performance by the Russian Ballet at the Opera House, Paris, 3 June 1922, conducted by Gregor Fitelberg. A manuscript copy of the Overture belongs to M. Ernest Ansermet. A sketch book is in Robert Craft's collection. Other manuscript material is in the composer's collection [C 40] and [C 94].

---

[1] It seems that in transposing this March from C major to B major, Stravinsky had at the back of his mind the effect of the modulation from F sharp minor back to F major in the finale of Beethoven's Eighth Symphony (see *Dialogues*).

Original Compositions

Composition

Mavra dates back to the summer of 1921, when Stravinsky and Diaghilev were staying at the Savoy Hotel, London (*Exp*).

Leonide Massine had just left the Russian Ballet; and in the absence of a leading choreographer, Diaghilev conceived the idea of reviving in the autumn Chaikovsky's full-length ballet *The Sleeping Beauty*, which had never been produced by his company and had in fact never been seen in Western Europe. He consulted Stravinsky on the music; and at his request Stravinsky agreed to orchestrate two of the numbers which were to be found in the piano reduction, but appeared to be missing from the only copy of the full score which Diaghilev had been able to lay hands on.[1] He undoubtedly enjoyed this experience; and a few weeks before the first performance of the ballet at the Alhambra Theatre, London, he wrote an open letter to Diaghilev (reprinted in *The Times*,[2]) extolling the virtues of Chaikovsky's music, which was then severely underrated in Western Europe, particularly France.

The following extract shows the lines on which he was thinking:

> Chaikovsky's music, which does not appear specifically Russian to everybody, is often more profoundly Russian than music which has long since been awarded the facile label of Muscovite picturesqueness. This music is quite as Russian as Pushkin's verse or Glinka's song. While not specifically cultivating in his art the 'soul of the Russian peasant', Chaikovsky drew *unconsciously* from the true, popular sources of our race.

And this is what Stravinsky decided himself to do in his new composition – to produce a music influenced by Italo-Slav culture that would be as Russian as Pushkin's verse or Glinka's song.

He decided the new work should be an *opera buffa*, and he found the subject he wanted in Pushkin's rhymed story, *The Little House in Kolomna*. Diaghilev was interested in the project, and his personal secretary, Boris Kochno, was chosen as librettist. The course of the action and the sequence of the musical numbers were worked out in London by the two of them, after which Stravinsky retired to Anglet near Biarritz to await the arrival of the libretto. Kochno produced a Russian verse text which was gay and (according to Stravinsky) 'musical' (*Exp*). The verses were a perfect pretext for the purpose he had in mind. He made a straightforward setting of them, without apparently feeling any need to cut across the sense by 'syllabising' as was to be the case later on in *Persephone*. But all the time he kept Pushkin's original text firmly in mind. This served him as a base; and in his music he tried to recreate what some years later in a lecture on the Russian poet he was to call the 'zephyr' of his verse.[3]

---

[1] 'Aurora's Variation' from Act II and the symphonic entracte preceding the finale of Act II. See p. 546.
[2] See Appendix A (1).
[3] *Pushkin: Poetry and Music.* 1940. See Appendix A (8).

2. Register of Works

Parasha's aria was the first part of the music to be written; but Stravinsky's work on the opera was soon interrupted by the necessity of going over to London for the first performance of *The Sleeping Beauty* at the Alhambra (2 November 1921). On his return he settled down with his family at Biarritz and resumed his composition. The opera was finished by March 1922. The overture was added a few weeks later while Stravinsky was visiting Monte Carlo, Marseilles and Paris.

The action of *Mavra* takes place in a small Russian town at the time of Charles X. The curtain rises on the living-room of a middle-class family, where Parasha, the daughter, is working at her embroidery. Her neighbour, Basil, a handsome hussar, appears outside the window; and the lovers sing a duet. When he has gone, Parasha's mother enters and laments the fact that she is without a servant, her old cook Thekla having recently died. Parasha goes off to see if she can engage someone; and while she is away, a neighbour calls for a gossip about the weather, servants and clothes. Parasha returns with the hussar wearing women's clothes and introduces him as the new cook – Mavra. The mother is delighted by her good fortune. After all four have joined in a quartet praising the virtues of the departed Thekla, the neighbour takes her leave and the mother goes upstairs to dress before going out. The two lovers, left alone, sing an impassioned love duet. Then Parasha joins her mother for a walk. With the house empty, Mavra decides it is expedient to shave; but Parasha and her mother return unexpectedly early from their walk and discover the new cook in the middle of this masculine operation. In her alarm, the mother faints, but recovers consciousness just in time to see the hussar leap out of the window and to hear her daughter crying after him 'Basil! Basil!' as the curtain falls.

The musical scheme consists of formal numbers separated by brief passages of dialogue, which are treated, not as recitative, but as fully composed declamation.

Overture
    I. 'Parasha's Aria'
    II. 'The Hussar's Gypsy Song'[1]
    III. 'Dialogue' (The Mother and Parasha)
    IV. 'The Mother's Aria'
    V. 'Dialogue' (The mother and the neighbour)
    VI. 'Duet' (The mother and the neighbour)
    VII. 'Dialogue' (The mother, the neighbour, Parasha and Mavra)
    VIII. 'Quartet' (The mother, the neighbour, Parasha and Mavra)
    IX. 'Dialogue' (The mother, the neighbour, Parasha and Mavra)

---

[1] This song alternates with passages from Parasha's aria, until after a brief duet the Hussar goes away, leaving Parasha to finish her aria alone.

  X. 'Duet' (Parasha and Mavra)
 XI. 'Dialogue' (Mavra, Parasha and her mother)
XII. 'Mavra's Aria'
XIII. 'Coda' (Mavra, Parasha, her mother and the neighbour)

Music

With the composition of *Mavra,* Stravinsky assumed a conscious esthetic standpoint; and when the initial production of this *opera buffa* proved a failure, he took great pains to explain, argue and defend his position. Important sections of his *Chronicle, Poetics of Music* and *Expositions* are devoted to this purpose; and a kind of supplementary apology is provided by his son Theodore in his book *Le Message d'Igor Strawinsky.*[1]

In the first place, he wanted to show that in the course of time he had grown thoroughly antagonistic to the picturesque nationalist element in Russian music as typified by the works of the Mighty Five (i.e., Balakirev, Mussorgsky, Borodin, Rimsky-Korsakov and Cui) and wished deliberately to align himself with the opposite tradition in Russian art which 'united the most characteristically Russian elements with the spiritual riches of the West' (*Chr*). In this connection (as he pointed out in his letter to *The Times*) he was thinking particularly of Pushkin, Glinka and Chaikovsky; and to this triumvirate he decided to dedicate his new work.

Secondly, he wanted to revive the form of the old Russo-Italian opera as a counterblast to the music drama of Wagner 'which represented no tradition at all from the historical point of view and which fulfilled no necessity at all from the musical point of view' (*Poetics*).

Kochno's libretto provided him with an excellent framework. The action of this little skit demanded a straightforward musical setting, and there was no question (as had been the case with *The Nightingale* and *Reynard*) of putting the singers in the pit and replacing them by actors or dancers on the stage. As for the question of style, his recent experience in adapting Pergolesi's music for *Pulcinella* had not only stimulated in him a new historical awareness and interest, but had also convinced him that certain idioms and procedures current in the music of earlier periods could be adapted and transmuted for his own creative needs. He accordingly seized on the vocal style of the operas of Glinka, Dargomisky and Chaikovsky as a model and produced a free flowing melos of his own that showed clear affinities with Italian *bel canto*. The modes employed are the major and minor – particularly the latter. Much use is made of traditional figures of accompaniment, consisting frequently of chords of the dominant, sub-dominant and tonic. The following example from Parasha's opening aria shows a characteristic asymmetric melodic phrase repeated with variants and embellishments over an ostinato accompaniment made up of two

---

[1] Lausanne, Librairie F. Rouge et Cie, 1948.

repeated figures of different lengths. (The time signatures of the accompaniment have been altered to make this point clear.)

The fitting-together of these three metrical schemes:

3/4 + 5/8 + 3/4 + 5/8 *et seq.*
3/4 + 3/4 *et seq.*
4/4 + 4/4 *et seq.*

each of which carries the simplest dominant and tonic implications, inevitably produces dominant/tonic superimposed harmonies at various nodal points in the pattern.

The more closely the score is examined the more one is astonished by the richness and flexibility of the melodic line. The Russo-Italian *bel canto*, of which Parasha's aria is a typical specimen, is varied by the introduction of gypsy elements for the hussar, with abrupt contrasts of long and short notes. The trick which Stravinsky used in the works of his Russian popular period, of restricting the melody to a limited number of notes and then ringing the changes by permuting their order and value, has completely disappeared.

The seemingly inexhaustible flow of melody in *Mavra* spills over into contrapuntal richness. The quartet (no. VIII) is of a polyphonic complexity that is novel in Stravinsky's music; and there are numerous passages where the solo voices are accompanied by two-, three- or four-part counterpoint in the orchestra. This often imitates the vocal line; and the following extract from the Mother's lament for the dead cook Thekla (no. IV) shows a characteristic layout.

There is one other element that enters into this *opera buffa* and is used to underline its satiric content – ragtime. A touch of it is to be found in the accompaniment to the duet between the mother and the neighbour (no. VI) and the quartet (no. VIII). But its main appearance is in the Coda (no. XIII) where (as in the Sacrificial Dance in *The Rite of Spring*) an interrupted cadence is repeated over and over again in different fragments until it finally makes a complete statement in the last few bars.

Metrically, the work appears almost orthodox. The restless time changes of *The Rite of Spring, The Soldier's Tale* and the *Symphonies of Wind Instruments* have almost completely disappeared; but what the work loses in metrical complexity, it gains in rhythmic subtlety.

Although tonality is everywhere clearly established by a strong and vigorous bass, the wealth of modulation within the various movements is something quite new in Stravinsky's music, as is also the wealth of suspended modulations in a number like the love duet (no. X). Changes of key are often ranged round a polar note – for instance, the G that dominates the Overture appears in different episodes as tonic (of G minor), mediant (of E flat major), dominant (of C); and although the Overture modulates ultimately to B flat to lead directly into Parasha's opening aria (in B flat minor), the G makes an occasional reappearance there too as major sixth in the vocal line (see Ex. 42). This device helps to articulate the different limbs of the music, giving a feeling of variety subject to unified control.

The instrumentation is somewhat unusual, for the orchestra is really a wind ensemble with a few strings added. The sound it makes is fiery and truculent. Stravinsky says he used it 'because the music whistled as wind instruments whistle, and also because there was a certain jazz element in it – the quartet especially – that seemed to require a "band" sound rather than an "orchestral" sound' (*Exp*).

First Performance

As *Mavra* had been planned from the beginning with Diaghilev's full knowledge and approval, arrangements were made for the Russian Ballet to produce it as soon as it was ready; but once again a serious miscalculation was made about the scale of the work. Whereas in the case of *Pulcinella* it had proved possible to adjust most of the choreographic errors before the work came to actual performance, with so small-scale a work as *Mavra* it was vital to find an intimate setting if the little *opera buffa* was to make its point. But Diaghilev had secured the Paris Opera House for his summer season, and it was in this thoroughly inappropriate and overpowering setting that, willy nilly, it had to be produced. For this purpose Diaghilev paired it with *Reynard*, both chamber works without chorus, and each with only four solo singers; and then, as if to emphasise their miniature proportions even further, included two of Stravinsky's most spectacular ballets, *Petrushka* and *The Rite of Spring*, in the same programme. The producer was Nijinska. The four singers – Oda Slobodskaia, Sadovène, Soia Rosovska and Bélina Skoupevski – did their best, but they failed to carry out Nijinska's choreographic ideas. Scenery and costumes were by Léopold Survage;[1] and Gregor Fitelberg conducted.

The result of the first performance (on 3 June 1922) was a ghastly flop. Stravinsky has described how anxious Diaghilev was 'to impress Otto Kahn, who attended the première in Diaghilev's box and who was to have brought the

---

[1] Bakst was originally chosen as designer, but Diaghilev quarrelled with him over money.

company to America. Otto Kahn's only comment was: "I liked it all, then 'poop' it ends too quickly" ' (*Con*). According to Robert Siohan,[1] the following witticism was bandied about the corridors during the interval, 'Ce Mavra, c'est vraiment mavrant'; and as the audience dispersed after the show Francis Poulenc overheard a couple saying to each other, 'Splendid! At last a work of Stravinsky's fit for our daughter's ears!'[2] Vuillermoz wrote so violent an article about the work in the press that (according to Darius Milhaud)[3] Stravinsky cut it out and mounted it in his manuscript score.

Not unnaturally it has taken *Mavra* a long time to recover from this false start. It was given a good production in Berlin (Krolloper, 23 February 1928); but other stage productions have followed reluctantly and slowly, partly because it is so short that it can be fitted into an opera company's repertory only as a single item in a mixed bill of three or four one-act operas, and this type of programme has the reputation of being particularly unpopular with the opera-going public. Perhaps in course of time it will be found to be an ideal length for television. The cosy bourgeois setting and intimate nature of the action ought certainly to come over well on the screen.

The first performance at the Paris Opera was preceded by a private audition at the Hôtel Continental, Paris, on 27 May 1922 with the composer at the piano. The first public concert performance was given at a Jean Weiner concert in Paris on 26 December 1922, conducted by Ernest Ansermet. In 1942 it was staged as a ballet at the Opera House, Rome, with choreography by Aurel Milloss.

Arrangement and Transcriptions

An extraordinary arrangement of part of *Mavra* was made in (or about) 1930 by Jack Hylton with Stravinsky's agreement. He took the middle section of the opera, including the duet and quartet (nos. VI and VIII), replaced the voices by instruments and arranged the music for his jazz band (including saxophones). According to Stravinsky, Hylton actually conducted this *Mavra* potpourri in the Paris Opera House about 1932, and 'it was an awful flop' (*Exp*). It seems strange that the composer should have consented to such a travesty of his music.[4]

Chanson Russe ('Russian Maiden's Song')

Arranged for violin and piano by I. Stravinsky and S. Dushkin, New York, April 1937. Published by Edition Russe de Musique, 1938 (later Boosey & Hawkes). MS comp. [C 60].

---

[1] *Stravinsky*. Paris, 1959.
[2] Quoted by Theodore Stravinsky in *Le Message d'Igor Strawinsky*.
[3] *Etudes*. Paris, 1927.
[4] There is a photograph (reproduced in Friedrich Herzfeld's book on Stravinsky, Berlin, 1961) showing Stravinsky, Jack Hylton, Ansermet, and one or two saxophonists at a recording session of this arrangement.

2. Register of Works

Chanson Russe ('Russian Maiden's Song')

For 'cello and piano by I. Stravinsky and D. Markevitch. Edition Russe de Musique (later Boosey & Hawkes).

51. OCTET

For wind instruments (1 flute, 1 clarinet in B flat, 2 bassoons, 1 trumpet in C, 1 trumpet in A, 1 tenor trombone, 1 bass trombone). Started at Biarritz, late 1922 and finished in Paris on 20 May 1923. Published by Edition Russe de Musique 1924 (later by Boosey & Hawkes).[1] Edited by Albert Spalding, New York. Duration 16 minutes. First performance, Concerts Koussevitzky, Opera House, Paris, 18 October 1923, conducted by the composer. The manuscript, which formerly belonged to Werner Reinhart, is now in the Stiftung Rychenberg, Winterthur. Other manuscript material is in the composer's collection [C 41].

    I. *Sinfonia*

        Lento, ♪=76, leading to *Allegro moderato* ♩=104

    II. *Tema con variazioni*

        'Tema' *Andantino* ♪=92
        Variation A ♪=126
        Variation B ♩=120–126
        Variation A ♪=126
        Variation C ♩.=63
        Variation D *Tempo giusto* ♩=189[2]
        Variation A ♪=126
        Variation E *Fugato* ♪=84
        A bridge passage *Moderato* ♩=116 leads to

    III. *Finale Tempo giusto* ♩=116

Composition and Treatment

In the late summer of 1922 Stravinsky made a journey to Germany to meet his mother, who was due to arrive at Stettin on a Soviet boat that was bringing her from Leningrad. While staying in Berlin at the Russischer Hof, he was approached by an enthusiastic young American musician, George Antheil, who introduced himself and spent some time in Stravinsky's company during the tedious period of waiting. According to Antheil,[3] Mozart was at that time

---

[1] The published score bears no dedication; but in *Dialogues* Stravinsky states that the work was in fact dedicated to Vera de Bosset, who later became his second wife.
[2] ♩ = 160 is the metronome marking in the revised version of 1952.
[3] *Bad Boy of Music.* London, 1947.

Original Compositions

Stravinsky's special musical love, and he quotes him as saying, 'If I had my way I would cut all the development sections out of Mozart's symphonies. They would be fine then!' Whether this story is true or apocryphal, it throws a sidelight on the nature of the problem that confronted Stravinsky later that autumn when on his return to Biarritz he started to compose an instrumental piece in sonata form.

There is a slight discrepancy between the two accounts he has given of the genesis of the *Octet* and of the circumstances that led to his choice of a wind ensemble. In his *Chronicle* he states: 'I began to write this music without knowing what its sound medium would be – that is to say, what instrumental form it would take. I only decided that point after finishing the first part, when I saw clearly what ensemble was demanded by the contrapuntal material, the character and structure of what I had composed.' The following account, however, as given in his *Dialogues*, could be interpreted as meaning that the composition was the immediate consequence of a dream about a wind music concert.

> The *Octuor* began with a dream, in which I saw myself in a small room surrounded by a small group of instrumentalists playing some attractive music. I did not recognise the music, though I strained to hear it, and I could not recall any feature of it the next day, but I do remember my curiosity – in the dream – to know how many the musicians were. I remember, too, that after I had counted them to the number eight, I looked again and saw that they were playing bassoons, trombones, trumpets, a flute, and a clarinet. I awoke from this little concert in a state of great delight and anticipation and the next morning began to compose the *Octuor*, which I had had no thought of the day before, though for some time I had wanted to write an ensemble piece – not incidental music like the *Histoire du Soldat*, but an instrumental sonata.

The truth is likely to reside in a conflation of the two statements, for it seems reasonable to assume that after drafting the first movement in short score and casting about in his mind for the ideal instrumental ensemble, he embraced with alacrity the wind octet cue offered by his dream.

The *Octet* marks his rediscovery of sonata form. Tonality and modulation are fundamental to the structure of the first movement; and repetition and imitation are consciously used as elements of symmetry, balance and contrast in the formal design.

According to Stravinsky, the *Sinfonia* was written first, and then the waltz in the second movement. It was at this point that he recognised that the waltz tune would make an ideal theme for variations: so the rest of the second movement was planned accordingly. It was the first time he had used the element of variation in his compositions; and it is interesting to know that when nearly thirty years later he was describing his variation technique, he said: 'In writing variations my method is to remain faithful to the theme as a *melody* – never mind the rest! I regard the theme as a melodic skeleton and am very strict in exposing it in the variations.'[1]

In the second movement of the *Octet,* the fourteen-bar theme is based on the second mode of limited transpositions.

Ex. 44

The first part of the theme (i.e., the first eight bars) starts in D minor and ends in D major. The second part (i.e., the last six bars) modulates to C major and back to D major. It is interesting to find that the tonic note (D) lies outside the

Ex. 45

range of the scale. It will be seen that the first six bars of the theme are built on the first four notes of the scale. The way in which Stravinsky rings the changes on these four notes is strongly reminiscent of his manner during his Russian national period. But after the opening bars the tune moves further afield, showing its readiness to modulate, and the intervals become bolder.

The notes are here numbered 1 to 33 (ignoring the two *gruppetti*) to show how he erects this series into a kind of system for the purpose of his variations. For instance, Variation A, a movement with rushing demisemiquaver scale passages that carry the notes of the theme up or down an octave at a time,[2] starts with the first nineteen notes transposed a semitone higher, followed by 20–24 a tone higher. Then 25–28 (a tone higher on the 2nd bassoon) overlap 29–32 (a tone higher on the 1st bassoon), and the 33rd note (also a tone higher) becomes the third of the staccato E major chord in the opening accompaniment to Variation B. Here the notes of the theme are embedded in a March, which

---

[1] Quoted by Robert U. Nelson in 'Stravinsky's Concept of Variations' printed in *Stravinsky: A New Appraisal of His Work* (edited by Paul Henry Lang) New York, 1963.
[2] 'Ribbons of scales' is Stravinsky's description (*Dia*).

Original Compositions

carries other melodic material unrelated to the artificial scale on which the theme is based (Ex. 44). Some idea of the impatient modulatory character of the variation can be gathered from the way the theme is laid out. Notes 1–14 appear a fifth higher, notes 11–19 a semitone higher, notes 15–19 then appear at the original pitch, notes 20–26 a fourth higher, and notes 27–33 at actual pitch. Without carrying out similar analyses for the remaining variations, enough has been said to show that Stravinsky regarded these 33 notes as a series which he treated with considerable freedom and boldness.

Writing about the *Octet* shortly after its first performance, Stravinsky said:[1] 'Form, in my music, derives from counterpoint. I consider counterpoint as the only means through which the attention of the composer is concentrated on purely musical questions. Its elements also lend themselves perfectly to an architectural construction.' Although it would be hard to maintain that the form of all Stravinsky's previous major compositions had been governed primarily by contrapuntal considerations, there is no doubt that counterpoint is a fundamental feature of the *Octet*. Sometimes the music is laid out on the lines of a vigorous two-part invention (e.g., portions of Variation D in the second movement and the opening subject of the Finale); and there are places where the contrapuntal treatment becomes quite dense and complicated. This is particularly true of the four-, five- and occasionally six-part writing in the fascinating fugato that serves both as Variation E and bridge passage to the Finale.

The work is written in metres that are sometimes simple and sometimes compound. For instance, the irregular barring of the woodwind passage in the *Lento* introduction to the *Sinfonia* (2/8, 3/8, 3/16 etc.) is nearly equivalent to a regular 7/16 metre; and the fugato is written in an almost uniform 5/8. Elsewhere simple metres prevail. There is an interesting variation in the Finale, where the basic metre is 2/4 and a flute solo marked *espressivo* introduces a compound metre of 3 + 3 + 2 quavers that is fitted into two-bar units.[2]

This compound metre returns in the last bars of the Finale,[3] where it is treated chordally and gives the coda a curiously attractive, hesitant, slightly breathless effect (See Ex. 47). The final chord is a second inversion which (as Stravinsky says) 'suffices to indicate *finis* and at the same time gives more flavour than the flat-footed tonic' (*Dia*).

---

[1] From *Some Ideas about my Octuor*. See Appendix A (2).
[2] Fig. 64. [Fig. 66 in the revised version of 1952.]
[3] Figs. 71 and 72. (Figs. 73 and 74 in the revised version.)

311

Ex.47

As will be noticed from the specification of the movements given above, the metronome markings are precise, and the work is nearly as carefully geared to interlocking speeds as *The Wedding* and the *Symphonies of Wind Instruments*.[1]

There is a curious passage in Stravinsky's article on the *Octet*[2] where he says: 'I have excluded all nuances between the *forte* and the *piano*. Therefore the *forte* and the *piano* are in my work only the dynamic limit which determines the function of the volumes in play.' An examination of the score will show that this is not true. The dynamic markings for the instruments are carefully specified and range widely from *ff* to *pp*. In order to achieve a proper balance and to obtain the light, dry and short degrees of accentuation that he needed, the score is also liberally marked with directions – *leggierissimo, staccatissimo, marcatissimo, très sec, très court, très marqué*, and the like.[3]

It is interesting to find that a few passages in the *Octet* are prophetic of *Oedipus Rex*. For example, the layout of Variation A with its rushing octave demisemiquaver scale passages is similar to that of the Messenger's announcement 'Divum Jocastae caput mortuum'; the *brillante* treatment of flute and clarinet in the vertiginous Variation D forecasts Jocasta's Aria; and there is a striking moment in the Finale when a new episode with bustling quaver figuration is prefaced with the call[4]

Ex.48a

which rings out with the peremptory insistence of Creon's '*Respondit deus*'.

---

[1] Care should be taken at the change of tempo at the beginning of the fugato (fig. 51). Early editions of the original 1923 score marked the change from ♪ = 126 to ♪ = 84 with the explanatory signs ♩ = ♪♪♪♪ and ♪♪♪♩ = ♪♪ Both were incorrect and should be replaced with ♪♪♪ = ♪♪
[2] See Appendix A (2).
[3] The French directions were omitted in the revised version of 1952.
[4] Fig. 61.

Ex. 48b

Re - spon-dit de-us

First Performance

After the *débâcle* of the *Symphonies of Wind Instruments,* Stravinsky was doubly nervous about the part that could be played by a conductor in 'interpreting' a musical work. Much of his article *Some Ideas about my Octuor*[1] is taken up with an argument that seeks to show that in this composition the play of movements and volumes is so compelling that it 'could not, indeed, admit the introduction of the element of "interpretation" in its execution without risking the complete loss of its meaning. To interpret a piece is to realise its portrait, and what I demand is the realisation of the piece itself and not of its portrait.' From this standpoint it was a short and obvious step to decide that he would conduct the *Octet* himself. But this was more easily said than done because in the first place the players found the style of the work unusual and the music tricky to perform, and then by Stravinsky's own admission (*Chr*) he was only just beginning his career as a conductor and had not yet acquired the necessary technique.

He conducted the first performance at a Koussevitzky Concert at the Paris Opera House on 18 October 1923. Once again the extravagant scale of the auditorium can hardly have been the ideal setting for the launching of a piece of chamber music; and to some of those who were present, the sight of Stravinsky's insect-like gesticulations in front of an intimate group of eight players set off by screens must have given the impression they were viewing the performance through the wrong end of a telescope. Jean Cocteau, however, found that Stravinsky's back reminded him of 'an astronomer engaged in working out a magnificent instrumental calculation in figures of silver';[2] and Stravinsky himself thought 'the sound was well balanced' (*Dia*).

Revised Version (1952)

The changes in the revised version of 1952 (published by Boosey & Hawkes) are minimal.

The repeat of 16 bars in the Finale is written out in full, and this accounts for the renumbering of the figures in the score after 62.

A different metronome marking ($\quad$= 160 instead of $\quad$= 189) is given for Variation D; and three notes have been altered in the clarinet part one bar before the fugato.

Various misprints (including 'Variazione' instead of 'Variazioni' in the title

---

[1] See Appendix A (2).
[2] *Le Coq et l'Arlequin* (*Appendice 1924: Stravinsky Dernière Heure*).

of the second movement) have been corrected. The numbers of the movements are omitted, but the letters of the variations retained. The French directions (*très sec, très court* etc.) have been dropped.

A number of small changes have been made in the interests of clearer accentuation and better balance. The *fp* sign is frequently used. A note has been elided from the clarinet part in the eleventh bar after fig. 33. Another note has been elided from the clarinet part at fig. 65 (fig. 67 in the revised version). The brass is marked *p* instead of *mf* at fig. 52. The final chord of the first movement has been shortened to a staccato quaver instead of a staccato crotchet; and the bassoon parts which were crotchets at fig. 67 (1923 version) become staccato quavers followed by quaver rests at fig. 69 (1952 version).

There is some rebarring (a doubtful improvement) in the flute bridge passage leading from the fugato to the Finale.

Ballet Productions

The score was used for two ballet productions in 1958. First, by the New York City Ballet with choreography by William Christensen: second, under the title *Agrismene* by the American Ballet Theatre with choreography by William Dollar. Both productions were given in New York.

52. CONCERTO

For piano and wind instruments[1] (3.3.2.2 – 4.4.3.1 – timpani – contrabassi). Composed at Biarritz, mid 1923 to April 1924. (The orchestral score is dated Biarritz, 21 April 1924.)[2] Dedicated to Mme. Natalie Koussevitzky. Published by Edition Russe de Musique 1924 (later by Boosey & Hawkes). The reduction for two pianos by the composer was published in 1924; the full score in 1936. Edited by Albert Spalding, New York. Duration: *c.* 20 minutes. First performance, Concerts Koussevitzky, Opera House, Paris, 22 May 1924, conducted by Serge Koussevitzky with the composer as soloist. The manuscript full score is in the composer's collection, together with other manuscript material [C 43].

    I. *Largo – Allegro*
    II. *Larghissimo*[3]
    III. *Allegro*

Composition and Treatment

Whereas for a considerable part of Stravinsky's residence in Switzerland during the First World War the cimbalom had been the instrument to which

---

[1] The original French title was 'Concerto (pour Piano suivi d'Orchestre d'Harmonie).
[2] The printed score is dated 21 *August* 1924; but this seems to have been a misprint for *April*.
[3] Marked *Largo* in the revised version of 1950.

Original Compositions

he seemed to turn most naturally when he needed a continuo part (as in *Reynard*, the *Rag-Time* and some of the Russian Songs), the necessity to decide on a definitive instrumentation for *The Wedding* when Diaghilev decided to mount it in 1923 and the difficulty in any case of finding suitable cimbalom-players led him to a reconsideration of the piano. His interest in that instrument was rekindled to such a degree by his piano adaptation of *Three Movements from Petrushka* (1921) for Artur Rubinstein and the score of *The Wedding* (1922/23) that he made up his mind to write a piano concerto for performance at one of Koussevitzky's Paris concerts. True to his predilection for wind instruments as manifested in such recent scores as the *Symphonies of Wind Instruments*, *Mavra* and the *Octet*, he decided to omit all strings from his orchestra, with the exception of double basses; and when the *Concerto* was nearly ready, he fell in with a suggestion of Koussevitzky's that he should play the solo part himself.

In the *Piano-Rag-Music*, the *Three Movements from Petrushka* and the score of *The Wedding*, the piano is used primarily as an instrument of percussion; and that is the aspect of the instrument that predominates in the first and last movements of the *Concerto*. In the first movement, the piano is given a three-part toccata-like theme with obvious affinities to Bach and Scarlatti.

Ex. 49

A counter-theme, first heard *cantabile* on a solo flute,[1] is the sole prerogative of the orchestra. Apart from this brief gesture of independence, the orchestra spends most of its time borrowing, adapting and developing material derived from the piano toccata theme: so the main focus – both here and throughout the *Concerto* – is not in the contrast of different material given to the solo piano and the orchestra, but in the contrasted sound of similar material shared between a percussive keyboard instrument and a wind ensemble.

Quite apart from the dotted quaver *Largo* introduction which recurs at the end as a coda, the movement is given a strong feeling of ternary form by the repetition of the greater part of the exposition (some 74 bars) in the same key almost without change. (This is the first time since *Petrushka* that Stravinsky has literally repeated so substantial a chunk of music.) This repeat leads to a point where a piano cadence[2] is lifted a semitone in its resolution, which is a

[1] See fig. 13, and subsequently figs. 21 and 25.
[2] Two bars before fig. 17, and two bars before fig. 38.

signal for the piano to shake off the orchestra and run into a headlong cadenza where common chords in the right hand alternate with single notes (or octaves) in the left. By shifting the accents, Stravinsky obtains a splendid effect of continuous syncopation. The beat is constant, and the metre is rendered irregular by the introduction of 3/16 bars that help to shift the stress from one hand to the other.

Ex.50

After this magnificently vital movement, the second movement with its extremely slow, *legato*, rather viscous melody accompanied by thick rich chords like folds of stiff drapery comes as a complete change of mood. Apparently Stravinsky was reading a novel by Leskov at the time he was composing it;[1] and it seems as if at some level of consciousness or subconsciousness the continuity of inspiration must have been broken. 'Some pages of the manuscript disappeared mysteriously one day, and when I tried to rewrite them I found I could remember almost nothing of what I had written. I do not know to what extent the published movement differs from the lost one, but I am sure the two are very unlike' (*Exp*). This interruption of the musical argument may have been partly the cause of his lapse of memory at this point during the first performance. (See below.) There are two cadenzas for piano in this movement, during which the right hand imitates the left hand at a bar's interval with groups of accelerating arpeggios, the effect of which is to produce two unsynchronised but overlapping waves of notes, that end, the first time in a *legato*, the second time in a *staccato* downward run for the right hand. The *Più Mosso* section in the centre of this movement harks back to the toccata theme of the first movement for its subject.

The final cadence of the *Larghissimo* played about five times as fast forms the opening bar of the third movement. Although this too is an *Allegro* with bustling semiquaver figuration, it shows none of the assurance of the first movement. In fact, the first 52 bars sound like an improvisatory passage, in which neither piano nor orchestra knows what it really wants to do. The piano then has a descending scale passage of 24 semiquavers, grouped first in threes and then in twos, which gives the impression that there is going to be a change of tempo;[2] but this is an illusion, there is no change of tempo, and the

---

[1] The authority for this statement is André Schaeffner.
[2] Fig. 68.

Original Compositions

piano enunciates a new theme which turns out to be closely related to the toccata material of the first movement. This helps to give an impression of stability to the movement, especially when after repetition by the piano it is taken over by the orchestra in augmentation.[1] But scraps of other material intervene, including fragmentary references to the piano cadenza in the first movement, and lead to an unexpected *fugato* in the remote key of A flat major with a somewhat pompous theme.[2] The music begins to disintegrate in a passage marked *Agitato*;[3] but some feeling of order is restored in the coda. This is in two parts: the first refers to the dotted quaver *Lento* introduction to the first movement and brings back the fundamental tonality of A minor; the second, which follows after a general pause, consists of eight bars marked *Vivo*[4] with the piano making a final *marcatissimo* reference to the two-part theme derived from the toccata and the orchestra accompanying with chords on the off-beats until the interpolation of a penultimate 5/8 bar turns the final orchestral off-beat into an on-beat.

The insertion of an occasional 3/16 or 3/8 bar in simple duple or triple time is a special feature of this score. A good example of 6/16 (3/8) + 3/16 occurs in Ex. 50 above. Another characteristic metrical grouping is 6/8 (3/4) + 4/8 (2/4) + 3/8. This is to be found several times in the *Più mosso* section[5] of the piano cadenza in the first movement, and also in the slow movement.[6]

Although there is a close relationship of texture, speed and sound between the outlying movements, there is no doubt that the third movement, in contrast to the impressive organisation of the first, produces an effect of disorder and disarray, and the balance of the Concerto is affected accordingly.

First Performance

When Koussevitzsky persuaded Stravinsky to undertake the solo part of the *Piano Concerto* himself, he was helping to launch his friend on an active subsidiary career as concert pianist that lasted for the next fourteen or fifteen years. He appeared as soloist in each of his two subsequent piano concertos – the *Capriccio* of 1929 and the *Concerto for Two Solo Pianos* of 1935 – and also undertook a concert tour in 1932/33 with Samuel Dushkin as violinist and himself as pianist.

Although Stravinsky had appeared as a solo pianist as far back as 1908 when he gave the first performance of his *Four Studies for piano* in St. Petersburg, he had not kept his piano playing up to concert standard. So, early in

[1] Fig. 75.
[2] Marked 'majestueux' in the piano reduction for four hands.
[3] Fig. 84.
[4] *Stringendo* in the revised 1950 version.
[5] *N.B.* The effect of this *Più Mosso* direction is *Meno Mosso*, because the unit of the cadenza changes at the same time from a semiquaver to a quaver.
[6] The three bars before fig. 48.

1924, he started to devote several hours a day to refurbishing his technique and acquiring the necessary endurance for a performance of this scale. 'I began, therefore, the loosening of my fingers by playing a lot of Czerny exercises, which was not only very useful but gave me keen musical pleasure' (*Chr*).

The first performance of the *Concerto*[1] took place at one of Koussevitzky's Concerts at the Paris Opéra on 22 May 1924. Although Stravinsky's performance of the piano part was excellent – dry, percussive, authoritative – there was a moment when he suffered some discomfort from a lapse of memory. 'After finishing the first movement and just before beginning the *Largo* which opens with a passage for solo piano, I suddenly realised that I had completely forgotten how it started. I said so quietly to Koussevitzky, who glanced at the score and hummed the first notes. That was enough to restore my balance and enable me to attack the *Largo*' (*Chr*).

This was not the only occasion on which he had this sort of mental black-out. 'Another time, while playing the same concerto, I suffered a lapse of memory because I was suddenly obsessed by the idea that the audience was a collection of dolls in a huge panopticon. Still another time, my memory froze because I suddenly noticed the reflection of my fingers in the glossy wood at the edge of the keyboard' (*Exp*).

For the next five years Stravinsky retained for himself the exclusive right of performing the *Piano Concerto*, and in that period he played it about 40 times.

Revised Version (1950)

Stravinsky's reduction of the work for two pianos, which includes the piano solo part, is dated April 1924 and was published the same year by Edition Russe de Musique with an extraordinary number of errors and misprints. The manuscript orchestral score is dated 21 April 1924. When the full score was printed by Boosey & Hawkes some years later, it was described as the revised (1950) version. The piano solo part seems to be identical in the two versions, with the exception of an octave B added on the first beat of the bars at figs. 7 and 29 in the 1950 version. Otherwise, the changes refer partly to minor points of instrumentation, but particularly to tempo markings, as can be seen from the following comparative table on page 281,

It will be noticed that at several points the markings of the 1924 reduction are at fault. The *Doppio Movimento* at the end of the first movement fails to restore the speed of the original *Largo*; and the slow movement – quite apart from the misprint of the initial metronome marking – does not obtain the right differentiation of speeds between its different sections. The situation is

---

[1] It was preceded by a private performance the previous week (? 14 May) at the Princess Edmond de Polignac's, at which Stravinsky played the solo part and Jean Wiener played a reduction of the orchestral score on a second piano.

1924 *Version*	1950 *Version*
I. *Largo* ♪=98 (96–100) *Allegro*[1] ♩=104 *Più Mosso* ♩=166 *Doppio Movimento* ♪=♪	**I.** *Largo* ♩=48 . *Allegro* ♩=104 *Più Mosso* ♩=166 *Maestoso* (*largo del principio*) ♩=48
II. *Larghissimo* ♩=84[2] *Cadenza* (*poco rubato*) ♪=♪ [at the end of the cadenza, no marking] Fig. 54 ♬=♪ *Cadenza* (*poco rubato*) ♪=♪ *Doppio movimento* ♩=♪	**II.** *Largo* ♬=84 *L'istesso tempo, ma poco rubato* [at the end of the cadenza] ♪=63 *Più Mosso* ♩=84 *Cadenza* (*poco rubato*) ♪=84 *Doppio valore* (*tempo primo*) ♬=84
III. *Allegro* ♩=112 *Agitato* ♩=120 *Lento* [no metronome marking] *Vivo* ♩=132	**III.** *Allegro* ♩=104 *Agitato* ♩=112–120 *Lento* ♪=96 *Stringendo* ♩=132

not made any simpler by the fact that the note values of the first cadenza are half those of the second cadenza, though the actual speed of the two cadenzas is intended to be the same.

Ballet Production

Under the title *Treize Chaises*, this score was used for a ballet with choreography by Aurel Milloss produced by the Bühnen der Stadt Köln in 1960.

53. SONATA

For piano. Composed at Biarritz and Nice in 1924. Dedicated to Princess Edmond de Polignac. Published by Edition Russe de Musique, 1925 (later by

---

[1] The early editions of the piano reduction completely omit the *Allegro* direction and metronome marking.
[2] Obviously a misprint for ♪=84. When playing the Concerto, Stravinsky used to start this movement at a speed of ♪= *c.* 60.

2. Register of Works

Boosey & Hawkes). Edited by Albert Spalding, New York. Duration: *c.* 10 minutes. First performance, Donaueschingen, July 1925.[1] MS comp. [C 44].

I. $\decrescendo$ = 112 (completed at Biarritz on 21 August 1924)
II. *Adagietto* (completed at Nice, 6 October 1924)
III. $\decrescendo$ = 112 (completed at Nice, 21 October 1924)

Return to Beethoven

After the *Concerto for Piano*, Stravinsky's interest in that instrument continued unabated; and the last few months of his residence at Biarritz in 1924 were devoted to writing a *Piano Sonata*. In his *Chronicle* he explains: 'I gave it that title without, however, wishing to give it the classical form that we find in Clementi, Haydn and Mozart, and which (as is generally known) is conditioned by the use of the so-called Sonata Allegro. I used the term *sonata* in its original meaning, as being derived from *sonare*, in contrast to *cantare* and its derivation *cantata*. Consequently I did not feel myself restricted to the form that has become customary since the end of the eighteenth century.'

When the *Sonata* was published and performed, most critics looked on it as a linear contrapuntal work close to the spirit of Bach, and there was considerable talk of a 'Return to Bach'. Schoenberg, for instance, certainly had Stravinsky in mind when in 1925/26 he wrote a little squib entitled 'Vielseitigkeit', which he set as a mirror canon and published as the second number of *Drei Satiren* (op. 28).

> *Ja, wer tommerlt denn da?*
> *Das ist ja der kleine Modernsky!*
> *Hat sich ein Bubikopf schneiden lassen;*
> *sieht ganz gut aus!*
> *Wie echt falsches Haar!*
> *Wie eine Perücke!*
> *Ganz (wie sich ihn der kleine Modernsky vorstellt),*
> *ganz der Papa Bach!*[2]

It is true that in the *Piano Sonata* Stravinsky continued the exploitation of

---

[1] Although this performance at the Donaueschingen Festival was not advertised as a first performance, it preceded by nearly two months the widely publicised performance by the composer at the I.S.C.M. Festival, Teatro la Fenice, Venice, on 8 September 1925.

[2] *Why, who's coming here?*
It's little Modernsky!
He's had his hair cut in an old-fashioned queue,
And it looks quite nice,
Like real false hair –
Like a wig –
Just like (at least little Modernsky thinks so
Just like Father Bach!

(Trans. E. W. W.)

certain eighteenth-century technical devices that he had already started to use in the *Octet* and *Piano Concerto*; but the really striking thing is the way parts of it, particularly the *Adagietto*, reveal an interest in romantic procedures as exemplified in Beethoven's music at the beginning of the nineteenth century. This return to Beethoven after a return to Bach was unexpected, since it was common knowledge that in the past he had felt an antipathy to Beethoven's music.

In his *Chronicle* he describes how in his youth he was surfeited by Beethoven's works and revolted by sentimental talk about the *Weltschmerz* of his music. His dislike of Beethoven was intensified during the War, possibly for non-musical reasons; but according to Ramuz,[1] the vigour of his opposition was an indication of the need he felt to defend and assert his own musical nature – it was the attitude of a creator and not a critic.

In 1924, when planning the composition of his *Piano Sonata*, Stravinsky showed he was quite prepared to revise his own judgment. Wishing 'to examine more closely the sonatas of the classical masters in order to trace the direction and development of their thought in solving problems of form', he replayed a large number of Beethoven's sonatas, among others, and renewed his acquaintance with a composer who he now agreed 'must be recognised as one of the world's greatest musical geniuses' (*Chr*).

The effect of this return to Beethoven can perhaps be most clearly seen in the Adagietto of the *Piano Sonata*. Even the relationship of the key (A flat major) to the C major of the first movement and the E minor of the third and final movement is symptomatic of Beethoven's propensity to use some of the movements in his later sonatas as an excuse for exploring remoter keys. As can be seen from the following quotation,[2] the mood is lyrical, almost elegiac, and the melodic line fluent but capricious, starting slowly and gradually proliferating into passages of varied ornamentation and decoration. (See Ex. 51.) 'Beethoven frisé' was the expression used by Stravinsky himself to describe this effect – a far call from the simple restricted melodies he had been using only a few years previously during his Russian popular period.

This sounds a new note in Stravinsky's music and one that was to recur in the slow movements of some of his later compositions, such as the *Capriccio* and the *Symphony in C*.

The first and third movements are not so strongly evocative of Beethoven as the Adagietto. They are closely related to each other by having the same metronome marking and by the use of material common to both. The first opens with a 32-note theme arranged in quaver triplets doubled at the distance of two octaves. This recurs in the course of the movement, and also at the end.

---

[1] *Souvenirs sur Igor Strawinsky*, 1929.
[2] This is taken from the recapitulation of the main theme (bars 40–43). In two places the notation has been corrected by writing groups of *hemi*-hemidemisemiquavers instead of hemidemisemiquavers.

Ex.51

The same theme appears in the coda to the third movement; but there it is grouped in semiquaver quadruplets and its character is changed by the altered incidence of the accents.

In the first movement the harmonic implications of the right hand melody and left hand accompaniment are pursued independently of each other and frequently fail to coincide. This gives the music, despite its metrical rigidity, a curiously blurred registration.

The third movement is, for the most part, a bustling two-part invention. The principal theme is enunciated solo and appears later accompanied by itself in augmentation. There are a sentimental chromatic subsidiary theme (bar 26 *et seq.*)[1] derived from a motive in the Adagietto (bars 24 and 25) and a hesitant vacillating middle section that do not seem to fit in with the taut muscular vigour of the rest of the movement.

An early performance of the *Piano Sonata* was given by this composer at the Teatro la Fenice, Venice, on 8 September 1925 during the I. S. C. M. Festival.[2]

---

[1] In his book on Stravinsky, Casella suggests this theme might be attributed to Saint-Saëns!
[2] For Malipiero's account of Stravinsky at the salon of the Princess Edmond de Polignac in Venice, see p. 88.

Original Compositions

Although Stravinsky had to ask for the indulgence of the audience as he had a severe and suppurating abscess in his right forefinger, he seems to have given an excellent performance. His own account was that, as soon as he touched the keys, the festering finger was healed – a 'minor miracle' he called it (*Dia*).

54. SERENADE IN A

In four movements for piano. Composition begun in April 1925 and finished in the autumn at Nice.[1] Dedicated to his wife. Published by Edition Russe de Musique 1926 (later by Boosey & Hawkes). Edited by Albert Spalding, New York. Duration: *c.* 12 minutes. MS comp. [C 45].

I. *Hymne* ♩. = 58[2]
II. *Romanza* ♪ = 96
III. *Rondoletto* ♩ = 92
IV. *Cadenza Finala* [*sic*] ♩ = 84

Composition and Treatment

During his first American tour in the early months of 1925, Stravinsky made a contract with a gramophone company to record some of his music. This gave him the idea of writing a piece that would be exactly the right length for recording purposes; and the *Serenade* was planned so that each of its four movements would fill one side of a 10-inch record.

Not only did he entitle the piece *Serenade* 'in imitation of the *Nachtmusik* of the eighteenth century, which was usually commissioned by patron princes for various festive occasions and, like the Suites, consisted of an indeterminate number of pieces' (*Chr*), but he gave titles to each of the four movements as well. He looked on the opening movement as 'a solemn entry, a sort of hymn'; the *Romanza* was 'a solo of ceremonial homage paid by the artist to the guests'; the *Rondoletto*, 'with its sustained and rhythmic movement, took the place of the various kinds of dance-music usually intercalated in the serenades'; and the *Cadenza Finale* was an epilogue intended to be 'tantamount to a signature with numerous calligraphic flourishes' (*Chr*). But in some ways these titles seem hardly apt. In the first place, there was no special occasion for which a festive 'evening' composition of this kind was required: so the entry, act of homage, dance and final flourish had no particular point. Then, Stravinsky chose to condense his composition 'into a small number of movements for a single polyphonic instrument' (*Chr*); and while the choice of piano may have been convenient from certain points of view, it was certainly not the ideal

---

[1] In the manuscript the Hymne is dated 3 August 1925 and the Romanza 9 October 1925.
[2] This metronome marking was misprinted ♩ = 58 when the *Serenade* was first published: but the dotted crotchet is quite clear in the manuscript, the first page of which was reproduced in *Cahiers de Belgique* for December 1930.

instrument for the sort of festive occasion he seems to have had in mind. There was the added disadvantage that as a hymn implies something that is sung by one or more voices, so a hymn for piano solo sounds like a transcription – just the sort of error he had been so careful to avoid when planning the instrumentation of *The Soldier's Tale*.

If anything, these titles are an obstacle to the proper appreciation of a work, which it is more satisfactory to regard merely as a piano suite in four movements.

The 'A' of the title is important. It means, not that the *Serenade* is in the key of A, but that A is the tonic pole from which the music radiates and towards which it tends. There is an A at the beginning of each movement and an A at the end of each: the note appears at various times as dominant, mediant and tonic. Each of the first three movements ends with a cadence where a halo of overtones is caused by depressing one or more of the A keys on the piano, thereby raising the dampers and allowing the undamped strings to pick up sympathetic vibrations.[1]

The opening[2] of the *Hymn* has a choral dignity that seems prepared to modulate into the majestic opening of *Oedipus Rex*.

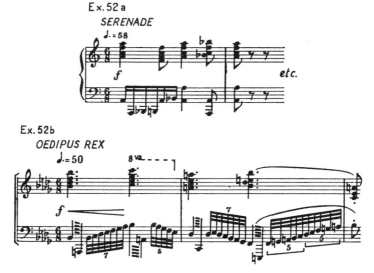

And even the following cadence in the *Serenade* has the same cut as the following cadence in *Oedipus Rex*.

---

[1] This device had already been used by Arnold Schoenberg in the first of his *Drei Klavierstücke*, 1910.

[2] In his book on Stravinsky, Casella points out the resemblance between this motive and Chopin's second *Ballade* (bar 7).

Ex. 53a
SERENADE

Ex. 53b
OEDIPUS REX

In the second part of this opening movement, the 6/8 theme is extended and developed over a running semiquaver arpeggio accompaniment full of harmonic suspensions. The 6/8 metre is varied by the introduction of occasional 9/8 bars; at bar 64 a passage of syncopation leads to the interpolation of a single 7/8 bar, but this change of time is not marked.

The *Romanza* opens and closes with a fine rhetorical cadence that recalls the cimbalom cadences in *Reynard*. The staccato passages that form an almost guitar-like accompaniment to the legato writing for the right hand demand crisp dry playing.

The *Rondoletto* is a two-part invention, in which the right hand theme (in A major) in the manner of Scarlatti is accompanied by rather turgid, close-set arpeggios (in C sharp minor) in the bass. The piece has something of the character of a *moto perpetuo*.

The *Cadenza Finale,* which was the first part of the *Serenade* to be composed, is a delightful fantasy on a kind of descending chimes motive. It is unusual in Stravinsky's music of this period to find a parallel stream of chords[1] – it is almost like an echo of Debussy, and the pianistic effect is attractive.

Ex. 54

legato   etc.

---

[1] In the musical illustration, the notation has been slightly changed in order to make this point clear.

The *Serenade* is perhaps the most satisfactory of all Stravinsky's works for solo piano. In it he showed he was no longer interested solely in the instrument's percussive qualities. It reveals a deeper sensibility than the earlier keyboard works, and a much wider range of texture and timbre. It is also a more grateful work to perform from the pianist's point of view.

SUITE (no. 1)

For small orchestra, 1925 – see no. 28 (A).

55. ОТЧЕ НАШЪ – PATER NOSTER

For mixed choir *a cappella* (S.A.T.B.) Composed in 1926. Published by Edition Russe de Musique, 1932 (later by Boosey & Hawkes). Duration: *c.* 1 minute 10 seconds. MS comp. [C 47].

The words of this unaccompanied setting of the Lord's Prayer are in Slavonic. In his *Expositions* Stravinsky recalls how when he was a boy in St. Petersburg, he and his brothers were occasionally allowed to join their parents for a late meal after one of their father's opera performances. 'After these late dinners, Mamma or Bertha came to see us in bed and to hear our prayers: "Our Father which art in Heaven..." – "Otchey nasch eezshey yehsee na nehbehsekh..."' (This is Slavonic – I do not know how to say it in Russian.)'

The *Pater Noster* was his first religious composition. In his *Memories* he says, 'In accordance with liturgical tradition, and in view of the Eastern Church fiat prohibiting the use of musical instruments (even of pitch pipes), the music is a simple harmonic intonation of the words.' But at a later date he admitted that at that time he knew nothing of the traditions of Russian church music and suggested that the *Pater Noster*, together with the other two sacred choruses composed a few years later – *Credo* (no. 63) and *Ave Maria* (no. 65) – probably fused 'early memories of church music in Kiev and Poltava with the conscious aim to adhere to a simple and severe harmonic style, a "classical" style but with preclassical cadences.'

The first time he heard the *Pater Noster* was in June 1937, when it was performed by the Afonsky Choir at the Alexander Nevsky Church in the Rue Daru, Paris, at the Requiem Service for his sister-in-law, Ludmila Beliankin.

There is also a sketch for a *Church Prayer* dating from about 1930 among his manuscripts; but this is unfinished and unpublished.

New Version with Latin Text (1949)

There are only minor changes in the new version with Latin text made in March 1949 and published by Boosey & Hawkes. These result from the necessity of adjusting the harmonies to the different number of syllables in the Latin text. The metronome marking of ♩ = 72 is given. A final *Amen* is added. MS comp. [C 95].

Original Compositions

56. OEDIPUS REX

Opera-oratorio in two acts after Sophocles by I. Stravinsky and J. Cocteau (Latin translation by J. Daniélou) for tenor (Oedipus), mezzo-soprano (Jocasta), bass-baritone (Creon), bass (Tiresias), tenor (the Shepherd), bass-baritone (the Messenger), narrator, male chorus and orchestra (3.3.3.3 – 4.4.3.1 – percussion, timp., harp, piano – string quintet). Composed at Nice between 11 January 1926 and 14 March 1927. The instrumentation was completed at 4 a.m. on 10 May 1927. Published by Edition Russe de Musique, 1927 (later by Boosey & Hawkes). Vocal score by the composer. Duration: *c.* 52 minutes. First performance (as an oratorio) by the Russian Ballet, Théâtre Sarah-Bernhardt, Paris, 30 May 1927, conducted by the composer. First performance (as an opera), Vienna, 23 February 1928. The manuscript full score is with Boosey & Hawkes, New York. The manuscript vocal score is in the Library of Congress, Washington D.C. Other manuscript material is in the composer's collection [C 49].

Genesis, Choice of Subject, and Libretto

This work stands almost at the midpoint of Stravinsky's creative output. It is true that it comes comparatively early in his 'neo-classical' period, which may be regarded as running from *Mavra* (1922) to *The Rake's Progress* (1948–51); but the intensity of his activity as a composer, which had been particularly marked in the years 1910–20, was slightly relaxed as soon as he launched out on his subsidiary careers as solo pianist and conductor. *Oedipus Rex* is the first masterpiece of his 'neo-classical' maturity.

In both his *Chronicle* and *Dialogues*, he has given detailed accounts of the genesis and composition of *Oedipus Rex*. It appears that for some years he 'had been aware of the need to compose a large-scale dramatic work' (*Dia*), but now that he had become an expatriate, the problem of language was foremost in his thoughts. This was solved by a lucky find. 'Returning from Venice to Nice in September, 1925, I stopped for a few days in Genoa to renew memories of the city where I had spent my fifth wedding anniversary in 1911. There, in a book kiosk, I saw a life of Francis of Assisi, which I bought and, that night, read' (*Dia*). The volume was a French translation of the monograph by Johannes Joergensen; and he was immediately struck by the following passage:

> French was, for St. Francis, the language of poetry, the language of religion, the language of his best memories and most solemn hours, the language to which he had recourse when his heart was too full to express itself in his native Italian,[1] which had become for him vulgarised and debased by daily use; French was essentially the language of his soul. Every time he spoke French, those who knew him realised he was happy.

---

[1] There is a misprint in the English translation of Stravinsky's *Chronicle*, where it says 'the familiar speech of the Saint was Provençal'. For 'Provençal' read 'Italian'.

2. Register of Works

This gave Stravinsky the idea that if he were to choose a sublime subject for his new work, he would be wise to express it, not in the vernacular, but in a special language, something older and partly sanctified, which might contain an incantatory element he could exploit in music. Latin seemed to offer the required qualities; and in his *Chronicle* he states, 'The choice had the great advantage of giving me a medium not dead but turned to stone and so monumentalised as to have become immune from all risk of vulgarisation'.

On his return to Nice, he continued to meditate on choice of subject. Turning to the myths of ancient Greece and remembering the impression made on him in his teens by Gneditch's Russian translation of Sophocles, he decided on *Oedipus Rex*. Here, as he explains in his *Dialogues*, was a universal plot, or, at least, one so well known that he would not have to elaborate its exposition. 'I wished to leave the play, as play, behind. I thought to distil the dramatic essence by this, and to free myself for a greater degree of focus on a purely musical dramatisation.'

Oedipus Rex: a page (dated 16 November 1926) from the fair copy of the vocal score

Original Compositions

At this point, he turned to his friend, Jean Cocteau, and invited his collaboration. They had known each other since the pre-war seasons of the Russian Ballet in Paris. Cocteau had dedicated *Le Potomak* to Stravinsky in 1914 when visiting him at Leysin with the idea of persuading him to collaborate on a new ballet to be entitled *David*. This scheme came to nothing; but late in 1922 or early in 1923 Stravinsky saw and admired the contraction of the *Antigone* of Sophocles that Cocteau mounted at l'Atelier, Paris, and now he decided to entrust him with the libretto for *Oedipus Rex*. He told him that what he wanted was not an action drama, but a 'still-life', and that the libretto must be a conventional one. Apparently the first draft Cocteau produced was precisely what Stravinsky did *not* want – it was 'a music drama told in a horribly meretricious prose' (*Dia*). After the book had been rewritten twice and subjected to 'a final shearing',[1] it was handed over to the Abbé Jean Daniélou, who translated it into Latin. Stravinsky received the first part of the final text early in 1926 and set to work immediately on the music. It was the collaborators' intention that the completed work should be a present for Diaghilev to commemorate the twentieth anniversary of his theatrical activity in 1927.

Cocteau published only a very brief comment on this collaboration. After recalling how he used to pay evening visits to Stravinsky and his family in Montboron near Nice, returning late at night to Villefranche on foot, he wrote: 'In February (1926) we made an excursion together in the mountains. Our guide spoke in oracles. We called him Tiresias.' It sounds like the setting for a scene in one of his films.

Whatever may have been Cocteau's own views, Stravinsky had very definite ideas about the staging of his composition. He was determined there should be a minimum of action on the stage. He envisaged the chorus seated in a single row, reading from scrolls with their faces concealed by cowls, while the singers stood on elevated platforms each at a different height. A note prefixed to the score specifies: 'Except for Tiresias, the Shepherd and the Messenger, the characters remain in their built-up costumes and masks. Only their arms and heads move. They should give the impression of living statues.' He wanted the singers to be illuminated during their arias. Creon and Jocasta were to be revealed on the stage, instead of making entrances. Oedipus would remain on the stage throughout, and his blindness in the final scene would be made manifest by a simple change of mask.

The idea of the Speaker was Cocteau's – a commentator in contemporary evening dress who would give an advance commentary on the action scene by scene in the language of the audience. Years later (in his *Dialogues*) Stravinsky was to express his detestation of this convention and his dislike of some of the

---

[1] From his draft for *Oedipus Rex*, Cocteau drew his play *Oedipe-Roi* (published in 1928). A few years later he reworked the Oedipus story into his four-act play *La Machine Infernale* (1934).

Speaker's lines. But he accepted it at the time; and the device certainly has its advantages. It helps the audience to keep its distance from the stage spectacle, which can be presented, not only at a language remove, but also as a kind of illustration of the dramatic theme, the successive stages of which are explained in advance so that the element of surprise is removed and the audience left free to concentrate on the purely musical (or operatic) progress of the score.

Although Stravinsky conceived the work as an opera and wrote into the score numerous directions for its staging, it is clear he was doubtful whether it would have much chance of consolidating its position on the operatic stage: so he aimed at making it viable in the concert hall as well and called it by the hybrid term of 'opera-oratorio'.

The progress of the composition can be followed in one of Stravinsky's notebooks.[1] The word *Serva* written beneath a chord with an indication of ternary rhythm was entered on 11 January 1926. The following day he noted the beginning of Oedipus's first solo. The opening chorus was sketched out between 13 and 15 January. After an interruption, he began Creon's aria in April; Tiresias's oracular pronouncement followed in August; Jocasta's aria in October. The duet between Jocasta and Oedipus was completed on 16 November;[2] and the last chorus on 14 March 1927. He finished the instrumentation on 10 May at four in the morning, just twenty days before the first performance.

Setting and Music

It is difficult to comment on the Latin libretto insofar as it is a translation from the French, since Cocteau's original text is not available. Daniélou's idiom is distinguished by brief, bold, block statements and occasional looseness of construction. Some examples of happy phrasing or neat word-play stick in the mind, e.g., 'Liberi, vos liberabo'; 'Audituri te salutant'; 'Solve, Oedipus, solve' followed by 'Salve, Tiresia, salve'; 'Ego exul exsulto'; 'Foedissimum monstrum monstrat'. In his *Dialogues*, Stravinsky has spoken of how when he composes words in music his musical appetite 'is set in motion by the sound rhythms of the syllables'. This may have been true of his Russian texts, whether in an onomatopoeic verse form like the *pribaoutki* or in more conventional verse patterns like Kochno's libretto for *Mavra*; but in the case of *Oedipus Rex*, he was confronted by a text that had no direct oral quality, as it could not be related to any living conversational tradition. Knowledge of Latin prosody being theoretic, he may be forgiven some of the false quantities in his setting. To one of these he has made public confession in his *Memories*. 'The line *Ego senem cecidi* accented on the *ce* as I have it means "I fell the old man",[1] whereas

---

[1] This notebook ('un registre commercial') was examined by André Schaeffner, when he was writing his monograph on Stravinsky in 1931.
[2] See illustration on page 328.
[1] This is not quite exact. *Cado* being intransitive, *cecĭdi* means 'I fell down' and the accusative *senem* is left in the air.

it should be accented *Ego senem cecídi* and mean "I killed the old man".' But given his need for musical freedom in syllabic setting, the effects in *Oedipus Rex* are not too upsetting. It is true that, whether judged by syllabic or verbal standards, the following passage from the big penultimate chorus – Stravinsky calls it a 'mortuary tarantella' – seems rather tortured, particularly when it is remembered that the tempo at which it is sung is nearly *presto*:

Ex. 55

Mu - li - er in ves - ti - bu - lo, in ves - ti - bu - lo

Yet the apparent awkwardness of the contradictory settings of *in vestibulo* is perhaps not inappropriate, since in its mood of frantic terror and excitement the chorus would be quite likely to trip over itself. As against this, the score contains a number of definitely felicitous passages, such as the whining note in Oedipus's voice when he appeals to the men of Thebes to place their confidence in him:

Ex. 56

A - mi - ki, a - mi - ki

An instance of a word proving germinal is *oracula*. Its setting in Jocasta's aria is the cue for a metrical development where rapid repeated notes in both voice and accompaniment produce an alarming tattoo like a warning tomtom and prove as memorable as the fate motive in Beethoven's Fifth Symphony. Another case is *trivium* – the crossroads near Thebes where Oedipus met and killed Laius. The word first appears, rather innocuously, in the *oracula* passage of Jocasta's aria; but later it is picked up by the chorus and repeated until it begins to beat out a warning message like a morse signal.

Stravinsky himself has pointed out one or two linguistic mistakes – 'mentiantur' for 'mentiuntur' in Jocasta's aria ('Oracula quae semper mentiuntur'); 'miki' for 'mihi' in Oedipus's comment to the chorus after Creon's aria ('Mihi debet se dedere'); and 'Vale!' for 'Ave!' when the chorus hails the arrival of Creon.

At this point it may be helpful to set out a schematic representation of the way the score is constructed with an indication of the key sequence. (Keys given within parentheses show some of the more important key changes in subsidiary sections of the various musical numbers.)

Act One

I. Speaker's Commentary

Chorus (Ai) 'Caedit nos pestis', B flat minor
    (Bi) 'Oedipus, adest pestis', B flat minor (A minor – C sharp minor)
Aria: Oedipus (1a) 'Liberi vos liberabo' E flat minor (F minor)
Chorus (Bii) 'Serva nos adhuc', B flat minor
Aria: Oedipus (1b) 'Uxoris frater', B flat minor
Chorus: quasi recitative 'Vale, Creo!', C major

II. Speaker's Commentary

Aria: Creon 'Respondit deus', C major (E major – E flat major – F minor – C major)
Aria: Oedipus (2) 'Non reperias', E flat major (E flat minor)
Chorus: quasi recitative 'Solve, Oedipus', E flat major

III. Speaker's Commentary

Chorus (Biii) 'Delie, exspectamus', B minor
Chorus: quasi recitative 'Salve, Tiresia', B minor/G major
Aria: Oedipus (3) 'Invidia fortunam odit', E flat major (C minor)
Chorus (C) 'Gloria', C major modulating to G major

Act Two

IV. Chorus (C) 'Gloria' (repeated), C major modulating to G major
Speaker's Commentary

Aria: Jocasta 'Nonn'erubescite', G minor (D minor – F minor – D minor – B minor – G minor)
Ensemble: Jocasta and three (four) part male chorus 'Laius in Trivio', G minor (C minor – E flat minor – A flat minor)
Ensemble: Oedipus and Chorus 'Pavesco subito' B flat major
Arietta: Oedipus (4) 'Ego senem cecidi', C minor
Duet: Jocasta and Oedipus, C minor (E flat major)
Ensemble: Oedipus, Jocasta and Chorus 'Volo consulere', B flat major (G major)

   V. Speaker's Commentary

      Chorus: quasi recitative 'Adest omniscius pastor', G minor
      Aria: Messenger (1) 'Mortuus est Polybus', A minor
      Ensemble: Messenger and Chorus 'Falsus pater', E minor
      Aria: Messenger (2) 'Reppereram in monte', G minor
      Chorus: 'Resciturus sum', G minor
      Recitative and Aria: Shepherd 'A patre, a matre', B flat major
      Aria: Oedipus (5) 'Nonne monstrum', F major
      Ensemble: Shepherd, Messenger and Chorus 'In monte reppertus est',
        D minor
      Arietta: Oedipus (6) 'Natus sum', D minor/major

   VI. Speaker's Commentary – intercut with trumpet fanfares

      Aria: Messenger (3a) 'Divum Jocastae', G minor
      Chorus (Di) 'Mulier in vestibulo', C minor
      Aria: Messenger (3b) 'Divum Jocastae', G minor
      Chorus (Dii) 'Et ubi evellit', E flat major
      Aria: Messenger (3c) 'Divum Jocastae', G minor
      Chorus (Diii) 'Sanguis ater', C minor
      Aria: Messenger (3d) 'Divum Jocastae', G minor
      Chorus (Aii) 'Ecce regem', G major
      Chorus (Biv) 'Ellum regem', E minor
      Chorus (Aiii) 'Adest ellum', G minor
      Chorus (Bv) 'Vale Oedipus', G minor

It will be noted that the action is broken without destroying its continuity by repeating the final chorus of Act One at the beginning of Act Two. This overlap device was also used by Cocteau in his play *Orphée* (1926) described as a tragedy in one act and an interval; and Stravinsky expressed his approval of it in his *Dialogues*, though he seems to prefer the repetition of the *Gloria* chorus to come after and not before the speaker's commentary. 'I like to go directly from *tutti* G major to *solo* flute and harp G minor. I also like to acknowledge the audience's apprehension that the Queen Mother must have a lot to say by giving them a pause before she says it.'

It will be seen from the key indications that the minor mode is predominant throughout the opera. The sombre tangle of the Oedipus/Jocasta/Laius relationship and its implications is treated mainly in the minor. The chorus of men of Thebes bewailing the plague that scourges the city (Ai and Bi and ii) is in the minor too; and although the opening chorus recurs in the major towards the end, when the riddle is solved and the guilty king reappears, blinded, on his way into exile (Aii), the respite is temporary, the same powerful chorus is repeated in the minor mode (Aiii), and the final chorus of farewell is also in the minor (Bv). As for Oedipus, he strives continuously towards the affirmation of major keys; but generally they prove elusive and evade his grasp. A good example is the way the leading E flat major phrase of his 'Invidia fortunam odit' aria gravitates inevitably towards C.minor after less than two bars.

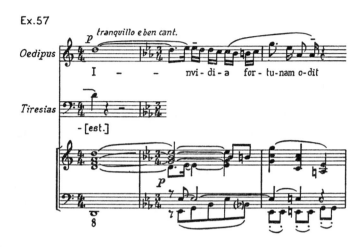

Ex.57

Oedipus's keys are flat keys. His final but vain attempt to escape his doom is made in the F major 'Nonne monstrum rescituri' aria (see Ex. 59b); but with the final revelation and realisation, he emerges at last out of flat keys and minor modes into a blindingly clear D major close (See Ex. 58).

Generally speaking, the flat keys, both major and minor, are geared closely to the Oedipus complex, while the sharp keys relate to the world of normality. The tonality of the opera radiates backwards and forwards from the still point of its centre – the magnificent C major chorus hailing Queen Jocasta at the end

Ex. 58

of Act One and beginning of Act Two. The score is an inspired example of the use of mode and key to achieve psychological insight in musical terms.[1]

Oedipus (unconsciously) attempts to evade the consequences of his secret crimes and affirm his integrity as a man and king by a somewhat arrogant and ostentatious style. His vocal line shows a tendency towards florid decoration in the form of descending and ascending scale passages, the notes of which are sometimes repeated and give a kind of hesitant, hobbled effect. This can be seen clearly in his promise to solve the riddle of Laius's murderer, 'Ego divinabo',[2] and also in the vocal line of 'Invidia fortunam odit' (see Ex. 57 above). When he wants to give his self-assurance an extra boost and to impress others, he is apt to repeat or imitate a phrase a semitone or a tone higher; and it is typical that after Tiresias's accusation 'Rex peremptor regis est', he should attempt to extricate himself by pushing the tonality up a semitone from Tiresias's D Minor close to the E flat major opening of the 'Invidia' aria (see also Ex. 57 above).

A minor mannerism deserves notice at this point. The trill, with its wavering oscillation between two neighbouring notes a semitone or a tone apart, is not a feature of Oedipus's vocal line; but trills appear once in the accompaniment to his 'Liberi vos liberabo' aria and three times in his 'Non reperias' aria with somewhat disquieting effect – like the revelation of a hidden flaw. This means that the significance of the clarinet trill in the last bar but two of his final 'Lux facta est' phrase (see Ex. 58 above) is particularly striking, for the two notes in the trill (E sharp and F sharp) can be interpreted as the minor and major third of the ultimately achieved tonality of D.

Much of the score represents the summation and consummation of his neo-classical discoveries of the last four years or so.[3] There are close resemblances to passages in the *Octet* and *Serenade* (see Exs. 48, 52 and 53 above) and to the contrapuntal style of accompaniment already tried out in *Mavra* (see Ex. 43 above). If outside influences are to be looked for, they will be found, not in eighteenth-century composers like Pergolesi or Handel or Bach – nor even in Beethoven – but in nineteenth-century Italian opera. Jocasta's great aria has been not inappropriately described as sounding 'like the finest milk of Verdi curdled into cheese'. But certain passages – particularly some of those connected with the Messenger and the Shepherd – revert to Stravinsky's earlier

---

[1] A fascinating examination of the tonal lay-out of *Oedipus Rex* has been made by Wilfrid Mellers in 'Stravinsky's Oedipus as 20th-Century Hero' printed in *Stravinsky: a new appraisal of his work* (edited by Paul Henry Lang), New York, 1963. There he suggests that 'the opera is dominated by the search for D major, which is the key of the inner light; and the tonal scheme of the work has a symmetry that is simultaneously musical and doctrinal'.
[2] Figs. 58 to 60.
[3] In this connection, it should be remembered that shortly after the first performance of *Oedipus Rex*, Stravinsky published a warning about the so-called reversion to classicism (see Appendix A (3)), pointing out that true classical music was based on musical form and eschewed ultra-musical elements.

2. Register of Works

Russian popular style with tunes of restricted range relying on metrical variation and permutation; and the central *Gloria*, is definitely music that has been influenced by Russian Church ritual.

Referring to the score as a whole, Stravinsky himself admits that 'a great deal of the music is a *Merzbild*, to borrow Schwitters's term. I put it together from whatever came to hand' (*Dia*). There should therefore be little call for surprise when one finds an underlying relationship between Oedipus's 'Nonne

monstrum rescituri' aria and the Lanner waltz that accompanies the Ballerina in Scene Three of *Petrushka*[1] (see Ex. 59a and b above).

---

[1] This parallel was pointed out to me by my wife in 1946, and I mentioned it in my book on Stravinsky published the following year. Since then it has been repeated by various critics; and in his *Dialogues* Stravinsky writes, 'Curious that a Soviet musicologist visiting me recently was convinced that I developed this melody from the cornet waltz tune in *Petrushka*.'

Original Compositions

The transformation of a Styrian Waltz into a Greek king's cry of defiance – whether a consciously premeditated, or an involuntary act on Stravinsky's part – is just as much a matter for speculation as the process of reversion which led Hamlet to contemplate the possibility of the noble dust of Alexander stopping a bunghole.

In this score, special attention has been paid to the handling of rhythm. Apart from the Messenger's 'Reppereram in monte' aria and the subsequent 'reppertus est', the metres are regular – Stravinsky calls them 'static' (*Dia*). Of major importance is the ostinato that is first heard accompanying the chorus (Bi) 'Oedipus adest pestis'. At that point, timpani, harp and piano are used to produce a slow sombre pulse emphasising the interval of the minor third,

Ex. 60

and the same pulse underlies three of the choruses in the first act (nos. Bi, Bii, and Biii) and returns at the end of the opera (Biv and Bv) to bring the work to its conclusion. The rhythmic force with which the 'oracula' episode in Jocasta's aria is handled has already been commented on; and there are similar instances of compulsive rhythms in the arias of Creon and Tiresias. The 6/8 of the 'Mulier in vestibulo' chorus (Di, Dii, Diii) has been a stumbling block to some people – the iambic jogtrot has been looked on as a Gilbert and Sullivan chorus, 'as a piece of inappropriate gaiety, as a ballet coda, even as a can-can' (*Dia*). But in reality it is a marvellous example of almost breathless mass hysteria under full musical control.

Production and Performance

Oedipus Rex was intended by Stravinsky and Cocteau as a present for Diaghilev in honour of the twentieth anniversary of his theatrical activity. Although to begin with, Diaghilev was not told about the work, the moment came when he had to be let into the secret, since it was part of the collaborators' plan that the opera-oratorio (so-called) should be presented by his company. The project seems to have met with a certain lack of enthusiasm; and according to Stravinsky, Diaghilev referred to the offering as 'un cadeau très macabre' (*Dia*). Whereas he had taken considerable pains over the mounting of Stravinsky's other two operas (*The Nightingale* and *Mavra*), he was puzzled by *Oedipus Rex* and could not decide who should be engaged to design the production. His régisseur, Grigoriev, thought it extravagant to order scenery and costumes for a work that was to be performed only three or four times and said so to Diaghilev at Monte Carlo sometime during the spring of 1927.

2. Register of Works

In his history of the Russian Ballet,[1] he describes how the next day he met Diaghilev 'on the terrace looking uncommonly pleased with himself. "Well – I've thought of the way to do *Oedipus*," he said. "We'll simply give it a concert performance – no *décor*, and the cast in evening dress, sitting on the stage in front of black velvet curtains. Musically it will even gain." ' Grigoriev congratulated him on this bright idea.

The decision to give the work in concert form was more or less inevitable, since time was short and Stravinsky was so late in finishing the score 'that the singers had hardly learned the notes before the piano preview performance which took place at Edmond de Polignac's house a few days before the public one' (*Dia*). Stravinsky conducted this private run-through himself and handed over his fee (of 12,000 francs) to Diaghilev to help defray the expenses of the public performances. According to Grigoriev, the work produced little impression on the first night audience. 'Compared to *L'Oiseau de Feu*, which was in the same programme, it seemed very tame. We gave it exactly three times, after which it was heard no more; so that it was just as well that Diaghilev had not spent much on its production.' Stravinsky's own comment was: 'When my austere vocal concert was programmed next to a very colourful ballet, the failure was greater than I had anticipated. The audience was hardly polite' (*Dia*).

It was a serious error of judgment to allow the first performance of *Oedipus Rex* to be given in concert form. In fact, any performance of it as a concert oratorio, however well prepared, must fail to do the work full justice. Stravinsky has chosen a great drama as his theme, and the musical content of the score is dramatic throughout. A non-dramatic presentation stultifies the significance of the music. A moment's thought will show, for instance, that the overwhelming effect of the chorus's G major outburst (Aii) 'Ecce regem Oedipoda' when Oedipus reappears blinded is almost completely thrown away in the concert hall. The truth is the work is an opera and not an oratorio.

It took *Oedipus Rex* a long time to recover from this faulty start. There were stage productions in Vienna and Berlin early the next year, and the Berlin one at the Krolloper was distinguished by the brilliant musical direction of Klemperer. Although Stravinsky has expressed his horror of the visual side of this production, it was sufficiently good as a whole for the true value of the work to come through with overwhelming force to most of the audience (though not to Schoenberg who was apparently present at the first performance on 25 February 1928). Nevertheless, other stage productions followed reluctantly, and it has taken a considerable time for it to win acceptance as one of Stravinsky's masterpieces and one of the great operas of the twentieth century.

---

[1] *The Diaghilev Ballet, 1909–1929*. London, 1953.

Original Compositions

New Version (1948)

The new version of the score made in 1948 is really a revised version, incorporating a number of small changes and improvements made after the first performance. There are, for instance, an added trumpet part in Oedipus's 'Nonne monstrum' aria, and added horn and tuba parts in the 'Aspicite' chorus. The idea that Oedipus should take over the last note (D) of Tiresias's aria in the bar immediately preceding the opening of his own 'Invidia fortunam odit' aria (see Ex. 57) is an afterthought – as are also the repeats marked in Jocasta's aria and her duet with Oedipus.

Certain misprints have crept into this revised version – for instance, the indication ♩= 88 at fig. 110 should be ♪= 84–88. There is also confusion over the time at fig. 133. The change of time signature from 3/4 to 2/4 comes at the end of a line, and the indication ♪= ♩ is printed at the end of one line and is followed by ♩= ♪ at the beginning of the next. The correct indication (in both places) should be ♪= ♪

The revised edition prints an unidiomatic and inadequate English translation of the original French note. But this unfavourable criticism does not apply to the English translation of the Speaker's commentary by E. E. Cummings. There is another English translation of the commentary by Carl Wildman (published by the Oxford University Press).

57. APOLLON MUSAGÈTE – APOLLO MUSAGETES

Ballet in two scenes for string orchestra (Vl. I, Vl. II, Vle., Vcl. I, Vcl. II, CB.)[1] Composed at Nice between July 1927 and January 1928. Published by Edition Russe de Musique, 1928 (later by Boosey & Hawkes). Piano reduction by the composer. Duration: *c.* 30 minutes. First performance at the Library of Congress, Washington D.C., 27 April 1928. First European performance, Russian Ballet, Théâtre Sarah-Bernhardt, Paris, 12 June 1928, conducted by the composer. One manuscript of the piano reduction (dated Nice 9 January 1927 [*sic*]) is with Boosey & Hawkes, London; another is in the collection of Dr. Paul Sacher, Pratteln, Basel. The manuscript of the full score (dated Nice, 20 January 1928) is in the Library of Congress, Washington D.C. Other MS material is in the composer's collection [C 50].

---

[1] In his *Chronicle* Stravinsky suggests an orchestra of 34 players (8.8.6.4.4.4). This replaced an orchestra of 54 players (16.14.10.4.4.6) proposed by Klemperer for a concert performance at the Krolloper, Berlin, in the summer of 1929.

2. Register of Works

Composition and Treatment

Early in the summer of 1927, Stravinsky received a commission from the Elizabeth Sprague Coolidge Foundation to provide a ballet score for a festival of contemporary music to be held at the Library of Congress, Washington D.C. He was given a free hand as to subject; but it was stipulated that the ballet should require only half a dozen dancers and should last for not more than half an hour. The commission fee was $1,000. In his *Chronicle* he explains how he decided to carry out an idea that had attracted him for some time, namely, 'to compose a ballet founded on moments or episodes in Greek mythology plastically interpreted by dancing of the so-called classical school'.

As theme, he chose Apollo, leader of the Muses, and for his purpose reduced their number from nine to three: Calliope personifying poetry and rhythm, Polyhymnia representing mime, and Terpsichore combining the rhythm of poetry and the eloquence of gesture in the revelation of the dance. The birth of Apollo on Delos is shown in a prologue according to the legend that 'Leto was with child and, feeling the moment of birth at hand, threw her arms about a palm-tree and knelt on the tender turf; and the earth smiled beneath her, and the child sprang forth to the light. . . . Goddesses washed him with limpid water, gave him for swaddling clothes a white veil of fine tissue, and bound it with a golden girdle.' This is followed by a sequence of nine allegorical dances for Apollo and the three Muses in the course of which he presents them with appropriate emblems and finally leads them away to Parnassus.

Fortified by his admiration for classical ballet, Stravinsky saw *Apollo Musagetes* in his mind's eye as a *ballet blanc* and found that 'the absence of many-coloured effects and of all superfluities produced a wonderful freshness' (*Chr*). He also remembered (according to Schaeffner)[1] that one day Derain had mentioned to him the difficulty a painter experienced in depicting rocks, since their resemblance to each other and lack of individuality made impossible any effect of contrast. This difficulty attracted him, and in his *Poetics of Music* he carries further the argument in favour of unity rather than variety:

> Contrast produces an immediate effect. Similarity satisfies us only in the long run. Contrast is an element of variety, but divides our attention. Similarity is born of a striving for unity. . . .Variety is valid only as a means of attaining similarity. Variety surrounds me on every hand. So I need not fear that I shall be lacking in it, since I am constantly confronted by it. Contrast is everywhere. One has only to take note of it. Similarity is hidden; it must be sought out, and it is found only after the most exhaustive efforts. When variety tempts me, I am uneasy about the facile solutions it offers me. Similarity, on the other hand, poses more difficult problems but also offers results that are more solid and hence more valuable to me.

[1] In *Stravinsky*. Paris, 1931.

Original Compositions

In the case of *Apollo*, this led him to the conclusion that the music for this *ballet blanc* must be diatonic in character and that all extrinsic effects of instrumental contrast and variety should be avoided. He accordingly set aside the ordinary orchestra with its various instrumental departments because of its heterogeneous character. He also felt that ensembles of woodwind and brass had been sufficiently exploited in recent years and decided to use only a string orchestra. This was to be a sextet with 1st and 2nd violins, violas, 1st and 2nd cellos, and double-basses.

At the same time his attitude to string writing seemed to have changed. Recalling in his *Chronicle* that the original purpose of the strings was the cultivation of melody, he made plain his delight in composing music where 'everything revolved about the melodic principle' and in immersing himself 'in the multi-sonorous euphony of strings and making it penetrate even the innermost polyphonic recesses'. This was very different from his attitude to string writing as revealed in the *Concertino for String Quartet* of 1920.

As soon as he had accepted the commission from the Elizabeth Sprague Coolidge Foundation, he seems to have realised that the new ballet might suit Diaghilev's requirements as well and that the first performance in Washington could easily be followed by a Russian Ballet production in Europe. He happened to be in London during the last fortnight of June 1927, when the Russian Ballet was appearing at the Prince's Theatre; and after the first night of *The Cat* (14 June) in which Serge Lifar scored a great personal success, he seems to have had a talk with Diaghilev at his hotel. According to Lifar,[1] Diaghilev came to his room in great excitement later that night and said: 'Let me congratulate you, Seriozha. Stravinsky has been saying the most astonishing things about you. He's so pleased with you that he's going to compose a ballet especially for you, even though he's working overtime on a commission for America.' Whether Diaghilev really believed at that stage that Stravinsky was proposing to write a ballet score for the Russian Ballet as well as the Library of Congress commission is not clear; but the work of composition started very soon after their London talk for (according to Schaeffner[1]) the chord accompanying Apollo's birth

Ex.61

was entered at the back of Stravinsky's *Oedipus Rex* notebook on 16 July, and four days later the first bar of the prologue was composed. The dance of the two goddesses who attend Apollo after his birth was written between 29 and

---

[1] This conversation is quoted in Lifar's *Serge Diaghilev*. London, 1940.
[2] *Op. cit.*

341

31 July; and by the end of September the prologue must have been complete together with the two following movements, for on 30 September Diaghilev wrote to Lifar from Monte Carlo describing a visit he had just paid to Stravinsky in Nice.

> I spent the whole day with him, and at five saw him off at the station. It was an eminently satisfactory meeting.... After lunch he played me the first half of the new ballet. It is, of course, an amazing work, extraordinarily calm, and with greater clarity than anything he has so far done; and filigree counterpoint round transparent, clear-cut themes, all in the major key; somehow music not of this world, but from somewhere above. It seems strange that, though the tempo of all this part is slow, yet at the same time it is perfectly adapted to dancing. There is a short, fast movement in your first variation – there are to be two for you, and the opening is danced to an unaccompanied violin solo. Very remarkable! On the whole, one feels it is part Glinka and part sixteenth century Italian, though without any intentional Russianising. He played it over to me three times running – so that I have the clearest idea of it now. The Adagio (*pas d'action*) has a broad theme very germane to us today; it runs concurrently in four different tempos, and yet, generally speaking, the harmony is most satisfactory. I embraced him and he said: "It's for you to produce it properly for me: I want Lifar to have all sorts of flourishes...." When the train was already moving out, he shouted to me: "Find a good title!"

The title was soon found, and the work completed less than four months later.

Music

Diaghilev was right insofar as calmness, clarity and almost transcendental serenity are salient characteristics of the music of *Apollo Musagetes*: but the suggested resemblance with Glinka and sixteenth-century Italian music is not so convincing – closer stylistic affinities are to be found in the music of some of the French composers from Lully to Delibes. The fact that there is no element of conflict in the action is reflected in the music's close adherence to diatonicism; and after the intensive use of the minor mode in *Oedipus Rex* to express the sombre tangle of that drama, it is significant to find a much greater reliance on the major mode in *Apollo*. Throughout the score there is a preoccupation with problems of versification, which manifests itself in numerous iambic metrical patterns.

First Scene (prologue): 'Apollo's Birth'. A slow dotted quaver introduction leads to a spacious dignified theme in E major.

After a cadential passage based on Apollo's birth chord (Ex. 61), there is an Allegro dance for the two attendant goddesses written as a duet, which leads to a reprise of the spacious theme (in C major) as the goddesses lead Apollo away to Olympus.

Ex. 62

Second Scene: 'Apollo and the Muses'. The first *Variation* for Apollo starts as a cadenza for unaccompanied violin solo and is elaborated into a rather hesitant duet for two solo violins with pizzicato accompaniment.

After this *pas seul*, Calliope, Polyhymnia and Terpsichore appear; and there is a *pas d'action* for the four of them, towards the end of which occurs the stretto mentioned by Diaghilev in his letter to Lifar quoted above, the main theme being played in canon, while it appears simultaneously in augmentation and in diminution.

Ex. 63

Calliope's 'Variation' is a curious conceit, being based on the rhythm of the Alexandrine and prefaced by the following quotation from Boileau:

Que toujours dans vos vers le sens coupant les mots
Suspende l'hémistiche et marque le repos.

The melody is divided into 12-note phrases, usually grouped as six iambic feet, with a heavy (D minor) caesura between the lines. The rhythm of the cello solo[1] was suggested by a Russian Alexandrine written by Pushkin.

Polyhymnia's *Variation* is an Allegro with a scurrying semiquaver line which is sometimes theme and sometimes accompaniment.

Terpsichore's *Variation* is a graceful Allegretto characterised by dotted semiquaver writing. Towards the middle of its course it is punctuated by four fermatas, which correspond in the ballet to a succession of attitudes held for a brief moment by the dancer.

A second *Variation* for Apollo follows, a slow movement for the full string orchestra with passages of resonant chording and a brief episode for solo quintet.

The *pas de deux* for Apollo and Terpsichore is an Adagio of great expressiveness written for muted strings throughout (with the exception of the double-bass).

The dance *Coda* for Apollo and the three Muses is a vivacious movement which generates considerable drive. Its speeds are most ingeniously geared. The 2/4 introduction marked *Vivo* (♩=76) leads to a 6/8 Tempo sostenuto (♩. =112), which means that the fundamental unit (♩.) is half as fast again as the ♩ of the introduction. At times the 6/8 bars alternate with 3/4 bars with constant quaver values (i.e. ♩=168), and this tempo, which is also half as fast again as the preceding one, is established for the last section of the movement.[2]

The *Apotheosis*, in which Apollo leads the Muses towards Parnassus, reverts to the tranquil mood of the introduction in the Prologue. The spacious theme (Ex. 62) reappears in D major; and there is a six-bar musical coda in which four different ostinato figures of varying lengths are gradually augmented, until the stream of the music broadens out into a delta of great serenity and calm.

This score is perhaps the best exemplar of Stravinsky's dictum about classicism in his *Poetics of Music*, where he says: 'The clear integration of a work of art and its crystallisation demand that all the Dionysian elements, which stimulate a composer and set in motion the rising sap of his imagination,

---

[1] At fig. 41.
[2] In the original 1928 version the metronome marking at figure 86 is given as ♩. = 160 and there is a footnote to explain that the ♩. is slightly slower than the previous ♩; but the metronome marking is altered to ♩. = 168 in the revised 1947 version.

be adequately controlled before we succumb to their fever, and ultimately, subordinated to discipline: such is Apollo's command.'

Productions

The original production of *Apollo Musagetes* at Washington D.C. on 27 April 1928 had choreography by Adolph Bolm and décor and costumes by Nicholas Remissoff. Ruth Page danced the role of Terpsichore.

The first European performance was given by the Russian Ballet at the Théâtre Sarah-Bernhardt, Paris, on 12 June 1928 with choreography by George Balanchine. For this production Diaghilev insisted, despite Stravinsky's disapproval, on basing the scenery on two landscapes by André Bauchant, whose naïve work was considered to be fashionable at that moment in the manner of le douanier Rousseau. (These inappropriate settings were dropped in subsequent revivals.) Apollo was danced by Lifar, and the three Muses were Danilova, Tchernicheva and Dubrovska.

Although in public Diaghilev was ready to hail *Apollo* as one of Stravinsky's major works – 'a product of true artistic maturity', he called it – he apparently decided during rehearsals that the variation for Terpsichore was too long and tedious and, according to Lifar,[1] advised the composer 'either to omit it completely, or to make a number of cuts'. On Stravinsky's refusal to do so, he ordered the variation to be omitted at the second performance on the pretext of the dancer's indisposition. When Stravinsky protested and asked for it to be restored, Diaghilev apparently agreed: but at the third performance, it was still missing, and certain informed persons in the audience began to protest. Ultimately Stravinsky got his way; but it is curious to find that when the first German concert performance of *Apollo* was given by Klemperer at the Kroll-oper, Berlin, in the autumn of 1928, this particular movement was still missing from the score.

This was not the first time Balanchine had choreographed music by Stravinsky. While still a member of the Imperial Ballet School, Petrograd, in the early 1920's he had devised some dances to the score of *Pulcinella* for his fellow students; and shortly after joining Diaghilev's company at the age of twenty in 1924, he was allowed to prepare a new version of *The Song of the Nightingale* as a choreographic exercise (1925). His work on *Apollo* set the seal on his reputation as a choreographer and was the beginning of an artistic partnership that was to lead directly or indirectly to the creation of other important ballets including *The Card Party*, *Orpheus* and *Agon*.

Balanchine has said that he thought of Stravinsky's music for *Apollo* as 'white on white';[2] and later he wrote: '*Apollo* I look back on as the turning

---

[1] *Op. cit.*

[2] From *The Dance Element in Strawinsky's Music* by George Balanchine, printed in the *Strawinsky in the Theatre* symposium in Dance Index, 1948.

point in my life. In its discipline and restraint, its sustained one-ness of tone and feeling, the score was a revelation. It seemed to tell me that I could dare not to use everything, that I too could eliminate.' It is true that the original version of his choreography was disfigured by certain extravagances such as the tableau at the end of the prologue where the two goddesses lying prone on the stage lifted their legs from the knees to form a pedestal on which Apollo balanced himself in an attitude of swimming through the air; but small blemishes like these were later removed to reveal the choreography in all its originality and beauty. Stravinsky was particularly satisfied by the results.

Balanchine's version was subsequently mounted by the Royal Danish Ballet in Copenhagen (1931), by the American Ballet in New York (1937), in Rio de Janeiro (1941) and Buenos Aires (1942), by the Ballet Theatre in New York (1943), by the Paris Opera (1947), and by the New York City Ballet, New York (1951). Other choreographers have also worked on the score at different times, but none has ever come near to rivalling Balanchine's supremacy.

Revised Version (1947)

The piano reduction (made by the composer) provides evidence of an earlier state of the full score than the version published in 1928. It looks as if this included a three-note phrase for the 2nd cellos in the fourth bar of the *Prologue*, and a trill for the 1st cellos in the bar before fig. 28 in the *pas d'action*, both of these features being missing in the 1928 edition.

The revised version of the score published in 1947 incorporates very few alterations. The change of metronome marking (from ♩. = 160 to ♩. = 168) at fig. 86 has already been mentioned. In the same movement (*Coda*), the repeat of the section figs. 89 to 92 inclusive was not in the original score. The remaining changes mainly affect directions for the string players – accentuation, phrasing, bowing, dynamics etc.

Despite the care taken over this revised version, Stravinsky has made it clear in his *Dialogues* that there are still a number of changes he would like to carry out. For instance, the dotted phrases appearing in the introduction as far as fig. 6, (including Ex. 62) and reappearing later between figs. 15 and 19, and from a bar before fig. 99 to the end, should be double-dotted; and the demi-semiquavers in the accompanying chords (as illustrated in Ex. 62) should be hemi-demi-semiquavers. The same double-dotting should apply to the upbeat of the first solo violin at fig. 21, the first cello at fig. 59 and the double-bass solo four bars before fig. 63. The fermata four bars before fig. 23 is intended to apply only to the two solo violins (with a suitable rest marked for the cellos and double-basses); and the fermata two bars before fig. 67 should apply only to the first cellos (with a suitable rest for the remainder of the orchestra). The violin cadenza at fig. 23 should be fitted into a strict 3/8 bar, with the first seven notes equivalent to a quaver, and the values of the subsequent notes (the two trilled phrases) halved.

Towards the end of his life Stravinsky preferred the shortened form of the title, i.e. *Apollo*.

58. LE BAISER DE LA FÉE – THE FAIRY'S KISS

Allegorical ballet in four scenes, inspired by the Muse of Chaikovsky (3.3.3.2 – 4.3.3.1 – timp., percussion, harp – string 5tet). Composed at Talloires and Nice, April to October 1928. (The MS full score is dated 30 October 1928 – midnight – Nice.) Dedicated to the memory of Peter Chaikovsky. Published by Edition Russe de Musique, 1928 (later by Boosey & Hawkes). Piano reduction by the composer. Duration: *c.* 45 minutes. First performance, Ballets Ida Rubinstein, Opera House, Paris, 27 November 1928, conducted by the composer. The full score, with other manuscript material, is in the composer's collection [C 52] and [C 53].

The published score is prefaced by the following note signed by the composer:

> *Characters.* A Fairy, a Young Man, his Fiancée, the Child's Mother, Creatures attendant on the Fairy, Villagers, Musicians at the Fête, Friends of the Fiancée.
>
> *Argument.* A fairy marks a young man with her mysterious kiss while he is still a child. She withdraws him from his mother's arms. She withdraws him from life on the day of his greatest happiness in order to possess him and preserve this happiness for ever. She marks him once more with her kiss.
>
> *Dedication.* I dedicate this ballet to the memory of Peter Chaikovsky by relating the Fairy to his Muse, and in this way the ballet becomes an allegory, the Muse having similarly branded Chaikovsky with her fatal kiss, whose mysterious imprint made itself felt in all this great artist's work.
>
> *General Note.* The strict and precise indications for the movements of the characters in this ballet as given in my score are intended to form *a fixed basis* for the producer. On the other hand, the vagueness and imprecision of my directions concerning the place and period of the action are meant to give designer and producer full freedom to construct a choreographic spectacle based directly on the character and style of the music.

Genesis of the Work and Synopsis

Towards the end of 1927, the dancer Ida Rubinstein, who was making plans to launch a ballet company of her own in Paris, approached Stravinsky's publishers, the Edition Russe de Musique, to enquire whether she might include his new ballet, *Apollo Musagetes*, in her repertory. On being told that the European rights belonged to Diaghilev, she offered to commission a new work; and Benois, who was acting on her behalf, submitted two plans to Stravinsky, one of which appealed to him at once. 'The idea was that I should compose something inspired by the music of Chaikovsky. My well-known fondness for this composer, and, still more, the fact that November, the time fixed for the performance, would mark the thirty-fifth anniversary of his death, induced me to accept the offer. It would give me an opportunity of paying my heartfelt homage to Chaikovsky's wonderful talent' (*Chr*). The fee offered was $7,500.

He was free to choose both subject and scenario; and as he had decided not only to dedicate his score to the memory of Chaikovsky, but also to base it on a selection of that composer's non-orchestral pieces, i.e., piano music and songs, he turned to a great literary artist of the same period, Hans Christian Andersen, whose power of imagination he felt was remarkably akin to Chaikovsky's. In the course of rereading Andersen's stories, he came across *The Ice Maiden* and decided that the theme was most suitable since it could also be looked on as an allegory applying to Chaikovsky himself.

When twenty years earlier Stravinsky had gone to Andersen for the libretto of his first opera, he had chosen *The Nightingale*, a comparatively brief and succinct story. *The Ice Maiden* is a much longer and more diffuse affair, which can almost be regarded as a short novel set out in fifteen chapters. It tells the story of a Swiss boy, Rudy, son of a postilion, who when a baby is taken by his mother across the Gemmi towards Grindelwald. There has been a recent fall of snow; and she falls into a concealed crevasse and dies. The child is rescued by two chamois hunters, but not before he has been kissed by the Ice Maiden, the Glacier Queen. 'To crush and to hold, mine is the power!' she says. 'They have stolen a beautiful boy from me, a boy whom I have kissed, but not kissed to death. He is again among men: he keeps the goats on the mountains, and climbs upward, ever higher, far away from the others, but not from me. He is mine, and I will have him!' Years pass, and Rudy grows up, becoming a celebrated marksman, hunter and climber. He falls in love with Babette, a miller's daughter. The evening before their wedding, they row out to a little island near Chillon, their skiff breaks loose from its moorings, and in swimming out to retrieve it, Rudy is drowned in the waters of Lake Geneva. The Ice Maiden has reclaimed him. 'I kissed you when you were little, kissed you on your mouth. Now I kiss your feet, and you are mine altogether!'

Stravinsky condensed Andersen's story into the following simple scenario:

Scene I (Prologue). Pursued by spirits in a storm, a mother is separated from her child, who is found and kissed by a fairy. A group of villagers passing by discover the abandoned child and take him away.

Scene II. Eighteen years later the young man and his fiancée are taking part in a village fête. They join in the country dances. When his fiancée and the villagers have gone home, the young man is approached by the fairy disguised as, a gypsy. After reading his hand and promising him great happiness in the future, she brings him to a mill.

Scene III. There he finds his fiancée surrounded by her friends. The lovers dance together; but when his fiancée retires to put on her bridal dress, the fairy reappears disguised as the bride and carries him off to her everlasting dwelling-place.

Scene IV (Epilogue). She then kisses him again, this time on the sole of his foot.

Music

At first sight it looked as if when Stravinsky agreed to base the score of his new ballet on existing piano and vocal music by Chaikovsky, he had taken on a task similar to his *Pulcinella* commission from Diaghilev. But, in effect, there was one considerable difference. In 1919 he had been a comparative stranger to the music of Pergolesi – in his *Expositions* he confesses that at that time he knew only the *Stabat Mater* and *La Serva Padrona*, neither of which seems to have excited him in the least – but with Chaikovsky's music he had been intimate since childhood. Performances of Chaikovsky's ballets that he had seen at the Maryinsky Theatre, St. Petersburg, were still fresh in his memory, as was also Diaghilev's revival of *The Sleeping Beauty* at the Alhambra Theatre, London, in 1921. It is true that Chaikovsky's music was undervalued in Western Europe then as it still is to a considerable extent today; but that seems to have made Stravinsky only the more determined to back his favourite Russian composer. In 1921 he had instrumented two of the numbers of *The Sleeping Beauty* for the London revival and written a letter in general praise of Chaikovsky as a composer for publication in the press;[1] and the following year he had chosen him as co-dedicatee together with Glinka and Pushkin when he composed his opera buffa *Mavra*. Not only did his search through Chaikovsky's piano and vocal music for suitable material for his new ballet prove a congenial task, but when he came to assemble his pickings, he found his appetite as a composer so quickened by contact with Chaikovsky's individual genius that he was able to continue quite fluently in the same vein where Chaikovsky had left off. This was something he had never attempted to do with Pergolesi. The result was that although the major part of the score of *The Fairy's Kiss* consists of authentic borrowings from Chaikovsky, there are also numerous passages and fragments of his own invention.

Stravinsky's check list of Chaikovsky sources for *The Fairy's Kiss* (as printed in his *Expositions*) is as follows:

Piano pieces:

    Scherzo à la russe op. 1, no. 1
    Humoresque op. 10, no. 2
    Evening Reverie op. 19, no. 1

---

[1] See Appendix A (1).

Scherzo humoristique op. 19, no. 2
Feuillet d'album op. 19, no. 3
Nocturne op. 19, no. 4
The Mujik plays the Harmonica op. 39, no. 12
In the Village op. 40, no. 7
Danse Russe op. 40, no. 10
Salon Valse op. 51, no. 1
Nata Valse op. 51, no. 4

Songs:

Painfully and sweetly op. 6, no. 3
None but the lonely Heart op. 6, no. 6
Winter Evening op. 54, no. 7
Lullaby in a Storm ('Berceuse') op. 54, no. 10
Serenade op. 63, no. 6

For some time it was thought (on Schaeffner's authority) that his only invention was the passage at fig. 14 where the spirits pursue the mother; but in his *Expositions* he also claims the following passages as his own:

The melody at fig. 2
The music at fig. 11
The music at fig. 27
The solo string quartet at the beginning of Scene Two
The music at fig. 70
The development at fig. 99
The music at fig. 108
The beginning of Scene Three
The rhythmic development at the second bar after fig. 134
The cadenza at fig. 168
The Variation at fig. 175.
The Coda at fig. 181 (see Ex. 64)
The horn solo at the end of the Epilogue[1]

As for the music at figs. 37 and 213, he was unable to recall whether it was his or Chaikovsky's.

The *Polka peu dansante* (op. 51, no. 2) should be added to the piano pieces listed above.[2] In addition to these direct borrowings, there is a passing reference (at fig. 174) to bar 25 of the Andante cantabile of Chaikovsky's String Quartet op. 11; and there are occasional echoes of passages in the symphonies, particularly Symphony no. 5.

---

[1] The score carries the following direction for the first horn one bar before fig. 227: 'ad libitum si le si ♭ aigu dans ce *P* ne gêne pas l'éxécutant.'
[2] See also p. 356 n.

Original Compositions

Stravinsky was truly inspired by Chaikovsky's music; and the process of assimilation was complete. The melos may remind one of Chaikovsky; but the total music is Stravinsky's. Even where such Chaikovskyan characteristics as sequences abound, 'instead of being Chaikovsky's inevitable squares, they are Stravinsky's rhomboids, scalenes, trapeziums, or trapezoids – shapes somehow stretched or shrunken into asymmetry and arranged in unpredictable combinations. Chaikovsky's faults – his banalities and vulgarities and routine procedures – are composed *out* of the music, and Stravinsky's virtues are composed *into* it.'[1] The resulting score is a complete unity of conception and realisation.

Stravinsky's original idea was that the ballet should be presented in classical form. He pictured all the fantastic roles as being danced in white ballet tutus, and the rustic scenes as taking place in a Swiss landscape with some of the dancers dressed like early tourists and mingling with the villagers (*Chr*). (In his *Expositions* he recalls how fascinated he had been by the English tourists who spent part of their time looking at the Jungfrau through telescopes, when he first visited Switzerland as a boy of thirteen.) But the music did not really serve this purpose. It is true that there is a distinctive idiom for the popular music of the village fête; but the suite of dances for the Young Man and his fiancée in Scene Three calls for classical dance treatment just as much as the episodes with the fairy.

In fact, his main problem was how to construct a full-length ballet – *The Fairy's Kiss* is longer than *The Rite of Spring*, *Pulcinella* or *Apollo Musagetes*, and about the same length as *The Firebird* and *Petrushka* – out of comparatively short pieces originally intended for salon purposes. So long as the mood remained lyrical, there was little or no difficulty. The suite of four dances intended as a *pas de deux* in Scene Three is successful partly because in the last of these (*Coda*) he breaks through the formal limitations of the type of song and piano piece he has been using to construct a bolder movement of dynamic impulse with just sufficient contrapuntal tension to lift the whole suite on to a higher level of organisation (see Ex. 64). The 'Village Fête' in Scene Two is also a most effective composition. The way this sequence of popular dances is framed by fragments of Chaikovsky's *Humoresque* and each individual number is floated off recalls the last scene of *Petrushka* and shows perhaps even greater cunning in the manipulation of the material.

But the dramatic crux of the composition comes at the end of Scene Three, where the fairy claims the bewildered young man, who tries at first to escape, but ultimately succumbs to her supernatural powers; and here it may be thought that Stravinsky has placed a greater burden on Chaikovsky's song *None but the lonely Heart* than it is capable of bearing. In order to obtain the

---

[1] Lawrence Morton, 'Stravinsky and Tchaikovsky: Le Baiser de la Fée', printed in *Stravinsky: A New Appraisal of His Work* (edited by Paul Henry Lang). New York, 1963.

climax he needs, he inflates the song with a thickened harmonic treatment spiced with chromatics.[1] The climax is brief and does the trick – after all, it is one of the few moments in the score when the full orchestra is unleashed – but it leaves behind it the impression of a trick.

The music recovers its ascendancy in the *Epilogue*, where the opening theme of Scene One ('Berceuse') returns in augmented guise to form a refrigerated musical coda that depicts the fairy's everlasting dwelling-place in all its glacial chill.

The orchestration marks a further step in the *concertante* style of instrumentation that Stravinsky embarked on when he rescored *The Song of the Nightingale* in 1917. Although a big symphony orchestra (with triple woodwind) is specified, the full orchestra is hardly ever used as such. Even at important climaxes, he rarely writes a full *tutti*: usually certain instruments are withheld, particularly those that are going to be heard immediately after the climax, and this helps to lighten the texture and refresh the ear. In fact, he uses the symphony orchestra both as a symphony orchestra and as a chamber orchestra, and a considerable part of the musical argument is carried out by small groups of instruments or single instruments conversing on chamber music lines.

Productions

Originally it had been suggested that Fokine should do the choreography for *The Fairy's Kiss*; but finally Bronislava Nijinska was engaged to do it, to Stravinsky's considerable relief, for not only did he feel critical of some of Fokine's choreography for *The Firebird* and *Petrushka*, but he was also exasperated by Fokine's habit of referring to the score of *The Firebird* as Stravinsky's 'musical accompaniment' to *his* 'choreographic poem' (*Mem*). As events turned out, however, Stravinsky was so busy during the summer and autumn of 1928, working on the composition and completing the instrumentation, that he was unable to supervise Nijinska's choreography in its early stages; and when he came to Paris to attend the final rehearsals he found that, while some of the scenes were successful and worthy of her talent, there was a great deal of which he could not really approve. But by then it was too late for him to attempt to interfere (*Chr*). In the circumstances, it is not surprising that the first performance in the Paris Opera House on 27 November 1928 was not a great success.

A fascinating account of the occasion was given in a letter[2] Diaghilev wrote to Serge Lifar, who was then touring with the Russian Ballet in England. He was furious at what he considered to be Stravinsky's defection.

I'm just back from the theatre, with a fearful headache, as a result of all the horrible things I've been seeing. Stravinsky's was the only new ballet,

---

[1] Fig. 210.
[2] Quoted in Serge Lifar's *Diaghilev*.

352

the other promised novelties not being ready. . . . It's difficult to say what it was meant to represent – tiresome, lachrymose, ill-chosen Chaikovsky, supposedly orchestrated by Igor in masterly fashion. I say "supposedly", because it sounded drab, and the whole arrangement lacked vitality. The *pas de deux*, however, was quite well done to a beautiful theme from Chaikovsky. . . . That, and the coda in the style of *Apollo* were really the only bright spots (though the latter, too, was somewhat melancholy). But what went on on the stage, it is impossible to describe. Suffice it to say that the first scene represents the Swiss mountains; the second a Swiss village *en fête*, accompanied by *Swiss* national dances; the third, a Swiss mill; and the fourth, back again to mountains and glaciers. The heroine was Shollar, who danced a long *pas de deux* with Vilzak, to Petipa's choreography, or at least a *pastiche* of his work. Bronia[1] showed not the least gleam of invention, not one single movement that was decently thought out. As for Benois's décor, it was like the sets at the Monte Carlo Opera House: these Swiss landscapes were worse than anything by Bocharov or Lambin. . . . The theatre was full but as for success – it was like a drawing-room in which someone has suddenly made a bad smell. No one pretended to notice, and Stravinsky was twice called to the curtain. The whole thing was still-born. . . .

Diaghilev was intensely indignant that Stravinsky and some of his other former collaborators should have deigned to associate themselves with so inferior an undertaking as the new Ida Rubinstein Company. His final, somewhat hysterical comment was 'Stravinsky, our famous Igor, my first son, has given himself up entirely to the love of God and cash.'[2]

After two performances in Paris, one at Brussels, one at Monte Carlo and one at Milan, *The Fairy's Kiss* was removed from the repertory of Ida Rubinstein's Company. In 1933 the Nijinska version was revived at the Colon Theatre, Buenos Aires. Subsequently, Balanchine made a new choreographic version, which was mounted by the American Ballet in New York (1937), the Ballet Russe de Monte Carlo in New York (1940), the Paris Opera House (1947) and the New York City Ballet (1950). In England, Frederick Ashton did the choreography for a production by the Sadler's Wells Ballet in 1935, and Kenneth MacMillan did new choreography for a production by the Royal Ballet in 1960.

Revised Version (1950)

The revision of the score was completed in 1950, a year later than the revision of the *Divertimento* (see below), and the revised version was published by Boosey & Hawkes in 1952. In the prolegomena, the General Note is omitted

[1] Nijinska.
[2] Serge Lifar *op. cit.*

and the Argument replaced by an extended synopsis. The scenes are given English titles (instead of French) as follows:

First Scene: (*Prologue*)
Second Scene: 'A Village Fête'
Third Scene: 'By the Mill'
Fourth Scene: (*Epilogue*) 'Berceuse of the Eternal Dwellings'

The changes in the score are small. A second flute part has been added at fig. 23, and parts for the second violins, violas and double basses at fig. 42. The tuba solo part at fig. 85 is marked *marcato in poco sfp* instead of *p accompagnando*. In the first number (*Entrée*) of the *pas de deux*, the accompanying semiquaver figures for clarinets (and, later, bassoons) have been lightened by the occasional omission of single notes; and the violas have been given a double-stopped passage at fig. 165. In the Coda, horn and trumpet notes have been shortened from dotted crotchets to dotted quavers (fig. 186), and the two final G major chords rescored. The repeats of figs. 110 and 111 and also of the four bars after fig. 180 are new.

Transcription

Ballad: transcription for violin and piano by I. Stravinsky in 1947, the violin part being established in collaboration with Jeanne Gautier. Published by Boosey & Hawkes, 1951. MS comp. [C 93]. An earlier version made with Dushkin in 1934 was not published. MS comp. [C 60].

58 (A). DIVERTIMENTO

Symphonic suite for orchestra (3.3.3.2 – 4.3.3.1 – timp., percussion, harp – string 5tet). Duration: *c.* 20 minutes.

1. *Sinfonia*
2. *Danses suisses*
3. *Scherzo*
4. *Pas de deux*

   (a) *Adagio*
   (b) *Variation*
   (c) *Coda*

As early as 1931 Stravinsky authorized the performance of extracts from the score of *The Fairy's Kiss* in the form of a concert suite. At a concert at Geneva in February of that year, Ansermet conducted a selection consisting of the whole of Scene One, Scene Two as far as fig. 96, and the *Pas de deux* in Scene Three. In 1934 Stravinsky settled the final shape of the concert suite, which he called *Divertimento*. The first movement (*Sinfonia*) contains the greater part of Scene One, but lacks the section from fig. 27 to fig. 39 inclusive in the ballet score. The second movement (*Danses suisses*) includes the whole of the second scene of the ballet as far as fig. 96. The third movement (*Scherzo*) is a slightly shortened version of the opening of Scene Three; and the fourth movement consists of the last three numbers of the *Pas de deux*, the first number (*Entrée*) being omitted. The *Coda* is given a concert ending. This 1934 version was published by Edition Russe de Musique in 1938.

The score of the *Divertimento* was revised in 1949, and this revised version was published by Boosey & Hawkes in 1950.

Transcription

A transcription for violin and piano was made by S. Dushkin and the composer in 1932 and published by Edition Russe de Musique (later by Boosey & Hawkes). MS comp. [C 60].

FOUR STUDIES

For orchestra, 1928 – see no. 33 (A).

59. CAPRICCIO

For piano and orchestra (3.3.3.2 – 4.2.3.1 – timp. – concertino string 4tet Vl. Vla. Vcl. C.B. and Ripieni string 4tet Vl. Vle. Vcl. C.B.) Composed at Nice and Echarvines between December 1928 and September 1929;[1] the orchestration finished on 9 November 1929. Published by Edition Russe de Musique 1930 (later by Boosey & Hawkes). Reduction for two pianos by the composer. Duration: *c*. 20 minutes. First performance, Paris Symphony Orchestra, Salle Pleyel, Paris, 6 December 1929, conducted by Ernest Ansermet with the composer as soloist. The manuscript full score is with Boosey & Hawkes, London, the first movement being dated, Nice, 26 October 1929, and the last movement, Nice, 9 November 1929. The manuscript of the two-piano reduction is in the collection of Nadia Boulanger. Other manuscript material is in the composer's collection [C 53].

Composition and Treatment

Since its first performance in 1924, Stravinsky had played the solo part of his *Piano Concerto* about forty times in Europe and America. He now thought the time had come to write a new piano concerto: so at Christmas 1928 he started to compose a movement for piano and orchestra that he labelled 'Allegro capriccioso'. His recent work on *The Fairy's Kiss* had not only confirmed his sympathy with Chaikovsky's music, but also aroused his desire to write a music of his own that would exhibit similar qualities of melodiousness, charm and variety. He had already produced something of this kind in those parts of

---

[1] The second movement was finished at Echarvines on 13 September 1929.

The Fairy's Kiss where, temporarily running short of suitable material by Chaikovsky, he had been impelled to have recourse to his own invention. A typical such passage was the *Coda* to the *Pas de deux* in Scene Three:[1]

Ex. 64

Keeping to the same key (G major) and pursuing the same idea of a rising motive distinguished by the rising appoggiaturas of the common chord being balanced by a falling motive, he now produced a subject that set the mood for a movement of capricious intent (Ex. 65).

This movement gave its title to the whole work. In his *Chronicle* Stravinsky explains that in naming his new concerto *Capriccio* he had in mind the definition of a 'capriccio' given by Praetorius – 'he regarded it as a synonym of the *fantasia* which was a free form made up of *fugato* instrumental passages'.

The form of the work may be free and capricious; but it is nonetheless very carefully organised.

The 'Allegro capriccioso' movement, which was written first and was the germ from which the rest of the concerto grew, is in rondo form; and the main subject (quoted above) proliferates into numerous related episodes. The tempo remains constant, the semiquaver figuration continues more or less unbroken, and the movement has all the verve of a *moto perpetuo.*

The main weakness of the 1924 Concerto had lain in the indeterminate construction of the last movement. By placing the 'Allegro capriccioso' as the last movement of the *Capriccio,* Stravinsky was able to ensure that his new

---

[1] But even here the trombone tune comes from Chaikovsky's *Polka peu dansante* (op. 51, no. 2).

Ex. 65

concerto would have a brilliant and unflagging finale. He added an opening movement in G minor with episodes in related keys (e.g., B flat major, E flat major, G major) and a slow movement in F minor with a leaning towards A flat major.

The tempo of the first movement is planned on more sober lines than that of the 'Allegro capriccioso' ($\downarrow$=66 as against $\downarrow$=96), and the piano is given a low-pitched percussive theme, based on the minor third, that acts as a kind of sheet anchor to the various flights of fancy that follow.

Ex.66

The accentuation is important, dividing the eight semiquavers into irregular groups of 3 + 3 + 2 or 2 + 3 + 3. This feature recurs constantly throughout the movement and is also to be found in the brief improvisatory introduction to the last movement. The free growth of musical ideas initiated by the inventive soloist is always kept within a rigid metric framework where $\flat = 264$, with the sole exception of a brief episode in E flat major, only ten bars long, marked *Poco più mosso*, where $\flat$ is stepped up to 352. Coming at the central point of the movement, this is intended to act as a kind of dorsal fin; but the mood and texture of the music (which is closely allied to the *Adagio* from the *Pas de deux* in *The Fairy's Kiss*) do not seem to make the point required, and the passage is strangely ineffective.

To complete the first movement, Stravinsky added a double introduction consisting of (*a*) a fast and loud statement for piano and orchestra, which is a succession of explosive cadences, and (*b*) a slow and soft passage given to the *concertino* string quartet and solo wind instruments. Each passage is repeated in an *abab* pattern. At the end of the movement the introductory material reappears, also in *abab* form, but this time the (*b*) passage is expanded into a coda in which an off-beat bass ostinato is provided by the solo piano, timpani and *ripieni* cellos and double-basses pizzicato, playing a low G, B flat and B flat in turn, an echo of the opening theme (see Ex. 66 above).

This leads without break into the second movement 'Andante rapsodico' where the solo piano gives a different context to the G–B flat interval by splitting it with an A flat.

Ex. 67

This piano statement in F minor is answered by a less rhetorical woodwind passage in A flat major. The piano part develops on rhapsodical lines, showing close affinity with the Adagietto of the *Piano Sonata*, and there is a brief cadenza towards the end.

Throughout the *Capriccio*, the writing for solo piano is less percussive and more graceful than in the *Piano Concerto*. A new technical feature makes its appearance: the use of repeated notes – occasionally, as in the 'Andante rapsodico', for emphasis; but more often, in order to prolong the auditory sensation of a held note.[1] This was to become a favourite device in later works for piano, particularly the *Duo Concertante* and the *Concerto for Two Solo Pianos*.

In this concerto the piano's discursive proceedings evoke friendly comment from the orchestra, but the argument never descends into a dispute. Chaikovsky's influence on the musical style has already been mentioned. After him, Beethoven and Weber are the two composers to whom the *Capriccio* seems to owe most.

---

[1] See figs. 27 and 84. This characteristic is reminiscent of cimbalom technique.

Original Compositions

Performance

The composition of the *Capriccio* was finished by the end of September 1929; the autumn was devoted to its orchestration; and the first performance took place on 6 December in the Salle Pleyel, Paris, at a concert of the newly constituted Paris Symphony Orchestra conducted by Ansermet, with Stravinsky himself as soloist. Although this performance went off without a hitch, Stravinsky's memory still continued to be unreliable. It will be remembered how at the first performance of the *Piano Concerto* he had had to ask Koussevitzky to remind him of the theme of the second movement. Robert Siohan recalls[1] a similar lapse of memory in the cadenza of the *Capriccio* during a performance he conducted at the Salle Pleyel, Paris, in 1934.

Revised Version (1949)

The revised 1949 version was published by Boosey & Hawkes in 1952. Changes are confined to the correction of misprints and omissions in the original 1929 score; but in the course of this reprint a few new mistakes have crept in.

In the first movement, the metronome marking for the change of time at fig. 14 has been altered from ♪. = 88 to ♪. = 80; but as the basic tempo of the movement is ♩ = 66 and at this point it is specifically stated that the new semiquaver equals the old, the original ♪. = 88 marking is to be preferred.

Ballet Productions

The score has been used twice for ballet productions – first by Leonide Massine, who choreographed it for the Teatro alla Scala, Milan, in 1947 with décor by Nicola Benois; second by Alan Carter, who mounted it with his own choreography, décor and costumes at the Bayerische Staatsoper, Munich, in 1957.

60. SYMPHONY OF PSALMS

For chorus of mixed voices[2] and orchestra (5.5.0.4. – 4.5.3.1 – timp., bass drum, harp, 2 pianos – Vcl. CB.). Composed at Nice and Charavines between Jan. and 15 Aug. 1930. Dedication: 'Cette symphonie composée à la gloire de DIEU est dediée au "Boston Symphony Orchestra" à l'occasion du cinquantaire de son existence.' Published by Edition Russe de Musique 1930 (later by Boosey & Hawkes). Duration: *c.* 23 minutes. First performance in Europe, Société Philharmonique de Bruxelles, Palais des Beaux Arts, Brussels, 13 December 1930, conducted by Ernest Ansermet. First performance in America, Boston Symphony Orchestra, Boston, 19 December 1930, con-

---

[1] *Stravinsky*. Paris, 1959.
[2] The score carries a note saying that the choir should contain children's voices, which may be replaced by female voices (soprano and alto) if a children's choir is not available.

ducted by Serge Koussevitzky. The manuscript of the full score belongs to the Boston Symphony Orchestra. Other manuscript material is in the composer's collection [C 55].

I.[1] ♩=92
II. ♪=60
III. ♩=48, followed by 𝅝=80

Analytical Note

At the end of 1929 Stravinsky was commissioned by Koussevitzky, the conductor of the Boston Symphony Orchestra, to write a symphonic work to celebrate the Orchestra's fiftieth anniversary in 1930. He was given a free hand regarding form and specification. Finding the traditional form of the nineteenth century symphony highly antipathetic, he decided 'to create an organic whole without conforming to the various models adopted by custom, but still retaining the periodic order by which the symphony is distinguished from the suite' (*Chr*). Gabriel Paichadze, his publisher, wanted an orchestral piece without chorus, '. . . . something popular': but Stravinsky had had the idea of a psalm symphony in his mind for some time, and that was what he insisted on composing (*Dia*). As he intended it to be a work of considerable contrapuntal development, he decided to choose 'a choral and instrumental ensemble in which the two elements should be on an equal footing, neither of them outweighing the other' (*Chr*). For his text, he selected from the Vulgate verses 13 and 14 of Psalm 38, verses 2, 3 and 4 of Psalm 39, and the whole of Psalm 150.[2] He prefaced the score with the direction that the words should always be sung in Latin.

The fast sections of Psalm 150 (the third movement) were the first to be written. Then he turned to the first and second movements. 'Psalm 40 is a prayer that a new canticle may be put into our mouths' (*Dia*). And the Allelujah at the beginning of the third movement was that new canticle. The rest of the slow tempo introduction, the 'Laudate Dominum', was originally composed to the Slavonic words of the 'Gospodi Pomiluy'. 'I decided to end the work with this music too, as an apotheosis of the sort that had become a pattern in my music since the epithalamium at the end of *Les Noces*' (*Dia*).

It has already been shown how important a part was played by the interval of a third in the musical structure of the *Capriccio*. In the *Symphony of Psalms*, he extended this idea to include the use of interlinked thirds. Throughout his career, he has been persistently preoccupied with this device. The division

---

[1] The programme of the first performance at Brussels carried the following subtitles for the three movements: I. *Prélude*, II. *Double fugue*, III. *Allegro symphonique*. These subtitles were not reproduced in the score.
[2] For the Authorised Version, the corresponding references are to verses 12 and 13 of Psalm 39, verses 1, 2 and 3 of Psalm 40, and the whole of Psalm 150.

of an augmented fourth into a major third interlinked with a minor third is fundamental to *The Firebird* score; and two such widely separated works as the *Two Poems of Balmont* (1911) and the *Double Canon* (1959) show other variants of the idea. In the first of the Balmont Songs, two descending major thirds

Ex. 68

Voice

form part of the opening phrase; and the same intervals reappear in the Gipsy music by Chaikovsky that he arranged at the end of Scene Two of *The Fairy's Kiss*.[1] Pairs of interlinked minor thirds are also to be found embedded in the series used in the *Double Canon* (i.e., an overlapping pair, 1 and 3, 2 and 4, followed by a consecutive pair, 7 and 8, 9 and 10):

Ex. 69

In the *Symphony of Psalms* a similar motive appears in the accompaniment to the first movement (minor thirds):

Ex. 70

etc.

In the second movement, the theme of the instrumental fugue recalls one of the motives in the second of the *Three Pieces for String Quartet*, which had just appeared in its instrumental form as the movement entitled *Eccentric* in his *Four Studies for Orchestra* (1928), and shows some of the thirds inverted into sixths (see Exs. 21 and 22). In the last movement, the opening 'Laudate' reveals a different treatment, with interlinked overlapping major and minor thirds, the revelation of the minor third being delayed until the end of the phrase, when it is harmonised with the major third:

[1] Fig. 102.

Ex.71

Lau-da-te, lau-da-te, lau-da-te Do - mi - num

The climax of this movement is reached in a 3/2 coda where the sopranos explore the contents of the interval of a minor third with calm unshakeable intensity:

Ex.72

Lau-da-te E- um in cym-ba-lis, be - ne so-nan-ti - bus

This preoccupation with the interval of the third is not erected into a system like those used in *The Firebird* and *The Wedding*. Instead, it is used to help interrelate the material in the Symphony's different movements and to achieve an impression of stylistic unity.

Although the descriptive titles of the three movements as given in the programme of the first Brussels performance (*Prélude; Double Fugue; Allegro symphonique*) were subsequently dropped, they nevertheless provide a helpful indication of the way this symphonic work was constructed.

The opening *Prelude*, which was composed 'in a state of religious and musical ebullience' (*Dia*), starts with an orchestral introduction whose somewhat stiff arpeggio arabesques are punctuated several times by a short sharp chord of E minor. The altos enter with a prayer that is almost a lamentation – 'Exaudi orationem meam, Domine' – in which the vocal part is confined to the interval of a minor second (E rising to F, and F falling back to E). This lamentation alternates with phrases for the full chorus, rising to a climax at 'Ne sileas', which is punctuated by the same E minor chord. More extended treatment for the full chorus leads to a passage where the lamentation theme passes from the tenors to the trebles; and in the final bars the key swings upwards from E minor, through F to G major.

Original Compositions

The *Double Fugue* opens with the instrumental fugue (already referred to) in C minor. This is in four parts and is built up into a knot of considerable contrapuntal complexity. The fugal exposition lasts nearly two minutes; and in view of his life-long love of concision and compression, it is interesting and hardly suprising to find that thirty years later he was ready to admit that it was really 'altogether too obvious, too regular, and too long' (*Exp*). It leads directly to the choir's entry with the second four-part fugue (in E flat minor) – 'Expectans expectavi Dominum' – which is developed over an orchestral accompaniment containing the subject of the first fugue. After the complete exposition of the second fugue, the choir has a *stretto*, with entries of their fugal subject spaced more closely and the orchestra silent. This is followed by an orchestral *stretto* of the first fugue, with the chorus silent. After a general pause, the final episode – 'Et immisit in os meum canticum novum' – begins vigorously with full choir and orchestra fortissimo. The trebles and tenors are given a theme which is partly a retrograde and partly a direct statement of the choir's fugal subject. This is accompanied by a *stretto* of the orchestral fugue in dotted rhythm. (This passage is strangely similar in musical feeling to Nick Shadow's song of defeat and defiance at the end of the Graveyard scene in *The Rake's Progress.*) For the last five bars of the movement, the temperature drops to a sudden piano, the choir sings 'Et sperabunt in Domino' softly in unison on E flat, and an attenuated echo of the subject of the first fugue is heard in the cellos and double-basses, and from a high-pitched trumpet.

Allegro symphonique is a somewhat inappropriate title for the last movement, which is not written in recognised sonata form. It is a movement of dramatic contrasts starting with a slow section which opens with a whispered *Alleluia*

Ex. 73

like a sigh – and leads to the devout 'Laudate' passage quoted above (Ex. 71). This is followed by a splendidly vigorous, almost barbaric fast section, distinguished by horns raucously barking out the rhythm of the words 'Laudate Dominum' in repeated staccato chords.

363

Ex. 74

sf sub p e stacc

This rhythmic phrase, which was the first passage in the Symphony to be composed, is as insistent in its message as the 'Oracula, oracula' passage in Jocasta's aria in *Oedipus Rex*. The analogy with *Oedipus Rex* persists, for a few bars later a wild whirling triplet figure in the woodwind sweeps up suddenly and as suddenly subsides; and this proves to be closely related to the duet in *Oedipus Rex*, where Oedipus sings of his fear, 'Pavesco maxime', and Jocasta tries to reassure him, 'Oracula mentiuntur'.

When the rush of triplets is over, the trebles enter softly and sweetly, followed by the altos, with a phrase that seems distantly related to the opening lamentation in the first movement: but now the minor seconds have changed to major seconds. The material is extended and developed, reaching a climax of great power and splendour – 'Laudate Eum in sono tubae' – which is broken short by a brief return to the slow tempo of the beginning of the movement.[1] This is just long enough for the choir to repeat their whispered 'Alleluia' (Ex. 73); and then the fast barbaric tempo is resumed.

This brief break in the centre of the movement is astonishingly successful. Although musically the passage is very slight (only five bars long), its effect is to maintain unimpaired the feeling of humility set forth at the beginning of the movement, and never really forgotten, despite all the brassy excitements that have intervened. It gives the movement a real centre of gravity – something the composer had tried to do in the first movement of his *Capriccio* the previous year without real success.

With the resumption of the barbaric *Allegro*, much of the earlier material is recapitulated and developed; but when the triplet passage returns, the first wave of E major arpeggios leads to a baroque flourish from the horns[2] based on the notes of the common chord of E flat major, a tune that somehow calls to mind the trumpet solo (also in E flat major) that bursts out in the Jocasta/ Oedipus duet in *Oedipus Rex*.[3] This is the passage that Stravinsky says was inspired 'by a vision of Elijah's chariot climbing the Heavens. Never before had I written anything quite so literal as the triplets for horns and piano to suggest the horses and chariot' (*Dia*). The wave of E major triplets returns, but the modulatory passage is carried a stage further so that the climax is a

---

[1] Fig. 12.
[2] 'A la Strauss', says Ernest Ansermet in his *Fondements de la Musique dans la Conscience Humaine*. Neuchatel, 1961.
[3] One bar before fig. 126.

tone higher than before. At this point the speed slackens,[1] and a fugal episode, starting with a tranquil canon between the trebles and basses at the thirteenth, leads to the coda 'Laudate Eum in cymbalis bene sonantibus'. (There are no cymbals in the orchestra!) This is built up over an ostinato bass (harp, two pianos and timpani) moving in fourths like a pendulum.

Ex.75

Combined with the trebles' six-bar phrase (Ex. 72), this implies a periodicity norm of twelve bars. The coda is in fact built up as follows: (i) 6 + 6 bars (Ex. 72 repeated), (ii) 8 bars (tenors and basses) + 4 bars (full choir) variant passage, (iii) 6 + 6 bars (Ex. 72 repeated), (iv) 6 bars postlude for orchestra alone. The movement ends with a final reference to the whispered 'Alleluia' (Ex. 73) and the unison 'Laudate' from the opening (Ex. 71).

This coda is one of the most striking passages in all Stravinsky's music. The basic ideas are simple but original, and the harmonisation so rich that at one point there are no fewer than ten independent parts. As the bulk of these are woodwind playing in the upper register, a halo of overtones hovers round the trebles' calm, unhurried, swinging melody like a nimbus. A Byzantine basilica would seem to be the ideal setting for this music, as it floats slowly upwards towards the figure of the Pancrator dimly discernible at the apex of the dome.

A Question of Faith

There is no doubt about the authenticity of Stravinsky's personal faith at the time the *Symphony of Psalms* was written. He had become a regular communicant of the Orthodox Church in 1926[2]; and both he and his friends have testified to the strength of his belief. That does not necessarily mean the *Symphony of Psalms* should be looked on as a personal confession of faith.

Shortly after the first performance of the Symphony, a criticism was forwarded to Stravinsky in which its author asked: 'Has the composer attempted to be Hebrew in his music – Hebrew in spirit, after the manner of Ernest Bloch, but without too much that is reminiscent of the synagogue?' In refuting this suggestion, Stravinsky says: 'All these misunderstandings arise from the fact

---

[1] There is a divergence here between the original and revised versions. For details of the change in directions see the section on *Revised Version (1948)* below. And for an examination of the different tempi used for this coda in the various recordings, consult David Hamilton's article, 'Stravinsky and the Microphone' in *High Fidelity*, June 1967.
[2] See *Pater Noster* no. 50.

that people will always insist upon looking in music for something that is not there' (*Chr*).

Ansermet probably comes near the heart of the matter, when he writes:[1]

As Stravinsky, in response to some form of inner compulsion, does not make of his music an act of self-expression, his religious music can reveal only a kind of 'made-up' religiosity. The *Symphony of Psalms*, for instance, expresses the religiosity of others – of the imaginary choir of which the actual singing choir is an *analogon*: but it must be agreed that the expression of this religiosity is itself absolutely authentic.

The *Symphony of Psalms* represents a projection of Stravinsky's own faith through the imagined faith of an anonymous congregation. His personal faith can only be guessed at through this projection; but, as he says in his *Dialogues*, 'one hopes to worship God with a little art if one has any'.

Revised Version (1948)

As in the case of *Apollo Musagetes*, the piano reduction of the *Symphony of Psalms* (made by Stravinsky's son Sviatoslav and published by Edition Russe de Musique in 1930) seems to be based on an earlier version of the full score than that published by Edition Russe in 1932. A clear indication of this is to be found at the bar immediately before fig. 6 in the opening movement, which is a 4/4 bar in the piano reduction and a 3/4 bar in the full score, the last two quavers having been excised. It looks as if the second figure for the harp and 1st piano in the first bar after fig. 9 has been changed too, and also the accompanying interlinked thirds for woodwind and harp four bars after fig. 12.

The 1948 revisions are mainly corrections of misprints and additions of omitted phrasing marks, accents, accidentals etc. At figs. 4 and 7 in the first movement, the woodwind figuration is given a lighter texture by the omission of occasional doubled notes. There is a material change in the first two bars after fig. 14 in the second movement, where a part for tuba in the first bar has been deleted, and new parts for the three trombones and tuba added, together with a part for the timpani.

The most important thing to notice, however, is the revised tempi markings for the last movement. These seem to represent second thoughts on the composer's part and affect the speed of the coda.[2]

---

[1] *Les Fondements de la Musique dans la Conscience humaine.*
[2] 'At first, and until I understood that God must not be praised in fast, *forte* music, no matter how often the text specifies "loud", I thought of the final hymn in a too-rapid pulsation' (*Dia*).

Third Movement	
1930 *Version*	1948 *Version*
Tempo ♩=48	Tempo ♩=48
Fig. 3 Tempo 𝅗𝅥=80	Tempo 𝅗𝅥=80
Fig. 12 Tempo 1° ♩=48	Tempo 1° ♩=48
Fig. 13 Tempo 𝅗𝅥=80	Tempo 𝅗𝅥=80
4 bars before Fig. 20 } Rallentando	Meno Mosso 𝅗𝅥=60
Fig. 20 Tempo 𝅗𝅥=48	Tempo 𝅗𝅥=48 (♩=96)
Fig. 22 [no change]	Molto meno mosso ♩=72 rigorosamente
Fig. 29 Doppio movimento 𝅗𝅥=48	Tempo 1° 𝅗𝅥=48

61. CONCERTO IN D

For violin and orchestra (3.3.3.3 – 4.3.3.1 – timp. – string 5tet[1]). Composed at Nice and Voreppe in the spring and summer of 1931. Published by Schott's, 1931. Reduction for violin and piano by the composer. Duration: *c.* 22 minutes. First performance, Berlin Funkorchester, Berlin, 23 October, 1931, conducted by the composer, with Samuel Dushkin as soloist.

   I. *Toccata* Tempo ♩=96
  II. *Aria I* Tempo ♩=116
 III. *Aria II* Tempo ♪=48
 IV. *Capriccio* Tempo ♪=120

The score bears no dedication; but there is the following prefatory note signed by Stravinsky:

> *Cette oeuvre a été créée sous ma direction le 23 octobre 1931 au concert du Rundfunk de Berlin par Samuel Dushkin auquel je garde une reconnaissance profonde et une grande admiration pour la valeur hautement artistique de son jeu.*

The violin part was written in collaboration with Dushkin. The manuscript full score, together with other manuscript material, is in the composer's collection [C 56]. The first movement was finished at Nice on 20 May 1931,

---

[1] The numbers of the string players are specified as follows: I Vl (8), 2 Vl (8), Vla (6), Vcl (4), Cb (4).

the second at Nice on 20 May 1931, the third at Nice on 10 June 1931. The completed score is signed and dated 'Voreppe (Isère) la Vironnière, 13/25. Sept. 1931'.

Composition and Collaboration with Dushkin

The idea that Stravinsky should compose a violin concerto came from Willy Strecker, one of the directors of the music publishing house of B. Schott's Soehne, Mainz. Stravinsky had met him in London during the summer of 1929; and shortly after this Schott's took over the publication of some of his earlier compositions including, *Fireworks, Scherzo Fantastique* and the instrumental version of *Pastorale*.[1] At the beginning of 1931 Strecker suggested that Stravinsky might care to write something for a young violinist friend of his called Samuel Dushkin, who had been adopted in early childhood by the American composer Blair Fairchild and trained in the school of Léopold Auer. In his *Chronicle* Stravinsky says that at first he felt doubtful about the proposal. Though he had successfully presented the rustic asperities of the fiddle as a concertante instrument in the small-scale ensemble of *The Soldier's Tale*, he was not at all sure about his capacity to write a full-scale virtuoso work for violin. 'I hesitated because I am not a violinist and I was afraid that my slight knowledge of that instrument would not be sufficient to enable me to solve the many problems which would necessarily arise in the course of a major work especially composed for it. But Willy Strecker allayed my doubts by assuring me that Dushkin would place himself entirely at my disposal in order to furnish any technical details which I might require.' He also consulted Paul Hindemith, asking him whether the fact that he did not play the violin would make itself felt in his composition. Not only did Hindemith reassure him on this point, but he added that it would be a positive advantage, as it would make him 'avoid a routine technique and would give rise to ideas which would not be suggested by the familiar movement of the fingers'.

Stravinsky accordingly agreed to Strecker's proposal; the Concerto was formally commissioned by Blair Fairchild; and the meeting between Stravinsky and Dushkin took place at Wiesbaden early in 1931. Stravinsky was delighted to find that, in addition to being a brilliant violinist, Dushkin was a cultured musician of great sensibility and understanding, and he invited him to visit him during the composition of the concerto so that he could benefit from his comments and advice. Dushkin fell under the spell of Stravinsky's charm; and the collaboration started under the most favourable auspices.

Some years later Dushkin wrote a most interesting account of the period when they were working together.[2]

---

[1] See also the section dealing with the publication of *Saucers* (no. 30).
[2] 'Working with Stravinsky', published in the Merle Armitage book on *Stravinsky* edited by Edwin Corle. New York, 1949.

During the winter I saw Stravinsky in Paris quite often. One day when we were lunching in a restaurant, Stravinsky took out a piece of paper and wrote down this chord

Ex.76

and asked me if it could be played. I had never seen a chord with such an an enormous stretch, from the E to the top A, and I said 'No'. Stravinsky said sadly 'Quel dommage'. ('What a pity.') After I got home, I tried it, and, to my astonishment, I found that in that register, the stretch of the eleventh was relatively easy to play, and the sound fascinated me. I telephoned Stravinsky at once to tell him that it could be done. When the Concerto was finished, more than six months later, I understood his disappointment when I first said 'No'. This chord, in a different dress, begins each of the four movements. Stravinsky himself calls it his 'passport' to that Concerto.

From Paris the scene of the collaboration moved to Nice, where the first two movements and part of the third were written; and the end of the third and the whole of the fourth were written at the Château de la Veronnière near Voreppe in Isère (where Stravinsky had taken a property for the summer) 'among half unpacked trunks and boxes and coming and going of removers, upholsterers, electricians, and plumbers' (*Chr*).

At this stage, Dushkin's function was to advise the composer how best his ideas could be adapted to the exigencies of the violin as a concert display instrument. As and when the composition progressed, Stravinsky would show him what he had written, and Dushkin's comments and suggestions would be discussed. 'Whenever he accepted one of my suggestions," says Dushkin,[1] 'even a simple change such as extending the range of the violin by stretching the phrase to the octave below and the octave above, Stravinsky would insist on altering the very foundations correspondingly. He behaved like an architect who if asked to change a room on the third floor had to go down to the foundations to keep the proportions of his whole structure.'

On one occasion, Dushkin noticed that a certain rhythmic accompaniment Stravinsky had written 'was at first somewhat symmetrical. After he had altered it, the number of pulsations remained the same, but the symmetry was completely gone and the personality of the rhythmic pattern was new'. At this point, Dushkin asked if he could define rhythm, and Stravinsky replied that a comparison between rhythm and mathematics would perhaps explain what he had in mind.

---

[1] S. Dushkin, *op. cit.*

'In mathematics,' he said, 'there are an infinite number of ways of arriving at the number seven. It's the same with rhythm. The difference is that whereas in mathematics the *sum* is the important thing; it makes no difference if you say five and two, or two and five, six and one or one and six, and so on. With rhythm, however, the fact that they add up to seven is of secondary importance. The important thing is, is it five and two or is it two and five, because five and two is a different person from two and five.'

Although Dushkin does not specify the particular passage that prompted this conversation about metrics, it would not be too fanciful to imagine Stravinsky taking a simple symmetrical figure of accompaniment adding up to seven bars like this –

Ex.77a

and teasing it into the following shape:[1]

Ex.77b

According to Heinrich Strobel,[2] Stravinsky examined all the important violin concertos in the classical repertory before beginning to compose his own; but none of these seems to have had so much effect on the work as his own *Capriccio*. The last movements of these two compositions are closely related in mood and style, and each bears the 'capriccio' label. As was the case with the *Capriccio*, reciprocity between the solo instrument and the orchestra is an essential part of the Concerto, and much of the material used by the solo violin or orchestra is interchangeable. This can be clearly seen in the opening Toccata, where the main subject in thirds, which seems to have a keyboard derivation, is accompanied by a counter-subject based on the arpeggio of the common chord prinked out with rising appoggiaturas, and each subject is equally suitable for presentation by the solo instrument or the orchestra (Ex. 78). This particular lay-out should be compared with the *allegro brillante* passage in the last movement of the *Capriccio* (Ex. 65).

---

[1] Violin Concerto, first movement, fig. 19.
[2] 'Stravinsky privat' in *Melos*, October 1931.

Ex.78

Instead of the single slow movement of the *Capriccio*, the violin concerto has two contrasted Arias. The first (in D minor) starts as a fast-moving two-part invention between the solo violin and the cellos, accompanied by occasional outbursts of repeated semiquavers played *spiccato* by the other strings. A syncopated passage marked *dolce tranquillo* leads to a *Più mosso* section, after which the two-part invention returns. Throughout this movement the solo violin has a most extended part, covering a very wide range. By way of contrast, the second *Aria* (in F sharp minor)[1] is a beautiful slow lyrical cantilena for solo violin, the compass of which is much more restricted and, with the exception of a few gratuitous octaves added towards the end of the movement, almost within the range of a human voice. The orchestral accompaniment is entrusted to the strings, and the rocking bass figure (in the cellos) recalls the style of some of J. S. Bach's slow movements.

Although there is no cadenza as such for the solo violin, the Presto coda to the fourth movement (*Capriccio*) is a kind of extended cadence with virtuoso passages of double-stopping for the soloist.

The first performance of the concerto took place in Berlin on 23 October 1931. Although Dushkin played brilliantly, the orchestral performance was poor; and in his *Memories*, Stravinsky recalls how Hindemith 'bravely chastised[2] the Berlin Radio Orchestra for its bad playing' of his new work. Dushkin retained the sole rights of performance for a period of about two years, during which he played it throughout Europe.

Ballet Production

George Balanchine used the score for a ballet called *Balustrade* that he produced for de Basil's Original Ballet Russe in New York in 1941, with décor and costumes by Pavel Tchelichev. He composed the choreography while listening to a recording of the Concerto; and Stravinsky 'could actually observe

[1] The bass is shy about confirming this tonality, and although the dominant (C sharp) is much in evidence, the tonic (F sharp) appears only once at the end of the first strophe and once at the end of the last strophe.
[2] The phrase in the American edition of *Memories* is '...bravely bawled out the Berlin Radio Orchestra...'

371

him conceiving gesture, movement, combination, composition' (*Dia*). The composer judged the result to be one of the most satisfactory visualisations of any of his works.

57. DUO CONCERTANT

For violin and piano in five movements. Composed at Voreppe, December 1931 – 15 July 1932. Published by Edition Russe de Musique 1933 (later by Boosey & Hawkes). Duration: *c.* 16 minutes. First performance by Samuel Dushkin and the composer at the Funkhaus, Berlin, 28 October 1932. MS comp. [C 57].

    I. *Cantilène*
   II. *Eclogue I*
 III. *Eclogue II*
  IV. *Gigue*
   V. *Dithyrambe*

When the *Duo Concertant* was published, Stravinsky explained its origin in the following note:

> After the Violin Concerto, which is orchestral as well as instrumental, I continued my researches in the domain of the violin and turned to its functions in the chamber-music ensemble. For many years I had taken no pleasure in the blend of strings struck in the piano with strings set in vibration with the bow. In order to reconcile myself to this instrumental combination, I was compelled to turn to the minimum of instruments, that is to say, only two, in which I saw the possibility of solving the instrumental and acoustic problem presented by the strings of the piano and those of the violin. Thus originated the idea of the *Duo Concertant* for violin and piano. The mating of these instruments seems much clearer than the combination of a piano with several stringed instruments, which tends to confusion with the orchestra.

Subsequently, he reproduced the substance of this statement in his *Chronicle* and went on to say that the composition of the *Duo Concertant* was closely connected in his mind with his friend Charles-Albert Cingria's book on Petrarch, which had then just been published, and from which he quoted the following passage:

> Lyricism cannot exist without rules, and it is essential they should be strict. Otherwise there is only a faculty for lyricism, and that exists everywhere. What does not exist everywhere is lyrical expression and composition. To achieve that, a craftsman's skill is necessary, and that must be learned.

He considered that in the *Duo Concertant* he was aiming at creating 'a lyrical composition, a work of musical versification' and that its spirit and form were determined by 'the pastoral poets of antiquity and their scholarly art and technique'. He also stated that the theme he had in mind 'developed throughout the five movements of the piece which formed an integral whole' (*Chr*).

It is difficult to reconcile some of these utterances with the work itself. There is certainly a pastoral spirit in the opening of the first *Eclogue*, and possibly also in the galumphing *Jig*. The *Dithyramb* is a noble rhapsody, though whether it has any genuine Bacchic element in it is hard to say; and an element of dialogue is not absent from the Eclogues. As for musical versification, the first *Eclogue* begins with a lively bagpipe episode, with the violin playing the chanter above a pedal A on the open string, while the piano provides a figured drone and echoes the chanter tune in canon at the octave, while later the roles of Dux and Comes are reversed, and the episode ends with the violin following the piano in canon. Here indeed is an ingenious attempt at regular musical versification; and the same can probably be said of the *Jig* with its perpetual dactylic jogtrot. But the *Cantilena*, the second *Eclogue* and the *Dithyramb* are in a free form of musical versification; and though Stravinsky has always been a stickler for metrical and notational exactitude, it is interesting to find that in the *Dithyramb* he lands himself in notational difficulties by adopting so small a unit as the semiquaver.[1] He drops barlines altogether for a considerable part of the first *Eclogue* and the *Dithyramb*; but this seems to be done for no apparent reason, for neither passage needs to be emancipated from metre and each could easily and helpfully be barred.

In the long run, it is best to put Stravinsky's various explanations on one side and accept the work at its musical face value.

The first movement is hardly a *Cantilena* in the usual sense of that word. It consists of two contrasted ideas – the first, a series of arpeggio arabesques (somewhat in the manner of the introduction to the first movement of the *Symphony of Psalms*); the second, a slowly expanding fanfare theme expressed chiefly in double-stopping on the violin. These are presented separately, and also in conjunction.

The first *Eclogue* starts with the bagpipe episode referred to above. This is followed by an episode like a cadenza for the violin, accompanied by a running stream of semiquavers in the piano, the style of which recalls the violin part in the 'Ragtime' and the 'Triumphal March of the Devil' in *The Soldier's Tale*. The second *Eclogue* develops a stage further the *cantabile* style of the two Arias in the violin concerto.

Stravinsky is usually so pithy and succinct in his musical utterances that it is strange to come across a long garrulous movement like the *Jig* – particularly when it is built up largely of fourths, not one of Stravinsky's favourite or

---

[1] There are misprints in the piano part of the *Dithyramb* at the 5th quaver after the first double bar where the bass crotchet F should be a quaver, and similarly at the 12th quaver after the first double bar where the bass crotchet chord (C and B) should also be a quaver. Also, at the 9th quaver after the first double bar, the solo violin's tied quaver B is too long.

characteristic intervals. The torrent of triplets is twice interrupted by episodes like trios, the second of which recalls the mood of the *pas de deux* in *Apollo Musagetes*.

The *Dithyramb* is a movement of grave beauty. The high-pitched violin part leads the piano into an increasingly elaborate passage of four-part counterpoint like the instrumental fugue in the *Symphony of Psalms*. The effect is that of an exalted threnody.

Another reason that had led to the composition of the *Duo Concertant* was Stravinsky's wish to open up a wider field for his music through chamber music performances. He found such concerts 'much easier to arrange as they do not require large orchestras of high quality, which are costly and so rarely to be found except in big cities' (*Chr*). The *Duo Concertant* was to form the kernel of such a programme. Between them Dushkin and Stravinsky planned to make new arrangements of the Pergolesi and Chaikovsky material from *Pulcinella* and *The Fairy's Kiss* under the titles *Suite Italienne* and *Divertimento*; and they also prepared transcriptions of the early *Pastorale*, the 'Chinese March' and 'Nightingale's Songs' from *The Nightingale*, the Scherzo ('Dance of the Firebird') and 'Lullaby' from *The Firebird*, and the 'Russian Dance' from *Petrushka*. With this programme they toured Europe during the 1932/33 and 1933/34 seasons.

63. СИМВОЛЪ ВѢРЫ – CREDO

For mixed choir *a cappella* (S.A.T.B.). Composed in 1932. Published by Edition Russe de Musique, 1933 (later by Boosey & Hawkes). Duration: *c*. 3 minutes. MS comp. [C 47].

This is a plainsong setting of the *Credo* in Slavonic. Like the *Pater Noster* (no. 55), it is intended for liturgical use in the Russian Orthodox Church.

New Version with Latin Text (1949)

The music in the new version is notationally the same: only the pointing and phrasing have been changed to fit the Latin words. Published by Boosey & Hawkes.

New Version with Slavonic Text (1964)

In May 1964 Stravinsky rewrote the Slavonic version of this *a cappella* piece, mainly to fix the rhythms of the *faux bourdon*; but it was to some extent recomposed.

64. PERSEPHONE

Melodrama in three scenes for tenor, narrator, mixed chorus (S.A.T.B.), children's choir (trebles and altos) and orchestra (3.3.3.3 – 4.3.3.1 – timp., percussion, 2 harps, piano – string 5tet). French text by André Gide. Composed at Voreppe and Paris, May 1933 – 24 January 1934. Published by

Original Compositions

Edition Russe de Musique, 1934 (later by Boosey & Hawkes). Duration: *c.* 56 minutes. First performance, Ballets Ida Rubinstein, Opera House, Paris, 30 April 1934, conducted by the composer. The manuscript full score together with other manuscript material is in the composer's collection [C 62]. The MS vocal score was given by the composer to Victoria Ocampo, Buenos Aires. The published score carries the following prefatory note signed by Stravinsky:

> *La première représentation de Perséphone a eu lieu à Paris, au Théâtre National de l'Opéra, le 30 Avril 1934, avec Madame Ida Rubinstein et sa troupe, sous ma direction.*

Stravinsky and Gide

At the beginning of 1933, Ida Rubinstein asked Stravinsky whether he would be prepared to set to music a poem André Gide had written based on the Homeric Hymn to Demeter. She intended to mount it as a ballet; and the fee offered was the same as for *The Fairy's Kiss*, viz. $7,500.

Stravinsky already knew Gide slightly. They had first met in Paris in 1910; and in those pre-war years Stravinsky used occasionally to see him at rehearsals of the Russian Ballet. They also came across each other in Switzerland in the summer of 1917 when Gide was working on his translation of Shakespeare's *Antony and Cleopatra*; and there was some suggestion that Stravinsky should compose incidental music for its stage production. In his *Memories* Stravinsky says: 'I replied that the musical style would depend on the style of the whole production. Later when I suggested that the production be in modern dress, he was shocked – and deaf to my arguments that we would be nearer Shakespeare in inventing something new, and nearer him in every way than he was, veristically, to Antony and Cleopatra.'[1] In his *Journal* for 16 January 1923, Gide recalled this episode when commenting on the production of Cocteau's version of *Antigone*. 'Cocteau's play responds to the same feeling that made Stravinsky say he would willingly collaborate over *Antony and Cleopatra*, but only if Antony were dressed as an Italian *bersagliere*'. And at this point he added one of his most memorable apophthegms: 'La patine est la récompense des chefs-d'oeuvre'.

Gide travelled to Wiesbaden early in February 1933 to meet him and show him the poem on Persephone he had written before the first World War. This

---

[1] On one other occasion Stravinsky showed interest in a play of Shakespeare's, and then his choice was rather unexpected. Asked early in 1964 which was his favourite Shakespeare play and why, he replied: 'At present, my answer is *Coriolanus*, because Olivier's performance of it a few years ago has remained in my imagination more vividly than any other Shakespeare performance that I have seen in recent years, but also because the arguments of the play have always had a very special appeal to me and because they are formed with such perfect art. Incidentally, the play could be made into a fine libretto, though none of us has enough heroic sentiment to presume to use it.' (*Show*, Feb. 1964.)

375

was in the French Parnassian tradition, rich in rhyme and romantic in phraseo-logy. The meeting seemed to go off extremely well. 'Entente parfaite', noted Gide in his *Journal* for 8 February. In a letter to Stravinsky of the same date, he expanded on his treatment of the subject. This he explained was 'half way between a natural interpretation (the rhythm of the seasons; the corn falling in the soil must die to be resurrected through the sleep of winter) and a mystical interpretation; this way the myth is connected at the same time with both ancient Egyptian cults and Christian doctrine'. Stravinsky seems to have suggested that the work should be geared to the cycle of the seasons; but Gide pointed out that his idea of starting with Autumn was untenable. 'It would be cheating the Greek myth too outrageously. . . . Proserpina has nothing to do with Autumn. (Besides, the Greek year had only three seasons.) She is the purest personification of the Spring.' On the other hand, he agreed with Stravinsky that certain anecdotal episodes he had been tempted to insert, including a meeting with Eurydice, should be removed, and a narrator (Eumolpus, the founder and first officiating priest of the Eleusinian mysteries) added to the cast. It was understood that the part of Persephone, which was to be played by Ida Rubinstein herself, should be spoken and not sung.

Gide dispatched the first of the three scenes to Stravinsky later that month; and the second followed about the beginning of March. Stravinsky started the work of composition in May, and towards the end of that month he took Ida Rubinstein and Gide with him to the church of Saint-Louis des Invalides to hear a boys' choir which he thought of using in the third scene.[1]

The collaboration that had started so auspiciously now began to run off the rails. At Stravinsky's request, Gide apparently wrote some extra verses for the children's chorus in the third scene; and there was some correspondence between them on minor matters of prosody. But by the time the score was finished, they no longer saw eye to eye.

It seems probable that there was a run-through at Ida Rubinstein's house in the Place des Etats-Unis, Paris, late in January, 1934, when, according to Stravinsky, Gide's only comment on the music was 'c'est curieux, c'est très curieux' (*Mem*). Gide has left an extended account of the occasion in his last book *Ainsi soit-il*. He says that in addition to Ida Rubinstein, Stravinsky and himself, Jacques Copeau the producer and André Barsacq the designer were also present, and the discussion proceeded on the following lines. Copeau explained that in the forthcoming production there would be no question of presenting the action in realistic dramatic guise. His idea was that the setting should be a temple or a cathedral and the action would be reported by a commentator. Stravinsky was in full agreement. 'It will be just like the Mass,' he said, 'and that's what appeals to me in your piece. The action needs only to be implied.' Gide tried to protest and pointed out that he had given precise

---

[1] In fact, the Zanglust Choir of Amsterdam was engaged for the production in 1934.

indications of the different settings for the three scenes – for instance, how could they show in a cathedral that the second scene took place in the Under-world? 'My dear friend,' said Copeau, 'that can be played in the crypt'. At this point Gide was apparently so upset that on leaving the meeting, he decided to get out of Paris without delay and went off to Sicily for a month's holiday. On his return, he kept away from the rehearsals and did not attend the actual performance, though he seems to have been present at the preview given at the house of the Princess Edmond de Polignac.

Stravinsky, of course, noticed Gide's withdrawal and was aware of his disapproval. As he says in his *Memories*, Gide 'had expected the *Persephone* text to be sung with exactly the same stresses as he would use to recite it. He believed my musical purpose should be to imitate or underline the verbal pattern; I would simply have to find pitches for the syllables, since he con-sidered he had already composed the rhythm. The tradition of *poesia per musica* meant nothing to him.' At this point, feeling in need of an ally, he turned to his friend, Paul Valéry, and paid him a visit, during which this particular problem was discussed. He was reassured by Valéry's affirmation of 'the musician's prerogative to treat loose and formless prosodies (such as Gide's) according to his musical ideas, even if the latter led to "distortion" of phrasing or to breaking up, for purposes of syllabification, of the words themselves' (*Mem*). Fortified by this support, he composed a manifesto, which was published in *Excelsior* on the eve of the first performance, and which made his position clear.[1] This ends with the frequently quoted passage: 'All this is in no way due to caprice on my part. I am on a perfectly sure road. There is nothing to discuss or to criticise. One does not criticise anyone that is functioning. A nose is not manufactured – a nose just *is*. Thus, too, my art.'

Two days after the first performance, Valéry wrote an enthusiastic note on *Académie Française* notepaper, saying: ' . . . the divine detachment of your work touched me. It seems to me that what I have sometimes searched for in the ways of poetry, you pursue and join in your art. The point is, to attain purity through the will. You expressed it marvellously well in the article yesterday[2] which I immensely enjoyed. LONG LIVE YOUR NOSE.'

It is perhaps a little unfair of Stravinsky to talk of 'loose and formless prosodies' in connection with Gide's text and to suggest (as in his *Dialogues*) that the best thing for a revival would be to scrap Gide's text and substitute therefor a newly written libretto by someone like W. H. Auden. The poem by no means deserves these strictures, and within its particular conventions, it is full of felicities. Indeed, there is a kind of mnemonic quality about some of its phrases, e.g.,

> *Je vois ma mère errante et de haillons vêtue*
> *Redemander partout Perséphone perdue*

---

[1] See Appendix A (5).
[2] This refers to the *second* version of the manifesto. See Appendix A (5).

It is everywhere rich in rhyme, and usually regular in metre. But sometimes the poet achieves a striking effect with lines of varied length, e.g.,

> *Cependant sur la colline*
> *Qui domine*
> *Le présent et l'avenir*
> *Les Grecs ont construit un temple*
> *Pour Déméter qui contemple*
> *Un peuple heureux accourir.*
> *Triptolème est auprès d'elle*
> *Dont la faucille reluit,*
> *Et fidèle*
> *Le choeur des Nymphes les suit.*

It should be added that Gide published the text of *Persephone*[1] at the end of April 1934 with a dedication to Ida Rubinstein 'dont la ferveur a su animer un projet endormi depuis plus de vingt ans'. The text published the same year in Stravinsky's score contains a number of variants. These, though minor, are worth noting, particularly by Gide scholars, because in most cases they seem to be improvements, and so far none of them has been incorporated in the text of *Persephone*, as printed on its own or as reprinted in the Collected Plays.

Synopsis and Composition

Stravinsky was originally attracted to Gide's text not so much by its poetic quality as by the variety and strength of its syllables. This was the first time he had made a setting of French words since the *Two Poems of Verlaine* in 1910; and he made his syllabic preoccupations abundantly clear in the *Excelsior* manifesto. This document is of particular importance, because it explains in somewhat intransigent terms the position he had taken up as a composer. It was as if he realised in advance that the special circumstances in which the work had been conceived and produced – the unusual melodramatic form adopted to suit the requirements of Ida Rubinstein, the idiosyncratic syllabic setting of the text which so seriously disconcerted Gide, the nature of a production that had to be geared to the limited abilities of a non-permanent dance company – were likely to militate against any possibility of immediate popularity. His reference to 'this score, as it is written and as it must remain in the musical archives of our time', has a chilly, rather forbidding ring about it. Nevertheless, he was right; and the work languished for many years after its first production. An occasional concert or radio performance helped to keep it half-alive; but it was not until the Royal Ballet at Covent Garden had the courage to revive it as a ballet and include it in its regular repertory that the full stature of the work could be appreciated once again. Meanwhile, the

---

[1] Librarie Gallimard, Paris, 1934.

378

composer had not made the position any easier when in his *Conversations* (1959) he answered a question of Robert Craft's about 'the use of music as accompaniment to recitation (*Persephone*)' by saying: 'Do not ask. Sins cannot be undone, only forgiven.' This was a melodramatic attitude to take up over a melodrama; but since then his views have apparently been modified, as can be seen from his use of controlled melodrama in *A Sermon, A Narrative and a Prayer* and in *The Flood*.

There is one unusual feature that makes the score of *Persephone* of special interest in Stravinsky's general opus. According to Robert Craft,[1] three of its melodic and rhythmic ideas were drawn from an abortive work called a *Dialogue between Reason and Joy*,[2] a setting of a Renaissance text on the subject of music that he sketched out in 1917. In his *Dialogues*, Stravinsky specifically states that he 'grafted whole from a sketch book of 1917 the G minor flute

Ex.79

---

[1] 'A Personal Preface' by Robert Craft. *The Score*, June 1957.
[2] The manuscript of this *Dialogue* is in Robert Craft's collection.

379

and harp music in Eumolpus's second aria in Part II'.[1] He also mentions that the chorus 'Sur ce lit elle repose'[2] was originally written as a lullaby for Vera de Bosset in Paris during a heat wave and was a setting of his own (Russian) words. Both this chorus and the chorus 'Nous apportons des offrandes'[3] are based on simple diatonic themes, which are almost literally repeated over varying accompanying figures, very much in the style of some of his earlier Russian popular music, and in each case the setting is not literally syllabic, but one syllable is often spread over two or more notes. In both choruses, he has adopted a system of irregular barring in an attempt to move away from the conventional accentuation of the theme. The first bars of the 'Sur ce lit elle repose' chorus are quoted as an illustration of this process. Stravinsky's own barring is given at the head of the example, and the time signatures of the various motives have been altered to show how a basic 4/4 theme with bass accompaniment has been crossed with a swinging decorative figure that starts by being accumulative (3/4 + 4/4 + 5/4) and then becomes decumulative (5/4 + 4/4 + 3/4) by way of compensation (See Ex. 79).

The following synopsis of the stage action follows Gide's text closely:

Scene One During Eumolpus's invocation to Demeter, goddess of fertility and mother of Persephone, the curtain rises on a meadow by the seashore, with a rocky defile on one side leading to the Underworld. The goddess has entrusted her daughter to the care of the Nymphs, who sing of the beauty of the springtime of the world. They extol the flowers growing in the meadow, but warn Persephone not to pick the narcissus, for whoever breathes its fragrance is vouchsafed a glimpse of the unknown Underworld. But Persephone, bending over the narcissus, sees a vision of the hopeless, wandering Shades; and then she plucks the flower. Eumolpus tells her that the Shades await her coming, and that her compassion for them will lead her to become Pluto's bride. In this way, she will bring them solace and reign over them. Persephone of her own free will descends to the Underworld.

Scene Two The Elysian Fields. On one side, the entrance to Pluto's palace; on the other, the banks of Lethe overhung by the branches of an immense tree. Persephone is discovered asleep on a couch, still pressing the narcissus to her breast. Nearby, the chorus of Shades are asleep, while a group of Danaides, draped in ashen green, are drawing water from the river in their urns.

Persephone awakes; and the Shades sing of their plight. They are not unhappy, for they know neither love nor hate, grief nor desire, and they ask her to speak to them of springtime on earth. But as she begins to do so, Pluto

---

[1] One bar before fig. 145 *et seq.*
[2] Fig. 74 *et seq.*
[3] Fig. 207 *et seq.* Stravinsky calls this chorus 'Russian Easter music' (*Dia*).

calls. Eumolpus reminds her that it is her destiny to reign over the Underworld and not to show pity. He urges her to drink a cup of water from Lethe. Shades draped in black enter from Pluto's palace bringing jewels and fine garments which she rejects. The clouds at the back of the stage part to reveal Mercury, followed by a procession of the Hours clad in colours ranging from sunrise to sunset. Each brings a present to Persephone; but she refuses them all. Then Mercury tempts her with a ripe pomegranate. She bites it, and the taste brings back a longing for the world she has lost. Mercury and the Hours retire. The Shades advise her that if she gazes at the narcissus she has brought with her, she will behold her mother and the world above. She does so and sees nothing but the desolation of what appears to be eternal winter on earth and her desperate mother who seeks her everywhere in vain. It is Eumolpus who assures her that the terrestrial winter will not last for ever. He tells her how Demeter, after arriving at the palace of Eleusis, takes into her care King Seleucos's last born son, the infant Demophoon. Her design is to confer immortality upon him, and under the name of Triptolemus he will bring salvation to the earth by teaching men to till the soil, and through him Persephone will be brought back to the light of day, to be his bride and to reign over springtime on earth.

Scene Three A hill surmounted by a Doric temple. On one side is a mound with evergreen oaks growing on it, and a tomb built into it in the Etruscan style. In front of its stone portals stands the genius of death with an extinguished torch in his hand.

The Greeks have built this temple to Demeter, and men, women and children bring their offerings. They all call on Persephone to reappear; and Triptolemus strips off the mourning cloak that Demeter is still wearing and strews flowers before the tomb. The stone panels swing back on their hinges, and Persephone emerges. As she comes forward with faltering steps, roses spring up wherever her feet touch the soil. She joins Demeter, Triptolemus and the chorus of Nymphs at the top of the hill by the temple. Despite her joy at being restored to her mother and united with Triptolemus, she realises that henceforth nothing can stop the cycle of the seasons, and it will be her destiny in due course to return to the Underworld and descend again into that pit of human misery. She takes the lighted torch from Mercury, who guides her towards the door of the tomb, while Demeter, Triptolemus and the chorus remain on the hillside.

Stravinsky reduced this to the following musical scheme:

Scene One – The Abduction of Persephone
1. Aria (Eumolpus): 'Déesse aux mille noms', E minor
2. (a) Chorus: 'Reste avec nous', G major
   (b) Chorus: 'Ivresse matinale', D major

(c) Solo (Eumolpus) and Chorus: 'De toutes les fleurs', D major

(d) Recitation (Persephone): 'Je vois sur des prés', D flat major

(e) Chorus: 'Ne cueille pas cette fleur', G minor

(f) Chorus: 'Viens, joue avec nous', G major
   [reprise of 2(a)]

3. Aria (Eumolpus): 'Perséphone un peuple t'attend' C minor

Scene Two – Persephone in the Underworld

4. Orchestral Introduction, B major/B minor

5. Aria (Eumolpus): 'C'est ainsi nous raconte Homère', E minor

6. (a) Chorus (lullaby): 'Sur ce lit elle repose', D major

   (b) Chorus: 'Les ombres ne sont pas malheureuses', E major

   (c) Chorus and Recitation (Persephone): 'Parle-nous du printemps', G major

7. Aria (Eumolpus): 'Tu viens pour dominer', D major

8. Orchestral Interlude, D minor

9. Chorus: 'Viens, Mercure', C major

10. Aria (Eumolpus): 'Persephone confuse', C major

11. Chorus and Recitation (Persephone): 'Si tu contemples le calice', C major

12. (a) Aria (Eumolpus): 'Pauvres ombres désespérées', E flat major

    (b) Chorus and Recitation (Persephone): 'Ainsi l'espoir renaît',

    (c) Recitation (Persephone): 'Déméter, tu m'attends' , B flat major

Scene Three – Persephone Reborn

13. Orchestral Introduction, A major

14. Aria (Eumolpus): 'C'est ainsi nous raconte Homère', E minor

15. (a) Chorus: 'Nous apportons nos offrandes' A flat major

    (b) Chorus: 'Encore mal réveillée'

    (c) Chorus of Children: 'L'ombre encore l'environne', G minor/B flat major

16. Recitation (Persephone) 'Mère, ta Perséphone', G flat major

17. Solo (Eumolpus) and Chorus: 'Ainsi vers l'ombre souterraine', E minor

If the key system of *Persephone* is compared with that of *Oedipus Rex*, it will be seen that the minor mode is not nearly so prevalent as it was in the earlier work. Nearly all the choruses (even those of the Shades) are in the major. Flat keys are associated specially closely with Persephone herself. And Eumolpus has no fewer than four numbers (1, 5, 14, 17) in the key of E minor. Each of these is closely interrelated to the others in style; and in fact the opening bars of his first aria form a kind of leading motive for this narrative framework.

Ex. 80

Dé - esse aux mil - le noms

Original Compositions

This motive of a fourth divided sometimes into a minor second and major third, and sometimes into a major second and minor third, is not developed into a comprehensive system as in *The Wedding*; but it bears within it the seed of the myth, for while the flattened seventh in the key of E implies descent, the unflattened leading note implies ascent. It is appropriate to find the two combined in a happy false relationship in the accompaniment to the final chorus with its splendid peroration:

> *Il faut, pour qu'un printemps renaisse*
> *Que le grain consente à mourir*
> *Sous terre, afin qu'il reparaisse*
> *En moisson d'or pour l'avenir.*[1]

Ex. 81

Examples 79 and 81 give an idea of the extremes of choral writing in this work, ranging from one to four parts. There are also intermediate stages where

[1] In his *Dialogues*, Stravinsky stresses the importance of this chorus being 'played and sung in tempo, and quietly, without a general crescendo'.

two- or three-part writing is involved; but the effect is always that of a harmonised melodic line, and the choral writing is homophonic rather than
contrapuntal in effect. The harmonic range is on the whole traditional; but
Stravinsky's approach to even the most obvious harmonic progressions is
fresh and unhackneyed, and the effect of originality is heightened by his
refusal ever to fall into stale metric patterns. A simple example will suffice – the
beautiful phrase denoting the revival of hope that comes at the end of Eumolpus's great aria (12.a) 'Pauvres ombres désespérées':

With one exception, Eumolpus's airs, vigorous and varied though they be,
do not possess the weight and stature of the great airs in *Oedipus Rex*. The
exception is the air already referred to – 'Pauvres ombres désespérées'. Here a
grave melodic beauty is allied to polyphonic richness of texture in the orchestral
accompaniment. The air is not a closed number, for Eumolpus's final phrase,
'Ainsi l'enfant prospère et sourit à la vie' leads directly to the choral comment
'Ainsi l'espoir renaît dans notre âme ravie' just quoted above (Ex. 82); and it
also finds room for a short passage (four bars long) of recitation for Persephone:
so it may be said to approximate to a scena rather than an aria.

Persephone's part is of crucial importance. While the function of Eumolpus and the chorus is to comment and report, and certain characters like Pluto and Mercury are mute, Persephone is the sole vocal dramatic character in the action. On her lies the burden of reciting a large proportion of Gide's text; and it was Stravinsky's job to ensure that the words had a fair chance of coming over without being swamped by the music, and that at the same time the current of the music was not weakened or distorted by the undisciplined cadences of the spoken voice. He made no attempt to devise a *Sprechstimme* notation for the vocal part; and the actress/dancer is free to develop the recitation on lines suitable to the lyrical and dramatic nature of the part. In addition to passages of melodrama inserted in the various numbers for Eumolpus or the chorus, there are at least three extended passages where the music is definitely personal to Persephone (2d, 12c, and 16). The first of these is in Scene One where Persephone, after bending over the narcissus, sees a vision of the Underworld – 'Je vois sur des prés semés d'asphodèles'. The trailing clarinet line of dropping fourths recalls the Garden of Death passage in *The Nightingale* (Ex. 18)

The idea of this flute duet is extended in Persephone's last recitation (no. 16), where a lovely two-part invention for the two flutes over a gently rocking string accompaniment leads without break to a reprise of Ex. 83. The transcendental tranquillity of this passage rivals that of Gluck's Elysian Fields music in *Orfeo ed Euridice*.

A comparatively new feature in the score is the occasional use of an aerated style of writing, in which notes and phrases are separated and punctuated by rests and pauses that introduce silence as a musical element. Stravinsky had already experimented with this style in the duet between the Shepherd and the

Messenger in *Oedipus Rex*;[1] but now he made more extended use of it, particularly in some of the choruses (nos. 2b and 15c) and Eumolpus's aria (no. 14). In the chorus, 'Ivresse matinale' (no. 2b), the rests sometimes cut through the words and give an effect of consummate lightness and transparency. Elsewhere, the musical pauses coincide with the natural pauses of the words and phrases and help the meaning.

Just before the climax of Persephone's return in Scene Three there is a fascinating example (almost unique in Stravinsky's work) of a musical line being broken up into small fragments and tossed between the various voices in the chorus.[2]

Ex. 84

Trip-to-lème... ...le man-teau... ... Qui la
...ar - ra-che... ...de deuil...

couvre... ... et par-sème... ...l'a-len-tour...
...en-core... ...de fleurs... ...du cercueil.

There is great clarity and radiance about the music of *Persephone*, particularly in Scenes One and Three. The opening choruses (nos. 2a and b) seem to evoke the sort of landscape setting Stravinsky enjoyed so much during the years of his residence at Voreppe – mountain and meadow, sunshine and the cloud's moving shadows, and in springtime the profuse beauty of the wild flowers. The second part of Eumolpus's aria in Scene Three (no. 14) – 'Cependant sur la colline' – with its alternation of *forte* and *piano* chords sketches in terms of sound the pattern made by rows of marble columns against the sky. Here is a very different setting and a very different ritual from those of *The Rite of Spring*, and a very different score.

---

[1] *Oedipus Rex*, fig. 166.
[2] Something similar occurs in *A Sermon, a Narrative and a Prayer*. See ex. 176.

Original Compositions

Production

Persephone is a complicated stage work of varying degrees of tension. The vocal element ranges from words spoken over music, where the literary element is given full independence, to sung words where the text is consumed by the music in varying degrees. The action includes mime and dance and is imaginatively extended by the commentary of Eumolpus. It is no easy task to balance these different elements and make them fuse. Without stage presentation, however, the force of the myth is blunted. It is vital for the resolution of the different tensions that Persephone's reappearance in the third scene should have its full dramatic effect – otherwise the musical climax at this point is muffed, and the score loses a considerable part of its impact. This can never really be achieved in a concert performance. There are even certain passages in the score (such as Pluto's march-aria for oboe and bass instruments)[1] that make little sense except in a stage performance.

The première (on 30 April 1934) was preceded by a private audition of the score at the house of the Princess Edmond de Polignac, with the composer at the piano and the poet 'bridling more noticeably with each phrase' (*Dia*). There were three public performances at the Paris Opera House, with Ida Rubinstein in the title role and René Maison as Eumolpus. Scenery and costumes were by André Barsacq, and choreography by Kurt Jooss. The chorus did not move, though this (according to Stravinsky) 'was not in accord with any esthetic plan, but only because their union wouldn't let them' (*Dia*). Pluto and Mercury did not appear. Thereafter, *Persephone* was rarely seen on the stage, until the Royal Ballet mounted it at the Royal Opera House, Covent Garden, on 12 December 1961, with choreography by Frederick Ashton, and scenery and costumes by Nico Ghika. Svetlana Beriosova was cast as Persephone, and André Turp sang Eumolpus.

In his *Dialogues*, Stravinsky suggests that the best way of staging *Persephone* is for the title role to be shared by two performers – a mime and a speaker.

> The speaker Persephone should stand at a fixed point antipodal to Eumolpus, and an illusion of motion should be established between them. The chorus should stand apart from and remain outside of the action. The resulting separation of text and movement would mean that the staging could be worked out entirely in choreographic terms.

Revised Version (1949)

Although the current edition of the full score (published by Boosey & Hawkes) carries a note to say it was revised in 1949, it is difficult after comparing it with the 1934 score (in the piano reduction by Sviatoslav Stravinsky) to find evidence of any important changes, except for a few revised dynamic directions, as follows:

---

[1] Two bars before fig. 63 *et seq.*

1934 *Version*	1949 *Version*
One bar before fig. 41 *Ancora meno* ♪ = 50	*Ancora meno mosso* ♪ = 88–100
Fig. 43 No change of tempo marked	*Tempo* ♩ = 88
Fig. 74 *Poco meno* ♩ = 60	*Tempo 1°* ♩ = 60
At the beginning of Scene Three *Largo assai* ♩ = 50	*Lento* ♩ = 50
One bar before fig. 250 *Assai lento* ♩ = 50	*Assai lento* ♪ = 66
Fig. 257 *Un po' più mosso* ♪ = 72	*Un po' più mosso* ♪ = 84

65. БОГОРОДИЦЕ ДѢВО – AVE MARIA

For mixed choir *a cappella* (S.A.T.B.). The composition is dated 4 April 1934. Published by Edition Russe de Musique, 1934 (later by Boosey & Hawkes). Duration: *c.* 1 minute. MS comp. [C 47].

Like the *Pater Noster* (no. 55) and the *Credo* (no. 63), the words of this unaccompanied setting of the *Ave Maria* are in Slavonic. It is intended for use in the Russian Orthodox Church.

This is not so much a chant as a four-part setting of a simple four-note melody varied metrically in the style of Stravinsky's earlier Russian popular music. It is written in the mode of D Phrygian, though the altos occasionally modulate into the Aeolian mode by sharpening the second of the scale (from E flat to E natural) when approaching the third from below.

New Version with Latin Text (1949)

A new version with Latin text was made in March 1949 and published by Boosey & Hawkes. In this version the work is transposed a tone higher (to E Phrygian) and lengthened from 20 to 35 bars. The metronome marking of ♩ = 72 is substituted for the direction 'Slow' (in Russian). There is a final *Amen* on the chord of A major without the fifth. MS comp. [C 95].

DIVERTIMENTO

Symphonic Suite for orchestra, 1934 – See no. 53(A)

66. CONCERTO

For two solo pianos. The first movement was composed at Voreppe in the autumn of 1931; the remaining movements were written in Paris in 1934 and

1935,[1] and the concerto was completed on 9 November 1935. Published by Schott's, 1936. Duration: *c.* 20 minutes. First performance, Salle Gaveau, Paris, 21 November 1935, with the composer and Soulima Stravinsky as the soloists. MS comp. [C 63].

    I. *Con moto* ♩=108
   II. *Notturno – Adagietto* ♪=69
  III. *Quattro variazioni*
        Variation I ♪=76
        Variation II ♩=56
        Variation III ♩.=96
        Variation IV ♩.=96
  IV. *Preludio e Fuga*
        Preludio – Lento ♩=50
        Fuga a 4 *voci* ♩=66

The published score carries the following prefatory note signed by Stravinsky:

> *Ce Concerto a été exécuté par moi et mon fils, Sviatoslav Soulima-Stravinsky pour la première fois à l'Université des Annales à Paris en la Salle Gaveau, le* 21 *novembre* 1935.

Just as after the *Violin Concerto* Stravinsky wrote the *Duo Concertant*, a work that needed no orchestra for its performance, so he was anxious to follow up the *Piano Concerto* and the *Capriccio* with a work that would have an important *concertante* part for piano solo, but would do away with the orchestra. The answer was his *Concerto for Two Solo Pianos*, which could be performed by his son, Soulima, and himself in places which had no resident orchestra.

The first movement was written in Voreppe in the autumn of 1931 immediately after the *Violin Concerto*; but Stravinsky dropped the composition at that stage because he could not *hear* the second piano.

> All my life I have tried out my music as I have composed it, orchestral as well as any other kind, four hands at one keyboard. That way I am able to test it as I cannot when the other player is seated at another piano. When I took up the Concerto again, after finishing the *Duo Concertant* and *Persephone*, I asked the Pleyel company to build me a double piano, in the form of a small box of two tightly-wedged triangles. I then completed the Concerto in my Pleyel studio, test-hearing it measure by measure with my son Soulima at the other keyboard. (*Dialogues*)

Soulima had grown up to be an excellent pianist and musician. He had studied under Nadia Boulanger; and his father had entrusted him with the preparation of the vocal scores of the *Symphony of Psalms* and *Persephone*. His début as a concert pianist had been made at the age of twenty-three, when

---

[1] In the manuscript score the second movement is dated 13 July 1935, and the fourth (i.e., the *Prelude and Fugue*) 1 September 1935.

he played the solo part of the *Capriccio* under his father's direction at Barcelona in November 1933; and the following year he appeared in Paris as soloist in both the *Capriccio* and the *Piano Concerto*.

In the new concerto, the two soloists are on an equal footing; and the composition stands halfway between a concerto and a large-scale piano sonata. There are numerous occasions when the pianos are treated in *concertante* fashion, and one piano part is developed in apposition and even opposition to the other. Much of the material is interchangeable between the two soloists; but the particular effects of contrast between the solo instrument and orchestra that are usually to be found in a concerto are naturally lacking. Furthermore, there are moments when this particular concerto is laid out like a piano piece for four hands, and the keyboard coverage is so wide and the two piano parts so interwoven that the density of timbre and texture recalls the effect aimed at in the *Study for Pianola*.

It is interesting to find that when Stravinsky told Casella he was working on this concerto and mentioned various important works for two pianos by other composers, he did not seem to know of the existence of J. S. Bach's two-piano compositions.[1] By his own account, however, he steeped himself in the variations of Beethoven and Brahms, and in Beethoven's fugues, before writing the last three movements (*Dia*).

The *Concerto for Two Pianos* marks a further stage in Stravinsky's exploration of symphonic form. Although the first movement is in ternary form, with an extended middle section in a baroque lyrical vein, the opening section makes use of well contrasted first and second subjects –

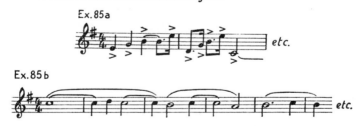

and the literal repetition of a substantial portion of the exposition (37 bars) at the reprise after the middle section, followed by further development and a coda built round the first subject (Ex. 85a) brings the movement very close to sonata first movement form.

The *Nocturne* is a slow movement of exquisite tenderness and feeling, closely related in style to the slow movements of the *Piano Sonata* and the *Capriccio*. Its ornamentation is particularly delicate and fresh.

As the work was originally planned, the *Prelude and Fugue* formed the third movement, and this was followed by the *Variations*; but after the concerto

---

[1] A Casella, *Stravinsky*, Brescia, 1951.

was completed, Stravinsky decided the *Prelude and Fugue* would provide a stronger close and changed the order.[1] This means that the *Variations* are on a theme that is implicit though not directly stated at the outset, and when finally the theme is heard in the *Prelude and Fugue*, it arrives and makes its point with added authority.

Ex.86

The use of a sextuplet grid of repeated semiquavers as background for the fugue and its inversion helps to make the texture tauter and more dynamic than was the case with the Double Fugue of the *Symphony of Psalms*.

The key system is of special interest.

The first movement opens and closes in E minor, the key of the first subject (see Ex. 85a). But the key of the second subject (Ex. 85b) is rather elusive and difficult to pin down, as can be seen from one of its later appearances:

Ex.87

---

[1] In 'A Personal Preface' (*The Score*, June 1957) Robert Craft says: 'The middle movements of the Concerto for Two Pianos were the other way round in the original manuscript'. But it is clear from the manuscript score that it is the order of movements three and four, not two and three, that was reversed.

The middle section is in the key of B flat major.

The *Nocturne*, which is also in ternary form, opens and closes in G major; and its middle section, like that of the first movement, is in the remotest possible key viz., D flat major.

The first Variation is in G minor modulating to B flat major; the second in B flat major modulating to C sharp minor; the third in C sharp minor modulating to A sharp minor (B flat minor); and the fourth has a ground bass rotating round G minor (or E flat major), while the harmonisation·of the theme implies the key of C major, but ultimately modulates to D major.

Ex. 88

The *Prelude* is in D, and so is the *Fugue*; but the coda (marked *Largo*) moves up a tone, and the Concerto finishes in E major.

From the last two examples it will be obvious that part of the concerto shows an extended use of bitonality; and this in its turn leads to outbursts of chromaticism. For instance, the third Variation with its humming chromatic accompaniment harks back to some of Stravinsky's early scherzo-like movements, and in particular the last of the *Four Studies for Piano* (op. 7).

The fact that this concerto approximates so closely to a rather more than life-size piano sonata should not blind one to its great qualities. It is bold in design, resolute in purpose, ingenious and sensitive in execution, and most impressive and moving in effect. It was the first composition Stravinsky finished after becoming a French citizen (10 June 1934).

Its première was sponsored by l'Université des Annales, a literary lecture society; and on that occasion Stravinsky introduced the music with a fifteen-minute talk.[1] He performed the concerto frequently with his son, Soulima, in Europe and South America during the years immediately preceding the second

---

[1] Reprinted in Appendix A(6).

World War, and several times with the American pianist Adele Marcus in the United States during the war.

Ballet Production

In 1960, it was mounted as a ballet at the Staatsoper, Hamburg, with choreography by Gustav Blank.

67. JEU DE CARTES – A CARD GAME – DAS KARTENSPIEL

Ballet in three deals, the stage action realised by the composer in collaboration with M. Malaïeff (2.2.2.2 – 4.2.3.1 – timp., percussion – string 5tet[1]).Composed in the summer and autumn and finished on 6 December 1936.[2] Published by Schott's, 1937. Piano reduction by the composer. Duration: *c.* 21 minutes. First performance, American Ballet, Metropolitan Opera House, New York, 27 April 1937, conducted by the composer. The manuscript score, together with other manuscript material, is in the composer's collection [C 64].

Synopsis and Composition

When Stravinsky was in America in 1935, Edward Warburg and Lincoln Kirstein suggested he should write a ballet score for the recently formed American Ballet, with which George Balanchine was associated as choreographer. The choice of subject was left to him.

Apparently he already had in mind the possibility of writing a ballet with an interplay of numerical combinations – a kind of *Chiffres dansants*, not unlike Schumann's *Lettres dansantes*. The action was to be implicit in the music; and one of the characters would be a malignant force whose ultimate defeat would impart a moral character to the whole.[3] But when he came to draw up the scenario, the action took a different turn.

Certain games had always made a strong appeal to him. For instance, it had been his custom to relax after meals over a game of Chinese chequers; and in Hollywood in the 1940's he went so far as to present a set of Chinese chequers to Alexandre Tansman and his wife so that he could be sure of getting his game every time he was invited by them to a meal.[4] Poker was another game that he enjoyed; and it was on this game that he decided to base the scenario of his new ballet. At first he tried to enlist the collaboration of Jean Cocteau; but when nothing came of this, he worked out the action himself with the help of

---

[1] The score specifies twelve first violins, ten second violins, eight violas, six cellos and six double-basses.

[2] According to Stravinsky, the whole score was written in Paris, with the exception of the passage between figures 189 and 192, which was composed at sea when he was sailing to Buenos Aires on the *Kap Arcona*. This is one of the rare examples in his music of a passage not directly composed at the piano.

[3] This information is based on a note supplied by John N. Burk for the Boston Symphony Orchestra's concert programme of 13, 14 and 15 January 1944.

[4] Alexandre Tansman, *Igor Stravinsky*. Paris, 1948.

M. Malaieff, a friend of his elder son, Theodore.[1] The argument as printed in the score runs as follows:

The characters in this ballet are the chief cards in a game of Poker, disputed between several players on the green cloth of a card-room. At each deal the situation is complicated by the endless guiles of the perfidious Joker, who believes himself invincible because of his ability to become any desired card.

During the first deal, one of the players is beaten, but the other two remain with even 'straights', although one of them holds the Joker.

In the second deal, the hand that holds the Joker is victorious, thanks to four Aces who easily beat four Queens.

Now comes the third deal. The action becomes more and more acute. This time it is a struggle between three 'flushes'. Although at first victorious over one adversary, the Joker, strutting at the head of a sequence of Spades, is beaten by a 'Royal Flush' in Hearts. This puts an end to his malice and knavery.

The score gives the title of the ballet in three languages (French, English and German); but it must be admitted that the English version is something of a misnomer. *A Game of Cards* would be nearer the meaning than *A Card Game*; and the Americans have common sense on their side when they refer to it currently as *The Card Party*.

The action is in three deals, and each deal contains a card shuffle and a card play.

The ballet scenario runs as follows:

Deal I
   Introduction
   Pas d'action
   Dance of the Joker
   Waltz-Coda
Deal II
   Introduction
   March (Hearts and Spades)
   Four Solo Variations for the Four Queens
     (in the order Hearts, Diamonds, Clubs, Spades)
   Variation of the Four Queens (pas de quatre) and Coda
   March, and Ensemble
Deal III
   Introduction
   Waltz-Minuet
   Presto (Combat between Spades and Hearts)
   Final Dance (Triumph of the Hearts)

[1] 'The idea for this ballet entered my head one evening in a *fiacre* while I was on my way to visit some friends. I was so delighted that I stopped the driver and invited him to have a drink with me.' *Le Jour*, Paris, 3 February 1938.

The musical scheme runs as follows:

Deal I

Alla breve 𝅗𝅥=69 B flat major
Meno mosso ♩=108 D flat major
Moderato assai ♩=84 D flat major/D major
Stringendo ♩=108 F minor
Tranquillo ♩=84 D flat major/F major

Deal II

Alla breve 𝅗𝅥=69 B flat major
Marcia ♩=112 A major
  Variation I *Allegretto* ♩=58 B flat major
  Variation II ♪=116 A major
  Variation III ♪=116 A flat major
  Variation IV ♩=76 G major
  Variation V *Sostenuto e pesante* ♩=69–72 E flat major
  Coda *Più mosso* ♩=100 G major
Marcia (brief reprise) A flat major
[Finale] *Con moto* ♩=108 F major/F minor; B minor/B major; F major
  /F minor

Deal III

Alla breve 𝅗𝅥=69 B flat major
Valse ♩=184 E flat major
Presto 𝅗𝅥=88 C minor/B minor
[Finale] *Leggiero grazioso* ♩=120 E major/G major
[Coda] *Tempo del principio* 𝅗𝅥=69 E major

The music is continuous. The score is given a unified framework by the recurrence of the *Alla breve* processional at the beginning of each deal and also in the final coda where this B flat major theme has its E flat altered to E natural in order to achieve a modulatory twist to the E major close.

The scheme of tonalities calls for little comment, except insofar as the modulations show a tendency for keys to succeed each other at semitone intervals. This is particularly marked in the second deal where the dance variations and coda[1] follow the *March*. Two cadences are illustrated. The first is forthright and somewhat brash, rather like the sign-off at the end of a stretch of recitative: in the second the descending sequence of semitones forces open the major third of the following chord of B flat major.

---

[1] Although these are variations in the choreographic sense, the kinship of the material makes it possible to regard them as musical variations too.

Ex.89a

Ex.89b.

Var: I

This gay and carefree score bubbles with allusions. For instance, the first variation sounds like an alteration of the opening of the *Allegretto scherzando* movement of Beethoven's 8th Symphony, and in the fourth Variation the 1st violins have a grazioso counter-theme that stems from *Die Fledermaus*. The *Stringendo* section at fig. 21 reminded Casella forcibly of the sort of *Allegro agitato* passages to be found in the overtures of Jacopo Foroni;[1] the waltz in the third deal sounds like a light-hearted skit on Ravel's *La Valse*; and the theme of the following *Presto* recalls the overture to Rossini's *Il Barbiere di Siviglia*. Chaikovsky and Delibes are other composers who seem to have been laid under contribution. All these allusions give the impression of being drawn from a well stored mind. They are not used literally, but are rethought in the light of their new context, and Stravinsky completely succeeds in extracting their objective content. For instance, Rossini's theme in *Il Barbiere*

Ex.90a

---

[1] This unjustly neglected and almost completely forgotten Italian composer, who was born in the province of Vincenza in 1825 and died in Stockholm in 1858, wrote four operas and three concert overtures. Casella is likely to have heard Foroni's overtures performed when, as a young boy, he attended the Turin Popular Concerts conducted by Carlo Pedrotti, a native of Verona and formerly a pupil of Jacopo Foroni's father. He refers to Foroni in his monograph on Stravinsky and is reminded of his music by this particular passage in *The Card Party*.

becomes the following in Stravinsky's score:

Ex.90b

and the altered notes (ringed) are important to its new role. In fact, the metrical formula of the last four repeated notes becomes a dominant feature of the whole of the following finale.

It should not be thought, however, that the musical allusions are only to the works of other composers. Stravinsky lays himself under contribution as well, and there are numerous echoes of *Mavra, The Fairy's Kiss*, the *Capriccio* and the concertos for violin and for two solo pianos as well.

The music is light-hearted and witty, and leaves a carefree impression. The instrumentation is masterly. Nevertheless, the fact that the Joker, though ultimately worsted, is a potential devil, emerges not from the music itself, but from a quotation from La Fontaine's sinister fable of *The Wolves and the Sheep* suffixed to the Argument:

> . . . *il faut faire aux méchants guerre continuelle*
> *La paix est fort bonne de soi,*
> *J'en conviens; mais de quoi sert-elle*
> *Avec des ennemis sans foi?*[1]

At the time this ballet was composed, the political situation in Europe was rapidly degenerating, and the warning conveyed by these line proved prophetic.

It should be added that when *The Card Party* was first performed in Great Britain at a Courtauld-Sargent concert at the Queen's Hall, London, on 18 and 19 October, 1937, Stravinsky, who was conducting, authorised two repeats which are not marked in the score: fig. 99–105, and the first two bars of fig. 202.

Production

Balanchine's choreography for the ballet was about half done when Stravinsky arrived in New York early in 1937. According to Lincoln Kirstein,[2] it was his habit to 'appear punctually at rehearsals and stay on for six hours. In the evenings he would take the pianist home with him and work further on the tempi. . . . During successive run-throughs of the ballet he would slap his knee like a metronome for the dancers, then suddenly interrupt everything,

---

[1] La Fontaine is one of Stravinsky's favourite French authors. See also the quotation from La Fontaine's fable of *The Serpent & the File* used as a scourge for critics in his letter to the Editor of *Cahiers d'Art* reprinted in Appendix A (4).
[2] The quotations are from Lincoln Kirstein's article 'Working with Stravinsky' printed in *Modern Music* Vol. XIV no. 3, March 1937.

rise and, gesticulating rapidly to emphasise his points, suggest a change. This was never offered tentatively, but with the considered authority of complete information. Thus at the end of the first deal, where Balanchine had worked out a display of the dancers in a fanlike pattern to simulate cards held in the hand, Stravinsky decided there was too great a prodigality of choreographic invention. Instead of so much variety in the pictures he preferred a repetition of the most effective groupings'. Kirstein makes it clear that these changes were not the result of mere caprice on Stravinsky's part, and that he was always most helpful and co-operative. He recalls, for instance, how on one occasion Stravinsky composed some additional music to allow for a further development in the choreography.

The original intention of the directors of the American Ballet had been to adapt the costumes from a set of medieval Tarot cards, and the settings and about forty costumes had been designed before Stravinsky's arrival in New York. But when he saw them, he objected that they would 'place the work in a definite period and evoke a decorative quality not present in his music': so they were scrapped in favour of a new set of designs by Irene Sharaff based on an ordinary pack of cards.

After careful deliberation, Kirstein, Balanchine and Stravinsky decided that at its première *The Card Party* should be partnered by *Apollo Musagetes* and *The Fairy's Kiss*. For this purpose, Balanchine revived his 1928 version of *Apollo* and prepared a new choreographic version of *The Fairy's Kiss*, which until then had never been seen in North America.

The first performance of *The Card Party* took place at the Metropolitan Opera House, New York, on 27 April 1937. Stravinsky conducted; and the part of the Joker was danced by William Dollar. Balanchine's version has also been mounted by the Ballet Russe de Monte Carlo (1940) and the New York City Ballet (1951). John Cranko made a version for the Stuttgart Ballet (1965), which was reproduced by the Royal Ballet at Covent Garden a year later.

Theatre Music and Concert Performance

All Stravinsky's previous ballet scores – from *The Firebird* to *The Fairy's Kiss* – had been heard for the first time in Paris in the theatre; but *The Card Party* was an exception to this rule. As it had been written for an American ballet company which was not planning to visit Paris and as no French company seemed able or willing to mount it, the score received its first performance in France in the concert hall.

On 3 June 1938 Stravinsky took part in a French broadcast, in which he answered questions put by Georges Auric. A reference to *The Card Party* gave him an opportunity to express his views on the concert performance of music originally intended for the theatre.

398

Whatever may be the destination of a piece of music – whether intended for the theatre, concert hall, or cinema – it is essential it should have its proper intrinsic value, its own existence, its *raison d'être*. Otherwise, it is demoted to a lower level and finds itself shorn of its independence, thereby becoming nothing better than a kind of *divertissement*.

That's why, when I am writing for the theatre, my first anxiety is to make certain my music has an independent existence and to guard it from the danger of subjecting itself to the demands of the other theatrical elements involved. In my view the relationship between music and these extra-musical elements can be presented only in parallel, or in association. In this connection, I am in no wise disconcerted by the apparent lack of accord in classical opera between the form of the musical numbers (airs, duets, ensembles, and so on) and the demands of the dramatic action. If in earlier works like *The Firebird* I did not always follow the precepts I am now preaching, I quickly realised the vital need of doing so; and as early as *Petrushka* it will be found that the music is constructed on symphonic lines. My later scores are conceived and constructed as separate musical entities, independent of their scenic purpose; and because of that I attach as much importance to their concert performance as to their stage presentation.[1]

68. PRELUDIUM

For jazz band. This piece was written partly in Paris in December 1936 and partly in New York during Stravinsky's third American visit in 1937. It seems that at one moment he intended to add other movements in order to turn it into a suite. There is a piano reduction as well as the orchestral version. In 1953 Stravinsky made a new arrangement of the piece, which received its first performance at one of the Evenings-on-the-Roof concerts at Los Angeles (18 October 1953) with Robert Craft as conductor, and was published by Boosey & Hawkes in 1968. MS comp. [C 64] and [C 65]. The jazz-band version remains unpublished.

69. PETIT RAMUSIANUM HARMONIQUE

The *Petit Ramusianum* was a *jeu d'esprit* written by Charles-Albert Congria and I. Stravinsky for C. F. Ramuz's sixtieth birthday on 24 September 1938. Three quatrains with words and music by Stravinsky are interpolated in a piece of verse with short rhyming lines written by Cingria. These quatrains are set so that they can be sung (unaccompanied) by a single voice, or several voices in unison. Stravinsky's score is dated Paris, 11 October 1937; and the work was first published in *Hommage à C.-F. Ramuz* (V. Porchet & Cie., Lausanne, 1938). A facsimile of the manuscript appeared in *Feuilles Musicales*, Lausanne, March–April 1962.

---

[1] Translation by E. W. W.

2. Register of Works

One copy of the manuscript was given by Ramuz to the Neuchâtel publisher Richard Heyd on some date unknown and is now in the collection of M. André Meyer of Paris. Another copy is in the composer's collection [C 67].

The following quotation (the second of Stravinsky's three quatrains) gives some idea of the fresh and graceful nature of the compliment conveyed.

Ex.91

70. CONCERTO IN E FLAT

For chamber orchestra (1 flute, 1 clarinet in E flat, 1 bassoon, 2 horns in F, 3 violins, 3 violas, 2 cellos, 2 double-bass). Composition started at the Château de Montoux, near Annemasse, Spring 1937 and finished in Paris, on 29 March 1938. (The score bears the inscription 'Dumbarton Oaks, 8.v.38'). Published by Schott's, 1938. Reduction for two pianos by the composer. Duration: *c.* 12 minutes. First performance, Washington D.C., 8 May 1938, conducted by Nadia Boulanger. The manuscript full score, which formerly belonged to Mr. and Mrs. Robert Woods Bliss, is now in the possession of Harvard University and is housed at Dumbarton Oaks, Washington D.C. Other manuscript material is in the composer's collection [C 66].

I. *Tempo giusto* ♪ = 152
II. *Allegretto* ♪ = 108
III. *Con moto* ♩ = 160

While Stravinsky was in America in 1937, he received a commission to write a concerto for chamber orchestra from Mr. and Mrs. Robert Woods Bliss of Dumbarton Oaks, Washington D.C. Both Mr. and Mrs. Bliss were well known as generous patrons of the arts; and at various times their house and gardens at Dumbarton Oaks had provided a magnificent setting for many important functions and entertainments. The immediate purpose of this particular commission was to celebrate their thirtieth wedding anniversary, which fell due in 1938. Stravinsky visited them at Dumbarton Oaks while the new composition was being thought out. He particularly admired the beautiful gardens attached to the house; and it is thought that the architectural conception of the concerto owes a debt to their special form and layout.

The fact that in the spring of 1938 he was undergoing a cure for tuberculosis made it impossible for him to conduct the first performance in America. At his express wish, Nadia Boulanger was invited to take his place, and the concerto was played for the first time at Dumbarton Oaks under her direction on 8 May 1938.[1] Mrs. Bliss, who attended all the rehearsals and who subsequently heard numerous performances of the concerto elsewhere, considered Nadia Boulanger's interpretation to be the 'most subtly interesting' of the lot.

Sometime in 1937 André Schaeffner asked Stravinsky what he was then working on and received the reply 'A little concerto in the style of the Brandenburg Concertos'.[2] This, in fact, gives the key to the composition. The fifteen instruments in the chamber orchestra are all treated as solo instruments. Sometimes they elaborate motives and figures to produce considerable variety and freshness of textures. At other times they indulge in a fair amount of contrapuntal development, especially in the first and last movements.

In view of the importance to be assumed in the *Symphony in C* by the interval of the fourth divided into a major third and minor second, it is interesting to find the same intervals forming the opening phrase of the fugal subject in the first movement –

Ex. 92

and appearing prominently throughout that movement.

The slow movement, *Allegretto*, gives a striking 'white page' impression in the printed score, and its effect in performance is of an intense purity of line where the different instrumental strands or wisps – some of them no more than single notes – stand out with startling three-dimensional clarity in their atmosphere of enveloping silence. Casella has pointed out the resemblance between the main theme and the phrase to which Verdi has set Falstaff's words 'Se Falstaff s'assotiglia' in the first act of his opera.[3] It is difficult to be certain, but it seems likely that this correspondence is a fortuitous one. After all, only

---

[1] This was a private performance. The first public performance took place at a concert of *La Sérénade*, Paris, on 4 June 1938 with the composer conducting.
[2] From 'Critique et Thématique', by André Schaeffner. *Revue Musicale* (special Stravinsky number), Paris, May–June 1939.
[3] A. Casella, *Strawinski*. Brescia, 1951.

a year later Stravinsky was to say in one of his lectures on the *Poetics of Music* that *Falstaff*, 'if it is not Wagner's best work, is not Verdi's best opera either'. Nearly twenty years later he modified this view; and in his *Conversations* he emphasises the resistance to Wagnerism displayed in the opera, the originality of its instrumentation, harmony and part-writing, and of the way its musical monologues are presented, and admits that *Falstaff* and *Rigoletto* are the two operas of Verdi's that he loves the best.

The main theme of the third movement is a kind of march; but just as a fugue emerged from the rich polyphonic texture of the first movement, so here a theme emerges which is treated on contrapuntal lines and leads to a *fugato* climax where it has four entries in five bars, the second entry being inverted.

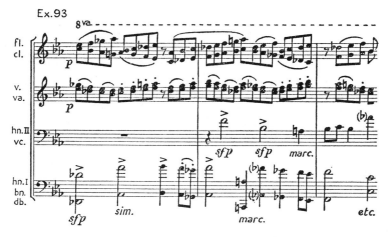

Ex.93

The three movements follow each other without pause and are bound together by quiet chordal cadences at the ends of the first and second movements.

This concerto is gay and exhilarating in its effect. It is curious to reflect that so innocuous a work should have aroused so much hostility and spleen at the time it first appeared. René Leibowitz attacked Stravinsky[1] for what he called his 'insolent borrowing of a theme from Bach' – he was presumably referring to a figure played by the violas in the opening bar, which is similar to one already quoted from the *Violin Concerto* (see Ex. 78) and which has been common musical currency for centuries – and Schaeffner spent a considerable part of his article mentioned above in refuting this charge and justifying Stravinsky.[2] In view of the continuous disparagement with which his new works were received at this time, it is hardly surprising that his ties with Western Europe

---

[1] In *Esprit*, Paris, 1 July 1938.
[2] André Schaeffner *op. cit.* Much of this special number of the *Revue Musicale* reads like an *apologia pro sua musica*.

and France were weakening and he was beginning to look increasingly to America for sympathy and support.

71. SYMPHONY IN C

For orchestra (3.2.2.2 – 4.2.3.1 – timp. – string 5tet). The first movement was composed in Paris in the autumn of 1938; the second was begun at Sancellmoz towards the end of March 1939 and finished there in August; the third was composed at Cambridge, Mass., during the autumn and winter of 1939/40; and the fourth at Beverley Hills, Hollywood, in the summer of 1940. The orchestral score is dated 19 August 1940. Its title-page bears the following dedication: 'This symphony, composed to the Glory of God, is dedicated to the Chicago Symphony Orchestra on the occasion of the Fiftieth Anniversary of its existence.' Published by Schott's, 1948. Duration: *c.* 28 minutes. First performance, Chicago Symphony Orchestra, Chicago, 7 November 1940, conducted by the composer. A pencil manuscript of the orchestra score is in the Library of Congress, Washington, D.C. A pencil manuscript ol the first two movements (also full score) is in the collection of Robert Craft. Other manuscript material is in the composer's collection [C 71].

    I. *Moderato alla breve* ♩= 66
   II. *Larghetto concertante* ♪= 50
  III. *Allegretto* ♪= 126
  IV. *Largo* ♩= 50
      Tempo giusto, alla breve ♩= 84

Stravinsky and Symphonic Form

Stravinsky's approach to symphonic form had been a rather devious one.

One of his earliest apprentice works was the *Symphony in E flat*, (1905–7),[1] an academic exercise deliberately modelled on the symphonies of Glazunov then in vogue; but thereafter by an accident of fate he was lured into the ambit of the theatre, and the tectonic form of his stage works, both opera and ballet, depended largely on the armature provided by the libretto or scenario. When the time came for him to write for an orchestra seated on the concert platform instead of in the theatre pit, he had to clarify his attitude to symphonic music and symphonic form as such. How original and unacademic was his initial approach can be seen from the unusual patterns evolved in his *Symphonies of Wind Instruments* (1920) where he deployed with mathematical skill a number of contrasting groups of themes, many of them expressed in the Russian vernacular idiom that he then affected.

His change of direction in the 1920's and his new-found allegiance to neo-classical material and procedures brought fresh problems of formal organisa-

---

[1] It is perhaps significant that Stravinsky conducted a performance of this symphony in Chicago on 22 January 1935.

tion in their train. These he tackled mainly through a systematic exploration of the principles of concerto form. The *Piano Concerto* (1923/4), the *Capriccio* (1929), the *Violin Concerto* (1931) and the *Concerto for Two Solo Pianos* (1935) mark successive steps in his attempt to reconcile the fundamental duality of this particular type of symphonic manifestation. But it seems as if he was not ready to write a straightforward symphony for orchestra until the 'Dumbarton Oaks' *Concerto* had cleared his mind and shown him how a symphonic work for chamber orchestra could be handled on freely varied *concertante* lines. So the commission from Mrs. Robert Woods Bliss for a symphony to commemorate the fiftieth anniversary of the foundation of the Chicago Symphony Orchestra came at just the right moment.

Although it may have been the right moment from the standpoint of his esthetic development, it happened to be a particularly disturbing one in public affairs and in his private life. The Munich crisis of 1938 showed that a fresh World War was imminent: and in the Stravinsky household in Paris, death struck down first his daughter Ludmila in 1938, and then his wife and mother the following year. The fact that no trace of personal unhappiness or grief is to be found in the symphony will surprise no one who knew Stravinsky's opinion about music and expression. In a much debated passage of his *Chronicle*, he wrote: 'I consider that music is, by its very nature, essentially powerless to *express* anything at all, whether a feeling, an attitude of mind, a psychological mood, a phenomenon of nature'. Subsequently (in his *Expositions*) he modified his standpoint and explained that this somewhat intransigent statement 'was simply a way of saying that music was supra-personal and supra-real'. This is particularly true of the *Symphony in C*. The music that was written during what was probably the unhappiest period of his life is extrovert and characterised by grace allied with strength, an uninhibited flow of ideas and a feeling of optimism. It is a true symphony both in stature and scale – in the dramatic exposition of the musical argument in the opening movement, the intensity of the mood of lyrical contemplation in the slow movement, the dynamic verve of the third movement, and the powerful summing-up and resolution of the last movement.

Stravinsky himself admitted that at the time he was writing the first two movements he had copies of symphonies by Haydn and Beethoven, and also Chaikovsky's no. 1, on his desk, and he may occasionally have turned to them as models[1]. He also suggests that the symphony falls into two parts, with a division between the European half (consisting of the first two movements) and the American half (consisting of the last two)[2] and calls attention to the

---

[1] From a sleeve-note for the *Symphony in C* written by Stravinsky and dated 12 December 1963.
[2] Stravinsky has suggested that the two bars before figure 104 would not have occurred to him before he had become acquainted with 'the neon glitter of the Californian boulevards from a speeding automobile.'

fact that 'the first movement is the only large one in the whole inventory of [his] mature works with no change of metre, whereas the third movement's metrical irregularities are among the most extreme in any of [his] compositions'. But this break in spirit is not really apparent to the listener. The third movement is like a suite of dances, and no one who is familiar with Stravinsky's ballet scores will be surprised by the compound metres he uses here; and the last movement is carefully dovetailed with the first by the simple device of introducing material from the last movement into the first, and *vice versa*, so that an overall feeling of unity is preserved.

Analytical Note

The *Symphony in C* is written for normal symphony orchestra and consists of the usual four movements.

In the opening movement, which is cast in traditional sonata form, there is a rich complex of material associated with the first subject, and much of this is related to the interval of a fourth divided into either a minor second and major third or a major second and minor third. Both forms of this motto are heard in the opening bars (as if the original statement were followed by an altered augmented echo).

Ex.94

Moderato alla breve

Presently the original form of the motto blossoms into a flowing but capricious theme (in C major) with a repeated quaver string accompaniment staccato, fastidiously punctuated in the bass.

Ex.95

There is a bridge passage (in G minor) in which a boldly moving bass implies both forms of the motto.

Ex.96

Above this bass a dotted crotchet motif is developed with Beethovenish intensity and leads to the second subject which appears in the key of F major. Here both accompaniment (staccato chords) and tune are entrusted to the horns, with subsidiary figuration in the strings and wind. A curiously brash sign-off is given by the trumpet four times, echoed by the first horn (in C major).

Ex.97

The music starts to modulate quite extensively as the material is developed; and when it reaches the comparatively remote key of E flat minor, the mood becomes more agitated (*Tempo agitato senza troppo accelerare*), and the strings have a new subject, based first on the falling and then on the rising scale, which turns out to be closely related to the main theme of the last movement. (See Ex. 20.) After this strenuous passage, there is a recapitulation of a considerable part of the exposition, with the first subject in C major as before. But the Beethovenish bridge passage is omitted; the second subject returns in C major (instead of F major); and the trumpet signs off in G major. The Beethovenish bridge passage follows at this point (in C minor instead of G minor), and the dotted crotchet rhythm leads to a coda where the first subject (Ex. 95) is heard once more played by solo flute and solo clarinet, spaced two octaves apart. Both versions of the motto are incorporated in the two *sff* chords that alternate in the final bars.

Ex.98

For the slow movement, *Larghetto concertante*,[1] the orchestra is reduced by omitting trombones, tuba, timpani, and one of the horns and trumpets. The main theme is shared between the oboes and first violins, with occasional

---

[1] According to Sol Babitz (writing in the *Musical Quarterly* of January 1941), Stravinsky described this movement as 'simple, clear and tranquil'.

assistance from the flutes and clarinets; and here too both forms of the motto are implied.

Ex. 99

Each instrument proceeds by way of individual elaboration, with highly graceful and ornamental results. A charming parenthesis only one (3/4) bar long marked *pp dolce contabile* for three solo violas is interpolated in the exposition and is taken over by three solo cellos in the reprise. The contrasting middle section, *Doppio movimento*, has a restless theme with dotted rhythm, the effect of agitation being accentuated by rapid demisemiquaver figuration for some of the strings and solo trumpet.

The third movement, *Allegretto*, follows without break, with the motive of the last three notes of the *Larghetto* transposed from F to G. It is a nervy, syncopated scherzo, with frequent changes of time signature. Its various episodes are punctuated by a cadence of *sforzato* string chords and a brief fanfare for wind. The last return of this fanfare ushers in a fughetta with a stretto marked *Più mosso*.[1]

A dialogue, *Largo*, between two bassoons in their low register punctuated by chords from horns and trombones, serves as introduction to the last movement.

Ex. 100

(Here too both forms of the motto are implied.)

---

[1] According to Sol Babitz (in the *Musical Quarterly* of January 1941), Stravinsky described this movement as 'white music'.

2. Register of Works

Such a sombre note had rarely been heard in Stravinsky's music before and was not to occur again until the Prelude to Act III Scene 2 of *The Rake's Progress*. The main theme of the following movement, *Tempo giusto alla breve* is based on the rising scale. (See Ex. 20.) The sprung nature of the rhythm of this phrase is underlined by syncopation. It leads directly to a passage where the first subject of the first movement (Ex. 95) returns in a new guise with its opening phrase altered to fit the second form of the motto.

Ex. 101

Later a *fortissimo* passage has the first subject of the first movement in its unaltered form (Ex. 95) as its bass (bassoons, cellos and double-basses).[1] This is broken off at the mid-point of the movement to allow eight bars of the bassoon dialogue from the introduction to be heard again, with the accompanying horn chords an octave higher. On the resumption of the *Tempo giusto*, there is a fugato[2] founded on the inversion of Ex. 20, at the climax of which the opening bar of the motto (Ex. 92) returns, harmonised by the dominant horn chord already heard in the *Largo* introduction (Ex. 100). This leads directly to the coda,

Ex. 102

a procession of slowly moving wind chords, with the motto in its original form heard in augmentation (Ex. 102). The final wind chord is echoed by the muted strings.

A Note on the Dialectics of Symphonic Form

Although one school of thought looks on this symphony as the summit of Stravinsky's achievement in symphonic form, another school considers that

---

[1] Figs. 159–161.

[2] 'The fugato in the fourth movement, abandoned there like a very hot potato, may or may not have been in my mind when I began the *Symphony in Three Movements*; I do not know.' From a sleeve-note for the *Symphony in C* written by Stravinsky and dated 12 December 1963.

behind its formal façade it is deficient in symphonic meaning. One of the most vigorous spokesmen of the latter view is Stravinsky's former friend and colleague, Ernest Ansermet. In his notes to *Les Fondements de la Musique dans la Conscience humaine*,[1] he develops the following argument:

> What allows a symphonic allegro to dispense with subject matter is the secret import brought into play by the sequence of harmonic tonalities and by binary form, for this secret import affects the structure of the melodies and prolongs their intrinsic meaning by adding a transcendental meaning due to the part they play in the global form. The fundamental motive or motives of melodic dialectic are then *thematized* in the sense that they carry a dialectical meaning that exceeds their intrinsic meaning as motives pure and simple. . . . They are no longer merely the 'motives' of a dialectical movement, but they become *the thematic premises of a dialectical act*, which poses a problem in the first stage, develops an argument in the second, and reaches dénouement in the third, so that when they reappear at the end of the work, they are charged with a new current from the internal dynamic power generated by the *formal dialectic* (and no longer merely by the melodic dialectic).

When he turns to the *Symphony in C*, he finds that its form is static and its motives fail to grow in meaning. 'On their reappearance,' he says, 'the fundamental motives are no more significant than they were on their first appearance; they simply return and prolong the dialectical movements by contributing to its unity of meaning and making us realise that its "subject" is constant.' His final judgment is that 'the Allegro of the *Symphony in C* is no more than the portrait of a symphonic allegro'.

Ansermet's general argument is undoubtedly sound; but its application to the *Symphony in C* seems to be open to dispute. He may feel that the main motives of the first movements – and here he is thinking primarily of the motto theme (Ex. 94) and its various metamorphoses – retain their literal meaning throughout the movement and do not get charged with dialectical meaning as a result of the varied experiences they undergo. But others may disagree and feel that such a change in meaning is precisely what does take place, not only in the first movement, but also in the course of the remainder of the symphony, so that when the motto that had opened the first movement reappears at the end of the fourth, it is charged with newly acquired power and significance, and the circle of symphonic experience is completed and closed.

72. TANGO

For piano solo. Composed at Hollywood, 1940. Published by the Mercury Music Corporation, New York, 1941. Duration: *c.* 4 minutes 30 seconds. MS comp. [C 70].

---

[1] Published by La Baconnière, Neuchâtel, 1961. (Translation by E. W. W.)

This rather attractive little dance number seems to be quite closely modelled on the earlier *Ragtime*. In order to maintain an almost unbroken flow of syncopation (though only occasionally in the characteristic tango rhythm), Stravinsky keeps the time signature to an unchanging 4/4. There is no variation of the basic metre, even during the (so-called) trio. Not only is the metre regular, but so is the musical paragraphing too – everything falls into 8-bar units.

A rhythmic introduction in D minor (A) leads to three different groups of closely related themes (Bi, ii, iii). The key changes to D major for the trio (Ci, ii); and a smoother, more *cantabile* melodic treatment recalls Chaikovsky in style. A literal repeat of part of the opening D minor material follows, and the work ends with a restatement of the introduction. The complete schematic shape is A, Bi, Bii, Biii, Bii, Biii, Ci, Cii, Bi, Bii, A – 88 bars in all.

Instrumentations

It is clear from the piano layout, with its occasional passages of rather dense counterpoint that do not easily fit the player's hands, that from the beginning Stravinsky had in mind some sort of instrumentation for this *Tango*.

The first instrumentation was for: 3.2.3.2 – 3 sax. – 2.3.3.1 – perc., guitar, piano – string 5tet. This version was scored, not by Stravinsky, but by Felix Guenther. Stravinsky examined and approved the instrumentation, and the score was published by the Mercury Music Corporation. The first performance was under Benny Goodman at Robin Hood Dell in July 1941.

The second instrumentation (Stravinsky's first) followed in 1953 for 4 clarinets, bass-clarinet, 4 trumpets, 3 trombones, guitar, 3 violins, 1 viola, 1 cello, and 1 double-bass. Here the music is transposed up a major second from D minor to E minor. This version was published by the Mercury Music Corporation in 1954. It was first performed with Robert Craft as conductor at one of the Evenings-on-the-Roof concerts, Los Angeles (18 October 1953).

In 1941, it was Stravinsky's hope that this work might be exploited in a number of ways. It was intended to publish a version for dance band, and even a quasi-popular-song vocal version. In the event, these attempts proved abortive. There is, however, a version for violin and piano (arranged by Samuel Dushkin) which is controlled by the Mercury Music Corporation, but has not been published. This manuscript is in the composer's collection [C 70].

73. DANSES CONCERTANTES

For chamber orchestra (1.1.1.1 – 2.1.1.0 – timp. – 6 Vl., 4 Vle., 3 Vcl., 2 C.B.). Composed at Hollywood, 1941/13 January 1942. Published by Associated Music Publishers, New York, 1942. Duration: *c.* 20 minutes. First performance, Werner Janssen Orchestra, Los Angeles, 8 February 1942, conducted by the composer. The manuscript full score is in Stanford University, California. Other manuscript material is with the composer. [C 74].

    I. *Marche — Introduction* ♩=96
   II. *Pas d'Action Con moto* ♩=104
  III. *Thème varié Lento* ♩=50
       Variation I *Allegretto* ♩=152
       Variation II *Scherzando* ♩=100
       Variation III *Andantino* ♪=104–108
       Variation IV [Coda] *Tempo giusto* ♩.=112
   IV. *Pas de Deux*[1] *Risoluto* ♩=66
     Andante sostenuto ♩=54
    V. *Marche – Conclusion* ♩=96

This work was commissioned by the Werner Janssen Orchestra of Los Angeles. Although it was intended for concert and not stage performance, Stravinsky cast it in the form of an abstract ballet. There is no specific subject, though it is clear from the layout that he must have had in mind the possibility that it might be choreographed some day. The variations, for instance, are variations in both dance and musical senses; and the opening and closing *March* serves the same function as the *March* in *Reynard* and can be used both to introduce the dancers and to get them off the stage.

Insofar as *Danses Concertantes* is conceived as a ballet score, it stems closely from *A Card Party*. It is interesting to find that whereas the variations in *The Card Party* followed a plan of keys arranged in descending semitones, the variations in *Danses Concertantes* follow a plan of ascending semitones (theme in G, followed by variations in A flat, A natural, A natural, and B flat). As a piece of music written for a chamber orchestra of 24 players, the score carries a stage further the special *concertante* style already initiated by the 'Dumbarton Oaks' *Concerto*. And the musical material is still close enough to the *Symphony in C* to be rather overshadowed by that great work. The opening of the *Pas d'Action*, for instance, is similar to the opening of the last movement (*Tempo giusto alla breve*) of the symphony.

Certain passages in this score reveal a growing tendency to avoid the strong accent at the beginning of a bar, either through a tied note or through a rest.[2] For instance, here are typical examples from the *Thème Varié* of the way the theme is stated, and one of the characteristic figures of accompaniment:

Ex. 103 a

---

[1] For some inexplicable reason, Helmut Kirchmeyer in his book *Igor Strawinsky: Zeitgeschichte im Persönlichkeitsbild* (Regensburg, 1958) confuses this *pas de deux* with the 'Bluebird' *pas de deux* from Chaikovsky's *The Sleeping Beauty*. (See Arrangements VIII (iii).)
[2] This tendency towards anacrusis becomes very marked in his later compositions.

Ex.103b

Ballet Productions

In 1944 *Danses Concertantes* was mounted as a ballet in New York by the Ballet Russe de Monte Carlo with choreography by George Balanchine, who found that, like *The Card Party*, this music was so rhythmically complex that he could use the 'bodies of dancers to feel out this volatile quality of the rhythm'.[1] Eugene Berman designed particularly striking scenery and costumes.

In 1955 Kenneth Macmillan made a new choreographic version for the Sadler's Wells Theatre Ballet, London, which was subsequently taken into the repertory of the Royal Ballet. Scenery and costumes were devised by Nicholas Georgiadis.

In 1959 *Danses Concertantes* was produced by the San Francisco Ballet with choreography by Lew Christensen and designs by Tony Duquette.

74. CIRCUS POLKA

For a young elephant. Composed in 1942[2] for the Barnum and Bailey Circus, New York, and first performed there by a Ballet of Elephants in the spring of 1942. (i) Version for wind band (flute, 2 solo clarinets, 2 clarinets, alto-saxophone, baritone-saxophone, 2 solo cornets, 3 cornets, 2 baritone-cornets, 2 horns, 4 trombones, 2 tubas, percussion (big drum, side drum, cymbals), and xylophone).[3] (ii) The symphonic version for orchestra (2.2.2.2 – 4.2.3.1 – percussion – string 5tet) was completed on 5 October 1942. Published by Associated Music Publishers, New York, 1944. Piano reduction by the composer. First performance, Boston Symphony Orchestra, Sanders Theatre, Cambridge, Mass., 13 January 1944, conducted by the composer. Duration of each version: *c.* 4 minutes. The manuscript full score, together with other manuscript material, is in the composer's collection [C 75].

The original commission for this ballet came to George Balanchine from Ringling Brothers of the Barnum and Bailey Circus, and he was entrusted with the choice of music. It is said that he immediately telephoned Stravinsky. 'What kind of music?' asked the composer. 'A polka.' 'For whom?' 'Elephants.' 'How old?' 'Young.' 'If they are very young, I'll do it.' They *were* very young, so Stravinsky agreed.

In this case he reverted to some of the *Easy Pieces for Piano Duet* (particularly

---

[1] From 'The Dance Element in Strawinsky's Music' by George Balanchine printed in the *Strawinsky in the Theatre* symposium in *Dance Index*, 1948.
[2] The piano version is dated Hollywood, 5 February 1942.
[3] The band score was made by David Reksin.

the *Polka* and *Galop*), not as a model for his new composition, but as a kind of spring-board. A consistent 2/4 time signature ($\downarrow$=100) forms the metrical framework of the *Circus Polka*; but in this score, unlike the 1940 *Tango*, the occasional use of elision breaks up the regularity of the barring and the musical paragraphs. It is interesting to observe that the characteristic polka rhythm emerges once only, and then it has a characteristic quotation from Schubert's *Marche Militaire* as countersubject, viz.:

Ex.104

This illustration gives a good idea of the carefree verve of the score.

Productions

At the première in the Madison Square Garden, New York City, in the spring of 1942, the circus programme carried the following billing:

Display No. 18 – "The Ballet of the Elephants"

Fifty Elephants and Fifty Beautiful Girls
in an Original Choreographic
Tour de Force

Featuring MODOC, première ballerina,

the Corps de Ballet and Corps des Eléphants

Directed by George Balanchine   Staged by John Murray Anderson

Music by Igor Stravinsky   Elephants trained by Walter McLain

Costumes designed by Norman Bel Geddes

In an interesting article,[1] George Brinton Beal refers to some of the difficulties involved in training and rehearsing the elephants. 'The first time Merle Evans, veteran bandmaster of the Big Show, put the music up on his rack and

---

[1] 'Entr'acte: Stravinsky and the Elephants' printed in the Concert Bulletin of the Boston Symphony Orchestra for 13, 14 and 15 January 1944.

started tooting away on his cornet, he knew there was trouble ahead. . . . Polite, as elephants always are, the big performers listened to the circus band, as it played their working music through. They listened, but with growing distaste and uneasiness, according to both the bandmaster and the super-intendent of bulls.' Beal explains that one of the main motives for staging this elephant ballet was to display the unique talents of Old Modoc, 'the best loved and most widely known elephant', whose solo dancing had long been featured by the Big Show. He goes on to say: 'Aside from the dancing of old Modoc, in center ring, the circus place of honor, "Display No. 18" was not a pretty act. The ballet skirts made the bulls appear ridiculous. The music didn't suit them. In spite of some of the stunts which they are made to perform, elephants are dignified animals. They respond instantly to waltz tunes and soft, dreamy music, even to some military numbers of a particular circusy tempo. The in-volved music of Stravinsky's "Elephant Ballet" was both confusing and frightening to them. It robbed them of their feeling of security and confidence in the world about them – so alien to their native condition of life. It would have taken very little at any time during the many performances of the ballet music to cause a stampede.'

No fewer than 425 performances were given of this act.

Sometime later, Paul Taylor made a new choreography for human dancers, which was seen in New York in 1935 and at the Festival of Two Worlds, Spoleto, in 1960.

Alan Carter used the music, together with the scores of *Fireworks*, *Ode* and the *Ebony Concerto*, as the basis for a ballet called *Feuilleton*, which was produced at the Bayerische Staatsoper, Munich, in 1957.

75. FOUR NORWEGIAN MOODS – QUATRE PIÈCES À LA NORVÉGIENNE

For orchestra (2.2.2.2 – 4.2.2.1 – timp. – string 5tet). Composed at Hollywood and finished on 18 August 1942. Published by Associated Music Publishers, New York, 1944. Duration: *c.* 8 minutes 30 seconds. First performance, Boston Symphony Orchestra, Sanders Theatre, Cambridge, Mass., 13 January 1944, conducted by the composer.

  I. *Intrada* ♩=106
  II. *Song* ♩=66
  III. *Wedding Dance* ♩=124
  IV. *Cortège* ♩=88

The full score together with other manuscript material is in the composer's collection [C 76].

Late in 1941 there was some talk of Stravinsky writing incidental music for a film on the Nazi invasion of Norway. He borrowed the themes he needed from a collection of Norwegian folk music his wife had just picked up in a second-hand bookshop in Los Angeles (*Mem*). But in the event Hollywood refused to accept his music in the form submitted; and as he refused to make any concessions, the material was withdrawn and turned into an independent concert suite.

In a communication about this composition that was printed in the Boston Symphony Orchestra programme for the first performance, Stravinsky stated that 'although based on Norwegian folk tunes, the title "Moods" must not be interpreted as "impression" or "frame of mind"'. It is purely a mode, a form or manner of style without any assumption of ethnological authenticity'. He went on to say that he had 'no more than followed the tradition of folklore treatment used by Joseph Haydn in his time', and had approached 'the given problems in formal order to reach the solution, using the folklore thematic only as a rhythmic and melodic basis'. Despite this statement, there are so few signs of the folk material having been fully assimilated that there might be a case for including this work among Stravinsky's adaptations rather than his original compositions.

76. ODE

Elegiacal chant in three parts (3.2.2.2 – 4.2.[1]0.0 – timp. – string 5tet). Composed at Hollywood and finished on 25 June 1943. Dedicated to the memory of Natalie Koussevitzky. Published by Schott's, 1947. Duration: *c.* 8 minutes. First performance 8 October 1943, by the Boston Symphony Orchestra conducted by Serge Koussevitzky. The manuscript score is in the Library of Congress, Washington D.C. Other manuscript material is in the composer's collection [C 77].

> I. *Eulogy – Lento* $\quad \downarrow = 50$
> II. *Eclogue – Con moto* $\quad \downarrow . = 92$
> III. *Epitaph – Lento* $\quad \downarrow = 46$

Through their firm, the Edition Russe de Musique, Serge and Natalie Koussevitzky had published the bulk of Stravinsky's music between *Petrushka* and *Persephone*. When Natalie died, her husband set up a Foundation to commission new compositions in her memory. In 1943 Stravinsky received one of these commissions and decided to write a triptych for orchestra. At that moment the *Eclogue* was already in existence, as it had been composed for an abortive film project. From his *Expositions* it appears that some time previously he had been approached by the agents of Orson Welles and urged to produce incidental music for *Jane Eyre*. 'As I was charmed by that book and

---

[1] The second of the B flat trumpets makes a very brief appearance, having two repeated notes to play in the first half dozen bars of the score and nothing else.

fascinated by the Brontës in general, I composed this piece for one of the hunting scenes.' But the suggestion that he should participate in this film came to nothing in the end; and the music of the Eclogue was salvaged to provide a pleasant interlude between the first and last movements of the *Ode*.

The *Eulogy* opens with a quiet call from three horns and two trumpets, preluding a short contrapuntal section which produces the impression of an accompanied fugue. The fugal subject is first enunciated by the various groups of strings; and each time its note lengths are altered and its rhythmic shape varied. Later the accompaniment moves from the wind to the strings, leaving the wind free to take over the fugal development.

The *Eclogue* is written in a bustling bucolic 6/8; and the rich independence of its part-writing recalls the 'Dumbarton Oaks' *Concerto*.

The opening phrase of the last movement (*Epitaph*), in which solemn triplets from some of the wind instruments revolve round the axis of an ostinato A, brings the same sort of tribute as a wreath of flowers and leaves. Halfway through, the tempo quickens slightly, and the music recalls the mourning mood of the *Symphonies of Wind Instrument*.

It is curious that the first performances of both these memorial works (the *Symphonies of Wind Instruments* and the *Ode*) were conducted by Koussevitzky, and in each case the result was unsatisfactory. In fact, Stravinsky has gone so far as to call the performance of the *Ode* 'catastrophic'. Apparently two serious miscalculations were made in the *Epitaph*. In the first place, the trumpet player read his part as if it were for a trumpet in C instead of B flat so that all his notes were out by a second. And then an unfortunate error occurred towards the end of the movement where 'two systems of score from the final page had been erroneously copied as one.[1] 'They were played in that way too,' continued Stravinsky, 'and my simple triadic piece concluded in a cacophony that would now win me new esteem at Darmstadt. This sudden change in harmonic style did not excite Koussevitzky's suspicion, however, and some years later he actually confided to me that he preferred "the original version".'[2]

Ballet Productions

In 1957 Alan Carter used the music, together with the scores of *Fireworks*, the *Circus Polka* and the *Ebony Concerto*, as the basis for a ballet called *Feuilleton*, which was produced at the Bayerische Staatsoper, Munich. Four years later (1961), *Ode* was produced as a ballet in its own right by the Western Theatre Ballet at Rotherham, Yorkshire, with choreography by Peter Darrell.

---

[1] This presumably refers to figures 43 and 44.
[2] 'Conductors: Good, Bad and Unspeakable' by I. S. *The Observer*, 24 June 1962.

Original Compositions

77. BABEL

Cantata based on words from the Book of Moses I.[1] Chapter 11, verses 1–9, for Male Chorus, with Narrator (male), and Orchestra (3.2.3.3. – 4.3.3.0 – timp. – harp – string 5tet). Composed at Hollywood and finished on 12 April 1944. Published by Schott's, 1953. Vocal score by the composer. Duration: *c.* 7 minutes. First performance (as part of the cycle 'Genesis'), Wilshire Ebell Theater, Los Angeles, 18 November 1945, conducted by Werner Janssen. The full score, which was in the composer's collection [C 80], is now in the Library of Congress, Washington, D.C.

Babel was the result of a rather unusual project. The music publisher, Nathaniel Shilkret, had the idea of commissioning a collective work based on the early chapters of *Genesis* and decided to invite a number of composers who had resided in America to take part. In the event, the *Prelude* was composed by Arnold Schoenberg; *Creation* by Shilkret himself; the *Fall of Man* by Alexandre Tansman; *Cain and Abel* by Darius Milhaud; the *Flood* by Mario Castelnuovo-Tedesco; the *Covenant* by Ernst Toch; and *Babel* by Stravinsky. Other sections were to have been written by Béla Bartok, Paul Hindemith and Serge Prokofiev.

The preliminary discussions were animated.[2] Shilkret wanted the music to provide a vivid, almost literal representation of the Biblical text. Doubtless he thought there were dramatic possibilities in the contrast between the chorus relating the story of the building and destruction of the Tower of Babel and the narrator speaking the words of God. But this ran absolutely counter to Stravinsky's ideas. As an orthodox Christian, he was opposed to the idea that the voice of God should be imitated by a human voice. In his cantata, he intended the words of God to be entrusted to the two-part male voice choir and the story to the narrator, and the construction of the score to be subject to purely musical considerations. He made it clear that not only did he think it wrong to attempt to illustrate the voice of God, but that music indeed ought not to attempt to illustrate anything at all. This was tantamount to an act of faith on his part; and in the end he had his own way.

Babel is in one movement, which can be conveniently divided into four sections. Robert Craft has described its general shape as 'that of a passacaglia in which a fugue serves as one of the variations'.[3]

In the earlier entry devoted to the *Symphony of Psalms*, attention has been drawn to Stravinsky's continuing preoccupation with the device of interlinked thirds. This recurs at the opening of the first section (*Largo*) of *Babel* where the interval of a fifth is divided into two interlinked major thirds.

---

[1] I.e., the first Book of Moses, called *Genesis*.
[2] See Tansman's *Igor Stravinsky*. Paris, 1948.
[3] From 'Music and Words' in *Stravinsky in the Theatre*.

Ex. 105

<p legato

etc.

In pitch and tone colour these opening bars recall the introduction to *The Firebird*; but the fact that the main interval subject to division is a fifth (E and B) instead of an augmented fourth implies a lesser degree of chromaticism and a stronger leaning towards tonality. The reciter, whose part carries no indication of specific stress, time or pitch, speaks the first five verses above an accompaniment consisting partly of variations on the above ground bass by strings, bassoons and bass clarinet and partly of a decorative oboe theme accompanied by three flutes and a trumpet in four-part harmony.

The second section (still *Largo*) is a two-part cantata for the tenors and basses (Voice of God) with a rather thick chordal accompaniment in which strings, woodwind and brass play strongly contrasted parts. Although the whole of this passage is diatonic, the final cadence resolves on a bitonal chord of C major superimposed on F sharp major.

This is the signal for a sudden change of time (*Con moto*) and an outburst of chromaticism. The new section, which opens with the Narrator's words

Ex. 106

'So the Lord scattered them abroad from thence upon the face of all the earth: and they left off to build the city', consists of an orchestral stretto in which repeated staccato chords on the horns that recall the *Laudate Dominum* passage in the last movement of the *Symphony of Psalms* introduce a rapid development of the ground bass theme from the introduction by variation, inversion and diminution. (See Ex. 106.) It is then treated fugally with entries allocated to horns, trumpets and trombones, reinforced by the strings which fill out the various note values with repeated semiquavers.

The fourth and final section (*Meno mosso*) is a coda where the work which started in the key of E is brought to a tranquil conclusion in the key of B.

Although *Babel* recalls the mood of the *Symphony of Psalms*, it also looks forward to other works to come and has a certain seminal quality about it. It was the first time Stravinsky set English words to music, so it is the forerunner of works like the *Cantata, Threni* and *The Flood*; the two-part setting of the words of God is a step in the direction of the *Mass* and *The Flood*; and the fragmentation of the *Con moto* section is a foretaste of the idiom that was to prove so successful in the Bacchantes' *pas d'action* in *Orpheus*.

The 'Genesis' suite (so far as it had been completed) was first performed under the direction of Werner Janssen at Los Angeles on 18 November 1945. It is difficult to imagine that a work conceived in such a curious way and carried out by seven composers of such different styles and temperaments can have been very effective as a whole. But Stravinsky's contribution is well able to stand on its own as a fascinating episode.

78. SCHERZO À LA RUSSE

(i) Original version for Paul Whiteman's Band. Composed in Hollywood, 1944, and performed on the Blue Network Programme. (ii) Symphonic version for orchestra (3.2.2.2 – 4.3.3.1 – xylophone, timp., tambourine, triangle, cymbals, side drums with and without snare, bass drum, piano, harp – string 5tet). Composed in Hollywood, 1943/44. Published by Chappell, New York, 1945. First performance, San Francisco Symphony Orchestra, San Francisco, March 1946, conducted by the composer. Duration: *c.* 4 minutes. The manuscript full scores of versions (i) and (ii), together with other manuscript material, are in the composer's collection (C 79].

The *Scherzo à la Russe* belongs to Stravinsky's abortive music for film use. It was originally intended for a war film with a Russian setting; but when that project came to naught, he re-orchestrated it for the Paul Whiteman Band, and in that version it was performed on the Blue Network Programme in 1944 (*Mem*).

It is closely related to the 'Russian Dance' in *Petrushka* and the 'Swiss Dances' in *The Fairy's Kiss*. In this Scherzo Stravinsky takes two streams of accordion-like triads and plays them off against each other. The key is G major; and the tune groups itself naturally into four-bar phrases. There are two trios: the first (in B major) has a close canon between piano and harp accompanied by three violins (muted) playing a rapid semiquaver figuration; the second is in simple ternary form with the first section in C major and the second in E flat major. The effect of the Scherzo as a whole is gay and un-inhibited in a rather conventional style.

The title is the same as Chaikovsky's op. 1, no. 1, which was one of the piano pieces laid under contribution in *The Fairy's Kiss*.

The first appearance of the Scherzo as a piece of symphonic jazz does not seem to have been a success, and the jazz version was speedily superseded by the version for symphonic orchestra.

79. SCÈNES DE BALLET

For orchestra (2.2.2.1 – 2.3.3.1 – timp. – piano – string 5tet). Composed in Hollywood and finished on 23 August 1944.[1] Published by Chappell, New York, 1945. Duration: *c.* 18 minutes. First stage performance in Billy Rose's revue *The Seven Lively Arts*, Philadelphia, 1944, conducted by Maurice Abravanel. First concert performance, New York Philharmonic Orchestra, New York, winter of 1945, conducted by the composer. The full score, together with other manuscript material is in the composer's collection [C 82].

Introduction: Andante ♪=92
Danses (Corps de Ballet): Moderato ♪=148
Variation (Ballerina): Con moto ♩.=74
Pantomime: Lento ♩.=74 leading to *Andantino* ♩=66
                                    and *Più Mosso* ♪=132
Pas de deux: Adagio ♩=58
Pantomime: Agitato ma tempo giusto ♩=74
Variation (Dancer): Risoluto ♩=86
Variation (Ballerina): Andantino ♩=63
Pantomime: Andantino ♩=72
Danses (Corps de Ballet): Con moto ♪=108
Apothéose: Poco meno mosso ♩=50

One day in the spring of 1944, Billy Rose telephoned Stravinsky and offered $5,000 for a fifteen-minute ballet suite to be incorporated in his new Broadway revue *The Seven Lively Arts*. The solo dancers were to be Alicia Markova and Anton Dolin, and Dolin was to compose the choreography. Stravinsky accepted; and as he composed the orchestral score page by page, his friend

---

[1] 'At the end of the manuscript score Stravinsky added the words "Paris n'est plus aux allemands"; the whole jubilant apotheosis was written on the day of the liberation.' Robert Craft in 'A Personal Preface' (*The Score*, June 1957).

Original Compositions

Ingolf Dahl arranged it for piano.[1] Billy Rose apparently liked the music in the piano version, but was dismayed by the sound of the orchestra. The preview of *The Seven Lively Arts* took place in Philadelphia; and after the first night Stravinsky received a telegram couched in the following terms: 'YOUR MUSIC GREAT SUCCESS STOP COULD BE SENSATIONAL SUCCESS IF YOU WOULD AUTHORISE ROBERT RUSSELL BENNETT RETOUCH ORCHESTRATION STQP BENNETT ORCHESTRATES EVEN THE WORKS OF COLE PORTER.' He telegraphed back: 'SATISFIED WITH GREAT SUCCESS.' After this it is not surprising to find that only fragments of the score were used during the revue's run on Broadway. The work was first performed in its entirety at a concert performance by the New York Philharmonic Orchestra in the winter of 1945.

Stravinsky himself has explained: 'This music is patterned after the forms of the classical dance, free of any given literary or dramatic argument. The parts follow each other as in a sonata or a symphony, in contrasts or similarities.'

Despite this warning it is evident that the ballet is not conceived in quite such abstract terms as the *Danses Concertantes*, for the specification of a ballerina and a leading male dancer shows that their relationship is a vital factor in the scheme, and the presence of passages of pantomime between some of the dance numbers helps to point the various changes in emphasis. In many respects the layout of *Scènes de Ballet* runs parallel to that of *Apollo Musagetes* for there is no element of conflict in the action and the anonymous protagonists dance their way through to some sort of final transformation.

It is typical of the score's metrical subtlety that the four opening chords of the Introduction are spaced with cunning irregularity.

Ex. 107

It is difficult for the ear to detect the basic compound 5/8 metre until the next number (*Danses*) gets under way. Here the characteristic, already noticed in *Danses Concertantes* (see Ex. 103), of avoiding the strong accent at the beginning of the bar becomes almost obsessive. The charming hesitancy of the main

---

[1] In at least one case, there has been confusion about Ingolf Dahl's role. A pupil of Schoenberg's noted in his diary on 16 September 1944 that he told Schoenberg that Dahl had orchestrated a piece that Stravinsky had written for Billy Rose. Not unnaturally Schoenberg was puzzled and replied: 'I do not understand this, to orchestrate for Stravinsky, for I have shown you how I compose for orchestra . . .'

theme – first played by four solo violas, then by all the strings, and on its reprise by oboes and horns – is due to the fact that its phrases, which would normally fit into 4/8, have become lengthened by a quaver's rest at the beginning of nearly every bar.

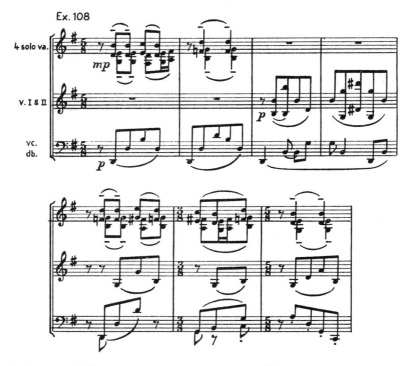

Ex. 108

At the end of this movement, an *accelerando* and upward runs in the clarinets lead to the ballerina's first dance variation, a coruscating *Con moto*, in which trills and repeated notes play an important part in the accompaniment, and brilliant commentary is provided by the wind instruments, and also the piano, which here has something of a *concertante* part.

The ensuing *Pantomime* enshrines two miniature episodes, of which the first[1] – an eight-bar *Andantino* – is especially charming, with a far-flung tune that covers a span of three octaves and is shared between horn, flute and piano.

The *Pas de deux*, which comes at the mid-point of the score, introduces a note of brash vulgarity, which though characteristic of such earlier scores as *Petrushka* and *The Soldier's Tale*, had been absent from his music for some years and had only recently made a reappearance in works like the *Circus*

[1] Fig. 58.

422

Polka and the *Scherzo à la Russe*. Yet the theme in itself is not so very different from the main subject of the opening movement of the *Symphony in C* (see Ex. 95). There is the same diatonic twisting round the triad of C major, the special effect in *Scènes de Ballet* coming from the scoring for solo trumpet (associated with the male dancer) imitated by solo horn (associated with the ballerina) and the rather sluggish triplet accompaniment given to the lower strings. Some critics have found this note of vulgarity rather incongruous. For instance, Lawrence Morton writes: 'In *Scènes de Ballet*, a work written for, of all people, Billy Rose, there is a trumpet tune of almost incredible sentimentality. . . . Remove from it the marks of genius, make it four-square, give it a Cole Porter lyric, and you have a genuine pop-tune. As it stands, however, it is a solemnisation of Broadway, a halo for a chorus girl, a portrait of Mr. Rose as Diaghilev.'[1] This is rather portentous. The tune is sentimental admittedly; but its delivery is so vigorous and exposed that its effect is like that of a strong spotlight thrown on the two main dancers – and this is just what is required at this particular point in the ballet.

Ex. 109

The ensuing *Pantomime* has a prominent dotted quaver theme and introduces a lively, resolute variation for the chief male dancer, in which the dotted quaver still plays an important part. A second dance variation for the ballerina follows, with a wistful theme in thirds (played by two solo cellos), which is threaded like a ribbon through the light string accompaniment. Another passage of *Pantomime* leads to a lively *Con moto* movement for the *corps de ballet*, which is like a dance coda with a strong ostinato bass for the cellos

---

[1] From 'Incongruity and Faith' printed in the Merle Armitage symposium edited by Edwin Corle and published in 1949.

and double-basses playing *pizzicato*. The theme is entrusted first to a solo clarinet, and later it is imitated by a solo horn and the first violin. The tempo slows up for the *Apotheosis*, at which point Stravinsky envisaged 'a stage full of groups twirling and mounting *delirando*' (*Dia*). The same theme augmented is played by oboe and bassoon above a tremolo accompaniment in the strings. The addition of a solo muted trumpet also playing tremolo gives this movement a shimmering radiance. The chords (all of them on off-beats) gather in strength like cumulus clouds at sunset; and the work ends in the same kind of transcendental splendour as *The Wedding* and *Apollo Musagetes*.[1]

Productions

The work was produced by the Sadler's Wells Ballet at Covent Garden, London on 11 February 1948.[2] The choreography was by Frederick Ashton, scenery and costumes by André Beaurepaire, and Margot Fonteyn and Michael Somes danced the leading roles. There have been subsequent productions at various places in Germany, including Berlin, Stuttgart and Hamburg, and by the Netherlands Ballet at the Hague.

80. SONATA

For two pianos. Composed at Hollywood, 1943/44. Published by Chappell, New York, 1945. Duration: *c.* 11 minutes. First performance by Nadia Boulanger and Richard Johnson at the Dominican Sisters, Madison, Wisconsin, July 1944. MS comp. [C 81].

    I. *Moderato* ♩=63
   II. *Theme with Variations*
        Theme: *Largo* ♩=40
        Variation 1 ♩=54
        Variation 2 ♪=126
        Variation 3 ♩=88
        Variation 4 (conclusion) ♩=40
  III. *Allegretto* ♩=80

This sonata was begun before and completed after *Scènes de Ballet*. It is on a much less extended scale than the *Concerto for Two Pianos* of 1935 and has

---

[1] There are some critics who disapprove of this work. For instance, Robert Siohan in his book on Stravinsky (Editions du Seuil, Paris, 1959) regrets that 'the score is so perfectly suited to the bombastic style of this type of show business' (i.e., the Broadway revue). He even says that he finds the Variations, the passages of *Pantomime* and the *Pas de deux* 'haunted by the ghost of Aubrey Beardsley, whose influence Stravinsky thought at one time he had detected in the text of Schoenberg's *Pierrot Lunaire*'. This seems a trifle far-fetched.
[2] This date was misprinted '11 February 1938' in the German translation of my book on Stravinsky (Claassen Verlag, Hamburg, 1950), and this misprint has unfortunately been followed by one or two books of reference.

Original Compositions

none of the *concertante* quality of the earlier work. The pianistic layout resembles that of the *Piano Sonata* of 1924 in that the writing for each pianist is predominantly two-part;[1] and it is interesting to find that in many places – particularly the first and last movements – the range of the two pianos overlaps so that the contrapuntal structure is quite closely knit.

The easy flow of the different strands making up melody, counter-melody and accompaniment in the opening *Moderato* is close in mood to the first movement of the 'Dumbarton Oaks' *Concerto*. It is written in sonata form, with its first subject in F major and its second subject in C major; but as the second subject is accompanied by a derivative of the first subject, the repeat of the exposition seems almost unnecessary. The development section shows signs of a more vigorous attitude with various spread *arpeggi*, some played *marcato sforzato* and others simply *staccato*, which is reminiscent of the first movement of the Two Piano Concerto. There is even a momentary modulation to the comparatively remote key of D flat major; and the gusto with which the new key is savoured reminds one of the gentle opening of the D flat major section in the Nocturne of the Two Piano Concerto. This episode lasts only about half a dozen bars, however, and proves to be the briefest of gestures, for it leads straight into the recapitulation of the first and second subjects in reversed keys, i.e., C major and F major.

The second movement is a set of variations. Unlike the Variations in the Two Piano Concerto, the G major theme is enunciated clearly at the outset, in canon by inversion. This canon is accompanied by a cantus firmus based on the notes of the common chord arpeggio. The value of these notes diminishes from breves at the start to semi-breves, minims and ends with crotchets. In the eleventh bar a bass enters, moving scalewise, and continues until the end. The illustration shows bars 11 and 12 where the canon by inversion is repeated, and the bass part makes its first appearance.

Ex. 110

[1] The Sonata began as a piece for one performer, but was redesigned for two pianos when I saw that four hands were required to voice the four lines clearly.' (*Dia*).

425

The result is richly polyphonic, as in the *pas d'action* in *Apollo Musagetes*.

The first Variation is a three- (occasionally four-) part harmonisation of the theme played above a simple *ostinato* accompaniment by the second piano[1] (Ex. 111). After nine bars the *ostinato* is interrupted for three bars, while the accompaniment gets drawn into the final cadence of the harmonised theme. When the *ostinato* is resumed, a single chord has its C sharp altered to C natural as if the key were going to modulate from D to G. But it does not modulate, and the C sharp is restored.

Ex. 111

In his *Poetics of Music*, Stravinsky has said of the composer in the act of composition: 'The least accident holds his interest and guides his operations. If his finger slips, he will notice it; on occasion, he may draw profit from something unforeseen that a momentary lapse reveals to him.' Was this C natural possibly such a lapse?

---

[1] In his book on *Erik Satie* (published by Dennis Dobson, 1948), Rollo H. Myers has drawn attention to the similarity between this and the accompaniment figure in the first of Satie's *Gymnopédies*.

In the second Variation, the theme is given a sharply dotted movement above (and below) a running stream of demisemiquavers. The third Variation is a gay little fughetta. In the fourth, the theme returns in the bass and is accompanied by a series of chords at three different (descending) levels in the treble – first, five chords whose top note is A in altissimo, then three chords whose top note is D in alt, and finally four chords whose top note is A in alt.

The *Allegretto* is in ternary form. Its initial phrase in G minor is immediately answered by a phrase in C minor, and the close involvement of these two neighbouring tonalities produces a curiously ambivalent effect. The middle section (*poco più mosso*) is a tender, rather wistful melody, which gives the impression that Stravinsky had suddenly been reminded of the period during the First World War when he was preoccupied with Russian folk lore and popular themes. The simple diatonic tune, doubled two octaves lower, is delightfully fresh, and its irregular phrasing most invigorating. It is as if an unexpected breeze from Volhynia had blown in through the open window of his study in California.

81. ÉLÉGIE – ELEGY

For unaccompanied viola (or violin) 'composée à l'intention de Germain Prévost, pour être jouée à la mémoire de ALPHONSE ONNOU fondateur du Quatuor Pro Arte'. Composed in 1944. Published by Chappell, New York, 1945. Duration: *c.* 4 minutes 30 seconds. The manuscript which was in the composer's collection [C 84], is now in the library of Congress, Washington, D.C.

This *Elegy* for unaccompanied viola (which may also be played a fifth higher by an unaccompanied violin) is a two-part invention in ternary form. There is no time signature; but according to the metronome indication, ♪ = 56 throughout. The first section is a kind of chant played above a simple flowing accompaniment. The middle section is skilfully written to give the impression of a fugue, though at no point are there more than two independent contrapuntal strands. At the climax the fugal subject is answered by its inversion at a distance of a single (2/4) bar. A (5/4) bar consisting of a rising sequence of a minor sixth followed by a fifth, a fourth, a major third and an augmented second forms a bridge leading to the recapitulation of the first section with an altered cadence in the last four bars. The viola (or violin) plays *con sordino* throughout.

Ballet Productions

In 1945 George Balanchine composed a dance to this score in which he tried 'to reflect the flow and concentrated variety of the music through the interlaced bodies of two dancers rooted to a central spot of the stage.'[1] This was

---

[1] From 'The Dance Element in Strawinsky's Music' by George Balanchine, printed in the *Strawinsky in the Theatre* symposium in *Dance Index*, 1948.

performed at the School of American Ballet. A professional performance was given three years later in New York by the Ballet Society with Tanaquil Leclercq and Pat McBride as the two dancers.

82. SYMPHONY

In Three Movements[1] for orchestra (3.2.3.3 – 4.3.3.1 – timp., big drum, piano, harp – string 5tet). Dedicated to the New York Philharmonic Symphony Society. Composed between 1942 and 1945. Published by Associated Music Publishers, New York, 1946. Duration: *c.* 24 minutes. First performance, New York Philharmonic Orchestra, New York, 24 January 1946, conducted by the composer. MS comp. [C 83].

    I. $\downarrow$ = 160
   II. *Andante* $\downarrow$ = 76
         Interlude: L'istesso tempo $\downarrow$ = 76
  III. *Con moto* $\downarrow$ = 108

Dionysiac or Apollonian? – Symphony or Concerto?

At the time of his seventy-fifth birthday in 1957, Stravinsky agreed to answer thirty-five questions posed by Robert Craft, and these were widely publicised at the time. Subsequently all this material was absorbed in the first volume of their published *Conversations*, with the exception of a single question[2] where Craft, after drawing his attention to the fact that W. H. Auden had called him an Apollonian, asked whether he recognised the other side of his nature, viz., the Dionysiac, and whether he was conscious of any internal conflict whereby sometimes the one element, sometimes the other, was in the ascendant – e.g., Apollo in *Persephone* and the *Symphony in C*; but Dionysus in the *Concerto for Two Pianos* and the *Symphony in Three Movements*. Stravinsky's characteristic answer was that he recognised both Apollonian and Dionysiac elements in all his works – for instance, the first part of *Orpheus* was Apollonian, the last part Dionysiac. Why this question and answer were dropped from the canon is not clear; but the presence of these two elements in varying proportions in most of Stravinsky's works is incontestable.

In his lectures on the *Poetics of Music*, he relates these elements to the concepts of classicism and romanticism and quotes with approval André Gide's saying that 'classical works are beautiful only by virtue of their subjugated romanticism'. The course of his argument leads him to the following conclusion: 'What is important for the lucid ordering of the work – for its crystallization – is that all the Dionysiac elements which set up the imagination

---

[1] 'Perhaps Three Symphonic Movements would be a more exact title.' (*Dia*).
[2] No. XIX in *Antworten auf 35 Fragen* as reprinted in *Igor Strawinsky: Leben und Werk*, published by Atlantis Verlag, Zürich, in conjunction with Schott's, Mainz, 1957.

of the artist in motion and make the life-sap rise must be properly subjugated before they intoxicate us, and must finally be made to submit to the law: Apollo demands it.'

The *Symphony in C* and the *Symphony in Three Movements* come so close together in Stravinsky's output – the *Symphony in C* was the first work he completed after moving from France to the United States in 1939; the *Symphony in Three Movements* was the first new work of his to be performed after his naturalisation as an American citizen (28 December 1945) – that it is naturally instructive to compare them and to see how far he has been successful in subjugating the Dionysiac elements in each to the Apollonian laws that govern classicism. But first it is necessary to ascertain whether the *Symphony in Three Movements* justifies its claim to be considered a symphony in the classical sense or not.

In his monograph on Stravinsky, Alexander Tansman recalls how as early as 1942 he heard the composer play some of the music that ultimately appeared in the first movement and thought it was then intended to be a symphonic work with a *concertante* part for the piano.[1] In his *Expositions*, Stravinsky says that at that time he looked on the work as a concerto for orchestra. A year later (1943) he was encouraged by Franz Werfel to try his hand at writing music for Werfel's *Song of Bernadette* film. Although in the end this turned out to be just as abortive as all his other film music projects, he actually completed a movement for the 'Apparition of the Virgin' scene, and this in due course was taken over as the slow movement of the new work. The fact that the *concertante* part was here entrusted to the harp, and not the piano, would seem to confirm the idea of the work being a concerto rather than a symphony.

The problem now arose of how to reconcile the two *concertante* instruments in the third and last movement – the piano which had appeared only in the first movement, and the harp which had appeared only in the second. His solution was not merely to combine them both in instrumental *tutti* passages, but also to spotlight them as the two leading voices in an *Alla breve* fugue[2] that he placed in the centre of the movement.

The attitude of some of the critics has been rather confusing. In his book on Stravinsky,[3] Alexandre Tansman maintains that the construction of the first movement, while rigorously following the pattern of sonata form, approaches closely the Beethoven conception, particularly as exemplified in the first Allegro of the Fifth Symphony. This claim has been repeated by subsequent critics like Roman Vlad and Robert Siohan, but without any attempt to substantiate it. Siohan, however, is nearer the heart of the matter when he says that as is the case with Beethoven's Fifth Symphony, the majority of the themes

[1] See Tansman's *Igor Stravinsky*. Paris, 1948.
[2] Fig. 170 *et seq.*
[3] Tansman, *op. cit.*

in Stravinsky's *Symphony in Three Movements* 'gravitate round a strictly limited number of notes and seem thereby to accumulate a reserve of energy which is revealed by interplay between the fixed elements and the moving elements.'[1]

On the other hand, Ernest Ansermet complains[2] that the listener to this symphony fails to establish an internal link between its various episodes because he is not carried from one to the other by an internal tonal movement which would create the form of the work from within, and furthermore because in it there is not the sort of complementary relationship between the episodes that there should be between the various movements of a symphony.

Sensitive perception of the issues involved is shown by Donald Mitchell[3] when he remarks that the true significance of the *Symphony in Three Movements* lies in 'the startling success with which Stravinsky's "dynamic" language serves a large-scale symphonic structure'. He admits that in comparison with the *Symphony in C* its melodic content is low,[4] but maintains that 'instead of its classicism breaking surface in the shape of defined melody, it is folded within the form, and to that degree is "concealed".'

Perhaps if the work is recognised as a concerto rather than a symphony, it is easier to understand why it is built up by the balance of contrasts rather than by the pursuit and resolution of the sort of dialectical argument proper to symphonic form.

Composition

In a programme note written for the first performance, Stravinsky said that while this symphony was absolute music which was not to be regarded as the expression of any particular 'programme', it was certainly possible to find in it traces of impressions and experiences coloured by 'this our arduous time of sharp and shifting events, of despair and hope, of continual torments, of tension, and at last cessation and relief'. In his *Dialogues*, he was more specific and explained that the score – in particular the first and third movements – was written under the sign of various world war events that when seen in films had often excited his musical imagination.

The first movement was inspired by a documentary film 'of scorched-earth tactics in China'; and the central episode for clarinet, piano and string 'was conceived as a series of instrumental conversations to accompany a cinematographic scene showing the Chinese people scratching and digging in their fields' (*Dia*).

It has already been mentioned how the second movement was derived from

---

[1] *Stravinsky*. Paris, 1959.
[2] In *Les Fondements de la Musique dans la Conscience humaine*. Neuchâtel, 1961.
[3] In *The Language of Modern Music*. London, Faber & Faber, 1963.
[4] In this connection, compare Ex. 113 with Ex. 95.

Original Compositions

an abortive project to write incidental music for the scene of 'The Apparition of the Virgin' in the film of Werfel's *Song of Bernadette.*

The beginning of the third movement was partly 'a musical reaction to the newsreels and documentaries that [he] had seen of goose-stepping soldiers'; and the latter part of the movement, from the exposition of the fugue to the coda of the Symphony, was associated in his plot with 'the rise of the Allies' after the overturning of the German war machine (*Dia*).

Analytical Note

The first movement opens with a vigorous skirl and flourish. Unlike the motto at the beginning of the *Symphony in C*, this motto is not germinal and has only a very minor part to play.[1]

Ex. 112

The contrasting sections of this movement are very striking. In (*a*) the opening section for full orchestra (♩=160), the piano is treated as an instrument of the orchestra; in (*b*) a *doppio movimento* section (♩=80), the piano becomes a solo instrument and the orchestra is broken down into small groups in the manner of a concertino. These two sections are interlocked in the following pattern *a(i) b(i) a(ii) b(ii) a(iii)*, where *a(i)* and *b(i)* give a full exposition of the music of each section, *a(ii)* and *b(ii)* briefly recapitulate part of the material, and *a(iii)* provides a coda by augmenting the chords of the opening theme (Ex. 113). None of the (*a*) or (*b*) material is interchangeable.

Whereas the *Symphony in C* was a predominantly diatonic work, the *Symphony in Three Movements* scintillates with a chromaticism derived from the sort of bitonality that had been comparatively rare in Stravinsky's music since the *Concerto for Two Pianos*. The chromatic clashes arising from two contrasting tonal strands are evident in the main theme of section (a).[2]

---

[1] Perhaps it should merely be looked on as a backward glance at the skirl with which the *fugato* opens in the middle of the last movement of the *Symphony in C* (fig. 163), or as an extension of the opening instrumental phrase in *Zvezdoliki.*

[2] For some reason hard to fathom, this passage is shorn of every alternative chord when quoted in Roman Vlad's study of the *Symphony in Three Movements* in his monograph on *Stravinsky* (*op. cit.*).

Ex. 113

There is a different sort of chromaticism in section (*b*), due partly to the extreme polyphonic development of the musical texture.

Ex. 114

Although the two illustrations just quoted are in regular metre, it is a feature of the development of both the (*a*) and (*b*) sections in the first movement that they embrace the use of irregular metres. The numerous changes of time

Original Compositions

signature in this movement should be contrasted with the uniform 2/2 time signature that runs through the whole of the long first movement of the *Symphony in C*.

Section (a) of this movement is divided into two parts by an extended ostinato based on an arrested cadence that is reiterated in slightly varying metrical patterns over a fixed ground bass.[1] Such a device was a typical feature in some of Stravinsky's early ballet scores, but is usually considered to be inimical to symphonic construction. The effect of such an ostinato passage is to arrest development and delay the launching of the following musical idea. It is as if the ostinato were a powerful spring, which increases the tension between the two parts that it joins (or separates) and affects the dynamic potential of the movement accordingly.

There is a magnificence of timbre in the climaxes of this movement that recalls the brazen glory of the *Symphony of Psalms*; and the level of the musical argument is generally an exalted one. Nevertheless, just as the first movement of the *Symphony in C* has its moments of occasional brashness (see particularly the trumpet signal Ex. 97), so this movement has a bathetic passage for strings[2] that sounds strangely pathetic in its context, particularly as the phrase has been elongated to fit into five bars instead of the more conventional four-bar pattern.

Ex. 115

mp dolce

After the stress of the first movement with its double exposition and multiple interlocking contrasts, the slow movement introduces an elegiac note. The harp, which takes over as *concertante* instrument from the piano, imitates and elaborates the business of an orchestra that has been reduced by the omission of all brass (three horns excepted) and percussion. The writing for harp is linear and avoids romantic affects such as thick chording, *arpeggi* and *glissandi*. The opening bars of the *Andante* show how delicately it is used to underline, reinforce and even to anticipate the flute melody (See Ex. 116.). As was the case with the slow movement in the *Symphony in C*, there is a charmingly expressive parenthesis just before the *Più mosso* middle section. These five bars (marked *dolce cantabile*) are for harp, four solo violins and two

---

[1] Figs. 7 to 12. A slightly shortened version (22 bars instead of 23) transposed a tone higher occurs at figs. 88 to 93.
[2] Fig. 52.

433

Ex. 116

solo violas; and when the passage is repeated at the end of the *Più mosso* section, the string parts are taken over by two flutes, two clarinets and two bassoons.

A brief cadential *Interlude*, seven bars long, leads directly to the third and last movement.

This combines the characteristics of both a scherzo and a finale. The opening statement (Ex. 117), a peremptory affirmation in C, harks back to Stravinsky's initial obsession with the division of the octave into major (minor) third and minor (major) sixth; and here the potential clash between major and minor becomes even more explicit and compelling. The basic idea is woven into a piece of figuration (Ex. 118) which is astonishingly close to the initial theme of *Babel* (see Ex. 105 above).

Shock tactics project irregular chordal cadences, punctuated by occasional explosions of sound, against this background. The fugue (mentioned above) provides a centre of gravity. The opening entry for piano (*Alla breve*) is echoed and underlined by a few fragmentary staccato phrases from solo trombone, a strange combination that foreshadows the single note treatment of the series that was later to emerge in a work like *The Flood*. The subsequent entries are entrusted to harp, bassoons and violins. A resumption of the agitated movement leads to further development of the dynamic potential as revealed in the earlier part of the movement, and an exhilarating *fff* close.

In 1943 Stravinsky had had the idea of revising and rescoring *The Rite of Spring*. He got no further than the final 'Sacrificial Dance'; but though this revised movement was published, it was never performed. Fresh contact with this heady score seems to have reintoxicated him with Dionysiac fumes. Some of the woodwind passages[1] in the symphony sound like the impressionist introduction to Part One of *The Rite of Spring*: the handling of the *ostinati* and the shock tactics of the last movement recall movements like the 'Glorification of the Chosen Victim' and the 'Sacrificial Dance'. The symphony also looks forward to a work like *The Rake's Progress*. For instance, the carefully pointed string accompaniment at the opening of the slow movement (see Ex. 116 above) is similar to that of Shadow's Act I aria, 'Fair lady, gracious gentlemen, a servant begs your pardon'; and even the cut of the opening phrase of the last movement (see Ex. 117 above) recalls that of the Act III Chorus of Madmen, 'Madmen's words are all untrue'.

This may not be a symphony in the orthodox sense of the word; but it is undoubtedly a work where even after the initial Dionysiac inspiration has been subjugated to Apollonian law and order, energy and originality remain unimpaired.

E.g., figs. 70–75, and fig. 131.

2. Register of Works

Ballet Production

In 1960, it was mounted as a ballet under the title *Par Flux et Marée* at the Bühnen der Stadt Köln (Cologne) with choreography by Aurel von Milloss.

83. EBONY CONCERTO

For solo B flat clarinet, 2 E flat alto saxophones, 2 B flat tenor saxophones, 1 E flat baritone saxophone, 1 B flat bass clarinet, 1 French horn, 5 B flat trumpets, 3 trombones, piano, harp, guitar, double-bass, tom-toms, cymbals, drums. Composed at Hollywood and finished on 1 December 1945. Dedicated to Woody Herman. Published by Charling Music Corporation, New York, 1946; reissued by Edwin H. Morris & Co. London, 1954. Duration: *c.* 11 minutes. First performance, Woody Herman's Band, Carnegie Hall, New York, 25 March 1946, conducted by Walter Hendl. The manuscript full score, which was in the composer's collection [C 85], is now in the Library of Congress, Washington, D.C.

> I. *Allegro moderato* ♩=88
> II. *Andante* ♩=84
> III. *Moderato* ♩=84
>   *Con moto* ♩=132

Just as the *Symphony in C* was flanked by two smaller *concertante* compositions – the 'Dumbarton Oaks' *Concerto* and the *Danses Concertantes* – so the *Symphony in Three Movements* was followed by the *Ebony Concerto* and the *Concerto in D* for string orchestra. The *Ebony Concerto* was in fact composed at the same time as the symphony; and in his monograph on Stravinsky, Alexandre Tansman has recorded his fascination at finding the composer engaged simultaneously on two works for a symphony orchestra and a jazz band. 'It was with surprise as well as intense admiration that I saw the greatest composer of our age, and one of the greatest of all times, put himself to school like a student to study this new problem, trying to extract all the latent possibilities from this new combination of instruments, working away at it with the same conscientious concentration that he had applied a few months previously to his great Symphony.'[1]

The blurb accompanying the publication of the score states that Stravinsky had been so favourably impressed by Woody Herman and his band, particularly in their recordings of *Bijou*, *Goosey Gander* and *Caldonia*, that he agreed to write a special composition for the band with a solo clarinet part for Woody Herman. According to his *Dialogues*, the only jazz he had heard in the United States had been in Harlem, and by negro bands in Chicago and New

---

[1] *Igor Stravinsky*. Paris, 1948.

436

Original Compositions

Orleans. His plan was to produce a jazz equivalent of a *concerto grosso*, with a blues slow movement. He studied recordings of the Herman band, added a French horn to the instrumentation, and enlisted the services of a saxophonist to demonstrate fingerings.

This is the most ambitious and most successful of his various flirtations with jazz. He managed to solve the problem of writing for a jazz-band without abdicating any part of his own artistic integrity, and at the same time exacted the maximum discipline from the players, refusing to make allowance for any improvisatory element in the performance. That the players did not always find it easy to meet his demands appears from his statement (printed in the English but not the American edition of his *Conversations*) that he was 'obliged to recopy the first movement of the *Ebony Concerto* in quavers, when the jazz musicians, for whom it was written, proved themselves unable to read semi-quavers'.

It is fascinating to see how Stravinsky adapts his 'classical' concerto technique to jazz purposes. The B flat major tonality of the opening *Allegro moderato* is firmly established by the first subject – a group of chords shaken together by vigorous syncopation. The second subject, where the melody of the solo trombone is followed and varied by the solo clarinet, is in E flat major. A brief cadenza for solo clarinet leads to a literal reprise (37 bars long) of the first subject; and a modulation brings back the second subject, presented this time by solo trumpet followed and varied by baritone saxophone, in the home key of B flat major. This is a good example of first movement sonata form.

The *Andante* is a 'blue' number in F minor ending in F major.

The final movement consists of a restrictive, intentionally monotonous theme (rather like that of the slow movement of the *Octet*) with variations and a coda. The last of the variations (marked *Vivo*) is treated as an opportunity for a virtuoso display by the solo clarinet. In the coda, a cadence of chords by the saxophones and trombones moving slowly through a barrage of sound produced by the French horn playing flutter-tongued and the five muted trumpets playing harmonics tremolo recalls the Apotheosis to *Scènes de Ballet*.

Ballet Productions

In 1960, the *Ebony Concerto* was produced as a ballet by the New York City Ballet, with choreography by John Taras, and décor and costumes by David Hays. In the first movement the dancers appeared in silhouette; the second movement was a *pas de deux*; and the finale proceeded at a hectic, staccato pace. The ballet was included in a programme with the general title of *Jazz Concert*.

In 1957, Alan Carter used the music, together with the scores of *Fireworks*, the *Circus Polka* and *Ode*, as the basis for a ballet called *Feuilleton*, which was produced at the Bayerische Staatsoper, Munich.

2. Register of Works

84. CONCERTO IN D[1]

For string orchestra.[2] Composed at Hollywood between the beginning of 1946 and 8 August 1946. 'Dedié à la Basler Kammerorchester et son chef Paul Sacher.' Published by Boosey & Hawkes, London,[3] 1947. Duration: *c.* 12 minutes. First performance, Basler Kammerorchester, Basel, 27 January 1947, conducted by Paul Sacher. The manuscript full score (in pencil) is in the collection of Dr. Paul Sacher, Pratteln, Basel. The manuscript dedication reads 'String Concerto in D dedicated to the Basler Kammerorchester and his conductor Paul Sacher'. Another copy of the full score was in the composer's collection [C 87] and is now in the Library of Congress, Washington, D.C.

   I. *Vivace* ♩. = 126
  II. *Arioso: Andantino* ♩ = 60
 III. *Rondo: Allegro* ♩ = 126

Composition

    The *Concerto in D* was Stravinsky's first European commission for over twelve years. Early in 1946 Paul Sacher asked him if he would write a piece to celebrate the twentieth anniversary of the Basler Kammerorchester; and on 6 April when Stravinsky wrote accepting Sacher's proposal, the composition was already under way.

    The 'Basle' Concerto is about the same length as the 'Dumbarton Oaks' *Concerto*, but of lighter weight. An obsession with the interval of the minor second pervades the musical material. In the first movement it appears in the main theme as the augmented second (E sharp) and major third (F sharp) of the key of D major; and this lilting 6/8 theme rides lightly over a galloping *spiccato* accompaniment.[4] There is a *Moderato* middle section with rather thick lush harmonies, where the key drops a minor second to D flat major, and the obsessive interval appears as between the augmented fourth (G natural) and fifth (A flat) of the tonic of the new key. In the *Arioso* (key of B flat major) it becomes the leading note (A natural) and tonic (B flat); and in the *Rondo* (key of D major) it is still the leading note (C sharp) and tonic (D), much use

---

[1] Frequently known as the 'Basle Concerto'.
[2] According to Helmut Kirchmeyer (*Igor Strawinsky: Zeitgeschichte im Persönlichkeitsbild*, Regensburg 1958), Stravinsky wrote to Sacher on 31 August 1946 making it clear that he intended this Concerto to be played by an orchestra of 8 first violins, 8 second violins, 6 violas, 6 cellos and 4 double-basses.
[3] This was the first new composition of Stravinsky's to be published by the firm of Boosey & Hawkes, which had just acquired all the works of his formerly published by Edition Russe de Musique. This gave him an opportunity to make revised editions of many of them and so to create fresh copyrights.
[4] It should be noted that whereas the first edition of the score carried the indication ♩. = ♩ at fig. 16 where there is a change of time signature from 6/8 to 9/8 = 3/4, there was no corresponding indication of ♩ = ♩. at fig. 17 where the tempo reverts from 2/4 to 6/8. This was corrected in later editions of the score.

being made of the clash between the two notes in the busy semiquaver figuration that persists throughout this spiky movement.

The string writing in this concerto is fastidious and of the utmost refinement. Stravinsky varies the articulation of the accompanying figures with great discrimination. He distinguishes carefully between *staccato, spiccato* and *ben articulato. Legato* phrases are frequently accompanied at the unison or the octave by *staccato* or *pizzicato* notes. The string layout is occasionally broken down into small groups of solo players.

Revised Version

A short time after the first performance of the concerto, Stravinsky made a revised version of the score. His changes affected only the *Rondo* and consisted of the repetition of some of the existing material. Nothing new was composed.

In the original version, the *Rondo* had 109 bars. In the revised version, bars 32, 33 and 34 are repeated after bar 34 (i.e., just before fig. 80). Bars 30 and 31 are repeated after bar 36 (i.e., two bars after fig. 80). Bars 16, 17 and 18 are repeated after bar 99 (i.e., just before fig. 97). Bars 102 and 103 are repeated after bar 104 (i.e., just before fig. 98). This extra material brings the revised version of the movement up to 119 bars in length.

Ballet Productions

Although to the average listener in the concert hall, this concerto seems to be a most amiable composition, Jerome Robbins found the music 'terribly driven and compelled' and was inspired to convert it into a ballet of considerable ferocity. Remembering that in certain forms of insect and animal life the female of the species looks on the male as prey, he devised a scenario, in which two male intruders, despite a momentary show of amorous weakness on the part of a female novice, are ultimately castrated and killed by the militant females. Under the title of *The Cage*, the ballet was originally mounted by the New York City Ballet in New York in 1951, with choreography by Jerome Robbins, décor by Jean Rosenthal, and costumes by Ruth Sobotka. Nora Kaye danced the Novice. Ten years later it was revived in Paris by the Ballets U.S.A.

Other ballets using the same score have been *Concerto in D* produced at the Hamburg Staatsoper in 1950 with choreography by Dore Hoyer, and *Attis und die Nymphe* produced at the Württembergische Staatstheater, Stuttgart, in 1959 with choreography by Werner Ulbrich.

85. LITTLE CANON – PETIT CANON POUR LA FÊTE DE NADIA BOULANGER

For two tenors. Words by Jean de Meung. Composed at Hollywood for Nadia Boulanger's birthday. Unpublished. One manuscript is in the collection of

Nadia Boulanger; another (dated 16 September 1947) is in the composer's collection [C 89].

86. ORPHEUS – ORPHÉE

Ballet in three scenes (3.2.2.2 – 4.2.2.0 – timpani, harp – string 5tet). Composed at Hollywood in 1947 and finished on 23 September 1947. Published by Boosey & Hawkes, 1948. Duration: *c*. 30 minutes. First performance, Ballet Society, New York, 28 April 1948. The manuscript full score is in the possession of the University of California at Berkeley; and some manuscript sketches are in the composer's collection [C 90].

Scene One

1.[1] Orpheus weeps for Eurydice. He stands motionless, with his back to the audience. Some friends pass bringing presents and offering him sympathy. *Lento sostenuto* ♩=69
2.   'Air de Danse': *Andante con moto* ♪=112
3.   'Dance of the Angel of Death.' The Angel leads Orpheus to Hades. *L'istesso tempo*
4.   *Interlude.*   The Angel and Orpheus reappear in the gloom of Tartarus. *L'istesso tempo*

Scene Two

5.   'Pas des Furies' (their agitation and their threats). *Agitato in piano* ♩=126. – *Sempre alla breve ma meno mosso* ♩=98
6(a) 'Air de Danse' (Orpheus). *Grave* ♪=63. *Un poco meno mosso* ♪=96
7.   *Interlude*   The tormented souls in Tartarus stretch out their fettered arms towards Orpheus, and implore him to continue his song of consolation. *L'istesso tempo*
6(b) 'Air de Danse' (concluded). Orpheus continues his Air. *L'istesso tempo*
8.   'Pas d'Action': Hades, moved by the song of Orpheus, grows calm. The Furies surround him, bind his eyes and return Eurydice to him. (Veiled curtain.) *Andantino leggiadro* ♪=104
9.   'Pas de deux' (Orpheus and Eurydice before the veiled curtain). Orpheus tears the bandage from his eyes. Eurydice falls dead. *Andante sostenuto* ♪=96
10.   *Interlude* (Veiled curtain, behind which the décor of the first scene is placed.) *Moderato assai* ♩=72
11.   'Pas d'action.' The Bacchantes attack Orpheus, seize him and tear him to pieces. *Vivace* ♩=152

---

[1] The different movements are not numbered in the score.

Original Compositions

Scene Three

> 12. 'Orpheus's Apotheosis.' Apollo appears. He wrests the lyre from Orpheus and raises his song heavenwards. *Lento sostenuto* ♩ = 69

Composition and Treatment

Since the Renaissance, every century has brought a new conception of the Orphic myth in terms of music in the theatre: Monteverdi's at the outset of the seventeenth century; Gluck's in the eighteenth; Offenbach's in the nineteenth; and Stravinsky's in the twentieth. This score was commissioned by Lincoln Kirstein for the Ballet Society of New York in 1947; and in composing it, Stravinsky worked in close collaboration with George Balanchine, who was responsible for the choreography. As will be seen from the above scenario, the neo-Orphic version of the legend was followed, which includes the episode where Orpheus, after Eurydice's second death, is dismembered by the Bacchantes.

About this time Stravinsky had been studying the music of Monteverdi and his contemporaries: so it is not surprising to find that his score has something of the same translucent emotion and noble proportions as Monteverdi's own *Orfeo*. Restraint is its distinguishing characteristic. With the exception of the Dance of the Bacchantes, all the music is pitched *mezza* or *sotto voce*. Even the music for the Furies (in Stravinsky's own words) 'is soft and constantly remains on the soft level, like most of the rest of the ballet'.

Orpheus's lyre is translated into sound in terms of the harp, which is treated as a *concertante* instrument, as in the slow movement of the *Symphony in Three Movements*. It is particularly to the fore in the second 'Air de Danse' (no. 6), where Orpheus moves Hades with his song. Stravinsky is most successful in rendering this song in ballet terms – that is to say, instrumentally, not vocally – and his success is even more striking when in the 'Apotheosis', after the death of Orpheus, the harp interrupts a fugue (between two horns) with two brief interjections that are intended to be a reminder of the earlier song. As Stravinsky said when he played this passage to Nicolas Nabokov at Christmas 1947, 'Here in the Epilogue it sounds like a kind of . . . compulsion, like something unable to stop . . . Orpheus is dead, the song is gone, but the accompaniment goes on'.[1]

Music

At the opening of the score, the mourning harp maintains an even pulse with slow descending scales in the Phrygian mode, while the strings provide a five-part hieratic chorale.

---

[1] Quoted in Nicolas Nabokov's *Old Friends & New Music*. Hamish Hamilton, London, 1951.

441

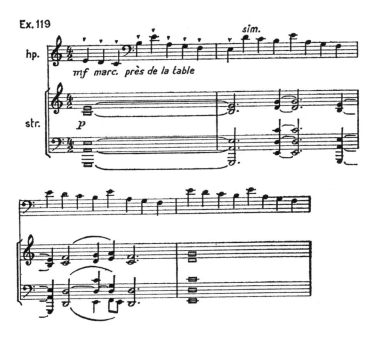

Ex. 119

In the following 'Air de Danse' the main theme is entrusted to a solo violin. This movement is in B flat minor; and as in the 'Basle' Concerto, the violin hesitates between two notes a semitone apart (E natural and F natural) before its melody gets properly launched. At first the violin's capricious arabesques are doubled by the flute; but later the two instruments imitate each other on independent though similar lines, with an effect of elaboration rather than counterpoint. After a middle section in D major with a horn solo, there is a reprise of the opening section, this time with a double spray of imitation by two flutes instead of one.

The next extended number is the 'Pas des Furies' at the beginning of the second scene. Its main theme is like a staircase with shallow risers and broad treads built on the ascending scale of G minor over a perpetually agitated *spiccato* quaver accompaniment from some of the strings. Halfway through the movement the key changes from G minor to C sharp minor, and the tempo slows down. The rising scale motive is still there; but now it is shadowed by the violas playing in C major. This independent C major line persists until the end of the movement – like a metal thread running through the paper of a banknote.

The second 'Air de Danse' is a recitative for harp accompanied by strings (one half playing with the bow, the other half pizzicato), followed by an air for two oboes accompanied alternately by harp and strings.

Ex. 120

Orpheus stops his song; but the lost souls in Tartarus implore him to continue (*Interlude*). He does so; and this time the air is entrusted to the harp, and there is canonic elaboration from the cor anglais and oboe.

A short 'Pas d'action' leads to the 'Pas de deux' for Orpheus and Eurydice. This is the climax of the ballet, a polyphonic Andante mainly for strings, in which the temperature rises only once above piano; and then a sudden short crescendo leads to a bar's silence, during which Orpheus tears the bandage from his eyes and Eurydice falls dead. This built-in silence is an integral part of the music.[1]

Ex. 121

[1] According to Robert Craft (in *Dialogues*) it was a suggestion of Balanchine's that led Stravinsky to extend the return of the F major string music at this point.

A brief *Interlude* (linked thematically with the *Interlude* between scenes one and two) leads to a 'Pas d'action', the 'Dance of the Bacchantes', who attack Orpheus and tear him limb from limb. The discords and violent syncopations of this powerful number recall parts of *The Rite of Spring*, but more particularly the last movement of the *Symphony in Three Movements*. The musical material is teased, worried and dismembered into twitching fragments. Finally, even the flesh disintegrates, and only the crunching of the bones remains. – 'Shall these bones live?'

Scene three follows with the 'Apotheosis of Orpheus'. The music of the opening scene returns; but this time the harp maintains its even pulse with slow ascending scales in the Dorian mode, while a muted trumpet doubled by a solo violin weaves its way through a majestic two-part fugue played by two horns,[1] the subject of which is an inversion of the violin part in the opening scene (see Ex. 119). This fugue is twice interrupted – or in Stravinsky's own words, 'cut off with a pair of scissors' – to make room for the two-bar harp solo previously mentioned. (In this illustration one of the fugal entries in the first horn part is marked with an asterisk.) The movement ends on a chord of D major with a flattened seventh.

Ex. 122

(*Ex. 122 continues on pp. 406*)

---

[1] Their parts are marked *cantabile maestoso ma sempre in mezza voce*.

Productions

In the case of *Apollo Musagetes* and *The Card Party* Balanchine had been presented with ready-made scores to work on; but for *Orpheus* he and the composer had ample opportunity to plan the ballet carefully together, scene by scene, number by number, with stop-watch exactitude. When the choreographing began, Stravinsky attended rehearsals to help ensure perfect coordination of music and dancing. The result of this collaboration was the sort of success that had occasionally been possible during the days of Diaghilev and his Russian Ballet, but had become extremely rare since Diaghilev's death. The choreography was one of Balanchine's best creations. Isamu Noguchi's scenery and costumes excited much praise. Nicholas Magallanes danced Orpheus, and Maria Tallchief Eurydice. After its first performance in New York on 28 April 1948, the Ballet Society toured the ballet extensively.

Other choreographers have worked on the ballet at various times – Aurel Milloss for the Festival of Contemporary Music, Venice, in 1948; David Lichine for the Ballets des Champs-Elysées, Paris, the same year; Rudolf Kölling for the Bayerische Staatsoper, Munich, in 1949; Erich Walter for Wuppertal in 1954; Yvonne Georgi for Hanover in 1955; and Tatjana Gsovsky for Frankfurt in 1961. A contemporary setting was devised for Alan Carter's adaption, *Herr Orpheus*, mounted at the Bayerische Staatsoper in 1957. But it was only right that in 1962 when the Hamburg Opera House wished to celebrate Stravinsky's eightieth birthday, it should have reverted to the original version in an all-Balanchine programme of *Apollo Musagetes*, *Agon* and *Orpheus*.

87. MASS

For mixed chorus and double wind quintet (trebles,[1] altos,[1] tenors, basses: 2 oboes – cor anglais – 2 bassoons – 2 trumpets in B flat – 3 trombones). The *Kyrie* and *Gloria* were finished in 1944.[2] The remaining movements followed in 1947, and the score was completed on 15 March 1948. Published by Boosey & Hawkes, 1948. Duration: *c.* 17 minutes. First performance, Teatro alla Scala, Milan, 27 October 1948, conducted by Ernest Ansermet. The manuscript full score is in the Library of Congress, Washington, D.C. Other manuscript material is in the composer's collection [C 91].

Kyrie ♩=66
Gloria ♩=72
Credo ♩=72
Sanctus ♩=56
Agnus Dei ♩=76

When Boris de Schloezer was writing the peroration to his monograph on Stravinsky (published in Paris in 1929), he could not resist trying to peep into the future. 'What ought we still to expect from Stravinsky, who is today in the prime of life and the full flowering of his genius? What will his next work be? In what new direction will he set out – to our pleasure and our surprise? Logically after *Apollo Musagetes* he ought to give us a Mass: but our logic is not necessarily his.'

Schloezer's prophecy was made shortly after Stravinsky had rejoined the Russian Orthodox Church in 1926; but in the event the direction taken by his music after *Oedipus Rex* and *Apollo* led, not to a Mass, but to the semi-dramatised *Symphony of Psalms*. It was not until 1942 or 1943 when by chance he came across some Masses by Mozart in a second-hand music store in Los Angeles that the idea of writing such a work himself began to take root. In his *Expositions* he writes: 'As I played through these rococo-operatic sweets-of-sin, I knew I had to write a Mass of my own, but a real one.' What he meant by a 'real one' was a Roman Catholic Mass that could be used liturgically, for the Orthodox Church proscribes musical instruments in its services and, as he explained in his *Expositions*, he could 'endure unaccompanied singing in only

---

[1] Children's voices are specified.
[2] See Robert Craft's 'A Personal Preface'. *The Score*, June 1957.

the most harmonically primitive music'. His views were expressed more fully in a conversation with Evelyn Waugh, as reported by Robert Craft.[1] 'My Mass,' said Stravinsky, 'was not composed for concert performances but for use in the church. It is liturgical and almost without ornament. In making a musical setting of the Credo I wished only to preserve the text in a special way. One composes a march to facilitate marching men, so with my Credo I hope to provide an aid to the text. The Credo is the longest movement. There is much to believe.' On another occasion he was reported as saying that he wanted to write 'very cold music, absolutely cold, that will appeal directly to the spirit'.[2]

The composition of the *Kyrie* and *Gloria* dates back to 1944; and there is a note by Robert Craft[3] mentioning that in Stravinsky's sketch-book the opening *a cappella* of the *Kyrie* differs from the score as finally printed in that it is accompanied 'by bassoons with a different bass from that of the chorus'. The remaining three movements followed in late 1947 and early 1948.

The *Credo* is the centre of the Mass, and the other movements are grouped, more or less symmetrically, round it. This was not the first time he had set the *Credo*; but his earlier composition (dated 1932) was a setting of the Slavonic words in plainsong, and his adaptation of this music to the Latin text was not made until 1949. The *Credo* in his Mass does not follow the plainsong treatment of the earlier *Credo*; but, as he rightly said, 'there is much to believe', and there are so many words to express this belief that in order to consume the words and their syllables, he had recourse to chanting, a device he had previously used to any marked extent only in *Zvezdoliki* and *Pater Noster*. The chords move slowly through their measured cadences, and the chanting goes on at a measured quaver pace and at an unvarying piano level, with the exceptions of three *marcato* passages (of two bars each) where the volume is increased to emphasis the words 'Ecclesiam . . . peccatorum . . . mortuorum', and of a crescendo passage at the words 'cujus regni non erit finis', after which the piano chanting recommences on the same chord as at the beginning of the movement. (See Ex. 123.) (Note the way the tenor line at 'Cujus regni non erit finis', moving in conjunction with the trebles, tries to reduce the interval between them from a tenth to an octave, but arrives at a minor ninth at the climax of the phrase and only reaches its octave goal when the music drops back to the E minor chanting as at the beginning.) The movement ends with an unaccompanied canonic 'Amen', like a separate porch attached to a building.

The main feature of the two flanking movements – the *Gloria* and *Sanctus* – is the deployment of solo voices. In the *Gloria*, a solo alto singing *mezzo forte*,

---

[1] In 'Stravinsky's Mass: A Notebook' printed in the Merle Armitage symposium on Stravinsky, New York. 1949.
[2] Quoted by Joachim Herrmann in a programme note for a Musica Viva concert, Munich, 6 July 1956.
[3] In 'A Personal Preface'. *The Score*. June 1957.

Ex. 123

with a long slow phrase that rises and then falls back, usually moving by consecutive steps of the scale, is answered by a solo treble, also singing *mezzo forte*, with an inversion of the theme. The two voices come together later in passages of conjunct movement, which are separated by soft passages of near-chanting in four-part harmony for the full choir. In the *Sanctus*, two solo tenors embellish the word 'Sanctus' with an uncial flourish and are answered by a loud snap 'Sanctus' from the whole choir. This snap rhythm is also a feature of the subject of the four-part fugue ('Pleni sunt coeli') for solo bass.

Ex. 124

Original Compositions

solo tenor, solo alto and solo treble, which is very close in mood to the two-part fugue in the final Apotheosis in *Orpheus* (see Ex. 122). There are two splendid *Più mosso* passages for full choir singing 'Hosanna' where the different limbs of the simple melody combine and mutate in a way that recalls the treatment of simple tunes in the Russian vernacular idiom used in *The Wedding*.

Ex. 125

The opening *Kyrie* contains about seven short contrasted episodes for full chorus accompanied by the orchestra, with cadences in at least seven different keys.

The final *Agnus Dei* consists of three *a cappella* passages for the choir introduced and separated from each other by a brief orchestral *ritornello* in ten parts, the mazy polyphony of which resolves each time in a straightforward D major triad. It ends with an orchestral coda, where one of the trombones picks up an unresolved seventh from the tenors and resolves it enharmonically through a final cadence in the form of a palindrome.

Ex. 126

2. Register of Works

The end of the *Sanctus* has elicited some rather surprising strictures from Ernest Ansermet, who was responsible for conducting the first performance of this *Mass*.[1] He says: 'The [*Sanctus*] ends with the chord of A major, in which a G/D fifth is inserted. This forms an agglomeration of notes, which the ear cannot take in and which is literally cacophonous. The fifth may be justified on paper by the movement of the parts leading up to the final chord; but once the auditor tries to analyse the sound, he has no idea what it really means. Perhaps Stravinsky intended to bring off some kind of effect; but such an effect is only justified in music (since music is a language) if it conveys a clear meaning to the auditor's conscious mind.' It is curious that Ansermet should take exception to this chord. The notes of the guilty fifth have been carefully approached by the two trumpets: the G comes at the end of a descending scale passage, the D at the end of a rising arpeggio passage based on the common chord of G major. When added to the A major chord, they suggest, instead of a full close, a modulation towards D with the tonic D anticipated in the chord of what now becomes the dominant seventh. If one of the cadences is to be queried, there might be better grounds for criticising the D major close to the three instrumental *ritornelli* in the *Agnus Dei*, for this triad seems almost too obvious and simple a solution to the maze of ten-part polyphony that precedes it and is apt (rather inappropriately) to remind the listener of the satirical treatment of the Lutheran chorales in *The Soldier's Tale*.

The instrumentation is most original – even for Stravinsky. In Robert Craft's words:[2] 'The orchestra which Stravinsky says "tunes" his choir never plays quite the same music. It adds tones, sounds different root tones than appear in the vocal parts, stresses, underlines, imitates, counterpoints, sets off and augments the chorus.'

Although it was Stravinsky's avowed intention that this *Mass* should be used for liturgical purposes, its first performance was in a theatre (the Teatro alla Scala, Milan), and performances as part of a church service have been comparatively rare. This is unfortunate in view of his hope that his sacred music would be found to register 'a protest against the Platonic tradition, which has been the Church's tradition through Plotinus and Erigena, of music as anti-moral' (*Con*).

---

[1] In *Les Fondements de la Musique dans la Conscience humaine*. Neuchâtel, 1961. His reference is actually to the *Gloria*: but this must be a misprint for the *Sanctus*.
[2] In 'Stravinsky's Mass: A Notebook', *op. cit.*

Original Compositions

88. THE RAKE'S PROGRESS – DER WÜSTLING – LE LIBERTIN – LA
CARRIERA D'UN LIBERTINO

An opera in three acts: fable by W. H. Auden and Chester Kallman. German
translation by Fritz Schroeder; French translation by André de Badet; Italian
translation by Rinaldo Küfferle. (2.2.2.2 – 2.2.0.0 – cembalo (pianoforte) –
timpani – string 5tet). The preliminary discussions with Auden about the
libretto took place in Hollywood in November 1947. Act I was written in 1948,
Act II in 1949/50, and Act III in 1950/51. The *Epilogue* is dated 7 April 1951.
Published by Boosey & Hawkes, 1951. Duration: *c.* 150 minutes. First performance, Teatro la Fenice, Venice, 11 September 1951, with chorus and
orchestra from the Teatro alla Scala, Milan, conducted by the composer. The
manuscript full score and summary sketches were given by the composer to
the University of Southern California, Los Angeles, on 9 December 1959.
Various manuscript sketches are in the collections of the composer [C 96] and
of Robert Craft, and a manuscript sketch of Act I was presented by the
composer to W. H. Auden.

Stravinsky on 'The Rake's Progress'

In his *Memories*, Stravinsky printed the letters he had received from Auden
during their collaboration over the libretto of *The Rake's Progress* and wrote
with considerable perspicacity about his librettist as a poet, thinker, moralist
and man. The following more general statement about the conception of the
opera was written for its first American production, in 1953.

For many years I have harbored the idea of writing an opera in English.
By this I mean a music originated in the English prosody and worked out in
my own way, as I did it before with Russian (*The Nightingale, Mavra, The
Wedding*), French (*Persephone*) and Latin (*Oedipus Rex, Symphony of
Psalms*) prosodies.

Six years ago [i.e. in 1947], in Chicago, at an exhibition of English paintings, I was struck by the various Hogarth series as by a succession of operatic
scenes. Shortly after, in conversation with my Hollywood friend and neighbour Aldous Huxley – who must be named godfather to my opera, for it
was he who suggested Wystan H. Auden as librettist – we discussed the
problems of English language opera.

In September 1947, having finished *Orpheus*, I informed my publisher,
the late Ralph Hawkes, of my plan to write a full length opera. The idea
pleased him very much and he later commissioned the libretto from Wystan
H. Auden. In November Auden joined me in Hollywood. We agreed on the
subject, a three-act moral fable, to be based on the *Rake's Progress* series
and drew up a synopsis of the plot, action, scene and characters. Returning

451

to New York, Auden took Chester Kallman as co-librettist. In March 1948, they delivered what is surely one of the most beautiful of libretti. The composition of the music occupied me three years.

When it was announced that I was at work on an opera, I read speculations in the press as to what I would do. These were invariably based on my two earlier 'operas' – *The Nightingale* and *Mavra*. *The Nightingale* seems more remote to me now than the English operas of three centuries ago or than the Italian-Mozartian opera which has been so neglected and misunderstood by the world of the musical dramatists. In so far as *Mavra* suggests any comparisons to my present work, it is in my conception of opera. I believe 'music drama' and 'opera' to be two very, very different things. My life work is a devotion to the latter.

The Rake's Progress is, emphatically, an opera – an opera of arias and recitatives, choruses and ensembles. Its musical structure, the conception of the use of these forms, even to the relations of tonalities, is in the line of the classical tradition.

Auden and Hogarth

William Hogarth was the first English painter to represent the life of his own days in a series of successive scenes. *The Harlot's Progress* (1731) was the first of these series; *The Rake's Progress* (1732–33) the second. Both sets were engraved and became very popular. The eight paintings of *The Rake's Progress*, at one time in the collection of Alderman William Beckford at Fonthill, were purchased by Sir John Soane in 1802 for £570 and are now in Sir John Soane's Museum, Lincolns Inn Fields, London. Their content may be briefly summarised as follows:

1. *The Heir*. Tom Rakewell on the death of his miserly father comes into his inheritance. The room where he is being measured for his suit of mourning shows everywhere signs of hoarded wealth. He is visited by a mother and her daughter, Sarah Young, whom he has seduced under promise of marriage and now proposes to buy off.
2. *The Levée*. The Rake appears in his ante-room surrounded by professors of dancing, fencing, music, prize-fighting and landscape gardening.
3. *The Orgy*. After a brush with the Watch, the Rake, who is drunk, spends the early hours of the morning with a bevy of whores at the Rose Tavern, Covent Garden.
4. *The Arrest*. The Rake, who has run through his first fortune, is about to be arrested for debt at the top of St. James's Street, when Sarah Young unexpectedly comes to his rescue with her slender savings.
5. *The Marriage*. To repair his fortune, the Rake marries an elderly, one-eyed, rich lady in the old parish church of St. Marylebone. Sarah Young,

with Tom's child in her arms, endeavours to enter the church in the hope of stopping the marriage.

6. *The Gaming House* (White's Club, St. James's Street). The Rake loses his second fortune in gambling.

7. *The Prison.* The Rake is committed to the Fleet Prison for debt. His enraged wife comes to taunt him, while Sarah Young, who is also visiting him with her child, is shown in a faint.

8. *The Madhouse.* The Rake has been removed to Bedlam, where he is visited by the still faithful Sarah Young, who weeps over him.

Auden's libretto[1] does not literally follow Hogarth's scheme. While Tom Rakewell is shown as a character vitiated by various kinds of dissipation, he is not really a debauchee; and it is typical of Auden's cast of mind – and it would have been quite foreign to Hogarth's conception – that one of the most moving moments in the whole opera is when in the middle of the brothel orgy the Rake recalls his broken lover's vows. To fit this conception, the figure of the town girl he had seduced (Sarah Young) must go, and her place is taken by the virtuous and constant country girl, Anne Trulove. Auden's view of the Rake's progress is fundamentally different from Hogarth's. Tom's fortune is not his inheritance from his father (as in the first of the Hogarth paintings), but is left to him unexpectedly by a rich uncle whom he hardly knows.[2] Auden diversifies the reasons for his downfall and shows him not only succumbing to the pleasures of the flesh (as in the brothel scene), but also indulging in the luxury of *l'acte gratuit* (his marriage to the monstrous Baba, undertaken not because he wanted her fortune, but in order to exercise a wanton freedom of choice) and in the megalomaniac belief that he could reform the ills of the world by exploiting a fantastic contraption for turning stones into bread.[3] To motivate these episodes, he invents a new character, Nick Shadow, who is meant to be the Rake's familiar, or *alter ego*, and ministers to his master's

---

[1] The libretto, which for the sake of brevity is here usually referred to as Auden's, was in fact a work of joint collaboration by Auden and his friend Chester Kallman. Kallman wrote the latter part of Act I Scene 1 (after the aria 'Since it is not by merit'), and the entire third scene; the first scene of Act II to the end of Tom's aria, 'Vary the song', and the entire second scene; the first scene of Act III (except for the off-stage lines of Tom and Shadow) and the card-guessing game in scene two. And Auden wrote the rest. A rough draft of part of Act 1 Scene 2 exists in one of Auden's poetry notebooks.

[2] This change was made after Auden had sketched the first outline of the libretto (printed as an appendix to Stravinsky's volume of *Memories*). As he wrote to Stravinsky on 20 November 1947, 'Je crois que ça sera mieux si c'est un oncle inconnu du héros au lieu de son père qui meurt, parceque comme ça, la richesse est tout à fait imprévue, et la note pastorale n'est pas interrompue par le douteur . . .' (The last two words must be misprints for 'la douleur'.)

[3] In the first draft of the scenario this was a device for making gold out of sea-water. (See Stravinsky's *Memories*.)

A page from W. H. Auden's notebook containing a rough draft of part of Act I
Scene 2 of the libretto for *The Rake's Progress*

three expressed wishes (spoken in the opera, not sung) – for wealth, happiness, and the power to become the saviour of mankind.

Shadow is a mixture of Mephistopheles, Mr. Hyde and the Admirable Crichton and displays remarkable ingenuity in keeping the plot in motion. But the ambivalence of the conception and the artificiality of the device are shown by the way the final catastrophe is precipitated.

In the penultimate scene, master and servant (now victim and devil) gamble for the Rake's soul. By sleight of hand, Shadow packs the cards against his opponent; but when by a sudden flash of inspiration the Rake evades defeat, the frustrated Shadow 'with a magic gesture' condemns him to insanity and sinks into the ground like a pantomime demon. Had the fable shown any tendency to build up a moral based on human behaviour, it would have collapsed at this point, for Tom is revealed as the victim, not of his own weaknesses and faults of character, but of an external malevolent supernatural power.

Nevertheless, the stage action as worked out by Auden is ingenious and varied. Sometimes the characters behave (in accordance with their names) like humours in a comedy; occasionally the action moves towards farce; and the final catastrophe of insanity, whatever its cause, does not fail to excite compassion and has the genuine ring of tragedy.

Auden's libretto is divided into the following scenes:[1]

Act I

Scene 1: The garden of Trulove's country cottage. (Spring afternoon)
Scene 2: Mother Goose's, a London brothel. (Summer)
Scene 3: Same as Act I, Scene I. (Autumn night)

Act II

Scene 1: The morning-room of Rakewell's house in London. (Autumn morning)
Scene 2: The street before Rakewell's house. (Autumn dusk)
Scene 3: Same as Act II, Scene I. (Winter morning)

Act III

Scene 1: Same as Act II, Scene 1. (Spring afternoon)
Scene 2: A churchyard. (The same night)
Scene 3: Bedlam

---

[1] It is worth mentioning that Stravinsky occasionally authorised a division into two acts instead of three, with the single interval coming after the street scene before Rakewell's house (II.2). This is the arrangement usually followed at Glyndebourne, for example.

Epilogue

The action, which in time covers the cycle of a year from spring to spring, can be summarised as follows:

Tom Rakewell (tenor), a young English gentleman, blessed by nature with good looks and a sound constitution, but loath to submit himself to the drudgery of discipline, is informed by a messenger, who calls himself Nick Shadow (baritone), that an unknown uncle of his has just died, making him his heir. He immediately engages Shadow as his servant and goes up to London from the country to take over his estate, leaving his sweetheart Anne Trulove (soprano) and her father (bass) behind. Once they are in London, Shadow introduces his master to the distractions of the metropolis, and when in due course Rakewell shows signs of becoming sated and bored, counsels him to secure happiness by acting in defiance of 'appetite and conscience'. Rakewell is persuaded by this paradoxical reasoning and on Shadow's suggestion decides to marry Baba the Turk (mezzo soprano), who by reason of her abnormally luxuriant beard has become one of the chief attractions of St. Giles's Fair.[1] Meanwhile, the deserted Anne has made up her mind to leave her home and come to London in search of Tom; but she arrives just after the wedding has taken place. The marriage, however, does not prosper, for Baba proves to be an incurable chatterbox, and Tom has no hesitation in leaving her. Egged on by Shadow, he sees himself in the role of a social reformer who, having invented and exploited an ingenious machine for converting stones into bread, is going to abolish want and poverty. His enterprise is duly floated, but collapses, and he himself becomes bankrupt. His house and chattels are sold up by Sellem[2] the auctioneer (tenor); Baba leaves him and returns to the Fair; and the final catastrophe comes when at the end of a year's service, Shadow leads him at midnight to a churchyard where there is a newly dug grave, reveals himself as the devil and claims as his wages his master's soul. After offering the unhappy Rake a choice of ways in which he can take his own life, the devil yields to his plea and agrees that his fate shall be decided by a game of cards. By amazing good luck, Rakewell wins; and the devil, baulked of his prey, curses him and condemns him to insanity. The final scene is laid in

---

[1] There is an important discrepancy between the stage directions of the full score and the vocal score at this point. In Act II Scene 1 Shadow brings Rakewell a broadsheet advertising Baba the Turk. In the full score (after fig. 47) there is the stage direction: *Rakewell looks at the broadsheet with his back to the audience in order that everyone in the theatre may see this broadsheet. He and Shadow look at each other. Then suddenly Rakewell begins to laugh . . .* Auden rightly objected to this in a letter to Stravinsky of 9 June 1951, which is printed in Stravinsky's *Memories*. A change was accordingly made in the vocal score, where the direction runs: *Tom looks up from the broadsheet. He and Nick look at each other. Pause. Then suddenly Tom begins to laugh. . . .*
[2] In some of his early music sketches, Stravinsky misspelled this name 'Selim'; but there is no oriental touch about the character!

Original Compositions

Bedlam,[1] where Rakewell, who thinks that he is Adonis and the other Bedlamites characters from classical mythology, awaits the visit of his beloved Venus. Anne finds him there; and Tom, after begging her forgiveness, dies.

In the *Epilogue*, Anne, Baba, Rakewell, Trulove (Anne's father) and Shadow come on the stage before the curtain without their wigs and point the moral of the fable in a kind of vaudeville finale.

> *So let us sing as one.*
> *At all times in all lands*
> *Beneath the moon and sun,*
> *This proverb has proved true,*
> *Since Eve went out with Adam:*

> *For idle hands*
> *And hearts and minds*
> *The Devil finds*
> *A work to do,*
> *A work, dear Sir, fair Madam,*
> *For you – and you!*

From this it will be seen that the only close borrowings from Hogarth are the general idea of the Rake's progress, his name of Tom Rakewell, and the brothel and Bedlam scenes.[2]

Composition and Treatment

It is interesting to find[3] that to begin with Stravinsky had the idea that just as in *The Soldier's Tale* the Soldier had his fiddle and in *Orpheus* Orpheus had his lyre (harp), so the Rake might be given a fiddle in the Bedlam scene;[4] and there was also the possibility that this instrument might (in Auden's words) have 'run through the story'. But as soon as the collaborators got together, the idea was dropped.

From the outset Stravinsky's guiding principle was to write an opera in what he called the 'Italian-Mozartian' style. To Nicolas Nabokov, who spent the Christmas of 1947 with him, he explained how he intended to treat Auden's

---

[1] When setting this scene, Stravinsky may have recalled Nikolai M. Karamsin's vivid account of his visit to Bedlam during his stay in London in July 1790 as described in his Letters of a Russian Traveller published in the Moscow Journal in 1791–92.
[2] In this, the opera differs from the ballet of the same title (now in the repertory of the Royal Ballet, Covent Garden), for Gavin Gordon's scenario and Ninette de Valois's choreographic tableaux are directly based on seven of the Hogarth pictures.
[3] From a letter written by W. H. Auden on 12 October 1947 and printed in Stravinsky's *Memories*.
[4] In Hogarth's picture, it is one of the Bedlamites, and not the Rake, who plays the fiddle, wearing a music book on his head like a hat.

libretto. 'I will lace each aria into a tight corset,' he said.[1] The link with Mozart was a strong one. While Auden was staying with him in Hollywood in the autumn of 1947, they attended a two-piano performance of *Così fan Tutte*; and the same opera provided almost the only music he would listen to, whether on the piano or on his gramophone, while he was composing the score.[2] There are also several close links with *Don Giovanni*.' The feeling of supernatural horror in the midnight scene in the churchyard, when the Rake and the devil gamble for Rakewell's soul, is similar to the atmosphere in the cemetery when Don Giovanni and Leporello confront the statue of the Commendatore; and the quintet in the *Epilogue* recalls the sextet at the end of *Don Giovanni*. In the course of an interview with Emilia Zanetti shortly before the première,[3] Stravinsky expressed the view that the Auden-Kallman libretto for *The Rake's Progress* was as good as, if not better than, da Ponte's libretto for *Don Giovanni*. High praise indeed!

The numbers of the opera are clearly marked in the score and consist of recitative (both dry and accompanied), arioso, airs, ensembles (such as duet, trio and quartet), and choruses. The types of aria include a cavatina (for Tom) and a cabaletta (for Anne). There is nothing to show that Stravinsky has been affected by any operatic developments subsequent to Donizetti and middle-period Verdi.

Although in *Babel* he had already tried his hand at setting two verses of the Bible in the English Authorised Version, *The Rake's Progress* was his first major assignment with the English language. When Auden handed over the final libretto of the opera to Stravinsky at Washington D.C. at the end of March 1948, he also introduced a friend of his, the twenty-four year old Robert Craft; and Stravinsky was so taken by Craft's enthusiasm that he invited him to join his household in Hollywood as a kind of secretary-assistant. Among other things, Craft was required to carry out certain jobs connected with *The Rake's Progress*, the most important of which was that he should pronounce and repeat the lines of the libretto. As Craft says,[4] 'Stravinsky's English was perhaps too original when I first knew him, and his Russian domesticity did little to vulgarize it . . . Stravinsky would invite comment on his settings of words and phrases but develop ingenious compromises rather than accede to suggestions. (For example, there were not enough notes to cover the final syllables of "questioning", "initiated", "gentlemen". When this was pointed out to him he added rhythmic stems in parenthesis. . . .) The claims of English stress and accent did not trouble him very deeply. He was far more concerned with singability, with vowel sounds in vocal ranges, with

[1] Quoted in Nabokov's *Old Friends and New Music*. Hamish Hamilton, London, 1951.
[2] See Robert Craft's 'A Personal Preface'. *The Score*, June 1957.
[3] *Guida al 'The Rake's Progress'*. XIV Festival Internazionale di Musica Contemporanea: Venice, 1951.
[4] Robert Craft. *op. cit.*

the effect of words on vocal quality and the other way round. . . . For example, whatever the last word of Act I may originally have been – it was not "heart" – Stravinsky, refusing to believe it was a good word for a final high C, wrote the lower C; the high C came at Auden's request and only after he had supplied a new rhyme. Stravinsky was keener than the librettists themselves that every word should be heard.'

The airs, ensembles and choruses are generally written in verse, the recitatives in prose. He adheres to the old distinction between dry and accompanied recitative; but although in the former he does not scruple to adapt the familiar cadential formulae to his own purposes,[2] they never degenerate into *clichés*. The various numbers in this score are bound together by a deliberate scheme of tonalities; and the modulations as cued by the passages of recitative play an important part in this. Each of the nine scenes is a separate entity. Apart from the flourish of horns and trumpets which introduces the opera – as the composer himself calls it, 'not an overture, or a prelude in the real sense, but simply the equivalent of *"on va commencer"* ' – the only scene to boast an instrumental prelude is Act III Scene 2.

The first scene of the first act is a clear and convincing piece of exposition. At the outset, the idyllic romance between Tom and Anne is briefly but firmly sketched; and the pastoral note of the rural setting is as successfully conveyed by the charming introduction (for oboe, English horn, and two bassoons) to the opening duet 'The woods are green' as in the 'Pastoral' movement of *The Soldier's Tale*. The slightly sinister arabesque on the cembalo that greets Shadow's sudden appearance

Ex. 128

should be compared with the cimbalom entry for the fox in *Reynard* (see Ex. 25). The chorus of Roaring Boys and Whores in the Brothel Scene is framed by a bustling instrumental setting of such light musical substance that Tom's C sharp minor cavatina, 'Love too frequently betrayed', with its burbling clarinet arpeggios, makes all the deeper impression when it comes. This, together with the following Gluck-like chorus of whores, 'How sad a

---

[2] Similar treatment of modulatory cadences in *The Card Party* is illustrated in exs: 89a and 89b.

song', is one of the most moving moments of the whole opera. The final *Lanterloo* chorus, with its distorted echo of 'Oranges and Lemons', has a wry folksong flavour about it. The third scene is an extended scena for Anne alone, ending with a brilliant cabaletta.

It must be admitted that the opera skates over some thin ice in Act II. Shadow's introduction of the idea of Rakewell marrying Baba the Turk leads to some rather light-weight note-spinning. The middle scene, with its sequence of arioso, duet and trio, is of greater interest – particularly the last number where Anne and Tom sing a serious duet, with grotesque interjections from Baba, who remains inside her sedan chair but pokes her head out of the curtains for each remark. Although the librettist has shown great ingenuity in writing a plethora of scatty lines for Baba's patter aria at the beginning of Scene 3 and the composer has matched it with a correspondingly fussy *moto perpetuo* accompaniment, the aria itself is not so effective as the stage action that accompanies the second part of it, where Baba strides about the stage smashing everything she can lay hands on. The pantomime of the stone-into-bread machine is accompanied by a strange squeaking piece of music that seems to be constructed to the same sort of formula as the Song of the Mechanical Nightingale in *The Nightingale*. But the final duet, 'Thanks to this excellent device', seems rather vapid; and the act ends on an anti-climax.

The opera makes a remarkable recovery in Act III. The auction is by far the most successful of the various fantastic episodes devised by Auden, and Stravinsky's setting of Sellem's aria and the bidding scene is a masterly piece of scherzo writing. Nonsense verses like the following:

> *La! come bid.*
> *Hmm! come buy.*
> *Aha! the it.*
> *This may be salvation.*
> *Poof! go high.*
> *La! be calm.*
> *Hmm! come on.*
> *Aha! the what.*

set him the same sort of problem as the Russian *pribaoutki* he had tackled thirty-five years previously, and he solves the conundrum with the same *éclat*. Now that there is no longer any need for Baba to behave grotesquely, she comes to life as a real character, and perhaps her most memorable moment is her exit:

> *You! Summon my carriage! Out of my way!*
> *The next time you see Baba you shall pay!*

The macabre Churchyard Scene is preceded by a brief instrumental prelude for strings (excluding double-basses). The dotted rhythm of the opening duet between Rakewell and Shadow recalls passages in some of Stravinsky's classical subject scores such as *Persephone* and *Orpheus*. The setting of the card game for cembalo solo is a masterly stroke; and every trick in the game comes off with startling musical effect.

Ex. 129

The opera rises to its greatest height in the final scene in Bedlam. In his madness, Tom believes himself to be Adonis; and when Anne comes to visit him, she humours his fancy by accepting the appellation of Venus and even adopts as her own the little melismatic trills with which he has started to decorate his song like wisps of straw. Her lullaby (accompanied only by two

Ex. 130

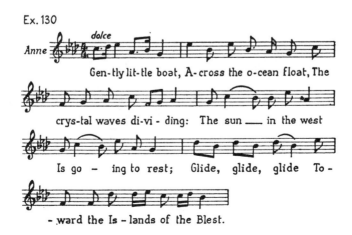

Gen-tly lit-tle boat, A-cross the o-cean float, The crys-tal waves di-vi-ding: The sun ___ in the west Is go - ing to rest; Glide, glide, glide To - ward the Is - lands of the Blest.

flutes) is a fascinating air, constructed of the simplest diatonic phrases assembled and put together with such strange irregularity as to contradict any implications of symmetry. It perpetually teases the mind with its unexpected turns of phrase.[1]

The final mourning chorus, 'Mourn for Adonis', could hardly be simpler or more moving. After its sombre close (on the first inversion of the chord of A minor), the A major *Epilogue* bursts out like a sudden squib. It goes off at a rattling pace; but lest the conductor, singers, players or public should think that everything is now straight-forward and they can afford to relax, the composer in teasing mood introduces a single bar of 5/8 in the middle of 158 bars of 2/4.

A Composer's Fingerprints

Since *Zvezdoliki* and *The Rite of Spring*, many of Stravinsky's works had shown a preoccupation with the oxymoron obtained by combining the major and minor modes, particularly as expressed by the simple statement of their thirds. In *The Rake's Progress* this device, resembling an appoggiatura, seems to be closely linked with the ill-fated love of Tom and Anne, and the score bears many marks of it – like fingerprints.

Right at the beginning of the opera, in the opening duet where Anne and Tom hail the springtime of the year, Anne's initial phrase shows a moment of minor hesitation followed by major resolution.

Ex. 131

Anne

The woods are green

---

[1] But in 1961 Robert Craft records Stravinsky as saying 'I shouldn't have repeated that flute lullaby *twice*' (*Dia*).

In the next stanza Tom's entry echoes her mood in a different key.

Ex. 132

And the device is cunningly used in the bridge passage leading to the reprise in the original key. (See Ex. 133.)

In the duettino towards the end of the scene, the minor third suffers an enharmonic change and becomes an augmented second; and it also appears in this form in the Brothel Scene. In the third and final scene of Act I, however, it reverts to the minor third. Between Anne's aria and cabaletta, there is a passage of recitative where she suddenly makes up her mind to leave her father and go to London in search of Tom. The passage quoted shows the minor third of G changing to the major third as she puts her trust in God, and the minor third of C changing to the major third as she is confirmed in her resolve (see Ex. 134).

There are a few traces of the minor/major appoggiatura in Tom's airs in Act II; and it returns with explicit emphasis in the Bedlam Scene where Tom's

Ex. 133

arioso opens in the same key as his duet with Anne at the beginning of the opera (see Ex. 135).

After the moving recognition scene between Anne and Tom and Anne's lullaby (see Ex. 130), Tom falls asleep. There follows a brief duettino between her and her father ('Every wearied body must late or soon return to dust').

Here the voices and part of the accompaniment are in the key of G major, while the bass line (cellos and double-basses) follows an independent course in B flat major. Consequently the minor third of G (B flat) is present or implicit all the way through – just like the C major strand in the violas that runs throughout the C sharp minor texture of the 'Dance of the Furies' in *Orpheus*.

Ex. 134

Ex. 135

2. Register of Works

The final appearance of the minor/major appoggiatura comes in Tom's last recitative just before his death. Above a shifting harmonic web provided by the orchestra, his melisma appears to be first in the key of A flat with minor third (C flat), then in A flat with major third (C natural); and ultimately these two notes have their bitter-sweet irresolution solved enharmonically when they become the fifth and minor sixth in the key of E minor.

Original Compositions

Productions

Any one of the great opera-houses of the world would have been proud to present the first performance of *The Rake's Progress*; but as Stravinsky said in his interview with Emilia Zanetti,[1] the work was written for modest forces, both vocally and instrumentally – '*musica da camera*' he called it – and that explains why for its première he preferred a modest-sized opera-house like the Teatro La Fenice, Venice, to the Metropolitan Opera House, New York, the Royal Opera House, Covent Garden, or the Teatro alla Scala, Milan.

The production formed part of the 14th International Festival of Contemporary Music, Venice. Carl Ebert was the producer. The Teatro alla Scala supplied the chorus and orchestra; and the cast was as follows:

Trulove	Rafael Ariè
Anne	Elisabeth Schwarzkopf
Tom Rakewell	Robert Rounseville
Nick Shadow	Otakar Kraus
Mother Goose	Nell Tangeman
Baba the Turk	Jennie Tourel
Sellem	Hugues Cuénod
Keeper of the Madhouse	Emanuel Menkes

The first rehearsals took place at the Scala; and later singers and players moved from Milan to Venice.

Robert Craft has written a very vivid account of the first night at the Fenice on 11 September 1951.[2]

'When the lights were dimmed and Stravinsky entered the pit, the applause that greeted him stratified into three areas: from the entire house, a general applause paid tribute to his great stature (what he would call his "credentials"); from the expensive seats, an applause of welcome for a major social event; from the galleries, the applause of expectancy in the promise of a master at the height of his powers presenting his largest work. Stravinsky conducted with his usual dignity, and with a firmness and intensity that no other conductor is able to bring to his work. This was the most memorable feature of a performance that – given the circumstances of a mere three weeks preparation – was less than ideal. . . . By the end of the second act there was an excitement and enthusiasm in the air appropriate to the first performance of a great opera. The Graveyard and Bedlam scenes are among the most moving ever written, and they did not fail to move that first audience. . . . Stravinsky was given an ovation. It was one a.m. before the theatre was cleared and six o'clock before we got to bed.'

---

[1] *Guida al 'The Rake's Progress'*. Venice, 1951.
[2] Robert Craft, ' "The Rake's Progress" in Venice.' Printed in the programme for the production by the Boston University Opera Workshop at the Esquire Theatre, Boston. (17 and 18 May 1953.)

Other productions of the opera followed speedily in Western and Central Europe; and Stravinsky thought particularly highly of Ingmar Bergman's production which he saw at Stockholm in September 1961. The opera reached the Metropolitan Opera House, New York, on 14 May 1953, the Opéra Comique, Paris, on June 18th of the same year, and the Glyndebourne Opera Company brought it to the Edinburgh Festival later that summer (25 August). Early in 1962 it entered the repertory of the Sadler's Wells Opera Company in London. It shares with some of the operas of Benjamin Britten the distinction of being one of the most successful operas written after the Second World War.

Transcription

Lullaby from 'The Rake's Progress' recomposed for two recorders (soprano and alto). Published by Boosey & Hawkes, 1960. Anne's lullaby from the third act (see Ex. 130), whose verses are accompanied by only two flutes, is here recomposed for two recorders. There is a very ingenious instrumental adaptation of the choral comment between the verses.

89. CANTATA

For soprano, tenor, female chorus, and a small instrumental ensemble (two flutes, oboe, English horn (doubling oboe II), and violoncello). Composed between April 1951 and August 1952. Published by Boosey & Hawkes, 1952. Vocal score by the composer. Duration: *c.* 30 minutes. The published score bears the following dedication in a facsimile of the composer's holograph: 'This Cantata is dedicated to the Los Angeles Symphony Society[1] which performed it under my direction and for the first time on November 11th, 1952.' The MS full score, which was in the composer's collection [C 98], is now in the Library of Congress, Washington, D.C.

    I. *A Lyke-Wake Dirge* (Versus I), *Prelude*: chorus ♩= 52
    II. *Ricercar I*[2] – 'The maidens came' . . . : soprano ♪= 69
    III. *A Lyke-Wake Dirge* (Versus II), *1st Interlude*: chorus ♩= 52
    IV. *Ricercar II* – 'Tomorrow shall be . . .' (Sacred History): tenor ♪= 108
    V. *A Lyke-Wake Dirge* (Versus III), *2nd Interlude*: chorus ♩= 52
    VI. *Westron Wind*: soprano and tenor ♩= 136
    VII. *A Lyke-Wake Dirge* (Versus IV), *Postlude*: chorus ♩= 52

In a programme note for the first performance by the Los Angeles Chamber Symphony Orchestra, Stravinsky wrote as follows:

---

[1] This is a misnomer for the Los Angeles Chamber Symphony Society.
[2] According to Helmut Kirchmeyer (*Igor Strawinsky: Zeitgeschichte im Persönlichkeitsbild*), the *Ricercar I* was the first part of the *Cantata* to be composed and was originally scored for two flutes and cello.

Original Compositions

My Cantata for solo soprano, solo tenor, female chorus, and instrumental quintet of two flutes, two oboes (the second interchangeable with English horn) and cello was composed between April 1951 and August 1952. After finishing *The Rake's Progress* I was persuaded by a strong desire to compose another work in which the problems of setting English words to music would reappear, but this time in a purer, non-dramatic form. I selected four popular anonymous lyrics of the fifteenth and sixteenth centuries, verses which attracted me not only for their great beauty and their compelling syllabification, but for their construction which suggested musical construction.

Three of the poems are semi-sacred. The fourth, *Westron Wind*, is a love lyric. The Cantata is, therefore, secular. It begins with a short instrumental prelude in the Phrygian mode, followed by the *Lyke-Wake Dirge*, a chorus whose seventeen bars, also modal except for the final cadence to D major, are repeated exactly to accommodate both the first and second stanzas. The next four stanzas of the Dirge are heard as first and second interludes, before and after the solo pieces for soprano and tenor. The music for all nine stanzas of the Dirge is the same, and the instrumental prelude is repeated before the third, fifth, and seventh stanzas. Then, after the duet for soprano and tenor, the last three stanzas form a postlude, with the rhythm of the last stanza changed slightly, and· the whole ending on an instrumental cadence to the 6/4 position of A major. Throughout, the chorus is in either two- or three-part harmony, with the sopranos and altos dividing alternately to form the third part.

The Maidens Came is a Ricercar for Soprano and instrumental quintet. I use the term '*Ricercar*' not in the sense that Bach used it to distinguish certain strict *alla breve* fugues, as for example the six-part Ricercar in the *Musical Offering*, but in its earlier designation of a composition in canonic style. In *The Maidens Came*, the canonic structure is obvious. In the first section, the English horn inverts the motion of the canon proposed by the flute. In the second section, the flute inverts a canon with the voice, while in the fourth bar the oboe takes up the canon in the original form, at the unison. Sectionally, in terms of A and B, the form of the piece could be charted like this: A, B, A, B, A, recitative, C (prayer). A is a section of ten bars in D minor, whose strong modal feeling is undissipated even by a strong cadence to A major in the fifth bar and a return to D in the tenth. B is in G minor, but with a modal feeling. The second A and the second B are shorter sections which recapitulate and develop. The final A begins with the first flute following the voice part with a canon at the octave, at the distance of an eighth note, which canon is simultaneously inverted in the oboe two octaves below. This is followed by a strict recitative, *Right mighty and famus Elizabeth*, etc. The last twelve bars have the function of a coda; they are a prayer, based on a tonal-modal A, which is only strengthened by the pull to B in the sixth and seventh bars (which the listener will recognise by the parallel fifths in the flutes). A cadence to A is followed by an *Amen* which has a Plagal flavour because of harmonic fourths in the wood-winds and the final melodic fourths in the voice.

Tomorrow will be my dancing day, for tenor, cello, and flutes and oboes in pairs, is also a Ricercar in the sense that it is a canonic composition. Its structure is more elaborate than that of *The Maidens Came.* The piece begins with a one-bar introduction by the flutes and cello, the statement of the canonic subject which is the subject of the whole piece. This subject is repeated by the tenor, over a recitative style accompaniment of oboes and cello, in original form, retrograde form (or cancrizans, which means that its notes are heard in reverse order – in this case, in a different rhythm), inverted form, and finally, in retrograde inversion. The second and third Cantus

Ex. 137

cantabile ma non *f*

T.

To — mor - row shall be, shall be   my dancing day,

I would my true   love did so chance to see   the le - gend

of my   play.

Cancrizans repeat respectively all and part of the first, but vary rhythmically; the second also adds imitation in the instrumental parts. The first two Ritornelli are each four-bars of 2/4; the last nine Ritornelli are each three bars of 3/4. The first two differ from the last nine in harmony, melody, and instrumentation (the two are scored for flutes and cello, and the nine for flutes, one oboe, and cello), but give the same sense of a refrain.

The fourth and sixth canons are nine bars long, the others are twelve bars long. The instrumentation of all of the canons is two oboes and cello. In the first canon, the second oboe proposes the original subject and the first oboe takes it up at the minor third above, while the tenor sings it in inverted form. The second canon begins with the voice singing the Cantus in cancrizans form, but transposed down a tone, with the first oboe, also in cancrizans form, a minor third below; the cello is in original form a fourth below. The third canon is identical with the first. In the fourth canon the first oboe follows the second at the interval of a second while the voice transposes the Cantus in inverted form down a minor third to A. In the three last bars, the cello, which has been accompanying with a new rhythmic figure, plays the

Cantus in F, original form, while the voice and first oboe play it in A, original form. The fifth canon is identical with the first. The sixth begins with the Cantus in the voice in original form, while the canon in the oboe, also in original form, florid and agitato, imitates the rhythmic figure of the cello which is playing the Cantus in inverted form. The seventh canon differs from the first only by some rhythmic variation in the voice part. In the eighth canon the voice has the Cantus first in cancrizans and then in original position, against which the oboe has it in retrograde inversion and then in cancrizans. While the oboe plays it in cancrizans, the cello plays it in retrograde inversion. Then in the second half of the canon everything is transposed up a half step to C sharp major, where the cello has the Cantus in original form, and the second oboe in cancrizans. The last canon is identical with the first.

Westron Wind is a duet in simple song-form for soprano and tenor accompanied by the instrumental quintet with the second oboist playing the English horn. Though it contains much imitation, it eschews in its sweep the formal canons of the other pieces. The cello's characteristic ostinato song-style accompaniment, the staccato pianissimo at the end, and the exactly recapitulated first part are features of this piece.

This long note has been reproduced in full, partly because it is of special interest to have so detailed an analysis of one of Stravinsky's works from the composer himself, and partly to show the great contrapuntal care he expended on the two Ricercars. Such an extended display of counterpoint was a new feature in his work and testified to his great love of Bach. (Otto Klemperer, who saw much of him in Los Angeles about this time, has left it on record that *Bach's Well-Tempered Clavier* was his daily fare.[1]) But from the way the Cantus in the second Ricercar makes various appearances in its original version, inversion, retrograde version and retrograde inversion, it seems as if he were beginning also to show an interest in serial processes of composition; and this is confirmed by Robert Craft's statement[2] that he heard Webern's Quartet, op. 22, several times in January and February 1952 (shortly before writing the second Ricercar) and was deeply impressed by it.

The second Ricercar is a long, intense, and most impressive movement, reminiscent at times of Couperin's *Leçons de Tenèbre*. It is also a very testing piece for the vocalist, for its melodic line is almost continuous for the whole of its 165 bars, and the singer must perforce snatch what breath he can between the limbs of the long interlocking phrases.

The wild agitation of the *Westron Wind* duet recalls the mood of the Jocasta/Oedipus duet in *Oedipus Rex*.

Although the setting of the *Lyke-Wake Dirge* is hauntingly simple, it must

---

[1] Otto Klemperer, *Erinnerungen an Gustav Mahler*. Atlantis Verlag, Zurich, 1960.
[2] In 'A Personal Preface'. *The Score*. June 1957.

be admitted that the device of splitting it into four parts separated by settings of three completely different poems does not do justice to the cumulative effect of this poem as a whole; nor do its slow, slightly monotonous stanzas provide an ideal framework for the two Ricercars, each of which proceeds at a rather similar pace. But the *Cantata* as a whole will always fascinate listeners with its glimpse of new musical horizons that were about to be opened up after Stravinsky's classical period had reached its apogee with *The Rake's Progress*.

90. SEPTET

For clarinet, horn, bassoon, piano, violin, viola and violoncello. Composed between July 1952 and February 1953. Dedicated to the Dumbarton Oaks Research Library and Collection. Published by Boosey & Hawkes, 1953. Reduction for two pianos by the composer. Duration: *c*. 11 minutes. First performance, Dumbarton Oaks, Washington D.C., 23 January 1954, conducted by the composer. In the printed score there are three movements – the first untitled and the last unnumbered, viz.

    I. ♩=88
   II. *Passacaglia* circa ♩=60
       Gigue ♪. =112–116

Perhaps it is best to think of the work as consisting of

    I. *Sonata Allegro*
   II. *Passacaglia*
  III. *Gigue*

Fifteen years after the 'Dumbarton Oaks' *Concerto*, this *Septet* was written for the Research Library and Collection at Dumbarton Oaks; and it is therefore appropriate to find that the opening of its first movement is not dissimilar in mood to the opening of the earlier concerto. (The clarinet part is also

Ex. 138

cl.

hn.
bn.

N.B. The piano and string parts are omitted.

distantly related to the main theme of *Pastorale*.) Familiar too is the hesitant alternation between the major and minor thirds of the key. The movement is governed by a carefully graded sequence of tonalities. After the first subject (Ex. 138), the piano introduces a second subject section with a series of syncopated E minor chords, and this leads to a fugue for all six instruments (excluding the piano). The first subject returns in its original key; the second subject section is in D minor instead of E minor; and a short coda (*Meno mosso*) brings the movement to a close on a chord of the second inversion of A major, with a G/D fifth added. (This is almost exactly the same chord that Ernest Ansermet took exception to at the end of the *Sanctus* in the Mass.)

With the *Passacaglia*, however, the composition begins to move in a different direction and plunges into the same sort of contrapuntal complexities that distinguished the two Ricercars in the *Cantata*. In the initial statement of the

Ex.139a

main theme, the different motives are shared out between clarinet, cello, viola and bassoon. The theme is then treated as a basic set of sixteen notes,

Ex. 139b

and the nine subsequent variations are for the most part built up from this set in its original version, inversion, retrograde version and retrograde inversion by canons of different kinds and at various intervals. In the eighth variation, for instance, the clarinet, bassoon, piano and cello present the original version – but each in a different rhythm – while the horn presents the inversion, the viola the retrograde version, and the violin the retrograde inversion.

In the *Gigue*[1] Stravinsky moves a step further. He takes the eight different notes from the *Passacaglia* theme and turns them into a note row, viz.

Ex. 139c

It is clear that this row has two tonal centres, E and A. It is written in the score above the parts of the instruments concerned, and its various transpositions are also indicated whenever the subject enters on a different note.

---

[1] 'He was probably influenced in the choice of a gigue for his Septet by the Gigue in Schoenberg's Suite op. 29.' Robert Craft in 'A Personal Preface'. *The Score*. June 1957.

In an excellent analysis of this work,[1] Erwin Stein describes the *Gigue* as follows: 'There are no less than four fugues in the *Gigue*. The first, for strings, is immediately repeated by the piano. Superimposed on the three-part keyboard fugue, however, is another fugue for wind trio, the subject of which is on the same notes, but in a different rhythm. This double fugue concludes the first part of the movement. The second part is built on similar lines, but the subject is inverted. We have again a three-part fugue for the strings, followed by a double fugue for the piano and wind. The latter, however, is still more elaborate than in the first part: the fugue of the wind, in 3/8, is in cross-rhythms with the 6/16 of the *Gigue*; the entries of the wind comprise the subject's retrograde motion and inversion; and finally there is a triple stretto of the subject and its inversion – the inversion of the inversion being identical, of course, with the subject's original form. The strings re-enter for the last two chords only, which express both keys, E and A.'

Few works by Stravinsky show greater mastery of counterpoint or better repay intensive study than this *Septet*.

91. THREE SONGS FROM WILLIAM SHAKESPEARE

For mezzo-soprano, flute, clarinet and viola. Composed in the autumn of 1953. Dedicated to 'Evenings on the Roof' (Los Angeles). Published by Boosey & Hawkes, 1954. Reduction for voice and piano by the composer. Duration: *c.* 6 minutes 30 seconds. First performance at one of the 'Evenings on the Roof' concerts, Los Angeles, 8 March 1954, conducted by Robert Craft. The MS score was presented by the composer to Oscar Moss.

    I. 'Musick to heare', ♪ = 69
   II. 'Full Fadom five', ♪ = 112
  III. 'When Dasies pied', ♪ = 92

This was the first set of songs to be composed by Stravinsky since the *Four Russian Songs* of 1919. Whereas most of the songs he wrote about the time of the First World War were settings of Russian nonsense jingles (*pribaoutki*) or popular verses intended to amuse children, this new set was a series of art songs, like the *Three Japanese Lyrics,* and was designed as a further exercise in the contrapuntal explorations he had started in the *Cantata* and *Septet.* For his text he chose Shakespeare's VIIIth Sonnet 'Musick to heare', Ariel's song 'Full Fadom five' from *The Tempest,* and the Cuckoo's song from the antic in *Love's Labour's Lost.* (In 'Full Fadom five', the 'Ding-dong' burthen is included in the setting.)

---

[1] Erwin Stein, 'Strawinsky's Septet (1953)'. *Tempo.* Spring, 1954.

The Sonnet is based on a brief row of four notes

Ex. 140a

and its inversion

Ex. 140b

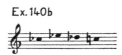

in various transpositions. The handling of this subdivision of the interval of a major third can be seen to advantage in the flute part in the introduction, where the clarinet and viola share a strangely simple little accompanying figure which consists of the first five notes of the scale of C major and provides a tonal framework.

Ex. 141a

The vocal part follows the flute part with various licences, e.g., octave transpositions and as much repetition of notes as is convenient in setting the words. Even so, it is curious to find the serial order lapsing in bars 26 and 27, and the insertion of an extraneous passing note (D natural) in the last bar but two of the vocal line,[1] viz.:

Ex. 141b

Sings this to thee _____ thou sin-gle wilt prove none _____

---

[1] Note that the printed score misprints this line: 'Sings this *for* thee thou single wilt prove none.' instead of 'Sings this *to* thee . . .'

2. Register of Works

The note rows of the other two songs carry quite strong tonal implications. In 'Full Fadom five', the only accidentals are flats; and this gives the music a slant towards the keys of D flat major/B flat minor and G flat major/E flat minor. In 'When Dasies pied', the note row for the voice is so contrived that the first half of it consists of notes from the scale of A flat major, while the second half consists of notes from the scale of C major. This dichotomy appears also in the accompaniment, where a feature is made of alternating fifths i.e., A flat/E flat followed by D natural/A natural, and A natural/E natural followed by E flat/B flat.

The songs contain a number of onomatopoeic effects. Bell sounds are suggested in Ariel's song, first by the *fp* attack of the viola on the minims of its opening theme accompanying the phrase 'Full fadom five they Father lies', and later by the two resonant pizzicato notes (at 'Ding dong, ding dong') on the viola's open D string. In the third song, the cuckoo is given its natural minor third (in the vocal part): but of greater interest is the nervous quavering trill (flute and clarinet) which is first heard during the line 'The cuckow then on everie tree', which is repeated between the two verses, and ultimately bursts out into a coda of flute arabesques spread over a bubbling clarinet tremolo that recalls the springtime ferment of 'Mazatsumi' (in the *Three Japanese Lyrics*) and the merry woodwind gurgles in some of the *Pribaoutki* and *Cat's Cradle Songs*.

When Stravinsky had finished these *Songs from Shakespeare*, he had a look at some of his earlier songs, and decided to instrument the *Two Poems of Balmont* for two flutes, two clarinets, piano and string quartet, and a selection of *Four Songs* from those composed during his Russian period for flute, harp and guitar.

FOUR SONGS

For voice, flute, harp and guitar, 1953/54 – see no. 43 (A).

92. IN MEMORIAM DYLAN THOMAS

Dirge-Canons and Song for tenor voice, string quartet and four trombones. Composed in February and March, 1954. Published by Boosey & Hawkes, 1954. Reduction for voice and piano by the composer. Duration: *c.* 6 minutes. First performed at one of the Monday Evening Concerts at Los Angeles, 20 September 1954, conducted by Robert Craft.

Stravinsky and Dylan Thomas

The score is prefaced by the following notes written by Stravinsky:

Since I began to get more and more acquainted with his work and later on, after I met him in person – in May 1953 – I cherished the project to compose an opera on a libretto to be done by Dylan Thomas.

He was as enthusiastic about it as I was and he wanted to arrange for his coming to visit me in California and put up the structure of this opera. In fact, he was on his way to meet me in Hollywood when he passed away suddenly after arriving in New York from England.

This was a terrible blow to me as well as to all those who knew Dylan Thomas's genius.

During the following months I thought of composing something to Dylan Thomas's memory. No poem of his could fit my purpose better than the one he had composed to the memory of his father.

I used these beautiful verses without changing them, of course.

Here my music is entirely canonic. It requires tenor voice and string quartet.

Having thus composed the Song I decided to add a purely instrumental prelude and postlude (called Dirge-Canons) which are antiphonal canons between a quartet of trombones and the string quartet.[1]

The complete name of the whole composition is:

In Memoriam Dylan Thomas
Dirge-Canons and Song

It was completed in the spring of 1954.

The world première was given by the Monday Evening Concerts at Los Angeles on September 20, 1954, Robert Craft conducting. Aldous Huxley pronounced a dedicatory address.

The opera project had been discussed at the first and only meeting between Stravinsky and Dylan Thomas, which took place in Stravinsky's bedroom at the Copley-Plaza Hotel, Boston, on the afternoon of 22 May 1953. This interview appears to have gone extremely well. 'As soon as I saw him,' says Stravinsky in his *Conversations*, 'I knew that the only thing to do was to love him. He was nervous, however, chain-smoking the whole time, and he complained of severe gout pains. . . . His face and skin had the colour and swelling of too much drinking.' There had already been an abortive attempt at joint collaboration early in 1952, when Michael Powell proposed that Stravinsky should write the music, and Dylan Thomas the verse, for a short film, 'a kind of masque, of a scene from the Odyssey', which would require 'two or three arias as well as pieces of pure instrumental music and recitations of pure poetry' (*Con*); but unfortunately the film plan came to nothing, as the necessary finance could not be found. This time, however, Stravinsky thought that Boston University

---

[1] 'While composing the *In Memorian Dylan Thomas* for his own choice of tenor and string quartet, Stravinsky requested a list of instruments expected to take part in the concert which would sponsor its first performance. When he knew for certain that four trombones would play in Schütz's *Fili Mi Absalon*, a cortège of mourning canons was added to the Thomas setting, canons for string quartet and four trombones.' Robert Craft, 'A Concert for St. Mark.' *The Score*. December 1956.

(whose Opera Workshop had just produced *The Rake's Progress*) would be prepared to assume responsibility for the commission.

According to Stravinsky, what Dylan Thomas had in mind was to write an opera 'about the rediscovery of our planet following an atomic misadventure. There would be a recreation of language, only the new one would have no abstractions; there would only be people, objects and words' (*Con*). John Malcolm Brinnin, who spent the evening with Dylan Thomas after he had returned from Stravinsky's bedside, says that seldom had he 'observed him in so buoyant a state of creative agitation;'[1] and Dylan Thomas gave him *his* version of the outline of the opera he had discussed with Stravinsky. 'They would do a "re-creation of the world" – an opera about the only man and woman alive on earth. These creatures might be visitors from outer space who, by some cosmic mischance, find themselves on an earth recently devastated and silenced by global warfare; or they might be earthlings who somehow have survived an atomic miscalculation. In either case, they would re-experience the whole awakening life of aboriginal man. They would make a new cosmogony. Confronted with a tree pushing its way upward out of radio-active dust, they would have to name it, and learn its uses, and then proceed to find names and a definition for everything on earth. The landscape would be fantastic – everything shaped and coloured by the dreams of primitive man – even the rocks and trees would sing.'

The idea was first-rate; and if the opera had come off, it might have had the same sort of relationship (in operatic terms) to *The Rake's Progress* as the *Symphony in Three Movements* had to the *Symphony in C* (in symphonic terms). But there were various snags.

Negotiations with Boston University for the commissioning of the new work fell through, and Stravinsky had to try to find financial support elsewhere. Meanwhile, Dylan Thomas's health was in a serious decline. Shortly after his conference with Stravinsky in Boston, he returned to Wales; but on 19 October he was back in New York for a number of public readings, after which it had been arranged that he should stay with Stravinsky in Hollywood. By then, however, he was in an advanced state of alcoholic poisoning, and this resulted in a severe 'insult to the brain', from which he never recovered. He died in St. Vincent's Hospital, New York, on 9 November.

Stravinsky was in Hollywood, awaiting a telegram that would announce the time of Dylan Thomas's arrival. 'On November 9th,' he writes in his *Conversations*, 'the telegram came. It said he was dead. All I could do was cry.'

Subsequently (in the course of an interview which the National Film Broadcasting Company filmed on the eve of his 75th birthday in 1957), he referred to Dylan Thomas as 'a wonderful poet', adding, 'I always have his portrait with me – I loved him very much'.

---

[1] John Malcolm Brinnin. *Dylan Thomas in America*. London, Dent, 1956.

Original Compositions

Composition

Dylan Thomas's poem 'Do not go gentle into that good night' has been much praised, and possibly over-praised. As can be seen from the use of 'gentle' and 'good night' in the opening line, sometimes the poet is able successfully to handle the ambivalence of words and phrases – sometimes not. Having adopted the form of the villanelle, he allows its highly organised scheme to dictate the poem's course, occasionally at the expense of poetic content. The opening exhortation to his father to rage against the approach of death emerges clearly; but the subsequent appeals to 'wise men', 'good men', 'wild men', and 'grave men' fail to provide satisfactory variations on the basic theme. Nevertheless, the main effect of the poem is unmistakable: an almost inarticulate cry of anger, despair, and fear – 'Rage, rage against the dying of the light'.

The formal pattern of the poem was a powerful stimulus to Stravinsky's appetite as a composer. The two reiterated lines (each of which has been quoted in the previous paragraph) gave him a cue for two refrains, which alternate at the end of each of the first five (three line) stanzas, and both of which appear at the end of the sixth and final stanza. For his setting, he chose a limited row of only five notes:[1] so, allowing for the inversion of the basic set, only nine out of the twelve notes of the chromatic scale are used.

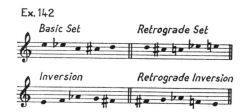

Ex. 142

Basic Set   Retrograde Set

Inversion   Retrograde Inversion

This restriction gives a vaguely tonal feeling to the work. The opening vocal phrase of the *Song* shows how the inversion (or retrograde inversion) at the augmented fourth can be made to overlap the retrograde set (or basic set).

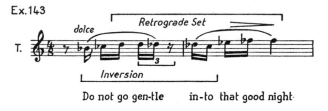

Ex. 143

dolce   Retrograde Set

Inversion

Do not go gen-tle   in-to that good night

---

[1] This row should be compared with the row used in the first of the *Three Songs from William Shakespeare* (see Ex. 140). In each case Stravinsky has confined his note row within the span of a major third. In the Shakespeare sonnet he has divided the third into only four notes; but in the *In Memoriam Dylan Thomas* composition he has used all the five chromatic notes.

2. Register of Works

Attention should be paid to the extraordinarily effective 'placing' of this phrase, with its rising cadence coupled with a diminuendo on the words 'good night', in the higher register of the tenor's voice. An identical cadence occurs at the end of the other refrain, 'Rage, rage, against the dying of the light'.

The whole composition is constructed according to the serial principle.

As mentioned in Stravinsky's notes prefixed to the score, the *Song* is for tenor and string quartet.

The instrumental *Prelude* and *Postlude* consist of antiphonal litanies that alternate between the trombone quartet (A) and the string quartet (B). In the *Prelude*, the scheme is A (i), B, A (ii), B, A (iii), the string quartet ritornello being constant, while the trombone canons are varied on each occasion. In the *Postlude*, the roles are reversed, the trombones taking the ritornello (B) and the string quartet taking over two of the canonic variations, viz. B, A (ii), B, A (i), B. A further variation on this symmetrical scheme is produced by the direction in the *Prelude* to the string quartet to play *in modo ordinario* and to the trombones to accentuate their notes as follows:

Ex. 144a

while in the *Postlude* the strings are muted and the attack of the trombones is altered by the addition of a staccato direction, viz.:

Ex. 144b

The score carries indications showing the theme and its inversions, reversions, and retrograde inversions in the Prelude only. Subsequently, in a letter of explanation the composer wrote, 'In correcting the proofs I forgot to erase in the Prelude these brackets left over from my final sketches where they were put *throughout* the work, thus complicating the reading of the instrumental and vocal score.'[1]

This work of compassionate homage transcends any weaknesses of Dylan Thomas's original poem and is one of Stravinsky's most moving compositions.

---

[1] This is quoted in Hans Keller's article 'In Memoriam Dylan Thomas: Strawinsky's Schoenbergian Technique', which appeared in *Tempo*, Spring, 1955, and contains an excellent analytic music example of the complete *Song*.

Original Compositions

93. GREETING PRELUDE

'For the eightieth birthday of Pierre Monteux.' – For orchestra (3.2.2.3 – 4.2.3.1 – timp., percussion, piano – string 5tet). Composed in 1955. Published by Boosey & Hawkes, 1956. Duration: *c.* 45 seconds. First performance, Boston Symphony Orchestra, 4 April 1955, conducted by Charles Munch.

This brief *jeu d'esprit* is based on the well-known tune '*Happy birthday to you*' by Clayton F. Summy. Stravinsky's account of its genesis runs as follows:

> I gave the downbeat to begin a rehearsal of Chaikovsky's Second Symphony in Aspen one day in the summer of 1950, when instead of the doleful opening chord, out came this ridiculously gay little tune. I was very surprised, of course, and quite failed to 'get it', as Americans say – the 'it' being that one of the orchestra players had just become a father. I confess that the shock of the substituted music and the change of emotions piqued me, and that for some time I considered myself the victim of a practical joke.

He remembered the tune, however, and in 1951, when invited to write a fanfare for a festival in North Carolina, set about composing canons on it. This particular project did not materialise; and in 1955 he turned it into what he called 'a kind of singing telegram' for the eightieth birthday of Pierre Monteux (4 April 1955).

The tune is stated by horns and piano, with each line (of the four-line stanza) echoed by the strings in diminution. It is then subjected to various typical serial devices. In the middle section, the tune moves to the bass (on bassoons, tuba and double-basses), while the cellos and violins play a rhythmically altered version of the tune in canon. The second violins break away from the first violins after three bars and provide a free counterpoint, while the violas start with the tune inverted and then run it in retrograde motion. The tune returns in the horns and piano, with a varied commentary from the strings.

A jovial, aphoristic work, but rather too short to make much effect.

94. CANTICUM SACRUM AD HONOREM SANCTI MARCI NOMINIS

For tenor and baritone soli, chorus and orchestra (1.3.0.3 – 0.4.4.0 – harp, organ – violas, double-basses). Latin text. Composed 1955. Published by Boosey & Hawkes, 1956. Vocal score by the composer. Duration: *c.* 17 minutes. First performance, St. Mark's Cathedral, Venice, 13 September 1956, conducted by the composer.

> *Dedicatio* ♩ = 60 (–69)
> I. 'Euntes in mundum' ♩ = 116
> II. 'Surge, aquilo' ♪ = 92

    III. *Ad Tres Virtutes Hortationes*
        Caritas ♩=108
        Spes ♩=108
        Fides ♩=108
    IV. *Brevis Motus Cantilenae* ♩=88
    V. 'Illi autem profecti' ♩=116

The manuscript full score is in the collection of Signora Adriana Panni, Accademia Filarmonica, Rome. The pencil manuscript of the piano reduction is in the Library of Congress, Washington D.C.

Stravinsky and Venice

VENISE INSPIRATRICE ETERNELLE DE NOS APAISEMENTS – these are the words inscribed on Diaghilev's tombstone on the island of San Michele. Like Diaghilev and all who are susceptible to the charms of Venice, who feel that, girt by the soft lapping water of the lagoons and canals, they have in some way re-entered the womb of our Mediterranean civilisation, Stravinsky had had a special affection for Venice for many years. Venice had witnessed an early performance of one of his neo-classical works, the *Piano Sonata*, in 1925; and just over a quarter of a century later it helped to launch his 'très grand bateau', as he called *The Rake's Progress*, one of the last works of his neo-classical period. He had conducted his *Capriccio* there as part of the 1934 Biennale, with his son Soulima as soloist.[1] The time had now come when Alessandro Piovesan on behalf of the organisers of the Venice Biennale International Festival of Contemporary Music wished to commission a new work from him and, in accepting this offer, he decided to make this composition particularly Venice's own – he would inscribe it to Venice's patron saint and design it for performance in the Saint's own cathedral.

Though he lacked direct practical experience of the acoustics of St. Mark's, he was certainly conscious of its special acoustical properties, and this awareness is shown in certain features of his composition. For instance, after *tutti* passages of some density and complexity he usually allows a pause for the sound to clear, and at such moments there may be a bass hangover from the previous block of sound. (See particularly the treatment of the *tutti* passages in the first movement.) He also employs antiphonal devices – sometimes (as in the first and last movements) between the orchestra and organ; at other times (as in the Spes section of the third movement) between the two solo voices and chorus. The mixed ensemble of instruments chosen for the orchestra (including organ) also conforms with Venetian tradition.

Some critics have suggested an analogy between the five movements of the *Canticum Sacrum* and the five domes of St. Mark's. What is evident is that the

---

[1] On this occasion he met Alban Berg in the green room at the Fenice after the performance (*Con*).

work is cyclical, the last movement being an almost exact retrograde version of the first, so that if a ground plan were to be sketched out, it would be something like this, with the *Dedicatio* as an entrance portico:

Composition

The *Dedicatio* runs as follows: 'Urbi Venetiae, in laude Sancti sui Presidis, Beati Marci Apostoli'. The text of the following five movements is taken from Vulgate.[1] (References to the equivalent passages in the Authorised Version are given in brackets.)

I. Evang. secundum Marcum XVI. 15. (*St. Mark XVI. 15*)
II. Canticum Canticorum IV. 16, V.1. (*Songs of Songs IV. 16, V.1*)
III. (a) *Caritas*
Deuter. VI. 5. (*Deuteronomy VI. 5*)
Prima Epistola Beati Joannis Apostoli IV. 7 (*I John IV. 7*)
(b) *Spes*
Libr. Psalm. CXXIV.1, CXXIX. 4, 5, 6. (*Psalms CXXV. 1. CXXX. 5–6*)
(c) *Fides*
Libr. Psalm. CXV. 10. (*Psalm CXVI. 10*)
IV. Ev. secundum Marcum IX. 22–23. (*St. Mark IX 23–24*)
V. Ev. secundum Marcum XVI. 20. (*St. Mark XVI. 20*)

The first and fifth movements deal with Jesus's exhortation to the eleven apostles (as recorded by St. Mark) – 'Go ye into all the world and preach the gospel to every creature' – and the fulfilment of his command. These movements are set for full chorus.

The second movement is lyrical in feeling. It is a dialogue between two lovers – the man who calls on the north and south winds to blow upon his garden; the woman who calls upon her beloved to come into his garden; and the man again, who after obeying her request calls on his friends to join him in eating and drinking. Stravinsky ignores the implications of this extract as a dialogue and sets it as a straightforward lyric for tenor solo.

The third movement is entitled *Ad Tres Virtutes Hortationes* and deals with the three Christian virtues of *Caritas, Spes* and *Fides.* Just as the central and longest movement of Stravinsky's Mass was the *Credo,* so here the central movement is the longest of the five, and by reversal of the usual Faith, Hope

---

[1] Some of the Vulgate references in the score are inaccurate.

and Charity order, special prominence is given to the Faith section with its emphasis on the importance of belief.

This serves as a direct cue for the fourth movement, which is a little scene illustrating the miracle of the casting forth of the dumb and deaf spirit:

> *Jesus said unto him, If thou canst believe, all things are possible to him that believeth. And straightway the father of the child cried out, and said with tears, Lord, I believe; help thou mine unbelief.*

Stravinsky calls this *scena* a *Brevis Motus Cantilenae*. He accepts its dramatic implications and sets it for baritone solo, with occasional support from the chorus.

As has already been mentioned above, the last movement represents the fulfilment of the Lord's command to preach the gospel, and the setting is identical with that of the first movement, except that it is in retrograde motion.

Ex. 145a

In the *Dedicatio*, the plainsong style of the vocal line is similar to that of the Mass, while the trombone accompaniment recalls the solemnity of the Dirge-Canons from *In Memoriam Dylan Thomas*. For the first half, the tenor and baritone soloists, singing in two parts, imitate the trombones which are also playing in two parts but in contrary motion. For the second half, the situation is reversed, and the trombones imitate the voices.

Ex. 145b

The first movement is built up by means of antiphonal contrasts between the chorus accompanied by full orchestra on the one hand, and the organ on the other. The opening chord (see Ex. 145a) is a bitonal aggregation of the first inversion of G minor (with the tonic omitted) and B minor. In conformity with Stravinsky's partiality for the third, the various harmonies oscillate round the two centres B flat and D natural. The final chord of the movement confirms the ascendancy of the key of D (see Ex. 145b). Within this broad wash of sound the chorus maintains a block of four-part hamony. The organ's ritornello, which twice breaks the continuity of the movement, is a nine-bar-long five-part modal invention (see Ex. 146b), where each part has its own limited note row, consisting of five, four, three, two and six notes respectively, moving from the upper line to the bass (see Ex. 146a).

Ex. 146a

Ex. 146 b
(♩=108)

org.

nonf e sempre legato

The music in this movement is closely linked with Stravinsky's neo-classical past.

The second movement takes a step forward into the serial future. At the same time it must be admitted that Stravinsky is writing a serial music that is still impregnated with tonal nuances. This is manifest from the series which is exposed in its original order by the tenor in his opening phrase:

Ex. 147 a
(♪=92)
mf

T. solo

Sur-ge a-qui-lo;___ et ve - - ni,ve - ni au-ster

Ex. 147 b

1 2 3 4 5 6   7 8 9 10 11 12

If the series is examined (see Ex. 147b). it will be seen that the notes of the first hexachord seem to group themselves round G as tonal centre, while the notes of the next hexachord group themselves round C. This sense of polarity is strengthened by the feeling that the penultimate notes in each hexachord (5 and 11) have something of the characteristics of a leading note, and also by the parallel relationship between notes 5, 6, 7, and 11, 12, 1, at the distance of a fifth. There are strong tonal implications in the two phrases formed by notes 2, 3, 4, and 7, 8, 9, where the interval of a fourth is divided into a second and minor third. However, there is no need to make a detailed analysis in order to appreciate the music's unity. As Erwin Stein says, 'the main thing is, that the song is a piece of great lyrical beauty'[1]. The accompaniment is confined to flute, English horn, harp, and three solo double-basses.

The third movement is like a miniature cantata within a cantata. The central Virtue, *Spes*, contains contrasted antiphonal liturgies: (*a*) The tenor and baritone soloists singing 'Qui confidunt in Domino etc.' in two parts (♪ = 108), accompanied by trumpets and harp (♪ = 108) and by bass and double-bass trombones (♪. = 72); and (*b*) four discanti and four altos singing 'Sustinuit anima mea etc.' in two parts (♪ = 144), accompanied by oboes (♪ = 144) and by tenor and bass trombones (♩ = 72). The scheme is *a b a b a*.

The core of the flanking Virtues is canonic. In *Caritas* there is a four-part canon between part of the choir (discanti, altos and tenors) and trumpet. This is sung first to the words from *Deuteronomy*, and then repeated to the words from the New Testament. According to Robert Craft, 'Stravinsky originally barred each canonic voice according to its own independent rhythm, which is how the piece should be performed, though in the published score all voices have been barred uniformly for conducting purposes.'[2] The score makes provision for optional viola parts (divisi a 3) to support the chorus and as an aid to pitch; but it was discovered in the performance at St Mark's that 'harmonic clarity and balance were better without this doubling'.[3] In *Fides*, a six-part canon for four-part chorus, trumpet doubled by double-bass trombone two octaves apart, and oboe doubled by bass trombone three octaves apart. Here too Stravinsky has cued in optional viola parts (divisi a 4) to support the chorus, but has added a footnote saying they are 'to be played only if required for acoustical reasons'. A three-part instrumental canon for two trumpets and organ follows the choral canon.

To bind the three Virtues together, he has devised an instrumental introduction to each of them, consisting of a ritornello for organ followed by a brief orchestral *sinfonia*. In each case the ritornello is a passacaglia-type theme, which turns out to be the retrograde inversion of the new series used throughout this movement. When used to introduce *Caritas*, it starts on A.

---

[1] From 'Igor Strawinsky: Canticum Sacrum ad honorem Sancti Marci Nominis'. *Tempo*, Summer, 1956.
[2] Robert Craft, 'A Concert for St. Mark'. *The Score*, December, 1956.
[3] Robert Craft, *op. cit.*

Ex. 148

For *Spes* its starting note is transposed to C; and for *Fides*, to B. After the three-part instrumental canon that follows the choral canon in *Fides*, the ritornello makes a final appearance; but this time it is played, not by the organ, but by the cellos and double-basses; and as it starts on B, it ends on A, which was its initial note at the beginning of the movement.

Whereas the series used in the *Ad Tres Virtutes Hortationes* movement is closely related to the series in the second movement, as can be seen by comparing the last four notes of Ex. 148 with notes 5, 4, 3 and 2 of the series given in Ex. 147b, the series used in the *Brevis Motus Cantilenae* is identical with that of the three Virtues, with the modification that the retrograde inversion of the earlier order (as shown in Ex. 148) has now become the original version of the new order. This little *scena* is divided into three parts: (i) After a brief instrumental introduction, the phrases of the baritone soloist's arioso written in near-recitative style are prolonged by echo effects from the chorus. A particularly beautiful example occurs with the setting of the words 'autem ait illi'.

Ex. 149

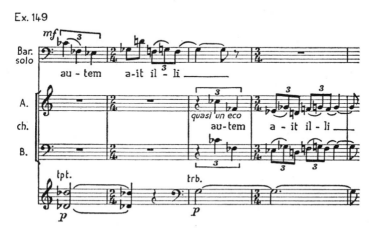

In this part, the baritone's arioso runs through the notes of the original order of the series followed by the retrograde version. As can be seen from Ex. 149, certain groups of contiguous notes, usually those at the distance of a second or a diminished second, are occasionally repeated. (ii) This part is followed by

487

2. Register of Works

a short four-part canon *a cappella*.[1] (iii) This leads to a resumption of the baritone recitative, with a particularly moving unaccompanied cadenza on the words 'cum lacrimis aiebat'. As the arioso continues (with trombone

Ex. 150 *quasi rubato discreto, non f*

cum la - cri-mis ai - e - bat

accompaniment) completing the inversion and the retrograde inversion of the series, it is underpinned by an octave D bass ostinato from the violas and double-basses pizzicato that is sounded on beats 1, 3, 6, 8, 11, 13 and so on. The coda is worth attention. The final cadence consists of the first eleven notes of the series played by the oboe and bassoons to form a descending arabesque; the organ picks out notes 1, 7, 8 and 11 and holds them as a chord; and the violas supply the final resolution by moving their ostinato note from D natural to F natural and so completing the twelfth note of the series.

Ex. 151

The organ chord in Ex. 151 is followed immediately by the chord for full orchestra with which the first movement ended (Ex. 145b). The music of the opening chorus returns in retrograde motion, with the organ ritornello (Ex. 146b) also in retrograde motion. Anyone who has heard recorded music played backwards will be familiar with the peculiar feeling of deflation that comes from the precision with which chords are usually attacked in performance as contrasted with the lack of precision with which they are terminated.

---

[1] Here too the score makes provision for the violas (divisi a 4) to support the voices as an aid to pitch if necessary.

Original Compositions

Stravinsky naturally takes care that his chords are exactly notated and expects accurate performance. In order to strengthen their armature in these two movements, he has introduced the device of breaking up some of the parts into rapidly repeated notes.[1] This pulsation works extremely well in propelling the music in either direction. As Robert Craft says,[2] 'Remembering the mechanical ugliness of most retrograde rhythms, Stravinsky's achievement in creating rhythms that work so fluently both ways ought to be remarked.'

The fifth movement concludes with the addition of a short *adagio* 'Amen'.

The music in the *Canticum Sacrum* is amazingly compact and varied. The idiom used ranges from long established, familiar modes to new experimental series. Its construction is sophisticated in detail, but observes closely the fundamental architectural principles of symmetry, proportion and balance.

The first performance in St. Mark's Cathedral had a mixed reception. According to Robert Craft, the critics 'proved they did not hear the masterpiece that was presented there. Instead, they noticed an "austerity", which is irrelevant, rather than a directness, which is profound; and they touted "influences", which are trivial, having failed to perceive inimitability.'[3] *Time* magazine was outspoken to the point of insult. 'Murder in the Cathedral' was their comment. But that may have been directed at the performance rather than the work.

At this time Stravinsky was much preoccupied by Webern and his music. There may be superficial resemblances between passages in the *Canticum Sacrum* and some of Webern's works; but as Robert Craft says, when referring to the *Canticum*,[4] 'The series intervals are not at all like Webern's and the melodic structure is wholly unlike the Viennese master's. More essentially still, Stravinsky's counterpoint is harmonic.' And this fits in with Stravinsky's own comments on composing with a series: 'The intervals of my series are attracted by tonality; I compose vertically and that is, in one sense at least, to compose tonally . . . I hear certain possibilities and I choose. I can create my choice in serial composition just as I can in any tonal contrapuntal form. I hear harmonically, of course, and I compose in the same way I always have' (*Con*).

95. AGON – 'ΑΓΩΝ

Ballet for twelve dancers (3.3.3.3 – 4.4.3.0 – harp, mandoline, piano, timpani, 3 tom-toms (or high timpani), xylophone, castanets – string 5tet). The com-

---

[1] A comparison between the manuscript full score and the published score shows that minor last-minute changes were made in the bassoon and trombone parts with a view to obtaining better stability and definition in the lower register.
[2] Robert Craft. *op. cit.*
[3] Robert Craft. *op. cit.*
[4] Robert Craft. *op. cit.*

2. Register of Works

position was started in December 1953, interrupted in 1954 by *In Memoriam Dylan Thomas* and in 1955 by the *Canticum Sacrum*, resumed in 1956 and finished on 27 April 1957. Dedicated to Lincoln Kirstein and George Balanchine. Published by Boosey & Hawkes, 1957. Reduction for two pianos by the composer. Duration: *c.* 20 minutes. First concert performance, Los Angeles, 17 June 1957, conducted by Robert Craft: first stage performance, New York City Ballet, New York, 1 December 1957. The manuscript full score is in the collection of Signora Adriana Panni, Accademia Filarmonica, Rome. The pencil manuscript of the two-piano reduction is in the Library of Congress, Washington, D.C.

Duodecimal Patterning

Usually the number of movements in a ballet score or song cycle seems to be fortuitous; but sometimes composers choose a deliberate pattern of multiples to form a kind of molecular grouping. For instance, Arnold Schoenberg's *Pierrot Lunaire* consists of settings of three times seven poems by Albert Giraud, while in William Walton's original *Façade* entertainment the Edith Sitwell poems are grouped in seven sections of three poems each. Benjamin Britten's *Spring Symphony* consists of settings of twelve different poems arranged in four parts of five plus three plus three plus one.

For *Agon* Stravinsky decided on twelve movements arranged in four sections of three, as follows:

I.   (i) *Pas-de-Quatre* (4m)
     (ii) *Double Pas-de-Quatre* (8f)
     (iii) *Triple Pas-de-Quatre* (4m 8f)

Prelude

II. (*First Pas-de-Trois* (1m 2f))

     (i) *Saraband-Step* (1m)
     (ii) *Gailliarde* (2f)
     (iii) *Coda* (1m 2f)

Interlude

III. (*Second Pas-de-Trois* (2m 1f))

     (i) *Bransle Simple* (2m)
     (ii) *Bransle Gay* (1f)
     (iii) *Bransle de Poitou* (2m 1f)

Interlude

IV. (i) *Pas-de-Deux* (1m 1f)
     (ii) *Four Duos* (4m 4f)
     (iii) *Four Trios* (4m 8f)

At first it looks as if the duodecimal scheme is broken by the *Prelude* and two Interludes; but when it is realised that virtually the whole of the music of I (i) is repeated in IV (iii) and the music of the two Interludes is identical with that of the *Prelude* (though somewhat differently scored), it can be reasonably maintained that the function of the *Prelude* and *Interludes* is caesural, and their contribution compensatory.

The duodecimal patterning is fundamental to the dance layout. From its title, it is clear that the ballet was conceived as a dance assembly or contest. The score specifies twelve dancers – four male and eight female – and the dance numbers are based on various groups of divisors, as set out in the parentheses above.

As was the case with the *Canticum Sacrum*, the musical idiom starts with a clear diatonic basis at the beginning of the score, but progresses towards chromaticism and serialism, returning to diatonicism at the end. Stravinsky shows an inclination to approach the twelve notes of the chromatic scale from two separate angles – first as an elaboration of diatonicism, secondly as the raw material of serialism; and there are times when the two are ingeniously combined together.

Composition and Treatment

Agon was commissioned by Lincoln Kirstein and George Balanchine as the result of a grant made to the New York City Ballet by the Rockefeller Foundation in 1954. When the news of the commission was bruited abroad, some persons seemed to think that the result was likely to be a score that, together with *Apollo Musagetes* and *Orpheus*, would complete a ballet triptych on classical themes. But that is not what happened. The subject chosen was an abstract one, without any semblance of plot: so the conception of the ballet lies closer to *Scènes de Ballet* than to *Orpheus*. Stravinsky found a prototype for some of the dance numbers (particularly those in the two middle sections) in the French Court dances of the seventeenth century as prescribed in de Lauze's *Apologie de la Danse* (1623) and Mersenne's musical examples (*Con*); and it is said that an engraving in the de Lauze publication showing two trumpeters accompanying a Bransle Simple suggested the instrumentation of Stravinsky's own *Bransle Simple*.

Agon had almost as disturbed a gestation as *The Nightingale*. It appears that composition was started as early as December 1953, shortly after the completion of the *Three Songs from William Shakespeare*, and more than a third of the score was completed before it was interrupted by *In Memoriam Dylan Thomas* and the *Canticum Sacrum*. When Stravinsky returned to *Agon* in 1956, he found he had to recast some of the early numbers so as to link them with a minimum of disturbance to the serial technique that by then was rapidly becoming his current idiom. For instance, there were three different versions of the introductory fanfare in I (i). The first – for three trombones – dates back to December 1953. The following year it was revised for trumpets and harp, and extended, and a guitar was specified for the following section (bars 10–13). In the final version, the fanfare was scored for trumpets and horns; and a mandoline, which had not appeared in any of Stravinsky's scores since *The Nightingale*, took the place of the guitar.

The fanfare appears four times in the first movement; and comparison of the first appearance with the third shows something of the speed with which the music is travelling from diatonicism (C major) to chromaticism (polytonality).

Ex.152a

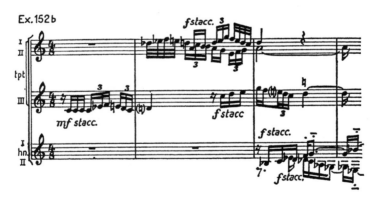

Ex.152b

The following movements – *Double Pas-de-Deux* (I (ii)) and *Triple Pas-de-Deux* (I (iii)) – should be taken together, for the second of these (marked *Coda* in the score) is, according to Stravinsky, an 'imitation' of the first. The tempo is brisk ($\flat$=116); the demisemiquaver triplet accompanying figure incisive. In his monograph on Stravinsky, Roman Vlad points out how 'in the first part the woodwind and strings gradually introduce the twelve different notes in the following order':[1]

---

[1] Roman Vlad, *Stravinsky*. Oxford University Press, 1960.

Ex. 153

But this is not really used as a series. It should be looked on as a juxtaposition of tetrachords, each of which consists of a sequence of four notes contained within the compass of a minor third. Twenty-four different permutations of such a four-note row are possible; and the rapid demisemiquaver figuration in these two movements takes full advantage of this. The appearance may at times be serial; but the intention is chromatic.

The following *Prelude* shows the same disposition as the opening movement to start from a diatonic basis and fill out with chromatics. It is in two parts: (i) a 3/4 ($\downarrow$ = 126) with semiquaver figuration is followed by (ii) a *Meno mosso*, also in 3/4, but with the metronome marking $\downarrow$. = $\downarrow$ = 84, a strange little march which enables the dancers to regroup before the next dance section. In (i) a rising semiquaver phrase of C D F G B C is reiterated by flutes and cellos, while bassoons, timpani, trumpets, tom-toms and violas gradually introduce most of the remaining notes of the chromatic scale, and the rhythmic pattern is underlined by the drumming. The march is played by flutes and bassoons accompanied by timpani, harp and three solo double-basses playing harmonics.

On its two subsequent appearances the *Prelude* is called *Interlude*. The first time a quaver C D F G B C phrase is added in augmentation; and the second time a tremolo figure for two trumpets playing the notes of the B flat minor and E flat minor triads makes its appearance. Otherwise the music is unchanged. The effect of these additions is barely noticeable in performance: but perhaps that is precisely the effect aimed at, for if the music of the *Prelude* had been literally repeated in the two *Interludes* without this stiffening, it might have begun to sound a little thin.

The dance movements in the second and third sections of the score all use French seventeenth century dance forms as their point of departure, though, as one observer of the ballet perspicaciously remarked[1], they recall 'a Court Dance as much as a Cubist still-life recalls a pipe or guitar'. Their instrumentation is varied and ingenious. A solo violin, xylophone and two bass trombones are the chief instruments in the *Saraband-Step* (II (i)); there is a canon between harp and mandoline (reinforced by flute) in the *Gailliarde* (II (ii)); flutes, mandoline and solo violin play the chief parts in the *Coda* (II (iii)); a canon for two trumpets is featured in the *Bransle Simple* (III (i)); the *Bransle Gay* (III (ii)) is written mainly for woodwind (flutes, clarinets, bassoons) with castanet accompaniment; and with the *Bransle de Poitou* (III (iii)) a line shared by solo trumpet and trombone is counterpointed against a line played by the violins in unison.

---

[1] Quoted in *Stravinsky and the Dance*. The Dance Collection of the New York Public Library, New York, 1962.

2. Register of Works

In these six dances Stravinsky makes free use of serial processes. Sometimes his note rows are based on a full series; sometimes he is content with a hexachordal group. In the *Coda* (II (iii)) he uses a full series that contains a striking number of contiguous intervals of a second; and the following illustration (Ex. 154) shows the original series accompanied by a chromatic non-serial theme played by the solo violin.

Ex. 154

In the *Bransle Gay* (III (ii)), there is a curious trick of notation where the castanets maintain a 3/8 rhythmic ostinato, while the rest of the music falls into 7/16 and 5/16 bars.

Ex. 155

Original Compositions

Ernest Ansermet is rather scathing about this polyrhythmic effect. He says that 'the simultaneous employment of two cadential structures in this number is due to deliberate calculation on Stravinsky's part, whereas the faculty of auditory perception is divorced from calculation' and adds: 'Here we touch on the defect of "intellectual" creative activity, which consists in manufacturing and elaborating structures that are *unnecessary* and add nothing to the musical substance of the work.'[1] It is true that the effect is for the eye, and the ear fails to apprehend the polyrhythmic subtleties. But in performance the auditor accepts the piece quite simply as being in 3/8 time, with syncopated phrasing that is more or less conditioned by the 7/16 and 5/16 bar-lines.

Apparently, Stravinsky's sketches show that at two points in this number (the first of which is to be seen in the last bar of Ex. 155) where the instruments stop and the castanets play alone, the ballerina is supposed to turn her head towards each of the two male dancers in turn.

The *Pas-de-Deux* (IV (i)) is the most highly organised movement in the score. It is subdivided into (a) an *Adagio* ($\flat$ = 112) in which a *concertante* part is played by the solo violin; (b) a variation for the male dancer marked *Più Mosso* ($\flat$ = 126); (c) a variation for the female dancer marked *L'istesso tempo*; (d) a refrain for the male dancer also *L'istesso tempo*; and (e) a *Coda* for both dancers, followed by a *Quasi stretto* bridge passage that leads directly to the subsequent *Four Duos* movement (IV(ii)). A new series (Ex. 156a) is used

Ex. 156a

in the *Adagio*; but the variations and refrain are content with shorter note rows. This series returns in monophonic form in the *Four Duos* (IV (ii)), lower strings pizzicato alternating with the tenor and bass trombones; and at the beginning of the following movement, *Four Trios* (IV (iii)) it expands into a four-part canon.

Ex. 156b

(Ex. 156b continues on p. 456)

---

[1] Ernest Ansermet, *Les Fondements de la Musique dans la Conscience humaine*. Neuchâtel, 1961.

495

At this point it is interrupted by a recall to diatonic order from the four horns, whose repeated chord proves to be the forerunner of the opening fanfare. The series (direct order followed by the retrograde version) is heard for the last time in the lower strings pizzicato; and the final note F natural (the initial note of the series) is absorbed into the opening fanfare chord. A reprise of the whole of the opening movement (I (i)) follows.

Productions

As in the case of *Orpheus*, there was close co-operation between Stravinsky and Balanchine over the production of this ballet by the New York City Ballet. The 'I B M ballet', as it was called, was described by Balanchine as being 'more tight and precise than usual, as if it were controlled by an electronic brain'.[1] Apart from the numbers of the dancers specified for the various movements, the only balletic indications in the score are the direction at the opening, 'As the curtain rises, four male dancers are aligned across the rear of the stage with their backs to the audience,' and a similar direction eighteen bars before the end, 'The female dancers leave the stage. The male dancers take their position as at the beginning – back to the audience.' Balanchine's choreography was abstract in the extreme – in fact, Stravinsky compared it to one of Mondrian's compositions. The ballet was danced in practice costume and scored a great success with the New York public at its première on 1 December 1957. The leading dancers were Diana Adams, Todd Bolender, Melissa Hayden and Arthur Mitchell.

Other choreographers have tackled the score at various times – Yvonne Georgi for the Landestheater, Hanover, in 1958 and the Vienna Staatsoper in 1959; Otto Kruger for the Deutsche Oper am Rhein, Düsseldorf, in 1958; Tatjana Gsovsky for the Berlin Staatsoper in 1958 and the Städtische Bühnen, Frankfurt, in 1959. Kenneth Macmillan's version for the Royal Ballet, Covent Garden (20 August 1958) was interesting in patches; but its duodecimal pattern was seriously flawed by the introduction of two extra dancers who were unnecessarily featured in the *Prelude* and *Interludes*.

---

[1] Quoted in *Stravinsky and the Dance*.

Original Compositions

96. THRENI: ID EST LAMENTATIONES JEREMIAE PROPHETAE

For soli,[1] mixed chorus and orchestra (2.3.3.0 and sarrusophone – 4.0.3.1 and contralto bugle in B flat (Fluegelhorn)[2] – timp., tam-tam, piano, celesta, harp – string 5tet). Latin text. Composition started in Italy in the summer of 1957 and completed on 21 March 1958. 'Dem Norddeutschen Rundfunk gewidmet.' Published by Boosey & Hawkes, 1958. Duration: *c.* 35 minutes. First performance (dedicated to the memory of Alessandro Piovesan), Sala della Scuola Grande di San Rocco, Venice, 23 September 1958, conducted by the composer. The manuscript full score is in Oberlin College Library, Oberlin, Ohio.

The Complete Serialist

The *Lamentations of Jeremiah* form part of the ritual of both the Jewish Synagogue and the Roman Catholic Church, where they are sung on certain occasions during Holy Week. Stravinsky had always hoped his Mass would be used liturgically; but he had no such aspirations for his *Threni*, which was why he did not style it a *Tenebrae* service. In his *Conversations* he says that he was already familiar with Palestrina's complete service, and the *Lamentations* of Tallis and Byrd; but none of these masters seems to have influenced his score.

For his text he went to the Vulgate and made the following selection from Chapters I, III and IV:

> Chapter I: verse 1, parts of verses 2, 5 and 11, verse 20.
> Chapter III: verses 1–6, 16–27, 34–36, 40–45, 49–66.[3]
> Chapter V: verses 1, 19, 21.

As in the *Canticum Sacrum* there is an introductory flourish sung by two soloists (in this case the soprano and alto); but here it is an *Incipit* instead of a *Dedicatio* – ('Incipit lamentatio Jeremiae Prophetae'). There is also a sung introductory title ('Oratio Jeremiae Prophetae') for the two bass soloists at the beginning of Chapter V (*De Elegia Quinta*). Throughout Chapters I and III the Hebrew letters, which mark the divisions of the text, are incorporated in the score and set for chorus. The musical layout is tripartite, corresponding with the three different Chapters laid under contribution; and as in the *Canticum Sacrum*, the middle movement is also divided into three parts, viz.

> [*Introduction*]
> *De Elegia Prima*
> *De Elegia Tertia*
>   1. *Querimonia*
>   2. *Sensus Spei*
>   3. *Solacium*
> *De Elegia Quinta*

---

[1] Soloists: soprano, contralto, two tenors, bass and basso profondo.
[2] Stravinsky's admiration for Shorty Roger's trumpet playing probably influenced him in the choice of this instrument (*Con*).
[3] In III 59 the words 'judica judicium meum' are omitted.

497

2. Register of Works

Whereas in the *Canticum Sacrum* and *Agon* the serial part of the scores had a tonal framework, *Threni* is a completely serial work. The original thematic idea consisted of the phrase sung in the *Introduction* by the soprano soloist accompanied by the alto soloist singing its inversion.

In fact, the whole work is based on the series derived from this thematic idea.

At the same time Stravinsky allows himself considerable licence in the use of the various rows. He exercises his right to repeat notes and groups of notes (see Ex. 157 above). He still savours with gusto the tonal implications of the intervals employed, even though the serial process inevitably contradicts these tonal implications in the long run. He is not even averse from introducing an occasional diatonic motive, as can be seen from the motive for tremolo strings in the following passage that occurs three times (with minor modifications) in the *De Elegia Prima* movement:

Ex. 159

At the end of the work it is fascinating to see how he achieves what Roman Vlad calls the 'tonal polarization of the twelve-note scale'.[1] The voices (first the chorus, then a quartet of soloists, and finally the chorus and soloists combined) present the original series together with its retrograde version, inversion and retrograde inversion in four-part harmony and are accompanied by horns playing, first in two parts and later in four. Example 160 shows the last three bars of the chorus, followed by the short coda for horns alone.

---

[1] Roman Vlad, *Stravinsky*. Oxford University Press, 1960.

Ex. 160

The simple harmonies of the final chord of the chorus and the final chord of the quartet of horns are achieved in an ingenious way. In the case of the chorus, the basic set and its retrograde version and retrograde inversion are given in the original form (see Ex. 158 above); but the inversion is transposed an augmented fourth, which makes the last note F sharp instead of C natural. In the case of the quartet of horns, the inversion (played by the first horn) is in its original form, ending on C natural, while the basic set is transposed down a major sixth, the retrograde version down a minor third, and the retrograde inversion down an augmented fourth to produce A natural, C natural and A natural in the final chord.

In the 'Audisti opprobrium eorum' passage in the *Solacium* section, Stravinsky uses interesting permutations of the basic series.

Ex. 161

By taking notes 1, 3, 5, 7, 9, 11, 12, 10, 8, 6, 4 and 2 from the R I of the original series and transposing them an augmented fourth, he creates the following new row

Ex. 162a

which is sung by the solo tenor, while the bass soloist sings the inversion. And the accompaniment is based on another row derived by a different system of permutation, notes 12, 9, 6, 3, 11, 8, 5, 2, 10, 7, 4 and 1 of the original series being combined to form

Ex. 162b

There are several instances of row lopping. Perhaps the most interesting of these is the passage towards the end of the *Solacium* section, where the omission of the eighth note from the original series (see Ex. 158), here transposed down a semitone, throws into relief a motive formed by notes 5, 6, 7 and echoed by notes 9, 10, 11.

Ex. 163a

It is curious to find that on one of its subsequent (transposed) appearances this lopped row has its second note changed from A natural to G natural (note 12), a procedure which creates a number of false relations within the row.

Ex. 163b

The canonic structure of *Threni* is even more strongly developed than in the *Canticum Sacrum*. The *De Elegia Prima* movement contains two *Diphonas* for two solo tenors unaccompanied, in each of which the four versions of the series (most of them in their original position; but some of them transposed) are shared by the two voices in a free contrapuntal manner. More complex is the treatment of the first section of the *De Elegia Tertia* movement, where the unaccompanied *Querimonia* builds up in magnificent cumulation from a monody for the second bass soloist (basso profondo) through a two-part canon for 1st tenor and 2nd bass soloists, and a three-part canon for 1st tenor and 1st and 2nd bass soloists, to a double four-part canon for 1st and 2nd tenor and 1st and 2nd bass soloists. In these two Diphonas, this monody and these three canons, there is no strict barring, and the voices are treated with great freedom. As Stravinsky explains in his *Conversations*, they 'are not always in rhythmic unison. Therefore, any bar lines would cut at least one line arbitrarily. There are no strong beats in these canons, in any case, and the conductor must merely count the music out as he counts out a motet by Josquin.'

This avoidance of rhythmic unison is also a feature of the blurred attack given to the pedal that underpins the passage of choral chanting without pitch at the beginning of the *De Elegia Prima* movement. (See Ex. 164.) This type of choral declamation is something new in Stravinsky's output. On its third (and last) appearance in the first movement – at the words 'Foris interficit gladius, et domi mors similis est' – the effect is made even more sombre by an adjunction

Ex.164

to the chorus 'abbassare la voce'. Chanting (still in equal quavers) is resumed in the *Sensus Spei* section of *De Elegia Tertia*; but here it is with specified pitch. There are three interjections from the 2nd bass soloist with a phrase introduced in each case by a falsetto note. (The same sort of device was used in the feast scene of *The Wedding*.) In *De Elegia Quinta* there is a brief resumption of choral chanting without pitch – just sufficient to recall the sombre tone colour of the opening movement.

One of the most striking features of the score is the setting of the letters of the Hebrew alphabet that designate the verses in the *De Elegia Prima et Tertia* movements. There are five of these in the *De Elegia Prima* movement. In the *De Elegia Tertia* movement, where each letter makes three consecutive appearances, there are four in the *Querimonia*, eight in the *Sensus Spei*, and three in the *Solacium* sections. None appears in the *De Elegia Quinta* movement. All are set for chorus. In the first movement they range from four to six bars in length. In the third, they are shorter – often no longer than a single bar containing a chord or a simple cadence. All are different, except in the *Sensus Spei* section where the repeated letters are identical. Usually they serve as a kind of marker, sometimes as introduction or ritornello, sometimes as caesura: but in the *Sensus Spei* section some of them are prolonged into pedal chords that accompany the following passages. In most cases Stravinsky directs that there shall be a vocal attack on the Hebrew letter followed by a rapid diminuendo. The effect is like that of a series of illuminated initials embellishing a manuscript; and the special cadential qualities of these brief harmonic glosses give them a curious kind of nimbus.

The orchestra specified is a big one; but it is nowhere used otherwise than as a series of continuously changing and shifting chamber music combinations. There are no *tutti* passages. This leaves the chorus and soloists continuously in the foreground so that the general impression is of a varied choral pattern of chanting and lamentation and polyphony, from which occasionally arises an anonymous solo interjection – such as the alto singing[1] 'Bonus est Dominus

---

[1] Bars 205–207 *et seq.*

sperantibus in eum' and the tenor responding in strangulated tones ('con voce strascicante') to the deep bass at the 'Ut contereret sub pedibus suis omnes vinctos terrae' passage[1] in the *Sensus Spei* section.

This is the longest score of Stravinsky's serial period. It is perhaps not surprising that he should have succeeded in unifying its diverse musical material – as Schoenberg said,[2] 'The main advantage of this method of composing with twelve tones is its unifying effect' – but what is especially remarkable is the way an entirely original form has been evolved to meet the exigencies of the serial organisation of the music.

Threni was intended to form part of the Venice Biennale programme for 1958; but shortly before the opening of the Festival, Alessandro Piovesan, its director since 1953, died. The first performance of *Threni*, which was given on 23 September 1958 in the Sala della Scuola Grande di San Rocco, was accordingly dedicated to his memory as a sign of friendship and esteem.

97. MOVEMENTS

For piano and orchestra (2.2.2.1 – 0.2.3.0 – harp, celesta – string 5tet).[3] Composition started in 1958 and completed on 30 July 1959. Dedicated to Margrit Weber. Published by Boosey & Hawkes, 1960. Reduction for two pianos by the composer. Duration: *c.* 10 minutes. First performance, Stravinsky Festival, Town Hall, New York, 10 January 1960, with Margrit Weber as soloist and the composer conducting. The manuscript full score and two manuscript piano scores are in the collection of Karl Weber, Zürich.

Composition and Treatment

This is one of the most hermetic of all Stravinsky's major works. Some of the difficulty in coming to terms with it resides in its brevity, for here the serial process has resulted in an even greater terseness and concentration than usual. The composition lasts ten minutes in performance, but has the specific gravity of a tonal work of three times that duration.

There are five movements in all; and these are separated from each other by four short sections which from the instrumental point of view serve as codas to the movements they follow, but as preludes to the movements they precede insofar as they anticipate the changes of tempo. These linking passages (in which the solo piano is silent) were called 'interludes' in the manuscript score; but subsequently this description was dropped. In some ways they are a development of the idea of setting the Hebrew letters in *Threni* as a kind of punctuation and marginal embellishment.

---

[1] Bars 218–221 *et seq.*
[2] From 'Composition with Twelve Tones', reprinted in *Style and Idea*. London, Williams and Norgate, 1951.
[3] Stravinsky specifies 6 first violins, 6 second violins, 4 violas, 5 cellos, and 2 double-basses.

The scheme of the work is as follows:

I. ♪ = 110 followed by *Meno mosso* ♪ = 72
   (interlude) ♩ = 52
II. ♩ = 52
   (interlude) ♩ = 72
III. ♪ = 72
   (interlude) ♪ = 80
IV. ♪ = 80
   (interlude) ♩ = 52
V. ♪ = 104

The serial process is used with remarkable freedom. In his *Memories* Stravinsky has stated that 'every aspect of the composition was guided by serial forms, the sixes, quadrilaterals, triangles etc. The fifth movement, for instance, uses a construction of twelve verticals. Five orders are rotated instead of four, with six alternates for each of the five, while at the same time the six "work" in all directions, as through a crystal.' This sounds extremely complicated: but a good example of how it works out in practice can be obtained from the opening of the first movement. The series used is the following:

Ex.165

The piano opens with a clear statement of the series in its original version.

Ex.166

A few bars later there is an extended flute solo, which is a kind of free montage of trichords and tetrachords drawn mainly from the original version and inversion of the series – sometimes in their original position, sometimes transposed. Some of the trichords and tetrachords overlap and cause a kind

505

of enharmonic modulation. There are even one or two unorganised notes that seem to serve as passing notes. For instance, the minor third (B flat followed by G natural) that occurs in the second bar is an interval that is foreign to the series.

Ex. 167

There is not so much canonic elaboration as in *Threni*, though a particularly complex passage is to be found at the end of the second movement 'where the four-part counterpoint is transmuted into a simultaneous statement of all four forms of the series, each passing freely from one part to another'.[1]

The series contains two perfect intervals – a fourth and a fifth – which provide harmonic points of reference. This is particularly noticeable in the fourth movement where both intervals are sustained as harmonic pedals on the high strings of the violas and cellos. Other tonal implications emerge, sometimes through the use of sustained or repeated notes or chords, sometimes because of a deliberate cadential twist. A good example of the latter occurs at the end of the first stanza of the fourth movement, where it is clear from the context that the piano is referring to the inversion of the series, but notes 7–11 appear in an altered order, viz. 7, 8, 9, 11, 10. The result is a moment of ghostly allegiance to the tonality of G major. The repeated chords in the last movement

Ex. 168

---

[1] Colin Mason, 'Stravinsky's Newest Works'. *Tempo*. Spring/Summer 1960.

Original Compositions

also set up tonal ripples. One such passage (bars 155 and 156) sounds strangely like the croaking of the toads in the penultimate scene of Berg's *Wozzeck*.

In his *Memories*, Stravinsky suggests that the rhythmic language of *Movements* is the most advanced he has so far employed. He goes on to say 'my polyrhythmic combinations are meant to be heard vertically' and quotes as parallels the second *Agnus Dei* (for three voices) in Josquin's *Missa l'Homme armé* and Baude Cordier's *pour le deffault du dieu Bacchus*. The rhythm of his phrases is subjected to contraction and expansion; and very little attempt is made to maintain the feeling of a regular pulse. Duodecimal and other mathematical patterns of apparent acceleration or deceleration frequently occur. The following example shows a simple duodecimal rhythmic scheme where contraction compensated for by expansion is mounted on a basic metre.

Ex. 169

When different patterns of this kind are interwoven, the polyrhythmic results are sometimes quite complicated, as can be seen from the following quotation (bar 39 preceded by part of bar 38) from the first movement. (Note that the bassoon part literally follows the pattern given in Ex. 169.)

Ex. 170

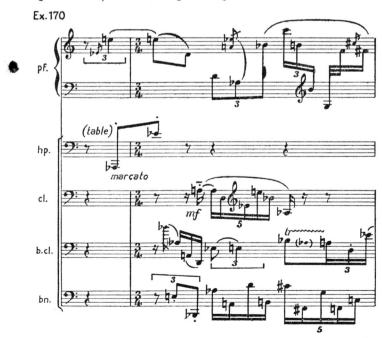

Stravinsky considers these rhythmic procedures are part of the general serial orientation – as are also the changes in instrumental specification between the five movements, and the confining of the four short interludes 'each to a defined timbre'.

Although the work was first thought of as a concerto – (its original title was Concerto for Piano and Groups of Instruments) – the piano part is not a *concertante* one in the usual sense of that expression. There is no real point of contrast between it as a solo instrument and the orchestra as an ensemble. Throughout the movements, the piano is the principal instrument in a series of continuously shifting chamber music ensembles.

Ballet Production

In April 1963 the New York City Ballet produced *Movements* with choreography by George Balanchine. It was danced by Suzanne Farrell and Jacques d'Amboise supported by a *corps de ballet* of six girls. According to the special correspondent of *The Times*, the ballet might be regarded 'as an essay in suspended motion. Its appeal is at once musical and spatial, and its dancers seem like a mobile caught in the breath of the music. The air is full of pauses.'

98. EPITAPHIUM

For flute, clarinet and harp. 'Für das Grabmal des Prinzen Max Egon zu Fürstenberg.' Composed in 1959. Published by Boosey & Hawkes, 1959. Duration: *c.* 1 minute 16 seconds. First performance, Donaueschingen Festival, 17 October 1959.

The harmony of this miniature *Epitaphium* is serially ordered throughout; and Stravinsky has given a fascinating glimpse of his composing process in his *Memories*. It appears that he began the work with a melodic-harmonic phrase for two flutes; and when he had composed about half of it, he saw its serial implication and began consciously to work towards that pattern.

The series that emerged was

Original Compositions

It is interesting to find that the first hexachord is closely related to the opening theme of *The Firebird*. If the notes are taken in the order 4 5 6 2 1 3, they will be found to spell out the initial phrase of the Introduction (see Ex. 2).

'Only after I had written this little twelve-note duet,' writes Stravinsky, 'did I conceive the idea of a series of funeral responses between bass and treble instruments and, as I wanted the whole piece to be very muffled, I decided that the bass instrument should be a harp. The first bar of the harp part was, however, written last. As I worked the music out, it became a kind of hymn, like Purcell's *Funeral Music for Queen Mary*. There are four short antiphonal strophes for the harp, and four for the wind duet, and each strophe is a complete order of the series – harp: O, I, R,[1] RI; winds; O, RI, R, I.'

Stravinsky explains that the constructive problem that first attracted him to the two-part counterpoint of the first phrase was the harmonic one of minor seconds. As can be seen, however, from the second harp strophe,

Ex. 173

hp.

the harp also exploits some of the major and minor thirds (tenths) and fifths implicit in the series.

The decision to substitute a clarinet for the second flute seems to have been taken when it was known that the completed work would be performed in a programme with Webern's songs op. 15 which use the flute/clarinet combination.

Prince Max Egon zu Fürstenberg was the patron of the Donaueschingen Festival; and Stravinsky was his guest during the 1957 and 1958 festivals. The Prince died in April 1959; and the *Epitaphium* was first performed at the 1959 festival. Each of the three concerts that year included a special musical tribute to the Prince, the other two being by Pierre Boulez and Wolfgang Fortner.

99. DOUBLE CANON

For string quartet. 'Raoul Dufy in Memoriam.' Composed in 1959. Published by Boosey & Hawkes, 1960. Duration: *c.* 1 minute 16 seconds. First performance, Stravinsky Festival, Town Hall, New York, 20 December 1959.

---

[1] There is a slight divergence from the series at the beginning of the third harp strophe; and the appoggiaturas do not always appear in their strict serial order.

According to Robert Craft, this *Double Canon* started life as an album-leaf duet for flute and clarinet and was composed in Venice in September 1959 in response to a private request for an autograph. It was later expanded into a *Double Canon* for string quartet. The music was not intended as a personal tribute to Dufy, for the two men had never met each other.

The series used in this work is given in Ex. 69. Both canons are strict. In the first, the first violin plays the theme twice in its basic version and twice in its retrograde inversion. The second violin follows the basic version, first at the major second below and then in unison, and the retrograde inversion, first at the major second above and then in unison. The second canon (between the viola and cello) starts at the end of the first statement of the theme by the first violin and consists of two statements of the retrograde version by the viola with the cello following, first at the minor seventh below and then at the octave. The second canon finishes just before the final statement of the theme in its retrograde inversion by the first violin.

100. A SERMON, A NARRATIVE AND A PRAYER

Cantata for alto and tenor soli, speaker, chorus and orchestra (2.2.2.2 – 4.3.3.1 – 3 tam-tams, piano, harp – string 5tet[1]). Composed at Hollywood in 1960/61 and finished on 31 January 1961. Dedicated to Paul Sacher. Published by Boosey & Hawkes, 1961. Duration: *c.* 16 minutes. First performance, Basler Kammerorchester, Basel, 23 February 1962[2], conducted by Paul Sacher. The manuscript full score (in pencil) is in the collection of Dr. Paul Sacher, Pratteln, Basel.

On 7 August 1961 Stravinsky sent Paul Sacher an explanatory note about this new cantata, saying that as *Threni,* the Lamentations of Jeremiah, went back to the Old Testament for its text, so *A Sermon, a Narrative and a Prayer* was a cantata of the New Testament. By faith and compassion, St. Stephen the first Christian martyr was led into the virtue of hope, the New Testament way to truth, so that he prayed for his oppressors, and followed in the path of his Master. The text was chosen from *St. Paul's Epistles,* the *Acts of the Apostles –* in the inspiring beauty of the Authorised Version – together with a prayer by Thomas Dekker[3] belonging to the same period as the Bible translation. 'And that is all that needs to be communicated to my audience,' was the conclusion of the composer's note.

The series used recalls the note row of *In Memoriam Dylan Thomas,* which consisted of the five notes contained within the interval of a major third. If the notes of the *In Memoriam Dylan Thomas* basic set (Ex. 142) are taken in

---

[1] The numbers of the string players are specified as follows: 1Vl (8), 2Vl (7), Vla (6), Vcl (5), C-B (4).
[2] The concert was preceded by a public rehearsal on 22 February 1962.
[3] Spelt 'Dekkar' in the score.

the order 2, 1, 3, 5, 4, they will be found to form the opening pentachord of the series used in *A Sermon etc.*, viz.

Ex. 174

Furthermore, it will be seen that the final pentachord of this series (viz., notes 8, 9, 10, 11, 12) consists of five notes contained within the interval of a major third – and this is also true of the preceding pentachord (viz., notes 3, 4, 5, 6, 7).

The use of the voices, both soloists and chorus, is varied and carefully calculated, ranging from melodrama in natural speech rhythm, through measured declamation without or with pitch, to normal *bel canto*. The gradations are managed with great skill.

For an example of speech leading by calculated overlap into *bel canto*, one turns to the *Narrative* movement.

Ex. 175

These four bars are immediately followed by a passage of measured pitchless declamation where the Speaker is accompanied by a canon of two trumpets playing the inversion of the series (Ex. 175b). It will be noted that shortened rows of the series are used in which the first trumpet omits the eighth note of the inversion of the series (C natural) and the second trumpet omits the seventh (G natural), and also the twelfth (D flat).

Ex. 175b

Further examples of co-ordination between the declamation of the Speaker and the recitative of the alto and tenor soloists are to be found in the *Poco meno* coda to the *Narrative*, which describes the stoning of Stephen (bars 187–206).

Just before this coda, Stravinsky evolves a new type of voice with an extended range of just over two octaves by joining the alto and tenor soloists, dividing the vocal line between them and using short overlaps to make certain the joins don't show. This enables the soloists to tackle a particularly spiky vocal line where many of the intervals of a second have been transformed to a

Ex.176

[N.B. The accompaniment to this duet is not shown.]

seventh or a ninth.

In *Movements*, the first movement was given an effect of formal symmetry by the literal repetition of the opening exposition. A similar effect is obtained in the *Sermon* by its division into two parallel and contrasting parts, followed by the same refrain – 'The substance of things hoped for, the evidence of things not seen, is faith. And our Lord is a consuming fire.' The parallelism of the instrumental introduction, the opening with the two soloists followed by the chorus, the brief instrumental interlude (no more than an arabesque of sound), the re-entry of the chorus, at first unaccompanied and then over a chord held

Ex.177

(Ex. 177 continues on p. 474)

513

by the horns – all this is imitated closely and varied in the second part. Only the refrain remains literally the same in both parts. Here it is interesting to see how the first half of the refrain shows the chorus starting with measured declamation, first without pitch and then with approximate pitch, leading to a fully sung cadence on the words 'is faith'. (See Ex. 177).

The *Narrative* is an elaborate *scena*. The chorus plays no part in it; but the Speaker sets the scene and comments on it and serves as a musical 'feed' for the soloists. The movement starts with declamation and recitative; and the musical texture becomes more closely knit towards the middle. New instruments are introduced for some of the canonic passages. Two oboes and two bassoons are heard for the first time in a double canon, where the Speaker describes the bringing to trial of Stephen ('Then there arose certain of the Synagogue . . .'[1]). A little further on, the piano and tuba are heard also for the first time in a three-part canon where, fortified by bass trombone, bass clarinet and cello, they imitate the tenor solo ('Ye do always resist the Holy Ghost . . .)[2], while the basic series is played twice in augmentation by clarinet and trumpet. Recitative and declamation return for the passage where Stephen is cast out of the city (see Ex. 176) and stoned. The words 'he fell asleep' are the cue for an instrumental coda eight bars long, a sequence of sombre chords in which all four forms of the series are combined; but the distribution of the notes is so complex and cunning that 'almost every note will bear alternative or complementary serial interpretations without any disruption of the strict order of any of the four forms of the series'.[3]

---

[1] Bar 113 *et seq.*

[2] Bar 142 *et seq.*

[3] From Colin Mason's excellent analysis of *A Sermon etc.* entitled 'Stravinsky's New Work'. *Tempo*, Autumn 1961.

The third movement starts with the alto soloist singing the first phrase of the *Prayer*. The tenor soloist takes over and begins a strict rhythmic canon, the alto soloist entering two bars later with the second part, the choral basses entering two bars after the alto soloist with the third part; and at this point the double-basses, harp and piano add another part in augmentation and

Ex. 178

are joined by three gongs (high, middle, and low), each note of the augmented theme being allocated to the gong with the appropriate pitch. The second phrase of this canon is quoted (Ex: 178) where the alto soloist leads and is followed by the tenor soloist. The rhythmic irregularity of the opening theme produces a metric counterpoint that is nearly as complex as in *Movements*; and at three points Stravinsky has recourse to a visual aid (see the last bar of Ex. 178), which is intended to elucidate the metric structure. Overlapping with the end of the canon, the chorus enters in four parts. The alto and tenor soloists introduce the final 'Alleluias'. Meanwhile, the bass movement of the double basses, harp, piano and gongs changes from an imitation of the canonic theme to a syncopated theme based on the first hexachord of the inversion of the series, which then reverses and returns to its initial E flat by way of the last hexachord of the retrograde inversion. Some of the two-note steps are repeated; and some of the single notes too. There is a final procession of chords alternating between strings and chorus. Here again, as Colin Mason points out,[1] all four forms of the series are combined; but he suggests – and he seems to have reason on his side – that in bar 267 the A flat of the viola part 'is either a misprint for G flat or a serial "error" that Stravinsky has permitted himself'. The measured syncopation of the gongs adds a note of solemn beauty to this peroration. 'For whom the gong tolls . . .' This movement is headed in the score 'In memoriam the Reverend James McLane (†1960)'.

101. ANTHEM 'The Dove descending breaks the air'

For chorus *a cappella* (S.A.T.B.). The words (Part IV of 'Little Gidding' in *Four Quartets*) by T. S. Eliot. Dated Hollywood, California, 2 January 1962. Dedicated to T. S. Eliot, to whom the manuscript was presented. First published by Faber & Faber as an appendix to the English edition of *Expositions and Developments*, and subsequently by Boosey & Hawkes. Duration: *c.* 2 minutes 10 seconds. First performance, Los Angeles (Monday Evening Concerts), 19 February 1962, conducted by Robert Craft.

Sometime in 1960 Stravinsky was invited to compose a hymn for a new English hymnal being planned by the Cambridge University Press. Shortly afterwards it was suggested by T. S. Eliot himself that the fourth section of 'Little Gidding', the last of the *Four Quartets*, would provide an appropriate text.

The work is based on the following tone-row:

Ex.179

Possibly taking his cue from the remarkable effect Eliot achieved by the repetition of key words as in . . . *Lies in the choice of pyre or pyre – To be redeemed from fire by fire* Stravinsky does not hesitate to repeat single notes and small note clusters. It should be noticed how in bars 26–32 where the following lines are set for tenors and basses alone—

> *Who then devised the torment? Love.*
> *Love is the unfamiliar Name*
> *Behind the hands that wove*
> *The intolerable shirt of flame. —*

---

[1] Colin Mason, *op. cit.*

Original Compositions

a complete sequence of the tone-row crosses from basses to tenors on the word 'Name', while the retrograde version followed by the inversion crosses from tenors to basses also on the same word.

EIGHT INSTRUMENTAL MINIATURES

For chamber orchestra, 1962 – see no. 49 (A).

102. THE FLOOD

A Musical Play[1] for tenor solo (Lucifer, Satan), two bass soloists (God), and chorus (S.A.T.), with speaking parts for Noah, Noah's wife, Noah's Sons, a Narrator, and a Caller, and for orchestra (4.3.4.3 – 4.3.3.1 – timpani, 3 tom-toms, xylophone-marimba, cymbal, big drum, celesta, piano, harp – string 5tet). Composed during 1961 and 1962 and finished on 14 March 1962. Published by Boosey & Hawkes, 1963. Duration: *c.* 24 minutes. First performance telecast by CBS Television Network, U.S.A., 14 June 1962. First stage performance, Staatsoper, Hamburg, 30 April 1963, conducted by Robert Craft.

Composition and Treatment

When Stravinsky, after being approached by Robert Graff in 1959, was invited by CBS Television through Sextant Inc. to write a special work for television, he thought of doing a kind of dance drama to the Biblical allegory of Noah and the Flood. Excellent texts existed in the various medieval mystery plays extant; but one of them (from the Chester Cycle of Miracle Plays) had already been most effectively set by Benjamin Britten in his *Noye's Fludde* (1957). In any case, Stravinsky wanted to give his work a wider ambiance by relating it to the Creation, and he saw the Flood as an image of catastrophe rather than a drama of antediluvian man.

> Why did I call my work *The Flood*, instead of *Noah*? Because Noah is mere history. As a genuine antediluvian he is a great curiosity, but a side-show curiosity. And even as 'eternal man', the second Adam, the – to Augustinians – Old Testament Christ image, he is less important than the Eternal Catastrophe. The Flood is also *The Bomb* (*Exp*).

In the event Robert Craft was responsible for the text, which is a conflation of passages from the York pageants of *The Creation and the Fall of Lucifer* and *The Fall of Man* and the Chester pageant of *Noah's Flood*, bound together with brief quotations from *Genesis*.[2]

---

[1] For the première recording, released before the publication of the score, *The Flood* was styled 'a Biblical Allegory based on Noah and the Ark'. For the telecast performance on 14 June 1962 it was entitled *Noah and the Flood* and subtitled 'dance drama'.

[2] The text has been considerably revised and altered to fit it for consumption by a television audience.

Such a scenario was bound to result in a mixture of musical methods. Certain passages from the Mystery Plays postulated a dramatic setting; others called for narration. And some episodes looked as if they could be better represented in terms of dance than song.

From the beginning, Stravinsky made a distinction between the celestials and the terrestrials, intending 'that the celestials should sing while the terrestrials should merely talk' (*Exp*). The terrestrials included a Narrator and a Caller as well as Noah and his family. There were only two celestials: God and Lucifer (Satan). Lucifer was cast as 'a high, slightly pederastic tenor'[1] (*Exp*); but God posed a problem. In *Babel* Stravinsky had avoided the anthropomorphic solution by setting God's words for male voice choir. In his second Canticle, *Abraham and Isaac* (1952), which was based on the pageant in the Chester cycle, Britten had had the genial inspiration of combining the voices of Abraham (tenor) and Isaac (alto) to create the voice of God. In *The Flood*, Stravinsky decided to use a duet of two bass soloists and, as a corollary, to exclude basses from the chorus. Commentary and narration were to be given in measured declamation (without pitch) or in free speech – sometimes to be accompanied by music (melodrama); sometimes not.

Two episodes – 'The Building of the Ark' and 'The Flood' – were to be solely instrumental (not choral) and were designed for choreography accordingly.

The audience sees only the builders (dancers) who carry invisible boards and beams and who hammer non-existent nails. I have already visualised[2] some of the dancers' movements – the men pulling over their shoulders on imaginary ropes, the women bending, tugging, dragging – and I have thought that the dancers should continue the rhythm of the music during the musical silences. The flood itself must be *altissimo*, not *fortissimo*, full and high, choked, unable to 'breathe' but not loud (*Exp*).

The relationship between the supernatural beings and the humans was satisfactorily established; but the problem of the animal world was not really resolved. It is true that the Caller catalogues the animals on their entry into the Ark; but it is a weakness in the action that, once there, they seem to be forgotten, for there is no further reference to them – not even to the special roles played by the raven and the dove.

The work is schematically set out as follows:

Prelude

    (i) Instrumental prelude
    (ii) *Te Deum* (Chorus)

---

[1] Whatever that may mean!
[2] Stravinsky wrote this passage in 1961, before the television production.

    (iii) Melodrama (Narrator)
    (iv) God's Word (2 basses)
    (v) Aria (Lucifer)
    (vi) Melodrama (Narrator)
    (vii) God's Word (concluded)

The Building of the Ark
(Choreography)

The Catalogue of the Animals
Melodrama (Noah and Caller)

The Comedy
Melodrama (Noah and his wife and sons)

The Flood
(Choreography)

The Covenant of the Rainbow
    (i) God's Word (2 basses)
    (ii) Melodrama (Noah)
    (iii) Reprise of instrumental prelude
    (iv) Aria (Lucifer)
    (v) *Sanctus* (Chorus)

This is a quite complicated scenario; and on the stage one would expect such an action to take well over an hour. The television screen, however, demands the speed of the cinema; and musically Stravinsky was able to meet the requirements of conciseness and concentration thanks largely to the use of the serial system. The score takes less than half an hour to perform.

As he worked on *The Flood*, he had a number of ingenious ideas about the screening of the action. For instance, when Lucifer is transformed into Satan ('Lucifer's negative polarity'), he imagined the singer 'made to seem transparent, like a scorpion' (*Dia*). And for the tempting of Eve, where Satan is seen in a transparent moth-bag serpent with reticulations, he insisted that 'the vermicular disguise must have an excremental shape, and Satan must appear unchanged and plainly visible within' (*Dia*). He also became fascinated by the possibility of a new musicodramatic form being developed through television.

Visually it [i.e. television] offers every advantage over stage opera, but the saving of musical time interests me more than anything visual. This new musical economy was the one specific of the medium which guided my conception of *The Flood*. Because the succession of visualisations can be instantaneous, the composer may dispense with the afflatus of overtures, connecting episodes, curtain music. I have used only one or two notes to punctuate each stage in The Creation, for example, and so far, I have not been able to imagine the work on the operatic stage because the musical speed is so uniquely cinematographic (*Dia*).

Music

Of all Stravinsky's serial works, *The Flood* is probably the one that shows the strongest feeling for harmony. The opening of the *Prelude*, which represents Chaos, is a twelve-note chord spanning five and a half octaves, built up symmetrically from its middle point (Ex. 180a). It is interesting to find that its component notes

Ex. 180

can be resolved into six fifths (Ex. 180b) though in the event little use is made of this version.[1] At the sixth bar of the *Prelude*, the chord of Chaos, which has been played tremolo by the strings, resolves into a clear statement of the series on which the score is based, the retrograde version being given to the harp in equal crotchets, while the original version is played by wood wind instruments in diminution in a series of rising arabesques, described by Stravinsky as a 'musical Jacob's Ladder'[2] (*Dia*).

Ex. 181

---

[1] See, however, bars 4 and 5 and bars 8–15. It is interesting that this is the same note-row as the one used by Benjamin Britten in *The Turn of the Screw* (1954).

[2] It is interesting to find that some critics – e.g. Anthony Payne in his article 'Stravinsky's "The Flood"' *Tempo*, Autumn 1964 – look on what I have called the original version of this series as the retrograde version, and *vice versa*. My own view is that just as in the expository introduction to *Threni* the original version is given to the higher voice (soprano) and the inversion to the lower voice (alto), so in *The Flood* the original version is heard in the higher notes of the woodwind and the retrograde in the lower notes of the harp of this 'musical Jacob's ladder'. According to my reading, the inversion is used to depict the rising of the flood, and this changes to the retrograde inversion as soon as the waters begin to subside. According to Payne, the opposite is the case. Perhaps, ultimately, it is not of much consequence, since the series is a closed system, the constituent parts of which are equally valid from whatever direction they are approached.

Original Compositions

But as soon as the chorus begins its *Te Deum* (at bar 8), it is apparent that the Jacob's Ladder series was in a distant key, and there has been a modulation up a fifth to reach the basic series (Ex. 182).

Ex. 182

The first six notes of the inversion of the series form the main theme of the *Te Deum*, the phrases of which are punctuated by chords, two of which have

Ex. 183

split away from the chord of Chaos, while a third is formed from the last six notes of the inversion of the series. It will be seen that Stravinsky repeats the first two notes to get an effect of chanting[1] – 'not Gregorian but Igorian chant' (*Dia*) – but unequal repetition results in a serial upset, as the third note of the inversion follows the first at the 've-' of 'veneratur' (Ex. 183).

God's voice as rendered by the two basses has an extra-dimensional quality caused by the dark shading of the lower line. As can be seen from the following excerpt (Ex. 184), chosen because it introduces the character of Lucifer, the upper voice starts with the second note of the retrograde version, while the

---

[1] The cut of this passage recalls the opening of the *Sustinuit anima mea* passage in the *Spes* section of the middle movement of the *Canticum Sacrum*.

lower voice starts with the second note of the retrograde inversion. (Both notes happen to be G natural.) Most of the notes in the phrase are repeated; the parts cross over once and cross back again; and each voice ends its phrase on the first note of the appropriate version/inversion (i.e., G sharp and F sharp). The bass chords are formed by combining the notes of the original version with the notes of the inversion played a second higher; and here too the parts frequently cross. The repeated notes of the bass drum provide a kind of sonorous nimbus.

The scene between Eve and the Serpent (melodrama) could hardly be simpler or more effective. The triplet accompaniment is based on notes 2 to 6 of the original version of the series, while the insinuating melody uses notes 1 to 6 of the retrograde version. Stravinsky's own comment on this passage is: 'The Tarnhelm music for two muted horns is likely to be my first and last attempt to compose a belly dance' (*Dia*).

Ex. 185

(N.B. The narration and declamation are not shown in this example.)

The Building of the Ark is a dynamic, percussive movement, where an urgent sense of hammering is conveyed by repeated chords, usually in groups of five. A cadence of *sforzando* chords[1] recalls similar passages in works as distant as the 'Danse Sacrale' of *The Rite of Spring* and the last movement of the *Symphony in Three Movements*. This is immediately followed by three bars of mixed wind arabesques, in which the time becomes as involved as passages in *Movements* (see Ex. 170), but even more so. Here the 3 + 4 + 5 grouping of notes already referred to in *Movements* (see Ex. 169) is much in evidence; and the bar illustrated (Ex. 186) is of extreme polyrhythmic complication.

---

[1] Bars 277–282.

Ex. 186

Should one wish to reduce these phrases at different speeds to mathematical order, this 4/8 bar must be subdivided into 1,680 equal beats (210 to each semiquaver). The schematic layout is then as follows:

Fl. I. Five notes of 168 beats, followed by four of 105 and three of 140.
Fl. II. Four notes of 105 beats, followed by three of 140 and five of 168.
Cl. I. Three notes of 140 beats, followed by five of 168 and four of 105.
Cl. II. A trill lasting 560 beats, followed by seven notes of 80 beats and two of 280 (one of them being a trill).
Cor I. & II. and Tr. I. Eight notes of 210 beats, of which the even numbers are tied to the following odd numbers.

This means that, if one ignores the notes of the two trills, there are separate notes being played on the following beats of this 1680/3360 bar:

1/106/141/169/211/281/316/337/421/505/561/589/631/641/673/701/721/
757/801/841/881/925/946/961/1009/1041/1051/1093/1121/1156/1177/
1261/1345/1366/1401/1471/1513/1541/1575

The climax of the work is the movement called *The Flood*. Here Stravinsky has produced a magnificent palindrome in musical terms. It is prefaced by a shrill sheet of lightning from the flutes, piccolo, marimba xylophone and piano, which is repeated but not reversed at the end of the movement. The twelve notes of the series are disposed as two successive but interlocking chords. These are like a mushroom of spreading sound, for from them is derived a seven-note chord which acts as a drone throughout the movement, while violins *flautando* and flutes weave a tremulous, whirling semiquaver pattern, and a trombone and a horn share an augmented statement of the series in all its four versions. The movement of the water reminds one of Leonardo da Vinci's amazing deluge drawings, on one of which he has written:

> Observe the motion of the surface of the water how it resembles that of hair, which has two movements – one depends on the weight of the hair, the other on the direction of the curls; thus the water forms whirling eddies.[1]

The opening glimpse of this vortex of sound shows how the violin and flute semiquaver motive, which never exceeds a tenth in compass, is made up out of fragments of the series eddying like flotsam above the strangulating sound of the seven-note chord.

Ex. 187

Towards the middle of the movement the series begins to emerge in its inversion in what proves to be the longest of the violin/flute cadences. The pattern is the following:

```
                             7
    1  2  3  4  5  6  7  8
    1  2  3  4  5  6  7  8  9
    1  2  3  4  5  6  7  8  9  10
    1  2  3  4  5  6  7  8  9  10  11
    1  2  3  4  5  6  7  8  9  10  11  12
    1  2  3  4  5  6
```

---

[1] Written by Leonardo da Vinci on his drawing 'Studies of an Old Man Seated and of Swirling Water'. Windsor Royal Library no. 12,579 *recto*.

When this cadence is interrupted, the ictus of the double chord (bar one of Ex. 187 above) is reversed, and the violin/flute cadence is resumed in its retrograde inversion, viz.

```
                    7  8  9  10  11  12
      1  2  3  4  5  6  7  8  9  10  11  12
         2  3  4  5  6  7  8  9  10  11  12
            3  4  5  6  7  8  9  10  11  12
               4  5  6  7  8  9  10  11  12
                  5  6  7  8  9  10  11  12
                  6
```

The rest of the movement then runs back to the initial flash of lightning. Stravinsky's own comment on this movement is:

> The music imitates not waves and winds, but time. The interruptions in the violin/flute line say: 'No, it isn't over.' As the skin of the sun is fire, so here the violins and flutes are the skin drawn over the body of the sound. This *'La Mer'* has no *'de l'aube à midi'* but only a time experience of something that is terrible and that lasts (*Dia*).

At the beginning of the Covenant of the Rainbow, God's voice is heard again; and there is a short passage of declamation for Noah ending

> *All beasts and fowls shall forth be bred*
> *And so a world begins to be.*

At this point, when the work was being planned, Balanchine had the idea that Satan's wing tips should be seen inching their way out of the squelchy ground, for he is 'another and unexpected survivor of the flood' (*Dia*); and to meet this suggestion Stravinsky agreed to repeat the Chaos music from the *Prelude* i.e. the first half dozen bars of the score ending with the musical Jacob's Ladder (see Ex. 181). A *quasi falsetto* aria for Satan follows; and here Stravinsky makes the interesting comment that as this aria 'is a prolepsis of Christianity, Satan must now be shown as Anti-Christ' (*Dia*). But this is beyond the power of the music; and for its effective realisation one has to rely on the screen or stage producer.

The score ends with a *Sanctus* for the chorus, which leads back to the original music of the *Te Deum*. The voices of the chorus die away and break off as a rearrangement of the original Chaos chord is heard, followed by the Jacob's Ladder music *rallentando*.

Productions

The American edition of *Dialogues and a Diary* reprints the working notes for *The Flood*. These were based mainly on two sessions that Stravinsky, Balanchine, and Craft had together in Hollywood (15–16 March and 11–12

April 1952) and show how much imagination and care were expended on the television production. This was designed by Rouben Ter-Arutunian, who made numerous sketches for gobos,[1] backgrounds, costumes, masks, and the settings for the choreographic scenes. The choreography was by Balanchine. The conducting was shared by Stravinsky and Craft; and the entire production was supervised by the composer. The première telecast took place on 14 June 1962.

The first stage performance was given at the Hamburg Opera on 30 April 1963 in the presence of the composer. Günther Rennert produced. Choreography was by Peter van Dyk, scenery and costumes by Teo Otto; and Craft conducted.

The telecast production, which was jointly commissioned and presented by Breck Shampoo and CBS Television, suffered from a preliminary build-up that was out of all proportion to the 24-minute-long work itself. There was 'a pseudo-profound anthropological prologue having to do with Flood Myths and a long, disorganised, totally inappropriate review of the Stravinsky-Balanchine collaboration. The remaining time was filled by Breck Shampoo commercials accompanied by their own distinctive, if uncredited, music'.[2] When one came to *The Flood* itself, some of the visual realisations were fascinating; but the choreographic numbers suffered from the inability of the television screen to cope adequately with ballet as a three-dimensional art. The mixture of conventions used in the production was teasing and at times confusing to the television audience; and the intimate scale of the screen dwarfed some of the effects. Although the music itself came over quite well, some of the critics gained the impression that the work was 'woefully inchoate'.

These deficiencies were not altogether remedied in the Hamburg stage production. The dancing made a greater impact, though Balanchine's choreography was missed; but trouble was caused by the fact that amplifiers were used for the Voice of God, the two basses being placed off-stage, and some of the music in the melodramatic passages was drowned by the declamation.[3]

Owing to the hotch-potch of conventions employed, *The Flood* is always likely to prove a difficult score to mount; but success is more likely to be achieved by simple than sophisticated means, and it may respond better to studio treatment than to stage production.

103. ABRAHAM AND ISAAC

A sacred ballad for baritone and chamber orchestra (2 fl., 1 fl. alto, 1 ob., 1 c.i., 1 cl., 1 cl. basso, 2 bn., 1 hn., 2 tr., 2 trb. (tenor and bass), 1 tuba, string

[1] Term used in television to designate a frame, foreground piece, or model.
[2] From 'Stravinsky: A Flood of Genius' by Benjamin Boretz. *The London Magazine*, January 1963.
[3] Part of the music accompanying the Comedy of Noah and his Wife was actually omitted.

5tet). Composition started in 1962 and completed on 3 March 1963. Dedicated to the people of the State of Israel. Published by Boosey & Hawkes, 1965. Duration twelve minutes. First performance, Binyanei He'Ooma, Jerusalem, 23 August 1964, and second performance at Caesarea the following day, by the Israel Festival Orchestra with Ephraim Biran as soloist, conducted by Robert Craft.

A Note on Language

Russian was Stravinsky's mother tongue; but he never used the work of Russian authors very extensively in his musical settings. As a comparatively young man, he wrote songs and a cantata to poems by Serge Gorodetzky and Konstantin Balmont, but was more at home with the sort of pan-dialectical folk-poems that he made up later for his 'Russian' style compositions. These belong mainly to the period of the first World War; and after 1922 (the year in which he completed *Mavra* to Boris Kochno's libretto after Pushkin) he never set another Russian text to music.

The years between the two Wars were a period of indecision. There are Italian texts in the ballet score of *Pulcinella;* but these are really Pergolesi's settings rather than Stravinsky's. Slavonic texts were used for the three *a cappella* pieces, *Paternoster, Credo,* and *Ave Maria.* As for French, after a preliminary essay in setting *Two Poems of Verlaine* in 1910, he accepted a French text from André Gide for *Persephone* in 1934, but was not encouraged to continue in this direction by the rather bitter controversy about French prosody that broke out between himself and the author. Latin provided a kind of refuge. *Oedipus Rex* represented a successful break-through into a dead language; and subsequently he used Latin texts culled mainly from the Scriptures for the *Symphony of Psalms,* the *Canticum Sacrum,* and *Threni.*

English he came to comparatively late in his career. The first English text he set was part of Genesis in the Authorised Version for *Babel* (1944); but after completing *The Rake's Progress* to W. H. Auden's libretto (1951), other English settings followed thick and fast. Several English medieval lyrics were used in the *Cantata;* there were settings of poems by William Shakespeare, Dylan Thomas, Thomas Dekker and T. S. Eliot; and the words for the first two movements of *A Sermon, A Narrative and a Prayer* were drawn from the Authorised Version, while the libretto for *The Flood* consisted of a conflation of passages from English medieval mystery plays and the Bible.

Russian; Slavonic; Latin; Italian; French; English. Now it was to be the turn of a seventh language – Hebrew.

When asked by the Israel Festival Committee to provide them with a new work, he agreed to make a setting of the story of Abraham and Isaac in Hebrew. As he was ignorant of this language, his friend Sir Isaiah Berlin helped him to understand the original Hebrew text and instructed him in the significance of its sounds and word structure. In an interview Stravinsky gave to the press

Original Compositions

shortly before the work's first performance in Jerusalem, he said:– 'Although I do not understand Hebrew, I have fallen in love with the language, which I have translated into music in my *Abraham and Isaac*. The only Hebrew word I know is "shalom", and it is the idea expressed in this word that my new work voices.'

Composition and Treatment

In a note for the Programme Book of the Festival of Israel, July – August 1964, Stravinsky wrote:

Abraham and Isaac is a sacred ballad for baritone and small orchestra composed on the Hebrew text of Genesis (B'RESHIT) Chapter XXII.

There are five parts[1] distinguished by changes of tempo and performed without interruption; and nineteen verses comprising ten musical units. Though, in the Bible, the verses are sometimes expressed in dialogue form, my setting does not impersonate the protagonists but tells the whole story through the baritone-narrator, underlining a change of speaker by changes in dynamics.

No translation of the Hebrew should ever be attempted as the syllables, both as accentuation and timbre, are a precisely fixed and principal element of the music. The verbal and musical accentuation are identical, incidentally, which is rare in my music. And though repetitions of words occur, they are never accompanied by exact musical repetitions. 'Abraham', the most often repeated word, is always sung without instruments.[2] The vocal line is partly *bel*-Cantor – melismatic – and partly an interval-speech of single syllables.

I do not wish the listener any luck in discovering musical descriptions or illustrations of the text. To my knowledge none were composed. Nor am I aware of musical symbolisms in my use of canons or 'expressive' rhythmic devices, and whoever pretends to hear them in, for example, the passage referring to Isaac and the two boys, is making too much of what for me could be no more than a coincidence.

A 12-note series is used but hexachordal and smaller units are stressed rather than the full orders. Octaves, fifths, and doubled intervals can be found but they are not in contradiction to the serial basis of the composition, being the result of concordances from the several serial forms, or what I call serial verticals.

Of the several origins of every work probably the most important cannot be determined. I may say, however, that I began to compose *Abraham and Isaac* because of the attractions of the Hebrew language as sound, because

---

[1] When this note was reprinted in *Themes and Episodes*, Stravinsky changed this 'five' to 'six'.

[2] In *Themes and Episodes* this was changed to '"Abraham" is the most often repeated word, and it is sung the first time without instruments.' There are also other minor changes of wording in the note as reprinted.

of the subject and, not least, because I wanted to leave a token of my gratitude to the people of Israel, to whom the music is dedicated, for their generosity and hospitality during my tour of their country in 1962.

In examining the score, it is convenient to subdivide it into seven sections, which are separated from each other by double-barring, rather than the five parts mentioned in Stravinsky's note above. Throughout the cantata, the part of the baritone soloist is central to the scheme; and the chamber orchestra is handled with care and restraint so as to throw the vocal line into maximum relief.

The series used is the following:

Ex. 188

Its most striking feature is the scale passage formed by the first five notes of the original version. This results in a tonal pull towards C sharp in the original and retrograde versions, and toward G natural in the inversion and retrograde inversion.

1. ♪ = 132. *Bars 1 – 11.* Instrumental introduction. *Bars 12 – 45.* The baritone starts *cantabile* and is at first accompanied by a single melodic line entrusted to the following solo instruments in succession: bass clarinet, oboe, bassoon, cor anglais, tenor and bass trombones, bass clarinet, bassoon, horn, clarinet, tenor and bass trombones. *Bars 47 – 51.* After a 2/8 bar of silence, there is a brief instrumental interlude. Note bar 49 (Ex. 189) where there are

Ex. 189

[N.B. The string parts are omitted]

groups of five, six and seven semiquavers to be played in the time of six by the bass clarinet, oboe, and clarinet respectively. *Bars 52 – 72.* This passage, in which the soloist sings of Abraham saddling his ass early in the morning and taking two of his boys with him as well as Isaac, has a two-part accompaniment. The top line (for flute and oboe) starts in even quavers, but changes to dotted quavers after half a dozen bars; and the bottom line (for bass trombone and tuba reinforced by bassoon and bass clarinet) starts in dotted quavers, but changes to even quavers. This results in a slightly hobbled effect. The final words of the section – 'of which God has told him' – are accompanied by the 1st and 2nd violins and violas playing *tremolo sul ponticello.*

2. ♪ = 132. (*Stesso tempo.*) *Bars 73 – 88.* Bassoon and solo violin sharing the retrograde version of the series closely follow the voice singing the retrograde inversion transposed up eight semitones. Two string chords punctuate the singer's closing cadence, and similar chords punctuate *bars 89 – 90* which is a melismatic flute cadenza marked *quasi rubato.*

3. ♪ = 120. *Bars 91 – 104.* The tempo quickens for this instrumental interlude, though as the musical unit changes from ♪ to ♪, no actual speeding up is perceptible. In this strange little march, the instruments are deployed in pairs – two bassoons; clarinet and bass clarinet; cellos and double-basses; flute and cor anglais; and any two of the following three: tenor trombone, bass trombone, tuba.

4. ♪ = 92 – 96. (*Meno mosso.*) *Bars 105 – 128.* The greater part of this section consists of unaccompanied declamation for the soloist, in which the phrases are punctuated by chords, brief cadences, or slight arabesques from the wind instruments. *Bars 129 – 162.* The soloist's part is marked *cantabile* for Abraham's speech 'My son, God will provide himself a lamb for a burnt offering'. It is accompanied by a two-part invention for trumpet and tuba; and henceforward for the rest of the section the accompaniment is again entrusted to instruments in pairs. It is in consonance with Stravinsky's usual reluctance to commit himself to expressive effects that no special emphasis, either vocal or instrumental, marks the passage where Abraham takes up the knife to slay Isaac.

5. ♪ = 76 (*Meno mosso.*) *Bars 163 – 181.* In the opening bars the soloist describes how the Angel of the Lord called out of heaven, and his vocal line is accompanied by flute (in inversion) and tuba (in augmented imitation). In the following bars he is for the most part unaccompanied, and his phrases are punctuated by *sff* chords from the strings. The section ends with a one-bar instrumental cadence for oboe and cor anglais stiffened by two muted trumpets.

6. ♪ = 72. (*Meno mosso*) *Bars 182 – 239.* There is a two-bar instrumental introduction consisting of a five-part phrase for strings followed by two chords scored for three flutes and two trombones. For the passage describing the ram caught in the thicket, clarinet and bassoon weave an accompaniment consisting of arabesques threaded on trills. Two chords for flutes, trombones and tuba

followed by a six-part phrase for strings make a brief instrumental caesura. A three-part canon for voice, horn and tuba leads to a close where the string phrase is brought in to provide a cadence leading to a final chord of C sharps (for flutes and trombones) extended over three octaves. A passage of declamation accompanied first by successive and then by overlapping notes from horn and tuba leads to the climax of the work: 'And in thy seed shall all the nations of the earth be blessed; because thou hast obeyed my voice.' Here eight chords are scored for woodwind (three flutes, clarinet, and bass clarinet) and muted brass (two trumpets, horn, tenor and bass trombones, and tuba) in which the woodwind is directed to play for a semiquaver's duration in all the chords, while in five of them the brass is sustained for varying periods. These chords provide a passage of maximum harmonic tension; and it is curious to find that these serial verticals carry such strong tonal implications with them. One feels that in a different context they might have fitted into one of the later neo-classical works such as the *Symphony in Three Movements*.

Ex. 190

[*N.B. The baritone part is omitted*]

7. ♪ = 60 (*Andante*) *Bars* 240 – 254. This coda, in which the tempo runs down to its slowest metronomic rate, starts with a five-bar introduction for a trio of solo string instruments. The voice enters *tranquillo* and is accompanied by solo viola, until in the last bar but two the bass clarinet takes over. It will be seen that the baritone's final phrase takes advantage of the peculiar structure of the series and can be construed as belonging to both the retrograde version and the inversion of the series.

Ex. 191

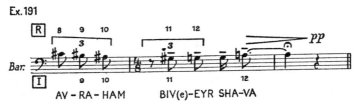

Original Compositions

104. ELEGY FOR J.F.K.

For baritone and three clarinets (two in B flat and one alto). Words by W. H. Auden. Composed in Hollywood, March 1964. Published by Boosey & Hawkes, 1964. Duration: *c* 1 minute 30 seconds. First performance, Los Angeles (Monday Evening Concerts), 6 April 1964, conducted by Robert Craft. A pencil version of the manuscript score is in the Library of Congress, Washington, D.C.

In common with hundreds of million people all over the globe, Stravinsky felt a deep sense of sorrow and loss when President John F. Kennedy was assassinated on 22 November 1963. A few months later it seemed to him that the events of the previous November were in danger of being too quickly forgotten and, wishing to anticipate (in his own words) 'the albatrosses of "epic" poetry and symphonic sentiment that the event [would] surely give rise to and for a certain time excuse', he turned to W. H. Auden for a 'very quiet little lyric', and Auden responded with a poem of four stanzas, each a free *haiku*, seventeen syllables in length. This was sufficient pretext for Stravinsky to write a short song for baritone accompanied by three clarinets.

The series used is a strange one, containing no fewer than three tritones; and as the third one (F natural/B natural) coincides with the sixth and seventh

Ex. 192

notes of the series, it acts as a pivot for the whole work, the same interval appearing with the notes unchanged (except for their order) at the same midpoint of the retrograde version, the inversion, and the retrograde inversion. Another feature of this series is the fact that the first five notes of the original version all belong to one of the whole-tone scales, and the next four notes belong to the other whole-tone scale.

This miniature work is most moving in its brevity and concision and has a projection much larger than its actual scale. Though lasting no more than a

Ex. 193

533

minute and a half, it has time even to achieve a formal perfection by repeating the opening stanza (*'When a just man dies, Lamentation and praise, Sorrow and joy are one'*) at the end and giving it an exquisite new instrumental cadence with a final whole-tone sigh. This leads to a 3/8 bar of silence, which is as much an integral part of the score as the built-in silences at the end of Act II and beginning of Act III of *Wozzeck*. (See Ex. 193.)

There is a version for mezzo-soprano (instead of baritone) with minimal changes in the clarinet parts. This version had its first performance at the Philharmonic Hall, New York, on 6 December 1964, when it was conducted by the composer.

105. FANFARE FOR A NEW THEATRE

For two trumpets. Composed in Hollywood, winter, 1964. Dedicated 'to Lincoln and George' (i.e. Lincoln Kirstein and George Balanchine). First performed at the New York State Theater in the Lincoln Center, 19 April 1964.

Although this is one of Stravinsky's shortest works, lasting no more than 30 seconds in all, it is one of the most compact and striking. The two trumpets, both in C, start in unison; and at various moments in this fanfare their repeated notes – A sharp to begin with, then D sharp, later G natural, and at one moment (near the centre of the work) F sharp – sketch a kind of tonal framework for a series that is put through its usual serial drill. This series, however, is remarkable in itself. In its original version each group of three consecutive notes is so arranged that it explores the interval of a second, and these groups follow each other in an ascending order. In the rather fast tempo required, the effect of the two trumpets is like that of two pennants flying and crackling in a brisk wind.

106. VARIATIONS (ALDOUS HUXLEY IN MEMORIAM)

For orchestra (3.3.3.2–4.3.3.0. – harp, piano – string 4tet[1]). Begun at Santa Fé in July 1963 and finished at Hollywood on 28 October 1964. Published by Boosey & Hawkes, 1965. Duration *c*. 4 minutes 45 seconds. First performance, Chicago, 17 April 1965, conducted by Robert Craft.

In this single movement of symphonic variations, Stravinsky carries a stage further the exploration of the possibilities of duodecimal patterning that he opened up in *Agon*. Not only is the work completely serial, the series used being the following:

---

[1] The score specifies 12 violins, 10 violas, 8 cellos, and 4 double-basses.

Original Compositions

but its central feature is a duodecet (if such a word may be coined), or twelve-part invention, that is fitted into a regular metrical framework of 4/8 + 3/8 + 5/8 bars. This 4 + 3 + 5 = 12 formula is used like a stanza twelve times in all with breaks after each group of four; and these three sections (here referred to as A, B, and C for ease of reference) are separated from each other by important musical episodes. For each section of the duodecet the instrumental layout is different. A is written for twelve solo violins and has a fairly high tessitura; B is for ten solo violas, and two solo double-basses, and its tessitura is correspondingly lower; and C features twelve wind instruments, *viz.* two flutes and alto flute, two oboes and cor anglais, two clarinets and bass clarinet, horn and two bassoons. The rhythmic articulation of each part throughout each section is idiosyncratic and completely different from the other eleven parts; but each part is isorhythmic within each section – that is to say, it adheres to the same rhythmic procedure when it reappears in the other two sections, though the actual notes are changed. The twelve parts are based on the versions of the original series and make extensive use of modulation; but each part is integrally different, so there is real twelve-part writing throughout the duodecet, with no literal repetitions of passages of close imitation. The point can be made clear by taking the third of the twelve instrumental parts and quoting the first few bars of its appearance from each of the three sections A, B, and C.

Ex. 195 a

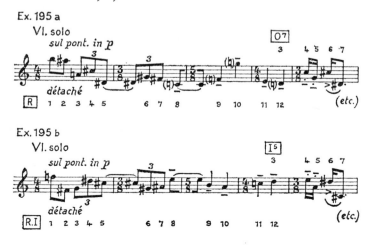

2. Register of Works

Ex. 195 c

The remaining music of these *Variations* is grouped round the three sections of the duodecet in what may be looked on as a prelude, two interludes and a postlude (here figured as I, II, III, & IV). The whole movement is geared to a metronome rate of 80; but the notation varies between ♩ = 80 and ♪ = 80.

I. After introductory chordal cadences, monodic phrases are presented, sometimes by single instruments, sometimes with doublings.

A. *Duodecet*, 1st section.

II. A short episode for flutes and bassoons, with oboe solo. (The first complete bar of the oboe solo is marked *più mosso* ♪ = 240; but the basic speed of ♪ = 80 returns in the next bar.)

B. *Duodecet*, 2nd section.

III. This is an extended section with five episodes: (*a*) It opens with a three-part invention for woodwind, trumpets and strings being added later. (*b*) Two chords sounded in quick succession (the first *forte*, the second *piano*) frame the phrases of a three-part invention for trombones. (*c*) A short contrapuntal episode for strings, clarinets, cor anglais, bassoon and horn leads to (*d*) a passage featuring staccato repeated chords from the trombones. This is followed by (*e*) a fugato for the strings reinforced by occasional dry comments from the piano.

C. *Duodecet*, 3rd section.

IV. Chordal cadences, similar to those in the prelude, recur in the postlude, framing monodic phrases from the flutes, piano, and harp. The final cadence of five chords is formed from eleven notes of the series. The missing note (G sharp) played solo by the bass clarinet constitutes the final bar of the movement.

These *Variations* are dedicated to Aldous Huxley, whom Stravinsky had originally met in London about the time of the publication of *Those Barren Leaves*. About twelve years later they met again in Hollywood, and their friendship became much closer. When Stravinsky wanted to find a suitable English libretto for his full-length opera, it was Huxley he consulted and Huxley who recommended W. H. Auden. By the summer of 1949 the two friends were meeting regularly for lunch several times a week. They went together to concerts, plays and film previews, and made joint excursions to explore

536

'Southern California's museums, zoological gardens, architectural oddities'. Stravinsky admired his friend, calling him 'an aristocrat of behaviour' and adding that he was 'gentle, humble, courageous, intellectually charitable' (*Dia*). When Huxley died on 22 November 1963 (the same day as the assassination of President J. F. Kennedy), Stravinsky was deeply grieved. He had already embarked on the composition of these *Variations* and decided to dedicate them to his friend's memory.

In a note dated 11 March 1965, just before the first performance, Stravinsky wrote:

> '*Veränderungen*' – alterations or mutations, Bach's word for the Goldberg Variations – could be used to describe my *Variations* as well, except that I have altered or diversified a series, instead of a theme or subject. In fact, I do not have a theme, in the textbook sense, whereas Bach's theme (for comparison) is a complete aria.
>
> Some of us think that the role of rhythm is larger today than ever before, but however that may be, in the absence of harmonic modulation it must play a considerable part in the delineation of form. And more than ever before, the composer must be certain of building rhythmic unity into variety. In my *Variations*, tempo is a variable and pulsation a constant.
>
> The density of the twelve-part variations is the main innovation in the work. One might think of these constructions as musical mobiles, in that the patterns within them will seem to change perspective with repeated hearings. They are relieved and offset by music of a contrasting starkness and even, notably in the first variation, by *Klangfarben* monody – which is also variation.
>
> The question of length (duration) is inseparable from that of depth and/or height (content). But whether full, partly full, or empty, the musical statements of the *Variations* are concise, I prefer to think, rather than short. They are, whatever one thinks, a radical contrast to the prolix manner of speech of most of the late last-century music which is the pabulum of our regular concert life; and there lies the difficulty, mine with you no less than yours with me.
>
> I do not know how to guide listeners other than to advise them to listen not once but repeatedly. . . . I may say that they should not look for the boundary lines of the individual variations, but try instead to hear the piece as a whole. And on second thought I *can* recommend one guide, the orchestra itself. The use of families and individuals in contrast is a principal projective element of the form, especially of its symmetries and reversibles. The leading solo roles are those of the flutes, bassoons, and trombones; and perhaps my economy is inconsistent in that the trumpet and horn families have in comparison so little to do; I needed only a spot of red, however, and a spot of blue. I might add that the orchestral *dramatis personae* is unusual in that four rather than the standard five string parts are required

2. Register of Works

(there is only one division of violins) and that each must be of equal weight. Percussion instruments are not used, but their position is occupied by the piano and harp which appear as a couple (married).

107. INTROITUS

(T. S. Eliot in memoriam) for tenors, basses, harp, piano, two timpani, two tam-tams, solo viola and double-bass. Composed in Hollywood early in 1965 and completed on 17 February. Published by Boosey & Hawkes, 1965. Duration *c*. three minutes thirty seconds. First performance, Chicago, 17 April 1965.

It is probable that towards the end of 1964 Stravinsky had in mind the idea that he might compose a Requiem Mass; but the death of his friend T. S. Eliot in London on 4 January 1965 precipitated the composition of a single movement entitled *Introitus*, which was completed six weeks later. Thereby T. S. Eliot joined the distinguished roll-call of those whom Stravinsky had already chosen to honour and commemorate – Rimsky-Korsakov, Debussy, Natalie Koussevitzky, Alphonse Onnou, Dylan Thomas, Prinz Max Egon zu Fürstenberg, Raoul Dufy, President Kennedy, and Aldous Huxley.

In lay-out the movement recalls the music for the Voice of God in *The Flood*. There God's words were set for two bass soloists, whose interlocking two-part chanting was doubled by harp and piano and accompanied by the strings (or, in the case of the Covenant of the Rainbow, by the flutes) and an undertow of rhythmic drumming. Here the solo viola and double-basses provide a two-part bass, which is closely imitated – and this imitation amounts almost to doubling – by two timpanists, whose basic unit of time is frequently broken down into semiquavers in sextuplets. One phrase is chanted by the tenors in unison, one by the basses in unison, one by the tenors and basses in two-part harmony; and these three phrases are separated from each other by two brief passages of rhythmic pitchless declamation marked *parlando sotto voce*, which recall similar passages in *Threni*.[1] The different sections of the work are punctuated by cadences of three chords for the harp and piano with off-beat accentuation from the gongs. These cadences contain some of the most brooding harmonic effects in the whole of Stravinsky's serial output. (See particularly the chords in bars 32 and 33.)

Ex. 196

[1] See ex. 164.

Original Compositions

The series employed is:

Ex.197

CANON ON A RUSSIAN POPULAR TUNE
For orchestra, 1965 – see no. 16(A)

108. REQUIEM CANTICLES
For contralto and bass soli, chorus and orchestra (4.0.0.2. – 4.2.3.0. – timpani (two players), xylophone, vibraphone, campane, harp, piano, celesta – string 5tet). Composed during 1965 and 1966 and finished at Hollywood on 13 August 1966. Dedicated to the memory of Helen Buchanan Seeger. Published by Boosey & Hawkes, 1967. Duration 15 minutes. First performance, Princeton University, 8 October 1966, by the New York Concert Symphony Orchestra, the Ithaca College Choir, Elaine Bonazzi and Donald Gramm as soloists. (The soprano and tenor soloists in the vocal quartet were Linda Anderson and Charles Bressler.) Conducted by Robert Craft.

Like most of Stravinsky's later serial works, the *Requiem Canticles* is a brief and pithy composition. For the most part its texts are no more than sentences or extracts from the words of the Requiem Mass. In *Themes and Conclusions* he had a word to say about the title. 'My original title was *Sinfonia da Requiem*, and I did not use it only because I seem to have shared too many titles and subjects with Mr Britten already.' Nevertheless, the title he ultimately chose seemed still to acknowledge some sort of link with Britten's *Sinfonia da Requiem*, and also with his various Canticles.

Its formal design is symmetrical – six vocal movements being separated at mid-point by an instrumental interlude and being flanked on either side by an instrumental prelude and an instrumental postlude.

A surprising technical feature of the work is the presence of two distinct series. In his fascinating article 'Some Notes on Stravinsky's Requiem Settings',[1] Claudio Spies, who copied the Requiem tables from Stravinsky's charts, suggested that the second series was probably formulated first, and

Ex. 198

First Series

Second Series

[1] Reprinted in *Perspectives on Schoenberg and Stravinsky*, ed. by Benjamin Boretz and Edward T. Cone. New York, Norton, 1972.

2. Register of Works

that Stravinsky may have composed the Prelude, which uses only the second series, before deciding to make use of another series in the composition. Both series start from F; F is the cellos' bass note at the opening of the Prelude, and F the bass note (played by horn, piano and harp) for the last chord of the Postlude.

Prelude (strings). In this movement the string contingent exploits a series of repeated notes played *marcato*. The notes are equal semiquavers, grouped roughly in fives. The sawing of the strings accompanies four inventions for solo strings: the first for violin solo, the second for two solo violins, the third for the solo violins and one solo viola, the fourth for solo quartet consisting of two solo violins, one solo viola, and a solo cello doubled by solo double-bass.

Exaudi (chorus and orchestra). The main theme is enunciated by the harp. A brief one-bar setting of the word 'Exaudi' for SAT chorus is followed by a four-bar setting for SAT chorus and a six-bar setting for SATB chorus covering the remainder of the sentence.

Dies Irae (chorus and orchestra). A fortissimo arpeggio (for piano, strings, and timpani) like a breaking wave ushers in the chorus's cry (Ex. 199a),

accompanied by trumpets, trombones, and horns. The tonal implication of the fifth (A sharp/E sharp) should be noted. The five lines starting *'Solvet saeclum in favilla'* are entrusted to the chorus *parlando sotto voce*. The metrical setting is exactly notated. The movement ends with a reiteration of the *Dies irae* motif. The echo effect is prolonged and leads into

Tuba Mirum (bass solo and orchestra). The effect of the two trumpets that open this bass solo reminds one for a moment of the *Fanfare for a New Theatre*.

Interlude (wind and timpani). The opening of this instrumental movement (Ex. 199b) recalls the *Dies irae*. (It will be noted that the tonal implications of the earlier movement have suffered an enharmonic change from sharps to flats.) There are several episodes for small groups of wind instruments, of

Ex. 199b

which perhaps the most delightful is an extended passage for flute quartet prior and subsequent to the caesura of a bar's rest at bar 184.

Rex Tremendae (chorus and orchestra). This movement starts with a massive four-part chorus in which the choral entries are accentuated by notes from trombone and trumpet; but soon the choral parts become looser and more varied, and some of them develop in odd and puzzling ways – as is the case, for instance, with the tenors in bars 210–213.

Ex. 200a

Lacrimosa (contralto solo and orchestra). This is a most serene and moving composition. The inflection of the word 'lacrimosa' in the opening bars sets a style of lamentation, and the vocal exploration of these low-pitched intervals

Ex. 200b

is of considerable poignancy, the voice being accompanied in the main by a quartet of flutes.

Libera Me (vocal quartet, chorus, and orchestra). Here the text is (exceptionally) complete and its setting is entrusted to a rapidly murmuring, rhythmically unnotated chorus marked *parlando in p*. Simultaneously a chorus of four soloists (SATB) chants the words in four-part harmony, which is doubled in the orchestra. Originally Stravinsky intended the doubled parts to be played by a harmonium; but subsequently – before the final rehearsal –

he changed this to four horns playing with mutes. The rustling of the *parlando* chorus leads directly to the

Postlude (for flutes, horn, piano, harp, celesta, campane, and vibraphone). In method and effect, this recalls other celebrated Stravinskyan codas like those to *Svadebka* and the Symphonies of Wind Instruments. In it a succession of five slow isolated chords (for flute quartet, piano, and harp) over a bass note for solo horn is interrupted by a stream of thirty-three chiming chords (for celesta, campane, and vibraphone). Nearly all of these chords are different, with the exception of the penultimate chord (for flutes, piano, and harp), which is exceptionally repeated before the final chord of death.

Ex. 201

CHOREOGRAPHIC VERSIONS

On 2 May 1968 Balanchine made a special ballet arrangement for the New York City Ballet, and this was given a single performance as a tribute to the memory of Dr Martin Luther King. Stravinsky, who had at first intended to compose an extra instrumental prelude to the *Requiem Canticles* for this performance, but abandoned it when he saw it could not be completed in time, sent Balanchine a message from Hollywood saying, 'I am honoured that my music is to be played in memory of a man of God, a man of the poor, a man of peace.'

A new choreographic version was made by Jerome Robbins for the New York City Ballet's special Stravinsky Festival at the New York State Theatre, when thirty-one ballets to Stravinsky's music were performed in seven programmes, twenty-one of them being ballet premières. *Requiem Canticles* was included in the last night's programme of the Festival on 25 June 1972. This version was taken into the repertory of the Royal Ballet at Covent Garden on 15 November 1972.

109. THE OWL AND THE PUSSY-CAT

For soprano and piano. Words by Edward Lear. Composed during 1965 and 1966. Dedicated 'to Vera'. Published by Boosey & Hawkes, 1967. Duration about two minutes forty seconds. First performance, Los Angeles (Monday Evening Concerts), 31 October 1966, with Peggy Bonini (soprano) and Ingold Dahl (piano). The manuscript sketches were given by the composer to Robert Craft.

In his Afterword to Arnold Newman's photographic album *Bravo Stravinsky!* Robert Craft has explained that *The Owl and the Pussy-Cat* was the first English verse that Vera Stravinsky learnt by heart. This simple quiet little song is a two-part invention, in which the gently rocking vocal line is accompanied by the piano with a line (also gently rocking) which is doubled at the octave, or sometimes at the double-octave. In his *Themes and Conclusions* Stravinsky traced its origins to the rhythm implicit in the title.

The rhythmic cell suggested a group of pitches, which I expanded into a twelve-note series in correspondence to the stanzaic shape of the poem. The piano octaves form a syncopated canonic voice as well as a double mirror, the vocal movement being reflected between both the upper and lower notes. Octaves are peculiarly pianistic. No other instrument produces them so well.

Stravinsky is said to have told Balanchine that the song 'should be impersonated: a little hooted, a little meeowed, a little grunted for the pig'.

B. Arrangements of Other Composers' Works

I. KOBOLD, by Edvard Grieg.

At Diaghilev's request, Stravinsky orchestrated this number for the score of *Le Festin*, produced by the Russian Ballet on 19 May 1909 at the Théâtre du Châtelet, Paris. It was danced by Nijinsky. Unpublished.

II. (i) NOCTURNE IN A FLAT, by Frederic Chopin.

(ii) VALSE BRILLANTE IN E FLAT, by Frederic Chopin.

At Diaghilev's request, Stravinsky orchestrated these two numbers for the score of *Les Sylphides*, produced by the Russian Ballet on 2 June 1909 at the Théâtre du Châtelet, Paris. 'Clarinet solo' type of music he calls these instrumentations in his *Conversations*. Unpublished.

III. TWO SONGS OF THE FLEA,

(i) by Ludwig van Beethoven (Op. 75 no. 3) instrumented for bass and orchestra (2.2.2.2 – 2.0.0.0. – string 5tet) and

(ii) by Modeste Mussorgsky, instrumented for baritone or bass and orchestra (3.2.2.2. – 4.2.3.1. – timp, arpa – string 5tet). Written in 1910. Published by W. Bessell & Co.,[1] later by Boosey & Hawkes.

Both songs are settings of Mephistopheles's song in the Auerbach cellar from Goethe's *Faust*. These instrumentations were made for a 'Goethe-in-music' concert in St. Petersburg conducted by Siloti (*Dia*).

IV. KHOVANSHCHINA, by Modeste Mussorgsky

At the beginning of 1913, Diaghilev commissioned Stravinsky to prepare a new version of Mussorgsky's opera *Khovanshchina* for production in Paris that summer. He wanted him to instrument those parts where Mussorgsky

---

[1] The Mussorgsky song has the plate number 7320.

544

had not completed the orchestration and 'to compose a chorus for the finale, for which Mussorgsky had indicated only the theme – an authentic Russian song' (*Chr*). Stravinsky was doubtful whether he had enough time to finish the job: so at his suggestion Ravel was brought in as collaborator. The work was carried out at Clarens in March and April 1913, Stravinsky's share consisting of the orchestration of Shaklovity's aria and various other sections, and the arrangement and orchestration of the finale. The work of the two collaborators was based on the version of the score edited by Rimsky-Korsakov and published by W. Bessel & Co. (Mussorgsky's original version was not published until 1931, when it was brought out by Pavel Lamm in Moscow.) A notebook containing Stravinsky's original sketches for the finale was given by him that summer to M. D. Calvocoressi: it is subscribed and dated Villa Borghese, Paris, 6 July 1913. This manuscript later passed into the collection of O. W. Neighbour, London. The manuscript of part of the orchestral score of Shaklovity's aria is in the composer's collection [C 5]. The Stravinsky/Ravel version of *Khovanshchina* was performed for the first time at the Théâtre des Champs-Elysées, Paris, on 5 June 1913; and it was heard in London at Drury Lane on July 1st.

In later years, Stravinsky was rather scathing about this arrangement. In his *Chronicle* he wrote: 'I have always been sincerely opposed to the re-arrangement by anyone other than the author himself of work already created, and my opposition is only strengthened when the original author is an artist as conscious and certain of what he was doing as Mussorgsky. To my mind that principle is as badly violated in the Diaghilev compilation as it was in Rimsky-Korsakov's Meyerbeerisation of *Boris Godunov*.' Presumably this objection was not felt to apply when in later years he rearranged music by Pergolesi and Chaikovsky in order to construct new scores like *Pulcinella* and *The Fairy's Kiss*.

The vocal score of the final chorus was printed at St. Petersburg and published by Bessel in 1914.[1] It bears the dedication 'A M-r S. de Diaghilew'. The opening of the chorus carried the following footnote:

> *Le choeur final n'a pas été composé par M. P. Moussorgsky, mais a été écrit par Igor Strawinsky sur le thème trouvé dans les brouillons de la Khov-anchtchina, d'après les anciens chants autentiques des sectaires 'vieux croyants' représenté dans les drames de Moussorgsky.*

It is worth noting that Stravinsky maintains a high A sharp cipher in the strings tremolo throughout the last 37 bars where the tonality sways between G sharp minor and D sharp minor.

---

[1] It has the plate number 7396.

2. Register of Works

V. SONG OF THE VOLGA BOATMEN – CHANT DES BATELIERS DU VOLGA[1]

At Diaghilev's request, Stravinsky arranged this Russian folksong for wind instruments and percussion (2.2.2.3 – 4.3.3.1 – timp., perc.) for a gala concert performance at the Costanzi Theatre, Rome. The score is dated 8 April 1917. The February Revolution had just taken place in Russia, and Diaghilev needed a substitute for the Russian National Anthem. Time was short: so throughout the evening preceding the performance Stravinsky 'sat at the piano in Lord Berners's apartment instrumenting and scoring the song for the orchestra, dictating it chord by chord, note by note, to Ansermet, who wrote it down' (*Chr*). The instrumental parts were quickly copied out; and he was able to hear this new version, conducted by Ansermet, at the orchestra rehearsal the following morning. Published by J. & W. Chester, 1920. Duration: *c.* 2 minutes [4 minutes]. Picasso painted a red circle or banner as a symbol of the Revolution on the title page of the manuscript score, which is in the composer's collection [C 20].

VI. PROLOGUE FROM BORIS GODUNOV, by Modeste Mussorgsky[2]

Piano arrangement of the Chorus of the Prologue made by Stravinsky for his children. Morges, 1918. Unpublished. MS comp. [C 25].

VII. LA MARSEILLAISE

Arrangement for solo violin (unaccompanied). Morges, 1 January 1919. Unpublished. MS comp. [C 33].

VIII. THE SLEEPING BEAUTY, by Peter Chaikovsky

(i) 'Variation d'Aurore' (Act II)

(ii) 'Entr'acte symphonique' (preceding the finale of Act II)

    At Diaghilev's request, Stravinsky orchestrated these two numbers for the revival of *The Sleeping Beauty* by the Russian Ballet at the Alhambra, London, on 2 November 1921. (Chaikovsky had made certain cuts after the first performance of the ballet in St. Petersburg. Diaghilev wanted to restore these two numbers; and Stravinsky had to instrument them from the piano score.) He also made a few changes in Chaikovsky's orchestration of the Russian Dance in the last act (*Exp*). Unpublished.

---

[1] The title in Stravinsky's manuscript score is *Hymne à la Nouvelle Russie.*
[2] In a letter to Vladimir Petrov dated 10 December 1962, Vera Stravinsky mentioned that after her husband's return to Russia in 1962, he considered the possibility of orchestrating Mussorgsky's *Sans Soleil* cycle.

Arrangements of Other Composers' Works

(iii) 'Bluebird Pas-de-Deux' (Act III)

This arrangement for small orchestra (1.1.2.1 – 1.2.2.0 – timp., piano – Vl, Vle, Vcl, Cb)[1] was made for Ballet Theatre in New York in 1941. At that time the full score of the ballet was not available in America, and Stravinsky had to work from a piano score. Wartime exigencies made it necessary to reduce the size of the orchestra. Published by Schott's, 1953. Duration: *c.* 5 minutes 15 seconds. MS comp. [C 72].

IX. THE STAR-SPANGLED BANNER

The third national anthem to be arranged by Stravinsky was *The Star-Spangled Banner*. This he harmonised and orchestrated at Los Angeles on 4 July 1941, and his version was performed for the first time, also in Los Angeles, where James Sample conducted it on 14 October 1941. When Stravinsky himself conducted it at a concert at Boston on 14 January 1944, a Police Commissioner appeared in his dressing room the following day and informed him 'of a Massachusetts law forbidding any "tampering" with national property'. The police had been instructed to remove his arrangement from the music stands (*Mem*). This version, which is for full orchestra (3.3.2.2. – 4.3.3.1 – timp. – string 5tet) and mixed chorus *ad lib.*, is published by Mercury Music Corporation. The manuscript score is in the Library of Congress Washington, D.C. Other manuscript material with the composer [C 73].

X. CHORAL-VARIATIONEN ÜBER DAS WEIHNACHTSLIED 'VOM HIMMEL HOCH DA KOMM ICH HER', by J. S. Bach

This arrangement for mixed chorus and orchestra (2.3.0.3 – 0.3.3.0 – harp – violas, double-basses) was made at a time when Stravinsky needed another work for performance with the *Canticum Sacrum* in St. Mark's, Venice, in September 1956. The ensemble for the Choral Variations is nearly the same as that for the *Canticum*. The first variation was written in New York on 29 December 1955, and the second during the next few days. The last three variations and the chorale followed in Hollywood between 20 January and 9 February 1956. When Stravinsky had completed the arrangement, he signed and dated the score, adding the words 'Mit der Genehmigung des Meisters'. The first performance, which took place in Ojai, California, on 27 May 1956, was conducted by Robert Craft, to whom the work is dedicated. Published by Boosey & Hawkes. Duration: *c.* 10½ minutes.

Bach wrote these Choral Variations on the occasion of his entry into Lorenz Christoph Mizler's Sozietät der musikalischen Wissenschaften, Leipzig, in

---

[1] To obtain a normal balance, Stravinsky recommends 5 violins, 4 violas, 3 cellos and 2 double-basses as a minimum.

1746/47; and they were published under the title *Einige canonische Veränderungen uber das Weynacht-Lied 'Vom Himmel hoch da komm' ich her'* for two-manual organ and pedals in 1748. Bach began his work with the first variation; but Stravinsky has introduced the *Vom Himmel hoch* chorale from one of Bach's settings in the Christmas Oratorio at the beginning of his arrangement.

The Bach Variations are all in the key of C; but Stravinsky uses the following plan of related keys:

Chorale	C major
Variation I	C major
Variation II	G major
Variation III	D flat major
Variation IV	G major
Variation V	C major

He brings in the chorus in Variations II to V, assigning the chorale melody to the voices in unison and thereby giving the work something of the characteristics of a cantata. He has not scrupled to add extra lines of independent counterpoint where it has suited his convenience to do so; and the most interesting of these additions are the new canons in the second and third Variations.

In the second Variation, he treats the chorale melody as four separate phrases; and he arranges for each phrase to be preceded by its inversion played by a trombone or trumpet. The inversions of the first and third phrases are sounded by the first trombone as a canon *alla quinta inferiora*; and the inversions of the second and fourth phrases by the second trumpet as a canon *alla quinta superiora*.

For a description of the additional canon in the third variation, one cannot do better than to quote Robert Craft:[1]

> The canon of the third variation is at the interval of the seventh. Stravinsky adds a new canon at the seventh, at the distance of a quaver after every note in all of the four phrases of the *cantus firmus*, It is compounded of two directions of interval and is sounded by trombone and trumpet, the latter always at the seventh above and the former always at the seventh below. This new canon has a different design in each phrase. In the first phrase one note in the trombone is followed by two in the trumpet, two in the trombone, two in the trumpet, and one in the trombone. The second phrase is confined to the trombone and the third phrase to the trumpet. The fourth phrase alternates one note in the trumpet and one in the trombone, with the last note producing the seventh in both directions so that the final chord contains a major second, in which the trombone is strengthened by violas.

---

[1] From 'A Concert for St. Mark'. *The Score*, December 1956.

Arrangements of Other Composers' Works

In Stravinsky's instrumentation, the handling of the brass deserves special attention, particularly in the fast and complex fourth variation.

The nature of the orchestral ensemble makes this a useful companion piece to the *Canticum Sacrum*; and it was included in the programme at St. Mark's, Venice, when the *Canticum Sacrum* received its first performance on 13 September 1956.

XI. TRES SACRAE CANTIONES, by Carlo Gesualdo di Venosa

(i) 'Da pacem Domine'
(ii) 'Assumpta est Maria'
(iii) 'Illumina nos'

In the third of these Sacred Songs, Stravinsky has supplied the missing sextus and bassus parts for 'Illumina nos,' which is the final motet in the book of twenty *Sacrae Cantiones* for six and seven voices printed in Naples by Constantino Vitali and published there in 1603 by Don Giovanni Pietro Cappuccio. This reconstruction was made in 1957 and published the same year by Boosey & Hawkes, with a preface by Robert Craft.

According to Craft, Stravinsky had been an admirer of Gesualdo and his music since about 1952; but it was not until 1956, when he received photostat copies of the partbooks of the *Sacrae Cantiones*, that he decided to try to complete the two missing parts in 'Illumina nos.' His intention was that the completed piece should be performed together with his *Canticum Sacrum* in St. Mark's, Venice; but the Venetians, who had buried Monteverdi as a Cremonese in a common grave in the Church of the Frari, would not hear of the works of a Neapolitan being performed in the precincts of St. Mark's. So the idea was dropped; and Stravinsky postponed the work of reconstruction until he had completed *Agon* in April 1957.

In September 1959, he picked two other songs – 'Da pacem Domine' (no. 2) and 'Assumpta est Maria' (no. 12) – from the same collection. Here too the sextus and bassus parts were missing. But in 'Da pacem Domine' the tenor part was marked 'in canon diapente' (at the interval of a fifth), and the canon could be resolved in the sextus part, while in 'Assumpta est Maria', the quintus part was marked 'in canon diapason et diapente' (at the intervals of a fourth and fifth), and the first canon could be resolved in the sextus (by Stravinsky) and the second had been resolved in the altus (by Gesualdo). So all Stravinsky had to compose afresh was the bassus part to each of these two songs.

The *Tres Sacrae Cantiones*, as completed by Stravinsky, were published by Boosey and Hawkes in 1960 to celebrate the 400th anniversary of Gesualdo's birth. This edition contains a preface by Robert Craft, which is different from the preface to 'Illumina nos', and in which he says:

549

Stravinsky has not attempted reconstruction. In fact, he seems to have avoided what in some cases might appear to be the prescribed solution. What he has done is to recompose the whole from the point of view of his added parts, with a result that is not pure Gesualdo, but a fusion of the two composers.

And in the preface to 'Illumina nos', he says:

Though Stravinsky's additions are all within Gesualdo's style, the listener who knows a great deal of Gesualdo will guess that the work is not purely his. For one thing, it is probably more complicated than the original, which is to say that it probably moves more rapidly harmonically and contains more musical ideas . . .

XII. MONUMENTUM PRO GESUALDO DI VENOSA AD CD ANNUM

Three madrigals recomposed for instruments (0.2.0.2 – 4.2.3.0 – Vl I, Vl II, Vla, Vcl). The score is dated Hollywood, March 1960. Published by Boosey & Hawkes, 1960. Duration: c. 7 minutes. First performed at the Venice Biennale on 27 September 1960 by the Orchestra del Teatro la Fenice, with Stravinsky conducting. The manuscript full score is in the Library of Congress, Washington, D. C.

    I. 'Asciugate i begli occhi', Madrigale XIV, Libro quinto
    II. 'Ma tu, cagion di quella', Madrigale XVIII, Libro quinto
    III. 'Beltà poi che t'assenti', Madrigale II, Libro sesto

This work is complementary to the *Tres Sacrae Cantiones*. The element of recomposition is comparatively small in the second and third madrigals. In one place in the second madrigal, Stravinsky echoes a two-bar cadence of Gesualdo's. 'Otherwise there are octave transpositions, exchanges of parts, harmonic doublings, occasional completions of the implied harmony, and one or two inserted passing-notes, but the substance of the two pieces remains essentially as it was.'[1]

The alterations in the first madrigal are more extensive. After the first nine bars, Stravinsky interpolates a passage in which he freely varies and repeats phrases that are anticipated from the following section of Gesualdo's madrigal (i.e., bars 19–22 of Stravinsky's recomposed version). From here to the end, there are numerous changes from Gesualdo's original, aimed partly at avoiding the monotony of Gesualdo's harmonic progressions by introducing suspensions and accented dissonances.

The tone quality of the three madrigals is subtly varied. No trumpets or trombones are used in the first; no horns or strings in the second; and the full ensemble is heard in the third.

In 1960 the New York City Ballet produced *Monumentum pro gesualdo*

---

[1] Colin Mason, 'Stravinsky and Gesualdo'. *Tempo*, nos. 55/56, Autumn/Winter 1960.

with choreography for seven couples by Balanchine. After 1963 it was always paired with *Movements*, and the two ballets were danced in succession.

XIII. CANZONETTA (op. 62a), by Jean Sibelius

This *Canzonetta*, originally written by Sibelius for strings, was arranged by Stravinsky in 1963 for eight instruments (4 horns, clarinet, bass clarinet, harp and double-bass). He was awarded the Wihuri-Sibelius Prize in 1963 and made his arrangement as a little act of homage. It was published by Brietkopf and Härtel in 1964.

When he visited Helsinki in 1961, he is quoted by Robert Craft in his Diary[1] as saying he was fond of this work – 'the first half of it, anyway. I like that kind of northern Italianate melodism – Chaikovsky had it too – which was a part, and an attractive part, of St. Petersburg culture'.

The manuscript is in the possession of Wihuri's Foundation for International Prizes, Helsinki. The first performance of this arrangement of the *Canzonetta* was given by the Finnish Broadcasting Company on 22 March 1964.

XIV. TWO SACRED SONGS from the 'Spanisches Liederbuch' of Hugo Wolf

These two songs – 'Herr, was trägt der Boden hier . . .' and 'Wunden trägst du . . .' with text by Paul Heyse and Emanuel Geibel – were instrumented by Stravinsky on 15 May 1968 in San Francisco for mezzo-soprano and three clarinets in A, two horns in F, and solo string quintet. Published by Boosey & Hawkes, 1969. First performance, the County Museum of Art, Los Angeles, 6 September 1968 with Christina Krooskos as the singer, and Robert Craft conducting.

According to Craft, Stravinsky made this instrumentation because he 'wanted to say something about death and felt that he could not compose anything of his own'.

---

[1] Entry for 10 September 1961.

Part Three

EPILOGUE

The Composer

Three stories provide evidence of Stravinsky's special interest in music as a child.

First, in his *Expositions* he recalls the summer of 1884 that he spent with his family at Lzy, and the attractive and restful song sung by the countrywomen as they returned in the evening from working in the fields. 'They sang it in octaves – unharmonized, of course – their high, shrill voices sounding like a billion bees. I was never a precocious child, and I have never enjoyed extraordinary powers of memory, but this song was branded on my ear the first time I heard it. My nurse brought me home from the village, where we had been perambulating one afternoon, and my parents, who were then trying to coax me to talk, asked me what I had seen there. I said I had seen the peasants and I had heard them sing, and I sang what they had sung:

Ex. 202

Everyone was astonished and impressed at this recital, and I heard my father remark that I had a wonderful ear.' This was certainly a remarkable feat for a boy of two. As he says in his *Chronicle* it marked the dawn of his consciousness of himself in the rôle of musician; and it is not surprising to find that subsequently, for about seven years of his musical career – i.e., from *Petrushka* to *The Wedding* – simple vernacular tunes like this one, whether borrowed or invented, formed an important part of his musical stock-in-trade.

Second, another childhood memory, probably also from the 1884 summer spent in Lzy. This is vividly described in his *Chronicle*.

It was in the country, where my parents, like most people of their class, spent the summer with their children. I can see it now. An enormous peasant seated on the trunk of a tree. The sharp resinous tang of fresh-cut wood in my nostrils. The peasant simply clad in a short red shirt. His bare legs covered with reddish hair, on his feet birch sandals, on his head a mop of hair as thick and as red as his beard – not a white hair, yet an old man. He was dumb, but he had a way of clicking his tongue very noisily, and the children were afraid of him. So was I. But curiosity used to triumph over fear. The children would gather round him. Then, to amuse them, he would begin to sing. This song was composed of two syllables, the only ones he could pronounce. They were devoid of any meaning, but he made them alternate with incredible dexterity in a very rapid tempo. He used to accompany this clucking in the following way: pressing the palm of his right hand under his left arm-pit, he would work his left arm with a rapid movement, making it press on the right hand. From beneath the red shirt he extracted a succession of sounds which were somewhat dubious but very rhythmic, and which might be euphemistically described as resounding kisses.

Here, one feels is the beginning of Stravinsky's love of nonsense jingles – of *pribaoutki*, for example – allied with his extraordinary sensitivity to simple, incisive rhythms, particularly when accentuated percussively. And it is typical that when he started to imitate this peasant's onomatopoeic performance at home and was promptly forbidden to make such indecent noises, the two dull syllables of the song, which were all that remained after the percussive element had been removed, lost their attraction for him.

Third, he remembered playing the scale of C major on the piano in his parents' apartment in St. Petersburg a few years later when he was about eight years old, and thinking, 'Who invented this scale? After all, someone must have done so; and if someone invented it, I can change something in it and invent something else . . .' So he played C, D, E, jumped to G and then came back to F. At this point one of his uncles, who was in the room, came over to the piano and asked. 'What's that you're playing? You start the scale quite decently with C, D, E, and then you jump to G.' The boy replied, 'My dear uncle, that's my own invention. Leave me alone.'[1] There spoke the embryo musical explorer and pioneer, with his unfailing curiosity about scales, modes, note rows and all the materials of his art.

Throughout his composing career, he never took anything for granted. For him the most obvious things in music, such as the intervals of the scale, needed a re-examination and testing that stripped them of their jejune academic attributes and gave them fresh life. Close examination of his output shows that it is the narrower intervals – particularly thirds and seconds – that fascinated him. When a wider interval, like a fourth or augmented fourth, seems to play an important part in his composition, it will usually be found that it really splits up into smaller component intervals, e.g., the division of the augmented fourth in *The Firebird* into interlinked major and minor thirds, and the division of the fourth in *The Wedding* into a major second and minor third. And the same observation is true of his use of the dodecaphonal series, which is frequently broken down into smaller groups of hexachords or tetrachords.

Ansermet relates[2] how one evening when he had been discussing with Ravel and Stravinsky Schoenberg's recent idea of using a major/minor chord – this must have been about 1913 or 1914 – Ravel said, 'But such a chord is perfectly

---

[1] Extracted from a filmed interview given by Stravinsky to the National Film Broadcasting Company just before his seventy-fifth birthday in 1957.
[2] In *Les Fondements de la Musique dans la Conscience Humaine*. Neuchâtel, 1961.

feasible, provided the minor third is placed above and the major third below.'
'If this arrangement is possible,' commented Stravinsky, 'I don't see why the
contrary shouldn't be possible too: and if I will it, I can do it.' ('Si je le veux,
je le peux.') He had in fact already used major/minor chords with the minor
third above the major third – as in the opening chord of the motto of *Zvez-*
doliki (see Ex. 12) and the Mystical Circles movement in *The Rite of Spring*.
Later on, he seems to have achieved his wish to reverse the position of the
thirds, for the 'Bell' motive in the opening bars of the *Symphonies of Wind*
Instruments shows the major third of G above the minor third, the B natural
being approached from the D above and the B flat from the G above.

Ex. 203

One can be sure that no interval or combination of intervals in the music
of his maturity was ever accepted by him without the most careful scrutiny
and consideration.

It is well known that he composed at the piano. (In his *Chronicle* he relates
how when he became Rimsky-Korsakov's pupil, he asked his master whether
he was right always to compose at the piano. 'Some compose at the piano,'
Rimsky-Korsakov replied, 'and some without a piano. As for you, you will
compose at the piano.') He enjoyed this direct contact with the physical
element of sound which enabled him to savour the vibrations of different
notes. He did not forget how the deaf Beethoven, to maintain some sort of
physical relation with the music he was writing but could no longer hear, used
to take a stick in his mouth which he placed in contact with the piano, because
(as Stravinsky said)[1] 'he needed to enjoy the vibrations – otherwise the music
was an abstract matter for him, and that was something he wanted to avoid.'

Stravinsky's own tests were rigorous and searching. In his *Conversations,* he
mentioned how at one point in his composition of *Threni* he was particularly
troubled by an interval. After working late, he retired to bed and dreamed
that this interval 'had become an elastic substance stretching exactly between
the two notes [he] had composed, but underneath these notes at either end was
an egg, a large testicular egg. The eggs were gelatinous to the touch and warm,
and they were protected by nests.' And he woke up knowing his interval was
right. The significant thing here would seem to be, not the possibility that

[1] Extracted from the National Broadcasting Company's filmed interview mentioned above.

certain chords contain a kind of glandular secretion or that the sex of intervals can be determined, but the sensitivity and potency of the terminal notes of an interval and the need for their protection.

The scales from which the intervals of Stravinsky's melos are drawn have varied at different times in his career. In his early works the major and minor modes predominated, and in scores like *Fireworks* and *The Firebird* they were sharpened and decorated by chromatic treatment; but by the time he reached *The Rite of Spring*, his melos was veering towards the modes that were current in Russian folksong and Russian Orthodox Church music. His subsequent attempt to adopt a more heterogeneous style (as in *The Soldier's Tale*) led to his conscious exploration and exploitation of the music of the past and a return of the hegemony of the major/minor modes. But occasionally the other modes were still laid under contribution, as can be seen in works like *Oedipus Rex*, the *Symphony of Psalms*, the *Mass*, and *Orpheus*.

His harmonic vocabulary was enriched by polytonal devices that made their first appearance in *Petrushka* and *The Rite of Spring*, and later by the deliberate amalgamation and synchronisation within the same tonality of different harmonic elements that had usually been kept separate in the past. The result is that some of the earlier works like *The Rite of Spring* contain dense chord clusters (see Exs. 13 and 14) and some of the neo-classical works show a combination of dominant and tonic elements in the same chord (see Ex. 41 from *The Five Fingers*). But even the simplest and most obvious chords were evolved and accepted only after considerable thought and care. In this connection, a typical story is told by Walter Piston,[1] who was at Harvard at the time Stravinsky held the Charles Eliot Norton Chair of Poetry (1939/40).

> Besides his series of lectures, now published under the title *Poetics of Music*, he held extremely rewarding meetings with the students, discussing their music and his own. In the course of a talk about *Oedipus Rex*, at one of these meetings, an observation that he made threw a bright light on a most important aspect of his artistic ideals. He said, 'How happy I was when I discovered that chord!' Some of us were puzzled, because the chord, known in common harmonic terms as a D-major triad, appeared neither new nor complex. But it became evident that Stravinsky regarded every chord as an individual sonority, having many attributes above and beyond the tones selected from a scale or altered this way and that. The particular and marvellous combination of tones in question owed its unique character to the exact distribution of the tones in relation to the spaces between them, to the exact placing of the instrumental voices in reference to the special sound of a given note on a given instrument, to the dynamic level indicated, and to the precise moment of sounding of the chord.

---

[1] From 'Stravinsky's Rediscoveries' printed in *Stravinsky in the Theatre*. Peter Owen, London, 1951.

Although Piston does not identify the chord in question, it is almost certainly the D major chord at the end of the *Lux facta est* cadence (see Ex. 58).

Fundamental to Stravinsky's musical behaviour, from his earliest compositions to *The Rake's Progress*, was his loyalty to the conception of tonality. Whatever complication may be provided by polytonal exploration, or the use of *ostinati*, or the synchronisation of separate harmonic procedures, the tonality of his music is usually clear and compelling, and so is the interrelation of tonalities between the different movements of his works.

A major change was embarked on when in the compositions following *The Rake's Progress* he began to experiment with serial processes. At first he showed considerable caution by using note rows that fell short of the full dodecaphonic series; and these were at times so closely related to his long established obsession with an interval like the third and its smaller component intervals that no substantial difference in his musical idiom could be detected. True, there was a greater insistence on counterpoint than ever before; but the net impression of works like the *Septet, In Memoriam Dylan Thomas* and the *Three Songs from William Shakespeare* was still a tonal one. It wasn't until he started to use the full series in parts of the *Canticum Sacrum* and *Agon* that the old tonal ties were seen to be loosening: but even here the construction of the works revealed a tonal framework and the deployment of the series showed traces of a lingering tonal cast of thought. As he said in his *Conversations*, 'the intervals of my series are attracted by tonality; I compose vertically and that is, in one sense at least, to compose tonally.'

At various times concern has been expressed at his attitude to the music of the past. Doubts set in after his flirtation with Pergolesi (in *Pulcinella*) when it was seen that in his neoclassical works he was deliberately using material and technical devices derived from earlier musical periods. 'Time travelling' Constant Lambert called it in *Music Ho!* – and so, in a sense, it was. When accused of *lèse-majesté* over his behaviour towards Pergolesi, Stravinsky replied with a spirited defence.

> Should my line of action with regard to Pergolesi be dominated by my love or by my respect for his music? Is it love or respect that urges us to possess a woman? Is it not by love alone that we succeed in penetrating to the very essence of a being? (*Chr*).

The copulative analogy provides a fetching argument, but is not really valid except where a living partner is involved. It can be fairly applied to works of genuine collaboration like *Petrushka* (Stravinsky/Benois), *The Soldier's Tale* (Stravinsky/Ramuz) and *The Rake's Progress* (Stravinsky/Auden). Elsewhere[1] Stravinsky has suggested that his interest in the music of the past can diagnosed as a rare form of kleptomania. The idea of his behaving like a *gazza ladra* is an amusing one, but it is not fair to suggest that his musical

---

[1] In *Memories*.

nests are made up entirely of bits and pieces stolen from here and there. The truth of the matter seems to be that certain music whetted his appetite. What he liked he consumed and by the process of assimilation or introjection made it his own. Immediately an important distinction becomes apparent. He was constitutionally incapable of reacting in this way to the work of any of his living contemporaries – to do so would have been a form of esthetic cannibalism. It was the music of the dead that appealed to him. Even in his apprentice days, the composition that most clearly showed his attachment to his master (*The Firebird*) was written not under Rimsky-Korsakov's direct supervision but after his death. The same is true of his conversion to serialism.[1] By his own admission, it was the music of Webern (who died in 1945) that triggered off his interest in the 'Method' and provided the 'Open Sesame' to the magic serial cave; but it is significant that this important move occurred only after the death in 1951 of Schoenberg, the pioneer and founder of the 'Method'. Berg had already died in 1936: so by the time Stravinsky was writing the important serial sections of *Canticum Sacrum* and *Agon*, the works of the 'Viennese Troika' had already taken their place in the perspective of musical history and were beginning to acquire the special patina that (according to Gide) is the recompense of masterpieces.

The adoption of the serial method had an important effect on Stravinsky's melos. Sometimes in the past critics had objected that his music lacked original melody; but such strictures were usually directed against quotations from popular music in a work like *Petrushka* or the limited range of the melos in works of the Russian period like *The Rite of Spring* and *The Wedding*. In both cases the restriction was a deliberate assumption on the composer's part. But even when his melos developed more freely in works of the neo-classical period, the originality of his tunes was rarely recognised, possibly because of their unusual asymmetrical shapes. Approaching the series as the extension of a germinal melodic idea, Stravinsky found that serial technique strengthened the melodic power of his music. The point is excellently argued by Donald Mitchell at the end of *The Language of Modern Music*,[2] where he draws attention to 'the richness and extent and strongly personal contours of his serial melody', adding: 'The Method, in fact, has made possible for Stravinsky a development of the very quality that his own "past", in some sense, may be said to have lacked: a strong melodic gift that owes its life exclusively to his own inspiration.'

At the beginning of his career, he was willing to accept the established symphony orchestra as the normal vehicle for his major scores. The *Symphony in E flat*, the *Scherzo Fantastique* and *Fireworks* all demand a full-scale orchestra for their concert performance. When Diaghilev's commissions for the Russian

---

[1] 'Stravinsky's absorption of Schoenberg's technique was arguably the profoundest surprise in the history of music.' Hans Keller, *Stravinsky at Rehearsal*. London, Dennis Dobson, 1962.
[2] Published by Faber & Faber, 1963.

Ballet introduced him to the world of the theatre, he clearly had in mind the sort of orchestra that was permanently attached to a theatre like the Maryinsky Opera House in St. Petersburg, or the Opera House in Paris, and may not have realised that Diaghilev's enterprise, so long as it remained a touring company without a permanent base, was bound to run into orchestral difficulties. The scores of *The Firebird*, *Petrushka*, *The Rite of Spring* and *The Nightingale* were written for an orchestra of nearly a hundred players – a formidable requisite when there was no resident full-scale orchestra in the theatres which the company was visiting – and occasionally some very bad musical performances resulted.

A reaction against the full symphony orchestra set in; and this manifested itself in different ways. In the first place, after *The Nightingale* he became convinced that the normal symphony orchestra could not provide him with the type of ensemble he needed for his next full-scale score for the Russian Ballet (*The Wedding*), and a nine-year search for the right combination of instruments ensued. Secondly, when he decided to adapt part of *The Nightingale* as a symphonic poem for orchestra, he not only chose a slightly smaller orchestra for the purpose (with double instead of triple woodwind, and other instruments scaled down in proportion), but also changed his attitude to the principle of orchestration. This change was typified by his growing interest in the *concertante* treatment of single instruments or small groups of instruments; and this in its turn, through the emphasis and prominence it gave certain instruments at certain moments, postulated their absence at many other moments. Instruments were no longer used as padding, or merely to fill in and inflate. The result was a purer palette of instrumental colours, lighter orchestral texture, greater variety and contrast in the use of tones, and less insistence on the importance of 'blend'. The orchestra no longer sounded like a gigantic organ playing in an over-resonant cathedral.

At the same time he paid special attention to matters of accentuation Between the extremes of *legato* and *staccato*, he was careful to specify various intermediate degrees and to differentiate between >, – , ⸗ , ▼ and • in his directions. He frequently favoured a 'half and half' mixture obtained by the doubling of *legato* and *staccato* notes. An obvious example is the use of divided strings with the same notes played *con arco* and *pizzicato*; and there are also cases of a *legato* wind instrument being accompanied by one playing *staccato* – a device which gives a special edge to the sound.

In arriving at his orchestral specifications, he was always prepared to accept conditions dictated by outside circumstances (as in *The Soldier's Tale*) or a series of self-imposed restrictions. Early in the 1920's, for instance, he concentrated on writing for ensembles in which wind instruments predominated (the *Symphonies of Wind Instruments*, *Mavra*, the *Octet* and the *Piano Concerto*). Later on, he began to treat the orchestra on chamber-music lines; and this is particularly noticeable in the big serial works like *Canticum Sacrum*,

3. Epilogue

Agon, Threni, Movements, A Sermon etc., and *The Flood*. In fact, every time he wrote a full-scale composition, he deliberately rethought his orchestra.

Arthur Honegger has told the story[1] of how he met Stravinsky at the Salle Gaveau, Paris, early in 1921, just after receiving a commission from René Morax to write a score for *Le Roi David* which was to be produced that summer at the Théâtre du Jorat, Switzerland, and mentioned how perplexed he was by the problem of having to balance one hundred choristers and seventeen instrumentalists (which was the size of the musical ensemble that had been imposed on him). 'It's very simple,' said Stravinsky. 'Act as if it were you yourself who had chosen this particular combination and compose for your hundred singers and seventeen instrumentalists accordingly.' Honegger's comment was that, although at first sight Stravinsky's advice might appear like a glimpse of the obvious, it taught him an excellent lesson – never to accept a given task as something imposed from outside, but to view it as a personal point of departure responding to inner necessity. It is perhaps only fair to add that Stravinsky usually seems to have had a fairly free hand when carrying out his numerous commissions; but when there were specific instrumental restrictions – as, for example, with the *Ebony Concerto* and *In Memoriam Dylan Thomas* – he invariably turned them to good account.

The effect of his style of orchestration has been not only to change the characteristic sound of twentieth century music, but also to help renew the sensitivity and perceptiveness of audiences whose taste had become debased as the result of a surfeit of the sweet clotted mess of sound that was the legacy of the late romantic composers. The adoption of a palette of pure tone colours and a 'dry' technique, whereby silence was allowed to fill the interstices between the instrumental sounds, thereby emphasising their relief, brought as great a revolution to twentieth century music as the change to impressionist technique did to nineteenth century painting.

Of equal if not greater importance was his attitude to time in music as exemplified in pulse, metre and rhythm.

In the compositions of the late romantic composers, the flow of music had become sluggish, if not stagnant; and abuse of *tempo rubato*, both in composers' directions and in execution, tended towards excessive morbidity. Stravinsky's first action was to try to restore a healthy, regular pulse. This was one of the most notable features of some of the *allegro* movements in his early compositions. In the Scherzo of the *Symphony in E flat*, in the *Scherzo Fantastique* and *Fireworks*, and in movements like the 'Princesses' Game with the Golden Apples' and the 'Infernal Dance of Kashchei's Subjects' from *The ·Firebird* and the 'Russian Dance' and the 'Dance of the Coachmen' in *Petrushka*, he used a *perpetuum mobile* technique to keep the pulse of the music running clearly, easily and regularly, and this produced a feeling of drive and exhilara-

---

[1] Arthur Honegger, 'Stravinsky, homme de métier'. *Revue Musical*, May–June 1939.

tion. It should be noted, however, that his time signatures were regular, and the musical phrases fell naturally into symmetrical groups based usually on four-bar units.

His next step was to break up metres into irregular patterns and so to disrupt the symmetry of his phrases.

All metres are ultimately reducible to duple and triple. The simple multiples are built up by addition of like figures, e.g. $2+2$, $3+3$, $2+2+2$, $3+3+3$, $2+2+2+2$, and so on. But Stravinsky wished to experiment with irregular compounds, and this led to combinations like $2+3$, $3+2$, $2+3+2$, $3+2+3$, and so on. The pulse remained regular, but the time signature changed continuously, and the effect was to produce a series of constantly shifting accents that disrupted the old symmetrical four-square patterns. This is the procedure he worked out in *The Rite of Spring*; and he was faithful to it in all the works of his Russian period up to and including the *Symphonies of Wind Instruments*. He also experimented with patterns made by the counterpointing of different metres, as can be seen from a work like *The Soldier's Tale* (see Ex. 32).

When in the 1920's his growing interest in classical procedures led to a change of style, he had to reconsider his attitude to metre and rhythm. In *Pulcinella* and *The Fairy's Kiss*, he was constrained to accept the original metres of Pergolesi and Chaikovsky, though he modified them by such devices as prolongation and elision; but his personal practice, as can be seen from *Mavra*, the *Octet* and the other neoclassical compositions, was to revert to greater regularity of metre while retaining an increasing measure of rhythmic freedom. As the years went on, irregular metres occurred less frequently; but greater resource and subtlety were shown in overall rhythmic treatment. For instance, although the first and last movements of the *Symphony in C* carry virtually no change of time signature,[1] their rhythmic variety and vitality are never in doubt. Even freer rhythms are to be found in the serial works; and the construction of some of the vocal canons in *Canticum Sacrum* and *Threni* leads to polyrhythmic combinations where barlines are no longer capable of serving as common denominators and are dropped accordingly.

Some of the works of his Russian period – particularly *The Wedding* and the *Symphonies of Wind Instruments* – were so carefully geared to different related speeds that their execution demanded a motor precision which was not always forthcoming. His distress at the inadequacy of some of the early performances of the *Symphonies of Wind Instruments* is referred to in the Register above. This was the moment when he hankered after near-mechanical solutions – hence his numerous experiments with mechanical pianos, and his almost neurotic anxiety that conductors and executants should literally follow the directions in his scores and refrain from imposing their own interpretation

---

[1] The first movement is marked 2/2 *moderato alla breve*; the last movement is marked ¢ *Tempo giusto, alla breve*, with the exception of the slow introduction which is a 4/4 *Largo*.

on the music. The intransigence of his attitude is well illustrated by the following story:

It appears that one morning in London – probably in the summer of 1914 – when he was listening to the bells of St. Paul's, he turned to Edwin Evans, who was with him in the taxi, and said: 'That is really the ideal way of making music. A man pulls a rope; but what happens at the other end of the rope is of no special significance to him. He cannot make the bells ring more softly or loudly; he cannot alter their rhythm; crescendos and diminuendos are beyond his scope. He has nothing to do, except to pull the rope – the bells do all the rest. The music is not in him; it lives in the bells. The man at the rope is the prototype of the ideal conductor.'[1]

Some people thought that his public performances, either as executant or conductor, were too mechanical and too inhibited; and Ansermet said that in 1925 Toscanini, who was preparing *The Nightingale* for production at the Scala, 'lost all confidence in his musicality when he heard him count the time out loud as he played through part of the score on the piano'.[2] But there is no doubt that as he gained more experience as conductor and executant of his own works, his views became modified. In his sixties he drastically revised the time signatures of the last movement of *The Rite of Spring* in order to facilitate the conductor's job; but in so doing he sometimes had to jettison an element of phrasing that was implicit in the barring of the earlier version, and this could be construed as a loss. About the same time he also altered some of the metronome markings in his other works; and his own recorded performances occasionally showed that a greater degree of latitude in tempo and interpretation was permissible than might have been expected after reading his intransigent public utterances.

Few composers (except possibly Webern) have wasted less time than Stravinsky. Balanchine, who collaborated with him on so many ballets, knew that to have all the time in the world meant nothing to him and quoted him as saying, 'When I know how long a piece must take, then it excites me.'[3] This respect for time has won the confidence of his audiences who know that in listening to his music they will get maximum value for the time they themselves sacrifice. It is only in exceptional cases – like the note-spinning *Gigue* of the *Duo Concertant* and certain passages in *The Rake's Progress* where Auden's weakness for the adolescent joke or fantastical quirk has tempted the composer to stray and loiter – that they may feel their attention is not being rewarded by music of full concentration. Time is golden; and nearly all Stravinsky's music is gilt-edged.

---

[1] See also p. 49.

[2] Ernest Ansermet, *Les Fondements de la Musique dans la Conscience Humaine*. Neuchâtel, 1961.

[3] George Balanchine, 'The Dance Element in Strawinsky's Music', *Strawinsky in the Theatre*. Dance Index, 1945.

The Composer

After his apprenticeship, there were no occasions when he showed himself prepared to accept an academic form in blank and attempt to fill it out. His approach to formal problems was always a fresh and original one. Sometimes his ballet music tried to create resemblances (as in part of *Petrushka*) or symbols (as in *The Flood*); but his more successful ballet scores are variations on the formal principle of the suite (as in *The Rite of Spring*, *Apollo Musagetes*, and *Agon*). Particularly fascinating and in some respects unique are the mosaic type of structure built up of various interlocking materials (as in the *Symphonies of Wind Instruments*) and the organic type of structure formed by proliferating, overlapping tissue (as in *The Wedding*). Sonata form made its appearance during the neo-classical period; and in works like the *Octet*, the *Concerto for Two Solo Pianos*, the *Symphony in C*, and the *Symphony in Three Movements*, he showed he had accepted it on his own terms. Cantatas and operas are impure forms because of their close dependence on the construction element postulated by the librettos. Stravinsky showed great ingenuity in arranging texts for himself, particularly in *The Wedding* and *Reynard* and in serial works like *Canticum Sacrum*, *Threni*, and *A Sermon, a Narrative and a Prayer*. With his opera librettists he had varying degrees of success. His obsessive hatred of 'music drama' drove him far in the opposite direction; and his operas have all been carefully constructed in terms of more or less closed musical numbers. It is interesting to find that in his *Dialogues* he abandons the old distinction between 'opera' and 'music drama' and replaces these terms with 'verse opera' and 'prose opera'.

He held strong views about expression in music; and these have been widely quoted and discussed – and frequently misunderstood. The argument started in 1934, when he wrote a strongly worded defence of his viewpoint at the time of the first performance of *Persephone*.[1] (It should be remembered that in this score he was setting a French libretto which postulated a stage action.)

> In music, which is regulated time and tone in contrast to the confusion of natural sound, there is always the syllable. Between the syllable and the general sense, there is the word, which acts as conductor to the flow of thought and helps to build up its discursive sense. But the word, acting as intermediary, is not so much a help as a hindrance to the musician . . . For music is not thought. One writes *crescendo*, one writes *diminuendo*: but the music that is real music does not swell out or contract according to the dictates of the action. *Je n'extériorise pas . . .*[2]

'I do not externalise . . .' 'Externalise' is a strange word to use, and this is a rather clumsy way of putting it; but it is clear that in this passage he is referring to the problem of expression. A year later he resumed the argument in his

[1] See Appendix A (5).
[2] English translation by E. W. W.

565

3. Epilogue

Chronicle. After referring to the special assonant and cadential qualities of the Russian popular verses he had decided to set in *Pribaoutki*, the *Cat's Cradle Songs* and *The Wedding*, he went on to say:

> For I consider that music is, by its very nature, essentially powerless to *express* anything at all, whether a feeling, an attitude of mind, a psychological mood, a phenomenon of nature etc. *Expression* has never been an inherent property of music. That is by no means the purpose of its existence. If, as is nearly always the case, music appears to express something, this is only an illusion and not a reality. It is simply an additional attribute which, by tacit and inveterate agreement, we have lent it, thrust upon it, as a label, a convention – in short, an aspect which, unconsciously or by force of habit, we have come to confuse with its essential being.

This doctrine of non-expression aroused considerable hostility and was frequently misunderstood, especially when quoted in a truncated form; and a quarter of a century later Robert Craft took advantage of the question and answer method used in his volumes of Conversations to revert to the subject and give Stravinsky a chance to explain himself further. In *Expositions*, Stravinsky says:

> That over-publicised bit about expression (or non-expression) was simply a way of saying that music is supra-personal and super-real and as such beyond verbal meanings and verbal descriptions. It was aimed against the notion that a piece of music is in reality a transcendental idea 'expressed in terms of music', with the *reductio ad absurdum* implication that exact sets of correlatives must exist between a composer's feelings and his notation. It was offhand and annoyingly incomplete, but even the stupider critics could have seen that it did not deny musical expressivity, but only the validity of a type of verbal statement about musical expressivity. I stand by the remark, incidentally, though today I would put it the other way round: music expresses itself.

That last phrase still seems to beg the question, though the rest of the passage is clear and convincing. Perhaps the final word was spoken by Stravinsky when he addressed the young readers of *Komsomolskaya Pravda* on the occasion of his return to Russia in the autumn of 1962[1]: 'The language of music is a special language; it is not the same as the language of literature.' And one might add that just as literature can express ideas in words, so music can express ideas in sound, but the ideas are different.

A vivid illustration of his views in action is provided by Maurice Perrin, who attended a composition class in 1935/6 arranged by the Ecole Normale de Musique in Paris under the joint direction of Nadia Boulanger and Stravin-

---

[1] See Appendix A (9).

sky himself. On one occasion, says Perrin,[1] Stravinsky told the class 'how in the first performance of [*Persephone*] at the Paris Opera in 1934, the singers used to treat the opening chorus – 'Reste avec nous' – in the most sentimental way. This displeased him very much, and he asked them why they did it. It seemed to them, they said, a particularly expressive chorus. "Then why do you want to *make* something expressive, when – as you yourselves say – it already *is* so!" And Stravinsky added, for our benefit: "It is as though one tried to sugar the sugar!" '

In discussing Stravinsky's attitude to composition and expression,[2] Ansermet claimed him to be the first of the great composers for whom creative activity was 'to do', while for all the others before him it had been 'to feel'. He said Stravinsky used to maintain that the chief problem of a composer was *how* to do it. 'But then,' Ansermet asked him, 'what is the "what" of music?' 'It's something,' Stravinsky replied, 'which comes of itself, which is given once and for all, and with which, in consequence, there is no need to preoccupy oneself, while there devolves on the composer the task of finding the "how".' Ansermet considered that in Stravinsky's earlier music (up to and including the *Symphonies of Wind Instruments*) 'the melodic dialectic and the unfolding of form had a *concrete significance*', which was missing in the works of pure music of his neo-classical and serial periods. But different persons read different meanings into the same work, or the same passage, or the same motive, at different times; and musical meanings are relative, not absolute.

Stravinsky's own attitude to the act of composition is set out at some length in the third and perhaps most valuable of his lectures on the *Poetics of Music*.

There he starts from the assumption that the act of composition is the result of the artist's exercise of the principle of speculative volition which is at the origin of all creation. He goes on to say that 'all creation presupposes at its origin a sort of appetite that is brought on by the foretaste of discovery'. In his case, this appetite is aroused 'at the mere thought of putting in order musical elements that have attracted [his] attention', and he finds that this responds to a habitual and periodic natural need. He admits that 'the idea of discovery and hard work' attracts him.

> The very act of putting my work on paper, of, as we say, kneading the dough, is for me inseparable from the pleasure of creation. So far as I am concerned, I cannot separate the spiritual effort from the psychological and physical effort; they confront me on the same level and do not present a hierarchy. . . The idea of work to be done is for me so closely bound up with the idea of the arranging of materials and of the pleasure that the actual doing of the work affords us that, should the impossible happen and my

[1] Maurice Perrin, 'Stravinsky in a Composition Class'. *The Score*, June 1957.
[2] In 'The Crisis of Contemporary Music: (II) The Stravinsky Case', a lecture given in London on 11 December 1963 and printed in *Recorded Sound*, April 1964.

3. Epilogue

work suddenly be given to me in a perfectly completed form, I should be embarrassed and non-plussed by it, as by a hoax.

Passing to the part played in creation by the imagination, he emphasises the importance of a composer profiting by the unforeseen, the accident, the obstacle. If by chance his finger slips, he will notice it in order possibly to profit by it at a later stage. 'An accident is perhaps the only thing that inspires us.' And here, one feels, he might have added to the accidental the subconscious.

It is strange how frequently dreams seem to have played an important part in directing Stravinsky's attention or resolving his doubts. The germinal idea of *The Rite of Spring* came from a dream. One of the key tunes in *The Soldier's Tale* was heard by him in a dream, and on awakening he was able to write it down.

Ex. 204

Sometimes they have provided solutions to particular problems. The idea of using a wind octet for his instrumental sonata came from a dream; and so did the confirmation of a difficult and unusual interval in *Threni*. 'My dreams are my psychological digestive system' he claims in *Expositions*.

The non-musical dreams are of interest too.

When he was living at Beaulieu in the early months of 1911, he had a nightmare, in which he thought he had become a hunchback. He awoke in great pain to discover that he was unable to stand or even sit in an erect position; and his illness was diagnosed as intercostal neuralgia caused by nicotine poisoning. At the moment he was still working on the last scene of *Petrushka*; and one cannot help wondering whether in some way he had identified himself with the sufferings of his puppet hero.

His autobiographical writings make it clear that at various times of life he was subject to a number of frustrations and inhibitions e.g., the long, exasperating Russian winters of his youth,[1] and the suffocating family ties. Something of this feeling is implicit in a nightmare he experienced once when sharing a bedroom with Ansermet. In his dream he found himself hiding in the grounds of a country house while an armed guard marched up and down a terrace facing the garden. He was trying to take advantage of a moment when the sentry's back would be turned, or his attention distracted, to slip into the house unobserved; and the agony of his situation caused him to wake up suddenly, bathed in sweat. (Or perhaps this reflects an exile's wish to return to his native country.)

---

[1] 'Winter, with its curtailing of liberty and amusements, with its rigorous discipline and interminable length' (*Chronicle*).

A recurrent episode in his dream life was that he was for ever trying to tell the time and for ever looking at his wrist watch, only to find it wasn't there (*Exp*). As time is the dimension within which he created his music – 'When I know how long a piece must take, then it excites me' – this dream would seem to reveal an anxiety neurosis connected with his creative potency.

But the creative effort continued unabated for more than sixty years. In that time he passed through a world of chaos, revolution, and change, remaining true to himself, his standards, and beliefs, and produced original music lasting for a total of about 1,500 minutes – a Stravinskyan day and night. The compositions of his different periods influenced musicians for over half a century. Those who experienced the exciting impact of the first performances of some of his major works when it seemed as if a new musical star had suddenly appeared in the firmament, who saw his short birdlike figure jigging on the podium as he conducted his own music with resilience and economy of gesture, occasionally inflecting one of his fingers or shrugging his shoulders or swaying his hips or cuing in an important new entry with a vigorous underarm bowling action, are not likely ever to forget the man or the music that is his legacy to the world.

Appendices

CONTENTS

572

Appendix A

VARIOUS WRITINGS REPRINTED

1

'THE SLEEPING BEAUTY'

(Open letter to Serge Diaghilev reprinted from *The Times* of 18 October 1921)

It gives me great happiness to know that you are producing that masterpiece *The Sleeping Beauty* by our great and beloved Chaikovsky. It makes me doubly happy. In the first place, it is a personal joy, for this work appears to me as the most authentic expression of that period in our Russian life which we call the 'Petersburg Period', and which is stamped upon my memory with the morning vision of the Imperial sleighs of Alexander III, the giant Emperor, and his giant coachman, and the immense joy that awaited me in the evening, the performance of *The Sleeping Beauty*.

It is, further, a great satisfaction to me as a musician to see produced a work of so direct a character at a time when so many people, who are neither simple, nor naïve, nor spontaneous, seek in their art simplicity, 'poverty', and spontaneity. Chaikovsky in his very nature possessed these three gifts to the fullest extent. That is why he never feared to let himself go, whereas the prudes, whether *raffinés* or academic, were shocked by the frank speech, free from artifice, of his music.

Chaikovsky possessed the power of *melody*, centre of gravity in every symphony, opera or ballet composed by him. It is absolutely indifferent to me that the quality of his melody was sometimes unequal. The fact is that he was a creator of *melody*, which is an extremely rare and precious gift. Among us, Glinka, too, possessed it; and not to the same degree, those others . . .

And that is something which is not German.

The Germans manufactured and manufactured music with themes and *Leitmotive* which they substituted for melodies.

Chaikovsky's music, which does not appear specifically Russian to everybody, is often more profoundly Russian than music which has long since been awarded the facile label of Muscovite picturesqueness. This music is quite as Russian as Pushkin's verse or Glinka's song. While not specifically cultivating in his art the 'soul of the Russian peasant', Chaikovsky drew *unconsciously* from the true, popular sources of our race.

And how characteristic were his predilections in the music of the past and of his own day! He worshipped Mozart, Couperin, Glinka, Bizet: that leaves us [in no] doubt of the quality of his taste. How strange it is! Every time that a Russian musician has come under the influence of this Latino-Slav culture and seen clearly the frontier between the Austro-Catholic Mozart turned towards Beaumarchais, and the German-Protestant Beethoven inclined towards Goethe, the result has been striking . . .

The convincing example of Chaikovsky's great creative power is beyond all doubt the ballet of *The Sleeping Beauty*. This cultured man, with his knowledge of folksong and of old French music, had no need to engage in archaeological research in order to present the age of Louis XIV; he recreated the character of the period by his musical language, preferring involuntary but living anachronisms to conscious and laboured *pasticcio*: a virtue that appertains only to great creative minds.

I have just read again the score of this ballet. I have instrumented some numbers of it which had remained unorchestrated and unperformed. I have spent some days of intense pleasure in finding therein again and again the same feeling of freshness, inventiveness, ingenuity, and vigour. And I warmly desire that your audiences of all countries may feel this work as it is felt by me, a Russian musician.

Yours ever,
Igor Stravinsky

Paris, October 10th, 1921

(*Translated by Edwin Evans*)

2

'SOME IDEAS ABOUT MY OCTUOR'

(Reprinted from *The Arts*, January 1924[1])

My Octuor is a musical object.

This object has a form and that form is influenced by the musical matter with which it is composed.

The differences of matter determine the differences of form. One does not do the same with marble that one does with stone.

My Octuor is made for an ensemble of wind instruments. Wind instruments seem to me to be more apt to render a certain rigidity of the form I had in mind than other instruments – the string instruments, for example, which are less cold and more vague.

---

[1] According to an editorial note, this was the first article Stravinsky had ever written for publication.

The suppleness of the string instruments can lend itself to more subtle nuances and can serve better the individual sensibility of the executant in works built on an 'emotive' basis.

My Octuor is not an 'emotive' work but a musical composition based on objective elements which are sufficient in themselves.

The reasons why I composed this kind of music for an octuor of flute, clarinet, bassoons, trumpets and trombones are the following: First, because this ensemble forms a complete sonorous scale and consequently furnishes me with a sufficiently rich register; second, because the difference of the volume of these instruments renders more evident the musical architecture. And this is the most important question in all my recent musical compositions.

I have excluded from this work all sorts of nuances, which I have replaced by the play of these volumes.

I have excluded all nuances between the *forte* and the *piano*; I have left only the *forte* and the *piano*.

Therefore the *forte* and the *piano* are in my work only the dynamic limit which determines the function of the volumes in play.

The play of these volumes is one of the two active elements on which I have based the action of my musical text (which is the passive element of the composition), the other element being the movements in their reciprocal connection.

These two elements, which are the object for the musical execution, can only have a meaning if the executant follows strictly the musical text.

My Octuor, as I said before, is an object that has its own form. Like all other objects it has weight and occupies a place in space, and like all other objects it will necessarily lose part of its weight and space in time and through time. The loss will be in quantity, but it can not lose in quality as long as its emotive basis has objective properties and as long as this object keeps its 'specific weight'. One cannot alter the specific weight of an object without destroying the object itself.

The aim I sought in this Octuor, which is also the aim I sought with the greatest energy in all my recent works, is to realise a musical composition through means which are emotive in themselves. These emotive means are manifested in the rendition by the heterogeneous play of movements and volumes.

This play of movements and volumes that puts into action the musical text constitutes the impelling force of the composition and determines its form.

A musical composition constructed on that basis could not, indeed, admit the introduction of the element of 'interpretation' in its execution without risking the complete loss of its meaning.

To interpret a piece is to realise its portrait, and what I demand is the realisation of the piece itself and not of its portrait.

It is a fact that all music suffers, in time, a deformation through its execution;

575

this fact would not be regretted if that deformation were done in a manner that would not be in contradiction to the spirit of the work.

A work created with a spirit in which the emotive basis is the nuance is soon deformed in all directions; it soon becomes amorphous, its future is anarchic and its executants become its interpreters. The nuance is a very uncertain basis for a musical composition because its limitations cannot be, even in particular cases, established in a fixed manner; for nuance is not a musical fact but a desideratum.

On the other hand, a musical composition in which the emotive basis resides not in the nuance but in the very form of the composition will risk little in the hands of its executants.

I have arrived at this conclusion: when the centre of gravity finds itself in the form considered as the only emotive subject of the composition, when the author puts into it such a force of expression that no other force could be added to it (such as the will or personal predilection of the executant) without being superfluous, then the author can be considered as the only interpreter of his musical sensations, and he who is called the interpreter of his compositions would become its executant.

I admit the commercial exploitation of a musical composition, but I do not admit its emotive exploitation. To the author belongs the emotive exploitation of his ideas, the result of which is the composition; to the executant belongs the presentation of that composition in the way designated to him by its own form.

It is not at all with the view of preserving my musical work from deformation that I turn to form as the only emotive basis of a musical composition; deformation is always fatal and inevitable. I turn to form because I do not conceive nor feel the true emotive force except under co-ordinated musical sensations.

These sensations only find their objective and living expression in the form which, so to speak, determines their nature.

To understand, or rather feel, the nature of these sensations according to that form (which is, as I said, their expression) is the task of the executant.

According to his temperament, the executant will bring out, more or less plainly, the sensations which have created that form. They will establish the form of the composition.

In this case the deformation that music will inevitably suffer through time, by the numerous successive manners of execution, will follow its normal path; and this path will be pointed out by the form of the composition. Then the deformation will not be in contradiction to the spirit of the music because its form will be the only guiding point for the executant.

Form, in my music, derives from counterpoint. I consider counterpoint as the only means through which the attention of the composer is concentrated on purely musical questions. Its elements also lend themselves perfectly to an architectural construction.

This sort of music has no other aim than to be sufficient in itself. In general, I consider that music is only able to solve musical problems; and nothing else, neither the literary nor the picturesque, can be in music of any real interest. The play of the musical elements is the thing.

I must say that I follow in my art an instinctive logic and that I do not formulate its theory in any other way than *ex post facto*.   Igor Strawinsky

3

'AVERTISSEMENT'

(Reprinted from *The Dominant*, December 1927)

On parle beaucoup à notre époque du retour au classicisme, et on classifie sous la rubrique néo-classique les oeuvres qu'on croit écrites sous l'influence des oeuvres dites classiques.

Il m'est difficile de dire si cette classification est juste ou non. En effet, ne s'agit-il pas plutôt, dans les oeuvres dignes d'attention – oeuvres qui subissent une influence évidente des oeuvres d'autrefois – d'une recherche plus profonde que la simple imitation du langage soi-disant classique? Il me semble que le gros public, et avec lui la critique, se borne à enregistrer des impressions superficielles de certains procédés techniques de la musique nommée classique.

Cela ne forme pas encore le néo-classicisme, car le classicisme lui-même ne se caractérisait pas du tout par ses procédés techniques, qui changeaient eux-mêmes autrefois comme maintenant à chaque époque, mais plutôt par ses valeurs constructives.

La chose en elle-même (par exemple, en musique, un thème ou un rhythme) n'est pas un matériel qui puisse suffire à l'artiste pour la création d'une oeuvre. Il est évident que ce matériel doit encore trouver sa disposition réciproque, ce qui en musique, comme dans tout art, porte le nom de la forme. Toutes les grandes oeuvres d'art étaient marquées par cette qualité – qualité de rapport des choses, rapport du matériel à construction; et ce rapport était le seul élément stable, toute autre chose étant, en dehors de lui, incompréhensiblement individuelle – en musique, élément extra-musical.

La musique classique – la vraie musique classique – avait comme substance à sa base la forme musicale, et cette substance, comme je l'ai définie plus haut, ne pouvait jamais être extra-musicale. Si ceux qui marquent du terme néo-classique les oeuvres de la dernière tendance musicale y constatent le retour salutaire à cette base unique de la musique, qui est la substance formelle, je veux bien. Je voudrais seulement savoir s'ils ne se trompent pas dans chaque cas particulier. Je veux dire par cela que c'est une tâche d'une difficulté énorme (et c'est là où la vraie critique peut se manifester) de se soustraire aux apparences trompeuses, qui mènent presque toujours à des constatations fausses.

Igor Strawinsky

'A WARNING'

There is much talk nowadays of a reversion to classicism, and works believed to have been composed under the influence of so-called classical models are labelled neo-classic.

It is difficult for me to say whether this classification is correct or not. With works that are worthy of attention, and have been written under the obvious influence of the music of the past, does not the matter consist rather in a quest that probes deeper than a mere imitation of the so-called classical idiom? I fear that the bulk of the public, and also the critics, are content with recording superficial impressions created by the use of certain technical devices which were current in so-called classical music.

The use of such devices is insufficient to constitute the real neo-classicism, for classicism itself was characterised, not in the least by its technical processes which, then as now, were themselves subject to modification from period to period, but rather by its constructive values.

The mere 'thing' – for instance, in music, a theme or a rhythm – is in itself not the sort of material that would satisfy an artist for the creation of a work. It is obvious that the constituents of such material must come into a reciprocal relation, which, in music, as in all art, is called form. The great works of art were all imbued with this attribute, a quality of interrelation between constituent parts, interrelation of the building material. And this interrelation was the one stable element, all that lay apart from it being unintelligibly individual – that is to say, in music, an ultra-musical element.

Classical music – true classical music – claimed musical form as its basic substance; and this substance, as I have shown, could never be ultra-musical. If those who label as neo-classic the works belonging to the latest tendency in music mean by that label that they detect in them a wholesome return to this formal idea, the only basis of music, well and good. But I should like to know, in each particular instance, whether they are not mistaken. By that I mean that it is a task of enormous difficulty, and one in which therefore serious criticism can show its worth, to achieve immunity from misleading appearances which almost inevitably lead to incorrect deductions.

Igor Stravinsky

4

'TRIBUTE TO PICASSO'
(Reprinted from *Cahiers d'Art*, 7e année, 1932)

Cher Monsieur,

Que ces lignes vous remplacent le mot que vous me demandez pour les *Cahiers d'Art* à l'occasion de la prochaine exposition Picasso dont vous me parlez.

Ne me sentant pas assez compétent pour me prononcer sur l'oeuvre magnifique de mon grand contemporain, je préfère me borner à vous dire simplement mon immense admiration pour ce très grand peintre.

Si j'admire quelquechose, je veux l'admirer intégralement et c'est bien le cas pour Picasso: je l'admire autant pour le présent et pour le passé que pour le futur. Alors je ne critique pas. Critiquer est le métier des critiques: or on ne sait que trop bien à quoi cela les mène, ce n'est pas un secret: cela les mène à embrouiller les choses, à supplanter l'enthousiasme par l'habitude et à retarder ainsi la compréhension des contemporains. Convenons que c'est un métier de méchants. Souvenez-vous seulement de ce que Picasso répondit, il y a bien longtemps, au *Serpent* de La Fontaine:

. . .
> *Pauvre ignorant! eh! que prétends-tu faire?*
> *Tu te prends à plus dur que toi,*
> *Petit serpent à tête folle:*
> *Plutôt que d'emporter de moi*
> *Seulement le quart d'une obole,*
> *Tu te romprois toutes les dents.*
> *Je ne crains que celles du Temps.*
> *Ceci s'adresse à vous, esprits du dernier ordre,*
> *Qui, n'étant bons à rien, cherchez sur tout à mordre.*
> *Vous vous tourmentez vainement.*
> *Croyez-vous que vos dents impriment leurs outrages*
> *Sur tant de beaux ouvrages?*
> *Ils sont pour vous d'airain, d'acier, de diamant.*

Espérant que ces lignes trouveront dans vos *Cahiers* un écho sympathique, car je sais l'admiration que, comme moi, vois portez à Picasso, je vous prie de trouver ici, cher Monsieur, l'expression de mes sentiments les meilleurs.

Igor Strawinsky

5

'PERSEPHONE'

(*NOTE: On Sunday 29 April 1934 a signed article appeared in* Excelsior *headed* 'Igor Strawinsky nous parle de "Perséphone"'. *On Tuesday May 1st* Excelsior *printed a fuller text of the article headed* 'M. Igor Strawinsky nous parle de "Perséphone",' *with a preliminary statement explaining that a paragraph had been omitted from the original article. For the purposes of this reprint, 'A' is the text of April 29th: 'B' the text of May 1st. The following text is based on 'B'. Text 'A' variants are shown in the footnotes.*)

Je dois, puisqu'on m'a proposé d'écrire sur la musique de Perséphone et que je n'ai guère le temps de le faire, attirer l'attention du publique sur un mot qui contient tout un programme : 'syllabe' et ensuite le verbe 'syllaber'.

Là réside ma préoccupation principale.

Dans la musique, qui est temps et ton réglé, par opposition au son confus qui est dans la nature, il y a toujours la syllabe. Entre elle et le sens tout à fait général – le mode qui baigne l'oeuvre – il y a le mot qui canalise la pensée éparse et fait aboutir le sens discursif. Or le mot, plutôt qu'il ne l'aide, constitue pour le musicien un intermédiaire encombrant. Je ne voulais pour *Perséphone* que des syllabes, de belles, fortes syllabes, et puis une action. Dans ce désir, je me félicite d'avoir rencontré Gide, dont le texte, hautement poétique, mais libre de sursauts, devait me fournir une structure syllabique excellente.

Car la musique n'est pas la pensée. On dit *crescendo*, on dit *diminuendo* : la musique vraiment musique n'enfle ni ne décroit selon les températures de l'action. Je n'extériorise pas. J'entends tout autrement qu'on ne le pense le rôle de la musique. Elle nous est donnée uniquement pour mettre de l'ordre dans les choses : passer d'un état anarchique et individualiste à un état réglé, parfaitement conscient et pourvu de garanties de vitalité et de durée.

Ce qui est le propre de mon émotion consciente ne peut, pour les autres et même pour moi, être réfléchi à l'état de règle. Dès l'instant qu'on prend conscience de l'émotion, elle est déjà froide : elle est comme la lave : elle devient un formalisme et l'on en fait des broches que l'on vend au pied du Vésuve.

Je crois devoir avertir le public que j'ai en horreur les effets orchestraux comme moyens d'embellissement et qu'il ne faut pas s'attendre à être ébloui par des sonorités séduisantes. J'ai depuis longtemps abandonné la futilité du brio. J'ai horreur de courtiser le public – cela me gêne. Que ceux qui font fonction de cette estimée besogne, soit en composant des partitions, soit en dirigeant, s'y adonnent à satiété. La foule exige que l'artiste fasse sortir et exibe ses entrailles. C'est cela que l'on prend pour la plus noble expression de l'art, le nommant personnalité, individualité, tempérament et autres titres du même acabit.

J'ai usé de l'orchestre normal, de choeurs mixtes, d'un choeur d'enfants. Comme soloistes, il n'y a qu'une voix chantante, qui est celle d'Eumolpe, maître des cérémonies du culte de Déméter à Eleusis. C'est lui qui expose l'action et dirige le drame. Le rôle de Perséphone est mimé, parlé et dansé. Il est remarquable de voir combien ce *parakataloghé* délicat s'accorde avec l'ensemble.

---

l.2 *et que je n'ai guère . . . faire* 'B'. Omitted in 'A'.
l.3 *et ensuite le verbe 'syllaber'* 'B'. Omitted in 'A'.
l.5 *qui est temps et ton réglé* 'B'. *dont les temps et le ton sont réglés* 'A'.
l.6 *il y a toujours la syllabe* 'B'. *il y a toujours le rhythme de la syllabe* 'A'.
l.7 *le mode qui baigne l'oeuvre* 'B'. *l'atmosphère qui baigne l'oeuvre* 'A'.
ll.23–31 *Je crois devoir avertir . . . du même acabit* 'B'. This paragraph is missing in 'A'
l.32 *normal* 'A'. *normand* 'B'.

Cette partition telle qu'elle a été écrite, telle qu'elle doit rester dans les archives musicales de l'époque, fait un tout indissoluble avec les tendances affirmées à plusieurs reprises dans mes oeuvres précédentes. Elle fait suite à *Oedipus-Rex*, à *Symphonie de psaumes*, au *Capriccio*, au *Concerto* pour violon et au *Duo concertant*, bref, à tout un acheminement où l'abstention de spectacle ne diminue en rien la vie autonome de l'oeuvre.

Perséphone, qui sera représenté le 30 avril 1934 par Mme. Ida Rubinstein et sa troupe au Grand Opéra de Paris, est la forme actuelle de cet acheminement.

Toute chose sentie et vraie est susceptible de donner des projections énormes. Ce ne sont pas des caprices de ma nature. Je suis sur un très sûr chemin. Ce n'est ni à discuter ni à critiquer. L'on ne critique pas quelqu'un ou quelque chose en état de fonction. Le nez n'est pas fabriqué : le nez *est*.

Ainsi mon art.
Igor Strawinsky

6

'QUELQUES CONFIDENCES SUR LA MUSIQUE'

Conférence de M. Igor Strawinsky
faite le 21 novembre1935 à 2 h. 45, répétée le même jour à 5 h.
et le 22 novembre

(reprinted from *Conferencia*, Journal de l'Université des Annales,
15 December 1935)

Mesdames, Messieurs,

L'Université des Annales vous a promis des confidences d'auteur. J'en ai déjà fait, de ces confidences, dans le premier volume de mes *Chroniques*, et vous en trouverez d'autres dans le second, qui est sous presse. La seule chose que je puisse faire aujourd'hui, c'est d'anticiper un peu en citant quelques pensées qui y sont développées et qui reflètent ma façon d'aimer la musique et de la cultiver. Vous y lirez, entre autres, ceci:

Pour moi, comme musicien créateur, la composition est une fonction quotidienne que je me sens appelé à remplir. Je compose parce que je suis fait pour cela et que je ne saurais m'en passer. Comme tout organe s'atrophie s'il n'est pas maintenu dans un état de continuelle activité, de même les facultés du compositeur faiblissent et s'engourdissent quand elles ne sont pas soutenues par l'effort et l'entraînement. Le profane s'imagine que, pour

1.5 *l'abstention* 'B'. *le défaut* 'A'.
11.13,14 *Le nez n'est pas . . . Ainsi mon art* 'B'. These two sentences are omitted in 'A'.

créer, il faut attendre l'inspiration. C'est une erreur. Je suis loin de nier l'inspiration, bien au contraire. C'est une force motrice qu'on trouve dans n'importe quelle activité humaine et qui n'est nullement le monopole des artistes. Mais cette force ne se déploie que quand elle est mise en action par un effort, et cet effort est le travail. Comme l'appétit vient en mangeant, il est tout aussie vrai que le travail amène l'inspiration, si celle-ci n'est pas apparue dès le commencement. Mais ce n'est pas uniquement l'inspiration qui compte, c'est son résultat, – autrement dit, l'oeuvre.

Après ce préambule d'ordre général, je me permettrai de vous dire quelques mots, d'abord des *Trois Mouvements de Pétrouchka*, qui seront exécutés par mon fils, et, ensuite, de mon dernier ouvrage, le *Concerto* qu'avec lui j'aurai l'honneur de vous présenter tout à l'heure.

C'est en été 1921 que j'ai fait cette transcription de *Pétrouchka*. Mon intention était de donner aux virtuoses du clavier une pièce d'une certaine envergure qui leur permettrait de compléter leur répertoire moderne et de faire briller leur technique. Ce travail me passiona beaucoup. Etant pianiste moi-même, je m'intéressais surtout à l'écriture spéciale que demande une oeuvre conçue à l'origine pour le piano, ainsi qu'aux multiples richesses sonores que nous offre la nature polyphonique de cet instrument. *Pétrouchka* se prêtait d'autant mieux à une pareille transcription que, dans son idée initiale ce morceau avait été conçu comme une pièce de piano avec orchestre, et que, dans la partition même de l'oeuvre, le piano joue un rôle important. Si j'emploie ici le terme courant, *transcription*, je tiens toutefois à prévenir un malentendu. Qu'on ne pense surtout pas que j'ai voulu donner avec le piano un *Ersatz* de l'orchestre et rendre, dans la mesure du possible, la sonorité de ce dernier. Au contraire, je me suis efforcé de faire de ce *Pétrouchka* une pièce essentielle-ment pianistique en utilisant les ressources propres à cet instrument et sans lui assigner en aucune façon un rôle d'imitateur. Bref, qu'on n'y voie pas une réduction pour piano, mais bel et bien une pièce écrite spécialement pour le piano, autrement dit, de la musique de piano.

J'insiste sur ce point. Les idées musicales peuvent naître d'une façon pour ainsi dire abstraite sans que le compositeur ait en vue, dès le début, leur expression instrumentale, c'est-à-dire sans qu'il pense à un instrument ou à un ensemble déterminés. Mais, dans une composition pour un instrument ou un ensemble choisis d'avance, ces idées sont *le plus souvent* suggérées par l'instrument lui-même et *toujours* conditionnées par les possibilités qu'il offre. Dans ce cas, la pensée du compositeur travaille, si j'ose dire, *en présence* de l'instrument. Combien cela se sent, par exemple, chez Beethoven! Comme il saute aux yeux que, dans sa musique instrumentale, les idées lui venaient de son ensemble, et, dans son immense oeuvre pianistique, de son clavier!

Voilà pourquoi les réductions pour piano sont absolument incapables de rendre sa pensée conçue pour un ensemble instrumental. Quant aux tentatives d'instrumenter ses oeuvres de piano, elles ne sauraient être qualifiées autrement que d'absurdes, tant elles dénotent un manque d'entendement fondamental. Il n'est pas exact d'appeler les oeuvres pianistiques de Beethoven des oeuvres *pour piano*. Il serait plus juste de dire: *de piano*. Car on peut écrire *pour piano* sans que de pareilles compositions soient des compositions *de piano*. Autrement dit, le fait qu'une oeuvre a été écrite pour être jouée par un instrument quelconque ne suppose pas encore qu'elle trouve dans cet instrument la plénitude de son expression. Ce fait indique seulement qu'on a écrit une musique en général, et que cette musique a été ensuite adaptée à un certain instrument ou à un certain ensemble.

J'ai cru devoir m'étendre sur ce sujet à propos de *Pétrouchka*, dans la supposition que, parmi mes auditeurs, il y en a certainement qui ont entendu cette oeuvre à l'orchestre et qui pourraient, en l'écoutant tout à l'heure, faire des comparaisons entre l'orchestre et le piano, comparaisons qui risqueraient de paraître désavantageuses pour ce dernier. Evidemment, il ne peut être question pour le piano de rivaliser avec l'orchestre. Au point de vue volume dynamique, ils sont certainement incommensurables. Il faut donc tâcher d'oublier la sonorité orchestrale et écouter simplement une pièce *de piano* qui n'est nullement une adaptation, mais une oeuvre essentiellement pianistique où toutes les ressources du clavier sont mises à contribution.

La piéce débute par un *allegro* qui, dans le ballet, est la *Danse russe* des trois pantins, par laquelle se termine le premier tableau. Ce mouvement est suivi de la scène intitulée: *Chez Pétrouchka*. C'est précisément de ce tableau, composé par moi en premier lieu, qu'est sortie l'oeuvre que vous connaissez sous le titre: *Pétrouchka, scènes burlesques en quatre tableaux*. J'écrivis cette scène à Lausanne, au début de l'automne 1910. J'avais en vue une oeuvre orchestrale où le piano jouerait un rôle prépondérant, une sorte de *Konzertstück*. En composant cette musique, j'avais nettement la vision d'un pantin subitement déchaîné qui, par ses cascades d'arpèges diaboliques, exaspère la patience de l'orchestre, lequel, à son tour, lui réplique par des fanfares menaçantes. Ce morceau burlesque achevé, il m'importait de lui donner un titre qui exprimerait en un seul mot le caractère de ma musique et, conséquemment, la figure de mon personnage. Je le cherchai longtemps. Et voilà qu'un beau jour, je sursautai de joie. Pétrouchka! l'éternel et malheureux héros de toutes les foires de tous les pays! C'était bien ça. Le titre était trouvé. Ce morceau devint, par la suite, le second tableau de mon ballet.

Pour le troisième mouvement, j'ai pris une grande partie de la musique du quatrième tableau. C'est, d'abord, le brouhaha de la foule en liesse, le tintamarre de la fête foraine brusquement interrompue par une série de divertissements. Parmi ceux-ci, vous retrouverez, tour à tour, la ronde des nourrices, l'entrée des tziganes enjôlant le marchand fêtard, les cochers entraînant les nourrices dans leurs danses massives; finalement, les déguisés et les masques avec l'apparition desquels l'allégresse générale atteint son apogée.

C'est par là que se termine cette composition qui – n'oublions pas – revêt une forme exclusivement musicale et où l'action dramatique n'entre pas en ligne de compte.

Passons, maintenant, au *Concerto* pour deux pianos solos.

L'histoire de la musique connaît, en somme, peu d'ouvrages écrits pour deux pianos sans orchestre. Quant à des concertos pour deux pianos, il n'en existe pas que je sache.

Au sens étymologique du mot, le concerto constitue une pièce musicale d'une certaine ampleur et en plusieurs parties, affectant la forme architectonique de la sonate ou de la symphonie, avec la différence que, dans cet ensemble instrumental, un ou plusieurs instruments – par exemple, dans le *concerto grosso* – jouent un rôle dit concertant. Cette dernière expression dérive du mot italien *concertare*, qui veut dire *concourir*, participer à un concours, à un match. Par conséquent le concerto présume logiquement une rivalité entre plusieurs instruments dits concertants ou entre un seul instrument et un ensemble qui lui est opposé.

Or, cette conception du concerto n'est plus appliquée dans les ouvrages portant ce nom, et cela depuis bien longtemps. Le concerto est devenu une oeuvre pour un instrument solo sans concurrent et où le rôle de l'orchestre se trouve généralement réduit à un accompagnement.

Dans les quatre concertos que j'ai composés – le *Concerto pour piano*, le *Capriccio*, le *Concerto pour violon* et, enfin, le dernier, le *Concerto pour deux pianos solos* – je me suis tenu à l'ancienne formule. Au principal instrument concertant, j'ai opposé, dans mon ensemble orchestral, soit plusieurs instruments, soit des groupes entiers, concertants eux aussi. Ainsi je sauvegardais le principe du concours.

Autant la conception la plus naturelle d'un accompagnement est d'ordre harmonique, autant le concours concertant, par sa nature même, requiert l'ordre contrapunctique. C'est ce dernier principe que j'ai appliqué à ma nouvelle oeuvre où les deux pianos, d'une égale importance, concourent l'un avec l'autre et assument ainsi un rôle concertant – et c'est cela, précisément, qui m'a permis de donner à mon ouvrage la qualification de concerto.

Cette oeuvre comprend trois mouvements. Le premier est un allégro de sonate. Le second mouvement, qui tient lieu d'andante, je l'ai intitulé *Notturno*, en pensant, non pas aux morceaux de caractère rêveur et sans forme déterminée que présentent, par exemple, les nocturnes de Field ou de Chopin, mais aux pièces du XVIIIe siècle appelées *Nachtmusik*, ou, mieux encore, aux cassations si fréquentes chez les compositeurs de l'époque. Seulement, chez moi, les différentes parties, qui formaient généralement les ouvrages de ce genre, sont condensées en une seule.

Le troisième mouvement, qui est le dernier, se compose d'un prélude et d'une fugue précédés de quelques pièces variées. Ces dernières sont, en quelque sorte, des variations sur deux motifs qui se retrouvent dans le prélude, mais dégagés et pour ainsi dire résumés; le premier de ces motifs sert de sujet à la fugue à quatre voix qui termine l'ouvrage. Le temps limité dont je dispose m'empêche de vous donner une analyse technique de mon concerto. Quant à des commentaires extramusicaux, de moi, vous n'en attendez pas, j'espère. Je serais vraiment bien embarrassé de vous en fournir.

Il y a différentes manières d'aimer et d'apprécier la musique. Il y a, par exemple, la manière que j'appellerai l'amour intéressé, celle où l'on demande à musique des émotions d'ordre général, la joie, la douleur, la tristesse, un sujet de rêve, l'oubli de la vie prosaïque. Ce serait déprécier la musique que de lui assigner un pareil but utilitaire. Pourquoi ne pas l'aimer pour elle-même? Pourquoi ne pas l'aimer comme on aime un tableau, pour la belle peinture, le beau dessin, la belle composition? Pourquoi ne pas admettre la musique comme une valeur en soi, indépendante des sentiments et des images que, par analogie, elle pourrait évoquer, et qui ne sauraient que fausser le jugement de l'auditeur? La musique n'a pas besoin d'adjuvant. Elle se suffit à elle-même. N'y cherchons donc pas autre chose que ce qu'elle comporte.

Rien n'est plus difficile que de parler musique. On ne peut le faire utilement qu'en se plaçant sur le terrain technique et professionnel. Dès qu'on abandonne ce terrain, on plonge dans le vague et . . . l'on divague. Un grand romantique, Robert Schumann, qui a beaucoup écrit et profondément réfléchi sur la musique et qu'on ne saurait en aucune façon accuser d'aridité ou de doctrinarisme, finit par déclarer qu'en musique rien ne peut être prouvé.

'La science,' dit-il, 's'appuie sur les mathématiques et la logique, la poésie sur la parole, les arts plastiques sur la nature, mais la musique est une orpheline dont personne ne saurait nommer ni le père ni la mère. Et c'est peut-être dans ce mystère de son origine,' ajoute-t-il, 'que réside l'attrait de sa Beauté.'

Après cela, il vaut mieux me taire et me mettre au piano.

7

'INTERVIEW AVEC SERGE MOREUX DE L'INTRANSIGENT
POUR LA RADIODIFFUSION, PARIS

(24 December 1938)

Question Beaucoup de questions me passent par la tête et par exemple celle-ci: vous qui êtes si souvent en contacte avec le public puisque vous dirigez partout vos oeuvres, quelles impressions avez-vous recueillies sur les réactions de ce public, c'est-à-dire, comment pensez-vous qu'il écoute la musique?

Réponse Tout d'abord il faut savoir qu'il y a écouter et qu'il y a entendre.

Ce n'est pas par hasard que j'ai toujours trouvé que la masse des auditeurs en écoutant ma musique que je lui fais entendre, l'entend infiniment mieux que ceux qui parlent ou croient parler en son nom et qui ainsi se substituent à elle. Cher ami, ce sont de mauvais bergers. Evidemment ils sont légion, mais malgré leur nombre on peut facilement en dégager deux types: il y a des pompiers qui ne sont pas d'avant-garde et puis il y a des pompiers d'avant-garde. Les pompiers d'avant garde parlent musique et Freud, parlent musique et Marx, parlent complexe et se laissent à contre-çoeur apprivoiser par Saint Thomas lui-même. Les pompiers tout court, eux parlent musique et mélodie, méditent inévitablement en musique, aiment le sentiment, ont le souci du noble, et risquent même l'aventure du pitoresque oriental. (Je pense à mon *Oiseau de feu*.) Ce n'est du reste pas pour cela que je les préfère aux premiers, vous pensez bien, mais je les trouve simplement moins dangereux; en effet quand on est pompier on est pompier et, qu'on le sache bien, on ne réussit jamais à le camoufler. Du reste messieurs les pompiers d'avant-garde, ne méprisez pas outre mesure vos pauvres collègues surannés: il est à craindre que vous ne vous démodiez beaucoup plus vite qu'eux; le temps vous menace plus, bien plus que le flair humain.

Q. S'il y a crise de jugement, ne croyez-vous pas qu'elle est l'expression d'une crise générale de l'art?

R. Il n'est pas étonnant que les critiques soient désorientés; la crise est bien plus générale que vous ne la voyez. En effet, la condition humaine elle-même est profondément affecté: on est en train de perdre la connaissance des valeurs et la sensation des rapports. C'est extrêmement grave, car cela nous mène à la transgression des lois fondamentales de l'équilibre humain. Appliqué à l'art musical, cela donne ceci: d'un côté on veut rabaisser l'esprit de ce que j'appelerai les hautes mathématiques musicales jusqu'à des applications serviles, et à le vulgariser par un utilitarisme élémentaire. De l'autre côté, comme lui-même l'esprit de notre époque est malade, la musique qui se croit pure porte en elle les germes d'une pathologie quelquechose comme un nouveau péché original.

Q. Votre première proposition ne demande évidemment ni précision ni développement; quant à la seconde, elle m'amène logiquement à vous demander quelle est cette pathologie, quel est ce nouveau péché original?

R. Vous comprendrez que je sois bref, n'espérant pas traiter ces questions à fond en quelques minutes. Le vieux péché original est essentiellement un péché de connaissance; le nouveau péché original, lui, est essentiellement un péché de non-reconnaissance et c'est la non-reconnaissance de la vérité et des lois qui en découlent, lois que nous avons dites fondamentales. Sur le plan musical quelle est cette vérité? Quelles sont ces répercussions sur l'activité créatrice? N'oublions pas qu'il est écrit: *'L'esprit souffle où il veut'*. Ce qui est à retenir dans cette proposition c'est le mot *veut*; l'esprit est donc doué de la capacité de *vouloir;* ce principe de volonté spéculative est un fait d'un ordre tel que le juger, le discuter est d'une inutilité manifeste. A l'état pur la musique est une libre spéculation; les créateurs de toujours portèrent précisément témoignage à ce concept là. Quant à moi, je ne vois aucune raison de ne pas essayer de faire comme eux. Créature moi-même, je ne peux pas ne pas avoir le désir de créer; je ne peux pas ne pas extérioriser ce désir. Mais pour l'extérioriser ce désir de création encore faut-il en posséder les moyens; ces moyens sont techniques, sont la *technique* au sens le plus précis du terme. La technique est donc postulée par le désir de créer et n'est pas cet ordre de choses subalterne que l'on croit. Il devient du reste pressant de reclasser une fois pour toute les notions tant méprisées de *technique, métier, artisan,* réalités que j'oppose fortement à une terminologie nébuleuse faite de mots tels que: *inspiration, art, artiste,* tous termes fumeux qui nous empêchent d'y voir clair dans un domaine où tout est calcul, équilibre et où passe le souffle de l'esprit spéculatif; c'est ce souffle qui ensuite, mais ensuite seulement, suscite l'émotion, cette émotion dont on a fait le principe de toute création, ce trouble dont on aime si impudiquement parler en lui donnant un sens qui vous gêne et qui compromet la chose même. Placée dans un temps directement dérivé de la spéculation, voyez, quelle valeur prend alors *l'émotion.*

Q. Que devient dans tout ceci ce qu'il est convenu d'appeler la personnalité?

R. D'abord j'oppose toujours *personnalité* et *individualité*; on les confond trop souvent et pourtant ils définissent des notions très distinctes: l'individualité est présomptueuse, la personnalité s'efface; celle-ci se soumet, celle-là se complait dans l'infatuation, la suffisance et la rebellion. Moi qui suis soumis parceque j'accepte l'ordre des choses créées, ordre dont je fais moi-même partie, je crois ne pas m'égarer en soumettant mon oeuvre aux disciplines qu'elle exige impérativement de moi, aux hiérarchies qu'elle m'impose.

Parmi toutes les disciplines, la plus importante, et cela peut paraître paradoxal, c'est le *goût.* On croit généralement que le goût est le privilège de l'individu qui se croit libre et indépendant. Eh bien, non: ce goût est un des privilèges de la seule personnalité, car c'est un moyen naturel de reconnaissance des valeurs, moyen qu'il s'agit de cultiver sans cesse, de vivifier sans cesse, moyen dont la perfectibilité prend naissance dans le principe de la soumission, la soumission éclairée, raisonnée, libre.

En terminant, laissez-moi vous confier que je médite souvent cette phrase de Sophocle tirée de l'Antigone si magnifiquement présentée en français par André Bonnard:

> Ce n'est pas la sagesse, c'est la sottise qui s'obstine. Regarde les arbres.
> C'est en épousant les mouvements de la tempête qu'ils conservent
> leur plus tendres rameaux; mais s'ils se cabrent contre le vent, les
> voilà emportés avec leur racines . . .
>
> Igor Strawinsky

8

'PUSHKIN: POETRY AND MUSIC'

(Printed for copyright purposes by Harvey Taylor,
New York and Hollywood, 1940)

Only three years ago the literary and musical worlds were enriched, during the
Centennial Commemoration of Alexander Pushkin's death, by some fifty
volumes in all cultural languages, which brought to light new data, a result of
patient, diligent research by scholars called 'Pushkinists'. Thousands of
Pushkin enthusiasts found answers to the hitherto unanswerable questions,
and other thousands learned, for the first time, of the existence of Pushkin,
the poet, pioneer-dramatist, historian and founder of the present Russian
language.

To the writer, however, this centennial did not constitute ordinary encyclo-
pedical data, not even a reminder of an historical fact, no matter how important
it might be to the history of Russian culture. Unfortunately, this latter point
has been adopted by the majority of my compatriots, who tenaciously hold for
Pushkin a school-boy's loyalty and sentiment of constancy, which are equally
traditional and superficial.

'Pushkin is our national glory . . .'

'Pushkin is our first classicist and romanticist, i.e. realist . . .' (The latter
definition depends upon the epoch, and also the temperament of the commentator.)

'Pushkin is the creator of that-or-the-other type, especially of Tatiana
Larina, the ideal Russian woman . . .'

And finally: 'Pushkin is the forefather of the Russian revolution . . .' as the
Russian Soviet critics are attempting to introduce him, and, by the way,
unsuccessfully.

What a lot of nonsense to fill, for a whole century, the brains of the public,
incidentally blissfully satisfied with such stencilled formulae!

Pushkinism, whose primary goal has been to re-create the precise understanding of the great poet's works, did not fulfil its aim, because it has taken
on an aspect of a dry, sterile bio-biographical science.

Fortunately I am not a professional Pushkinist, and it is permissable for me
to have, in regard to Pushkin, a feeling of a different sort. His poetry has
preserved for me its intrinsic value, and his personality remains to me alive
and intact, the personality of a man.

A strong, live bond connects me with Pushkin's creativeness. It was his
dramatic poem that inspired my opera *Mavra* in 1921. A young poet, Boris
Kochno, who is very loyal to Pushkin's style, transcribed the text of the opera,
but it was Pushkin's original text that served me as a base, and especially was

it the 'zephyr' of his lines that I tried to re-create in my music. That is the reason that the depth of Pushkin's dramatic poem, in a high degree lyrical, or rather its spiritual nucleus, as well as his method of transmitting this depth, i.e. Pushkin's poetic structure of rhymes, had interested me much more than the abstract ideas which one could draw from the story itself.

Incidentally, Pushkin himself has expressed strong contempt for such abstractness, as we learn from one of his letters: 'Poetry, may God forgive me, must be slightly stupid.'

But let this phrase not delude anyone! Pushkin was very far from being desirous of degrading the thought, the innermost thought which he exalted in one breath with exalting the Muses, and which he dared to exalt – an unprecedented event in the history of poetry – in a 'Bacchic Song'.

All of Pushkin's creations bear proof of a scrupulous commonsense and matchless lucidity, but being a poet to the finest fibres of his soul, Pushkin ridiculed all false, pseudo-philosophical ideologies, and adhered only to his art and true portrayal of his inner self.

Pushkin created 'pure poetry' not in Valéry's sense, but in the wide sense of the word: he coveted pure poetry, free from rhetoric – medieval or any other – he craved poetry reduced to pure art, to art alone, amply deep and amply mystical in itself.

'You are asking me: "What is the aim of poetry?" ' writes Pushkin to a friend. 'The aim of poetry is poetry.' Is it necessary to repeat how much such understanding of art is near and dear to me? All one has to do is to read the pages which I dedicated to Beethoven in my book *The Chronicle of my Life* (an autobiography). There one would learn that I profess the very same sentiment in reference to music. Those pages I can sum up in this manner: 'What is the aim of music? The aim of music is music.'

This confession of Pushkin puts many things into their places. What interest have we in all the elucidation of Pushkin's works which emanate from poetry critics and historians, beginning with the 'Ideal Types' by Bielinsky, and winding up with 'Class Conscience' by the Marxist Commentators. Incidentally, I do not deny that Pushkin's novels or dramatic poems contain a little of both, but the same ideas from the pen of anyone else would be insufficient to create *Eugene Oniegin* or *The Bronze Horseman*.

This reminds me of a conversation between Mallarmé and Degas, which has been preserved by Paul Valéry, and which I cited in my own *Chronicles*. I am permitting myself to re-cite it:

> Once Degas, who, as all know, loved to 'flirt with the Muses said to Mallarmé: 'I am unable to finish my sonnet. And yet I am not in want of ideas.' 'One does not create rhymes with ideas,' retorted Mallarmé quietly, 'but with words.'

However, let us return to Pushkin. The intimate bond which ties me to

Appendices

Pushkin and which I have mentioned above, does not efface for me the immense part which Pushkin has had in the domain of Russian culture. On the contrary, it only strengthens it. While Pushkin remains, in my mind, a live man and artist, he remains, at the same time, a symbol, if not a whole programme. I dedicated my opera, taken from *The Little House in Colomna* not only to the memory of Pushkin, but also to the two greatest composers of the nineteenth century: Glinka and Chaikovsky. My connecting these three names sufficiently proves how I have appreciated his genius, and what I have managed to gain from his creativeness or the creativeness of my glorious musical predecessors.

In reality those three names have many common points of contact. Pushkin's influence on Glinka and Chaikovsky supplies obvious proof: Glinka took Pushkin's text to create his opera *Ruslan and Ludmilla*; Chaikovsky availed himself of *Eugene Oniegin* and *The Queen of Spades*. That could have been a mere coincidence, i.e. the composers' choice of material while searching for a libretto, if the general character of the creativeness of those three [sic] composers would not categorically disprove such supposition. Their nature, as well as their creative mentality, places them into the most unusual category which Russia could have ever produced. Russia has always had representatives of that supreme category, and they are in existence today. I generate a fascination for them as soon as I meet them in life. Thus is explained my profound friendship to the late Diaghilev, who undoubtedly belonged to that class, and my fond memories of collaborating with him for many years. I have felt the 'germs' of this mentality, and have cultivated it, at first subconsciously, and later, most deliberately.

The actual progenitor of the above-mentioned category was Peter the Great, whose personality made such an impression on Pushkin. (*The Bronze Horseman, Poltava, Arap of Peter the Great* and many other ravishing lyrical poems prove the point.) The great monarch conceived a plan to melt together the most specific of Russia's civilization with intellectual wealth of the occidental world. Like Pushkin in poetry, so Chaikovsky in music succeeded in forming this fortunate alliance which lifts the Russian art to the all-highest level attained by the European art, at the same time permitting it to preserve its particular national characteristics. Much later some artists-folklorists reproached those three great Russians for calling their art 'cosmopolitism'. Nothing can be more unjust than this reproach. National elements in Pushkin, as well as in Glinka and Chaikovsky, have an important place. Only those elements leaked out spontaneously from their very nature, but not from doctrinal estheticism, which, at that time, was being forced on them by a group of 'Five' in the Beliaeff circle. This national ethnographic estheticism, in reality, is not far away from the films of our times, which portray the ancient Russia, its Czars and Boyars. This tendency is sterile and rather naive because it compels the artist to change the art which had instinctively been created by the genius of the people. I say 'sterile' because it does not hinder the piercing of certain occidentalism, and is rather dangerous because it does hinder the free and organic development of a culture which is forever tied to the culture of Europe.

Pushkin's tradition, while paving the way to the finest Western influences, leaves untouched the eminent Russian foundation of the Russian artists. Much was said about Pushkin's Byronism. *Childe Harold's* creator's influence on Pushkin is unquestionable. It is even permissible to add other influences upon Pushkin's creativeness: that of the eighteenth century, and later, in the epoch of his dramatic poems, [that of] Shakespeare.

Nevertheless, there is nothing more organically Russian than Pushkin's poetry, so typically Russian, that one hundred and three years after his death the foreign countries have not as yet estimated his real value. At the same time, when the works of Tolstoy, Dostoievsky, Turgenev were circulated with prodigious rapidity and left, quite justly, deep and indelible marks, there were very few translations, to the best of my knowledge, of Pushkin's poetry. Those that were available left the Western Europe quite indifferent.

Unfortunately, Pushkin's name itself, to the majority, remains another name in encyclopedias, and few suspect that, in justice, his name should be revered on the same plane with those of Dante, Goethe, Shakespeare.

(*From the French manuscript by Gregory Golubeff.*)

9

'LOVE MUSIC!'

(Reprinted from Komsomolskaja Pravda of 27 September 1962)

I am very glad that correspondents of *Komsomolskaja Pravda* have come to me. I know and love your paper and often read it. It is an important and useful thing to popularise music among youth. It would be excellent if everyone could learn the foundations of musical culture during their time at school. I have lived a long time in France and can appreciate how useful the teaching of the tonic sol-fa in French schools is. The first stimulus is important, the first contact with the great mystery of music; and then that wonderful world opens in front of the young man, and he can if he wishes comprehend its inexhaustible depths.

The language of music is a special language; it is not the same as the language of literature. It is not easy to know whether a piece of music has been written by a Russian or a person of some other nationality – a Frenchman or an Englishman. All my life I have spoken and thought in Russian. I have a Russian style. Perhaps this is not immediately apparent in my compositions; but it is there – latent in my music.

In general, it is best to judge the works of a composer through the perspective of time. It is necessary to stand a little way off in order to see and understand better.

I am very glad of this opportunity to send through *Komsomolskaja Pravda* my best wishes to the paper's young readers and to say to them – *Bravo*!

Igor Stravinsky

Moscow, 1962

(*Translated from the Russian by Sarah S. White*)

Appendix B

A SELECTION OF LETTERS WRITTEN TO STRAVINSKY IN 1913 BY CLAUDE DEBUSSY, FREDERICK DELIUS, MAURICE RAVEL AND JULES ROMAINS

FROM MAURICE RAVEL

4 *avenue Carnot, Paris* 17e
19.1.13

Vieux, —

des tas de voeux sincères, de nous trois à vous tous. Ils viennent en retard, mais je n'ai pas encore fini de corriger les épreuves de *Daphnis* où j'ai découvert des choses à faire dresser les cheveux sur la tête d'Astruc.[1] J'ai eu de vos nouvelles par Delage, qui était allé chercher dans les *Sacres du printemps* le contrepoison que réclamaient ses propres harmonies. . . . . Quand on songe que M. D'Indy dont j'entendais Fervaal l'autre jour, est en bonne santé! Il n'y a pas de justice. Vous a-t-on dit que M . . . e avait l'intention de divorcer, et qu'il avait été demander l'opinion de l'Abbé Petit sur ce projet? On m'assure que Nijinsky ne veut plus entendre parler de danse.[2] Allons, je le vois bien, il faut que M. Poincaré se mette à la chorégraphie.

A bientôt, affectueusement,

M. R.

FROM MAURICE RAVEL

4 *avenue Carnot, Paris* 17e
15.3.13

Vieux, —

voulez-vous me télégraphier l'adresse de l'hôtel où vous avez trouvé de la place pour nous? Cela m'est absolument nécessaire. Je fais déjà envoyer un peignoir à votre nom. Nous arriverons *Lundi soir*.[3] (Train de 8 h. du matin)

Affectueusement,

Maurice Ravel

---

[1] Gabriel Astruc, manager of the newly built Théâtre des Champs-Elysées, Paris.
[2] Nijinsky was experiencing considerable difficulty in working out the choreography of *The Rite of Spring*.
[3] Ravel was joining Stravinsky at Clarens in Switzerland in order to work with him on a new version of Mussorgsky's *Khovanshchina* for Diaghilev.

FROM MAURICE RAVEL

*[Paris – towards the end
of April* 1913*] Lundi*

Vieux, —

d'abord, admirez le papier – on portera beaucoup le quadrillé, cette année – et ensuite ma mémoire: Au milieu des plaisirs – comme vous le voyez, je suis chez le bistrot, à cause de la chaleur – je pense à la commission dont vous m'aviez chargé.

J'ai demandé les prix du Splendid-Hôtel: 2 chambres, l'une grande avec 2 lits jumeaux, l'autre plus petite mais très suffisante. Salle de bains (tout ça communiquant): 25 frs. Un supplément de 2 frs. pour mettre un lit dans la 2de chambre. Ça donne sur l'avenue Carnot. De mon balcon je plongerai dans votre appartement (je n'en abuserai pas). Dès le matin – vers midi ½ – nous pourrons échanger des 'gentillesses' en pyjama. Pas moyen d'obtenir une réduction: c'est le tarif. Vous trouverez ci-joint le plan. Seulement il faut vous décider tout de suite. Par retour du courrier écrivez-moi: ou, si vous préférez, écrivez directement à l'hôtel[1].

Il fait un temps splendide, que l'on eut souhaité au Lac Majeur.[2] Je vais demain au comité de la SMI,[3] où je vous fais bombarder membre. J'ai vu à mon arrivée Delage, qui est florissant et travaille. On a vidé entièrement Mme. C... et on a tout remplacé par de l'ouate hydrophile. Elle va tout-à-fait bien. Quant à Mme. S... l'opération a bien reussi; mais le chloroforme a causé une entérite. Ce n'est pas grave, heureusement.

Merci du petit bout de choeur.[4] Ne m'en envoyez plus, sans quoi je ne pourrais terminer la melodie n⁰ 2[5]... et d'autres choses.

Le théâtre Astruc est au-dessous de tout, parait-il..... Seulement, *il ne faut pas le dire*, assure Sert.[6] Je devais aller hier soir à *Benvenuto:* au dernier moment le coeur m'a failli.

Et ce grattage de nez? ça s'est bien passé? Je suis ravi d'apprendre que tout le monde va bien – je touche ma gueule, qui est de bois.

Je vais demain chez cette malheureuse Isadora Duncan. J'en tremble à l'avance. C'est vraiment trop affreux – et trop injuste.

A bientôt, vieux. — Mes respectueuses amitiés à Mme. Strawinsky, et à Mme. Belankine,[7] si elle est toujours à Clarens. Embrassez très fort les enfants

---

[1] Stravinsky booked in at this hotel and stayed there until the end of May.
[2] Stravinsky and Ravel had recently made a joint excursion to the Lago Maggiore and Varese from Clarens.
[3] Société Musicale Indépendante.
[4] This refers either to a chorus from *Khovanshchina* or to Stravinsky's cantata *Zvezdoliki*.
[5] The second of Ravel's *Trois Poèmes de Mallarm*é.
[6] Jose-Maria Sert, the Spanish theatre designer.
[7] Stravinsky's sister-in-law, to whom he dedicated the second of his settings of *Two Poems of Balmont.*

de la part de Madame Ravel – et de Monsieur – et croyez à l'affection de votre dévoué

Maurice Ravel

FROM MAURICE RAVEL

4 *avenue Carnot, Paris* 17*e*
5.5.13

Cher Igor, —
nous sommes ravis d'apprendre que le petit Nini a bien supporté son opération, mais regrettons l'augmentation de votre nez – mon frère surtout, qui ne recevra plus les gratulations qui vous étaient destinées.

En même temps que votre lettre, j'ai reçu l'heureuse nouvelle que MM. et Me. Miquel Alzieu[1] étaient condamnés à vous payer les 10,000 frs. Vous allez enfin pouvoir vous offrir l'auto et le yacht qui vous manquaient tant. Moi aussi, je pense, car je viens de recevoir la visite de M. Enckell-Bronikowsky,[2] lequel venait me demander, de la part du théâtre Sanine,[3] où en était l'orchestration du *Mariage*.[4] Je ne lui ai pas caché la vérité, et que je serais obligé de consacrer à ce travail mes trois mois de vacances. M. Enckell . . . &c. m'a dit que je recevrais sous peu de Berlin la confirmation de la commande, et que ces messieurs se considéreraient comme liés par ma réponse. J'attends cette lettre avec curiosité, car il n'a pas été question d'argent. Or je suis assez embarassé. Quelle doit être ma situation vis-à-vis de Bessel? Dans quelle mesure puis-je imposer des conditions au sujet d'un ouvrage qui appartient à son éditeur? J'espère que vous serez à Paris au moment où je recevrai des nouvelles de Berlin, et que vous m'apporterez le concours de ces lumières du Nord, que Voltaire nous a vantées.

Rassurez-vous: l'acoustique du théâtre des Champs-Elysées est parfaite, au point que l'on perçoit la finesse des harmonies de Berlioz. *Ce qui est au-dessous de tout*, c'est le spectacle, c'est les décors, c'est le public, c'est Van Dyck, c'est Gabriel[5] lui-même. Serge[6] et lui se sont quittés hier brouillés à mort. Tout était rompu. Ça s'est arrangé 5 minutes après.

---

[1] Madame Alzieu was a pianist who, wishing to undertake a concert tour of India, borrowed about 3,000 roubles from Stravinsky which he had recently received from Moscow as part of his commission fee for the completion of *The Nightingale*. He sued her for the return of this sum, but it was never fully repaid.
[2] An emissary of the music publishing firm of W. Bessel & Co., which handled the Stravinsky/Ravel version of *Khovanshchina*.
[3] A. Sanine was *régisseur* at the Maryinsky Theatre, St. Petersburg.
[4] It appears that Ravel had been invited to undertake the orchestration of Mussorgsky's unfinished opera *Zhenitba* (written to a scenario by Gogol). Although this project fell through, some years later he arranged Mussorgsky's music for a private performance in Paris (April 1923).
[5] Astruc.
[6] Diaghilev.

J'ai envoyé la lettre à *Musika*.[1] On va voir ce que ça donne.

Excusez-moi, j'avais tout-à-fait oublié la valise. Je vais vous la faire parvenir comme le désirez.

Contrairement à tout ce que l'on pouvait croire, la comtesse G. . . a toujours l'intention de donner ces concerts d'avant-garde internationale. Que voyez-vous pour l'école russe? Avez-vous autre chose que votre choeur?[2] *Prométhée* de Scriabine, ne tiendra-t-il pas la place des deux concerts? Et si vous voyiez quelquechose d'intéressant dans les écoles étrangères, en Allemagne par exemple, signalez-les moi en deux mots.

A bientôt, mon vieux. Mes respectueuses amitiés à Madame Strawinsky – embrassez les enfants et croyez à l'affection de votre

Maurice Ravel

Les chambres sont retenues pour le 13 mai.

FROM FREDERICK DELIUS

Grez sur Loing (*Seine et Marne*)
27.5.13

Cher Monsieur Strawinsky, —

Malheureusement il m'est tout à fait impossible de venir demain pour la répétition générale,[3] mais je viendrai certainement jeudi car je voudrais absolument entendre votre oeuvre: seulement, puisque je n'ai pas de billet, j'irai vous prendre à votre hôtel pour entrer avec vous comme je l'ai fait la dernière fois: s'il y avait quelques difficultés, écrivez-moi un mot 13 rue d'Alger, Paris. Votre musique m'intéresse énormément,[4] ce que je ne pense pas dire de la plupart de la musique que j'ai entendue depuis bien longtemps. Bien cordialement à vous,

Frédérick Delius

FROM CLAUDE DEBUSSY

[80 avenue du Bois de Boulogne, Paris]
31 *mai* 1913

Cher Strawinsky,

J'ai essayé vainement de vous téléphoner – il y avait peut-être quelqu'un dedans? – pour savoir quand vous nous ferez l'amitié (vous et votre femme)

---

[1] A music magazine published in St. Petersburg.
[2] *Zvezdoliki*.
[3] *i.e.* the dress rehearsal of *The Rite of Spring*.
[4] Delius had probably heard *Petrushka* in London earlier that year. (See the reference to Delius in Stravinsky's *Memories and Commentaries*.)

de venir diner. Il ne faut pas perdre les bonnes traditions[1]. Alors, répondez-moi le plus vite possible, et croyez-moi, comme toujours, votre vieux dévoué

Claude Debussy

FROM JULES ROMAINS

27 *bis avenue du Parc Montsouris, Paris*

Cher Monsieur,

Je serais très heureux d'aller applaudir et défendre, demain soir mercredi, le *Sacre du Printemps* aux Champs-Elysées.[2] J'ai trop souffert moi-même dans une circonstance analogue de la sotte incompréhension d'un certain public pour ne pas éprouver une vive sympathie à votre égard, et pour ne point désirer soutenir votre cause.

Si mon mot vous parvenait trop tard, ou si vous ne disposiez pas de deux entrées pour demain, je vous demanderais de penser à moi pour un jour de la semaine prochaine.

Merci d'avance, et bien confraternellement à vous

Jules Romains

FROM MAURICE RAVEL

[Paris]
5.6.13[3]

Vieux, —

Excusez n'être pas venu[4] . . . . Ça c'est bien passé . . . peine un peu de cha. . .
Enfin, on a entendu toute l'oeuvre.[5]

---

[1] It is perhaps strange that this *pneumatique*, written only two days after the scandalous première of *The Rite of Spring*, should make no reference to it. But by the time it was delivered, Stravinsky was sickening for typhoid fever, and it is doubtful whether he can have replied, for a few days later (probably on 4 June) Debussy's wife followed up her husband's invitation by sending the following *pneumatique* to Madame Igor Strawinsky:

Mercredi

Chère Madame,

Nous sommes très inquiets de ne pas avoir de nouvelles de vo [tre] mari et de ne mê [me] pas pouvoir aller vers vous, puisqu'on nous a dit que vous aviez quitté l'hôtel.

Si vous avez une minute, envoyez-moi une toute petite ligne, je vous en prie. Toutes mes fidèles amitiés.

Emma C. Debussy

[2] This (undated) letter was almost certainly written on Tuesday 3 June. (The Russian Ballet season at the Théâtre des Champs-Elysées ended on 17 June.)

[3] This was the date of the first performance of the Stravinsky/Ravel version of *Khovanshchina* at the Théâtre des Champs-Elysées. Stravinsky did not attend, because he had just succumbed to an attack of typhoid fever.

[4] The *pneumatique* has been torn; and this affects the writing in three places.

[5] The reference is to the performance of *The Rite of Spring* the previous evening.

Vous verrai demain à 2 heures au théâtre. Répétition du Pétrouschka. Saviez-vous ? Respects à Mad. Strawinsky.
Vous embrasse.

M. Ravel[1]

FROM MAURICE RAVEL

Ongi Ethori, 23 *rue Sopite, Saint Jean de Luz*
28.8.13

Vieux, —

Je ne vous fais aucun reproche; je pense que vous rossignolez[2] jours et nuits. Moi, je surgis de la croupe et je 'bonde' comme dirait notre confrère Tchérépnine. Entendez que je viens de terminer le 3e poème de Mallarmé. Je vais maintenant revoir le 2d et me mettrai aussitôt à *Zazpiac Bat*.[3] Je m'accorde un jour de répit, consacré à une vingtaine de lettres. Songez que des malheureux attendent, depuis plus de 2 mois, une réponse par retour du courrier.

Pour l'une de ces lettres, il faut que vous m'aidiez: j'ai besoin de savoir où gitent les russes[4] en ce moment. Depuis le mois de juin ces pauvres diables n'attendent qu'une lettre de moi pour m'envoyer de l'argent (droits d'auteur d'une 4e représentation). Ça, c'est pour Swietloff.[5] Je dois encore écrire à Diaghilew qu'il ne compte pas sur moi pour le ballet Scarlatti.[6] J'ai vraiment mieux à faire.

Donc, réponse *par retour du courrier* – pas à ma manière! Pas besoin de littérature: adresse de la saison russe, – nouvelles de la famille – Croyez &c. . . . signature.

Pour vous et autour de vous, le souvenir affectueux de votre dévoué

Maurice Ravel

Et puis, si vous avez un moment, écrivez-moi longuement.

---

[1] The signature is illegible, but could be construed as being 'M. Ravel'.
[2] Stravinsky had already started work on the second act of *The Nightingale*.
[3] This was the title of a piano concerto Ravel intended to write based on Basque themes.
[4] The Russian Ballet company had sailed for South America on August 15th.
[5] Valerien Svetlov, the ballet critic, who frequently managed Diaghilev's affairs in his absence.
[6] This presumably refers to the project that eventually resulted in Tommasini's adaptation of pieces by Scarlatti for *The Good-Humoured Ladies* (produced by the Russian Ballet in 1917).

Appendix C

A CATALOGUE OF MANUSCRIPTS (1904-1952) IN STRAVINSKY'S POSSESSION[1]

1. THE MUSHROOMS GOING TO WAR

Unpublished song for bass and piano. 10¼ by 15,[2] ink and pencil, signed and dated at top, 1904.

2. THE NIGHTINGALE (LE ROSSIGNOL)

Eight packets contained in a yellow paper envelope 10¼ by 15½.

(a) Forty sheets of full score in ink with sketches in pencil of the first scene, tied by a paper ribbon with the title and signature in blue crayon.
(b) Sixteen sheets of sketches in ink and pencil, varying sizes, and five sheets of libretto in Russian.
(c) A paper notebook, 8½ by 10½, containing part of the libretto in Stravinsky's hand, in ink.
(d) Three typewritten pages of the libretto of Act I.
(e) Seventy-two pages of sketches, in ink, many signed and dated.
(f) Nineteen pages of libretto.
(g) Three letters to Stravinsky concerning *Le Rossignol*.
(h) Twenty-six pages of bills for mailing *Le Rossignol* material.

3. THE RITE OF SPRING (LE SACRE DU PRINTEMPS)

(a) Edition Russe de Musique, orchestral score, 12 by 15½, 1921 edition. Markings in Stravinsky's hand on almost every page. Pages 112, 113 and 114 are entirely re-written by him, and pages 99, 100 and 101 are almost entirely in his blue- and red-pencil manuscript. Canvas bound, 139 pages.

---

[1] Not a catalogue in the sense of Köchel or Rufer, but a directory intended for Stravinsky's personal use; compiled by Robert Craft in 1954.
[2] Measurements in inches throughout.

(b) A white paper envelope, 4½ by 5½, containing two sketches of *Le Sacre du Printemps*, one on a Russian telegram blank, in pencil, the other on a *Taverne Parisienne* bill, in ink and dated Monte Carlo, 1912.

(c) An orange folder, 12½ by 9½, containing three pages of sketches and one page of full score, 18 by 13½, unsigned.

4. THREE JAPANESE LYRICS

(a) Three pages of ink sketches, 9½ by 12½, unsigned and undated, with Japanese characters in Stravinsky's hand.

(b) A notebook, twenty-eight pages, 5½ by 8¼, containing a few sketches for the 'Danse Sacrale' and 'Prelude' to the second part of *Le Sacre du Printemps*. On pages 4–9 are the complete sketches of the *Japanese Lyrics*. Page 10 contains a sketch of 'Le Corbeau' (*Three Little Songs*, 'Souvenirs de mon Enfance'). Pages 11–23 are covered with rough sketches of *Le Rossignol*. Pages 24 and 25 have sketches for *The Firebird Suite*, 1919 reduction, and pages 26 and 27 for the 'Chant dissident' (*Four Russian Songs*).

5. KHOVANSHCHINA (MUSSORGSKY)

A folder of violet paper, 12½ by 9½, with two pages of the 'Aria of Chaklovity', in Stravinsky's orchestration, and a sketch page for the same. Signed.

6. VALSE DES FLEURS

Two-piano score, three pages, signed and dated Clarens, 30 August 1914. Ink. 12½ by 9½ paper cover. An original, unpublished work.

7. 'UN GRAND SOMMEIL NOIR' (TWO POEMS OF VERLAINE)

An orchestration – 1 large folded sheet (four pages), ink, signed and dated Salvan, 27 July 1914.

8. THREE PIECES FOR STRING QUARTET (TROIS PIÈCES POUR QUATUOR À CORDES)

(a) Thirty pages of instrumentation, ink, 1914.

(b) A notebook, 10¼ by 7½, bound in oiled paper, containing a four-hand piano reduction, signed and dated 1914.

(c) Revised orchestrations, signed and dated 10 December 1918, 6 December 1918, and December 1918. (Substantially the same score as 8a.)

9. PRIBAOUTKI

(a) A copy of the full score, ink, signed and dated, bound in oiled paper, 12¼ by 9½.
(b) A sketch book, cover painted by Stravinsky, signed and dated Salvan, 1914, containing

> *Trois Pièces pour Quatuor à Cordes*
> *Renard*
> *Pribaoutki*
> *Berceuses du Chat (Cat's Cradle Songs)*

10. THREE EASY PIECES FOR PIANO DUET (TROIS PIÈCES FACILES)

(a) *Marche:* four sheets, complete sketch of the four-hand piano version.
(b) *Valse* and *Polka:* four sheets ,version for piano, four hands, dated 1914.
(c) *Valse* and *Polka:* two sheets, reduction for piano two hands, 1914–15.
(d) A notebook containing the *Marche*, full score for twelve solo instruments, signed and dated 25 March 1915, seven pages, ink, 8½ by 11. The yellow cover is painted by Stravinsky.

11. CHANTS GEORGIENS

Sixteen songs copied by Stravinsky, ca. 1915, from a Russian anthology. For his own use, Stravinsky devised a key to the differences of pronunciation in the Russian and Georgian alphabets. A notebook bound in old silver paper.

12. THREE TALES FOR CHILDREN

A single manuscript page of the 'Chanson de l'ours', 11 by 8, ink, signed and dated 30 December 1915.

13. SOUVENIR D'UNE MARCHE BOCHE

Ink, complete copy, 13½ by 10, but not in Stravinsky's hand, though signed and dated by him. A description of the Edith Wharton book in which the piece was published is found on the reverse.

14. CAT'S CRADLE SONGS (BERCEUSES DE CHAT)
FOUR RUSSIAN PEASANT SONGS
BERCEUSE (A MA FILLE MIKA)

(a) A blue notebook, 4½ by 7, cover painted by Stravinsky. Nineteen pages of sketches and 4 inserted sheets.

(b) One page of Berceuse, 10 by 13¼, ink, signed and dated 1917.

(c) *Berceuses du Chat*, arrangement for piano, two hands, 1915–16.

15. RENARD

(a) Vocal score, thirty-nine pages, signed in Russian and dated 'Morges, 1 August 1916, at noon, sky without clouds', ink, bound cloth over boards, 12½ by 13. This score does not contain the *March*, which was composed at a later date.

(b) Full orchestral score, four pages, of the *March* and of the first pages following the *March*, ink, unsigned, 11¼ by 8¼.

(c) A faded blue notebook containing eighteen pages of sketches, 8½ by 6½, pencil and ink, signed in Russian on cover.

(d) Forty pages of pen and pencil sketches on various sizes of paper.

(e) A proof cover of the piano score with corrections in Stravinsky's hand.

(f) An envelope containing two pages of vocal score, signed and dated Morges, 1916, 7¾ by 9¼, ink, unbound.

16. FOUR RUSSIAN PEASANT SONGS ('SAUCERS')

(a) Score, signed in Russian and dated Morges, December 1916, eleven pages, 7 by 9, ink, text in Russian.

(b) A sketch book of the choruses, and of *Renard* and the 'Chanson de l'ours', unsigned, ink and pencil, 5 by 6¼, bound in speckled-grey stiff Italian paper. The first of the choruses is dated Morges, 22 October 1916. Twenty-five pages.

17. VALSE POUR LES ENFANTS ('LA VALSE DU FIGARO')

(a) One page, 8¼ by 10¼, unbound and unsigned, but Stravinsky has written on the envelope 'sketch of the *Figaro Valse* composed at Morges, 1916 or 1917', pencil. On the reverse is a sketch for *Renard*.

(b) Clipping from the newspaper *Figaro* for Sunday, 21 May 1922, containing the '*Valse pour les Enfants* (une Valse pour les petits lecteurs du *Figaro*)'. A pencilled annotation in Stravinsky's hand corrects the printed statement that the *Valse* was 'improvised'. The piece is timed, in Stravinsky's hand, to 52 seconds.

18. FIVE EASY PIECES FOR PIANO DUET

An 8½ by 11½ yellow envelope dated Morges, 1917, containing seventeen pages of sketches in pencil, 9¼ by 7¼, several of them dated and signed.

19. THE SONG OF THE NIGHTINGALE (LE CHANT DU ROSSIGNOL)

(a) An envelope containing four sketch pages, 4½ by 6½, 1917, unbound.
(b) Six pages of full orchestral score in pencil, 14¼ by 10½, unsigned and undated, and eight pages, various sizes, of sketches.
(c) Orchestral score, ninety pages, signed and dated 'Winter-Easter – 4 April 1917, Morges', 12½ by 16¼, ink, corrections in pencil. Title in Russian and French.

20. SONG OF THE VOLGA BOATMEN (CHANTS DES BATELIERS DU VOLGA)

Manuscript score of Stravinsky's wind-instrument arrangement under the title *Hymne à la Nouvelle Russie*. A red banner has been painted on the cover by Picasso. A note on the cover reads: 'dictated in Rome by Stravinsky to Ansermet, April 8 1917'. At the foot of each page is a pencilled piano reduction by Stravinsky. Signed in Russian. Four pages and a fifth, smaller in size, with the last 8 measures of the piano arrangement.

21. STUDY FOR PIANOLA

A notebook containing the original manuscript of the score, complete except for first few measures; ink 9 by 10¼, bound cotton print cover, signed Morges, 10/11/17.

22. THREE TALES FOR CHILDREN (TROIS HISTOIRES POUR ENFANTS)

(a) Three printed scores (J. & W. Chester) with Stravinsky's notes for the Pleyela transcriptions in red, black, blue and orange pencils. Two of the copies are signed.
(b) A yellow paper envelope, 8½ by 11¼ containing: a page of a pencil sketch of *Tilimbom*, signed and dated Morges, 1917; the English text of the song by Rosa Newmarch; the piano and voice part of the song in ink, signed at top; English and French texts.

23. SKETCHES FOR A SETTING OF A DIALOGUE BY C. A. CINGRIA

Seven pages, 1917, 7¼ by 9¼. (Unpublished.)

24. THE SOLDIER'S TALE (L'HISTOIRE DU SOLDAT)

(a) A sixteen-page parchment-bound 5 by 7 notebook of pencil sketches, signed and dated '1 May, 1918'.

(b) A notebook, fourteen pages, ten of which contain sketches for the music, in ink and pencil. Stravinsky has pasted an old colour lithograph of a Barber Shop scene to the first page. On the second, third, and fourth pages are drawings by Auberjonois for the *Soldat* set.

(c) A manuscript of the arrangement for piano, clarinet and violin, dated 1918.

25. PROLOGUE FROM BORIS GODUNOV (MUSSORGSKY)

Piano arrangement of the Chorus from the *Prologue*, made by Stravinsky for his children, $10\frac{1}{2}$ by $13\frac{1}{4}$, ink, Morges, 1918. (Unpublished.)

26. RAGTIME

(a) A 'summary sketch[1]' – dated and signed 21 March[2] 1918.

(b) A copy of the *Ragtime* arranged for piano, twelve pages, ink, $13\frac{1}{4}$ by 10, signed and dated 1918.

27. THREE PIECES FOR CLARINET SOLO

Complete sketches, 1918.

28. DUET FOR TWO BASSOONS

Sketch, ca. 1918. (Unpublished.)

29. FOUR RUSSIAN SONGS (QUATRE CHANTS RUSSES)

(a) Complete sketch of 'Canard', 'Chanson pour compter', 'Le Moineau est assis', in a version for voice, cimbalom, and flute.

(b) Three pages in ink, 13 by $9\frac{1}{2}$, signed, and a small pencilled sheet of a flute part for a transcription of 'Chant dissident' for voice, flute and piano.

(c) The printed copy with Stravinsky's markings for the Pleyela transcription, which absorbs the voice in the piano part.

30. PETRUSHKA

(a) Five pages of an ink score, $13\frac{1}{2}$ by $10\frac{1}{2}$, of fragments of the 4th Tableau

---

[1] Stravinsky's term for *particell*.

[2] Stravinsky had therefore composed the piece long before the Armistice, at which time he was probably completing the 11-instrument score. (cf. 'Jazz Commercials', *Dialogues and a Diary*, p. 87.)

of *Petrushka* arranged for Pianola, signed and dated 'Morges, winter 1918'.

(b) An envelope containing three cardboards and two small paper sheets, drawings in colour by Stravinsky, 1919, titled *Les Cris de Pétrouchka*.

31. THE FIREBIRD (SUITE)

(a) Rough sketches, eighteen pages, 5½ by 8¼, 1919.

(b) Two sketches for the 1919 version of *Firebird*; one ink, one pencil, unsigned.

32. PIANO-RAG-MUSIC

Complete manuscript, signed and dated '28 June 1919' with a dedication to Artur Rubinstein.

33. LA MARSEILLAISE

Arrangement for solo violin, two pages, 4½ by 7; pencil, signed and dated Morges, 1 January 1919. (Unpublished.)

34. PULCINELLA

(a) An envelope, 6¼ by 10, containing eight sheets of sketches; pencil, one sheet signed and dated 1919.

(b) Orchestral score with reduction for piano two hands, 215 pages, 11 by 14½, signed and dated Morges, 20 April 1920, in black ink with red marks designating the cuts to be used for the *Suite*.

35. CONCERTINO FOR STRING QUARTET

(a) Full ink score, thirty-four pages, Société des Auteurs stamp, signed and dated Garches, 24 September 1920; bound in white stiff paper, 7½ by 6.

(b) A red paper folder, 9½ by 12½, with signature and title on cover, containing three pages of pencil sketches, signed.

(c) A blue folder containing the complete manuscript of Stravinsky's reduction for piano four hands; twenty-five pages, ink, 13 by 9¼, signed and dated 1920.

(d) A few sketches, ca. 1920.

(e) Sketch book, eighty-one pages of ink and pencil, 6½ by 8, bound in blue-gold patterned boards. Contains the first sketches of the *Concertino* as well as sketches of the *Ragtime*, dated 5 March 1918; *Berceuse* (for Mika Stravinsky) signed and dated 10 December 1917; the *Study for Pianola*, the *Quatre Chants Russes* and the *Piano-Rag-Music*.

(f) Fourteen large sketch sheets, in pencil, of the transcription for twelve instruments, 1962.

(g) Orchestral score of the transcription, fifty-four pages, ink on onion skins, 1952.

36. SYMPHONIES OF WIND INSTRUMENTS (SYMPHONIES D'INSTRUMENTS À VENT)

(a) An envelope, 6¼ by 10, with twelve sheets of sketches, mostly in ink, 8 by 11¼, unsigned. Also, J. & W. Chester's second proof of the separate 'Chorale', corrected and signed by Stravinsky.

(b) Orchestral score, thirty-four pages, signed and dated 20 November 1920 at Garches; 9¼ by 14, ink, with some corrections in pencil.

(c) Complete summary sketch score, ink, sixteen pages, signed and dated Carantec, 2 July 1920, 10 by 8½.

(d) Four pages, 12 by 9½, pencil sketches for the 1947 version.

(e) Full score of the 1947 version, ink on thirty-five unbound onion skins, 15 by 11.

37. CINQ PIÈCES MONOMÉTRIQUES, FOR INSTRUMENTAL ENSEMBLE

Six pages of an unfinished work, dated Garches, 1920–21.

38. PETRUSHKA

Seven small sheets of rough sketches of the arrangement of three movements for piano solo, 1921.

39. THE FIVE FINGERS (LES CINQ DOIGTS)

An orange notebook, 12 by 9½, containing all eight pieces, ink, fifteen pages. Each piece is signed and dated. The final date is 18 February 1921, in Garches.

40. MAVRA

(a) A small sketch of the Overture.

(b) Piano vocal score, 100 pages, signed in Russian and dated Biarritz, 7 March 1922; ink, bound in red stiff boards, black leather corners and fold; 8½ by 11½. This score does not include the Overture.

(c) A linen portfolio in which are:

1. An orange folder containing an orchestral score of Parasha's song; eighteen pages, signed, undated, ink, 9½ by 12¼.
2. The complete libretto and two pages of sketches, together with a clipping from the Paris *Journal* for 22 December 1922 announcing the *Mavra* performance at a Jean Wiener concert December 26.
3. A proof copy of the fly-leaf with the portraits of Glinka, Chaikovsky, and Pushkin.
4. The Programme of Diaghilev's concert on 29 May 1922 at the Hotel Continentale, announcing the preview performance of *Mavra* with the composer at piano. Containing remarks in Stravinsky's hand.
5. Sketch of orchestral score, in green folder, fifteen pages, ink and pencil, unsigned, 7½ by 10.
6. Twenty pages of libretto, in Russian, in the hand of Boris Kochno, the librettist; ink; Kochno's initials at bottom of one page.
7. Seventeen pages of the libretto in French translation, in the hand of Catherine (Mme.) Stravinsky, ink.
8. Nine sketch pages of unequal sizes.
9. Vocal score of the quartet, nine pages, 10½ by 14; ink.
10. Vocal score, ten pages, of the duet of Parasha and the Hussar, ink, 10½ by 14.
11. Fifty-four pages of sketches, various sizes.
12. A notebook containing the aria of the Mother and the duet with the Neighbour; ink, 9½ by 12¼, unsigned and undated.
13. A copyist's bill and a receipt from and for same.

41. OCTET FOR WIND INSTRUMENTS (OCTUOR)

(a) Summary sketch score, thirty pages, 11 by 14¼, in ink, bound in boards, and two separate sheets (three pages) of sketches in ink and pencil, and three pages of the Fugato in ink, dated and signed Paris, 20 mai 1923.
(b) Sixty-six pages, 6 by 10, bound in parchment and boards, of sketches for the first movement, mostly ink, several dated and signed.
(c) A white paper folder with an ink copy of the Fugato.

42. THE WEDDING (LES NOCES)

(a) Full score in ink of most of the first tableau in a version for eight woodwinds, eight strings, fourteen brass, percussion, harpsichord cimbalom, harp. Signed in Russian and dated 1914, 1915, and 1916; Russian and French texts; brown paper cover over twenty-one pages of unbound 12 by 16 manuscript paper.

(b) The full score, 11 by 14¼, ink with corrections in pencil, but without vocal parts, signed in Russian and dated Monaco, 6 April 1923. Title in Russian and French.

(c) Full score of the first Tableau and 3½ pages of the second tableau in the final, four-piano version, signed but undated, pencil, thirty-three pages of unbound 11½ by 8½ manuscript paper.

(d) Seven pages of a standard-orchestra score of the first tableau. (This was the first plan for the instrumentation. R.C.)

(e) An envelope containing 211 pages of sketches, some loose pages and some in notebooks, many with coloured inks for the text, designs for frontispieces, marginal rubrics. Signatures and dates on several entries.

(f) Full score, 13½ by 10½, ink, of first two tableaux in a version for two cimbaloms, pianola, harmonium, percussion. Eighty-eight pages, undated but signed on the blue paper cover. Russian and French texts.

(g) Four sheets of an orchestral score for the beginning, pencil. (Similar to (d) above.)

(h) Same thing in a carbon copy and with some additional notes in pencil.

43. CONCERTO FOR PIANO AND WIND INSTRUMENTS

(a) Fifty-two pages of summary sketches with two addenda sheets, signed and dated Biarritz, 13 April 1924, ink, 9 by 11½, bound in cloth with leather tips and endings.

(b) The orchestral score, ninety-five pages, signed and dated Biarritz, 21 April 1924, with notes for performance, at the end, in Stravinsky's hand; ink with corrections in pencil, 11 by 14¼.

44. SONATA FOR PIANO

(a) The complete manuscript, twenty-five pages, first movement dated and signed Biarritz, 21 August 1924; second movement dated and signed Nice, 6 October 1924; third movement dated and signed Nice, 21 October 1924; ink, bound in stiff paper cover with brown pattern, leather fold and corners.

(b) Complete sketch, nineteen pages, signed and dated Nice, 21 October 1924; pencil, 10½ by 13½ unbound manuscript paper. Most entries are dated.

45. SERENADE IN A

(a) The complete manuscript, twenty-four pages, 8¼ by 11¼, bound in green leather. The *Hymne* dated and signed Nice, 3 August 1925. The

Hymne, Romanza, and *Cadenza Finale* are in ink and the *Rondoletto* is in pencil.

(b) Twenty-seven pages of sketches, pen and pencil, various entries dated; the complete *Romanza* dated 9/10/25.

(c) Complete score, engraver's copy, 14 by 10½, six pages, ink, signed and dated 1926 on the cover.

46. SUITE NO. 1 FOR SMALL ORCHESTRA

The full score, in an orange wrapper, twenty-four pages, 14 by 10½ manuscript paper, ink, signed and dated Nice, 31 December 1925.

47. AVE MARIA.   PATER NOSTER.   CREDO

A pale orange folder containing complete copies in ink of the three choruses in their original Russian versions; five sheets of 8¼ by 11 manuscript paper. Each chorus is autographed. There are also eleven sheets of sketches for the three choruses, in pen and pencil.

48. PULCINELLA SUITE FOR VIOLIN AND PIANO

(a) Nine pages of random pencil and ink sketches, and eight pages of ink for the *Gavotte and Two Variations,* dated London, 1921, and signed.

(b) Complete manuscript score, signed and dated Nice, 24 August 1925, ink, twenty-one pages, 14¼ by 11¼, bound in grey cloth with red leather tips and fold.

49. OEDIPUS REX

(a) Sketches; bound in brown leatherette and dated 1926–27.

(b) Complete sketch of the piano score with a frontispiece by Stravinsky; signed and dated 1927, in Nice; 128 pages, 9½ by 9¼, a coarse-paper book bound in Italian paper with white parchment endings.

(c) An orange folder, 12½ by 9½, containing five unsigned pages of full score in ink, and seven pages of sketch score, in pencil, unsigned.

50. APOLLO MUSAGETES

(a) A violet folder, 12½ by 9½, containing eleven pages of piano score, ink, signed at top.

(b) Four pages of full score, pencil, unsigned and undated, 13 by 14.

51. FOUR STUDIES FOR ORCHESTRA

Pencil manuscript of the full score; signed and dated in several places, and at the end, Nice, 2 October 1928; forty-seven pages, 14 by 10½.

52. THE FAIRY'S KISS (LE BAISER DE LA FÉE)

(a) Six sheets of pencil sketches and the copy of a letter from Stravinsky to Alexandre Benois describing the ballet in outline.
(b) Piano score, two hands, seventy-two pages in pencil, 7¼ by 11, signed Nice, 16 October 1928; bound in brown cloth over board with leather folds and corners.
(c) The manuscript of the orchestral score, 167 pages, 11¼ by 14½, signed and dated '30 October 1928, midnight, Nice.' Pencil.

53. CAPRICCIO

Sketch book in pencil, 7 by 9¼, bound in blue boards with leather corners and fold containing the complete *Baiser de la Fée* (sixty-eight pages), signed and dated 15 October 1928; and the complete *Capriccio* (fifty-six pages). The second movement of the *Capriccio* is dated 13 September 1929, Echarvines. One page of a sketch for the *Study for Orchestra No. 3*, and a one page sketch for the orchestration of 'Souvenirs de Mon Enfance' (*Three Little Songs*).

54. A CHURCH PRAYER

A short sketch for a projected work, *c.* 1930.

55. SYMPHONY OF PSALMS

Part of a summary-sketch score, thirteen pages, 11¼ by 17, ink, signed in Russian and dated 14–27 April 1930, Nice. Bound in boards.

56. VIOLIN CONCERTO

(a) An abbreviated score, fifty-three pages, the first movement dated and signed Nice 20/5/31, the second movement dated and signed Nice 20/5/31, the third movement dated and signed Nice 10/6/31, the fourth movement unsigned and undated. The last measures are in pencil, otherwise the score is in ink on thick Italian paper, bound in tan linen, 9½ by 11½. On a separate sheet Stravinsky has written, in French, 'to Samuel Dushkin, the first performer'.

(b) Orchestral score, ninety-one pages, 11 by 14, signed and dated Voreppe (Isère) la Vironnière, 25 September 1931; ink with additional indications and corrections in pencil.

An envelope with twenty-six sketch sheets of various sizes, unsigned and undated, ink and pencil.

57. DUO CONCERTANT

Complete summary-sketch score, thirty-two pages, $9\frac{1}{2}$ by $12\frac{1}{2}$, pencil, dated and signed 15 July 1932 and bound in blue boards.

58. THREE LITTLE SONGS ('SOUVENIRS DE MON ENFANCE')

The manuscript of the orchestral score, twenty-nine numbered pages, 7 by $10\frac{1}{2}$, pencil, signed and dated in ink on the cover '1913 and 1933'.

59. PASTORALE

A copy of the score (Schott Edition, Number 3399) with piano reduction showing numerous changes in black, blue, and red pencil by the author and S. Dushkin; 11 pages. This copy was used for the Columbia recording, in London in 1933, and it has been signed by the four wind instrumentalists.

60. THE DUSHKIN COLLABORATIONS

(a) The 'Scherzo' from the *Firebird* arranged for violin and piano by Stravinsky and S. Dushkin, seven pages, 14 by $10\frac{1}{2}$, ink, signed, undated.

(b) The *Divertimento* (*Baiser de le Fée*) for violin and piano, fifty-two pages, pencil, of unbound 14 by $10\frac{1}{2}$ manuscript paper, signed on the cover and first page, and dated 1928–1932.

(c) A standard Edition Russe de Musique copy of the piano score of *Baiser de la Fée* with marks in Stravinsky's hand and a note explaining that this copy was used for the arrangement of the *Divertimento* for violin and piano.

(d) The *Ballad* for violin and piano (*Baiser de la Fée*), a $10\frac{1}{2}$ by $14\frac{1}{2}$ envelope containing the proofs of the unpublished Dushkin version of 1934.

(e) 'Airs du Rossignol'; five pages, pencil and ink.

(f) 'Marche Chinoise' from *Le Rossignol*; nine pages, pencil and ink.

(*e* and *f* are dated Voreppe, 1932, and signed by Stravinsky: 'arranged for violin and piano by Igor Stravinsky and Samuel Dushkin.')

(g) 'Danse Russe' from *Petrushka*: 'Transcribed for violin and piano by Stravinsky and S. Dushkin.' Eight pages, 14 by 10½; ink, signed by Stravinsky, 17 April 1932, Voreppe. An eight-page, 14 by 10½, pencil sketch copy is also included, signed and dated 17 April 1932, Voreppe.

(h) 'Parasha's Song' from *Mavra*, 'Arranged for violin and piano by Stravinsky and S. Dushkin', six pages, signed and dated New York, April 1937, pencil, 7 by 10.

61. SUITE ITALIENNE (PULCINELLA)

A grey envelope containing a transcription for piano and cello by Stravinsky and Piatigorsky; twenty-seven pages, 14 by 10¼, pencil, Stravinsky's signature is in blue pencil on the first page.

62. PERSEPHONE

(a) The full score of the manuscript, 226 pages (forty-nine pages in ink, the others in pencil), 11½ by 16¼, signed and dated Paris, 24 January 1934.

(b) Complete summary sketch, seventy-four pages, in pencil, 10½ by 10½, dated and initialled Paris, 30 December 1933. Bound in stiff Italian paper with parchment ends.

63. CONCERTO FOR TWO SOLO PIANOS

(a) Score, sixty pages, Société des Auteurs stamp 19 November 1936, first movement signed and dated Paris, 10 June 1935; second movement signed and dated Paris, 13 July 1935; third movement (in this copy, the *Prelude and Fugue* movement is third and the *Variations* movement fourth) signed and dated Paris, 1 September 1935; the *Variations* movement is unsigned and undated. Ink on unbound manuscript paper, 10½ by 14.

(b) Seven pages of pencil sketches, assorted sizes, unsigned and undated.

(c) Summary sketches of the complete concerto, eighty-nine pages, 10 by 12, bound in blue-green boards with one loose sheet in pencil, dated and signed Saturday, 9 November 1935.

64. THE CARD PARTY (JEU DE CARTES)

(a) The manuscript of the orchestral score, 235 pages, 8½ by 11¼, signed and dated 6 December 1936, Paris. The score, with some instrumental indications, is in pencil, and the pagination in ink.

(b) The complete sketches, with many instrumental indications and some of the sixty-nine pages fully scored. Also, four pages – pencil sketch – of the *Preludium*. The *Jeu de Cartes* sketches are signed 3 December 1936, Paris.

(c) Three sketch sheets, signed, undated, pencil, uneven sizes, contained in a brown paper folder, 12½ by 9½.

65. PRELUDIUM

(a) Six pages of rough sketches in pencil, three pages of summary sketches in pencil, two pages of reduction for piano in pencil, five transparent pages of the piano arrangement.
(b) Full score, nine pages, signed and dated New York, 1937, pencil, unbound music paper, 9¼ by 14½. (Unpublished.)

66. CONCERTO IN E FLAT ('DUMBARTON OAKS')

An envelope containing two pages of sketches, in pencil, unsigned and undated.

67. PETIT RAMUSIANUM HARMONIQUE

The complete music on one page of 11 by 7½ manuscript paper, signed and dated Paris 11/10/37; pencil, title on the envelope in Stravinsky's hand.

68. ANDANTE, FROM THE FIVE EASY PIECES FOR PIANO DUET

An arrangement for piano (two hands) of the *Andante* from the *Five Easy Pieces* of 1917. (1940)

69. RENARD

Three pages of sketches for a replacement of the cimbalom part by piano, 1940. Incomplete.

70. TANGO

(a) Ten pages of sketches, signed and dated Beverly Hills, California, 1940.
(b) An envelope of sketches, 1940.
(c) Manuscript of violin and piano version, four pencilled pages of 13½ by 10½, unbound manuscript paper, signed and dated 1940.

71. SYMPHONY IN C

(a) Thirty-one pages of sketches for the first and second movements, pencil and some ink; eleven pages of sketches for the third and fourth movements, the whole collection signed and dated 1939–40 on the title page.

(b) Fifty-eight pages of summary sketches, in pencil, with indications of instrumentation, signed and dated 17 August 1940, Beverly Hills. Bound in imitation leather.

72. THE BLUEBIRD

(a) The manuscripts of the piano score and of the score for male chorus [*sic*].

(b) Twenty-six pages, 13½ by 11, full score, pencil of the 'Arrangement for small orchestra from the original Stravinsky orchestration' (!). Signed and dated New York, 1941.

73. THE STAR SPANGLED BANNER

(a) The manuscripts of the piano score and of the male chorus [*sic*] *a cappella*; six pages, pencil and ink, 12¼ by 9½, signed and dated 1941.

(b) A 14½ by 11½ envelope containing ink manuscript copies of (a) above, signed and dated 1941; a photostat of the piano version by Stravinsky; a published version of the music by Walter Damrosch; a photostat of Stravinsky's orchestral manuscript; a second photostat and a photostat of the first sketch of Stravinsky's harmonization; correspondence, adverse reviews, publicity, and programmes.

74. DANSES CONCERTANTES

(a) The complete summary sketches, undated, signed at top, sixty-eight pages; pencil, 7½ by 9½, black notebook.

(b) Sketches, pencil, 7½ by 10¼, notebook with some extra sheets pasted in, a total of fifty-one pages.

75. CIRCUS POLKA

(a) An envelope containing two pages of sketches, 12¼ by 9¼, unsigned, undated, in pencil.

(b) The manuscript of the piano version, fourteen pages, 12¼ by 9¼, ink, signed and dated Hollywood, 5 February 1942.

(c) Full orchestral score, twenty-eight numbered pages, in pencil, on 13½ by 11 manuscript sheets, signed and dated 5 October 1942.

76. FOUR NORWEGIAN MOODS

(a) An envelope containing 24 pages of unsigned and undated pencil sketches, most of them 19 by 13.

(b) Forty-seven numbered pages, 13½ by 11, of full orchestral score, pencil, signed and dated Hollywood, 18 August 1942.

77. ODE

An envelope containing twenty-three pages of 14½ by 11½ pencil sketches, dated and signed 25 June 1943.

78. 'DANSE SACRALE' (FROM THE RITE OF SPRING)

An envelope containing five pages of sketches for the 1943 version, pencil and ink; unsigned and undated.

79. SCHERZO À LA RUSSE

(a) An envelope containing sketches; six pages of orchestral score and thirty pages of two-piano and 3-stave score. The second trio is signed and dated January 1943; pencil and ink, unbound 14½ by 11½ music paper.
(b) Twenty-three manuscript pages of the full score, 15 by 11, in ink, of the 'Blue Network' version, signed and dated 1944; twenty-three transparent ink sheets, 15 by 11, of the full score symphonic version, signed and dated 1944.

80. BABEL

(a) Nineteen pages of summary sketch score, 12 by 9½, ink, transparents, signed and dated 29 March 1944.
(b) Six sketch sheets, pencil, signed and dated 29 March 1944.
(c) Twenty-three pages of full orchestral score, transparent sheets, 15 by 11; ink, signed and dated Hollywood, 12 April 1944.

81. SONATA FOR TWO PIANOS:

An envelope containing fifty-four pages of sketches, several of them dated (12 August 1943, 9–10 September 1943, October 1943, etc.), ink and pencil on 12 by 9½ music paper.

82. SCÈNES DE BALLET

(a) An envelope containing thirty pages of pencil sketches; undated and unsigned.

(b) Full orchestral score in ink on fifty-four sheets of 11 by 17 transparent paper, signed and dated 23 August 1944.

(c) An abbreviated full score, four to ten staves, with almost all instrumentation indicated, signed and dated '23 Aout 1944 à Hollywood – Paris n'est plus aux Allemands'; pencil, twenty pages, bound in blue leatherette, 9¼ by 12¼. The title *Scènes de Ballet* is not found in the manuscript and was added at a later date.

83. SYMPHONY IN THREE MOVEMENTS

(a) An abbreviated full score, with most instrumentation indicated. The first movement comprises fourteen pages and the second movement six pages; all on 12½ by 19 sheets. The third movement of thirteen pages is written on sheets of 11½ by 17½.

(b) An envelope containing 111 pages of sketches. One sketch for the first movement is dated 15 June 1942, and the last page of the first movement is dated 15 October 1942. The sketches are in ink and pencil.

84. ELEGY

Ink, 12 by 9½ transparent sheets, three pages of the violin version and three pages of the viola version signed and dated 1944; there are also three pages of a viola version written on two staves instead of the one staff as published.

85. EBONY CONCERTO

(a) Summary sketch score with instrumentation indicated and the last pages scored in full; twenty-six pages, signed and dated at the top 1945; ink, unbound, 12¼ by 9½ music paper.

(b) Forty-five pages, 15 by 11, of orchestral score; ink, transparent master sheets, signed and dated 1 December 1945.

(c) An envelope containing sketches with some instrumentation indicated, and a sixteen-page sketch score, signed and dated 1 December 1945; pencil, 11¼ by 17.

86. 'CHORALE' (*from* THE SYMPHONIES OF WIND INSTRUMENTS)

(a) Full score; six pages, 12 by 9½, pencil, signed 'New Version' and dated 11 December 1945.

(b) Score of the same version in an arrangement without clarinets for a concert with the *Symphony of Psalms*, seven pages, 15 by 11 transparents, ink, signed and dated 1945.

87. CONCERTO IN D FOR STRINGS ('BASEL')

    (a) Thirteen large sheets of pencil sketches, unsigned, dated 7 May 1946, in a 14½ by 11½ envelope.

    (b) Full score, fifty-seven pages, signed and dated 1946 at top; ink, unbound, 12½ by 9½ transparent music paper, last page signed and dated 8 August 1946.

    (c) Abbreviated score; eighteen pages, also signed and dated Hollywood, 8 August 1946; pencil, bound in blue leatherette, 12½ by 9¼.

88. PETRUSHKA

An envelope containing sketches for the 1946 orchestration.

89. LITTLE CANON (PETIT CANON POUR LA FÊTE DE NADIA BOULANGER *for two tenors*)

Dated 16 September 1947, poem by Jean de Meung; pencil manuscript and transparent master. (Unpublished.)

90. ORPHEUS

Sketches, 1947.

91. MASS

Kyrie: fourteen pages of full score and four pages of sketches.
Gloria: eleven pages of full score and six pages of sketches.
Credo: six pages of sketches.
Sanctus: four pages of sketches.
Agnus Dei: two pages of sketches.

All sketches are in pencil on 19 by 13 paper. The full scores of the *Kyrie* and *Gloria* are in ink, on 12½ by 9½ sheets of onion skin paper. The titles are calligraphically drawn by Stravinsky.

92. THE FIREBIRD (SUITE)

Full orchestral manuscript score of the 'Pas de Deux', 'Scherzo' and the 'Pantomimes'. Forty-five pages, 12 by 18¼, ink, signed and dated at the top, 1945.

93. BALLAD FOR VIOLIN AND PIANO (*from* BAISER DE LA FÉE)

Seventeen pages of transparent manuscript paper signed but undated; ink, 13 by 9½, in envelope. (1947.)

94. RUSSIAN MAIDEN'S SONG (*from* MAVRA)

The 1947 arrangement for voice and piano, seven sheets on transparent manuscript paper, 13¼ by 9½, ink, signed but undated; in envelope.

95. PATER NOSTER AND AVE MARIA

The Latin versions, six pages, signed at top and dated 1949, ink on 13 by 9½ transparent manuscript paper.

96. THE RAKE'S PROGRESS

Complete sketches; pencil, some sheets dated, 1948–1951.

97. TWO POEMS OF VERLAINE

(a) The 1951 orchestral version, four pages of pencil sketches and twelve pages of transparent manuscript full score.
(b) Transparent manuscript, ink, sixteen pages and a few sketches.

98. CANTATA

(a) Summary sketches, pencil, 1952.
(b) Manuscript of the full score on onion skins, ink, eighty-nine pages, 1952.

Appendix D

ARRANGEMENTS FOR PLAYER-PIANO

This book contains no list of gramophone records of Stravinsky's works. There are numerous published catalogues, guides and the like, which list current records, while particulars of withdrawn recordings can be obtained from the British Institute of Recorded Sound. But it seemed advisable to include a list of his arrangements for player-piano, since these rolls were withdrawn about the time of the Second World War and have now become obsolete. They have a special importance, since many of the Pleyela arrangements, 'especially of vocal works like *The Wedding* and the Russian songs, were virtually recomposed for the medium' (*Exp*).

Stravinsky's interest in player-pianos dated from 1914, when he attended a demonstration of the Pianola by the Aeolian Company in London. This led to the acceptance of a commission from the Aeolian Company to compose a work specially for Pianola. This was the *Study* of 1917. In 1923, he entered into a six-year contract with the Pleyel Company in Paris, under which he agreed to transcribe his complete works for Pleyela. In *Expositions* he wrote: 'I then discovered the chief problem to be in the restrictive application of the pedals caused by the division of the keyboard into two parts. . . . I solved this problem by employing two secretaries to sit one on either side of me as I stood facing the keyboard; I then dictated as I transcribed, from right to left and to each in turn.'

The following works were recorded at various times for Pianola (or Duo-Art), and the Pianola recordings were transferred to the Duo-Art (Aeolian) Company, London, in 1927:

Four Studies for Piano (op. 7) – Pianola T22596A, T22597B, T22598A, T22599B.
The Firebird: An autobiographical sketch of Stravinsky's life to the year 1910, with a literary and musical analysis of *The Firebird* and a complete performance of it played by Stravinsky – Duo-Art D 759, 761, 763, 765, 767, 769; Pianola D 760, 762, 764, 766, 768, 770.
The Rite of Spring – Pianola T24150/53C
Study for Pianola – Pianola T967B.
Concerto for Piano: the first movement, played by Stravinsky – Duo-Art 528G.

Sonata for Piano: the first movement, played by Stravinsky; annotated by Edwin Evans – Duo-Art D231; Pianola D232.

A dozen works were issued by Pleyela. They are listed here (with their French titles) in the order of recording:

Pulcinella (8421–8428)
Le Sacre du Printemps (8429–8437)
Piano-Rag-Music (8438)
Trois Pièces Faciles pour le piano (8439)
Cinq Pièces Faciles pour le piano (8440)
Pétrouchka (8441–8447)
Les Cinq Doigts (8448–8449)
Le Chant du Rossignol (8451–8453)
Histoires pour Enfants (8454)
Quatre Chants Russes (8455)
Concertino (8456)
Les Noces Villageoises (8831–8834)

The researches of Rex Lawson and others have shown that a number of rolls of early works were privately cut about 1915 by Esther Willis for Philip Heseltine, Alvin Langdon Coburn, and possibly Edwin Evans. These were unnumbered and included *Faun and Shepherdess, Two Melodies, Fantastic Scherzo, Fireworks*, and the Chinese March from *The Nightingale*. Two of these, *viz. Fireworks* and the Chinese March, were performed at recitals given by Alvin Langdon Coburn at the Aeolian Hall, London, on 5 and 15 May 1915.

Appendix E

BIBLIOGRAPHY

In 1940 Paul David Magriel compiled a bibliography of critical writings on Stravinsky's life, music and influence, which was published in the *Bulletin of Bibliography*, vol. 17, nos. 1 and 2, January / April and May / August 1940, by the F. W. Faxon Company, 83 Francis Street, Boston. Subsequently he revised and enlarged this bibliography, dividing it into five sections: (1) books devoted to Stravinsky, (2) special periodical issues devoted wholly to Stravinsky, (3) references to Stravinsky in other books, (4) references to Stravinsky in periodicals, (5) references to specific works by Stravinsky. In this form (comprising over 600 references) it was published in *Stravinsky in the Theatre*, edited by Minna Lederman, 1951.

A selected bibliography consisting of (1) books and articles by Stravinsky, (2) books about Stravinsky, (3) periodical articles devoted to Stravinsky, and (4) references to specific works in periodicals, was compiled by Carroll D. Wade for publication in *Stravinsky: a new appraisal of his work*, edited by Paul Henry Lang, 1963.

The bibliography in this Appendix includes (I) books by Stravinsky, (II) books on Stravinsky and his music, (III) other publications, including (a) special Stravinsky issues of periodicals, (b) guides, and (c) catalogues, and (IV) films.

I. BOOKS BY STRAVINSKY

1. CHRONIQUES DE MA VIE. (Two vols.) Paris, Les Editions Denoël et Steel, 1935 and 1936.

    Written in collaboration with Walter Nouvel.

    CHRONICLE OF MY LIFE. London, Gollancz ,1936.

    No translator's name given. The translation is not always completely reliable. A few short passages are missing.

    AN AUTOBIOGRAPHY. New York, Simon and Schuster, 1936. Reprinted, 1958. (A paper-back edition was published by the Norton Library, New York, in 1962.)

CRONICAS DE MI VIDA. (Vol. 1.) NEUVAS CRONICAS DE MI VIDA (vol. 2). Buenos Aires, Sur, 1935 and 1936.

Spanish translation by G. de Torre (vol. 1) and L. Hurtado (vol. 2).

ERINNERUNGEN. Zürich–Berlin, Atlantis Verlag, 1937.

German translation by Richard Tüngel. (See also LEBEN UND WERK, no. 4 below.)

N.B. – A Russian translation by L. Yakovleva-Shaporina, with an introduction by V. Bogdanov-Berezovsky, was published by the State Publishing House in the U. S. S. R. in 1964.

2. PUSHKIN: POETRY AND MUSIC. 1940.

The title-page of this rare little octavo pamphlet, the text of which is reprinted in Appendix A (8), runs as follows:

HARVEY TAYLOR / AUTHOR'S REPRESENTATIVE / (address) / OFFERS / Serial Rights / to / "PUSHKIN: Poetry and Music" / by / IGOR STRAVINSKY / *From the French manuscript by Gregory Golubeff* / (vignette) / Printed for copyright purposes only / Copyright, 1940, by IGOR STRAVINSKY / Printed in the U.S.A.

3. POETIQUE MUSICALE: sous forme de six leçons. Cambridge, Harvard University Press, 1942.

The Charles Eliot Norton lectures for 1939/40. Written in collaboration with Roland-Manuel.

POETIQUE MUSICALE. Paris, J. B. Janin, 1945. New and revised edition, Paris, Editions Le Bon Plaisir, 1952.

The 1945 edition, published in France just after the war, omits the whole of the fifth lecture, *Les Avatars de la Musique russe.*

POETICS OF MUSIC: in the form of six lessons. Cambridge, Harvard University Press, 1947. New York, Vintage Books, 1956.

English translation by Arthur Knodel and Ingolf Dahl. Preface by Darius Milhaud.

MUSIKALISCHE POETIK. Mainz, Schott's, 1949.

German translation by Heinrich Strobel. (See also LEBEN UND WERK, no. 4 below.)

4. LEBEN UND WERK. Zürich, Atlantis Verlag; and Mainz, Schott's, 1957.

This consists of a reprint of *Erinnerungen* and *Musikalische Poetik,* together with *Antworten auf 35 Fragen* (*Answers to 35 Questions*) translated from the American by Manfred Gräter.

5. CONVERSATIONS WITH IGOR STRAVINSKY, by I. S. and Robert Craft. New York, Doubleday, 1959. London, Faber and Faber, 1959.

These two editions are nearly identical. They include *Answers to 35 Questions* as reprinted in *Leben und Werk*, except for the omission of Question XIX.

6. MEMORIES AND COMMENTARIES, by I. S. and Robert Craft. New York, Doubleday, 1960. London, Faber and Faber, 1960.

There are a few short passages where these two editions are at variance. The American edition carries a footnote quoting an extensive passage from an article by Winfried Zillig about Schoenberg's preoccupaton with multiple orchestras, which does not appear in the English edition.

7. STRAWINSKY IN CONVERSATION WITH ROBERT CRAFT. London, Penguin Books, 1962. With a Preface by David Drew.

A reprint of the English editions of nos. 5 and 6 above. In this edition the dedication to Sir Isaiah Berlin appears for the first time.

STRAWINSKY: GESPRÄCHE MIT ROBERT CRAFT. Zürich, Atlantis Verlag, 1961.

A reprint of nos. 5 and 6 above in a German translation by Manfred Gräter, H. J. Schatz, G. W. Baruch, and Martin Hürlimann. The material was edited by Martin Hürlimann, who rearranged it in eleven sections.

8. EXPOSITIONS AND DEVELOPMENTS, by I. S. and Robert Craft. New York, Doubleday, 1962. London, Faber and Faber, 1962.

There are numerous points of difference between these two editions. The American edition has a long appendix, '*Slightly More of a Plague on One of their Houses*', only a brief extract from which is included in the English edition. The English edition carries the following three appendices, none of which appears in the American edition:

Appendix A *Berceuse:* words and music by I. S.
Appendix B *Anthem:* words by T. S. Eliot, music by I. S.
Appendix C Check List of Chaikovsky sources for *Le Baiser de la Fée*

In the English edition, the material has been slightly rearranged so that it falls into two parts: 1. *Expositions*, and 2. *Developments*. This differentiation has not been made in the American edition.

9. DIALOGUES AND A DIARY, by I. S. and Robert Craft. New York, Doubleday, 1963. London, Faber & Faber, 1968.

The English edition contains more material than the American edition, particularly a set of letters written by Stravinsky to Cocteau during the composition of *Oedipus Rex*.

10. DIALOGUES: MEMORIES, THOUGHTS, COMMENTARIES. Leningrad, 1971

   This is a Russian translation of nos. 5, 6, 8 and 9 above, rearranged and edited by Mikhail S. Druskin.

11. THEMES AND EPISODES, by I. S. and Robert Craft. New York, Knopf, 1966.

12. RETROSPECTIVES AND CONCLUSIONS, by I. S. and Robert Craft. New York, Knopf, 1969.

13. THEMES AND CONCLUSIONS, by I. S. London, Faber & Faber, 1972.

   This book consists of a reprint of Stravinsky's contributions to nos. 11 and 12 above, with the contents of no. 11 revised and the contents of no. 12 expanded, the Robert Craft diary contributions to nos. 11 and 12 being omitted.

II. BOOKS ON STRAVINSKY AND HIS MUSIC

ACKERE, JULES VAN. *Igor Stravinsky*. Antwerp, Standaard-Boekhandel, 1954.

ARMITAGE, MERLE (ed.). *Igor Strawinsky* – articles and critiques by Eugene Goossens, Henry Boys, Olin Downes, Merle Armitage, Emile Vuillermoz, Louis Danz, Jose Rodriguez, Manuel Komroff, Jean Cocteau, Erik Satie, Boris de Schloezer. New York, G. Schirmer, 1936.

ASAFIEV, BORIS. *A Book about Stravinsky*. Leningrad, 1977. A reprint of the 1929 edition published in Leningrad under Asafiev's pen name of Igor Glebov.

BORETZ, BENJAMIN and EDWARD T. CONE (eds.). *Perspectives on Schoenberg and Stravinsky*. Princeton University Press, 1969. London, Oxford University Press, 1969.

CASELLA, ALFREDO. *Igor Strawinski*. Rome, A. F. Formiggini, 1926.

—— *Strawinski*. Brescia, La Scuola, 1947. New edition, with an extra chapter by Guglielmo Barblan. Brescia, La Scuola, 1951.

CIRLOT, JUAN EDUARDO. *Igor Strawinsky: su tiempo, su significación, su obra*. Barcelona, G. Gili, 1949.

COLLAER, PAUL. *Strawinsky*. Brussels, Editions 'Equilibres', 1930.

CORLE, EDWIN (ed.). *Igor Stravinsky* – articles and essays by Boris de Schloezer, Erik Satie, Eugene Goossens, Jean Cocteau, Henry Boys, Aaron Copland, Arthur Berger, Nicolas Nabokoff, Merle Armitage, Edwin Corle, Robert Craft, Sir Osbert Sitwell, Samuel Dushkin, Cecil Smith, Lawrence Morton, David Hall. New York, Duell, Sloane and Pearce, 1949.
  Part of this material appeared in the Merle Armitage collection of 1936.

COSMAN, MILEIN. *Stravinsky at Rehearsal* – a sketch book by Milein Cosman, with text by Hans Keller. London, Dennis Dobson, 1962.

CRAFT, ROBERT. See I. Books by Stravinsky, nos. 5, 6, 7, 8, and 9.

CRAFT, ROBERT. *Stravinsky: the Chronicle of a Friendship, 1948–1971*. New York, Knopf, 1972. London, Gollancz, 1972.

CRAFT, ROBERT, with ALESSANDRO PIOVESAN and ROMAN VLAD. *Le Musiche religiose di Igor Strawinsky*. Venice, Lombroso, 1956.

DRUSKIN, MIKHAIL S. *Igor Stravinsky: his Character, Creative Work, Opinions*. Leningrad, 1974. A German translation was published by Verlag Philipp Reclam jun. at Leipzig in 1976.

FLEISCHER, HERBERT. *Strawinsky*. Berlin, Russischer Musik Verlag, 1931.

FODOR, ANDRAS. *Stravinszkij: szemtöl szemben*. Budapest, Gondolat Könyvkiadó, 1976.

GLEBOV, IGOR[1]. *Kniga o Stravinskom*. Leningrad, Triton, 1929.

GOZENPUD, A. *Feodor Stravinsky: essays, letters, reminiscences*. Leningrad, 1972. This contains the text of eight letters written by the young Igor to his parents from Ustilug (1899–1901).

HERZFELD, FRIEDRICH. *Igor Strawinsky*. Berlin, Rembrandt Verlag, 1961.

HORGAN, PAUL. *Encounters with Stravinsky: A Personal Record*. New York, Farrar Straus & Giroux, 1972. London, The Bodley Head, 1972.

KELLER, HANS. See COSMAN, MILEIN.

KIRCHMEYER, HELMUT. *Igor Strawinsky: Zeitgeschichte im Persönlichkeitsbild*. Regensburg, Gustav Bosse Verlag, 1958.

LANG, PAUL HENRY (ed.). *Stravinsky: a new appraisal of his work*. Contributions by Paul Henry Lang, Edward T. Cone, Wilfrid Mellers, Lawrence Morton, Robert U. Nelson, Boris Schwarz, Carroll D. Wade. New York, the Norton Library, 1963.
  The essays in this volume were originally written for a special issue of *The Musical Quarterly* to commemorate Stravinsky's eightieth birthday in 1962.

LEDERMAN, MINNA (ed.). *Stravinsky in the Theatre*. Contributions by Minna Lederman, Jean Cocteau, Emile Vuillermoz, Jacques Rivière, André Levinson, C. F. Ramuz, Arthur Berger, Ingolf Dahl, George Balanchine, Robert Craft, Nicolas Nabokov, Ernest Ansermet, Aaron Copland, Alexei Haieff, Carlos Chavez, Pierre Monteux, Walter Piston, Darius Milhaud,

---

[1] The pen-name of Boris Asafiev.

Appendices

Leonard Bernstein, Vittorio Rieti, William Schuman, Lincoln Kirstein, and Igor Stravinsky. New York, Pelegrini & Cudahy. London, Peter Owen, 1951.

LIBMAN, LILLIAN. *And Music at the Close: Stravinsky's Last Years.* New York, W. W. Norton & Co. Inc., 1972. London, Macmillan, 1972.

LINDLAR, HEINRICH. *Igor Strawinskys sakraler Gesang.* Regensburg, G. Bosse Verlag, 1957.

MALIPIERO, GIAN FRANCESCO. *Strawinsky.* Venice, Cavallino, 1945.

MEYLAN, PIERRE. *Une amitié célèbre: C. F. Ramuz/Igor Stravinsky.* Lausanne, Editions du Cervin, 1961.

MONNIKENDAM, MARIUS. *Strawinsky.* Haarlem, J. H. Gottmer, 1958.

MYERS, ROLLO H. *Introduction to the Music of Stravinsky.* London, Dennis Dobson, 1950.

NABOKOV, NICOLAS. *Igor Strawinsky.* Berlin, Colloquium Verlag, 1964.

OLEGGINI, LEON. *Connaissance de Stravinsky.* Lausanne, Foetisch, 1952.

ONNEN, FRANK. *Strawinsky.* Translated from the Dutch by Mrs. M. M. Kessler-Button. Stockholm, The Continental Book Company, 1948. London, Sidgwick and Jackson, 1948.

PAOLI, DOMENICO DE'. *L'Opera di Strawinsky.* Milan, 1931.

—— *Igor Strawinsky: da 'L'Oiseau de Feu' a 'Persefone'.* Turin, G. B. Paravia, 1934.

PIOVESAN, ALESSÀNDRO. See CRAFT, ROBERT.

RAMUZ, CHARLES F. *Souvenirs sur Igor Strawinsky.* Lausanne, Editions Mermod, 1929. Paris, Nouvelle Revue Française, 1929.
New editions by Mermod, Lausanne, 1946 and 1952.

—— *Erinnerungen an Igor Strawinsky.* German translation by Leonharda Gescher. Berlin and Frankfurt a.M., Bibliothek Suhrkamp, n.d. [c. 1956].

SAUGUET, HENRI and others. *Strawinsky.* Paris, Hachette, 1968. (Collection Génies et Réalités.)

SCHAEFFNER, ANDRE. *Strawinsky.* Paris, Editions Rieder, 1931.

SCHLOEZER, BORIS DE. *Igor Strawinsky.* Paris, Editions Claude Aveline, 1929.

SIOHAN, ROBERT. *Stravinsky.* Paris, Editions du Seuil, 1959. London, John Calder, 1966.

SMIRNOV, V. *Creative Formative Years of I. F. Stravinsky.* Leningrad, Muzika, 1970.

SOPENA, FEDERICO. *Strawinsky; vida, obra y estilo.* Madrid, Sociedad de Estudios y Publicaciones, 1956.

STRAVINSKY, THEODORE. *Catherine and Igor Stravinsky: A Family Album.* London, Boosey & Hawkes, 1973.

STRAVINSKY, VERA and Robert Craft. *Stravinsky in pictures and documents.* New York, Simon & Schuster, 1979.

STRAWINSKY, THEODORE. *Le Message d'Igor Strawinsky.* Lausanne, Librarie F. Rouge, 1948.

—— *Igor Strawinsky: Mensch und Künstler.* German translation by Heinrich Strobel. Mainz, Schott's, 1952.

—— *The Message of Igor Strawinsky.* English translation by Robert Craft and André Marion. London, Boosey and Hawkes, 1953.

The German and English translations include a small amount of new material that did not appear in the original French version.

STROBEL, HEINRICH. *Stravinsky: Classic Humanist.* New York, Merlin Press, 1955. Translated by Hans Rosenwald.

—— *Igor Strawinsky.* Zürich, Atlantis Verlag, 1956.

STUCKENSCHMIDT, HANS H. *Strawinsky und sein Jahrhundert.* Berlin-Dahlem, Akademie der Künste, 1957.

TANSMAN, ALEXANDRE. *Igor Stravinsky.* Paris, Amiot – Dumont, 1948.

—— *Igor Stravinsky: The Man and his Music.* New York, Putnam, 1949. Translated by Therese and Charles Bleefield.

—— *Igor Stravinsky.* Buenos Aires, Editorial Argentina de Música, 1949. Translated by Roberto García Morillo.

TOMEK, OTTO (ed.) *Igor Strawinsky: Eine Sendereihe des Westdeutschen Rundfunks zum 80 Geburtstag.* Contributions by Pierre Boulez, Jean Cocteau, Hans Curjel, Helmut Kirchmeyer, Heinrich Lindlar, Aurel von Millos, K. H. Ruppel, Paul Sacher, Leo Schrade, Reinhold Schubert, Oscar Fritz Schuh, Pierre Souvtchinsky, Roman Vlad. Cologne, Westdeutscher Rundfunk, 1963.

VAINKOP, Y. *Stravinsky.* Leningrad, Triton, 1927.

VERSHININA, I. *Stravinsky's Early Ballets.* Moscow, Nauka, 1967.

VLAD, ROMAN. *Strawinsky.* Rome, Giulio Einaudi, 1958.

—— *Stravinsky.* English translation by Frederick and Ann Fuller. Oxford University Press, 1960.

The English translation carries a new chapter on *Threni.* See also under CRAFT, ROBERT.

WHITE, ERIC WALTER. *Stravinsky's Sacrifice to Apollo.* London, The Hogarth Press, 1930.

—— *Stravinsky: a critical survey.* London, John Lehmann, 1947. New York, Philosophical Library, 1948.

—— *Strawinsky.* German translation by Gottfried von Einem. Hamburg, Claassen Verlag, 1950.

The German translation includes an extra chapter covering some of the more recent works.

YARUSTOVSKY, BORIS. *Igor Stravinsky*: a short essay on his life and work. Moscow, Soviet Composer Publishing House, 1964. Second edn., enlarged, 1969.

—— (ed.) *I. F. Stravinsky: Essays and Documents.* Moscow, 1973. This collection includes the text of 62 letters written in Russian by Igor Stravinsky between 1905 and 1932.

Appendices

III. OTHER PUBLICATIONS

(a) *Special Stravinsky Issues of Periodicals*

La Revue Musicale. Année 5, no. 2. Paris, December 1923. Contributions by Boris de Schloezer, Jean Cocteau, Michel Georges-Michel, André Coeuroy, André Levinson.

Contemporaneos. Tomo 5, no. 15. Mexico, August 1929. Contains *El Caso Strawinsky* by Samuel Ramos.

Cahiers de Belgique. Année 3, no. 10. Brussels, December 1930. Contributions by Raymond Petit, André Schaeffner, Arthur Lourié, Paul Collaer, Franz Hellens.

Neujahreblatt der Allgemeinen Musikgesellschaft in Zürich. No. 121. Zürich and Leipzig, 1933. Contains 'Igor Strawinski: Versuch einer Einführung' by Jacques Handschin.

La Revue Musicale. Numéro spécial. *Igor Strawinsky.* Paris, May–June, 1939. Contributions by André Schaeffner, Roland-Manuel, Roger Desormière, Arthur Honegger, Alfred Cortot, Darius Milhaud, P. Souvtchinsky, Serge Lifar, Olivier Messiaen, Georges Auric, C. A. Cingria, A. Hoérée, G. Pittaluga, André Boll.

Dance Index. 'Stravinsky in the Theatre'. Vol. VI, nos. 10, 11, 12. New York, 1945. Contributions by Minna Lederman, Ernest Ansermet, Jean Cocteau, C. F. Ramuz, George Balanchine, Arthur Berger, Lincoln Kirstein, Ingolf Dahl, Alexei Haieff, Pierre Monteux, Carlos Chavez, Aaron Copland, Walter Piston, Darius Milhaud, Vittorio Rieti, William Schuman, Leonard Bernstein, and Igor Stravinsky.

Tempo. Strawinsky Number. London, Summer 1948. Contributions by Tamara Karsavina, Cyril W. Beaumont, Henry Boys, Eric Walter White, Charles Stuart.

Musik der Zeit. Strawinsky Number. Bonn, 1952. Contributions by H. H. Stuckenschmidt, Jean Cocteau, Gian-Francesco Malipiero, Arthur Honegger, Will Grohmann, Tamara Karsavina, Igor Markevitch, Ferdinando Ballo, Henry Boys, Gottfried von Einem, Charles Stuart, Alfred Cortot, Ernest Ansermet, Werner Egk, Eric Walter White, Ferenc Fricsay, Paul Sacher, Emilia Zanetti, Max See, W. H. Auden, Hans Mersmann.

The Score & I.M.A. Magazine. Stravinsky Number. No. 20. London, June 1957. Contributions by Robert Craft, Henry Boys, Hans Keller, Roger Sessions, Roberto Gerhard, Maurice Perrin, David Drew.

Feuilles Musicales. Stravinsky Number. Lausanne, March–April 1962. Contributions by Yvonne Racz-Barblan, Pierre Meylan, Igor Stravinsky & Charles-Albert Cingria, Constantin Regamey.

The Musical Quarterly. Stravinsky Number. New York, 1962. The essays in this issue were reprinted in book form a year later. See the entry in section II above under Paul Henry Lang (editor).

Tempo. Stravinsky number. London, spring and summer, 1962. Contributions by Eric Walter White, Colin Mason, Donald Mitchell, Herbert Read, Benjamin Britten, Michael Tippett, A. Tcherepnin, Peter Wishart.

(b) *Guides*

Igor Stravinsky's 'Les Noces': an outline, by Victor Belaiev. Translated from the Russian by S. W. Pring. Oxford University Press, 1928.

Stravinsky: 'The Fire-Bird' and 'Petrushka', by Edwin Evans. Oxford University Press, 1933.

Petrouchka: the story of the ballet, told by Sandy Posner. Leicester, Newman Wolsey, 1945.

The Firebird [and Sheherazade]: the stories of the ballets, told by Marion Robertson. Newman Wolsey, London, 1947.

Guida a 'The Rake's Progress'. La Biennale di Venezia XIV Festival Internazionale di Musica Contemporanea, Venice, 1951.

Petrushka: an authoritative score of the original version, with backgrounds, analysis, essays, views and comments. Edited by Charles Hamm. New York, W. W. Norton & Co. Inc., 1967.

The Rite of Spring: Sketches, 1911–1913. Facsimile reproductions from the autographs. London, Boosey & Hawkes, 1969.

(c) *Catalogues*

Kostbare Autographen der neueren Musik und Literatur/A Unique Collection of Modern Music and Literary Manuscripts. L'Art Ancien S.A., Zürich, 1948.
This sale included holograph manuscripts of the full scores of *Perséphone* and *Pétrouchka* (1947 version), the instrumental score of *Les Noces,* and the piano reduction of *Apollon-Musagète;* and the catalogue contains brief notes (in German and English) on the works in question and reproduces the first page of the orchestral score of *Perséphone.*

Igor Strawinsky: a complete catalogue of his published works. London, Boosey & Hawkes, 1957.
—— A new edition with addenda. London, Boosey & Hawkes, 1962.

Stravinsky and the Dance: a survey of ballet productions 1910–1962. The Dance Collection of the New York Public Library, New York, 1962.
N.B. – A separate typewritten list was issued of the visual materials assembled for the exhibition held at the Wildenstein Gallery, New York, 2 May–2 June 1962.

Stravinsky and the Theatre: a catalogue of decor and costume designs for stage productions of his works, 1910–1962. The New York Public Library, New York, 1963.

Appendices

IV. FILMS

Stravinsky: a 16 mm film in black and white, 1,779½ ft. long (or 49′ 26″), co-sponsored by the National Film Board of Canada and the Canadian Broadcasting Corporation, and produced by the National Film Board of Canada.

Direction:	Roman Kroitor and Wolf Koenig
Location recording:	Marcel Carrière
Camera and editing:	Wolf Koenig
Sound editing:	Jean-Pierre Joutel
Sound recording:	Ron Alexander
Commentary:	Don Brittain
Production:	Roman Kroitor

This film is centred on a recording session of the *Symphony of Psalms* conducted by the composer with the C.B.C. Symphony Orchestra and the Mendelsohn choir in Toronto, 1963.

Stravinsky at Home: filmed in March 1965 by the Norddeutscher Rundfunk Television with Rolf Liebermann as director.

Stravinsky: an hour-long profile by C. B. S. Television, filmed in April-May 1965 with David Oppenheim as director.

Acknowledgements

Special acknowledgement has already been made in the Preface to the late Mr. Igor Stravinsky for his kindness in allowing me to quote extensively from his published writings, and also to the copyright holders for permission to reprint a number of letters addressed to Stravinsky in Appendix B. Further acknowledgements are due for permission to use copyright material from the following books and articles by way of brief illustration and comment:

A. BOOKS

ERNEST ANSERMET, *Les Fondements de Musique dans la Conscience humaine.* Neuchâtel, Editions de la Baconnière, 1961.

GEORGE ANTHEIL, *Bad Boy of Music.* London, Hurst & Blackett, 1947.

CYRIL BEAUMONT, *The Diaghilev Ballet in London.* London, Putnam, 1940.

CLIVE BELL, *Old Friends.* London, Chatto & Windus, 1956.

ALEXANDRE BENOIS, *Reminiscences of the Russian Ballet.* London, Putnam, 1941.

JOHN MALCOLM BRINNIN, *Dylan Thomas in America.* London, Dent, 1956.

ALFREDO CASELLA, *Strawinski.* Brescia, La Scuola, 1947.

EDWARD J. DENT, *Ferrucio Busoni.* Oxford University Press, 1933.

EDWIN EVANS, *Stravinsky: 'The Fire Bird' and 'Petrushka'.* Oxford University Press, 1933.

M. FOKINE, *Fokine: Memoirs of a Ballet Master.* London, Constable, 1961.

ANDRÉ GIDE, *Journal (1889-1939).* Paris, NRF, 1941.

EUGENE GOOSSENS, *Overture and Beginners.* London, Methuen, 1951.

S. L. GRIGORIEV, *The Diaghilev Ballet 1909-1929.* London, Constable, 1953.

HANS KELLER (& MILEIN COSMAN), *Stravinsky at Rehearsal.* London, Dobson, 1962.

SERGE LIFAR, *Diaghilev.* London, Putnam, 1940.

G. F. MALIPIERO, *Strawinsky.* Venice, Cavallino, 1945.

PIERRE MEYLAN, *Une Amitié Célèbre.* Lausanne, Editions du Cervin, 1961.

DONALD MITCHELL, *The Language of Modern Music.* London, Faber, 1963.

N. NABOKOV, *Old Friends and New Music.* London, Hamish Hamilton, 1951.

ROMOLA NIJINSKY, *Nijinsky.* London, Gollancz, 1933.

C. F. RAMUZ, *Souvenirs sur Igor Stravinsky.* Lausanne, Mermod, 1929.

ANDRÉ SCHAEFFNER, *Strawinsky.* Paris, Editions Rieder, 1931.

ARNOLD SCHOENBERG, *Style and Idea.* London, Williams & Norgate, 1951.

Acknowledgements

ROBERT SIOHAN, *Stravinsky*. Paris, Editions du Seuil, 1959.

OSBERT SITWELL, *Great Morning*. London, Macmillan, 1948.

THÉODORE STRAWINSKY, *Le Message d'Igor Strawinsky*. Lausanne, Librairie F. Rouge, 1948.

ALEXANDRE TANSMAN, *Igor Stravinsky*. Paris, Amiot-Dumont, 1948.

ROMAN VLAD, *Stravinsky*. Oxford University Press, 1960.

B. ARTICLES

ERNEST ANSERMET, *'L'Expérience Musicale et Le Monde d'aujourd'hui'*. Neuchâtel, Editions de la Baconnière, 1948.

—— 'The Crisis of Contemporary Music'. *Recorded Sound*, London, April 1964.

GEORGE BALANCHINE, 'The Dance Element in Stravinsky's Music', from *Stravinsky in the Theatre*, Dance Index, New York, 1948.

GEORGE BRINTON BEAL, 'Entr'acte: Stravinsky and the Elephants'. *Concert Bulletin*, Boston Symphony Orchestra, 13-15 January 1944.

BENJAMIN BORETZ, 'Stravinsky: A Flood of Genius'. *The London Magazine*, January 1963.

BENJAMIN BRITTEN, 'Britten Looking Back'. *The Sunday Telegraph*, 17 November 1963.

ROBERT CRAFT, 'Music and Words', from *Stravinsky in the Theatre*, Dance Index, New York, 1948.

—— 'Stravinsky's Mass: A Notebook', from the Stravinsky symposium edited by Edwin Corle, New York 1949.

—— ' "The Rake's Progress" in Venice', Boston University Opera Workshop programme, 1953.

—— 'A Concert for St. Mark'. *The Score*, London, December 1956.

—— 'A Personal Preface'. *The Score*, London, June 1957.

PRINCESS EDMOND DE POLIGNAC, 'Memoirs'. *Horizon*, London, August 1945.

SAMUEL DUSHKIN, 'Working with Stravinsky', from the Stravinsky symposium edited by Edwin Corle, 1949.

RALPH HAWKES, 'American Diary'. *Tempo*, London, March 1946.

ARTHUR HONEGGER, 'Strawinsky, homme de métier'. *La Revue musical*, Paris, May-June 1939.

ALEXIS KALL, 'Stravinsky in the Chair of Poetry'. *The Musical Quarterly*, New York, July 1940.

TAMARA KARSAVINA, 'Recollection of Stravinsky'. *Tempo*, London, summer 1948.

LINCOLN KIRSTEIN, 'Working with Stravinsky', from *Stravinsky in the Theatre*, Dance Index, New York, 1948.

COLIN MASON, 'Stravinsky's Newest Works'. *Tempo*, London, Spring/Summer 1960.

Acknowledgements

—— 'Stravinsky and Gesualdo'. *Tempo,* London, Autumn/Winter 1960.

—— 'Stravinsky's New Work'. *Tempo,* London, Autumn 1961.

WILFRID MELLERS. 'Stravinsky's Œdipus as 20th Century Hero', from *Stravinsky: a new appraisal of his work* (ed. P. H. Lang), New York, 1963.

LAWRENCE MORTON, 'Incongruity and Faith', from the Stravinsky symposium edited by Edwin Corle, New York, 1949.

—— 'Stravinsky and Tchaikovsky', from *Stravinsky: a new appraisal of his work* (ed. P. H. Lang), New York, 1963.

RALPH PARKER, 'Stravinsky in Russia'. *The New Statesman,* 2 November 1962.

ROLAND PENROSE, Introduction to Catalogue of Picasso Exhibition, Arts Council of Great Britain, London, 1960.

MAURICE PERRIN, 'Stravinsky in a Composition Class'. *The Score,* London, June 1957.

WALTER PISTON, 'Stravinsky's Rediscoveries', from *Stravinsky in the Theatre,* Dance Index, New York, 1948.

YVONNE RACZ-BARBLAN, 'Igor Stravinsky vu par le cymbaliste Aladar Racz'. *Feuilles Musicales,* Lausanne, March-April 1962.

BORIS SCHWARTZ, 'Stravinsky in Soviet Russian Criticism', from *Stravinsky: a new appraisal of his work* (ed. P. H. Lang), New York, 1963.

ERWIN STEIN, 'Igor Stravinsky. Canticum Sacrum ad honorem Sancti Marci Nominis'. *Tempo,* Summer 1956.

VIRGIL THOMSON, 'Stravinsky's Operas', *Musical Newsletter,* Fall, 1974.

CALVIN TOMKINS, 'Living Well is the Best Revenge'. *The New Yorker,* 28 July 1962.

JEAN VILLARD-GILLES, 'Souvenirs du Diable', from *Hommage à C.-F. Ramuz.* Lausanne, La Concorde, 1947.

In addition I acknowledge with gratitude permission to quote from T. S. Eliot's 'Little Gidding' (published in *Four Quartets* by Faber & Faber Ltd.), and from Amy Lowell's 'Stravinsky's Three Pieces "Grotesques" for String Quartet' (first published in *Some Imagist Poets 1916* by Constable & Co. Ltd.), and to reprint H. G. Wells's letter about the London première of *The Wedding* in 1926.

633

Index

This Index of names, places and works covers the three parts of the book, together with Appendices A to D – but not Appendix E.

The names included are mainly those of members of Stravinsky's family, and of musicians, writers and artists.

Place-names are given; but not necessarily the names of countries. Buildings are sub-indexed under the name of the city or town in which they are situated, *e.g.*

St. Petersburg,
Maryinsky Theatre

The titles of works are printed in italics, followed by the composer's (author's) name within parentheses. References to main entries in the Register are in bold type.

634

Index

Index

Index

Index

Index

Index

Index

Index

Index

Index

Index

Index

Index

Index

Index

Index